Preface

13 April 1970
Swigert: Okay, Houston, we've had a problem h
Lousma: This is Houston. Say again please.
Lovell: Houston, we've had a problem . . .

This exchange on April 13th 1970 marked the beginning of one of the most remarkable rescues of all time. An oxygen tank aboard *Apollo 13* had exploded. The space craft lost vital supplies of water power and oxygen when the side of the service module blew away. An hour after the explosion it was realised that the three crewmen would have to move into the lunar module, which had its own independent supplies; they made it with about fifteen minutes of power to spare. Using the module as a lifeboat had been discussed years before, but it was never considered a serious proposition. Unfortunately, the lunar module was designed for two, with supplies for just 45 hours, and without the heat shields necessary for earth landing. And so there they were, 200,000 miles from home, still on course for a moon landing, and without the power to turn around.

As Lovell later remarked in his usual understated style, 'To get Apollo 13 home would require a lot of innovation.' From our point of view the most important quote is Flight Director Gene Kranz's initial reaction: 'Okay, let's everybody keep cool . . . Let's solve the problem, but let's not make it any worse by guessing.'

Over the next days enormously complicated and interrelated problems were solved. Procedures which were normally written and tested over three months had to be ready in three days. As was said afterwards, failure was not an option; they had to get it right first time. Some operations were carried out with only minutes to spare. Some even involved the creative use of cardboard and duct tape - an improvised carbon dioxide filter was designed and prototyped on earth before being replicated and successfully deployed in space.

On April 17th, three very tired, hungry, cold, dehydrated astronauts returned to earth. In total, Haise, Lovell, and Swigert weighed 31.5 pounds less; Lovell alone had lost 14 pounds. Sometimes solving problems can be a truly heroic pursuit. (The full amazing story can be found in many accounts including a surprisingly accurate film. Innumerable detailed reports, sound and video recordings and flight logs are available online.)

Innovation is not just about solving problems and making effective decisions; it's also about finding opportunities. You don't have to work for NASA to show your ingenuity. In 2004 Californian Todd Basche beat over 8,300 other entries in a competition run by the office supplies company Staples with his invention of a combination lock which uses letters to spell easy to remember words rather than random numbers. As often seems to be the case, with hindsight the idea was ridiculously simple, but no one else had thought of it and so Todd profited to the tune of $25,000 plus royalties.

Innovations do not even have to be particularly useful. In August 2005 twenty-one-year-old student Alex Tew was trying to think of ideas to fund a debt-free further education: 'After an hour or two of jotting down random things on paper, the idea seemingly popped out of nowhere. Almost like my subconscious mind had been ticking over in the background, working it all out. So it just kind of happened. That's about it. I scribbled it down and within about ten minutes a picture of what needed to be done had emerged.' That idea was the Million Dollar Homepage, an Internet phenomenon that sold advertising at the rate of one dollar per pixel. Less than five months later the final one thousand pixels were sold in an online auction, and after costs, taxes and charitable donations Tew expected to net up to $700,000 profit from a start-up cost of €50.

- This is a book for people who are still astonished at the skills, resourcefulness and sheer determination of the *Apollo 13* team.

- This is a book for people who are amazed at the utter simplicity of the Million Dollar Homepage and say to themselves, 'I wish I'd thought of that.'

- It is also a book for people who are fed up with being told to be more creative, to 'think outside the box' or that 'you don't have to work harder, just work smarter' and just want to know *how*.

The standard response to 'problems' is often, *'Don't bring me problems, bring me solutions!* Decisions have to be made with speed and certainty. Action not words. If you have a problem, just think about it really hard and – *EUREKA!* – the solution will appear. And if at first you don't succeed then try, try and try again. If you don't succeed it's because you didn't want it enough. As for creativity, apart from the occasional genius, it's all a bit overrated and impractical really, isn't it?'

But as we shall see, the quick decision is not necessarily the best decision; ideas do not come out of thin air and 'creatives' are not special people.

Most of us have more than three days to work with and most of us are playing for lower stakes than the lives of three astronauts. Most of us have the luxury of seeing problems as opportunities and many of us enjoy the further luxury of choosing which problems/opportunities we care to address. We are not suggesting that reading this book will enable you to salvage a moon mission: there is no short cut to competence. But we *are* suggesting that invention, innovation, effective decision making and entrepreneurship share the same basic problem-solving process which we can analyse and deconstruct in order to understand better how ingenuity works so that we can all enhance our thinking skills.

In today's climate of uncertainty we see more clearly than ever the truth of the assertion that the greatest resource that humanity possesses is the human mind. It is readily available, inexhaustible and free at the point of use. The currency of the human mind is ideas. The effective generation and evaluation of ideas to solve problems, make decisions and exploit opportunities is the great challenge for the future; but it is also the greatest hope. How we produce ideas, good and bad, and how we use them are the subjects of this book. Our contention is that creativity is not the preserve of a few special people but a skill that can be taught and learned by everyone. The concept of 'Peak Oil' is well known; the concept of 'Peak Water' is gaining currency; but it would be a very dismal person indeed who would predict 'Peak Ingenuity'.

- So this is a book for optimists; people who still have a sense of wonder and possibility, or if they've lost it want to find it again.*

*About This Book

A few years ago the authors embarked on a project to explore opportunities in entrepreneurship education for the University of Nottingham Institute for Enterprise and Innovation (UNIEI since 2014 re-named The Haydn Green Institute for Innovation & Entrepreneurship). The key outcome of that project was the devising of a new creative problem-solving methodology: the Ingenuity Process. This methodology is used by all students entering the Nottingham University Business School (NUBS) in the United Kingdom and at campuses in China and Malaysia, as well as being a key part of our Executive Education provision. It is available in several forms. Readers who are only interested in the method are directed to the leaner versions, particularly 'Ingenuity in Practice – a guide for clear thinking' (second edition, 2011).

The process has as its core a three-fold structure: first defining precisely the problem to be solved, then discovering a wide range of possibilities before determining the most appropriate solution. This book is the fullest exposition of the process. It is a book about ideas, and as such is full of them. Ideas drawn from the arts and sciences as well as business and society in general. We juxtapose famous and not so well known examples of problem solving with other more commonplace, 'real life' instances drawn from case studies of our own. The book could be likened to an overheard conversation, but with the advantage that the reader can stop, pause and rewind at will. The conversation is long, and relaxed, with all kinds of voices, from many disciplines, past and present, but at its spine is the three fold Ingenuity Process, which is indicated by page headers/footers. Marshalling so many disparate voices has not been easy. Liberties have been taken; passages have been edited, in some cases spellings and punctuation have been standardised for the sake of clarity - to allow the conversation to flow: in others something like the original style has been preserved for precisely the opposite reason - to give an idea of the flavour and texture of the source material. This may appear arbitrary. The only reason anything has been included is that the authors find it interesting and/or amusing. Information included should be relied on in the same way that any overheard conversation would be trusted.

This book could not have been written only a few years ago and it is presumed that readers will have web access and the good sense to confirm and explore facts and quotations, always remembering that the Internet allows you to be both extremely well informed and totally wrong at the same time.

Ingenuity

© 2013 Paul Kirkham, Simon Mosey and Martin Binks. All rights reserved.

Published by the Haydn Green Institute for Innovation & Entrepreneurship.

ISBN 978-0-9563453-2-5

Designed and set by TCC
www.tccommunications.co.uk

Although every precaution has been taken in the preparation of this book, the publisher and authors assume no responsibility for errors or omissions. Neither is any liability assumed for damages resulting from the use of this information contained herein.

Contents

Overview

Planet Earth seen from Apollo 13

Why We Need Innovation – the scale of the challenge

Over the years there have been many philosophers and thinkers who have predicted the imminent downfall of the human race. Favourite reasons have been over-population, the depletion of vital resources and the collapse of the established order.

One of the earliest of these pessimists is the Chinese philosopher and statesman Han Fei Tzu (died 233 BC):

> Nowadays, however, people do not regard five children as many. Each child may in his or her turn beget five offspring, so that before the death of the grandfather there may be twenty-five grand-children. As a result, people have become numerous and supplies scanty; toil has become hard and provisions meagre. Therefore people quarrel so much that, though rewards are doubled and punishments repeated, disorder is inevitable.
>
> (tr. Wenkui Liao)

And yet it will not have escaped the readers' notice that civilisation is still here; for that matter so is China: and that cannot just be a matter of good luck. Humanity has survived against all expectation through intelligence, creativity, invention and innovation – in one word: ingenuity.

Now just because Fei Tzu and others have been proved wrong time and again does not mean we can ignore the gloom merchants – as we shall see, predictions based on past performance are far from guaranteed. Moreover, present-day doom-mongers have added considerably to the apocalyptic bill of fare – on top of the standard war, famine, pestilence and death, we have climate change, worldwide pandemics, loss of biodiversity, not forgetting asteroids and solar flares.

> It's being so cheerful as keeps me going.
>
> (1940s catchphrase, Mona Lott)

But if the challenges are greater than ever, so is the potential for dealing with them. If in the past we have relied upon human minds to solve problems, then we ought to remember that the number of minds has kept exact pace with the population and our access to them has increased beyond anything that has ever happened before. You could say that the World Wide Web represents the collective mind of humanity and the Internet our collective brain – we are all entering a new era whose possibilities we can scarcely grasp.

Doom-mongers

The first of the modern doom-mongers to take a scientific approach was Thomas Malthus:'I say, that the power of population is indefinitely greater than the power in the earth to produce subsistence for man.' This argument is as controversial today as when it was first published in 1798, in *An Essay on the Principle of Population*.

An early critic was Frederick Engels, writing in 1843: 'Malthus, the originator of this doctrine, maintains that population is always pressing on the means of subsistence; that as soon as production increases, population increases in the same proportion; and that the inherent tendency of the population to multiply in excess of the available means of subsistence is the root of all misery and all vice.'

For Engels this was palpable nonsense: 'The productive power at mankind's disposal is immeasurable. The productivity of the soil can be increased ad infinitum by the application of capital, labour and science.'

But over the last century population has been rising extremely quickly, probably a good deal faster than either Malthus or Fei Tzu predicted, and doubts are still being raised as to whether there is a limit to the technical solutions possible. Social solutions have their own difficulties: Garrett Hardin's 1968 essay 'The Tragedy of the Commons' describes the way in which individuals, acting independently and rationally, will bring about the depletion of finite resources in the full and certain knowledge that such a depletion is of long-term interest to no one. The forecast destruction of commonly held resources has the inevitability of Greek tragedy.

In the same year (1968), ecologist Paul Ehrlich wrote *The Population Bomb*, which opened thus: 'The battle to feed all of humanity is over. In the 1970s the world will undergo famines – hundreds of millions of people are going to starve to death in spite of any crash programs embarked upon now.'

In 1980, Ehrlich accepted a wager from economist Julian Simon that prices of raw materials would fall rather than rise. The commodities, chosen by Ehrlich and his colleagues, were copper, chromium, nickel, tin and tungsten. The period of the bet was ten years. Ehrlich lost; every one of the metals fell in price. Simon's explanation was:

> More people, and increased income, cause resources to become more scarce in the short run. Heightened scarcity causes prices to rise. The higher prices present opportunity, and prompt inventors and entrepreneurs to search for solutions. Many fail in the search, at cost to themselves. But in a free society, solutions are eventually found. And in the long run the new developments leave us better off than if the problems had not arisen. That is, prices eventually become lower than before the increased scarcity occurred.
>
> (*The State of Humanity*, 1996)

Since then the science of climate change has intensified the debate. The *Stern Review on the Economics of Climate Change* of 2006 argues that strong, early action is essential to obviate the consequences of climate change. Then Prime Minister Tony Blair stated the case plainly: 'This disaster is not set to happen in some science fiction future many years ahead, but in our lifetime.' 'Investment now will pay us back many times in the future, not just environmentally but economically as well.' (*BBC News, 31 October 2006*)

The extremes of the argument can be represented thus. The pessimistic view is that of scientist James Lovelock who wrote, 'Billions of us will die and the few breeding pairs of people that survive will be in the Arctic where the climate remains tolerable.' *(Independent, 16 January 2006)*

The optimistic view is that of 'cornucopians' who follow Julian Simon's 'mind-boggling vision of resources: the more we use, the better off we become – and there's no practical limit to improving our lot forever. Indeed, throughout history, new tools and new knowledge have made resources easier and easier to obtain. Our growing ability to create new resources has more than made up for temporary setbacks due to local resource exhaustion, pollution, population growth, and so on.' (*The Ultimate Resource 2*, 1998). A more temperate consideration of the situation appears in a report issued by the [British] Government Office for Science:

> The global food system will experience an unprecedented confluence of pressures over the next 40 years. On the demand side, global population size will increase from nearly seven billion today to eight billion by 2030, and probably to over nine billion by 2050; many people are likely to be wealthier, creating demand for a more varied, high-quality diet requiring additional resources to produce. On the production side, competition for land, water and energy will intensify, while the effects of climate change will become increasingly apparent. The need to reduce greenhouse gas emissions and adapt to a changing climate will become imperative. Over this period globalisation will continue, exposing the food system to novel economic and political pressures.
>
> (*Foresight. The Future of Food and Farming (2011)*)

So on the one hand it is indisputable that we are still here and that for many people things have never been better in terms of health, life expectancy, material possessions, etc. There is, however, plentiful evidence of societies that have failed. For the Saxon poet surveying the ruins it was fate which destroyed Roman culture in Britain ('weird wrecked it' – *'wyrde gebrǣcon'*). In his poem 'Ozymandias', Shelley contrasts the arrogance of Rameses with the broken remnants of Egyptian civilisation, around which 'the lone and level sands stretch far away'. Modern scholarship provides compelling, well-documented examples throughout history of societies and civilisations that have finally collapsed, sometimes in the space of a couple of generations, despite having made successive innovative leaps of technology and organisation.

Moreover, from Easter Island in the Pacific to the Viking settlement of Greenland in the far north, the reasons why some civilisations fail is becoming clearer; it seems that factors like population pressure, environmental depletion and climate change, singly or in combination, are responsible.

Whatever turns out to be correct, whether it is fate or arrogance or ignorance, one thing all parties do agree on: innovation has been and will continue to be essential to human progress and/or survival. Innovation in business; innovation in finance;

innovation in technology; innovation in science; innovation in politics; innovation in organisations; indeed innovation in all walks of life: carrying on in the same old way is simply not an option (and, as we shall see, probably never has been).

It is ingenuity that has kept us ahead of catastrophe and it is the optimism engendered by ingenuity that continually leads some of us to expect things to get better, not worse. We progress by solving the problems life throws at us.

Take for example the story of Will Chase who was feeling detached from his end customers after twenty years of growing potatoes on his Herefordshire farm:

> With the continual price pressure from the supermarkets as well, I realised I had to change direction. I wanted to remain in farming and produce a great tasting product we could make from potatoes.
>
> *I was hit one day with the eureka moment to turn my potatoes into chips.*

Tyrrell's Hand Cooked Potato Chips went on sale to the public in 2002. Six years later Chase sold three-quarters of the business for £30 million.

But even highly successful businesses have problems – what to do with all those potatoes which are too small to be made into chips (a.k.a. crisps)? For Chase the answer is to turn another problem into another opportunity. It's an old adage that 'When life gives you lemons you should make lemonade.' What could you make from 'small potatoes'? In 2010, Chase Vodka was awarded the accolade of World's Best Vodka at the San Francisco World Spirits Competition.

With hindsight, it is easy to see what Will Chase has done: he has turned a cheap commodity into a premium product and reaped the reward. So did he just get lucky? Twice? Or did he, in essence, take advantage of an opportunity that he recognised simply by looking at things from a different point of view?

We are not suggesting that reading this book will enable you to make yourself a fortune or salvage a moon mission: there is no short cut to competence and hard work is going to be required to nurture the germ of an idea into reality. But we *are* suggesting that these things do not depend upon luck either – invention, innovation, effective decision making and entrepreneurship all share a similar basic problem-solving process that we can analyse and deconstruct in order to understand better how ingenuity works, so that we can all enhance our thinking skills.

Take this more mundane problem as another example: despite or perhaps because of the information technology revolution, the developed world seems to be disappearing under a mound of paperwork. More time seems to be spent target-setting, form-filling, and box-ticking than actually doing the job in hand. There must be a better way.

Our approach would be first of all to try and understand why we seem to need so much paperwork: is it accountability or transparency; is it a substitute for trust or common sense? (It must be more than something to pass away the long winter nights.)

Having identified the purpose of so much paperwork, we would ask whether there is not a more imaginative way to achieve that same purpose. What actually happens if we 'think the unthinkable': what if offices were to disconnect their printers; what if they banned e-mails and insisted on face-to-face meetings; what if you were limited to one phone call? Might that sort of 'off the wall' thinking actually allow you to re-order your priorities and re-focus on the purpose rather than the process? And if it turns out that there really is no alternative, then surely there must be a more practical way of doing it.

And finally we would insist on examining the potential impact of new schemes *before* they are implemented. Hindsight is a wonderful thing; forethought is much more difficult and a lack of it can be very expensive and often terminal for the project.

In Belfast on January 28th 2009, Lord Robin Eames, the former Anglican Primate of Ireland, launched the *Report of the Consultative Group on the Past* (otherwise known as the *Eames Bradley Report*). The purpose of the group was to examine ways of dealing with the legacy of conflict in Northern Ireland:

> We all come from different backgrounds, we came with varying experiences of the conflict, with different political outlooks, but we have accepted our differences. We faced many contentious issues and we knew it would not be easy. But this Report, whether people agree with what they read or not, represents an integrity which comes from honest dialogue and a willingness to think 'outside the box'.

The report contained 31 recommendations, of which the most controversial, which had been leaked several days previously, was for £12,000 to be paid to the relatives of each person who had died in the 'troubles', irrespective of whether they were victim or perpetrator. The reasoning was that 'There is no difference in a mother's tears' and that every loss ought to be acknowledged.

Eames recognised the controversy, but defended their position:

> Maybe this gesture for those outside of our group is too sudden. Maybe we did make a mistake in our timing. Maybe we forgot that we had been at this for eighteen months. If so, we apologise. It is not that we wouldn't stand by the recommendation. We would and we do. But maybe we forgot that we have been at this for eighteen months and during that time we had the opportunity to reach that conclusion.

But they were unable to make their case in the whirl of publicity and within a month the British government had rejected the payment plan. The rest of the report, along with thirty other less contentious recommendations, fell by the wayside and shows little sign of being implemented. Eighteen months' work by eight intelligent and well-intentioned people fell at the first hurdle because they had no adequate response to the question, 'What will happen when we announce our findings?'

'Thinking outside the box' is all very well but, as we will demonstrate, solutions that do not fit 'back in the box' pose special difficulties. (It is a supreme irony that the keynote address as they began to consider their report was given at the Innovation Centre in the Titanic Quarter, Belfast. There are few areas of public policy more iceberg strewn than the north of Ireland.)

All innovation comes at a price and that cost is not just financial, although it is often expressed as such – time, after all, is money. Even 'goodwill' sometimes has a price attached. But as we have seen, there are some non-financial costs with quite limited resources. The 'credibility budget' of the *Eames Bradley Report* was almost all spent at the launch event. Of all the costs of innovation, we would contend that investment in ideas is the most cost effective. Ideas don't cost anything other than a bit of time and brainpower. As we will show, generating ideas is what humanity does best.

Much of the literature of innovation starts from that 'eureka moment' when an idea, solution or concept appears; we, on the other hand, will be starting earlier: *pre-concept*, that 'Houston, we have a problem' moment. We are going to try to solve problems and not make things worse by guessing.

Innovation, Entrepreneurship and Creative Problem Solving: The UNIEI approach

Innovation is the process whereby new concepts are introduced. In the business world this might be referred to as 'bringing a new product to market'. But that 'product' is not necessarily a physical object; it may be a new technique or procedure, it may be a new policy initiative, and the 'market' is not necessarily a financial one. The essence of innovation is the successful introduction of new ideas so as to change a situation for the better: what economists call 'welfare generation' has a broader application: to bring 'value' to a particular domain in terms which that domain values.

Much of the discussion of innovation starts with the 'concept' and debates how best to realise that new idea or invention, how it can be developed, designed and deployed. There is a tendency for individuals and organisations to rush to judgement – straight from problem to solution, straight from invention to implementation. Not only does this often result in a sub-optimal solution with a sub-optimal chance of success, it usually brings forward the expenditure of sunk costs. We will be concentrating on the area *before* the idea is fully formed – *pre-concept* – enhancing the quality of the invention before many resources are spent on implementation. There is a cost but we can look upon it as borrowing time and effort which would otherwise be spent later in bitterness and recrimination as the concept is found wanting.

The Process of Innovation

C O N C E P T

Need
Problem
opportunity

DEFINE

DISCOVER

DETERMINE

DEVELOP

DESIGN

DEPLOY

Innovation
Improvement
Exploitation

The Costs of Innovation

Pre-concept relevance
determines the quality
of ideas generated

Post-concept relevance
determines the extent
to which the potential of
new ideas is realised

Time

In the course of a fairly wide-ranging ramble through the world of ingenuity it may appear at times that we ask more questions than we give answers. But at the core of the book you will find a straightforward procedure for clear thinking that, we consider, has general relevance, from business innovation to choosing your next holiday, from coping with global warming to organising your office. We will demonstrate a technique for solving problems and for recognising and evaluating opportunities that allows us to take time to examine the situation, come up with alternatives and choose the right one. We will reveal where ideas come from and demonstrate how to come up with new ones. We feel that this practical technique leads to a higher abstraction; an understanding of the commonality of problem solving as a universal proficiency, generic rather than particular. Moreover, we will insist that 'creativity' is this practical skill that can be taught and learned by everyone and that opportunities for innovation are to be expected; that's the nature of creative problem solving.

That Eureka Moment

'EUREKA!' is the archetypal expression of discovery. It is associated with one of the greatest of the hero inventors of the ancient world and the story bears retelling.

King Heiro of Syracuse had ordered a new crown in the shape of a laurel wreath. Although it weighed the same as the gold he had given for it to be made, the king wondered whether the goldsmith had robbed him by replacing a certain proportion of the gold with less valuable silver.

Luckily the greatest scientist, engineer and inventor of the age, Archimedes (died c. 212 BC), lived in Syracuse. Heiro asked him to investigate, but of course forbade him from damaging the crown.

Archimedes knew how to tell the difference between silver and gold by comparing their relative densities. Density is calculated by dividing the mass (weight) of an object by its volume, so Archimedes's problem was how to measure the volume of an irregular object, i.e. the crown.

The solution came to Archimedes as he relaxed in the bath and noticed the water level go up as he got in. His irregularly shaped body had displaced a measurable amount of water.

He was so excited he ran naked down the street shouting, *'Eureka!'* (I have found it). That's the legend.

More than two thousand years later, on Monday, September 10th 1984, at 9:05 a.m., Alec Jeffreys (now Sir Alec) had what he described as a eureka moment when he took an X-ray photograph of his assistant's genetic code from the developing tray. Seeing the similarities and differences in the results of experiments on his technician's family made him realise that he could trace the links between their unique genetic profiles.

Within an hour, he and his immediate team had sketched out most of the applications of what would become known as genetic fingerprinting.

The First of Many Digressions

Since one of the themes of this book will be to warn of the danger of false assumptions and to challenge what we know and what we think we know, it would be best to start as we mean to go on and take a step to one side and consider the word eureka itself and how we use it. There will be many of these diversions and the reader ought to know what to expect.

The story told above comes from the works of the Roman architect and engineer Marcus Vitruvius Pollio a couple of centuries after the supposed event. We have no way of knowing whether the tale is true or whether anyone at that time possessed the technology to measure weight and volume accurately. But a couple of clicks on the Internet can bring us several translations and the original Latin and we can make our own judgement. It seems to be a story told to illustrate the most extraordinary circumstances of Archimedes discovery. With the problem still on his mind, he went by chance to take a bath (*'casu venit in balineum'*) and was so astonished at the sudden appearance of the answer to his problem that he returned home naked, shouting that he had found it ('. . . *nudus vadens domum . . . clamabat ευρηχα ευρηχα'*).

There is a subtle difference in the way Alec Jeffreys uses the expression: it was not the surprise appearance of a solution made when he was doing something else but the unexpected realisation of how enormous were the possibilities of the results of an experiment. He wasn't relaxing in the bath; he was in his lab, doing his job. As we shall see, chance played little part in the discovery of DNA fingerprinting.

So the question to ask is how an ancient Greek expression comes to be used in much the same way more than two thousand years later. The first thing to note is that there is no continuity of use between Archimedes and Alec Jeffreys. The works of Vitruvius lay dormant for a millennium before being rediscovered in the fifteenth century. As we shall discover, invention and innovation were looked upon with some suspicion in the intervening years; for a long time revelation was far more Saint Paul than Archimedes. Vitruvius' views on proportion inspired Leonardo Da Vinci's famous drawing showing a man with arms and legs stretching to fit in both a square and a circle. Interestingly although the drawing was made around 1487 this most iconic image of both Vitruvius and Leonardo was not known or used by anyone before it was published in 1811.

Vitruvius was championed by the Venetian architect Andrea Palladio who developed the Palladian style so beloved of English aristocrats on the Grand Tour, but eureka did not enter the English language that way. A couple of clicks on the Oxford English Dictionary website show that the word was known to Elizabethan mathematician and astrologer John Dee in 1570. A couple more clicks reveal that Shakespeare did not use it, neither did Samuel Johnson think fit to include it in his *Dictionary* of 1755 – and yet within a hundred years it was being used by gold miners in California and Australia to describe a 'lucky strike'.

A 'eureka moment' enters English in 1906 through a translation of a largely neglected essay by a French psychologist.

So words can change their meaning; they can be lost and found again; they can die out and be resurrected or re-created and used for the 'wrong' purpose.

But in order to make that point do we really have to cite works in Latin and French, with translations; together with web addresses that might well not exist by the time the reader looks for them? Obviously the authors find all this reasonably interesting, although how germane it is to the argument of the book might be questionable. We leave it to the reader to decide which to trust and which to check.

Overview

What can we learn from studying innovation?

Where do those great leaps forward, those eureka moments, come from? Do they happen by chance or is 'progress' inevitable? Do they only happen to special people, those whom we call geniuses, or can *anyone* be 'creative'? Where exactly do new ideas come from and what do we mean by creativity anyway?

A quick look at a single area of human ingenuity reveals the power of creative problem solving.

Shipbuilding

Humanity has spread all over the earth, from Africa to the Arctic; from Tierra del Fuego to Easter Island. And in order to get there we have had to cross water. Obviously, we can ford rivers, and have done so for hundreds of generations, following herds of animals. We can swim if we have to, but if we want to *use* water as a resource or as a means of transport we have to exercise our ingenuity.

Much of the development of water transport must have happened bit by bit, almost accidentally. Let's start with a floating log. The idea of tying two or more logs together to form a raft is fairly obvious and has occurred to people all over the world.

But it is quite an imaginative leap to shape a piece of wood into a paddle to help you along, and another enormous leap to hollow out the log and make a canoe. A 9,500-year-old paddle has been found, although the earliest canoe yet found is only 8,300 years old. (Paddles can be used on logs so we probably don't have a break in invention like that mysterious gap between cans and can openers.)

Dugout canoes are of course limited in size, although they could be paired together. What about another imaginative leap; split the logs into planks and then fix them together with pegs or with rope to make a wider canoe? Remains of boats up to 16 metres long, with room for eighteen paddlers, have been found at North Ferriby on the banks of the River Humber: one of them is more than 4,000 years old.

But what if there are no logs? How about using bundles of reeds? Quite clever, and invented at least twice: in the Middle East and later in South America. After a while, the reeds will soak through, so why not waterproof them using bitumen? The obvious point of reference is Moses in the bulrushes.

There are plank boats from a 5,000-year-old tomb in Egypt but the oldest evidence of seafaring yet discovered comes from Kuwait, where a 7,000-year-old ceramic model boat has been found together with pieces of bitumen indented with reeds on one side and barnacles on the other.

It must have occurred to lots of people that anything that holds water *in* can keep water *out*, and indeed we find some nomads in Central Asia using inflated animal skins to cross rivers just as their ancestors did when Marco Polo passed through. It is possibly still the most cost-effective way to get to the other side.

But it is surely an act of genius to realise that animal skin can be used to cover a wooden frame and make an open boat. Whether such technology is diffused or discovered independently is a matter for debate, but skin boats in one form or another have been around for a long time. And if skins are not suitable you could use fabric or even the bark of the birch tree. Modern coracles and curraghs, kayaks and canoes might be made with modern materials such as glass-fibre or Kevlar but they still owe their existence to a leap of imagination from an unknown age.

And which whiz kid was it who invented the outrigger? Magellan and his crew were reduced to eating leather from the rigging as they 'discovered' the Pacific in 1519. The indigenous people island-hopped at will, navigating by the ocean swells and the winds, coping reasonably well without the 'superior' technology of fixed stars and compass.

Generation after generation of shipwrights have honed a few basic designs into the diversity we see today. And don't forget the countless men and women who developed all the allied technologies: weaving, tanning, rope making.

Most of these changes are gradual; some are revolutionary. Sail technology surely extends all the way from someone holding an animal skin aloft right up to the twentieth-century rip stop nylon spinnakers. But again it is hard not to describe as genius whoever it was who first discovered how to sail into the wind, or whoever it was who applied the magnetic compass to navigation.

These enormously practical individuals are rarely celebrated; but up in the Northlands, where word-fame used to be prized above anything, they were more likely to remember the names of extraordinary individuals. So let the story of Thorberg Skavhogg stand for all those uncommon 'common' people.

In 998, near Trondheim, a king, who shall remain nameless for once, commissioned a new dragon ship. One morning, when it was nearing completion, it was found that someone had hacked great notches in the planking from stem to stern. The culprit was Thorberg, who had only just returned to the project and wasn't pleased by what he saw (cf. the quality-control methods of Josiah Wedgwood, who used to leave imperfect work smashed in pieces on the bench of the potter responsible). Upon pain of death, Thorberg completed his improvements and was promoted to head shipwright. According to the sagas, everyone agreed that the *Ormen Lange* (Long Serpent), with 34 benches and gilded head and tail, was the best fitted and costliest ship ever built in Norway.

By the time of the Industrial Revolution, we start to see more and more inventors and entrepreneurs getting individual recognition, and it is one of these, John Wilkinson, who finally showed the wider world quite how clever the shipbuilders had been, by demonstrating that ships that are heavier than water can still float. 'Iron-mad' Wilkinson was so keen to promote his product that in 1787 he built an iron boat. He also had an iron desk and was eventually buried, after a great deal of effort, in an extremely heavy iron coffin.

In spite of resistance from those who spoke of iron ships and wooden men, the future was clear and another era began. In America, Robert Fulton and others successfully introduced steam power to ships, starting another branching tree of incremental and revolutionary change; from paddle steamers to hydrofoils, interacting all the time with other technologies, sometimes on purpose but also sometimes by chance. The story is rarely simple: gradual, step-by-step improvements in wooden ship design powered by more and more efficient sail technology may have been no match in the commercial arena for steam-powered iron vessels, but in fact the earliest practical steamship, the *Charlotte Dundas* (1803), had a wooden hull, while *Cutty Sark* (1869), the epitome of the sailing ship, was built with iron frames and bulkheads.

'Madeira, My Dear?'

From early times it was realised that ships need weight to maintain stability. Cargo ships have to be 'trimmed' regularly by replacing cargo with ballast and vice versa. And ocean-going ships need supplies.

Ships used to visit the island of Madeira to take on wine both for export and for their own supplies. Contrary to all expectations, it was found that conditions in the ship's hold actually improved the wine. The oxidation improved the flavour and the humidity seemed to strengthen the alcohol content, which helped preservation, especially if the wine was also fortified with spirit. Such was the success of this process that wines were sent on voyages as ballast simply in order to mature them. The most prized were *vinho da roda* – round-trip wines. Quite why rolling around in bilgewater at tropical temperatures should be better than keeping the wine still in a cool cave as the rest of the world does is a bit of a mystery, but Madeira is certainly one of the longest-keeping wines. Bottles 150 years old have been found to be perfectly drinkable. Demand for Madeira was so strong that the winemakers began imitating the special conditions by constructing sauna-like buildings called *estufas*, which mature the wine faster and more consistently. Madeira is still the aperitif of choice for many in the southern states of America, having been popular in pre-revolutionary days and becoming extremely fashionable after being used to toast the Declaration of Independence.

By looking at just one strand of technology from the Stone Age to the present day, we can see human ingenuity in all its variety from the gradual to the radical: incremental change, revolutionary change, planned progress and chance discovery; the interplay of different people with different skills.

Throughout this book we will be using stories like these to illustrate ingenuity in action, but they are not told simply to inspire all of us. They represent a tiny fraction of the collective past experience of humanity: ideas, both successes and failures, which are a very real resource for the creativity of the future.

When ideas are applied – that is, put into action – they bring about change and, as we noticed with shipbuilding, there is a difference between gradual and radical change. Before we look at ideas, we first need to look more closely at our perception of the nature of change.

The Nature of Change

We tend to see change over time in one of two ways: either as a circle, turning and returning to the same spot; or as a line with a beginning and an end.

How are we to reconcile the cyclical nature of the world, 'time's cycle', with notions of continuous progress, 'time's arrow'? Is progress gradual or step by step: is it continuous or discrete?

The work of economist and political scientist Joseph Schumpeter brings the two together: time's arrow of economic progress meets time's cycle of the market. The market with perfect circular flow is going nowhere. What propels it forward is innovation.

> Capitalism, then, is by nature a form or method of economic change and not only never is but never can be stationary. And this evolutionary character of the capitalist process is not merely due to the fact that economic life goes on in a social and natural environment which changes and by its change alters the data of economic action; this fact is important and these changes (wars, revolutions and so on) often condition industrial change, but they are not its prime movers. Nor is this evolutionary character due to a quasi-automatic increase in population and capital or to the vagaries of monetary systems, of which exactly the same thing holds true. The fundamental impulse that sets and keeps the capitalist engine in motion comes from the new consumers, goods, the new methods of production or transportation, the new markets, the new forms of industrial organization that capitalist enterprise creates.
>
> (*Capitalism, Socialism and Democracy*, 1942)

Schumpeter identifies two different responses to changes in the business environment: an 'adaptive response', which is an adjustment of existing practice; or a 'creative response', which comes from outside existing practice. The *adaptive* is incremental change; the *creative* is revolutionary. The creative response destroys; old ideas, technologies, products, skills and equipment become obsolete. For Schumpeter the 'creative response is an essential element in the historical process: no deterministic credo avails against this'. It is the entrepreneur who disturbs the equilibrium and is the driving force of economic development. The entrepreneur identifies and creates opportunities and then takes action to realise those new ideas.

This breaking of the circle is happening continuously in different domains, along several time scales, interacting with economic cycles and fluctuations to cause a veritable 'gale of creative destruction'.

In 2004 this statue (a gift from the Government of India) was unveiled at the European Organisation for Nuclear Research (CERN) in Geneva. Shiva Nataraja, the Lord of Dance, holds both the drum of creation and the fire of destruction at the same time: creation and destruction are inextricably linked, two sides of the same coin. In Europe, creation and destruction have different aspects according to which is placed first. The phoenix has to die before it can be hatched in the ashes of its own destruction; Oedipus, on the other hand, has to be fully grown before he acts out his destiny and destroys his own father. When the nineteenth-century anarchist Mikhail Bakunin recognised that the destructive passion was also a passion for creation he was surely thinking of the phoenix, but only a few years later it is Oedipus who casts his long shadow across western thought. European interpretations of Hinduism and classical Greek tragedy; the birth of archaeology; the rise and fall of ancient empires; psychoanalysis and economics; nihilists and Nazis: it's a heady brew with far-reaching influence. Nietzsche was obsessed by the dynamic between creation and destruction and even today there's more than a slight odour of the *Übermensch* in some modern depictions of the entrepreneur as warrior hero.

The distinction between creative and adaptive responses is resonant with the views of Cambridge academic William Beveridge:

> Scientific research may also be divided into the exploratory type which opens up new territory, and the developmental type which follows on the former. The exploratory type is free and adventurous; occasionally it gives us great and perhaps unexpected discoveries; or it may give us no results at all. The developmental type of research is more often carried on by the very methodical type of scientist who is content to consolidate the advances, to search over the newly won country for more modest discoveries, and to exploit fully the newly gained territory by putting it to use. This latter type of research is sometimes spoken of as 'pot-boiling' or 'safety first' research.

(*The Art of Scientific Investigation*, 1957)

'Pot boiling' sounds somewhat disparaging but the point is also made by the biologist Edward Menge in a lecture published in 1930, which is worth quoting for its wider relevance to our studies:

> But merely extending knowledge a step further is not developing science. Breeding homing pigeons that could cover a given space with ever-increasing rapidity did not give us the laws of telegraphy, nor did breeding faster horses bring us the steam locomotive. The so-called improvements of the microscope pertain to improving the stands that hold the lenses. Until a new principle of optics is discovered, the microscope remains what it is.*

In 1962, Thomas Kuhn published *The Structure of Scientific Revolutions*, arguing that science does not progress by a simple linear accumulation of knowledge, but is characterised by periodic revolutions. 'Normal Science' represents a linear progression of successful problem solving, until the pressure of unsolved puzzles or anomalies builds up, causing a 'crisis', which is resolved after a period of 'Revolutionary Science' that overturns some or all of the previously accepted principles. The discovery of new facts and the invention of new theories mark these changes. For example, the earth-centred model of the universe was replaced by the sun-centred model. The new worldview accommodates the problems of the old worldview better and more fully, while setting a completely new array of puzzles to be solved.

It is difficult for two views that lack a common measure to co-exist. They look at the same thing in fundamentally different ways. It is important to understand that the new worldview may not necessarily explain everything that the old one did; there may actually be a loss of explanation.**

*It was the very next year that Ernst Ruska started work on the electron microscope.

**This is fascinating since it subverts that version of history which suggests a steady cumulative progress towards an ideal 'truth'. It is an issue we will return to towards the end of the book.

Kuhn argues that the revolutionary nature of change is sometimes rendered invisible. Science is taught through texts which have to be rewritten after each revolution. These will tend to concentrate on problems that are solved by the new science; problems of the old science will be ignored as irrelevant.

Kuhn would be little known outside the philosophy and history of science but for his first use of two key terms which have entered popular culture. He describes the web of interwoven assumptions and beliefs that underlie normal science as a *paradigm* and the revolution that overturns it as a *paradigm shift*.

Take this extremely simple example of differing perceptions of the same data: a car park full of cars.

We can classify them according to colour:
so many red ones, so many blue, etc.

We can classify them according to size:
large, medium or small.

We can classify them according to country of origin:
British, German, Japanese, etc.

We can classify them according to manufacturer:
Ford, BMW, Toyota, etc.

Which method is 'best'?

You cannot compare the different systems because they each use completely dissimilar measures; colour does not measure size. It all depends on your point of view.

Kuhn used this famous image to illustrate the difficulties of shifting perceptions. Is it a duck, or a rabbit? Can it be both? Is it neither?

If we simply replace one system with another we lose some of the explanations of the old one. A full understanding of the array may well have to take into account all of these points of view. (As individuals we alter our personal paradigms over time; for example, our preferences might change from a red sports car to a family hatchback, then from a people carrier to a 4x4 off-roader until a mid-life crisis brings a return at last to the red sports car.)

If that is too frivolous then take another example: the plant kingdom. You might think that the modern cladistic (family) classification is best. It explains the relationships and ancestry of plants far better than older arrangements. But that is because our civilisation is obsessed with genetics. In the past plants have been arranged differently.

Theophrastus (third century BC) grouped plants according to their sizes: trees, shrubs, grasses, etc; but also by their shapes; where they grew; how they grew; and their practical uses.

Dioscorides (first century AD) placed together plants with similar properties: oily, resinous, aromatic; or by their roots or their seeds, only occasionally by form: the umbrella-like umbelliferae or the daisy-like compositae. But that is because Dioscorides was a doctor and he was looking at plants through a pharmacologist's eyes. His measure is not the same as a modern botanist's.

Classification by form became dominant in western science providing the basis upon which the phylogenetic system developed.

The old ways are still useful, however; ecologists may be more interested in which plants grow where, while garden designers will still want catalogues arranged by colour.

The palaeontologists Niles Eldredge and Stephen Jay Gould have attempted to resolve the gradual/step-by-step dilemma in evolutionary biology with their theory of punctuated equilibrium ('Punctuated equilibria: an alternative to phyletic gradualism', 1972). The concept of gradual, almost imperceptible change interrupted by sudden episodes of revolutionary change echoed the nineteenth-century accommodation between 'uniformitarians', who saw the present as the key to the past, and 'catastrophists', who saw the past as a very different place, filled with volcanoes, floods, earthquakes and ice ages.

So is change continuous or discrete? We can distinguish them both in action: adaptive and creative; developmental and exploratory; normal and revolutionary; uniform and catastrophic. We can even observe the particular situation where continuing change suddenly becomes cataclysmic – the commonplace expression is 'the straw that breaks the camel's back'; scholars may follow the lead of French mathematician René Thom and call it 'catastrophe theory'.

The challenge of trying to make sense of shifting paradigms and gales of creative destruction is illustrated by looking at just one industry with which we are all familiar.

The music industry

The music industry has a long history; it's safe to say that people all over the world have been singing for their supper since time immemorial. If we exclude performers for the moment, the history of European music publishing starts with the Italian Ottaviano Petrucci, who in 1501 produced the first book of sheet music using movable type. From the start there were copyright issues: Petrucci had a monopoly in Venice; in England, Queen Elizabeth I gave Thomas Tallis and William Byrd the exclusive right to print and import music in 1575. Lyrics, however, were not covered by copyright and 'Broadside Ballads' were sold widely.

By the late nineteenth century in Western Europe and North America, there was a thriving industry selling sheet music to the general public. This 'do-it-yourself' home consumption of music was itself quite a novelty, but the invention of the phonograph was something else. The original machine, however, was not even designed for music reproduction. In 1878 Thomas Alva Edison listed ten possible applications of his invention, only two of which were music related. But playing music was the application that drove the technology. By the 1890s, the average price of a wax cylinder was 50 cents, well within the reach of a mass market, but, in what we will recognise as a familiar feature of the industry, a rival system appeared. In 1887 Emile Berliner had patented the gramophone, which played discs. Flat discs were easier and cheaper to manufacture, although purists insisted that cylinders produced a superior sound. The two systems carried on side by side until Edison finally withdrew cylinders in 1929. Disc continued as the most popular format for recorded music through incremental improvements in manufacture and technology; from clockwork to electricity as the power source; from brittle shellac to flexible vinyl as the material used for the disc.

But alongside the disc, another technology which owed nothing to the wax cylinder had been developing. Magnetic recording was first demonstrated with metal wire as long ago as 1898. It can then be traced through a different series of incremental changes; from wire to steel tape, then coated tape; from ferric to chrome; from reel-to-reel to compact cassettes and eight-track cartridges. These last two competed for a while until the cassette won a brief victory before another revolution came along. Just as there is no connection between groove and tape, there is no continuity with compact-disc manufacture and anything which had come before; likewise the technology which leads to the MP3 player.

Each development in popular music recording has been subject to the critical judgement of the marketplace. Some have succeeded and others have failed. Eight-track cartridges and minidisks fell by the wayside but not necessarily because of any inherent faults in invention. The industry does not seem to tolerate radically different systems for long: uniformity is the norm.

And so we can trace threads of innovation both incremental and revolutionary: successive waves of creation and destruction. We can even note another of Schumpeter's predictions, the corporatisation of innovation, where the larger companies will produce several products in direct competition with themselves so that they won't be caught out. (Soap powder manufacturers have been delivering the same basic product in different formats under different brand names for years. For instance Persil, Daz, Ariel, Surf, Bold, Fairy, Dreft, Lux and Tide are available as powders, liquids, tablets and flakes and yet all of them are manufactured by either Unilever or Proctor & Gamble.)

A common feature of innovation is that it is often resisted by vested interests. Recorded music was seen to be a threat to live music back in the 1920s. 'Home taping is killing music' was the industry mantra in the 1970s and 80s.

Another upheaval is taking place; a 'disruptive innovation' from outside the industry. The digital revolution did not confine itself to the music industry; personal computer ownership has soared, a myriad of bedroom producers are selling or giving away their music on the Internet. The music industry is now desperately playing 'catch up', having lost control of both the means of production and the means of distribution. Home taping (and all forms of non-industry copying) did not kill music, it encouraged it. The future of music was never in doubt; the future of the music industry is not so certain: the pie is greater than ever but the slices are much thinner. Ironically, the best money-spinner for musicians has been a return to playing live.

There is an important qualification to make before we leave the music industry. Tracing innovation back through a narrative of connections (and disconnections) and rivalries is a very simplistic method of study. Innovation does not happen in isolation; the breaking of the circle (as we said before) happens continuously in different domains, along several time scales, interacting with economic cycles and fluctuations. Those 'gales of creative destruction' exist in a context. Back in the 1880s, there was a background of mechanical reproduction of music other than by the direct recording of performance: music boxes, steam organs and player pianos. In the 1920s, the problems of synchronising sound with moving pictures influenced innovation both ways. The rival technologies interacted; the last cylinders were actually reproductions of disc recording. Vinyl microgroove discs were reproductions of tape recordings. Tape allowed editing of the recording and so we see a shift away from live performance. In the 1970s, transistor radios, increasing car ownership and a growing concept of portable music all had parts to play in the development of cassettes and cartridges, which in turn brought about another revolution, the personal stereo. Today, the switchover from analogue to digital radio is likely to be influenced by whether the automotive industry fits DAB devices in new cars.

We have already noted the digital revolution which brought the MP3 player, but consider this: the present context includes millions of mobile phones with access to the Internet, which is capable of the simultaneous streaming of every music track ever recorded. Not only is the mighty iPod threatened, but the very concept of ownership is brought into question. When the rental is so cheap, what is the point of *ownership*, whether physical or virtual?

The often complex relationship between all these different kinds of change form the view that underpins this book: that periods of incremental advance, stability, certainty, even stagnation are interrupted by tempests that permanently alter the status quo, ushering in a brave new world.

From within the storm it's quite difficult to see what's going on and even more difficult to predict the outcome. Once the dust has settled, it should be possible to see what went on but there is a further complication. Humans, consciously and unconsciously, have a tendency never to let the truth stand in the way of a good story. The story we want to tell is always going to reflect the wider context in which we tell it. We write and re-write history to reflect our ever-changing notions of change. Heroes and villains are cast and re-cast anew.

The introduction of sound to film is regarded as a great paradigm shift that swept away the silent era in one fell swoop. According to one popular version of history, the silent star John Gilbert could not survive the transition because of his squeaky voice. In fact no one mentioned Gilbert's voice at the time; it was the dialogue that was squeaky. Elements of the legend are re-told and thereby reinforced in the 1952 film *Singin' in the Rain*. But there is a germ of truth in the story; there were winners and losers in the changeover: when Howard Hughes spent a fortune re-shooting *Hell's Angels* with sound, he sacked Greta Nissen because of her Norwegian accent, which gave Jean Harlow her big break.

Early sound-recording kit was, just like early camera equipment, not particularly mobile or robust. This led to a temporary loss of sophistication in film; early talkies* are comparatively static: no one moves far from the microphone.

There was a longer-lasting loss in this paradigm shift. The essential features of cinema today – narrative structure, rapid cutting between multiple points of view, tracking shots, special effects – all were created in an international market. The first world-famous film star, Max Linder, whom Charlie Chaplin acknowledged as 'The Master', made films which could be enjoyed far from his native France. The talkies fractured that internationalism. As the medium developed, the diffusion of new ideas, and even plots, has tended to be conducted at 'expert' level rather than directly through a common audience. Thus Akira Kurosawa's *Seven Samurai* is transmuted into *The Magnificent Seven* without the audience needing to know.

Retronyms

New products and processes bring new names to get used to. One of the attractions for first adopters of anything new is the jargon that goes with it and the exclusivity that accompanies the jargon. You can always tell that radical innovation has been in action when we have to invent new names to describe old products.

- The first motion pictures were 'movies'. Then 'talkies' came along and by the time most movies had become 'talkies' the term 'silent movie' had had to be invented.

- What we call a 'penny farthing' was just a bicycle before the introduction of the 'safety bicycle', after which it was retronymed an 'ordinary'.

- Before retail parks came along, 'high street shops' used to be just 'shops'.

- 'Reel-to-reel' used to be just 'tapes' before the invention of cassettes.

- The ubiquity of mobile phones means that an ordinary telephone is now a 'landline'.

- Pocket watches were just watches before the wristwatch.

- 'Analogue' watches used to be just 'watches'.

- The first digital watches referred to the display rather than the mechanism.

- Digital technology (which pedants insist should properly be called 'binary') is now the norm in photography and so 'ordinary' cameras are now also called 'analogue'.

- In America, before the advent of fast food, all restaurants were 'sit-down restaurants'. (In Europe we use this linguistic variation to assert our 'superiority' over those New World upstarts by insisting that any restaurant worthy of the name should have cutlery and not serve food in a bucket.)

Lots of paradigm shifts pass almost unnoticed by outsiders; never mind the distinction between incremental and abrupt changes, sometimes we don't even notice the storm; for example, knowing that the world is round is of no real relevance when you are putting up a shelf; we're all flat-earthers then! Although some changes may go unnoticed at the time in our own personal narratives, in general the more radical the change the greater the cry of 'Eureka!' from those concerned and the even greater cry of eureka from the rest of us when we finally catch up.

Sometimes paradigm shifts are chronicled that may never have even happened: Bob Dylan's decision to 'play electric' in 1965–6 is a case in point; did the audience jeer him because he had abandoned 'folk music', or because the music was too distorted to be heard or because he wouldn't play another encore? There seems to have been a part of the crowd who thought that booing Bob Dylan was part of the occasion, much like punk bands would spit and be spat at only a dozen or so years later.

The narrative is very different depending on who is telling the story. It is only to be expected that witnesses to particular events will have different perceptions of what happened, especially when that event was not perceived at the time to be as important as it later transpired. When the story is retold, the narrator tends to settle for the version most in tune with the story they wish to tell.

The Duke of Wellington, who has been described as a man who raised common sense to the level of genius, heard many different versions of the 'truth': 'The history of a battle, is not unlike the history of a ball. Some individuals may recollect all the little events of which the great result is the battle won or lost, but no individual can recollect the order in which, or the exact moment at which, they occurred, which makes all the difference as to their value or importance.'

This is a far more innocent phenomenon than history being written by the winners but can be just as misleading. The American historian Frederick Jackson Turner was also very aware that history is a movable feast: 'Each age tries to form its own conception of the past. Each age writes the history of the past anew with reference to the conditions uppermost in its own time.'

A Red Shift

In October 1562 Queen Elizabeth I fell sick with a raging fever. A German physician, Dr Burcot (a.k.a. Burchard Kranich, sometime mining engineer, alchemist and suspected charlatan), diagnosed smallpox. For his pains he was peremptorily dismissed: 'Have the knave out of my sight.' But by the next day the Queen lay close to death, her own doctors were in despair and the Council had been summoned to discuss the succession. As a last resort, the reluctant Burcot was recalled, one account says at knifepoint. He had the Queen placed by the fire, wrapped in red cloth and given a potion of his own devising. By midnight she was conscious and able to speak. As her rash faded she was left unmarked. In contrast, Lady Mary Sidney, who had been her chief companion, caught the disease and was so disfigured that she retired from the Court. (We ought to bear in mind that stories about the notoriously vain, image-conscious Queen Elizabeth, known for her heavy make-up, are not the most reliable of evidence.)

Burcot was said to have found the treatment in a 200-year-old text, the *Rosa Anglica* compiled by John of Gaddesden. John was court physician to King Edward I and claimed to have cured his son of smallpox by covering the patient and his surroundings in red. *('Deinde capiatur scarletum rubreum et involvatur variololus totaliter vel in panno alio rubeo sic ego feci de filio nobilissimi Regis Angliae quando patiebatur istos morbos et feci omniaesse rube . . .')*

So where did Gaddesden get the red treatment from?

A clue can be found in *The Canterbury Tales*, where Chaucer describes his 'verrey parfit practisour' the 'Doctour of Phisyk':

> Wel knew he the olde Esculapius,
> And Deyscorides, and eek Rufus,
> Olde Ypocras, Haly, and Galyen,
> Serapion, Razis, and Avycen,
> Avervois, Damascien, and Constantyn,
> Bernard, and Gatesden, and Gilbertyn.

Chaucer is listing the doctor's authorities from the ancient Greek god Aesculapius right up to the latest, Gaddesden [Gatesden] and Gibertus Anglicus. In amongst the others we might recognise Dioscorides, Hippocrates and Galen but it is some of the Arabic scholars who are more interesting to us on this occasion.

Avervois or Averroes is Abū 'l-Walīd Muhammad ibn Ahmad ibn Rushd, a twelfth-century Andalusian polymath.

Avycen or Avicenna is Ibn *Sīnā Balkhi, born in Bukhara, who flourished in the eleventh century.*

Razis or Rhazes is Abū Bakr Muhammad ibn Zakariyā Rāzī, who first differentiated smallpox from measles in tenth-century Baghdad.

These Islamic practitioners thought that red cloth and even red foods and drinks would draw heat out from the body and restore balance. In turn they may have been influenced by teachings from even further to the east, where the colour red is still associated with smallpox.

By the time of Elizabeth I, the Galeno/Arabic theory of medicine was in decline. Perhaps the 'red treatment' seemed a little too close to magic and that's why it had been forgotten by all but the arcane and distinctly dubious Dr Burcot. We don't hear much of it again, except in folklore. Inoculation and later vaccination became the preferred preventatives.

By the turn of the twentieth century, however, the red treatment rises from obscurity. Possibly in tune with photography and all things optical, there was an increasing interest in the therapeutic qualities of light during the nineteenth century, resulting in a short-lived craze for *blue* glass in the U.S.A.

Red light achieved respectability in 1903 when Niels Ryberg Finsen was awarded a Nobel Prize 'in recognition of his contribution to the treatment of diseases, especially *lupus vulgaris*, with concentrated light radiation, whereby he has opened a new avenue for medical science'. Specifically, red light was said to reduce smallpox scars by improving the speed at which the skin heals. All of a sudden the medieval red treatment seemed explicable in the context of modern science. Light therapy is nowadays used for all sorts of conditions from seasonal affective disorder to acne.

So we can see how a remedy which was once perfectly in tune became incommensurable with the new paradigm, before being reassessed when 'modern' science seems to offer an explanation of *how* it worked. But did the 'red treatment' actually work? Red light is, after all, very different from red bedclothes.

The short answer is of course that we will never get the chance to find out because no one catches the disease any more. We will revisit the defeat of smallpox but for the moment suffice it to say that it wasn't done by wearing a red nightshirt and drinking pomegranate juice.

Motive forces

Thomas Kuhn writes of the 'essential tension' between innovation and orthodoxy. In 2001, the American sceptic Michael Shermer, writing of 'the exquisite balance' between heresy and orthodoxy in science, coined the term 'heretic personalities' to describe those who know the rules well enough but are driven by their creative imagination to challenge assumptions and bring about paradigm shifts.

Which brings us to another serious question: what is the motive force behind change? Does change happen by chance or is it inevitable? Is it driven by individuals, whether we call them heretics, geniuses or entrepreneurs? Or is it forced by circumstance?

Traditionally, 'necessity is the mother of invention' and the arguments of Han Fei Tzu and Malthus are particularly resonant today because of worries that the limits of the earth's resources are in sight. But as this remark, widely attributed to Saudi Oil Minister Sheikh Zaki Yamani during the oil crisis of the 1970s, points out: 'The Stone Age did not end because of a lack of stone.'

We will examine the interaction of chance and inevitability later but it might be worth also starting to think about the character of innovators themselves. Why is it that certain people respond creatively rather than adaptively? This creative response is what Schumpeter identifies as the entrepreneurial spirit.

As to those individuals who are moved by this spirit, Schumpeter had this to say:

> Everyone is an entrepreneur only when he actually 'carries out new combinations,' and loses that character as soon as he has built up his business, when he settles down to running it as other people run their businesses. This is the rule, of course, and hence it is just as rare for anyone always to remain an entrepreneur throughout the decades of his active life as it is for a businessman never to have a moment in which he is an entrepreneur, to however modest a degree.
>
> (*The Theory of Economic Development*, 1934)

A popular view of the entrepreneur is of an innovator driven by personal gain, but money is rarely the exclusive or even the prime motivation of many famous serial inventors and discoverers. For example, the Wright Brothers already had a successful bicycle business from which they diverted time and money to pursue the uncertain returns of powered flight. Steve Jobs, the CEO of Apple Inc., was quoted as saying, 'Being the richest man in the cemetery doesn't matter to me . . . Going to bed at night saying we've done something wonderful . . . that's what matters to me.' Alec Jeffreys shares the sentiment: 'I never came into academia and scientific research for money, I did it for love.'

According to American academic Scott A. Shane (*The Illusions of Entrepreneurship*, 2008), typical entrepreneurs work longer hours for less money than had they worked for someone else and the most common reason people start businesses is to avoid working for somebody else.

There are those, like Shane, who define entrepreneurship as almost synonymous with business start-ups. But not everyone who starts a business is avoiding working for somebody else – some people do not have that option. A recent worldwide study of people who survive on less than a dollar a day points out that 'The poor don't see becoming an entrepreneur as something to aspire to.'

'Perhaps the many businesses of the poor are less a testimony to their entrepreneurial spirit than a symptom of the dramatic failure of the economies in which they live to provide them with something better.'

Entrepreneurs like these would happily trade their independence for the stability of a salary: 'The enterprises of the poor often seem more a way to buy a job when a more conventional employment opportunity is not available.' (Abhijit Banerjee and Esther Duflo, *Poor Economics*, 2011)

It is quite limiting to measure entrepreneurial success solely in monetary terms.

The authors take a broader view: just as the costs of innovation are not necessarily financial, so the benefits of innovation are not always expressed as the bottom line in an account book. For example, where welfare is the prime consideration, the term 'social entrepreneurship' is used to describe actions which increase 'social capital'. Lower crime figures, more jobs, less pollution, increased life expectancy, quality of life, even world peace, liberty and the pursuit of happiness can be the goals of social entrepreneurship.

The authors describe the entrepreneurial spirit as that which identifies and creates opportunities and then takes actions to realise new ideas in an appropriate domain. *

So now we have an awareness of the way change seems to occur and a suggestion of the reasons why certain humans act as the agents of change; we might even have begun to wonder whether *anyone* can be like that. But we are getting ahead of ourselves. First we need to look at the nature of orthodoxy. *We need a deeper understanding of the difference between what we know and what we think we know.*

*In such a way as to bring value to that domain in terms which that domain values.

Orthodoxy and common sense

> The greatest obstacle to discovery is not ignorance – it is the illusion of knowledge.
>
> (Daniel J. Boorstin)

The simplest way we learn is by trial and error, and about the first thing we notice is cause and effect. We string these causes and effects into a narrative, which, as we have seen, may or may not be particularly reliable.*

When we gather new experiences we compare them to old experiences, look for analogies and use metaphors and similes to describe them. (Quite how limited we are is confirmed by the number of times we use the phrase 'Tastes like chicken.')

The distinction between metaphor and simile is quite fine: take the story of Phaeton, the first boy racer, as told in Ovid's *Metamorphoses*: 'My dad's the sun-god,' Phaeton boasted to his friends, who didn't believe him. When his dad Helios (or Phoebus or Apollo in other versions) promised him anything as proof, Phaeton took the sun's fiery chariot for a spin. He drove too high, freezing the world, and then too low, burning the deserts of Africa. Eventually Zeus had to intervene and Phaeton crashed into a river and drowned. It is a sad story and a cautionary tale.

The point is, from the ancients, who may have believed that the sun was literally a fiery chariot, to some moderns, who believe the story may actually be a folk-memory of an asteroid impact, most of us in between use the story to describe something similar. The sun is a fiery chariot (metaphor) or the sun is like a fiery chariot (simile); Phaeton is like a boy racer or Phaeton is a boy racer. Quite how alike things may be is the realm of analogy, where, as will be seen, we find our best ideas.

With the story of Phaeton we also see that people tend to describe the world by use of metaphors that reflect the society they come from and the technology they use every day. The word technology is used here in its widest sense, both concrete and abstract; thus the technology seen in a pencil is not just the pencil itself. It

---

*The ability to link cause and effect erroneously is not limited to humanity. Ivan Petrovich Pavlov was awarded a Nobel Prize in 1904 in recognition of his work on the physiology of digestion which included his observation of 'conditioning' in his subsequently famous dogs. In 1947 the American behavioural psychologist B. F. Skinner described an experiment in which he showed how 'to demonstrate a sort of superstition' in pigeons. *Time* magazine (September 20th 1971) records him explaining one of his techniques for conditioning behaviour:

> One of the most powerful schedules, the variable-ratio schedule, is characteristic of all gambling systems. The gambler cannot be sure the next play will win, but a certain mean ratio of plays to wins is maintained. This is the way a dishonest gambler hooks his victim. At first the victim is permitted to win fairly often. Eventually he continues to play when he is not winning at all. With this technique, it is possible to create a pathological gambler out of a simple bird like a pigeon.

Skinner had 'previous' with conditioned pigeons, having suggested using them as a guidance system for missiles during the Second World War. He later complained: 'Our problem was no one would take us seriously.'

includes both the ability to make one and all of the allied technologies used in its manufacture, and also the knowledge of what one can be used for. (Although sucking a pencil as a source of inspiration doesn't count: that's not technology; that's just wishful thinking.)

So-called primitive societies are comfortable with natural metaphors such as fire, clay, rivers, trees, animals, etc. Philosophies developed from nature are with us to this day. Wood and water; light and dark (and twilight); metal and fire. In western civilisation, the ancient division into earth, air, fire and water pervaded science, particularly medicine, well into the Enlightenment and still exists in popular culture from daily horoscopes to an ordinary pack of playing cards. For all those things with which we have difficulty there is the fifth element, *the quintessence*, the void, the world of ideas.

As technology develops so metaphors change: we've seen the chariot; what about *Bifrost*, the rainbow bridge in Norse mythology? One metaphor, the bow, is joined by another, the bridge. And the eyes could never be the windows or mirrors of the soul before those last were invented. If the technology is short lived, an apposite metaphor can soon be dated in both senses of the word: in the 1850s Walt Whitman referenced early photography to describe his poetry as 'a daguerreotype of inner being'.

Spinning wheels and looms are joined by more complex machinery; mills which grind slow but exceeding small. The cogs and gears of mills are also used on a smaller scale to measure the sun and moon and stars. The astrolabe that measures also becomes the model of the universe in the form of the orrery. Clockwork technology shows the movement of heaven's crystal spheres.

The technology of the pump describes the circulation of the blood, replacing the tidal ebb and flow. The steam engine provides the power.

As the pace of change increases, it is harder and harder to keep up with the fashions in metaphors. Electricity replaces steam, nuclear replaces the internal combustion engine.

The world we see today is described in terms of *our* latest technology, primarily computers and genetics. We describe ourselves as hardwired or genetically programmed.

It is not too much to generalise that *the worldview of any society resonates with the technology of that society*. But metaphor is merely a language we use to explain the world; it is not a model of the world. If we confuse the two we will remain no different from the peasant who imagined his life as a thread, being spun, woven and eventually cut off by the Fates on an eternal loom.

We use lines of narrative and metaphor to connect our experience and observation in the simplest way possible to form a view of the world that works for us and call it common sense. With hindsight, it is easy for us to see how people are 'mistaken' in

Overview

their worldview and even sneer at their 'ignorance' but we have to remember what Kuhn called the 'incommensurability of paradigms'. What seems like common sense to us would not be common sense to them. The widely quoted L. P. Hartley said plainly in *The Go-Between* (1953), 'The past is a foreign country, they do things differently there.'

Ancient peoples all over the world looked to the heavens and joined the dots of the stars into shapes and pictures that reflected their worldview. Of course from any other place in the universe these stars do not even appear to be connected. The constellations tell us far more about the peoples who named them than about actual astronomy.

Graphic artists are well aware of the human tendency to join up the dots prematurely. For example, an established technique to make it easier to copy an image accurately is to turn the original upside down. Because the artist does not immediately recognise the image, they are more likely to draw what they actually see rather than what they think they see. The technique also removes fear: most artists would hesitate to copy, for example, a line drawing by Albrecht Dürer or a print by Hokusai but are in fact quite competent to copy the lines as long as they don't know what they represent.

As will become apparent, one of the central themes of this book is the importance of the ability to look at things from a different point of view.

When our worldview alters we rewrite the narrative and change the metaphors. In 1961 Serge Moscovici published *La psychanalyse, son image, son public*, a study showing how the ideas of psychoanalysis were received in very different ways by different segments of French society. Moscovici identified two universes: the *reified* one of science where procedures and rules give rise to knowledge and the *consensual* one of 'social representation' where the ideas from the world of science are transformed into 'common sense'.

Common Sense

Surely we know what that means; it's *common sense*, isn't it? Common sense is usually understood as the direct opposite of whatever blindingly obvious stupidity is being perpetrated by any given politician/child/motorist at any particular time.

In fact common sense is quite hard to pin down, because the word 'common' has several meanings in English. It can mean 'shared by', 'ordinary', or 'inferior'.

When Leonardo Da Vinci says, 'Common sense is that which judges the things given to it by other senses,' he is following in the steps of Ibn Sina (Avicenna) and Aristotle in identifying the *sensus communis*.

Later philosophers use a different common sense against sceptics who insist that we can never be sure of anything. When G. E. Moore says (to paraphrase),

'When I wave my hands in front of me it's bloody obvious that they exist,' he is making a philosophical claim that you can know something without proving it.

But it's the everyday, practical and anti-intellectual sense that Lord Chesterfield means when he says, 'Common sense is the best sense I know of,' and it's frustration at human folly that makes people from Voltaire to Frank Lloyd Wright and Will Rogers claim that 'Common sense ain't that common.'

The French distinguish between *sens commun* and *bon sens*, good judgement. As Raymond Chandler points out, however, that sort of common sense 'always speaks too late. Common sense is the guy who tells you ought to have had your brakes relined last week before you smashed a front end this week.' It's that hindsight bias again.

When Thomas Huxley read *Origin of Species*, he couldn't believe he had been so stupid as not to have thought of it himself. That common sense is the expression of a paradigm shift, recognised by Henry Ward Beecher: 'The philosophy of one century is the common sense of the next.'

Common sense is also a collection of those beliefs that can be held by all of us without resort to too much philosophy or religion: 'common knowledge'.

The danger of relying on common sense is the certainty that usually comes with it.

Dr Samuel Johnson (not generally thought of as a fool) was certain that swallows were hibernating birds. Linnaeus shared the opinion. Gilbert White, the father of English natural history, who was well aware of migration, nevertheless spent many fruitless hours digging sand martin burrows, trying to discover the truth.

After all, what is more ridiculous: that birds might hibernate as other creatures were known to, or that they should be able to navigate their 'bird-brains' all the way, thousands of miles to Africa, in the space of a few weeks, non-stop?

Albert Einstein (among others) is supposed to have defined common sense as 'the collection of prejudices acquired by age eighteen'.

A final observation from René Descartes: 'Nothing is more fairly distributed than common sense: no one thinks he needs more of it than he already has!'

Common sense must be one of those irregular grammatical expressions:

- I have plenty of common sense.
- You haven't got enough common sense.
- They haven't got any common sense.

Our mindset changes along with what we call our common sense. As Kuhn pointed out, there is a tendency to rewrite the narrative to render such changes invisible. Occasionally we find a snapshot of the past that reveals the distance travelled.

In the early twelfth century the English monk Adelard of Bath returned to his native country after years of travel and study. The Norman web of power and influence stretched throughout the Mediterranean, interacting with the Arab world from Spain through Sicily all the way to Antioch in Asia Minor. Adelard translated Euclid into Latin from an Arabic version of the Greek original. He wrote treatises on the abacus and the astrolabe. He was the final link in a long chain that brought the concept of zero to Britain from India.

A fascinating glimpse into the worldview of one of the finest minds of the age can be found in the dialogue *Quaestiones Naturales*. Adelard lists 76 questions representing the cutting edge of his knowledge. They show what he knows and what he wants to know. Some appear to be simple with hindsight; some seem bizarre; while others are still hard to answer.*

- He wants to know why the sea is salty, and where the winds and the tides come from.
- He wants to understand the relationship between thunder and lightning.
- He knows that the earth is spherical but how does it move and why is it held in space?
- He asks whether the stars are animate and if so what do they eat?
- How can we blow both hot and cold from the same mouth?
- He wants to *comprehend* plant propagation: he knows that cuttings and grafts work; he doesn't know how.
- He wonders whether beasts have souls and why all men die.

Adelard's world of four elements, humours and crystal spheres may have been superseded but we can help him with quite a few of his questions. We can tell him how plant grafting works, we can explain sound waves and echoes and we can even give an account of our progress in the field of atomic motion. But some of the basics remain elusive.

Adelard knew that reason, imagination and memory are functions of the brain but it is only recently that serious scientific progress has been made in explaining how the brain works and what exactly we mean by intelligence.

Adelard may seem a distant figure but on at least one point he connects with us directly. He translated some of the works of the ninth-century mathematician and astronomer Al-Khwarizmi, who was responsible for introducing the joys of algebra *(al-jabr)* to the west, and whose name was translated as Algoritmi, the origin of our *algorithm,* which brings us right back to problem solving.

*The reader might care to consider which questions Adelard *fails* to ask? What questions would represent the cutting edge of our knowledge?

Problem Solving

A better understanding of our worldview (our orthodoxy) allows us to seek answers beyond it, while designing solutions that will resonate within. So now we are in a position to ask the simple question, 'Where do ideas come from?' (The question of precisely what ideas are is way beyond the scope of this book!)

It is sometimes thought that ideas come out of thin air; that genius is 'inspired' from the outside. Poets and painters seek their 'muse'. Words like 'insight' and 'illumination' are used, providing neither insight nor illumination nor any real explanation of *how* the process works.

But there is a more practical and straightforward way of studying human ingenuity.

If for a moment we put to one side the notion that these moments of discovery are the result of some kind of outside intervention, and if we assume that these innovators are not *fundamentally* different from the mass of humanity, and instead examine *how* we think, we may understand a little better how we solve problems, how we make decisions and why we make so many mistakes.

Not only should we be able to explain exactly where ideas come from but we might begin to pin down that elusive concept, creativity.

How we solve problems

We have pointed out that we learn by trial and error. Ordinarily we re-use previous experiences to solve problems; we do what was successful last time.

The psychologist Max Wertheimer (1880–1943) called this 're-productive thinking'. All of which sounds like 'common sense'.

What about when this repetition does not work, when we are faced with a problem we have not seen before? We need to discover a different response.

First, it is impossible to deny the role of accidental discovery. The Austrian physicist and philosopher Ernst Mach states the argument unequivocally:

> We see, thus, it is by accidental circumstances, that is, by such as lie without his purpose, foresight, and power, that man is gradually led to the acquaintance of improved means of satisfying his wants. Let the reader picture to himself the genius of a man who could have foreseen without the help of accident that clay handled in the ordinary manner would produce a useful cooking utensil! The majority of the inventions made in the early stages of civilisation, including language, writing, money, and the rest, could not have been the product of deliberate methodical reflection for the simple reason that no idea of their value and significance could have been had except from their practical use.
>
> (Inaugural lecture delivered on assuming the Professorship of the History and Theory of Inductive Science in the University of Vienna, October 20th 1895)

We can see, for example, that a tree that has fallen across a stream by accident solves the problem of crossing the stream. Where the problem has not been solved in this way, an intelligent person might move a fallen log or even chop one down specially to make a bridge deliberately. Thus reason builds on chance to hone and improve innovation. This sort of thinking requires imagination in that we can *see* the solution but it is still repetition and is not what we commonly mean by creativity.

The pioneer French psychologist Théodule-Armand Ribot put his finger on a defining quality of creativity – it has to be new: *'L'imagination créatrice exige du nouveau: c'est sa marque propre et essentielle'* (*Essai sur l'imagination créatrice,* 1900).

So when trial and error does not work we must look for new solutions by re-presenting the problem, restructuring it, using our imagination.

Wertheimer called this 'productive thinking'. This is the creative part of problem solving; this is when we say 'Aha!'

For some reason we don't call this 'common sense', but instead use words like 'insight', 'inspiration', even 'genius', depending on how good an idea we think it is. Genius is a very troublesome word, which we will return to later. For now, however, let's note that we use the word when we are taken aback by ideas of such quality that we cannot measure them in ordinary terms. We use the word at the very moment of our changing perception, precisely because of the incommensurability of paradigms. But we shall see that ideas do not 'come out of nowhere': when someone says 'new' they nearly always mean 'new to me'. Also, when we look back we shall see that although what we call genius is always characterised by extraordinary quality, that very quality is often simply the result of a selection from quantity.

All of us (or very nearly all) use imagination to create new concepts from old. *Therefore: we are all creative, to a greater or lesser extent.*

Most of the time we do this automatically and almost unconsciously.

From our bank of experience we generate and evaluate ideas so quickly that the process seems almost instantaneous. If we don't like the idea, we think again, gathering more facts, searching our memory, finding similarities and analogies, generating more ideas and evaluating once more. We repeat this procedure until we reach a solution we do like.

This model sounds quite mechanical, so it might be worth asking the question:

How do machines solve problems?

Quite apart from the many myths and legends of statues that come to life, there has been a long history of machines that mimic humans.

There is an account written in China in the third century BC of a mechanical man built by the artificer Yan-Shi at the court of King Mu Wang.

There is the story of the bronze giant Talos who guarded the island of Crete until the Argonauts discovered how to drain the molten lead-like blood from his vein.

We are on more certain ground looking at the achievements of Al-Jazari, the author of a *Book of Knowledge of Ingenious Mechanical Devices* in 1206, which gives descriptions and drawings of fifty devices, ranging from clocks and fountains to a band of programmable robot musicians. Although some of his devices appear frivolous, the design and construction techniques illustrate groundbreaking innovation. For example, Al-Jazari is the first engineer to demonstrate the use of crankshafts and connecting rods. But automata imitate bodies not minds. The fascination of Mary Shelley's *Frankenstein* (1818) is the creation of a new mind in a reconstructed body. The subtitle 'The Modern Prometheus' reveals the scale of Victor Frankenstein's ambition; Prometheus was the Titan who gave fire to mankind after stealing it from the gods. In both cases arrogance and pride result in inevitable unpleasantness; *hubris* brings forth *nemesis*.

In Victorian times, Charles Babbage's Difference Engines were the first programmable devices, but it was only in the twentieth century that artificial intelligence became a realistic prospect.

Alan Turing, famous for his part in code-breaking exploits at Bletchley Park during the Second World War, is also regarded as a founder of computer science. In the 1930s he recognised that any mathematical problem ought to be solvable by a theoretical machine following a specific series of instructions or algorithms. Advances in electronics made the construction of such machines possible and Turing was at the heart of the development of the first true computers.

In 1950, Turing proposed the test of artificial intelligence which bears his name: if a human, communicating by text only, cannot tell whether the correspondent is human or machine, then that machine can be said to be thinking.

Advances in neuroscience, the development of information theory, an understanding of feedback loops and cybernetics and, most significantly, the invention of the digital computer led to serious research into artificial intelligence.

The term 'artificial intelligence' was first coined for the Dartmouth College Summer Research Project on Artificial Intelligence in New Hampshire, USA in 1956. John McCarthy, then in Dartmouth's mathematics department, chose the name so that there would be no doubt about the dynamic, new scientific field's objective: to simulate human intelligence.

The conference proposal included the statement: 'Every aspect of learning or any other feature of intelligence can be so precisely described that a machine can be made to simulate it.'

By the 1960s, these pioneers had high hopes: 'Machines will be capable, within twenty years, of doing any work a man can do' (H. A. Simon). 'Within a generation . . . the problem of creating "artificial intelligence" will substantially be solved' (Marvin Minsky).

The early optimism of A.I. researchers was blunted by the funding/breakthrough dynamic that so bedevils innovation. (As research reveals the complexity of the task, the hoped-for breakthrough recedes and funding disappears.) Their ambition, however, is undiminished as they seek to replace questions such as 'What sort of things are emotions?' with 'What process does each emotion involve?' and 'How could machines perform such processes?'

A model of problem solving which has been very successful for machines is case-based reasoning, originally developed by Roger Schank and others at Yale University as part of their work on artificial intelligence. When faced with a problem, the first reaction is to recall a similar case and approach the problem accordingly. This is formalised into four stages:

1. RETRIEVE (from memory) the most similar case or cases.

2. RE-USE the information and knowledge in that case to solve the problem.

3. REVISE the proposed solution (effectively, create a new solution by adjusting an old one).

4. RETAIN (commit to memory) the parts of this experience likely to be useful for future problem solving, i.e. learn.

A machine can do this effectively by the sheer power of its computation but is limited by the quality of its knowledge base. Where the knowledge base is finite, computers ought to outperform humans every time; their capacity for error is smaller, their logic inexorable. That is why they're so good at chess, but the ability to play chess at grandmaster level is one that most of us throughout history have managed quite well without.

For more abstract problem solving, computers are still some way behind humans, despite the fact that humans are far less logical than machines.

A simple sentence such as 'Get, set, go' reveals the extent of the computer's task. Without knowing any context, virtually all English speakers understand the meaning immediately. However, there are 289 definitions of 'get' in the *Oxford English Dictionary*, 464 for 'set' (the most for any word) and 368 for 'go'. That produces 49,347,328 combinations from three words. What the computer needs is what we call 'common knowledge'. And that is why A.I. researchers are interested in building up databases of 'common-sense knowledge'.

Most of us accept that a computer can only be as good as the information programmed into it: the GIGO principle (Garbage In Garbage Out). This would seem obvious but it has needed explanation from the very start of computer science.

> On two occasions I have been asked, – 'Pray, Mr. Babbage, if you put into the machine wrong figures, will the right answers come out?' – I am not able rightly to comprehend the kind of confusion of ideas that could provoke such a question.
>
> (Charles Babbage, 1864)

So what about humans? Babbage's visitors might have been particularly stupid but they're not the only ones with a 'confusion of ideas'. The underlying rationale behind much of our behaviour is little understood.

Evolutionary psychologists see human behaviour developing as a reaction to changing environmental conditions.

Cultural materialists, following the lead of American anthropologist Marvin Harris see human cultures as a product of problem solving in response to Malthusian pressures.

Cost/benefit analyses of behaviour lie behind numerous game theories and some, such as 'the prisoners' dilemma', have risen to the giddy heights of the television game show.

The prisoners' dilemma describes a situation where partners in crime are each separately offered clemency in return for betraying the other. They know that if both of them stay silent then they will both probably go free – but if both of them betray then both will lose. The scenario is similar to that of the tragedy of the commons described earlier – narrow short-term self-interest leads to mutual betrayal. If, however, the game is repeated, the tendency is to temper self-interest with the fear of punishment in the next round. As well as offering us all hope for the future, for some, this 'iterated prisoners' dilemma' suggests an evolutionary driver of altruism.

There is a whole branch of economics seeking to explain everyday decision making in logical, usually monetary terms. Steven D. Levitt and Stephen J. Dubner (authors of *Freakonomics*, 2005) call themselves 'rogue economists' while journalist Tim Harford prefers the tag 'undercover'. In their book *Nudge* (2008), Richard Thaler and Cass Sunstein seek to alter social behaviour through behavioural economics.*

*An eminently sensible overview of this branch of social engineering can be found within a discussion document commissioned by the [British] Cabinet Office entitled MINDSPACE: Influencing behaviour through public policy (Institute for Government, 2010).

The relationship between emotion and cognition complicates matters enormously. Any proficient salesman or conjuror is able to exploit our unreasonable reasoning. On top of which most of us are able to hold at least two or more conflicting opinions at the same time; cognitive dissonance must be very difficult for a computer to understand.

> The most important thing to understand is that the brain is 'context bound.' It is not a logical system like a computer that processes only programmed information; it does not produce preordained outcomes like a clock. Rather it is a selectional system that, through pattern recognition, puts things together in always novel ways. It is this selectional repertoire in the brain that makes each individual unique, that accounts for the ability to create poetry and music, that accounts for all the differences that arise from the same biological apparatus— the body and the brain. There is no singular mapping to create the mind; there is, rather, an unforetold plurality of possibilities. In a logical system, novelty and unforeseen variation are often considered to be noise. In a selectional system such diversity actually provides the opportunity for favorable selection.
>
> (American neuroscientist and Nobel Laureate Gerald Edelman, speaking in 2004)

The very fact that this whole area is so new and controversial exposes the limitations of the brain-as-computer metaphor. For a machine truly to replicate human decision making, all the nuances of emotion and instinct would have to be digitised and it could be said that the society which possessed that capability might have achieved its ends with yet to be imagined technology and would have little need for simulated human minds with all their inconsistencies.

> It would be possible to describe everything scientifically, but it would make no sense; it would be without meaning, as if you described a Beethoven symphony as a variation of wave pressure.
>
> (Albert Einstein)

Using a technology undreamt of at the time, however, digitised Beethoven is now available to all at the click of a mouse. It was probably inconceivable to Einstein that anyone would *want* to listen to a full symphony orchestra playing 'Beethoven's greatest hits' while jogging or travelling on the Tube, while you're stuck in a lift or, even worse, while you're hanging on the telephone to a call centre half a world away.

Once more we can see the incommensurability of paradigms, with a warning for us all: if the past is 'another country' then we ought to recognise that the future will be just as 'foreign' and when we get there they also will do things differently.

On a far less accessible subject (quantum electrodynamics), the mathematician Paul Dirac offered this advice: 'If one is a research worker, one mustn't believe in anything too strongly; one must always be prepared that various beliefs one has had for a long time may be overthrown.'

The British philosopher of science Nicholas Maxwell takes changes in physics to illustrate the logical, if somewhat uncomfortable, conclusion:

> A glance at the history of physics reveals that ideas have changed dramatically over time. In the seventeenth century there was the idea that the universe consists of corpuscles, minute billiard balls, which interact only by contact. This gave way to the idea that the universe consists of point-particles surrounded by rigid, spherically symmetrical fields of force, which in turn gave way to the idea that there is one unified self-interacting field, varying smoothly throughout space and time. Nowadays we have the idea that everything is made up of minute quantum strings embedded in ten or eleven dimensions of space-time.
>
> Some kind of assumption along these lines must be made but, given the historical record, and given that any such assumption concerns the ultimate nature of the universe, that of which we are most ignorant, *it is only reasonable to conclude that it is almost bound to be false*. [Our emphasis]
>
> (*From Knowledge to Wisdom*, online extract, 2010)

Knowledge and knowing

No one teaches us how to think, we do it unconsciously. Just as our hearts pump and our lungs breathe, our brains think and learn. And the knowledge that we pick up as we go through life is not all the same; we accumulate skills as well as facts. Teaching and learning are subtly different.

Here is the philosopher Ludwig Wittgenstein on acquiring the sort of knowledge that leads towards 'expert judgment':

> Can one learn this knowledge? Yes; some can learn it. Not, however, by taking a course of study in it, but through *'experience'*. – Can someone else be a man's teacher in this? Certainly. From time to time he gives him the right *tip*. – This is what 'learning' and 'teaching' are like here. – What one acquires here is not a technique; one learns correct judgments. There are also rules, but they do not form a system, and only experienced people can apply them rightly. Unlike calculating rules.
>
> (*Philosophical Transactions*, 1953 tr Anscumbe)

Rules, or procedures, do play a large part in transferring knowledge. This example is from the social services: 'The most obvious strength of procedures is that they are a way of formulating best practice in carrying out a task so that the wisdom of experienced staff is readily disseminated throughout the organisation and variation in the quality and type of service received is reduced.'

But: 'The strength mentioned above that newcomers can quickly learn to follow procedures even when they do not understand them is also a weakness. It can lead to people just following procedures and not trying to become better' (Professor Eileen Munro, *The Munro Review of Child Protection – Interim Report*, 2011).

So it is possible to have knowledge without understanding; for example, is it possible to learn to cook from the manual alone? Boiling an egg could be described like a scientific experiment: the result should be predictable and repeatable. But frying an egg to the required standard would surely involve a deal of trial and error before you got it right.

Some recipe books are extremely prescriptive – exact quantities, timings and temperatures – and many people swear by them. But, just like the artist copying a classic line drawing, what you are aiming for is the faithful replication of someone else's creation.

Other recipe books, however, are far looser and more open to interpretation; they assume a certain level of competence.

The following is taken from the collection of medieval recipes known as *The Forme of Cury:*

Tart de Bry: Take a Crust ynche depe in a trape. take zolkes of ayren rawe & chese ruayn & medle it & þe zolkes togyder and do þerto powdour gyngur sugur safroun and salt. Do it in a trape, bake it and serue it forth.

(Brie Tart: take an inch deep crust in a tray. Take raw egg yolks and [ruayn] cheese. Mix the cheese and yolks together and add powdered ginger, sugar, saffron and salt. Bake it in a tray and serve it forth.)

There is very little information in terms of method and no information at all in terms of quantities, times or temperature. Some recipes in *The Forme of Cury* include actual quantities of ingredients but these can be less helpful than was originally meant, as, for example, one which includes two pennyworth of anise. For this one you are expected to know what 'ruayn' cheese is and possess the skills required to cook the tart; if you don't have that understanding you have no business reading the book. Any cook worth their salt will be able to cook from this recipe and yet every tart will be different.

As a contrast we can go back another thousand years to the second-century Greek physician Galen in his treatise on the power of foods. Galen gives more explicit instructions because he is addressing a wider audience with a different agenda. When he gives a recipe for eggs with olive oil, wine and fish sauce, he insists that the eggs should not be overcooked as that would be bad for the digestion. He gives an unambiguous description of the method, what we would call a bain-marie; and tells us when they're done: moderately firm.

(Eggs in wine and fish sauce sounds pretty unpalatable but think of prairie oysters or bull shots; anything with Worcestershire Sauce, which, among other ingredients, contains fermented anchovies.)

So when we are trying to transfer knowledge it might help to be conscious of what is expected of the recipients. If we expect them to know next to nothing then detailed instruction is essential – and if so that explicit information has to be absolutely correct.

It used to be said it was not possible to pin down experiences such as colour and taste and that they could only be described to someone else by reference to a mutually recognised standard; and so we commonly use expressions like 'pillar-box red' and, once more, 'tastes like chicken'. Stricter definitions are available. It is now possible to define the colour red scientifically, as for instance, radiant energy of wavelengths between approximately 630 and 750 nanometres, although even that definition is less than precise as it does not include variations in shade, hue, gloss, etc. But artificial flavours and scents can have an existence as mere formulae: Colonel Sanders keeps his recipe written down and knows exactly what chicken should taste like. In theory it may be possible to describe everything scientifically but the potential for error is enormous: two pennyworth of anise is hardly an S.I. unit of measurement; even 'one egg' is variable according to the chicken. And it is still difficult to know exactly how different minds perceive identical experiences.

If, conversely, we expect a certain level of proficiency then we have to trust the recipients to interpret the knowledge effectively, while tolerating or indeed expecting some creative input.

The Good Soldier Švejk (commonly spelled Schweik) is a character created by Czech writer Jaroslav Hašek (1883–1923). As a soldier of the Austro-Hungarian Army during the First World War, Schweik continually undermines authority by the simple expedient of doing exactly what he is told to do. Whether this is through stupidity or as a deliberate act of subversion is not always clear.

Any organisation with inflexible procedures can be destroyed by the actions of a few Schweiks. There is a view that their survival depends upon the regular and often tolerated disregard of those rules. The most famous example is probably the disabled British seaman Admiral Lord Nelson during the battle of Copenhagen in 1801. When his commanding officer signalled to 'leave off action', he responded, 'Well, damn me if I do! . . . I have only one eye – I have a right to be blind sometimes.' Raising his telescope to the blind eye, he added, 'I really do not see the signal!' At the end of the day he prepared to face the music with the words 'I have fought contrary to orders and I shall perhaps be hanged.' Had he lost he probably would have been court-martialled; as it was the Danish surrendered and Nelson's reputation was further enhanced.

But we ought to bear in mind that individuals and groups vary: the competence of a Chinese noodle chef is quite unlike that of a French patissier, even though both of them are using the same basic materials, fat, flour and eggs.

The scientist and philosopher Michael Polanyi (1891–1976) formed the concept of 'tacit knowing'. It is summed up by his aphorism 'We know more than we can tell.' Tacit knowing is often described as *know-how* as opposed to *know-about*.

Tacit knowledge and knowing must be learnt; it cannot simply be taught. An easy example is swimming: all the instruction books in the world will not *teach* us to swim; it is only by practical experience that we can *learn* to swim. And it is only with continuing practice that we improve our skill. *We have to get our feet wet*.

Tacit knowledge and knowing becomes even more interesting when we look beyond individuals and recognise the phenomenon within groups and organisations. Tacit skills can vary between groups which are superficially similar. For example, every orchestra will interpret an identical score in a very different fashion, even when the same conductor wields the baton. And the tacit knowing of a group can produce a qualitative difference in performance. Every week we see sports teams that somehow perform beyond expectations. The team which exceeds the sum of its parts can defeat the team which does not play together.

The concept of tacit knowing raises some interesting questions:

- To what extent can tacit knowledge be codified or articulated and so become explicit knowledge?
- How can we assess the house style or ethos of a group of individuals?
- How do we pass on skills that we find difficult to measure or even define?

In practice the challenge must be to balance the need for actual experience with the expectation that explicit knowledge can be effectively interpreted. It might be a complex calculation: we may wish to take into account the creative possibilities and encourage innovation, or, for perfectly understandable reasons, we may not. (There are plenty of times and circumstances when the last thing we need is free-thinking creativity – the dentist's chair, for example, is not an ideal place for improvisation.)

Most fundamental, however, is the ability to recognise when we do not possess the knowledge, of whatever kind, to make progress, and for that we need the acquisition and retention of an open mind.

Practical common sense

Having recognised our own difficulties, it's worth returning once more to artificial intelligence researchers to see how they respond to the limitations of computer reasoning. As we saw, they are building up databases of 'common-sense knowledge' to use in what they call 'common-sense reasoning':

- Reasoning with knowledge that we cannot *prove*.

- Tolerating that uncertainty in our knowledge.

- Coming to conclusions without complete knowledge.

- The ability to revise those decisions or beliefs as better knowledge becomes available.

Human Common-Sense Reasoning

An incident on the football field: the striker goes down, rolling and writhing into the penalty area; the defender backs out of the area protesting his innocence; the ball rolls free, the linesman's flag stays down and the referee waves play on. The crowd is in uproar, the commentators are in uproar as well; either it was a foul or it was not. Either the defender gave away a free kick or he did not; and if he did it inside the area then it's a penalty. If it wasn't a foul then the striker is guilty of simulation and must receive at least a yellow card, if not a sending off. The referee has obviously 'bottled it' by failing to make a decision.

But let's look at it from the referee's point of view. It's a prime case of having to reason with incomplete information. He cannot prove who was at fault; his assistants did not see anything and this sport does not allow referral to a video umpire. He needs to make a decision quickly and so he looks at the bigger picture. Will the outcome of the match be affected either way by his decision? Quite possibly, especially if he awards a penalty or a sending off. But the incident occupied fewer than 30 seconds out of 90 minutes. And as the match progresses he can use the information gained to make a better assessment of the players involved and referee accordingly. And so he *does* make a decision, which is to tolerate uncertainty, trusting that the refereeing panel will agree with him and give him the next match. Of course, what often happens is that with the players, coaches and crowd all baying for his blood and with the whole incident being replayed in slow motion on the big screen, the referee, in a vain attempt to restore his authority, totally overreacts to the next incident and once more calls his parentage into question. That's common-sense reasoning, and that's what machines find so hard to do. And that's why, despite all the emphasis on winning or losing, it is in fact *how* the game is played that keeps us humans watching. That and of course the pleasure of having someone to blame!

The structure of intellect

Despite the theoretical similarities between human brains and computers, in practical terms we have to acknowledge the differences. For a start we have very different origins. The history of computers is well documented; we know how they work. The study of how the brain works is really still in its infancy. The first undergraduate course in neuroscience was only offered as recently as 1973. (Amherst College, USA.) The structure and processes of the brain, its relationship to the mind and the nature of consciousness itself are at the absolute cutting edge of human understanding, and interpretations of neuroscience are bound to leave the 'reified' world and try to enter the 'consensual' public domain. Recall our assertion that 'the worldview of any society resonates with the technology of that society'. One example would be the study of differences between the two hemispheres of the brain which won Roger Wolcott Sperry the Nobel Prize for Medicine in 1981. Moscovici and Hewstone (1983) studied the social representation of split-brain research, as a *prime* case of how science may find itself transformed into an ideology far removed from the original findings.

Advances in neuroscience are going to change the way we think about ourselves, but we don't *need* to know all about frontal lobes, cortices or synapses to be able to use our brains more effectively. After all you don't need to understand how a bicycle works in order to ride one.

But we will need a working hypothesis and will use the following description of the functions of intelligence as a basic model. J. P. Guilford (1897–1987) proposed a structure of intellect divided into general processes or operations:

- Cognition: the ability to recognise, discover and comprehend information.
- Memory: the ability to record, retain and recall information.
- Divergent production: the ability to produce multiple solutions to a problem.
- Convergent production: the ability to deduce a single solution to a problem.
- Evaluation: the ability to assess the validity of a solution.

Guilford felt that creativity was to be found in divergent thinking and was characterised by fluency (the creation of a large number of ideas), flexibility (simultaneous production of a variety of approaches), originality and elaboration.

How we make mistakes: 'it seemed like a good idea at the time'

If we apply the GIGO principle to Guilford's structure we can see the potential for error in all parts of decision-making:

- Errors of cognition, where we fail to recognise and fail to comprehend the basic facts before us.

- Errors of memory, when we record information incorrectly and recall information incompletely.*

These errors are magnified in productive thought where we rely on experience (our own and others'), to re-present the argument. Faulty input at this stage is bound to lead to faulty problem solving. Conversely, sound cognition and sound experience (through memory) must lead to better problem solving.

Errors of evaluation, when we fail to foresee the likely consequences of our decisions.

Errors of application, when we try to impose a successful solution from one domain upon another quite different domain; this is little better than trial and error.

Finally: the persistent application of failed solutions. As is often said, if we do not learn from history we are condemned to repeat it, first as tragedy and then as farce. This last case is not clever people doing stupid things; it is rather clever people revealing themselves not to be so clever after all.

> 'Insanity is doing the same thing over and over again but expecting different results' (American novelist Rita Mae Brown). This is reminiscent of *folly*, as defined by Barbara Tuchman in her history of stupid decisions from the Trojan Horse to the Vietnam War as 'A perverse persistence in a policy demonstrably unworkable or counter-productive. It seems almost superfluous to say that the present study stems from the ubiquity of this problem in our time'
>
> (*The March of Folly*, 1984).

*Copying errors may sometimes work as an improving mechanism:

In the individual, invention is as natural as imitation. Indeed normal imitation is rarely free from invention!

> In all the processes of social absorption and imitation, therefore, we find that the individual thinks and imagines in his own way. He cannot give back unaltered what he gets, as the parrot does. He is not a repeating machine. His mental creations are much more vital and transforming. Try as he will he cannot exactly reproduce; and when he comes near to it his self-love protests and claims its right to do its own thinking. So the new form, the personal shading, the embodiment of individual interest, the exhibition of a special mode of feeling – all these go to make his result a new thing which is of possible value for the society in which it arises.
>
> (J. M. Baldwin, *The Individual and Society*, 1911)

The evolutionary scientist J. B. S. Haldane was quite brutal about the limitations of human intelligence:

> Man is after all only a little freer than a barnacle. Our bodily and mental activities are fairly rigidly confined to those which have had survival value to our ancestors during the last few million generations. Our own appraisement of these activities is dictated to some extent by other considerations than their survival value, but their nature is limited by our past. We have learned to think on two different lines – one which enables us to deal with situations in which we find ourselves in relation to our fellow-men, another for corresponding situations with regard to inanimate objects. We are pretty nearly incapable of any other types of thought. And so we regard an electron as a thing, and God as a person, and are surprised to find ourselves entangled in quantum mechanics and the Athanasian Creed. We are just getting at the rudiments of other ways of thinking. A few mystics manage to conceive of God as such, and not as a person or a substance. They have no grammar or even vocabulary to express their experience, and are generally regarded as talking nonsense, as indeed they often do. We biologists, or some of us, are managing to think about an organism neither as a mere physico-chemical system, nor as something directed by a mind. We also tend to contradict ourselves when we try to put our ideas into words. On the other hand, our way of thinking has led some of us to a very shrewd idea of how an organism will behave in given circumstances, and to making experiments which throw a good deal of light on the nature of an organism. But I do not feel that any of us know enough about the possible kinds of being and thought, to make it worth while taking any of our metaphysical systems very much more seriously than those at which a thinking barnacle might arrive. Such systems seem to be helps to the imagination rather than accounts of reality. Yet it is of fundamental importance that metaphysical speculation should continue. The only alternative to this appears to be the adoption of some rather crude metaphysical system, such as Thomism or materialism, and regarding it as commonsense.
>
> (*Possible Worlds and Other Essays* 1927)

Haldane was writing in the 1920s – many would say that metaphysical speculation has indeed advanced our understanding at least somewhat.

Globalisation is going to bring about sudden and exponential growth of ideas and technology, opening up the potential for errors of a hitherto unimagined magnitude. Our ability to deal with the vicissitudes of the new world will be called into question. Both the global banking crisis and the disruption of European air travel by volcanic ash show the inadequacy of existing structures when they find themselves applied on a worldwide scale.*

As we suggested earlier, our minds are shaped by our experiences; and our ancestors' minds were shaped by their experiences. If a sabre-toothed tiger is chasing you, thinking quickly is the name of the game. The system is built for speed and perhaps this is why ideas sometimes seem to come 'out of the blue', when we are no longer thinking actively; maybe the computation needs time to catch up.

The other consequence of this need for speed is that we apply the principle of least effort; we nearly always go for the first acceptable solution to a problem rather than wait for what we perceive to be only a marginally better one.

There is a tendency to equate good decision making with rapid decision making. The 'alpha male', or female, will invoke Winston Churchill's habit of labelling documents 'Action This Day'. Unfortunately, they ignore the fact that Churchill also used tags reading 'Report in Three Days' and 'Report Progress in One Week'. Bearing in mind the pressures of time, we ought perhaps to remember the old Hollywood adage, 'You can have it good or you can have it on Tuesday.'

*An interesting response to the banking crisis has been the rise of 'peer-to-peer' lending online. The pioneer in this field is ZOPA (named after the negotiating term Zone Of Possible Agreement). Lenders and borrowers do so at superior rates by cutting out the middlemen – banks. Lenders do, however, have to accept the risk of bad debts, although they can spread the risk by sharing loans with other investors, each only contributing a small amount. Similar organisations, such as Kiva, exist with more altruistic aims – microfinance for would-be entrepreneurs in developing countries. This sort of personal engagement is a very real illustration of how the World Wide Web can function as a 'global village'.

Overview

Acceptable or Optimal?

At this point we cannot avoid taking a brief excursion into the world of bell curves and long tails.

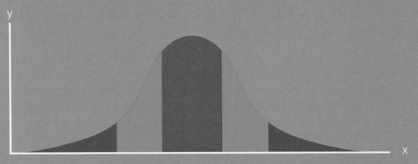

Illustration of Bell Curve Distribution

The bell curve above illustrates a statistical normal distribution of, for example, packets of biscuits, where *y* is the number of varieties and *x* the price. As can be seen, the easiest place to find biscuits is in the red zone. But the graph only describes the biscuits according to price, so if you're looking for value for money or fat content or any other variable you're going to have to look more closely. But you're still unlikely to get beyond the green zone before you find an acceptable choice. Supermarkets know this; that's why they display the products they want to push on the middle shelves. Less popular (and less profitable) products are placed on the highest and lowest shelves. Your favourite biscuits, however, may be more difficult to find. You might have to look in the blue or even white zones to find best value or least additives or whatever. You may *not* find them there; your best choice could be in the red zone after all, but you won't know unless you look. And that's the difference between acceptable and optimal. (And yes, as it happens, there are some people who are better off shopping on their own.)

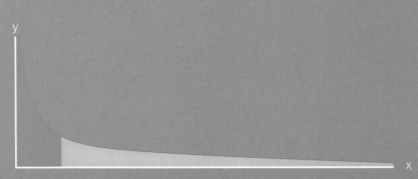

Illustration of Power Law Graph

This power-law graph illustrates a similar feature – the long tail. If the graph represents, for example, popular book titles, it is clear to see that a bookshop with limited shelf space would stock mostly green titles. An online bookshop, however, can stock the full range and therefore supply rarer yellow titles as well. Chris Anderson coined the phrase in an article for the online magazine Wired in 2004 which was expanded into a book two years later *The Long Tail: Why the Future of Business is Selling Less of More*.

As with the bell curve, the optimal solutions are not necessarily to be found in the easiest places.

The graph also shows a popular misconception known as the Pareto Principle or '80/20 Rule'. This is commonly used to state, for example, that 80% of your problems are caused by 20% of your customers, or that 20% of your advertising attracts 80% of responses. The fact that there are also so-called 90/10 and 70/30 rules only goes to demonstrate the inadequacy of the rule. It was named after the Italian economist Vilfredo Pareto (1848–1923), who noted that 20% of Italians controlled 80% of the wealth. There really is no use for this 'law' outside the study of nineteenth-century Italian economics. It is an example of social *mis*representation. The numbers do not even have to add up to 100, as they are measuring entirely different things. For example, in the 1960s the notorious Dr Beeching reported that 95% of UK rail traffic was carried on just 50% of the network, leading him to recommend swingeing cuts; whatever his other sins, no one has accused Beeching of coining a spurious '95/50 rule'. It should be noted that Vilfredo himself is totally innocent of this particular piece of nonsense: Pareto indices, Pareto efficiency and Pareto charts are all perfectly sound.

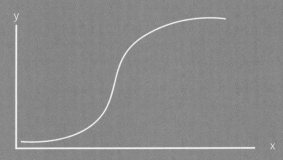

Illustration of Sigma Curve

A final graph explains one example of why we are so often taken by surprise. The S-shaped line describes the common growth pattern of many phenomena: a long slow build up followed by a steep rise before a long slow levelling off. The bottom two thirds of the curve is often used to illustrate exponential growth. If, however, observation of such phenomena is incomplete, the middle section seems to show a sudden spurt of growth apparently from nowhere.

One of the first great Internet phenomena in modern music (as opposed to the many faux phenomena that followed) was the British rock band the Arctic Monkeys. The press and music business were shocked by the appearance of a group of musicians of considerable originality and enormous appeal, and the wholly predictable media bandwagon started to roll. (When he was British prime minister, even Gordon Brown was said to have them on his iPod.) The speed of their success probably took the band by surprise but they certainly didn't come from nowhere. Their GCSE coursework is proof of that and their original fans certainly thought they were the best thing since sliced bread. The only reason the music business didn't see them coming was that they weren't looking in the right place. The next big thing is already out there; we just haven't noticed it yet. Stephen Jay Gould called this kind of error 'a sigmoid fraud'.

The expenditure of time is of course a cost; in much decision making it seems to be the only cost. But the consequences of sub-optimal decision making can be very time consuming. It's clear that rushing to judgement is a major and easily avoided cause of error; it is epitomised by the age-old injunction 'Less haste, more speed.'

If we dissect the thinking process we should be able to see more clearly.

- We would have time to adopt a more analytic approach.
- We would have time to adopt a more imaginative approach.
- We would have time to search for creative possibilities.
- We would enhance our chance of finding the optimal rather than the acceptable.

It's a lot cheaper in time as well as money to make a little extra effort at this pre-concept stage and take a little more trouble at the planning stage than to rush into a project and find yourself saying, 'Of course, if we had the chance to do it again . . .'

> Sir Amice Pawlet, [1532–1588], when he saw too much haste made in any matter, was wont to say 'Stay a while, that we may make an end the sooner.'
>
> (Recalled by an old pupil of his – Francis Bacon *Apothegms,* 1624)

When you invest in pre-concept ideas you are generally expending nothing more than brainpower and, as we will demonstrate, generating ideas is what humanity does best.

Problems, Needs and Opportunities

Crisis and opportunity

危
机
'When written in Chinese, the word "crisis" is composed of two characters – one represents danger and one represents opportunity.' (John F. Kennedy, 1959)

Unfortunately for J.F.K. and a succession of speakers following in his wake, the expression rendered in pinyin as *wēijī* means no such thing – it makes slightly less sense than the cliché 'There's no I in team.' But the fact that the etymology is suspect does not mean that the sentiment is not sound.

'You never want a serious crisis to go to waste,' Rahm Emanuel, President Obama's first Chief of Staff, said in 2009. Emanuel illustrated this sentiment by referring to the oil crisis of the early 1970s, which he saw as a lost opportunity to address the serious problems of fossil fuel dependency by building new solutions rather than patching up the old system.

And once more we can say that this is hardly new: as the old rhyme shows, when 'London Bridge is falling down', we build it up again in a new and improved manner until we find a solution that works. The Great Fire of London was a disaster which turned into an opportunity for Christopher Wren. Out of the ashes a phoenix is born. Even when we deliberately recreate something that has been destroyed, we take the opportunity to improve it. Buildings destroyed in the Second World War might have been reconstructed brick by brick but it would be bizarre to reconstruct lead plumbing or antiquated electric wiring. But 're-creations' are still liable to be controversial: following the reunification of Germany in 1990, there was an impetus to rebuild the Dresden Frauenkirche, which had lain in ruins as a memorial since its destruction in 1945. While the rebuilding was based on the original eighteenth-century plans, the reconstructed church has attracted criticism as an 'improved' version.

It is important to emphasise that entrepreneurial thinking, along with creativity in general, is *amoral*. It brings *value* to a domain in terms which that domain values.

On September 11th 2001, shortly after the twin towers of the World Trade Center in New York had been attacked by hijacked aircraft but before they collapsed, Jo Moore, a British government adviser, sent an e-mail: 'It's now a very good day to get out anything we want to bury. Councillors' expenses?' The next day a minor U-turn on councillors' allowances was indeed announced and largely ignored by the British press, which was concentrating, quite naturally, on the terrorist outrage.

Overview

It was a month before the e-mail became public and scandal ensued. 'A good day to bury bad news' is now a byword for the dark arts of the spin doctor.

What passes as opportunity for some is seen as opportunism by others. Some, happily, are plain common sense: when volcanic ash forced the closure of East Midlands Airport in 2010, the management used the time, and 5,000 litres of paint, to renew all the runway markings in one go.

The authors make no apology for using the word problem to describe the needs and opportunities that arise and the decisions that need to be made when crises occur. After all, the word *problem* itself simply means something which has been *thrown forward*.

Once again, we are not the first to do so: in 1890, French philosopher and pioneer sociologist Gabriel Tarde wrote in *Les lois de l'imitation*: '*Toute invention, comme toute découverte, est une réponse à un problème.*' (Every invention, like every discovery, is a response to a problem.)

There are, however, many different types of problem.

In 1974, Hungarian architect, engineer and sculptor Ernő Rubik invented the puzzle which bears his name. The 3x3x3 cube has 43,252,003,274,489,856,000 possible combinations on its six faces. The first international competition was held in Hungary in 1982 and was won in a time of 22.95 seconds. Nowadays under ten seconds is the benchmark for serious puzzlers. While most of us are amazed by such abilities, the problem itself is a simple one – despite the enormous number of combinations it is a *finite* number and there is only *one* solution.

'Real life' is not like a Rubik's Cube – there are innumerable combinations and more than one way forward. In real life we may have to accept that there is no 'correct' answer.

Take, for example, a more commonplace problem – what to have for breakfast. Apart from those poor souls who literally have nothing to eat, this is a problem addressed by everybody throughout the world every single day.

It is fair to say that solutions vary, from smoked salmon with quails' eggs to a can of Coke and a packet of potato crisps. The staple food will vary – rice, wheat, oats, maize – as will the form it is processed into. There is clearly more than one 'solution' to the problem of what to have for breakfast and those solutions depend upon cost, availability, convenience. Moreover the problem area exhibits *polytely* (multiple goals). There are several 'stakeholders', not just the consumer and the provider – there may, for instance, be social implications, health, welfare, child protection. Each of these stakeholders will have their own agenda; their objectives may be very different and not all will be financial.

And so what appears to be a simple problem (breakfast) is in fact enormously complicated, whereas the apparently complicated Rubik's Cube puzzle turns out to be simple.

The contrast is succinctly explained in the abstract of a paper entitled 'Dilemmas in a General Theory of Planning':

> The search for scientific bases for confronting problems of social policy is bound to fail, because of the nature of these problems. They are 'wicked' problems, whereas science has developed to deal with 'tame' problems. Policy problems cannot be definitively described. Moreover, in a pluralistic society there is nothing like the undisputable public good; there is no objective definition of equity; policies that respond to social problems cannot be meaningfully correct or false; and it makes no sense to talk about 'optimal solutions' to social problems unless severe qualifications are imposed first. Even worse, there are no 'solutions' in the sense of definitive and objective answers.

> (Rittel and Webber, 1973)

Note: the terms simple or complex, tame or wicked, bear no relation to the ease or difficulty of solving the problem. What to have for breakfast, a complex problem, is solved every day, whereas decoding the human genome, a simple problem, is taking a little longer. What Beveridge somewhat disparagingly called 'pot boiling' science is of course a long and difficult enterprise. But as an opportunity for creative problem solving and entrepreneurial enterprise what to have for breakfast is a far more attractive area.

The British Plain English Campaign annually announces a 'Foot in Mouth' award 'for baffling quotes by public figures'. The 2003 award went to the following:

> Reports that say that something hasn't happened are always interesting to me, because as we know, there are known knowns; there are things we know we know. We also know there are known unknowns; that is to say we know there are some things we do not know. But there are also unknown unknowns – the ones we don't know we don't know.

> (US Defense Secretary Donald Rumsfeld, February 12th 2002)

A spokesperson from the organisation waggishly said: 'We think we know what he means, but we don't know if we really know.'

But some things *are* difficult to understand; some sentences need to be read several times if you don't understand them. Among his other misdemeanours, Rumsfeld may have been arrogant in assuming that the press could keep up with him, but he was expressing a profound truth about the limits of knowledge in the real world.

It is the uncertainty of real life which makes it so difficult – if it was easy we wouldn't need a guide to try and help us.

Overview

The contrast between simple problems in a certain environment, which we know how to solve even though working them out might be extremely difficult and laborious, and complex problems in an uncertain environment, where we don't even know what the problem is never mind how to solve it, is illustrated by referring to two seemingly contrasting quotes.

At a press conference in 1929, Thomas Alva Edison said, 'None of my inventions came by accident. I see a worthwhile need to be met and I make trial after trial until it comes. What it boils down to is one per cent inspiration and ninety-nine per cent perspiration.'

In 2004, following a winning World Cup campaign, England rugby football coach Clive Woodward described his approach to innovation: 'Find out "what" I wanted to do, set it all up and then find a way to make it happen. Some people consider that a bit frustrating. To me, it's just getting my priorities straight. It's the "what" that takes most of the ingenuity. The "how" is easy.'

The two are resolved when we consider that both Edison and Woodward are highlighting the importance of the concept: for them the most important thing is to identify what needs to be done; the rest, although it may well be very hard work, is comparatively straightforward. Success depends upon direction – if we begin by recognising the 'severe qualifications' required even for 'wicked problems', we may in fact be able to work towards optimal solutions.

If there are many different types of problem, there are also different kinds of opportunity.

Geoff Kirk, former chief designer at Rolls Royce, uses the graphic illustrated below to describe innovation.

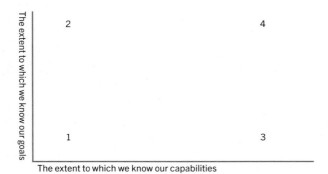

The vertical axis describes the extent of our knowledge about the problem/opportunity/need. (It is this axis that Edison found straightforward: 'I see a worthwhile need to be met . . .')

The horizontal axis describes the extent of our ability to address the problem/opportunity/need. (This is the one that Woodward found trouble-free: 'The "how" is easy.')

Our everyday 'what to have for breakfast' example initially appears thus: vertical axis is the need – hunger; the horizontal axis is the capability – whatever's in the cupboard.

Most problems start off in and around the bottom left-hand corner (1): we know there's a problem but we're not quite certain what it is and we are not especially sure how to solve it.

Other problems can be placed nearer the other corners. Top left (2), the end of the vertical axis, is where we have a clear and unequivocal idea of the problem to be solved – where we want to be.

For example: on May 21st 1961, President Kennedy proclaimed to the United States Congress that 'This nation should commit itself to achieving the goal, before the decade is out, of landing a man on the moon and returning him safely to the earth.' At the time NASA had only very sketchy ideas on how that might be done but, in July 1969, *Apollo 11* fulfilled the aspiration with five months to spare.

More prosaic examples of this kind might take the form of almost any given imperative, from the social – better housing, improved health, etc.; to the commercial – cutting budgets, marketing products, etc.

Bottom right (3), the end of the horizontal axis, is where we have a clear understanding of our capabilities and are looking for ways of using them.

For example: the discovery of genetic fingerprints – a 'solution' without a problem. As we have related, it took Alec Jeffreys and his team less than an hour to see most of the possibilities which have been developed in the years since.

This is the area of technology transfer – the recognition that capabilities and competencies may have relevance beyond their point of origin.

The top right (4) is where we know what we want to achieve and we know how to achieve it. It is the acme of optimal utility – the problem is solved! At this 'bliss point' stands James Henry Atkinson (1849–1942). *Who?*

> 'Build a better mousetrap, and the world will beat a path to your door.'*
>
> (Emerson)

---

*As with most of the clichés of innovation it turns out not to be quite true. In his journal in 1855 Emerson did write, 'I trust a good deal to common fame, as we all must. If a man has good corn, or wood, or boards, or pigs to sell, or can make better chairs or knives, crucibles or church organs than anybody else, you will find a broad hard-beaten road to his house, though it be in the woods.' This was misquoted in 1889 as: 'If a man can write a better book, preach a better sermon, or make a better mousetrap than his neighbor, though he builds his house in the woods the world will make a beaten path to his door.'

So why has no one heard of James Henry Atkinson, never mind know where he lived so that we could visit him and see? Because there is little doubt that James Henry Atkinson *did* build a better mousetrap. (Actually, even then it could be argued that what he did was to perfect a pre-existing snap-trap design.) Nevertheless, at the turn of the twentieth century Yorkshire ironmonger Atkinson patented his design (GB 13277). Ten years later he registered the trademark 'Little Nipper'. Around 1913 he is supposed to have sold the rights to manufacturers Procter Brothers for £1,000. What is absolutely certain is that almost a century later Procter Brothers still manufacture and market the 'Little Nipper'.

It is said that over 4,400 US patents for mousetraps have been issued since the 'Little Nipper', with only twenty designs actually making any money. Which is not surprising when you consider that the snap-trap design reportedly accounts for 60% of the market. Newer designs appeal to the humane, non-lethal market or to those too squeamish to empty the trap. The traditional product is now so cheap that it has been re-marketed as 'disposable' to answer the concerns of the latter.

This way of looking at things is perfectly comprehensible in the terms of ancient Greek philosophy if we rename the vertical axis *telos* (τέλος) and the horizontal *techne* (τέχνη). The *telos* is the goal – 'What do we want?' – and the *techne* is 'How are we going to get it?'

What we do, in this book, is strive for a perfect balance between *telos* and *techne* – to have a clear vision of the problem, need or opportunity we wish to address and certain knowledge of how we can try to solve it. By improving the quality of the concept we are bound to enhance its chances of success.

Entrepreneurial Education

The German philosopher Arthur Schopenhauer is credited with this observation: 'Talent hits a target no one else can hit; genius hits a target no one else can see.'

In order to gain that precious 'know how' as well as the 'know about' of entrepreneurship, every student entering Nottingham University Business School is expected to come up with brand new concepts in areas such as ageing populations, sustainable local energy supplies, shortages of fresh water, etc.

We use Kirk's Space to illustrate entrepreneurial opportunities and issue challenges.

The extent to which we know our goals

The extent to which we know our capabilities

- 4. Top right: the opportunities are restricted; the problem seems to have been solved already. There is an existing market but the budding entrepreneur is going to have to make a compelling case to customers why they should change – price, quality, efficacy, service, etc. Plus the existing solution provider is likely to react to competition. For example, 'How can we persuade home owners to consider domestic wind turbines as a source of power?'

- 3. Bottom right: the opportunity is to identify objectives that can be attained with a particular capability, e.g. 'What are the possible industrial uses of microwave heating?'

- 2. Top left: the opportunity rests with identifying the capabilities needed to achieve the stated objective, e.g. 'How can we encourage car-sharing among commuters?'

- 1. Bottom left: this is the area of most opportunity; the area where the entrepreneur 'carries out new combinations' matching goals with capabilities in a hitherto unrealised fashion, e.g. 'Can we identify the unmet needs of an ageing population?'

Most importantly, students are challenged to look for opportunities beyond well-known problem areas because the most radical innovations are in solving the problems no one else can see . . .

For example, so-called latent or dormant needs. Fifteen or twenty twenty years ago no one 'needed' a mobile phone and yet nowadays mobiles are 'essential' accessories for at least half the people in the world and are seen as a key element in economic development in the poorest countries.

> The principal goal of education in the schools should be creating men and women who are capable of doing new things, not simply repeating what other generations have done; men and women who are creative, inventive and discoverers, who can be critical and verify, and not accept, everything they are offered.
>
> (Jean Piaget 1988)

Problem solving and effective decision making

In the last hundred years or so, an increasing number of formal problem-solving methodologies have been developed across a wide range of domains, from industry to advertising.

- George Polya's *How to Solve It* (1945) has been enormously influential far beyond its original domain of mathematics.

- The Theory of Inventive Problem Solving or TRIZ, the heuristic/algorithmic system developed by Genrich Altshuller in post-war Russia, has a devoted following outside engineering.

- In the area of creative idea generation, Alex Osborn's 'brainstorming' has entered the language as has Edward de Bono's 'lateral thinking'.

- Edward Lumsdaine and Martin Binks (2003, 2005) highlight the importance of recognising and balancing different thinking styles, and also lay particular emphasis on entrepreneurship.

It is probably fair to say that some problem-solving techniques have become more detailed and specific as time has gone on. Some of the most interesting deserve to be better known beyond their particular sphere. For example, those who are intrigued by ad-man James Webb Young's *A Technique for Producing Ideas* (1940), which emphasises incubation, ought to be just as interested in William Beveridge's insistence on the importance of chance in scientific progress.

It is no criticism to say that some problem-solving techniques have become more detailed and specific as time has gone on. Many design and management methodologies show signs of cross-pollination. Some techniques are public domain, others are quite strictly copyrighted. Some are more useful than others. Some are at best the 'professionalisation of common sense' (Ben Goldacre, *Bad Science*, 2009). Others are fairly dubious.

About Learning (2005), the Report of the Learning Working Group of the respected think tank Demos, quotes Harvard professor Howard Gardner's concerns about the representation of his (itself controversial) theory of Multiple Intelligences (MI): 'I learned that an entire state in Australia had adopted an educational program based in part on MI theory. The more I learned about this program, the less comfortable I was. While parts of the program were reasonable and based on research, much of it was a mishmash of practices, with neither scientific foundation nor clinical warrant. Left-brain and right-brain contrasts, sensory-based learning styles, "neuro-linguistic programming," and MI approaches commingled with dazzling promiscuity.'

Our purpose is not to replace or reject any of these techniques but to reference them while offering a broader guide for clear thinking which should enhance creativity, innovation and effective problem-solving right across the board from business to politics, from arts to science.

Before setting out our methodology, it is worth reviewing some of our observations so far:

- We have seen that change and innovation have both incremental and revolutionary characteristics.

- We have hinted that what we call 'common sense' is often merely a reflection of the orthodoxy of the time.

- We have concluded that we have to tolerate uncertainty in our reasoning, suggesting indeed that in many cases there may be no such thing as one single *correct* answer.

- We have demonstrated that all of us display a creative element in our everyday thinking and therefore that the agents of change, those people with their eureka moments, are not fundamentally different from the rest of us.

- Despite the difficulties inherent in passing on tacit knowledge, we contend that almost anyone can enhance their own creativity with practice.

And so, against a background of the storms of destruction and creation, and very conscious of the uncertainties of both men and machines, we will use a fairly simple model linking reproductive and productive thinking with convergent and divergent elements as a practical framework with which to solve problems. Having said that, the structured thinking process described below does not depend upon theory. As we remarked earlier, this is not a theoretical but a practical book. Although it came out of interplay between theory and practice, it is ultimately to be judged by whether or not it works. Even when we put forward possible explanations of the hows and whys of ingenuity and suggest fruitful areas for research, *reason must always triumph over 'authority'*.

We propose a relatively straightforward three-phase process:

1. Definition; spending more time finding root causes, understanding how problems are constructed and interrelated.

2. Discovery; making the effort to look as widely and as imaginatively as we can for ideas that we can engineer into creative possibilities.

3. Determination; using appropriate judgement to foresee the likely consequences, turning possibilities into probabilities.

Each of these phases should be separated to allow ideas to incubate, to soak. Quite apart from the story of Archimedes in his bath, there is far too much anecdotal evidence of the benefits of incubation to ignore. 'Sleep on it' has always been good advice. So, whenever possible, we should take our time. When we separate and slow down the thinking process, this does not necessarily mean postponing or delaying decision making. When we 'put something on the back-burner' it's in the full expectation that when we return to it, it will have cooked. Incubation is not the same as procrastination; the former happens after the hard work, the latter precedes it.

In addition, as the inevitable by-product of creative problem solving, we ought to be able to spot a few good ideas that may be applicable elsewhere. Some people call this serendipity; entrepreneurs call it 'opportunity recognition'. Finally, we will demonstrate a specific technique to take this further: *entrepreneurial problem finding*.

Fractals

As we were designing this problem-solving process a pattern began to emerge. The pattern is a consequence of our particularly straightforward analysis of the way we think and solve problems; i.e. the interplay of convergent and divergent thinking styles. Deliberately separating these basic modes of thought, together with an insistence on allowing space for reflection, results in the three distinct phases to virtually all the non-automatic thought processes we describe.

1. We pose a question.

2. We look at the alternatives.

3. We choose from the alternatives.

A good analogy might be decision making in a committee: we start with an agenda, follow up with a discussion and finally come to a conclusion or plenary. The next meeting will start with an agenda based upon the conclusion of the last meeting and so on. Thus we make progress in a structured manner. This threefold structure seems to exhibit fractal characteristics.

Fractals are a fascinating and it must be confessed extremely fashionable branch of mathematics, the term itself being coined by Benoit Mandelbrot in 1975 as part of the mathematical description of recursive self-similarity. In popular usage self-similarity is when a pattern can be successively broken into smaller parts, each of which exhibits the same qualities as the one before.

Fractals in nature – Romanesco broccoli. It might *look* complex but it's broccoli all the way through!

Each of these phases seems to exhibit the following characteristics:

1. **Definition** is all about preparation. Setting the agenda. What do we know and where do we want to be? Questioning, investigative, diagnostic, methodical, analytic. Clarity of vision.

2. **Discovery** is about discussion. Idea generation. How can we engineer possibilities? Free-thinking, open-minded, relaxed, uncritical, non-judgemental. Fuzzy and tolerant of uncertainty.

3. **Determination** reflects the conclusions we have come to. Idea evaluation. Assess the possibilities; have we made progress? Judgement and choice. Critical, logical, reasoned. Re-focus the vision.

The results of phase 3 (evaluation) should form the basis of phase 1 (preparation) of the next cycle.

A useful analogy might be a series of meetings to monitor a project: we start with an agenda, which forms the basis of discussion. The meeting ought to end with decisions and actions. The consequences of those decisions and actions will then appear on the agenda for the next meeting. If they are unsound or not carried out then we end up repeating ourselves.

This methodology is an iterative process, but it ought not be a repetitive one.

Thus we flip/flop using both convergent and divergent thinking styles, with the all-important element of soak time in between. The rest of the book will follow this structure: three sections – define, discover and determine – with numerous discursions and digressions to act as soak time, but always progressing towards some sort of conclusion.

'L'esprit d'escalier' is a phrase associated with French philosopher Denis Diderot; it means the experience of thinking of what you should have said, just a little too late, when you have left the room and are at the foot of the stairs.

Interlude: why bother?

Before we embark on the rather severe and narrow road of problem definition ('so thick beset with thorns and briars'), let's find the time for another brief excursion.

Imagine that you are in a spaceship travelling towards some distant star.

One day you look in the equivalent of your rear-view mirror and see a faster vessel overtaking you.

This vessel, oddly enough, is from your own planet; it set out years after your departure and is the result of enormous improvements in space technology since your day.

What was the point of you setting out at all? Why bother?*

The second spaceship ought to pick you up and continue before it is overtaken in turn and everybody climbs aboard the latest technology, just as happens in practice with any radical innovation – sooner or later we all jump ship, whether it be from vinyl to digital or fountain pen to Biro.

At the time of writing, five spacecraft are heading away from the solar system. The first two, *Pioneer 10* and *11*, each bore a plaque with some basic information about their place of origin.

The second two, *Voyagers 1* and *2*, enlarged the idea, sending more information – this time on a phonograph disc engraved with instructions on how to play it back!

The fourth to be launched (*Voyager 1*) is now the furthest from the sun, travelling fastest and is the first man-made object to reach interstellar space, while the fifth, *New Horizons*, despite being launched around thirty years after the others, will surely outdistance them. None of them, however, will overtake another – they are all going in different directions.

*There is a parallel with the very down-to-earth problem of personal pension provision – when is the best time to start saving for your retirement?

At the start of your working life, when it seems a long way off and you are comparatively poor?

Towards the end, when you begin to panic but are, with any luck, more able to afford it?

There ought to be a perfect moment, or moments; a sliding scale of increasing contributions based on projected earnings and life expectancy – the sort of complex calculation so beloved of financial advisers. And indeed such speculative calculations can be used to predict the best time to set off to another planet, but the resolution of this paradox is surely that the second spaceship would never have been invented but for your efforts: this is one of the things we mean when we say that we see further because 'we stand on the shoulders of giants'.

Overview

But the paradox also suggests a more general question about waiting for someone else to solve our problems. Why not call in the experts? American writer Paul Lutus (b. 1945) addresses the consequences of this attitude; he divides us all into people who know how to think, 'idea producers', and those who do not think for themselves, 'idea consumers'. He is especially hard on the latter: 'The content of their experience is provided by television, the Internet and other shallow data pools. These people believe collecting images and facts makes them educated and competent, and all their experiences reinforce this belief. The central organising principle of this class is that ideas come from somewhere else, from magical persons, geniuses, "them".'

Our book is about consuming ideas in order to produce more and better ideas. Lutus highlights that fundamental distinction between ideas and facts. And before we start having *ideas*, we might find it useful to establish some *facts*.

PHASE ONE:
Problem Definition

'All we want is the facts . . .'
(Sgt Joe Friday, *Dragnet*, 1950s television series).

This section is all about preparation. We need to establish the facts.

Where are we and where do we want to be?

The mood should be focused and analytic; linear, logical, sequential algorithmic processing; the thinking style popularly associated with the left hemisphere of the brain. Because our problem-solving methodology takes its form from machines (case-based reasoning) rather than brains (neuroscience), we shall be using left/right thinking styles as a metaphor rather than as established fact, but it would help to be aware of the science as currently understood:

> If you think about a bird trying to eat a little piece of grain against a background of pebbles, it's got to have a very focused, detailed attention to be able to seize it, and it knows exactly what it's after before it even starts focusing; but it's also got to keep a very broad, open attention for whatever might be, a completely uncommitted attention, otherwise it's going to end up being someone else's lunch. So it has to do a rather difficult thing – in fact impossible probably in one lump of neuronal tissue which is probably why we have two – it has to keep a very broad, open attention, an uncommitted attention, and a very narrow focused, detailed one.
>
> (Neuroscientist Iain McGilchrist speaking on BBC Radio 4, November 15th 2010)

We will therefore try to keep our attention narrow and focused.

Before we start, let's look at a case of what happens if you do not take the time to explore a problem properly.

New Coke; a cautionary tale

> There is a twist to this story which will please every humanist and will probably keep Harvard professors puzzled for years.
>
> (Donald Keough, President Coca-Cola)

There will almost certainly never be a definitive account of the introduction of New Coke if only because of that hindsight bias we noted earlier, whereby each of us tends to construct our own narrative, but a quick look at the story provides a wealth of interest to anyone who wonders how the world works.

The bare bones of the tale are as follows:

In the 1970s, Coke's great rival Pepsi started an advertising campaign, 'The Pepsi Challenge', in which Pepsi was consistently preferred over 'other leading brands'.

By the 1980s, Coke was running scared, seeing significant inroads into their market share, especially in supermarkets.

Coke's response was to reformulate the taste of Coca-Cola, which they launched on April 23rd 1985.

Less than three months later, following a public outcry, the company announced the re-introduction of the original formula.

To this basic narrative you may wish to pick and mix from the following facts:

In 1982, Coca-Cola had introduced Diet Coke. Diet Coke was not merely original Coke without sugar; it was a new formulation with a 'Pepsi-like' flavour and was a great success.

New Coke was essentially Diet Coke with sugar and it consistently beat both old Coke and Pepsi in taste tests.

One factor which might be relevant is that Coca-Cola had for years been sold as 'The Real Thing', incapable of improvement.

The press conference to launch New Coke was less than a triumph. The company appeared uncomfortable and arrogant under questioning by Pepsi-primed reporters.

Pepsi's response was to claim victory in the cola wars.

New Coke was sold as Coca-Cola until 1992 when it was rebranded as Coke II.

Old Coke was re-introduced as Classic Coke.

After the dust had settled, Coca-Cola was left with a larger market share than before.

In this version of the story, Coca-Cola does everything right up until the launch, which is simply a marketing disaster, turned around with a dash of humility amidst publicity you could not buy.

So what went wrong?

Coca-Cola underestimated brand loyalty and competitor's reaction, says the standard version.

Nothing went wrong, say the conspiracy theorists, pointing out that no one seemed to be sacked or disciplined and market share actually went up. It was all a publicity stunt.

Upon reflection, however, the story becomes more complicated, but perhaps clearer.

The taste tests, which yielded such remarkably consistent results, may have been flawed. Specifically, there is an enormous difference between sip tests and home trials; a sweet sip may become sickly after a glassful. Perhaps most significantly, 'blind tastings', by their very nature, ignore the fact that nobody (not even the sightless) tastes anything 'blind': the style, colour and texture of the packaging, even the glass it is served in, make up a complete experience – a 'whole product' – and that is what people buy.

Pepsi's supermarket share may well have had a lot more to do with price and negotiations about shelf space rather than flavour.

Coca-Cola was reluctant to dilute their brand by introducing too many variants.

Another less obvious consideration may be important: this all happened before the Berlin Wall came down; a cold-war mentality permeated business as well as politics. Fear may have led Coca-Cola to afford far too much respect to the market research of their rival.

> There is always a well-known solution to every human problem — neat, plausible, and wrong.
>
> (American writer H. L. Mencken)

Conclusion

Coca-Cola never really identified the root cause of its loss of market share and jumped to a solution to a problem that was not there; in the process it opened a marketing Pandora's Box.

Its real problem was the perennial 'How do we maintain and increase our market share?' and was eventually answered by doing the one thing it did not want to do, namely increase its line. Nowadays the shelves are filled with variations: Cherry, Caffeine-free, Diet, with lemon, with lime and Coke Zero.

Donald Keough's response to speculation has been, 'We're not that dumb and we're not that smart.' So did Coca-Cola learn from its mistakes?

In January 2004, Coca-Cola launched the Dasani brand of bottled water in the United Kingdom. Despite the fact that all of their drinks are overwhelmingly water based, they were taken aback by customers who insisted on the word 'spring'.

After a media backlash led by the piranha-like tabloid press, the product was withdrawn by March 2004. Meanwhile, the flavoured-water market in the UK goes from strength to strength, without Dasani, which nonetheless enjoys considerable success in the rest of the world.

The Big Picture

Despite tabloid opinion, there is more than just water in bottled drink water. There is the design, packaging and advertising which make up the 'total product'. There are processing costs, also transport and retail costs getting the water from cloud to customer. And it takes much more than one litre of water to produce a one-litre bottle of water. Water is used in the manufacture of everything from the bottle to the truck that delivers it. The concept of such embedded or virtual water results in a 'water footprint' to go along with the more familiar carbon footprint. Once you start adding flavourings, the water footprint goes up considerably: for example, according to figures from *The World's Water 2008–2009*, by Peter H. Gleick et al., it takes 300 units of water to produce one unit of beer; coffee requires even more – 1,120 cups for one cup. You can calculate your personal water footprint online, but beware – the figures are far from consistent. There are three *colours* of water, *green*, *blue* and *grey*, and measuring the balance between these can be contentious. Also the value of these different waters must vary: some places have very little water, some have plenty and some have too much.

Carbon footprints are a bit clearer but are far from set in stone. The comparative footprints of apples from New Zealand and Europe vary over the year, as storage costs gradually overtake the cost of air freight. Similarly, artificial heat used to grow crops in temperate zones may have a greater impact than the transport costs from warmer climates. Imported vegetables may actually incur smaller CO2 emissions than home-grown ones. The latter are often grown under intensive cultures using oil-based fertilisers and pesticides as well as diesel power for ploughing, harvesting, spraying, etc.

As Gareth Thomas, Minister for Trade and Development, pointed out, 'Driving 6.5 miles to buy your shopping emits more carbon than flying a pack of Kenyan green beans to the UK' (*Observer*, March 23rd 2008).

At which point the final tally is calculated should also be taken into account: there are *upstream* and *downstream* components. The carbon footprint of a tin of chickpeas is much higher than a similar quantity of dried, but the latter has not reached its end user until the chickpeas are cooked, which may very well involve much more unit energy than tinned, which benefit from economies of scale when cooked in bulk.

Even after a product reaches its end user there are further *downstream* consequences. For example, it is possible to calculate the carbon footprint of an incandescent lightbulb thus:

Raw materials and manufacture – 1%; logistics and distribution – 1%; retail – 1%; recycling – 1%; leaving a whopping 96% for actual consumer use.

All of which goes to show both how difficult it is to appreciate the whole of a problem and the dangers that ensue when we generalise.

So how can we avoid solving the 'wrong' problem and identify the 'right' one? We need to explore the nature of the problem beyond our immediate perceptions; we need to *drill down* and find the root causes. And to do that we need to look at the nature of information.

The idea of drilling down to root causes is not new. We all remember:

> For want of a nail the shoe was lost.
> For want of a shoe the horse was lost.
> For want of a horse the rider was lost.
> For want of a rider the battle was lost.
> For want of a battle the kingdom was lost.
> And all for the want of a horseshoe nail.

The Nature of Information

In 1948, Claude Elwood Shannon published 'A Mathematical Theory of Communication', coining the term 'bit' (binary digit), essentially a yes/no answer.

For example, it takes on average 5.7 bits or yes/no questions to find a card picked from a pack of 52 (the power to which 2 must be raised in order to result in 52 alternatives).

The sequence is 2, 4, 8, 16, 32, and 64. Since 52 lies between 32 and 64, the number of bits must be between 5 and 6, in this case, on average, 5.7.

Twenty bits of information, or 2 raised to the power 20, discloses 1,048,576 possibilities.

And so twenty questions simply answered, yes or no, have the potential to find one answer in a million.

This idea, of course, was not new in 1948. A radio game show called *Twenty Questions* had already been on the air in the USA for two years. Members of the public sent in suggestions to be guessed by the panel. (Apparently the most popular submission was Churchill's cigar.)

But the game itself is even older. In Charles Dickens' *A Christmas Carol* (1843), Scrooge's nephew plays the yes/no game, much to the chagrin of the unseen Scrooge, who finds himself the butt of the joke.

There is an account of George Canning (Britain's shortest-serving prime minister), and William Huskisson (the world's first passenger railway accident victim), playing Twenty Questions in 1827. The object discovered then was 'the wand of the Lord High Steward', which shows what kind of people we're dealing with.

We can follow a trail even further back, from Budapest in 1961, where Hungarian mathematician Alfréd Rényi used the Bar Kochba Game to introduce students to information theory.

The game reflects a gruesome legend associated with the leader of a revolt against the Emperor Hadrian in 132 AD. Bar Kochba is one of many variants of the name of Shimeon bar Kosiba (tr Yigael Yadin) who established and ruled an independent Jewish state for three years before a bloody and pyrrhic reconquest by the Romans.

The story goes that Bar Kochba came across a man whose tongue had been cut out and his hands cut off. The victim managed to identify his assailants by answering questions which only required a nod or shake of the head. In another version the wretched man is Bar Kochba's own spy, who had been caught and mutilated by the enemy but still managed to complete his mission.

Bits and bytes are binary numbers but since we are not limited to base two we should be able to drill down even faster. We should be able to come up with a series of diagnostic questions which will expose the structure of the problem and drill down to the root causes.

Were we to use the number of letters in our alphabet for a base we could solve any word puzzle simply by asking, what's the first letter? What's the second letter? And so on. Galileo, in his *Dialogue Concerning the Two Chief World Systems* (1632), puts the joke in the mouth of one of his protagonists, Sagredo.

'I have a little book, much briefer than Aristotle or Ovid, in which is contained the whole of science, and with very little study one may form from it the most complete ideas. It is the alphabet, and no doubt anyone who can properly join and order this or that vowel and these or those consonants with one another can dig out of it the truest answers to every question, and draw from it instruction in all the arts and sciences.'

You can take this sort of thing too far:

I've always enjoyed reading dictionaries and they are far more interesting than people give them credit for. And I think everything you find in a great book you would find in a great dictionary, except for the plot.

All the normal emotions – grief, happiness and loss – exist in a dictionary but not necessarily in the order that you would think.

(Author Ammon Shea, after reading all 20 volumes of the *Oxford English Dictionary*)

British readers will no doubt be reminded of the celebrated exchange between conductor and composer André Previn and Eric Morecambe as the inept pianist in the 1971 *Morecambe and Wise Christmas Show*.

Previn: You're playing all the wrong notes.

Morecambe: I'm playing all the right notes – but not necessarily in the right order.

Definition

Algorithms and heuristics

To understand our decision-making processes it is useful to distinguish between two sorts of diagnostic questions.

An algorithm is a finite series of unambiguous instructions, which will lead inevitably to a predetermined solution. Algorithms form the basis of most mathematical and computer-processing problem solving.

Heuristics are far more loosely defined. From trial and error to an educated guess, heuristic questions will tend to reduce or simplify the search for solutions. They are particularly useful in revealing complexities about problems, which may allow a better algorithm to be selected. Heuristics guarantee neither optimal nor feasible solutions, but will usually help with problem definition.

For example, 'How are we going to settle this restaurant bill?' A simple off-the-shelf algorithm might be to divide the total by the number of diners. This is rarely satisfactory, of course. Heuristics will reveal quite how unsatisfactory: 'Shall we share it equally?' is not acceptable to the family of four who didn't have fillet steaks and brandy; 'Let's all pay for our own' is far too meticulous, and that's before we get to the service charge and the tip, if any. And so the complexity of the problem is revealed and we need to select a solution with more care. 'I'll pay; you paid for the theatre tickets'; 'Count two kids for one adult'; 'Ten pounds each and share the rest'; 'I wonder if we can put this on expenses?' and finally, 'I've paid it, now for goodness sake, CAN WE GO?'

(Working backwards reveals another dynamic: if people know in advance how the bill is to be paid then they might be tempted to alter their order so as to maximise their share. We are back with the tragedy of the commons and the prisoners' – or diners' – dilemma. And so everyone has starters and fillet steak, liqueur coffees, etc. That's how projects spiral out of control, especially when someone else is picking up the tab.)

Before your doctor attempts a diagnosis, never mind a cure, he or she will always want to ascertain the facts. Taking a patient's medical history is taught as a skill of its own, with rules and structures and mnemonics. The ability to discover and describe the symptoms and history of a complaint, together with an understanding of the wider implications, is essential. As well as providing the basis of thousands of jokes, these Q and A sessions are one of the fundamentals of medicine. And as we will see, merely establishing the facts accurately often points the way forward with blinding clarity.

Diagnostic questions are used routinely by professionals from botanists to motor mechanics.

For instance, if you want to identify a plant, how do you go about it? You could thumb through a catalogue until you find an illustration: acceptable perhaps for the amateur gardener, but there are better methods. You could perhaps look in a directory organised by colour or habitat. As mentioned earlier, botanical classification is nowadays cladistic, that is by genetic similarity, but identification is usually carried out by studying shape and form. If you are a botanist, however, you would use a diagnostic flora. The best of these will ask a series of dichotomous questions, each answer reducing the number of possibilities. For example, is it vascular or non- vascular? That gets rid of mosses and lichens. Is it flowering or not? Is it bi-laterally or radially symmetrical? For trees you could ask whether deciduous or evergreen. In a remarkably short time the plant will be identified; *if* it is there, because we are in a limited system.

Similarly a motor mechanic should be able to pinpoint a problem in the restricted system of a car engine. Within any finite system it should be possible to devise and use diagnostics and construct algorithms. That is why, as we pointed out earlier, the Rubik's Cube, for all its daunting statistics, is a *simple* problem.

Over the years a number of formal heuristics has been developed in a variety of domains from engineering to creative writing. Obviously not all the questions are relevant in different domains but the similarities that all problems have in common are remarkable. Also remarkable is the way that some widely differing domains provide insights into each others' problems. Checking fuel and battery levels are the first thing a roadside repairman does, just as an accountant will check the balance and cash flow.

It sometimes helps to adopt the attitude of an insistent child who keeps asking the same question over and over again – Why? Why? Why? – until they have extracted every last jot of information.

The Japanese inventor and industrialist Sakichi Toyoda formalised this as '5 Whys' and used it as part of Toyota's problem-solving process, although the first thing to be said is that five is not the definitive number of times you should ask 'Why?' You may need fewer, you may need more. You have to make a judgement as to when to stop. For example, let's have a look at that byword for disaster, RMS *Titanic*. What was the root cause of the problem? Most people are happy to start by blaming the iceberg; some will mention the decision to steam so far north; others will point to the construction of the ship itself. But surely, for practical purposes, the root cause of the loss of so many lives was the fact that no one had thought the unthinkable. None of which was of any use on the night of 14–15 April 1912; they had to deal with the situation as it was: lifeboats places for only 1,178, around half the number of passengers and crew aboard. Even then only just over 700 survived the disaster and over 1,500 perished, suggesting, incidentally, that the chosen heuristic, *women and children first*, was probably not the best one.

Most problems do not have guaranteed solutions. As we saw with the concept of common-sense reasoning, quite often we have to tolerate uncertainty, just as we often end up telling the insistent child that they might have to find out for themselves.

To *describe* a problem, what better start than the classic six questions every junior reporter is told to ask: who? what? when? where? how? and why? (We, of course, will need to be far more accurate in our answers than the average tabloid journalist.)

Because our problem-solving process is so wide ranging, not all the questions we suggest will be as relevant as others; two contrasting cases will illustrate this.

First case history:

a fictional account of an all too common true-life situation

Imagine that you are an adviser of small businesses and your good friend James rings you up one morning in a state of absolute panic.

James is one of the cleverest people you know; he has been developing innovative products for years for one of the biggest multinationals. He recently branched out on his own in an unrelated field with his best invention yet. His company is expanding, his order book is overflowing and, last time you heard, his wife had given up her job to help with the admin. Everything was looking marvellous.

James's problem turned out to be very simple: a tax demand for £38,000 with a week to pay. So let's ask the journalist's six questions:

1. Who? Who does the problem affect? James, his wife and family, their workforce, their customers; in fact everyone.

2. What? A £38,000 tax demand!

3. When? This morning!

4. Where? Through the [expletive deleted] letterbox!

5. How? How is more revealing: a quick chat with James's bookkeeping wife shows that he has been trading in the VAT, i.e. failing to pass on to the government the percentage he has been charging his customers.

6. Why? This is the key question and each iteration of it reveals more:

    *   Why did this come as a surprise? 'I thought I had a year to pay.'

    *   Why were you so naïve? 'I'm not very good at the finance.'

    *   Why didn't you go on a course or something? 'I haven't had the time.'

    *   Why haven't you had time? 'I have to manage the rest of the business.'

    *   Why haven't you delegated? 'I have, but my wife is only just beginning to get the accounts in order.'

Five whys and we begin to see the problem in perspective.

At first the solution seemed easy: beg, borrow or steal £38,000 to pay the debt.

As we look deeper, James's financial incompetence is revealed and the best solution might be to crawl back to his former employers with his tail between his legs.

But after discovering all the facts, we can define the root cause of James's problem.

The skills which served James so well in his career so far have proved inadequate for the circumstances he now finds himself in. But there are positives: James has realised that he needs to delegate and the core of the business remains sound. We can now revisit some of our questions to seek solutions to a problem which has been properly defined.

When can we negotiate a stop-gap payment?

Might it be possible to restructure the business to make the most of the (considerable) skills that we know are in the company?

And so we can see that the first solution would actually make things worse, but a proper appreciation of the situation turns a potential disaster into a salutary experience.

Second case history:
the true story of one of the greatest detective stories in the history of medicine

Remember detective Joe Friday - all we want is the facts:

Who? The people of the Soho district of london.

What? Cholera.

When? 1854.

On 31 August 1854, a terrible outbreak of disease struck Soho. Three days later 127 people were dead and most of the residents were fleeing. By the end of the epidemic, 616 men, women and children had died.

Where? Dr John Snow, with the assistance of the Revd Henry Whitehead, traced the source of the outbreak to the public water pump at Broad Street and persuaded the authorities to remove its handle on 8 September, after which the outbreak declined. (The legend has Snow heroically removing the handle himself against a background of hostility.)

How? The prevailing theory of disease was miasma: that illness was spread by pollution in the air. This view had been dominant since ancient times, giving its name to malaria, and seemed confirmed by the sanitary reforms of the likes of Florence Nightingale. The rival germ theory, proposed by Snow and others, was unproven.

Why? Investigation revealed that the water was polluted from a nearby cesspit.

The solution to this problem came with the answer to the question 'Where?' How and why then disclosed the root cause and helped to prove the germ theory, giving impetus to the construction of a modern sewage system.There is a memorial to these events at the corner of Broad Street (now Broadwick Street), in the form of a replica pump, which stands opposite a pub, the John Snow.

Definition

Define – gather the evidence, analyse the facts

The fractal nature of the problem-solving process means that each phase will *tend* to reflect the overall structure. Thus within 'Problem Definition' there will be three smaller phases of definition, discovery and determination, which should be characterised by alternating convergent and divergent thinking styles.

1. **Define:** *a rigorous analysis of the evidence. Describe the symptoms.*

- How does the problem manifest itself?
- Who does the problem affect?
- What is the impact of the problem?

2. **Discover:** *an open-minded exploration of the structure of the problem. Find the cause.*

- How does the problem work?
- Is it simple or complex?
- What are the root causes?

3. **Determine:** *a judgement and a plan of action to seek a cure.*

- What are the criteria for success?
- What are the constraints in both time and resources?
- What are the priorities?

Because our problem-solving process is so wide ranging, not all the questions we suggest will be as relevant as others.

How does the problem manifest itself?

('Houston, we have a problem')

- How did it come to your attention? Was it a sudden failure or did you feel it coming? Letters in the post or a phone call, or is it one of those nagging problems that has always been there? Make sure you get input from those who first noticed the problem.

- What are the symptoms? For example, 'I feel ill' is not enough; exactly *how* do you feel ill? You have to give the doctor more information. Similarly, 'My car won't go' needs qualifying: does the engine turn over at all or does it start and then stop? You have to describe the problem.

- For Dr Snow it was people dying. For Coca-Cola it was declining sales in supermarkets, confused with a caning in the 'taste tests'. For James it was a nasty letter in the in-tray.

> Problems are like greatness in this regard:
>
> - Some we are born with, from the basics such as providing food, water and warmth to more complicated desires: what we want as well as what we need.
>
> - Some we achieve, that is they are specific to our particular interest; we seek them out as part of our job, be it organising a distribution network or solving Fermat's Last Theorem.
>
> - And those that are thrust upon us, from the unexpected tax demand to a collapse in sales; when whatever it might be hits the fan.

Who does the problem affect?

- Whose problem; yours or someone else's?

  In a business context that someone else is your customer.

  In a health context it is your patient.

  In education it would be your student.

The end user of whatever activity you are involved in. The point being emphasised is the possibility that you might attempt to solve a problem according to your criteria rather than the criteria of the actual 'sufferer', e.g. artificial limbs which *solve* aesthetic problems may be addressing the problems of society rather than the limbless person, who might not necessarily want to carry around an essentially useless appendage. It's always best to ask the end user: their perception of what the problem is may be different from yours.

- Can you get rid of the problem by outsourcing a solution? Much in the same way as King Hiero passed his problem on to Archimedes.

For example, 'the roof is leaking' so 'call the builders'. If you do, you face another series of questions:

- How will you monitor the situation?
- How will you resource the project?
- Can you trust your sub-contractor to deliver on time?

If you cannot answer these questions the problem is likely to bounce right back at you just when you've stopped worrying about it. Also you should consider the degree to which you may become dependent on experts.

What is the impact of the problem?

For the people of London the impact of the Broad Street cholera outbreak was dramatic and immediate. But even a potential small business failure has a larger knock-on impact. Your problem may be about to become someone else's problem. What will happen when they find out? Will they panic and send your credit and reputation down the drain; or might they be persuaded to help? Understanding the potential impact is essential when planning to solve a problem.

- What are the consequences?

  For example:

  'Our despatches are getting later and later.''So?'
  'Our customers are complaining.'
  'So?'
  'They might take their business elsewhere.'
  'So?'
  'Our business will suffer.'
  'So?'
  'You will lose your job!'

  And so on.

If problems are also opportunities and a problem shared is a problem halved then an opportunity shared ought to be an opportunity doubled. Which leads on to all sorts of possibilities – alliances, partnerships, symbiotic relationships, etc.

Discover – explore the structure of the problem, find the root causes

Former criminal and first director of the *Sûreté Nationale*, Eugène François Vidocq (1775–1857) is widely regarded as the world's first private detective.*

'The Murders in the Rue Morgue' by Edgar Allan Poe, published in 1841, is widely regarded as the world's first detective story.

Here is the fictional detective Auguste Dupin criticising the actual detective Vidocq. He 'was a good guesser and a persevering man. But . . . He impaired his vision by holding the object too close. He might see, perhaps, one or two points with unusual clearness, but in so doing he, necessarily, lost sight of the matter as a whole. Thus there is such a thing as being too profound. Truth is not always in a well. In fact, as regards the more important knowledge, I do believe that she is invariably superficial . . . To look at a star by glances . . . is to have the best appreciation of its lustre.'

Poe is comparing the *number-crunching* Vidocq with the *big picture* Dupin: Vidocq can't see the wood for the trees. They exhibit contrasting modes of thinking; indeed Dupin could be paraphrased as promoting 'a different point of view'. Nowadays only two thinking styles would be unimaginable. To quote once more from the Demos report *About Learning*, a list of terms they had come across: 'activists, theorists, pragmatists, reflectors, divergers, convergers, assimilators, accommodaters, verbalisers, imagers, analytics, wholists, analysts, changers, realists, visual, auditory, kinaesthetic'. Clearly some of these words describe the same or very similar aspects of thinking.

As with the various problem-solving methodologies, our purpose is not to reject or replace these formats, but to refer to them as part of a broader guide. There can be no doubt that different people have different thinking preferences, from those who have to write everything down to those who have to pace up and down. It makes perfect sense to be aware of the wide range, especially of your own limitations.

So, while remaining analytical, you need to relax somewhat and look *around* the problem. Step back and try to see the 'big picture'; look at it from different points of view. You need to understand the problem in its broadest context before you decide what to do about it.

Definition

*Vidocq is also notable as the inspiration for *both* protagonists in Victor Hugo's *Les Misérables*.

'Headline news'

We've already pointed out the rush to judgement which leads to so many poor-quality concepts which are half-heartedly and/or expensively applied and very often entirely fail to solve a problem. The sequence seems to be Scandal! – Outrage! – Action! It is best exemplified nowadays in tabloid journalism:

- Day One – Scandal! The headline writer: 'Shock Horror!'

- Day Two – Outrage! The columnist: 'Why oh why? Something must be done!'

- Day Three – Action! The response: 'Something WILL be done' – a cobbled together initiative.

Take, for example, 'Teenage Binge Drinking'. The first three questions of our process are quickly answered:

- How does the problem manifest itself? Easy – just go into any UK city centre on a Saturday night.

- Who does the problem affect? Again quite easy – for a start the teenagers, then all the people who have to deal with the problem, from parents to police to street cleaners and the health services.

- What is the impact of the problem? A little harder but still quite straightforward as we look at the consequences of the problem – health and safety; public order and respect for the law; the knock-on effect on other users.

The headline writer and columnist can usually manage this between them. But any snap judgement will tend to be based upon what has been discovered thus far, tempered by whatever knowledge and experience are immediately available.

The first solution to jump to is usually 'Ban it!' and if that is not feasible then 'Control it!'

But neither of these solutions is as easy to do as to say.

Total prohibition has a poor record. America was left with a legacy of organised crime and corruption after their 'noble experiment'. As John D. Rockefeller Jr wrote in 1932:

> When Prohibition was introduced, I hoped that it would be widely supported by public opinion and the day would soon come when the evil effects of alcohol would be recognised. I have slowly and reluctantly come to believe that this has not been the result. Instead, drinking has generally increased; the speakeasy has replaced the saloon; a vast army of lawbreakers has appeared; many of our best citizens have openly ignored Prohibition; respect for the law has been greatly lessened; and crime has increased to a level never seen before.

It is ironic that in a nation committed to the free market there should have been such an innocent appreciation of the principles of supply and demand. Reducing the supply would certainly increase the price and theoretically reduce demand, but the increased price would just as certainly encourage the interest of criminals. As we pointed out earlier, entrepreneurial thinking is amoral; Al Capone recognised opportunities in the domain of alcohol consumption in the same way as General Booth (founder of the Salvation Army) but with totally different ideas of what constituted 'value'.

The history of prohibition in the USA covers far more than the lifespan of the Volstead Act from the eighteenth amendment in 1919 to the twenty-first in 1933. Their earliest anti-alcohol laws date to seventeenth-century Massachusetts and some counties are still 'dry'. Mississippi was the last state to repeal prohibition in 1966. Kansas, which had outlawed alcohol in 1881, finally allowed sale of alcoholic beverages 'by the drink', i.e. on the premises, in 1987.

In fact alcohol is controlled throughout most of the world to some degree or other, from the almost total ban in the Arabian Peninsula to the severe restrictions in Sweden, which from 1917 to 1955 tried rationing: eligible citizens were issued with booklets, which were stamped to record purchases up to a monthly allowance. Even today alcohol purchase is only permitted in government-run stores called *Systembolaget.* In these, strict controls apply. In addition to age limits, special discounts are prohibited; no product can be sold at an advantage, for example all beer must be refrigerated or none, usually meaning that all is sold warm; and most products are sold individually. Taxation is solely based upon alcohol content. According to the Swedish government, in the ten years following accession to EU membership in 1995, which resulted in more permissive regulation, consumption rose by 30%.

But we are falling into the very trap we are warning of – we are discussing possible solutions before we have finished exploring the problem. For example, the relationship between price and consumption is not a simple one, complicated as it is by another dynamic between tax revenue and public expenditure on policing and health care; which in turn is complicated by potential lost revenue from those affected by the problem. Any in-depth discussion of binge drinking should explore the reasons why people drink 'antisocially'. And so we try to look at the bigger picture by posing another three questions: How does the problem work? Is it simple or complex? What are the root causes?

How does the problem work?

- Is there some sort of internal dynamic?
- For example: low performance = low remuneration = low morale = low performance. How can you reverse a spiral of decline?
- Is there a string of consequences?
- For example, housing chains: 'I can't move in until you move out.' How can you get the market moving?
- Can you draw a flow chart to illustrate the structure? Or even make a model?

Is it simple or complex?

Again we return to the issue of speed, or as we suggest is often the case, haste. As we mentioned earlier, prompt decision making is perceived as somehow better than slower (and, we would contend, more considered) judgement. And so it is with much else: fast food; rapid transit; express delivery. Speed is one of those factors which have become more and more attractive, a 'must-have'. And yet we know that the race is not always to the swift. As we will examine in more detail later in the book, during the 1960s and 70s the future of aviation was predicted to be supersonic but it is the jumbo jet that has succeeded while Concorde is the museum piece. Similarly, the Channel Tunnel offered the quicker journey between England and France but for many long-distance drivers the cross-channel ferry gave them the chance to take their mandatory break in more pleasant circumstances than a lay-by on the M20, especially when the ferry companies started offering free breakfasts. This is why it is so important to explore the context of a problem – bacon and eggs and tachographs were not quite as irrelevant as might be thought.

- How do different elements interact?
- For example, is there a knock-on effect within your organisation in terms of morale or allocation of resources?
- Obviously the larger the project the more complex it is but apparently simple problems can have complications.
- For example, how can I carry out market research on my new product without disclosing it to my competitors?
- Even the simplest of situations have snags.
- For example, five of us can drive to the party but if we decide to leave the car the taxi home can only carry four.

What are the root causes?

It is nice to think that there is a single root cause for any phenomenon; that any proposition should be reduced to its simplest expression. That may be to rush to judgement, however. Bear in mind that an apparently complex problem might in fact be a combination of relatively uncomplicated ones, which may or may not be interdependent.

- Each question 'Why?' may have more than one answer; each answer forming a new branch of the root network. Or you may find a string of single answers forming a 'tap root'; a single unambiguous cause.

For example:

'Why is there so much litter?'
'Because people drop it.'
'Why?'

Here we have two possible answers, which we will follow in turn:

1. 'Because people don't care.'
   'Why?'
   'Because they're detached from the consequences.'
   'Why?'
   'Because they're ignorant.'
   'Why?'
   'Because we haven't educated them.'

2. 'Because there are no litter bins.'
   'Why?'
   'Because we haven't put any there.'
   'Why?'
   'Because we haven't the resources to empty them.'
   'Why?'
   'Because we have other priorities.'

It's easy to say that you must drill down to the root cause of your problem; but it is harder to judge when to stop. The final 'Why?', which led to a full appreciation of the sequence of cause and effect which ended in the failure of the oxygen tank aboard *Apollo 13* was not answered until some time after the rescue was completed; they simply did not have the time. But what they did achieve was a comprehensive understanding of the situation as it was and they did not make it worse by guessing.

The idea that there should be one single root cause to any problem comes from *lex parsimonia* (the law of parsimony), which insists that we should seek explanations that rely on the least possible number of assumptions. It is better known as Ockham's Razor (or Occam's Razor) after the fourteenth-century English monk William of Ockham, who used the principle to *shave* away unnecessary suppositions in logic. A modern acronym is KISS: Keep It Simple Stupid. But the principle is hard to justify rationally; it is only a rule of thumb.

In medicine there is a desire to find a unifying diagnosis to explain a range of symptoms. But John Hickam, an American doctor, pointed out that 'a patient can have as many diseases as he damn well pleases'. Thus a patient reporting a headache, fever and cervical muscle spasm may be suffering from meningitis (one cause) or may be a chronic migraine sufferer with a throat infection and a stiff neck (three causes). The ability to choose when to apply Hickam's Dictum over Ockham's Razor is one of the reasons that medicine is called an art as well as a science.

Determine – decide how to attempt a solution

We now need to become more judgemental, fixing upon a plan of action.

Is it possible for a complex problem to be broken into manageable parts? Are the constituent parts separable or interdependent?

What are the criteria for success?

- How will you know if you have found the right solution?

- Criteria might include effectiveness, acceptability, ease of implementation, profitability, etc.

- You need to decide these now. They make up the target you are aiming at, which you will have to recall at the end of the problem-solving process to judge the likely success of your potential solutions.

In many ways you are listing the *minimum* requirements for the project to proceed. (Although we always hope to exceed our expectations.)

What are the constraints in both time and resources?

- **Is it important or is it urgent?**

  There is a real distinction. Urgent problems need solving straight away: important ones deserve more attention. The underlying causes of the *Apollo 13* emergency were important to the continuation of the programme: getting the astronauts home safely was urgent.

  Is a stop-gap solution feasible to give you enough time to create a permanent solution? For Dr Snow, removing the pump handle was most effective. (To continue the medical theme, sticking-plasters are both cheap and effective in the appropriate circumstances: a tourniquet is sometimes an absolute necessity.)

- **What can you afford to spend in terms of time and money? Would a cost/ benefit analysis help?**

  To return to the restaurant where we were dining on page 80, if your food order is beyond your means, then you might have solved one problem, i.e. you're no longer hungry, but you have caused another problem, i.e. how to pay for it.

What are the priorities?

We have already mentioned Churchill's method of prioritising: 'Action This Day', 'Report in Three Days' and 'Report Progress in One Week'. Another method is to split a pile of problems into three smaller piles: 'Things I have to deal with now', 'Things I have to deal with soon' and 'Things I can't do anything about and will probably just have to live with'. In management-speak this is *triage*. As with a lot of management-speak, the term is borrowed from elsewhere and should be treated with a certain amount of caution. For a start, triage has nothing to do with three; it comes from the French *trier* – to sort or select. It is a medical term used primarily in mass casualty situations such as war or civil disaster. As such the divisions tend to range from 'walking wounded' to 'dead' and can be used to select casualties using more complicated criteria than mere urgency. For instance, in a disaster 'walking wounded' would be treated last since they are likeliest to survive; but in a combat situation they might be treated first so that they could return to the battlefield. The distinction between important and urgent is dependent upon the circumstances.

- **Can you set sub-goals on the way to a complete solution?**

  That is, can progress be gradual, can it be step by step, or does it have to be all at once? Very often you can make the choice yourself; for example, it is possible to introduce reforms into an organisation gradually; a new product might be launched region by region. (But if you're building a bridge or an air terminal, it had better be ready once it's opened.)

- **What are the consequences of partial solution?**

  Partial solutions allow a cybernetic approach; being flexible enough to react to feedback, adjusting your solution if necessary. Would that help or hinder a complete solution?

  By the end of this phase you should have a good understanding of the problem; its structure, its dynamics, its complexity.

You should have a fair idea of where you are on the vertical axis of Kirk's Space.

You should not necessarily be thinking of a solution to the problem yet but should be formulating a plan for how to tackle it – what sort of solutions you are looking for and the order in which you need to find them.

You should be formulating a concise definition of the problem – or definitions if you decide to break it down and solve it bit by bit.

Very often defining a problem is half of the solution; sometimes indeed it is the whole of the solution. If, for instance, you have realised that the root cause of your car's breakdown is the failure of a particular component, then a solution is available quite literally 'off the shelf'. You need look no further; the problem's solved.

Definition

Problem Solved?

Occasionally a proper consideration of a 'problem' will reveal that it might not actually exist –any impartial study of the Bermuda Triangle, for example, will reveal that unexplained disappearances are no more frequent than in similarly busy areas elsewhere. The killer fact confirming that there is no problem is that insurance companies, who would if they could, as the cynics amongst us suggest, do not impose extra premiums for travellers through the area.

For difficult problems we need to ask 'Why?' a few more times.

On January 28th 1986, the Space Shuttle *Challenger* disintegrated shortly after take off, killing all seven crew members. The root cause of the disaster was the failure of one component due to cold weather – an O-ring seal in one of the rocket boosters. A stop-gap solution would have been to replace the component and reschedule launch dates to avoid cold weather. But it was realised that the problem was far more important than urgent when it emerged that the design was known years before to be potentially catastrophic. Root causes included NASA's organisational procedures and decision-making processes, and issues of workplace ethics and whistle blowing were exposed. The Rogers Commission, set up to investigate the disaster, characterised it as 'an accident rooted in history'.

On the other hand some problems are still difficult to solve even when the solution is perfectly obvious. The major cause of lung cancer is smoking tobacco; the solution is simple: stop smoking. So why is it so difficult?

If you are unable to come up with a concise definition, you have to ask whether you know enough about this problem to attempt a solution.

For example, look at these statistics from the UK National Health Service:

- In 1948 the death rate from cancer was 16%.
- In 2008 the death rate from cancer was 27%.
- Conclusion: an 11% increase despite 60 years of the NHS. A real problem.

Consider these figures, however:

- In 1948 average life expectancy was 67 years.
- In 2008 average life expectancy was 78 years.

Conclusion: the situation is more complicated than it first appears. Maybe there is more cancer than there used to be. Perhaps diagnoses have changed over sixty years. Perhaps people in 1948 used to die of other causes before they had a chance to die of cancer. Perhaps there isn't a problem at all; perhaps it's a success story. The fact is we simply don't know; we haven't got enough information to form any sort of judgement.

Lack of knowledge concerning all the factors and the failure to include them in our integral imposes false conclusions.

(Buckminster Fuller, 1975)

For instance, in relation to our problem of binge drinking, it is to be hoped that we would already have made ourselves aware of similar situations during the discovery phase of definition. We will, of course, have looked at the 'Gin Craze' in eighteenth-century England and its manifestation of the triple dynamic of individual liberty, Puritanism and tax. The modern dynamic is additionally complicated by the 'nanny state', leading to the curious circumstance where alcoholics, and smokers, can try to argue that their tax contributions more than outweigh the cost to the state of their addictions; further, it can be argued, their early death is a positive boon to an ageing and infirm society!

(Researchers from the Erasmus University in Rotterdam concluded that costs to society would actually rise if more smokers gave up since an increasing population of healthier individuals would be left to succumb eventually to the relatively expensive diseases of old age. They assessed the average lifetime costs of a non-smoking male to be nearly 15% greater than his smoking neighbour.)

We might have noticed the political origins of the gin distillery and even its relationship to the cultivation of 'bad' barley. We will probably have gone from there to a discussion of the absinthe craze and its relationship to the devastation of European, especially French, viticulture by the *phylloxera* epidemic at the end of the nineteenth century. We will know that the tee in teetotalism is nothing to do with tea, although we will have observed the effects of tea drinking on public health. We may even have come across the idea that the late nineteenth-century rise in ether abuse and coal-gas bubbled through milk (the 'corporation cocktail') was the result of pleasure/oblivion seekers being unwilling to break the soul-threatening oath of abstinence. We will know why Britain introduced limited licensing hours during the First World War. We may know about the failure of Gothenburg public houses as a solution to drunkenness and possibly have come across the encouragement of beer as an alternative to spirits, from Hogarth to the 'beer parties' of modern Eastern European politics.

By this time we will, at the very least, have an answer to the question, 'Is the problem simple or complex?'

If you don't have a proper understanding of a problem you don't have much chance of finding a solution. Go back and start again.

Another hazard of problem solving is when we think that we have a solution and so rush to implement it without reflection.

Very often we feel pushed for time and under great pressure to DO SOMETHING! Then we are tempted to make an educated guess, trusting our 'gut instinct'. But we can fall into the trap that Gene Kranz warned of: we can make things worse, in some cases fatally.

Definition

On January 8th 1989, British Midland Flight 92 crashed while attempting an emergency landing at East Midlands Airport. Initial reports were that both engines had failed. Modern airliners are designed with the capability to fly safely on just one engine; for both to fail on the same flight was almost inconceivably unlikely. And so it proved. The awful truth was that one engine had malfunctioned but the pilots had shut down the working one. The official report could not be clearer: 'The cause of the accident was that the operating crew shut down the No 2 engine after a fan blade had fractured in the No 1 engine.'

As the fan blade fractured, there were severe vibrations and smoke poured into the cabin. The captain made an educated guess, based on his knowledge of the Boeing 737, and shut down the right-hand engine; the smoke disappeared and the vibrations reduced. Unfortunately, this model of the 737 was different from the one the captain was familiar with and the disappearance of the smoke and vibration was coincidental, due to cutting the autothrottle rather than shutting off the engine. The plane crashed just yards from the runway. Of the 126 people on board only five escaped with minor injuries, 74 were seriously injured and 47 died.

Although the disaster was exacerbated by other factors, including failure to complete review procedures, the simple fact remains that nobody checked the original diagnosis. Passengers and cabin crew had seen with their own eyes smoke and flames coming from the left-hand engine but assumed that the pilots knew what they were doing, not realising that the engines were not visible from the cockpit. Under extreme stress they had fallen into the error known as confirmation bias: seeking a simple explanation of what had happened, they tended to over-emphasise supporting evidence while ignoring contradictory data.

The flight crew overrode procedures and, in the words of the report, 'reacted to the initial engine problem prematurely and in a way that was contrary to their training'.

Confirmation bias is the modern phrase but the error has been well known for centuries. In 1759, Laurence Sterne has his hero Tristram Shandy describe his father thus: 'He was systematical, and, like all systematic reasoners, he would move both heaven and earth, and twist and torture every thing in nature to support his hypothesis.'

As long ago as 1620, Francis Bacon pointed out that once the human intellect has adopted a position, it draws to it only that evidence which supports it, neglecting anything to the contrary. Bacon concluded that it is a great failing of human understanding to be more excited by affirmatives than negatives when they ought to be treated equally.

And yet in proving or disproving an axiom it is the negative which has the greater weight. If that last observation sounds familiar it is because the asymmetry between verification and falsifiability lies at the heart of Karl Popper's philosophy of science.

To get some idea of the stress those pilots were under we ought to remember that only eighteen days previously 270 people had died in the then still unexplained Lockerbie bombing. Very few of us indeed are under that sort of pressure. So before we begin the next phase, find time to pause and have another look at your problem definition; you can modify and repeat as many times as it takes to make it possible to attempt a solution: creative problem solving is an iterative process; you can always return to GO.

If possible get someone else to review your progress. It is very easy to become fixated with one particular idea. Confirmation bias is particularly powerful in a group; favourite ideas attract more support than criticism. It is perfectly understandable; most of the time it is commendable to avoid conflict and to reach consensus. It is hard to be the only critic in the group when everyone else is swept along on a wave of enthusiasm. It's always easy to go with the flow, and intellect is certainly not a barrier:

> One has to belong to the *intelligentsia* to believe things like that: no ordinary man could be such a *fool*.
>
> (George Orwell, 'Notes on Nationalism', 1945)

When things go wrong with group decision making, the rest of us can see immediately that the Emperor never had any clothes – 'What were they thinking of?' It's hard to imagine that the *Eames Bradley Report* would not have benefited from 'a fresh pair of eyes'. The more formal of us use the word 'groupthink',* always pejoratively and with hindsight.

Fine discriminations of definition need not concern us here, nor the ways in which groupthink operates. We need only to be aware of it and have strategies to avoid it.

It is easy to say, 'Get someone else to review your progress'; more difficult to do in highly cohesive goal-driven teams engaged in often secret or confidential projects – precisely the sort of people most prone to groupthink. But it can be done, by each team member taking turns to play devil's advocate, for example, or by inviting expert opinion on a confidential basis.

---

*Groupthink has changed its meaning over time.

Sociologist William H. Whyte coined the expression in 1952, writing that, 'We are not talking about mere instinctive conformity – it is, after all, a perennial failing of mankind. What we are talking about is a rationalised conformity – an open, articulate philosophy which holds that group values are not only expedient but right and good as well.'

By the 1970s, psychologist Irving Janis had redefined it as 'A mode of thinking that people engage in when they are deeply involved in a cohesive in-group, when the members' strivings for unanimity override their motivation to realistically appraise alternative courses of action.'

Definition

There are, of course, some people who consciously reject the involvement of others and make a virtue of an individual vision. The fashion designer Manolo Blahnik works without assistants or apprentices, controlling every aspect of his highly successful shoe business, from the initial sketches, through hand carving the master lasts, to supervising the manufacturing process.

He would probably agree with Sir Alec Issigonis: 'A camel is a horse designed by committee.' (Of course if they were crossing a desert, most people would choose a camel every time.)

The iconoclastic Issigonis dismissed market research as 'bunk', insisting that 'The public don't know what they want; it's my job to tell them.' He thought that mathematics was the enemy of creativity and dismissed experts as people who tell you 'why you can't do something'.

Three of the most successful cars in post-war Britain – the Morris Minor, the Mini and the Austin 1100 – all bore his personal stamp on almost all aspects of design. The Mini was so innovative (not least by having its engine mounted sideways) that it has become an icon itself. Such fierce independence is all very well, but Issigonis wouldn't have sold so many cars had his rejection of radios and comfortable seats as 'luxuries' not been overruled.

A more recent example of the highly successful designer with absolute confidence in his own judgement was the late Steve Jobs who, like Issigonis, was occasionally just plain wrong. His opinion of e-readers, specifically Amazon's Kindle, was quoted in 2008: 'It doesn't matter how good or bad the product is, the fact is that people don't read anymore . . . 40% of the people in the U.S. read one book or less last year. The whole conception is flawed at the top because people don't read anymore.'*

At the very least you should take a break to allow you to refocus on the problem when you return. If you find it difficult to do nothing for a while then do something else. This is what we shall do now.

*In October 2011 the biggest-selling book on Amazon was Jobs' biography – so someone must still be reading books.

Interlude: the multi-disciplinary imperative

This diversion will take as its starting point a 1952 editorial in *History Today*, which observed that 'One of the chief tragedies of twentieth-century life is the lack of any form of coordination between intelligent men of goodwill, who, if they are engaged in different fields of research, inevitably speak in different languages and are almost incapable of associating for any common purpose.'

The physicist Robert Oppenheimer remarked in a 1954 speech:

> The specialization of science is an inevitable accompaniment of progress; yet it is full of dangers, and it is cruelly wasteful, since so much that is beautiful and enlightening is cut off from most of the world.

> The truth is that this is indeed inevitably and increasingly an open, and inevitably and increasingly an eclectic world. *We know too much for one man to know much, we live too variously to live as one.* Our histories and traditions – the very means of interpreting life – are both bonds and barriers among us. Our knowledge separates as well as it unites; our orders disintegrate as well as bind; our art brings us together and sets us apart.

Charles Percy Snow coined the phrase 'Two Cultures' in a 1956 article, which he expanded in a lecture some three years later. C. P. Snow was both a scientist and a novelist and so thought he knew what he was talking about when he said he believed that 'the intellectual life of the whole of western society is increasingly being split into two polar groups . . . Between the two a gulf of mutual incomprehension – sometimes (particularly among the young) hostility and dislike, but most of all lack of understanding.'

He placed physics at one pole and, at the other extreme, literary intellectuals ('who incidentally while no one was looking took to referring to themselves as "intellectuals" as though there were no others'.) This last crack aroused the ire of the literary critic and academic F. R. Leavis who repudiated Snow in such vituperative terms that the resulting debate still reverberates, still generating more heat than light. Snow achieved further fame when he coined another phrase, 'the corridors of power'. Leavis's lasting fame, like all critics', rests on his assessment of the efforts of others.

Oppenheimer compared professional critics to popularisers and promoters of science and it must be said that scientists themselves have made significant progress in explaining their work to the wider public. The world of literary criticism still awaits a Dawkins or Sagan to put their world into plain words for the rest of us.

There is no point for us in arguing whose culture is more worthy – we have nailed our colours to the mast already by describing them all as problems waiting to be solved. Our concern is Snow's explanation of the consequences:

> At the heart of thought and creation we are letting some of our best chances go by default. The clashing point of two subjects, two disciplines, two cultures – of two galaxies, as far as that goes – ought to produce creative chances. In the history of mental activity that has been where some of the breakthroughs came. The chances are there now. But they are there, as it were, in a vacuum, because those in the two cultures can't talk to each other.

Even within disciplines there is often a 'hostility and dislike' between 'pure' and 'applied' knowledge. So there are far more than two mutually incomprehensible cultures at work these days and some seem to be deliberately impenetrable.

Specialisation is, as Oppenheimer said, the inevitable accompaniment of progress, but there is more to the cultural divide than mere specialism and obscure language. The differences between art and science are deep rooted – they seem to look at the same information in different ways, from different points of view.

In order to trace the estrangement of art and science, we shall return to that article in *History Today*, which issued this question as a challenge: 'When did it become impossible for an educated man to grasp, at least in its broader and more general outlines, the entire extent of European learning?'

For a long time Aristotle was thought to be the man who knew everything worth knowing, despite being wrong in many respects: for example, he believed men had more teeth than women. It was Bertrand Russell who suggested that he could have checked by asking Mrs Aristotle.

By the sixteenth and early seventeenth centuries it was certainly still possible for an individual to be familiar with the major works of art, science and philosophy from both the modern and classical worlds. We think of course of Leonardo and Galileo, but also of Bacon and Newton.

Separation in the European tradition seems to have started in the mid-seventeenth century with the growth of the study of Natural Sciences and the increasing rejection of 'old knowledge'. Reason rather than classical authority became the guiding principle of what became known as the Enlightenment. Astronomy disconnects from astrology; chemistry replaces alchemy. The Royal Society, instituted in 1660, was dedicated to the propagation of new knowledge; its motto *'Nullius in Verba'* suggests that we should take nobody's word for anything and put our trust in experiment rather than written authority. (Adelard would have been proud of them.) As the Enlightenment went on it was still possible, even desirable, to be a polymath. Natural Philosophy was a gentlemanly pursuit, as popular as art or music. In the Midlands, the spirit of the gentleman amateur was carried forward by the Lunar Society, a collection of industrialists and intellectuals who used to meet once a month when the full moon would see them safely home along the unlit country roads. (They cheerfully referred to themselves as Lunaticks.) But as the industrial revolution progressed, technology became less fashionable. James Boswell was clearly impressed by his visit to Birmingham, where the engineer and inventor Matthew Boulton told him, 'I sell here, Sir, what all the world desires to have – POWER,' but he showed no interest in becoming *engaged* with technology. (His friend and mentor, one of the greatest intellects of the time, the lexicographer Dr Samuel Johnson, didn't even bother to make the short trip.)

Gentlemen would send their sons, and very occasionally daughters, on the Grand Tour, but it was for culture rather than science. The technology needed to translate the art and architecture from the Grand Tour into the reality of northern Europe was not the particular concern of *gentlemen*. There is almost certainly an element of old-fashioned snobbishness about this; technology being a little too close to 'trade' for some of the ruling classes. An honourable exception to this generalisation is the extent to which the landed gentry were often very interested in improvements in agriculture.

The social-climbing provincial magnates of the Industrial Revolution appreciated art and poetry, and in return some painters were certainly inspired by science and technology.

Paintings by the English artist Joseph Wright of Derby hang in the Hermitage in St Petersburg, the Louvre in Paris and the Getty in Los Angeles. Famous in his lifetime as a portrait and landscape artist, he specialised in painting light and shade, using his own innovative techniques. But he is best known today for his innovative choice of subjects; he was one of the first painters of the Industrial Revolution. His 1768 work, *An Experiment on a Bird in the Air-Pump* (National Gallery, London), depicting the marvels of science being demonstrated to a contemporary audience with mixed reactions – wonder, horror and boredom – is nowadays seen as one of the great evocations of the Enlightenment. The equally iconic *A Philosopher Giving that Lecture on the Orrery, in which a lamp is put in place of the Sun* (1766) has pride of place in the Derby Museum and Art Gallery. Close by *The Orrery* is a third masterpiece of special interest to students of the history of ingenuity, *The Alchymist*.

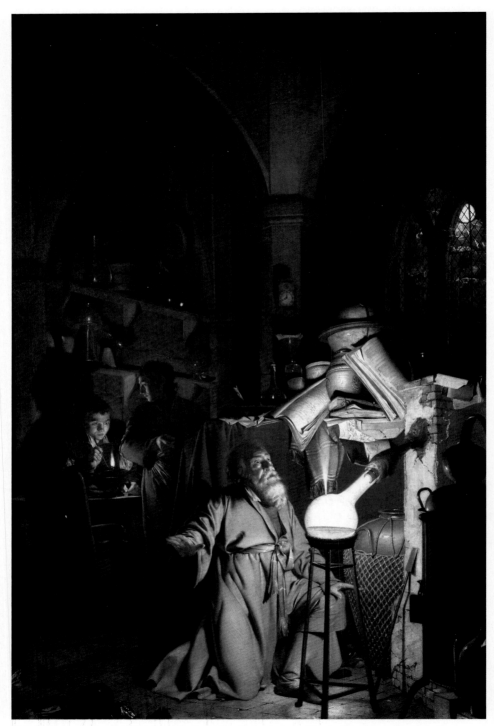

The Alchymist by Joseph Wright of Derby by kind permission of Derby Museums and Galleries

To the modern viewer, especially anyone interested in innovation, the picture is a magnificent exposition of a eureka moment in all its glory, the genius awestruck by the wonder of his discovery. The full title, *The Alchymist, in Search of the Philosopher's Stone, Discovers Phosphorus, and prays for the successful Conclusion of his Operation, as was the custom of the Ancient Chymical Astrologers*, suggests that the picture depicts an actual event: the curious experiment of Hennig Brandt in Hamburg in 1669, in which he boiled down and distilled an enormous quantity of putrefied urine. To discover a substance as remarkable as phosphorus from a material derived from living creatures must have led Brandt to think he was close to his dream of finding the very essence of life – the philosopher's stone. When we look at the painting in our terms, with our hindsight, we share the wonder of Brandt's discovery but we are also aware that we are witnessing a paradigm shift; we see Brandt as simultaneously the last of the alchemists and the first chemist.

The Alchymist was painted in 1771; the same year that Wright's friend and patron Sir Richard Arkwright opened that landmark of the Industrial Revolution, Cromford Mill, just a few miles up the River Derwent from Derby. It was an exhibition piece, with no particular customer in mind, and originally priced at £105. Wright seems to have been unsure about the picture from the beginning and indeed it remained in his possession, even travelling to Italy and back to Derby. So what was it about *The Alchymist* that made it so difficult to sell to enlightened gentlemen? The painting had been offered to his friend Josiah Wedgwood, who thought it 'inappropriate' and preferred the more romantic *Corinthian Maid* (a picture of the daughter of a classical potter). What was it that was inappropriate about the subject during Wright's lifetime?

Alchemy, in the latter half of the eighteenth century, was a delicate subject, which still attracted controversy. Ben Jonson's play *The Alchemist* remained popular, representing alchemists as mere charlatans. In 1783, a fellow of the Royal Society, James Price, had committed suicide by drinking prussic acid in front of three of his fellows, who had insisted on a demonstration of his purported method of producing gold and silver from base metals. We can speculate that an alternative reading of Wright's painting would be more critical; we might echo Francis Bacon and see alchemists as seeking to replace honest human sweat and endeavour with a few drops of elixir. Why should we be celebrating an old fool with no methodology, who only discovered anything by accident? Magic and superstition would have no place on the walls of hard-nosed rationalists, who left nothing to chance and whose achievements came from pure cold reason and the free exchange of ideas. Perhaps the comfortably distant classical world was 'art' but alchemy was a little too recent.

Thirty-five years after he painted it and nearly four years after his death, *The Alchymist* was finally sold by auction at Christies on 6 May 1801 for the respectable sum of £80 17s 0d,* reflecting that renewed interest and appreciation of an artist which often seems to come posthumously.

*It must now be regarded as priceless.

But also perhaps there was an acceptance of the subject matter; science was more secure in its separation from alchemy; discussion of their relationship could be more relaxed and the image was quite suitable and appropriate.

In 1807, Humphry Davy (a provincial like Wright) isolated both potassium and sodium through electrolysis, using very scientific methodology. One account states that 'Davy danced about the room in ecstatic delight; he likened the potassium to substances imagined by alchemical visionaries.'

It is not too much to speculate that Davy, who was aware of Brandt's experiment and whose acquaintances ranged from the poets Southey and Coleridge to the Wedgwoods, would have seen the painting. In his *Elements of Chemical Philosophy* (1812), Davy reviews the history of chemistry. He is happy to look as far back as the 'Egyptian priests, and the Brahmins of Hindostan'. He criticises the Greeks, dismisses the Romans and marks the beginnings of chemistry as an experimental science in the seventh and eighth centuries. He is well aware of the Arabic origins of chemistry.

He condemns all alchemists for following 'the pursuit as a secret and mysterious study' and in general finds little to 'instruct or amuse an intelligent reader'. Of all the alchemists, 'Paracelsus alone deserves particular notice, from the circumstance of his being the first public lecturer on chemistry in Europe, and from the more important circumstance of his application of mercurial preparations to the cure of diseases' but he too is condemned: 'He pretended to confer immortality, by his medicines, and yet died at the age of 49.' A sad irony is that Davy also died prematurely at the age of 51, almost certainly poisoned by his own experimentation like Paracelsus.

It would be unthinkable today, but in the 1790s when Erasmus Darwin published his translation of Linnaeus' classification of plants it was as verse; and it was well received as both art and science. The leading poets of the day, many of them personal friends of Davy, admired Darwin's poetry and had undoubtedly been fascinated by Galvani and Mesmer, but they were increasingly estranged from science, having developed fundamentally different viewpoints. William Wordsworth states the new romantic point of view in 'The Tables Turned': 'Enough of Science and of Art', he says, 'Let Nature be your Teacher.'

> Sweet is the lore which Nature brings;
> Our meddling intellect
> Mis-shapes the beauteous form of things: -
> We murder to dissect.

Why did Wordsworth fall out of love with science? Why does Keats accuse science of trying to 'unweave the rainbow'? 'Do not all charms fly at the mere touch of cold philosophy?'

In England, Enlightenment ideas had been fatally associated with both the American and French revolutions – the pioneer chemist Joseph Priestley was burnt out of his house by a counter-revolutionary mob in 1791. The birth of Romanticism, however, was a reaction to other perceived shortcomings of the Enlightenment.

In 1965, a series of lectures by Isaiah Berlin examined *The Roots of Romanticism.* Berlin first enumerated three propositions:

1. That all questions can be answered and a question that cannot be answered is not a genuine question.

2. That there are ways and means by which we (humanity) can discover these answers.

3. That all these answers must be compatible.

'The general pattern, I wish to stress, of this notion is that life, or nature, is a jigsaw puzzle. We lie among the disjected pieces of this puzzle. It is like a hunt for some kind of concealed treasure. The only difficulty is to find a path to the treasure.'

From Aristotle onwards, Berlin maintained, these are:

. . . the general presuppositions of the rationalist Western tradition, whether Christian or pagan, whether theist or atheist.

The particular twist which the Enlightenment gave to this tradition was to say that the answers were not to be obtained in many of the hitherto traditional ways . . . The answer is not to be obtained by revelation, for different men's revelations appear to contradict each other. It is not to be obtained by tradition, because tradition can be shown to be often misleading and false. It is not to be obtained by dogma, it is not to be obtained by the individual self-inspection of men of a privileged type because too many impostors have usurped this role – and so forth. There is only one way of discovering these answers, and that is by the correct use of reason, deductively as in the mathematical sciences, inductively as in the sciences of nature. That is the only way in which answers in general – true answers to serious questions – may be obtained. There is no reason why such answers, which after all have produced such triumphant results in the worlds of physics and chemistry, should not equally apply to the much more troubled fields of politics, ethics and aesthetics.

It was this dissection and measurement that Romantics so despised, and as science, engineering, economics and architecture continued their 'improvements' through the accumulation and interpretation of cold hard facts, the separation of reason and imagination became pronounced.

At a meeting of the British Association for the Advancement of Science in 1834, the word 'scientist' was proposed to describe 'students of the knowledge of the material world' in a direct analogy with artists.*

In 1847, the Royal Society decided to elect future fellows solely on their scientific worth; the days of the interested gentleman amateur were over. There was no Victorian equivalent to the Lunar Society.

By 1854 the divorce was complete. In *Hard Times*, Charles Dickens contrasts *fact* and *fancy*. Fact is exemplified by Mr Gradgrind: 'NOW, what I want is, Facts. Teach these boys and girls nothing but Facts. Facts alone are wanted in life. Plant nothing else, and root out everything else. You can only form the minds of reasoning animals upon Facts: nothing else will ever be of any service to them.'

Mr Gradgrind is led through experience to know the error of this point of view and will henceforth make 'his facts and figures subservient to Faith, Hope, and Charity'. (It's probably no surprise that F. R. Leavis regarded *Hard Times* as Dickens' only masterpiece.)

Fact versus fancy; and yet we need both. Oppenheimer contrasted artists and scientists but concluded that they had much in common.

Both the man of science and the man of art live always at the edge of mystery, surrounded by it; both always, as the measure of their creation, have had to do with the harmonization of what is new and what is familiar, with the balance between novelty and synthesis, with the struggle to make partial order in total chaos.

The great storm kick-started by Copernicus** had broken into myriad fierce squalls; each different discipline able to develop exclusive of the rest. Art, science, technology, politics and philosophy all embarked on separate courses, undergoing their own paradigm shifts, losing sight of one another and abandoning any unifying ideals. Only a few disciplines such as architecture or design still require both art and

*It was in a letter that same year that Alexander Humboldt wrote of his ambition to encapsulate all *he* knew into one volume: *'Ich habe den tollen Einfall, die ganze materielle Welt, alles was wir heute von den Erscheinungen der Himmelsräume und des Erdenlebens, von den Nebelsternen bis zur Geographie der Moose auf den Granitfelsen, wissen, alles in Einem Werke darzustellen, und in einem Werke, das zugleich in lebendiger Sprache anregt und das Gemüth ergötzt.'* (I have the extravagant idea of describing in one and the same work the whole material world all that we know to-day of celestial bodies and of life upon the earth from the nebular stars to the mosses on the granite rocks and to make this work instructive to the mind, and at the same time attractive, by its vivid language.)

The resulting work, *Kosmos*, had run to four published volumes by the time of Humboldt's death in 1859, the very year that Charles Darwin published *On the Origin of Species*.

**Ironically the heliocentric model is no more accurate than the geocentric in locating the centre of the universe. Bearing in mind that sun and earth are constantly moving in relation to each other, at different times each will be nearer to any other hypothetical centre, so they're both wrong. The Big Bang theory insists, however, that the universe came into being everywhere at once and can therefore have no centre, since there was nowhere for a centre to be before space came into existence – so the geocentric/heliocentric debate is irrelevant. But it seemed important at the time.

science. During the Victorian era the very idea of possessing knowledge beyond one's immediate sphere became ripe for satire: Gilbert and Sullivan's 1879 Modern Major-General is so filled with binomial theory and Babylonic cuneiform that he has no room for practical military understanding.

Since we cannot know everything, we have to trust experts in fields other than our own. The astronomer Carl Sagan told of a discussion with an expert in ancient history concerning Immanuel Velikovsky's controversial revision of world history. Each expert found the theory quite persuasive in the other's field, yet totally ridiculous in their own.

So how can the layperson proceed?

> *Douter de tout ou tout croire, ce sont deux solutions également commodes, qui l'une et l'autre nous dispensent de réfléchir.* (To doubt everything or to believe everything are two equally effortless solutions; they both exempt us from thinking.)
>
> (Henri Poincaré, *La Science et l'Hypothèse* 1901)

If we think of depth of knowledge as a vertical axis and breadth of knowledge as a horizontal axis, we have to recognise that vertical pre-eminence counts for nothing on the horizontal axis. If we try to leap from one height to another we may fall, but bearing in mind that we are 'pre-concept', we have nothing to lose; we might even enjoy the trip!

Vertical knowledge is built up slowly from first principles; every mathematician should have crossed Euclid's *pons asinorum*. Most musicians know their scales, and every architect *ought* to be able to build a garden wall.

When we look horizontally for the greatest breadth of ideas, we must be aware that we are more likely to find shallow and half-understood concepts. There is a distinction between shallow and surface knowledge – shallow knowledge implies no profundity; whereas surface knowledge recognises that there is great depth to the subject.

In his autobiography, the great Victorian inventor and entrepreneur Sir Henry Bessemer showed no fear of this:

> I may here remark that I have always adopted a different reading of the old proverb, 'A little knowledge is a dangerous thing'; this may indeed be true, if your knowledge is equally small on all subjects; but I have found a little knowledge on a great many different things of infinite service to me.

On the subject of sugar-cane milling, he saw a certain ignorance as a positive benefit:

> I had an immense advantage over many others dealing with the problem under consideration, inasmuch as I had no fixed ideas derived from long-established practice to control and bias my mind, and did not suffer from the too-general belief that whatever is, is right. Hence I could, without check or restraint, look the question steadily in the face, weigh without prejudice or preconceived notions, all the pros and cons, and strike out fearlessly in an absolutely new direction if thought desirable.

As for the field where he gained lasting fame:

> My knowledge of iron metallurgy was at that time very limited, and consisted only of such facts as an engineer must necessarily observe in the foundry or smith's shop; but this was in one sense an advantage to me, for I had nothing to unlearn. My mind was open and free to receive any new impressions, without having to struggle against the bias which a life-long practice of routine cannot fail more or less to create.

Bessemer is not a lone voice. In a 1963 essay Michael Polanyi said of one of his scientific projects:

> I would never have conceived my theory, let alone have made a great effort to verify it, if I had been more familiar with major developments in physics that were taking place. Moreover, my initial ignorance of the powerful, false objections that were being raised against my ideas protected those ideas from being nipped in the bud.

> It seems to me what is called for is an exquisite balance between two conflicting needs: the most skeptical scrutiny of all hypotheses that are served up to us and at the same time a great openness to new ideas . . . If you are only skeptical, then no new ideas make it through to you . . . On the other hand, if you are open to the point of gullibility and have not an ounce of skeptical sense in you, then you cannot distinguish the useful ideas from the worthless ones.
> (Carl Sagan, 'The Burden of Skepticism' 1987)

But the tide of nonsense is relentless:

> 'No matter how cynical you become, it's never enough to keep up.'
> (American comic Lily Tomlin, written by Jane Wagner)

Opportunity Recognition: write it down!

Before moving on to look for possible solutions, be sure to note down any interesting thoughts; seemingly irrelevant ideas which might be useful in other areas are the inevitable by-product of structured thinking. If there is one thing as inevitable as death and taxes it is that *you will forget unless you write it down*.

It is obviously very difficult to come up with examples of really good ideas that have been forgotten but the phenomenon has long been recognised. Back in the sixteenth century, Michel de Montaigne complained that his best ideas came to him when he least expected them, whether at dinner or in bed, but especially when out riding, and that they vanished before he had a chance to record them. He describes the frustration of sensing good ideas going down the drain: *'Plus j'ahane à le trouver, plus je l'enfonce en l'oubliance.'* (The more I struggle to find them, the deeper I sink them into oblivion.)

The seventeenth century antiquary John Aubrey relates a story of the habit of Montaigne's English contemporary Sir Philip Sidney 'as he was hunting on our pleasant plains, to take his table book out of his pocket, and write down his notions as they came into his head'. Aubrey notes wryly that he never actually completed his most ambitious work, *Arcadia*.

The educationalist Graham Wallas confessed: 'I myself find that my newest, and therefore, most easily forgotten thoughts tend to present themselves under the stimulus of the first spongeful of water in my bath; but I have never had the courage to search in the stationers' shops for a waterproof writing-tablet and pencil' (*The Art of Thought*, 1926).

So write it down, and while you're at it, back it up.

Modern technology means that nearly all of us have experienced at some time the sheer horror of losing a document. Nowadays, the worst we have to fear is the pitying looks of 'technical support'; in the past things were different, especially the level of horror!

Imagine the scene – 1869, Highgate Cemetery in London, late at night; an exhumation is taking place. The grave of Elizabeth Rossetti (née Siddall) is being opened in order to retrieve a notebook that had been buried with her seven years previously. Her body was reported to be perfectly preserved and her long red hair had continued to grow after death. In attendance as the initiator of proceedings, the thoroughly disreputable figure of Charles Augustus Howell. Howell was immortalised by Arthur Conan Doyle as the very thinly disguised 'king of blackmailers', Charles Augustus Milverton, to whose murder Holmes and Watson are witnesses and accessories after the fact: 'It was no affair of ours; that justice had overtaken a villain.'

Howell was said to have died in the gutter outside a public house, his throat slit and a coin placed in his mouth – the sign of a slanderer – but at the time of the exhumation he was building a reputation as a 'fixer' for the artistic community of London. James McNeill Whistler later said that 'It was easier to get involved with Howell than to get rid of him.'

Lizzie Siddall had been working in millinery when she was 'discovered' and became entangled with the Pre-Raphaelite Brotherhood. She became seriously ill after floating in an unheated bathtub while modelling for John Everett Millais' painting of Ophelia; her father forced Millais to pay the doctor's bill. She became an accomplished artist in her own right and married the poet and painter Dante Gabriel Rossetti in 1860. Less than two years later she was dead from an overdose of laudanum. There is a suspicion that a suicide note was found but suppressed by her husband. Her death affected Rossetti badly; the growing craze of spiritualism allowed him to try and contact her at séances.

By 1869, Rossetti himself was also a drug addict, in his case chloral and alcohol. Involved in a messy affair with Jane, the wife of his friend and business partner William Morris, he was also desperate to revive his reputation as a poet. And so, at the behest of Charles Augustus Howell, he allowed his wife's repose to be violated in order to retrieve that slim volume of handwritten love poetry he had, in his grief, placed in those famous red locks. The water-damaged and worm-eaten volume was disinfected by a physician and the text reworked by Rossetti. It was published the next year to mixed reviews. In the years that followed Rossetti suffered a mental breakdown and was cut out of the company by Morris. As a guilt-ridden near recluse, he continued and increased his chloral intake before he eventually died in 1882, described as 'a man grown old long ages before his due time'.

There are numerous morals to be drawn from this cautionary tale, mostly about fidelity, choosing your friends wisely, avoiding bad company, the perils of substance abuse and the fickle nature of fame. But the one we wish to highlight is the need to back up your files.

PHASE TWO:
Discovery

This section is more relaxed, what Guilford identified as divergent production, generating multiple solutions. How might we get where we want to be?

> . . . what we are about to consider is that kind of change arising from within the system *which so displaces its equilibrium point that the new one cannot be reached from the old one by infinitesimal steps.* Add successively as many mail coaches as you please, you will never get a railway thereby. [Original emphasis]
>
> (J. Schumpeter The Theory of Economic Development, 1934)

We need to explore broadly; gathering ideas as widely as we can; horizontal rather than vertical thinking: the style of thinking popularly associated with the right hemisphere of the brain. Remember Iain McGilchrist's description, 'a very broad, open attention for whatever might be, a completely uncommitted attention . . .'

This is the point where the authors can imagine a great many very successful people – managers, engineers, academics, businessmen and women – are likely to paraphrase Reggie Perrin's stereotypical boss CJ and say, 'I didn't get where I am today by adopting a completely uncommitted attention.' And yet we maintain – and will demonstrate – that is exactly the sort of approach that has yielded the most radical solutions throughout much of human history.

The Hungarian mathematician George *Polya* (1887–1985) took a no-nonsense approach to problem solving. His 1945 book, *How to Solve It*, contains a series of heuristics designed to help the solver through a four-stage process:

1. Understand the problem.
2. Devise a plan.
3. Carry out the plan.
4. Review your results.

And yet he prefaces his volume thus: 'A great discovery solves a great problem but there is a grain of discovery in the solution of any problem.'

Unfortunately, as we have seen, imaginative thinking has received a bad press over the years. This has not been helped by the kind of half-explained gobbledegook and nonsense available under the banner of 'creativity'. As we move through this section, we would ask the reader to keep an open mind – there will be plenty of time for making judgements later.

Lateral Thinking

In 1967, the Maltese writer and thinker Edward de Bono coined the term 'lateral thinking' in contrast with what he perceived as the 'vertical' style of 'traditional thinking'. The term has since entered the language to describe an unconventional approach to problem solving. Mr de Bono does not suffer from false modesty: 'I am one of the very few people in history to have had a major impact on the way we think – rather than on what we think. For the first time in history it has become possible to see creativity not as a mystique [sic] process but as the behaviour of a self-organising information system formed from neural networks.'

He can be criticised, however, for being very good at generating alternative ideas while not concerning himself too much with the practicalities of putting them into effect. For example, he was reported as suggesting (to the British Foreign Office) that the solution to the problems of the Middle East could be addressed by shipping out large quantities of yeast extract.

> The logic, briefly, is this. A lack of zinc makes men irritable and belligerent. You get zinc in yeast . . . But in the Middle East, the bread is unleavened. Ergo, the great man says, Marmite is the answer to easing the way to peace . . . He was confident his zinc theory would be proved if only hospitals in the Middle East would co-operate in tests. But he conceded they probably would not.
>
> (*Independent*, December 19th 1999)

Mr de Bono has written 62 books.

Thinking 'Outside the Box'

Most lateral-thinking puzzles rely for their solution upon looking from a different point of view and so from the outset will direct the puzzler's attention in the 'wrong' direction. Misdirection is the secret behind the nine-dot puzzle, which is also a contender for the origin of the phrase 'outside the box'. You have to join all the dots with only four straight lines, never removing your pen from the paper. The solution requires you to ignore the 'box' formed by the nine dots; no one told you to stay within them.

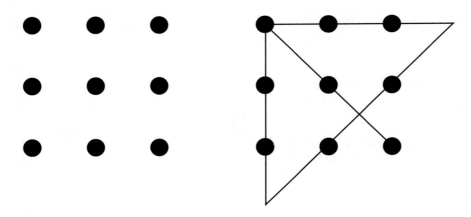

The worst sort of mystery story is the one with the preposterous solution, which you have no realistic chance of solving; the murderer turns out to be the long-lost identical twin or something equally unlikely. Sherlock Holmes's dictum that 'Once you have eliminated the impossible, whatever remains, however improbable, must be the case,' is neither fair to the puzzler, nor of that much use in an imperfect world, where the *impossible* seems to happen with frightening regularity.

Many so-called lateral-thinking puzzles are like this; the old, politically incorrect, favourite, for example, where a man who lives in a skyscraper uses the lift every morning to go down to street level but always climbs the stairs to return home, except when it's raining. The answer to this puzzle, that the man is a dwarf who can only reach the high buttons in the lift with an umbrella, is an insult to the intelligence. The dwarf would have to be short witted as well as short in stature; frustrating when you don't know the answer, pointless when you do. Entertaining enough if you don't find it offensive, possibly worthwhile as a loosening-up exercise, but once you know the answer to puzzles of this type, they have very little to offer. Others are mere tricks.

Consider the following:

The secretary of the local tennis club wants to know how many matches there will be in this year's tournament. 'There are 157 entrants so obviously we need to start organising ourselves.'

The linear thinker retires to the corner with pen and paper and starts analysing.

The lateral thinker immediately comes up with the answer: 'Easy, really. All you have to do is remember that there will only be one winner, all the others are losers, and they only lose once. So, one winner, 156 losers, therefore 156 matches.'

And that's that; the members retire to the bar congratulating the lateral thinker on his brilliance.

But – some time later, the linear thinker comes in with his little piece of paper. He too has the correct answer, and because he worked it out analytically he also knows how many rounds there will have to be: working backwards from one final, two semi-finals, four quarter-finals and so on. Crucially, the linear thinker has also identified the number of entrants who will have to be given 'byes' into the second round, raising further potential problems of selection.

Who do you think the club secretary is buying drinks for?

By misdirection, the puzzler has led us to an easy answer to what is only one aspect of a much more complex problem.

But we mustn't be too dismissive. Some puzzles are genuinely insightful. Here, making his only appearance in this book, is the novice monk.

One day a young novice monk leaves his monastery at dawn to climb up the holy mountain to visit the temple at the top. It is a cold day so he walks briskly to start with. As the day wears on, he tires and rests a while before finally hurrying to get to the temple just before sunset.

The next morning, as the sun rises, the monk returns homeward down the same narrow path. This day however is warmer and even though the journey is downhill he walks quite slowly. In the afternoon he has to shelter from a thunderstorm and so ends up having to run the last mile to reach the monastery before it gets dark.

Is there any point on the mountain path that he occupied at exactly the same time on each day, and can you prove it? *Clue: H. G. Wells.*

Here are two similar problems:

- A farmer and his dog are returning from the market with their purchases: two hens and a bag of corn. They have to cross a river but there is only a small boat available. The boat can carry only the man and one of the others – either the hens, the corn, or the dog. How can he get all three across without leaving the hens with the corn or the dog with the hens? For the purpose of the puzzle the farmer is not allowed to do anything sensible such as tying up the chickens, wrapping up the corn, muzzling the dog. Or asking a passer-by for help, or getting a bigger boat, or wading across, or making the dog swim, or doing any of the myriad common-sense solutions which apply in the real world.

- In the land of 'Kleptomania' a wife wishes to send some valuables to her husband. The postal service is notoriously corrupt as are all the security guards. She has a secure iron chest with a padlock, which could not be stolen or broken into, but her husband doesn't have a key. If she sent the key separately it would certainly go missing. How can she deliver the treasure without having to accompany it herself?

Clue: both these problems are similar to the mathematical puzzle 'The Tower of Hanoi'.

None of these problems seems to have any practical application but, in the case of the last one, substitute 'password' for 'padlock' and the 'Internet' for 'Kleptomania' and you begin to see how some puzzles may have their uses.

Solutions:

The Monk and the Mountain

An analytic solution might be to draw a graph using time and distance as axes. Even though we have no measurements to tell us the exact crossing point, it would be clear that plotted lines of the two journeys must intersect somewhere on the chart.

A lateral solution requires imagination: simply use a time machine. If the monk travels in time back one day and sets off down the mountain, then at some place and time he is bound to meet himself on the way up! That's thinking outside the box.

The Farmer and the Boat

The farmer takes the hens across first, leaving the dog and the corn.
Next he takes the corn but brings back the hens.
Then he takes the dog across leaving the hens.
Finally he returns to collect the hens.

The Locked Box

The wife sends the treasure in the padlocked box and keeps the key.
The husband returns the box, having added a padlock of his own, and keeps his key.
The wife removes her padlock and re-sends the box, which is now secured by her husband's key.

Finally a slightly different one. This is your situation:

- You are a member of a fire-fighting crew which has been parachuted into the wilderness to tackle a forest fire.

- You have a considerable amount of equipment (which you are responsible for): food, water, first aid, as well as heavy tools for fire fighting – saws, axes and shovels.

- You are miles from anywhere, without radio communication, when you realise that the forest fire you have been sent to fight has spread further than you expected. (The fire is spreading at an estimated rate of 120 ft per minute.)

- You start to head downhill towards the safety of a river.

- Suddenly the fire 'jumps'; blazing brands fly up into the air and land on the tall, dry grass on the slope below you.

- Your route to the river is blocked by fire and the fire is moving rapidly uphill. (Fire will spread at least twice as fast in grass as in timber.)

- At the top of the slope is the comparative safety of bare rocks.

- You realise that you have little chance of outrunning the fire in the grass.

- What do you do?

The fire is about 200 yards away: the clock is ticking!

> Answer. You set fire to the grass immediately around yourself and then lie down within the burnt area until the fire flashes over the unburnt grass all around you and moves on.

This one is different because it actually happened – on August 5th 1949 at Mann Gulch in the Helena National Forest in Montana, USA.

Some bare facts from the subsequent investigations:

- The crew started up the hill at 5.45 – the fire reached that point four minutes later.

- The crew was ordered to drop their heavy tools at 5.53 – the fire reached that point just one minute later. This was probably the moment when the crew members fully appreciated their predicament.

- The foreman lit his escape fire at 5.55.

- By this time the fire was moving at between 360 and 610 ft per minute; that's up to 10 ft per second.

- By six o'clock it was all over.

- Of the sixteen men on the mountain that afternoon eleven were dead. Two more died from their burns next day. Twelve of the dead were firefighters who had been parachuted into the area to fight the fire; the thirteenth was a park ranger.

- Only three of the 'smokejumpers' survived: two teenagers who managed to reach the rocks by taking a short but steep climb, and the foreman Wagner Dodge who lit the escape fire. (The two fittest and the one cleverest survive.)

- Although it was widely thought to be an on-the-spot invention, it may be that Dodge had heard of the technique being used by Native Americans.

- The disaster was the spur for the wholesale reappraisal of firefighting strategy in the US. Issues of leadership and logistics were highlighted – Dodge did not know his crew that well and they did not understand his strategy. Also it was realised that the long dry grass was only there because grazing had been stopped as a conservation measure.

Mann Gulch is a *true* example of lateral, counter-intuitive thinking carried out under extreme pressure. Rather than quoting fictional puzzles we shall try to illustrate lateral thinking through more real life examples.

Example: the Netflix Prize

How much would you pay to have nearly 50,000 computer programmers working for you? From 184 different countries? (Bear in mind that the US State Department only recognises 194 independent countries.)

Established in 1997, Netflix is an online DVD and Blu-ray Disc rental service, offering flat-rate rental-by-mail and online streaming to customers in the United States. Netflix asks users to review and grade the movies that they watch and builds up unique customer profiles which they use to recommend further rentals. Automated recommendation algorithms offer a key competitive edge in e-commerce, giving retailers the chance to predict the products and services customers might buy by examining their past behaviour. Netflix recognised that its movie recommendation system Cinematch could be better but, as an alternative to in-house research and development, took the unusual step of holding a competition.

Launched on October 6th 2006, the prize offered a million dollars to anyone who could demonstrate a 10% improvement in performance using Netflix's own metrics and training data. In addition, each year that the competition ran, a $50,000 progress prize was to be awarded. A leader board monitored progress and collaboration was encouraged. The winners have to share the method with Netflix and publicise how and why their algorithm works. All participants gain kudos, shared expertise and a possible prize, while Netflix gains both publicity and a bargain.

The company told *Wired* magazine, 'A 10 percent improvement on its algorithms could help move substantially higher numbers of movies and increase customer satisfaction, with a direct boost to profits.'

Clearing the 10% hurdle wasn't easy. Thousands of teams tackled the problem for more than three years, sharing their results and algorithms along the way. Improvements would come in spurts, followed by long periods of no gains, or slow ones.

The culmination of the race came about through the union of the two leading teams. The finale was announced on their website (July 5th 2009): 'There are currently 49796 contestants on 40893 teams from 184 different countries. We have received 42092 valid submissions from 4770 different teams; 86 submissions in the last 24 hours.'

On 21 September 2009, Netflix awarded the $1m Grand Prize to team 'BellKor's Pragmatic Chaos'.

Example: the Nullarbor Links

Here's the problem: you own a roadhouse on one of the longest roads in the world, the Eyre Highway which crosses the Nullarbor plain in Australia. About 300 cars per day pass by; a few of them stop to refuel or grab a bite to eat but few of them stay for long. How can you get people to stay longer and spend more money? For members of the trade association, the Eyre Highway Operators Association, the answer has taken nine years of hard work to come to fruition but has made headlines around the world.

The world's longest golf course, the Nullarbor Links, opened in October 2009. The par 72 course spans 1,365 kilometres from Kalgoorlie to Ceduna with a hole in each participating town or roadhouse. Golfers can obtain scorecards and certificates at either end. Tourists are enthusiastically booking up accommodation along the course. Any golf club in the world knows the value of the 'nineteenth hole' – the Nullabor Links has eighteen 'clubhouses'!

'Thinking outside the box' has its own pitfalls:
Creativity and Sport
(Thinking outside the box with William Webb Ellis and others)

A plaque at Rugby School reads as follows:

THIS STONE COMMEMORATES THE EXPLOIT OF WILLIAM WEBB ELLIS WHO WITH A FINE DISREGARD FOR THE RULES OF FOOTBALL AS PLAYED IN HIS TIME FIRST TOOK THE BALL IN HIS ARMS AND RAN WITH IT THUS ORIGINATING THE DISTINCTIVE FEATURE OF THE RUGBY GAME A.D. 1823

The key words here are 'with a fine disregard for the rules' – our hero W.W.E. invents the game of rugby football in a moment of creative genius. But this is a perfect illustration of the perils of 'thinking outside the box': when Ellis picks up the ball and runs, he at once destroys the game as it was 'played in his time'. The Lord Shiva dances, Schumpeter strokes his chin and the new world is born. William Webb Ellis is lucky in that everyone seems to give him a hearty clap on the back in a manly fashion and adopt his new way of playing with nary a backward glance. Of course that was the golden age, but an equally likely response might have been to flatten Ellis without the option: try that sort of innovation in a game today and see what happens! (It has been said that even if his fellows had flattened Ellis then they would *still* have invented rugby football.)

All of which is very appealing but there is next to no evidence at all that William Webb Ellis did anything of the sort. The 'rules of football as played in his time' were very informal, often being finalised just before the kick-off, and they nearly always allowed players to handle the ball. The school rules were only written down in 1845 and the split between what became Rugby Football and Association Football did not occur until 1863, and that was largely a dispute over hacking your opponents' shins. In fact it was soccer that progressively limited handling the ball until at last only the goalkeeper was left. It's all a myth, known to be false for many years, with as much truth in it as the one that says Abner Doubleday invented baseball. But the narrative bias is so strong that the truth is wilfully ignored. As was said in *The Man Who Shot Liberty Valance*, 'When the legend becomes fact, print the legend.' In the case of the origin of rugby, the fable is so attractive that it is not only printed or even carved in stone; as recently as 1987, the words 'The Webb Ellis Cup' were engraved in silver on the trophy of the Rugby World Cup.

In fact, contrary to the legend of William Webb Ellis, that sort of entrepreneurial creativity has always been frowned on. Because sports represent a closed world with fixed rules and 'correct' answers, they are inherently conservative. The rules of sports and games have evolved rather than sprung forth fully formed. After all, as a solution of the problem of 'What to do with 24 men on a summer's afternoon', cricket would seem about as likely as those monkeys with typewriters hammering out Shakespeare. (It is better described as an 'emergent phenomenon', of which more later.)

It is the arguments caused by radical actions that often lead to an entrenchment of the status quo, and at least an extra line or two in the rule book. Consider these incidents, more than two centuries apart:

In 1771, a certain Mr White (nobody's sure of his first name) took the field against the famous Hambledon Club wielding a bat as wide as the wicket. A law was quickly introduced limiting the width to 4¼ inches.

In 1979 the Australian fast bowler Dennis Lillee tried to get away with an aluminium bat he was promoting. Again there was a swift change in the laws to preserve the sound of leather on willow.

Cricket has been altered to provide variants, 20/20, ODI, Test and County (5- or 3-day), but nearly always against concerted opposition. The entrepreneur Kerry Packer was responsible for introducing many characteristics of the modern game (coloured outfits, white balls, floodlit games) but nearly split the cricket world in two in the process.

People are very attached to their 'boxes' and have no interest in destroying them. Sport is so much more than a book of rules; it is a whole product just like Coca-Cola and you meddle with it at your peril. This isn't quite 'If it ain't broke don't try to fix it' but it is something similar: if you 'improve' something to the point where it no longer resembles the original then the other parts of the whole product may desert you.

So when thinking outside the box in search of innovative solutions, you have to remember that those solutions should match your criteria for success; they should be *appropriate* – they must fit back inside the box. A modern instance occurs in rugby and soccer today: soccer has discipline problems and has looked to the more restrained order of Rugby Union for inspiration. But rugby is a game of phases; there are plenty of stoppages and so the innovation of video referees has been accepted without much complaint; the same is true of cricket. On the other hand, soccer is perceived as a free-flowing game which would be ruined by delay, so that solution to disputed refereeing decisions is not considered appropriate; it's the wrong box. (Ironically, it is the lack of stoppages that has held back soccer in the USA; not enough room for advertising, that and the American intolerance of the notion of a draw.)

Even if an innovation is within the rules, creative change in sport is never likely to be the result of an individual's moment of genius, although it may appear to be just that. In 1968, Richard Douglas Fosbury won the high jump gold medal at the Olympic Games in Mexico with a record-breaking height, using a technique which became known as the Fosbury flop. Once the rest of the world caught on to the new style, they all started using it. A clear case of paradigm shift; but as you might guess it wasn't quite like that. Fosbury had been developing his new style for some time; he had used it in the Olympic trials earlier that year. Neither was its adoption as swift as we think; ten years later the world record was broken by an old-fashioned straddle jumper. The flop was not that new at the Mexico games but it was new to most of the people watching; it's that sigmoid fraud again. The innovation that was really behind the Fosbury flop was the replacement of the sawdust pit with thick foam mattresses to land on.

Define – prepare to find solutions

Again the fractal nature of the problem-solving process means that we start from the focused problem statement, going into the deliberately unfocused, fuzzy generation of as many ideas as possible, before starting to draw these together into possibilities.

1. **Define:** *preparation*

- Present a clear explanation of the problem.

- Construct a strategy to tackle the problem.

- Compose a short, concise statement of the problem or part of the problem to be addressed.

2. **Discover:** *exploration*

- Seek analogies from other domains.

- Generate non-obvious ideas.

- Find as many ideas as possible.

3. **Determine:** *assessment*

- Reflect upon the nature and diversity of those ideas.

- Have all the permutations and combinations been explored?

- Have enough ideas been produced for novel concepts to emerge?

The first section is actually a final iteration of the last section of Phase One. We are setting an agenda for the discussion of possible solutions to follow. We should have established the facts, where we are and where we want to be; now we need a plan.

This is where we have to define the limitations of our 'box', not only so that we can think outside it but also to recognise that any solution we come up with must fit back inside it. Anything else, however innovative, is not a solution to our problem; it is something else, an opportunity which should be properly assessed another time.

This may well be the most difficult part of the problem-solving process. If we've been lucky, a straightforward definition of the problem has set us well on the way to a solution but quite often the definition will only have made us realise quite how hard it's going to be to solve. Nobody said it was easy! We might identify a root cause of a problem but it might be too late to do anything about it.

We might come to the conclusion that the problem is in fact adequately solved already and that any improvement is not justified in cost/benefit terms. If we are looking for opportunities rather than having a specific problem to solve, we might well decide that there is no profit in pursuing anything in this particular area and decide that 'if at first we don't succeed' we are going to give up and take our talents elsewhere. As we pointed out earlier, a 'better mousetrap' will bring neither fame nor fortune when the existing need is met by a near perfect product at a disposable price.

In 2005, W. Chan Kim and Renée Mauborgne published their book, *Blue Ocean Strategy*. The book was the result of a ten-year study of strategic moves over the last century in more than thirty industries. The underlying concept almost explains itself in the title – existing markets are the red ocean, filled with sharks. The aim of the strategy is, in their words, 'Not to out-perform the competition in the existing industry, but to create new market space or a blue ocean, thereby making the competition irrelevant.'

Kim and Mauborgne are primarily concerned with large corporations but their description of the red ocean is immediately recognisable for the smallest of businesses. A case study from a UNIEI problem-solving workshop illustrates a familiar scenario.

Kay and Jonathan are in the floristry trade in a large provincial market town. Although they own the freehold to four shops, inherited from Kay's father, life is increasingly tough. Their problem statement reflected their concerns: 'How to compete effectively in a market with low profit margins'.

The solutions generated split into two categories – those which concentrated on more efficient use of their staff and premises, and those which sought to add value by expanding the services they could offer to differentiate them from the competition, using facilities and competencies that were unavailable to their rivals. Examples included diversification of the business into provision of flower-arranging classes, a café/teashop and an expanded delivery service.

But it was the definition phase which was of almost morbid interest to the other participants. It became obvious that floristry was a cut-throat business resulting in an extremely bloody ocean. Profit margins were around 16%, while wastage in raw materials could easily top 10%. The competition came from both sides: large supermarkets, where economies of scale forced down prices, and also smaller, home-based enterprises with minimal overheads. Remember Scott A. Shane's typical start-up 'entrepreneurs' who work longer hours for less money. Add to this his observation that many such businesses start with around $25,000 worth of investment and only last for about two years and the picture becomes even grimmer. For not only are Kay and Jonathan competing against the might of big business, they are also competing against individuals working out of their spare rooms and garages, a considerable number of whom, despite their best efforts, after a period of operating at a loss on the margins of legality, are statistically certain to go bust.* When an inefficient business goes under there is a knock-on effect as the remaining, more efficient competitors find their market swamped with bankrupt stock and second-hand machinery. Competition of this sort can easily drag down whole areas of business.

The situation is reminiscent of the old joke about the lost car driver who asks for directions, only to be told, 'I wouldn't start from here.' For those of us looking for opportunities and not in the unenviable situation of being stuck in the red ocean, it is essential not to 'start from here'; we after all are still 'pre-concept' and have invested next to nothing but a little brainpower.

Present a clear explanation of the problem

During the definition stage we looked at the structure of problems; we should by now have a better understanding of how any particular problem works, the root causes and the way that different elements interact. We now have to start looking for a way in, an angle, an edge.

- Are the constituent parts separable or interdependent?

To what extent are the different parts of a problem related? Can we attack it bit by bit or does it have to be all at once? Certain situations are such a tangle of cause and effect that they seem intractable. For example, inner-city deprivation; crime, unemployment, poverty and poor health are so interrelated that any positive initiatives in one area are overwhelmed by the negative remainder. It might appear that the first issue to be addressed must be how to coordinate a response across the widest range: the multi-agency approach. But conversely, there is a silver lining to the difficulties of complex systems, which is the very fact that they are so interrelated. Just as we saw the negative consequences of the loss of a horseshoe nail, might we not engineer massive positive consequences from similarly small events? The 'broken windows' approach is just such a plan: by concentrating on easily dealt with small problems like litter and vandalism there will be a knock-on effect on the larger problems of crime and antisocial behaviour. The far more prescriptive and controversial zero-tolerance programmes have their roots in the broken-window theory. Both want to achieve big results from small actions; they're looking for chain reactions: the 'butterfly effect'.

---

*A colleague, reading this case, remarked that having to compete with people who were going bust was not limited to the finances of small business. Many professionals in high-pressure jobs are called upon to keep up with co-workers who are without doubt heading for early burn-out.

'The butterfly effect', 'tipping points'; chaos and catastrophe*

We hinted earlier that the distinction between the continuous and the discrete is problematic when discussing the nature of change: gradual or step-by-step, incremental or revolutionary. The change from red to blue along the spectrum is continuous; we have to introduce arbitrary boundaries to separate colours. Other changes, however, are most definitely discrete; most obviously there *is* a last straw which breaks the camel's back; an accelerating aircraft does at some stage actually leave the ground. As we mentioned earlier, catastrophe theory seeks to describe such sudden shifts mathematically. The expression 'tipping point' is often applied to any process that suddenly and dramatically changes or increases. In relation to some domains such as marketing, however, the phrase 'take-off point' might be more accurate.

Chaos theory describes dynamic systems which are very sensitive to initial conditions. The 'butterfly effect' originates in the work of meteorologist Edward Lorenz who postulated situations with initial conditions so susceptible that the flap, or not, of a butterfly's wings might lead to totally different weather systems. (This is one reason why, despite the stupendous technology available to them, most meteorologists no longer attempt long-range forecasts.) 'Chain reaction' and the 'domino effect' similarly describe small causes leading to large effects, opposing the 'drop in the ocean' view that small changes will always be ineffective against the mass.

*Again a massive health warning: the social representation of higher mathematics is not the same as actual higher mathematics.

Construct a strategy to tackle the problem

- Is it possible for a complex problem to be broken into manageable parts?

Complex situations do not necessarily have complex mechanisms.

In 1970, the British mathematician John Conway published a model of a self-replicating machine as a mathematical game. The game consisted of a regular two-dimensional grid, each 'cell' being surrounded by eight neighbours. An initial simple pattern of 'live' cells is imposed on the grid. The cells then react with their neighbours according to simple rules. Over successive steps in time each cell either switches on (is 'born') or switches off ('dies') according to the number and status (live or dead) of their neighbours. Some configurations are static, some become stable in relatively few generations, but others 'emerge' as self-organising systems, which reproduce infinitely. The earliest patterns were produced manually, using graph paper or the Japanese board game 'Go', but Conway's 'Game of Life' really took off with the home computer revolution. The results of thousands and millions of generations can be seen in seconds. More intricate initial configurations and the grids in which they operate can be produced relatively easily.

The behaviour of a flock of birds seems to exhibit an intelligence far beyond the capacity of the 'bird-brained'. The same is true of a shoal of fish. This 'swarm intelligence' has naturally attracted the interest of A.I. investigators.

In 1986, the computer programmer Craig Reynolds designed a programme to replicate the behaviour of birds. Each individual manoeuvres according to only three criteria:

Separation – *steer to avoid collision.*

Alignment – *steer in the same direction as local neighbours.*

Cohesion – *steer towards the average position of neighbours.*

These three 'rules' result in remarkably bird-like behaviour.

Demonstrating the rich wit that humans possess, and thus far is absent from artificial intelligence, Reynolds called his creations 'boids'.

Reynolds' boids entered the public arena with the appearance of flocks of swarming bats and penguins in Tim Burton's 1992 film *Batman Returns*. (Such computer-generated images are not only realistic, they are cheaper than traditional animation.)

Adopting the right strategy goes a long way towards the solution. Some problems can be approached gradually, others step by step, but some have to be dealt with all at once. Top down or bottom up. As has been pointed out by many, it is hard to cross a chasm in two jumps.

Choosing the Right Strategy

In 1798, Edward Jenner showed exactly why milkmaids were renowned for their clear complexions. Those who had contracted the relatively harmless cowpox had developed immunity to the often lethal smallpox. Using the established technique of variolation, Jenner proposed deliberate infection with cowpox (vaccine and vaccination have their roots in the Latin for cow) as a preventive for smallpox. He was immediately hailed as a hero and saviour; fans included Thomas Jefferson, Napoleon and the Empress of Russia. It was confidently predicted that the dread disease would soon be just a horrible memory. But vaccination was a preventive rather than a cure and it proved impossible to treat 100% of the population of the world; there were never enough field workers and vaccine at the same time. By the late 1960s, a new strategy was adopted. 'Ring vaccination' emphasised the early detection and control of each outbreak. If surveillance was meticulous enough, then the mere preventive could actually be used to attack and defeat the disease itself with far lower levels of vaccination. By 1980, the World Health Organisation was able to announce the end of smallpox; the first ever global eradication of any disease known to man.

Around the same time that smallpox was being defeated, another lethal disease was rampant, this one affecting trees rather than humans. As with smallpox, there is no cure but, unlike smallpox, there is no guaranteed preventive and so Dutch Elm Disease caused the death of around 25 million trees in England. Nevertheless one place at least has managed to resist the epidemic. Learning from failures elsewhere and assisted by their geographical seclusion between the sea to the south and the treeless downs to the north, the arboriculturists of Brighton and Hove adopted a determined strategy of resistance. Early identification, isolation and eradication are the key factors, together with public funding of the work. Constant alertness has kept 15,000 mature trees safe, among them the oldest elms in Europe.

Two diseases, two strategies; one for attack, the other in defence, but both sharing similar tactics – divide, isolate and destroy.

Compose a short, concise statement of the problem or part of the problem to be addressed

- For multiple problems you will need to address each element in turn with a separate problem statement. Your first statement might well be 'How can we integrate this?' You may be able to control an explosion of problems by looking at them fractally and taking them each in turn.

You will probably find yourself returning to this point. (Again and again.)

Discover – generate multiple solutions

This is the creative filling in the problem-solving sandwich.

> Intelligent people can juggle a half-dozen concepts simultaneously and make good decisions rapidly – and many of them seldom have a creative moment. They are so good at the standard answers and so eager to move on to the next decision that they never play around with nonstandard possibilities . . . There is such a thing as being 'too good' because, in much of life, there are no correct answers. You have to invent new ones and contemplate them for some time.
>
> (W. H. Calvin, *A Brief History of the Mind* 2004)

The ability to make rapid decisions based on the standard answers is one that is rightly admired and rewarded but it is *not* an ability which will create or even recognise new and radical responses. New and radical responses are not necessarily required – as we said towards the end of the definition stage, if an off-the-shelf solution is available then the problem disappears. With hindsight, it was a 'tame' problem. We are concerned with 'wicked' problems which are still there; for those we need to generate alternative solutions to choose from. How thick the creative filling needs to be we do not know but it has to be there – to recall Polya's metaphor: 'There is a grain of discovery in the solution of any problem.'

The place of imagination in the scientific method

Science is one of those domains in which some say that there definitely are 'correct answers' and so there is no room or need for creativity; all we have to do is uncover the truth step by step by use of the 'scientific method'. (Observation of phenomena; formulation of hypotheses and testing of those hypotheses by experimentation.)

In his 1713 essay 'General Scholium', Isaac Newton asserted *'hypotheses non fingo'*, which has been variously translated as 'I form no hypotheses' or 'I do not construct hypotheses' or even 'I do not imagine hypotheses'.

> I frame no hypotheses. For whatever is not deduc'd from the phenomena, is to be called an hypothesis; and hypotheses, whether metaphysical or physical, whether of occult qualities or mechanical, have no place in experimental philosophy. In this philosophy particular propositions are inferr'd from the phenomena, and afterwards render'd general by induction.
>
> (1729 translation)

The authors' reading of this is that Newton is insisting that the propositions of his scientific method are *deduced* from phenomena: he does not *make them up.* Such propositions are then subjected to experiment and proved or not. This passage is taken to show that deductive and inductive logic are all that are required for science – there is no room for guesswork. But surely any proposition is a hypothesis, a supposition, a guess, an act of imagination. In its most basic form, trial and error, experimentation still involves an act of imagination; albeit a fleeting one.

In his 1957 book *The Art of Scientific Investigation*, William Beveridge writes, 'It is scarcely possible to foresee a discovery that breaks really new ground, because it is often not in accord with current beliefs.' To formulate his hypothesis, the investigator has to take an imaginative leap: 'for usually discovery is beyond the reach of reason'.

He quotes British scientist T. H. Huxley in support:

> It is a favourite popular delusion that the scientific enquirer is under a sort of moral obligation to abstain from going beyond that generalisation of observed facts which is absurdly called 'Baconian' induction. But anyone who is practically acquainted with scientific work is aware that those who refuse to go beyond fact, rarely get as far as fact; and any one who has studied the history of science knows that every great step therein has been made by the 'anticipation of Nature', that is by the invention of hypotheses, which, though verifiable, often had very little foundation to start with; and, not unfrequently, in spite of a long career of usefulness, turned out to be wholly erroneous in the long run.

Philosophy is for the Birds

Bertrand Russell illustrates the limits of inductive reason (*The Problems of Philosophy*, 1912). He suggests that a chicken who is well fed every day by the farmer might expect, from all the evidence available, that the future looked bright but as Russell so elegantly and drily puts it,

More refined views as to the uniformity of nature would have been useful to the chicken.

The mere fact that something has happened a certain number of times causes animals and men to expect that it will happen again. Thus our instincts certainly cause us to believe that the sun will rise to-morrow, but we may be in no better a position than the chicken which unexpectedly has its neck wrung.

Western philosophers from Aristotle to Hume had long observed that, despite the fact that every swan they had observed was white, they could not *prove* that 'all swans are white', when their theoretical position was complicated in 1790 by the actual discovery of black swans in Australia. In the twentieth century, Karl Popper used the swans to illustrate his position that science proceeds by constructing theories that can be falsified. In his 2007 book *The Black Swan*, Nassim Nicholas Taleb coins the phrase 'Black Swan events' to describe those times when assumptions are turned on their heads with extreme consequences (and later rationalised by narrative bias).

In a stroke of the pen, Russell's chicken is turned into Taleb's turkey: *'fed for a 1000 days – every day confirms to its statistical department that the human race cares about its welfare "with increased statistical significance". On the 1001st day, the turkey has a surprise.'*

So the philosophers would advise us that we cannot be certain of very much. (Ironically, we are surely using inductive reasoning to suggest that we should expect the unexpected, i.e. we cannot 'prove' that black swans will be found either.) We cannot carry on with the certainty of turkeys; nor can we allow uncertainty to prevent progress: that would be a final avian parallel – the suitably mythical ostrich with its head in the sand.

If we have to rely on the certainty of our premises (even if, like Nicolas Maxwell, we acknowledge that our assumptions are almost bound to be false), we are unlikely to find anything which does not agree with our paradigm. If we are uncertain of everything, we cannot proceed at all.

The relentlessly optimistic Norman Vincent Peale (author of The Power of Positive Thinking, 1952) puts it plainly: 'If you put off everything till you're sure of it, you'll get nothing done.'

Hamlet (another fairly unsound role model) states the dilemma more poetically:

> Thus conscience [doubt and uncertainty] does make cowards of us all;
> And thus the native hue of resolution
> Is sicklied o'er with the pale cast of thought,
> And enterprises of great pitch and moment
> With this regard their currents turn awry,
> And lose the name of action.

But another poet, Keats, realises the *power* of uncertainty: '. . . it struck me, what quality went to form a Man of Achievement, especially in literature, & which Shakespeare possessed so enormously – I mean Negative Capability, that is when man is capable of being in uncertainties, Mysteries, doubts, without any irritable reaching after fact & reason'.

Lest it be thought we have wandered a long way from our brief of entrepreneurship and problem solving, let one of the founders of the Chicago School of economics remind us why this is important:

> It is a world of change in which we live, and a world of uncertainty. We live only by knowing something about the future; while the problems of life, or of conduct at least, arise from the fact that we know so little. This is as true of business as of other spheres of activity. If we are to understand the workings of the economic system we must examine the meaning and significance of uncertainty; and to this end some inquiry into the nature and function of knowledge itself is necessary.

> (F. H. Knight, *Risk, Uncertainty and Profit*, 1921)

We shall indeed have to examine risk and what has become known as 'Knightian uncertainty' but before that it might be best to have some ideas and projects to be uncertain about.

Keats makes it plain that he, as our representative Romantic poet, dislikes facts and we know that many consider poets the least practical of people, yet his concept of negative capability is an extremely neat and practical way for us to progress 'beyond the reach of reason' – to 'think outside the box'. We can use our common-sense reasoning: tolerating uncertainty; reasoning with knowledge that we cannot *prove*; reasoning rapidly across a wide range of domains; and coming to conclusions without complete knowledge, with the ability to revise those decisions or beliefs as and when it becomes necessary.

It's worth reminding ourselves of what Keats's contemporary Humphry Davy thought: 'Imagination, as well as reason, is necessary to perfection of the philosophical mind. A rapidity of combination, a power of perceiving analogies, and of comparing them by facts, is the creative source of discovery.'

If we accept that Davy's view that creative problem solving is reliant upon imagination and reason, the next question is: 'Can anybody do that?'

Can *anybody* be creative?

We have already demonstrated that we all use our imagination to create new concepts from old in our everyday thinking. So let's start by dismissing, again, the idea that 'creatives' are 'special people'. A very simple example will confirm that we are all 'creatives'.

We all know that we should engage our brain before opening our mouth, but we rarely do. When we start to speak, we seldom have any real idea of how the sentence is going to end, or even *if* it is going to end.

We may set out with a plan in mind, but in conversation, even with ourselves, we are constantly subject to interruption.

We revise what we might have been going to say as we see other people's reaction. The feedback loop makes our speech cybernetic; one of the most significant stages of child development. And of course sometimes we just tail off into inconsequence from lack of interest (other people's as well as our own).

So creativity is there every time we open our mouths. We are all creative; we are all making it up as we go along, and we can usually tell when someone isn't. We admire mellifluous eloquence but are suspicious of too smooth snake oil. The distinction between honey-tongued and serpent-tongued can be quite fine. From chat-up lines to telesales, we hope that we can recognise *spiel* for what it is – a game.

We distrust people who sound too pre-prepared. We think they're trying to fool us.

The well-directed heckle tests any speaker's reliance on the script, while we warm to a genuine ad-lib; it makes the speaker more human.

The best actors are those who can make every line sound fresh. That's why it's so difficult to stage the classics. Every time *The Importance of Being Earnest* is staged, we wait to see what Lady Bracknell is going to do with the line 'A handbag?' Every Hamlet has to try to make 'To be or not to be' sound as if it was the first time anyone had said it.

When we say that creativity is present almost every time we speak, we are not using language as a model but as an *example* of creativity in action. Stories, jokes, analogies, metaphors and similes all provide a rich mine for the study of creativity, not least because of the endless (truly endless and ever-increasing), seam of material.

As we have seen, our love of narrative often obscures rather than illuminates. Written language is very different from spoken language, innit? But the advent of audio and video recording allows us to study spoken vernacular and reveals quite how extraordinarily creative we all are in everyday conversation.

> As Ronald Carter has put it, 'Creativity is an all-pervasive feature of everyday language . . . Linguistic creativity is not simply a property of exceptional people but an exceptional property of all people.' So creativity is there every time we open our mouths. *We are all creative.*
>
> (*Language and Creativity: The Art of Common Talk* 2004)

Although Mozart was a super human he was not super-human. We are all creative to some degree . . .

> What Mozart was able to do was of the same kind as what all of us can do – only he could do it better.
>
> (Margaret Boden, *The Creative Mind*, 1990)

We *all* possess some of that tacit knowledge, that know-how. The very fact that we no longer speak as children shows that we have all (well, most of us) been able to create bigger and better sentences as we have grown up: sentences which are both new and appropriate to their context. We can also see that we all possess the capability to make up completely new words if we have the confidence to try and the fortune to find them accepted. We will return to notions of acceptability and appropriateness later, when we attempt to define more precisely what we mean by 'creative'.

So we can see where new ideas come from. Taking our cue from Wertheimer, we realise that all new experiences resonate in our memories of old experiences.

'New' ideas are simply restructured and developed old ideas.

It is important to remember we are leaving aside the traditional notion of 'inspiration', the perception that ideas are somehow injected into our minds from the outside.

Even more important is to remember that our methodology is not *dependent* upon such speculations: it is a mechanistic process derived from case-based reasoning – at the moment we are at the retrieve/revise stage of CBR.

Ex nihilo nihil fit (Out of nothing, nothing can be made)

Having shown that *all* of us create new ideas out of old we ought to take a brief diversion and ask whether *any* of us are capable of creating ideas out of thin air.

In the western tradition, the question of whether or not it is possible for something to be created out of nothing (*creatio ex nihilo*) has occupied the attention of sages for a long time, at least since Parmenides of Elea in the fifth century BC, who may (or may not) have suggested (among other things) that merely *thinking* of a thing gave that thing some sort of existence. More recently the question of what, if anything, preceded the 'Big Bang' has raised the issue for theoretical physicists.

With regard to the social representation of the principle (*ex nihilo nihil fit*), honourable mentions in between are due to King Lear ('Nothing can be made out of nothing') and Captain Von Trapp ('Nothing comes from nothing, nothing ever could').

Ideas of where ideas come from and what creativity is have changed considerably over time. The idea that creativity might be a universal faculty of humanity, even its defining characteristic, is really quite new. It always used to be thought that acts of creation were not the business of mortals. For most of the time the best one could hope for was to *re*-create: a painting, for instance, was not an object in its own right, it was an imitation. We hear the idea when a sculptor says that they are trying to find the statue that already exists within a block of marble and we hear echoes of the principle when we say there's nothing new under the sun.

> It is perhaps best to leave the finer points of *ex nihilo* creativity to the theologians and philosophers, who quite rightly preface every argument with 'It all depends what you mean by . . .' because words, as we know, change their meaning over time and it is hard to know exactly what each person meant by them. '"When I use a word," Humpty Dumpty said, in rather a scornful tone, "it means just what I choose it to mean — neither more nor less"'
>
> (Lewis Carroll, *Through the Looking-Glass*, 1871).

The etymology of words connected to creativity reveals how much the meanings have changed over the years. The word 'invention' originally had connotations of finding and discovery.

'Genius' once referred not to people but to supernatural spirits that might help or hinder – the obvious parallel is the Arabic djinn or genie, which is resonant, although the words have no shared etymology.

Long before it was used to describe a usually young and attractive sidekick to an old and curmudgeonly artist, a 'Muse' was a goddess.

'Inspiration' was something blown in from the outside by such mystical elements.

The recipients of this magical inspiration were almost exclusively artists, especially poets.

While some artists do indeed claim that they are inexplicably inspired and others are reluctant to discuss where they get their ideas from, perhaps fearing that *to dissect is to murder*, other eminent writers, poets and painters are happy to reveal their secrets.

In his collection of first-hand accounts of creativity, *The Creative Process: a symposium* (1952), the American poet and academic Brewster Ghiselin quotes Stephen Spender: 'Inspiration is the beginning of a poem and it is also its final goal. It is the first idea which drops into the poet's mind and it is the final idea which he at last achieves in words. In between this start and this winning post there is the hard race, the sweat and toil.'

Spender expands on where that first idea comes from:

It is perhaps true to say that memory is the faculty of poetry, because the imagination itself is an exercise of memory. There is nothing we imagine which we do not already know. And our ability to imagine is our ability to remember what we have already once experienced and to apply it to some different situation. Thus the greatest poets are those with memories so great that they extend beyond their strongest experiences to their minutest observations of people and things far outside their own self-centredness (the weakness of memory is its self-centredness: hence the narcissistic nature of most poetry).

That first idea can come from almost anything:

> As our friend Botticelli remarks . . . by throwing a sponge impregnated with various colours against a wall, it leaves some spots upon it, which may appear like a landscape. It is true also, that a variety of compositions may be seen in such spots, according to the disposition of mind with which they are considered; such as heads of men, various animals, battles, rocky scenes, seas, clouds, woods, and the like.
>
> (Leonardo da Vinci, Trattato della pittura, tr. J. F. Rigaud)

Leonardo does not think too much of the technique: 'Those spots may furnish hints for compositions, though they do not teach us how to finish any particular part; and the imitators of them are but sorry landscape-painters.'

Which is all very well for 'traditional' art: what about the modern variety?

> There is no abstract art. One must always begin with something. Afterwards one can remove all semblance of reality; there is no longer any danger as the idea of the object has left an indelible imprint.
>
> (Pablo Picasso, interviewed in 1934)

This trick of removing an original stimulus is used by modern poets:

> Sometimes when I'm trying to write, I'll think of a song, usually a pop song, and pretend that I'm writing new lyrics for that song. It's just a way of generating some language and getting language onto the page and then hopefully what happens is that the song dies away, the poem comes into the foreground and then eventually you can't even remember what the song was.
>
> (Simon Armitage, speaking on BBC Radio 4, 2011)

So we see that even the most 'creative' of people start from something. The Russian writer Anton Chekhov was forthright in his opinion: 'If an author boasted to me of having written a novel without a preconceived design, under a sudden inspiration, I should call him mad' (Letter, dated October 27th 1888, tr. C. Garnett). Chekhov suggests what that preconceived notion might be: 'An artist observes, selects, guesses, combines—and this in itself presupposes a problem: unless he had set himself a problem from the very first there would be nothing to conjecture and nothing to select.'

Towards the start of this book (p. 8), we suggested that 'invention, innovation, effective decision making and entrepreneurship all share a similar basic problem-solving process'. Is it possible that 'art' is also to do with problems? Chekhov certainly thought so, although he differentiated between *solving a problem* and *stating a problem correctly*. It is only the second that is obligatory for the artist. In "Anna Karenin" and "Evgeny Onyegin" not a single problem is solved, but they satisfy you completely because all the problems are correctly stated in them. It is the business of the judge to put the right questions, but the answers must be given by the jury according to their own lights. [Original emphasis]

All of which seems to show that ideas do not come out of thin air.

> What we call [creativity] is in reality a composition – a construction raised on ... material of the mind, which must be collected ... by the senses ... We are unable to 'imagine' things that don't actually present themselves to our senses.
>
> (Italian physician and educationalist Maria Montessori, 1870–1952)

With such luminaries as quoted above on our side, we shall proceed without the need to invoke *ex nihilo* creativity. There remains at least one case, however, where someone seems to have made something from nothing.

In 2002, there was a very public dispute between the musician Mike Batt (of Wombles fame) and the estate of experimental composer John Cage. Batt had separated some remixes from the main part of an album by a period of silence. The album was released with the track 'A One Minute Silence' credited to Batt/Cage as joint composers. Those in the know immediately understood the joke – in the 1950s John Cage had 'composed' a score in three movements which instructed the performers not to play for a total of four minutes and thirty-three seconds.

The joke took a surreal turn a few months later when Batt received a letter from the Mechanical Copyright Protection Society informing him that they would be upholding a claim from John Cage's publisher for half of the royalties from the track. After he finished laughing, Batt contacted them to say that he had in fact registered the pseudonym Clint Cage just in case he got in trouble. He challenged them to a duel, his performers versus theirs. The world's press duly turned up and the story went global. Batt eventually handed over a cheque as a 'donation' to settle the dispute. The press reported that Batt had paid over £100,000 for 'nothing'. In 2010, Batt finally came clean and revealed that much of the story was a publicity stunt by both parties to highlight the importance of copyright and that his 'donation' had been for £1,000.

So had anyone made 'something out of nothing'?

John Cage himself was making the point that there is no such thing as silence. In *Conversing* with *Cage* (Richard Kostelanetz, 2002) he says, 'When activity comes to a stop, what is immediately seen is that the rest of the world has not stopped.' The idea was that listeners would pay attention to the other sounds around them. Furthermore, he was aware of the likely reaction: 'I was afraid that making a piece that had no sounds in it would appear as if I were making a joke.'

His statement that 'In fact, I probably worked longer on my "silent" piece than I worked on any other. I worked four years,' leaves us in no doubt that he took things extremely seriously. Unlike Mike Batt:

> There was no court case, no serious litigation. Just a lot of fun between us and lots of press coverage. But let's get this straight: John's silence was inferior to mine. My silence was digital and his was analogue. Also, mine was not played by an eight-piece band and his was not played by a solo clarinet. I think my 1,000 quid was well spent – so long as it didn't subsidise some avant-garde ****er to write more silence and call it art.
>
> (Quoted in the *Daily Telegraph*, December 2010)

The press certainly went well beyond the facts and the lawyers were willing to go ahead – both parties maintained that theirs was a strong case – but they were not making something from nothing. They were making something from the *idea* of nothing, which brings us back to Parmenides, but also introduces us to the pleasures and perils of intellectual property.

The example of language shows us two distinct ways in which we solve problems. If we look upon a sentence as a solution to the problem of how to communicate an idea, we see that there are two elements – the words and the way that they are put together: content and structure. If the sentence does not solve the problem adequately, we need to improve it.

It is perfectly possible for someone to be creative by changing the structure, using the content in different or unusual ways which get the message across appropriately, but usually, to create 'better' sentences, people also seek to increase the content – the words from which to choose. When we add words to our vocabulary, or even create new ones, we rarely do so at random – we always look for relevance. If we are searching for new ways of saying something, we don't just flick through a dictionary; we use a thesaurus.

We are not only interested in simple problem solving and effective decision making, but also actively searching for new, creative solutions. So if we want to find relevant ideas we need to produce a *thesaurus of ideas*.

Novelty, as we know, is easy – appropriate novelty is more difficult. It is easy to produce novel ideas – just open that dictionary at random. A popular conception of infinite chance is the assumption that a monkey indiscriminately typing keys would be bound to produce the complete library of the British Museum, the plays of Shakespeare or any given text, given an unlimited amount of time. This may be the case but the problem immediately arises of how, out of an unimaginable number of texts, we would be able to find the one we wanted.

Richard Dawkins (*The Blind Watchmaker*, 1986) uses the Infinite Monkey Theorem to illustrate a common misconception about evolutionary change. By choosing not the complete works of Shakespeare, but one line, 'Methinks it is like a weasel' (demonstrating his often well-hidden sense of humour), he shows that cumulative selection takes far fewer steps to reach an objective than random selection. The programme starts with 28 randomly selected characters; the number of possible combinations being 27^{28}, a ridiculously large number. The sequence is repeatedly duplicated but with a deliberate element of error – a 'mutation'. For example, the programme could be written to produce a hundred 'offspring' of the 'parent' sequence with a 5% chance of any character being replaced at random by another. The computer selects the one of these progeny which most closely resembles the target phrase and runs the exercise again. In most cases the target will be reached in fewer than fifty 'generations'.

But for problem solvers the resonance is clear – creative problem solving uses cumulative selection in exactly the same way to build potential solutions. This is one of the ways in which we make our own luck by putting ourselves in the right place. But that is towards the end of the process and we need to return to it when we look at how concepts emerge. In the meantime, is it possible to reverse the process in order to increase the generation of ideas whose relevance has yet to manifest itself?

One of the defining characters of creativity is that it be neither obvious nor foreseeable from within the context in which the problem is identified. But with hindsight, once the paradigm has shifted, when we try to trace the genesis of concepts, we can see the relevance of all the paths and combinations which led forward. Remember Schumpeter's classic example: 'Add successively as many mail coaches as you please, you will never get a railway thereby.' Railways arose from the combination and modification of pre-existing elements whose relevance is clear with hindsight, but was simply not visible from the stable yard of any of the great coaching inns of Victorian England. Had we been able to ask the proprietor of one of those inns to carry out a 'SWOT' analysis, what would he come up with?*

If we asked him what would improve his business, he might have said better road surfaces, cheaper oats or even faster horses. If we asked where he thought the greatest threat to his livelihood was likely to come from, it is doubtful that he would have said the steam engine.

Let us be generous and accept that this opinion was not the result of lack of awareness. Like any well-informed businessman, he would be aware of the wonders of steam power. Let us imagine that in his youth he had seen Richard Trevithick's 'Puffing Devil' careering up and down Camborne Hill in Cornwall on Christmas Eve 1801 and not laughed a few days later when the vehicle was destroyed after the operators left the fire burning when they retired to the pub. Maybe, in 1808, he paid his shilling to see the 'Catch Me Who Can' running on a circular track at Trevithick's Steam Circus in London. A top speed of 12 mph was claimed but the cast-iron rails proved too brittle and investors withdrew their support, but let us suppose that our coach proprietor knew that locomotives were more successful in the mines. How could such engines rival a passenger-transport industry like his, which was at the peak of efficiency? After all, in 1831, the 'Wonder', a daily coach, ran from Shrewsbury to London via Wolverhampton, Coventry and St Albans, taking under 16 hours to cover the 158 miles.

And yet with hindsight we can see all the elements of the railway revolution coming into place through separate acts of creativity. The decision to run wagons on rails; the decision to replace horse/man power with steam haulage; the placing of the engine *on* the wagon; making flanged wheels rather than flanged rails; the introduction of passengers: all against a background of burgeoning capitalism and cheap labour. Looking at the context, it is difficult not to include seemingly diverse factors such as the Irish Potato Famine and the introduction of the Penny Post: the famine was behind the supply of cheap migrant labour, the Penny Post provided a rapidly expanding volume of business.

Another, more modern example of the unpredictability of change might be to contrast *The X-Factor* and *Strictly Come Dancing*, both highly rated TV shows, both based on old shows. *The X-Factor* lies on a direct line back through *New Faces* and *Opportunity Knocks* – it is basically a talent show and is reasonably predictable from

*A 'SWOT' analysis, for non-business readers, is a well-established, almost routine, strategic-planning technique which lists the Strengths, Weaknesses, Opportunities and Threats of an enterprise.

any of its precursors. *Strictly Come Dancing* is different. Its parent show – *Come Dancing* – ran off and on from 1949 to 1998 and went through many changes but at no stage could the present show be predicted from within its original context. But with hindsight we can see the context from which it emerged: format franchising; reality TV, celebrity culture, premium-rate phone voting (the truly radical element of both shows); kitsch; and so on.

So we return to the dichotomy between incremental change and radical change. There is a view that to some extent all change is radical – incremental innovation represents a sequence of small, but at their own level, radical steps. It is a question we will return to later but for the moment let us assume that radical change is that which is not apparent, sometimes even to those most concerned with the problem.

What we have to do is create a mass of ideas, some of which will have a relevance we hope will be revealed afterwards. Which is easier said than done. One of the consequences of studying and trying to teach creative problem solving is that one inevitably gets better at it. As with almost everything, generating 'lateral' ideas gets easier the more you do it.

Alice laughed. 'There's no use trying,' she said: 'one CAN'T believe impossible things.'

> 'I daresay you haven't had much practice,' said the Queen. 'When I was your age, I always did it for half-an-hour a day. Why, sometimes I've believed as many as six impossible things before breakfast.'
>
> (Lewis Carroll, *Through The Looking Glass*, 1871)

At about the same time as Carroll was writing, the great scientist John Tyndall defended using the imagination:

> How then are those hidden things to be revealed? How, for example, are we to lay hold of the physical basis of light, since, like that of life itself, it lies entirely outside the domain of the senses? Now philosophers may be right in affirming that we cannot transcend experience. But we can, at all events, carry it a long way from its origin. We can also magnify, diminish, qualify, and combine experiences, so as to render them fit for purposes entirely new. We are gifted with the power of Imagination . . . and by this power we can lighten the darkness which surrounds the world of the senses. There are tories [sic] even in science who regard imagination as a faculty to be feared and avoided rather than employed. They had observed its action in weak vessels and were unduly impressed by its disasters. But they might with equal justice point to exploded boilers as an argument against the use of steam. Bounded and conditioned by cooperant Reason, imagination becomes the mightiest instrument of the physical discoverer.
>
> (*The Scientific use of the Imagination* Lecture 1870)

If there is a secret to creativity it is this: we are not limited to our own experiences; we are not limited to our own minds. It is *our* minds which reach out and seize 'inspiration'; not the other way round: *we* are the motive force behind 'ingenuity'. From this standpoint we can either sit around waiting to take hold of 'inspiration' if it floats by, or we can go looking for it. We can search other people's minds, other people's experiences. We are not limited to our own species; neither do the ideas we find even need to be 'true'.

But it can be difficult to 'transcend experience' deliberately. Idea generation is a bit like dancing to pop music – we are always told to do it as if no one is watching. But we find it difficult to believe that no one's looking (they usually are!) and we end up even more self-conscious. So we might need to devise a few more formal dance steps to get ourselves started.

One set of 'dance steps' might be a method akin to homeopathic dilution.

(Homeopathic dilution works on the principle that water retains the memory of certain elements and compounds, which are successively diluted to such a degree that none of the original molecules are likely to remain – thus rendering them 'safe'. *If* it worked, homeopathic dilution would overturn most principles of both physics and pharmacology but that's by the by – it doesn't need to be true for us to use it as an analogy, and 'impossible things' are just what we are likely to find when we go 'beyond the reach of reason'.)

Dance step one is to seek analogies – this ought to generate relevant ideas by simple addition; synonyms and translations, if you like.

Dance step two is to look at this increased array of ideas in a different manner – this will multiply the array: anagrams, letter substitutions, rhymes and so forth, to continue the language example. Even when we apply an element of pure chance or 'nonsense', the idea we alter will still retain a relevant taint of the original.

Dance step three is to judge whether you have 'enough' – repeat as necessary.

Once we have enough ideas we will stop and try to pull them together. Because of the method used to generate them, each one will retain at least a trace or imprint of the original (like homeopathic dilution), which we hope will flocculate and can be squared and cubed back into something recognisably appropriate.

The Limitations of 'Learning'

An early exploration of this phenomenon appears in the sixteenth century text 'A Discourse of the Common Weal of this Realm of England'. (The discourse was written for private circulation in 1549. Its authorship is nowadays credited to Sir Thomas Smith who died four years before it was printed in 1581.)

'Theare maye be wise men enoughe, thoughe they be not learned. I haue knowne men verie wise and pollitique, that knowe never a lettere in the boke ; and contrarywise, as many other learned men, that haue bene verie Idiottes in maner for anie worldly pollicie that they had.'

Smith remarks that experience certainly furthers wisdom but asks what part 'book learning' may play. He answers: 'as experience dothe begett wisdome as a father, so memorie norisethe it as a mother; for in vayne should experience be had, if the same weare not kept in Remembraunce.'

In other words, experience is nothing if you cannot remember it, and you can share your memory if it is 'kepte in writinge' because: 'an old man seithe but only thinges of his owne time . . . [whereas] the learned man seithe not only his owne times experience, but also that that befell in a greate manie of his auncestors; yea, since the world began.'

The ability to pass on knowledge from one person to another is one of the distinguishing characteristics of humanity. One might suggest that each step in complexity in society has been accompanied by a radical innovation in communication: the development of spoken language, then writing, then printing has increased the sum total of ideas exponentially.

And it isn't just words: polyphonic music spread through the monasteries of medieval Europe through the invention of notation; the adoption of Arabic numerals was crucial to the spread of mathematics – they are all new information technologies.

In *A Brief History of the Mind*, W. H. Calvin quotes Galileo rejoicing in the IT of his day:

> But surpassing all stupendous inventions, what sublimity of mind was his who dreamed of finding means to communicate his deepest thoughts to any other person, though distant by mighty intervals of place and time! Of talking with those who are in India; of speaking to those who are not yet born and will not be born for a thousand or ten thousand years; and with what facility, by the different arrangements of twenty characters upon a page!

But, as Polanyi pointed out, there is a difference between practical experience and theoretical knowledge. Smith's *experienced* man could pass on his wisdom by word of mouth (explicit transfer) but he would also probably have a pupil who would be expected to learn through apprenticeship (tacit transfer). The *learned* man, even Galileo, relies on explicit transfer alone.

The limitations of writing were noted at the very time when it was first becoming commonplace for humans to record their ideas in text – fourth/fifth century BC Greece. In the dialogue 'Phaedrus', Plato has Socrates tell of the origin of writing in Egypt. Theuth (a.k.a. the god Thoth) claims that his invention will enhance the memory of humans. Thamus (a.k.a. the god Amun) disagrees: 'O ingenious Theuth, the inventor of an art is not necessarily the best judge of its usefulness.'

Writing will actually create forgetfulness because learners will cease to practise their own memory. Readers will have only the semblance of wisdom because they will read many things without understanding them properly.

Writing, Socrates continues, is very like painting – the images may be lifelike but they cannot speak. Words are only of worth if one can interrogate them.

Elsewhere (in his Seventh Epistle) Plato even suggests that because writing cannot defend itself, it might be advisable not to commit one's best ideas to paper for fear of being misunderstood and abused.

But an author can soon become an authority and *heretic personalities* are likely to face troubles when they question the accepted wisdom.

But we are not like the fellows of the Royal Society who took nobody's word for anything (*Nullius in Verba*) and tested theories in order to supersede them and establish a new authority. From our point of view (problem solving) it is not whether ideas were valid in the past that matters – it is whether they are appropriate in the present, and they might well be appropriate for purposes for which they were not designed.

> In order to develop better solutions . . . it is not primarily new knowledge that we need; rather what we primarily need is to act in new, appropriate ways. The fundamental intellectual task . . . must be to create and make available a rich store of vividly imagined and severely criticised possible actions, so that our capacity to act intelligently and humanely in reality is thereby enhanced.
>
> (Nicholas Maxwell, 1984)

Seek analogies from other domains [Dance step one]

The significance of analogies has been recognised for a long time, at least since Aristotle. We singled out Davy's opinion: 'A rapidity of combination, a power of perceiving analogies, and of comparing them by facts, is the creative source of discovery.' (*'Parallels Between Art and Science'*, 1807)

Théodule Ribot agrees: 'The essential, fundamental element of the creative imagination . . . is the capacity of *thinking by analogy*, that is to say through partial, often accidental similarity.' (*L'élément essentiel, fondamental, de l'imagination créatriee . . . c'est la faculté de penser par analogie, c'est-à-dire par ressemblance partielle et souvent accidentelle.*)[Original emphasis]

For Ribot analogy is an almost inexhaustible instrument of creativity (*'un instrument presque inépuisable de creation'*). Crucially he points out that 'It produces in equal measure absurd comparisons and very original inventions.' (*Elle produit également des rapprochements absurdes et des inventions très originales.*)

So we ought not to be alarmed if we produce *absurdity* as well as originality.

We are now in the white heat of a technological revolution unimaginable to either Plato or Harold Wilson; the Internet now offers more ideas than we can possibly cope with. It is actually impossible to cite all sources when the number of sources increases every single day.

So we have a lot to look at.

- A similar problem to yours may have been successfully solved in an entirely unrelated field.

   In postwar Russia, Genrich Altshuller (1926–1998) developed an algorithmic approach to invention and problem solving. The methodology, *Teoriya Resheniya Izobreatatelskikh Zadatch* (Theory of Solving Inventive Problems), better known as TRIZ, has a devoted following outside engineering, the field it was designed for. One of its very simplest aspects involves finding solutions by analogy: describing your specific problem as a general problem; finding a general solution, which can then be adapted as a specific solution.

We can apply this procedure outside the rigid worlds of mathematics and engineering thus:

What sort of problem is it?

For example, is it: product – process – service – manufacturing – marketing – communication – organisational – competitive – cooperative – transport – supply and demand – capacity – intelligence – political – reactive?

Most problems will show elements of several types of problem and this will serve to help deconstruct the problem.

Analogies Work Both Ways: sport and business

Sport and business have a lot in common quite apart from the fact that many sports are businesses generating vast amounts of income. There is the symbiotic relationship of sponsorship and hospitality – it must be symbiotic because it's often difficult to tell who is paying whom! But what can sport learn from business and what can business learn from sport?

Two success stories from English sport illustrate how much business practices have come to play a significant part in coaching sport.

Rugby: in 2003, England became the first northern-hemisphere team to win the Rugby World Cup, beating Australia in the final. For many casual spectators their achievement came as a surprise; five years previously they had been humiliated 76–0 in Brisbane. Australian Premier John Howard certainly looked shocked as he presented the trophy. It was England's greatest sporting success since the soccer World Cup in 1966. On a cold December day, at least three-quarters of a million people lined the streets of London to see the victory parade.

Cricket: between 1989 and the start of 2005, England and Australia played 43 matches. Australia won 28 of them; eight had been draws; England had achieved a mere seven victories, only one of which had come in a match when the Ashes were still at stake, the other six being consolation wins when the series had already been decided in Australia's favour. In 1999, England were unofficially rated bottom of the world rankings. Again it came as somewhat of a surprise to the population in general when England not only competed fiercely but actually regained the Ashes. Even taking into account their legendary 'sledging', it must have been a shock for Australian fast bowler Glenn McGrath, who had forecast a 5–0 whitewash, and to captain Ricky Ponting, who was forced to follow on for the first time in seventeen years. It did not, however, come as a complete surprise to the England squad – they knew they stood a good chance. Like the rugby team, they had been working towards it for some time.

Rugby coach Clive Woodward wrote in 2004 that 'There is absolutely no doubt in my mind that England won the World Cup because we applied business principles to the management of a professional sport. And I firmly believe the principles found in the England story can be applied to any sport or business situation.'

Woodward had started his working life in sales and he brought that target-driven culture to rugby coaching, along with an openness to innovation born of his experience running a successful small business of his own. He used techniques very similar to those espoused in Nottingham University Business School's Ingenuity Guide: a combination of vertical and lateral thinking, which took inspiration from the Royal Ballet as well as the Royal Marines to build an élite squad capable of peak performance under maximum pressure. (The team had trained to score a try in twenty seconds and so did not panic at the prospect of scoring the winning drop goal with 35 seconds to spare.)

Woodward saw the main barrier to his innovations as 'inherited thinking'. He thought that the governing body, the Rugby Football Union, was run by well-meaning amateurs and volunteers with the inherited ideals of an era when participation was more important than winning. In the words of American sports writer Grantland Rice, what mattered was 'Not that you won or lost – but how you played the Game.' This spirit dates from the latter days of the nineteenth century when there was a natural desire for skilful players who attracted large paying crowds to be paid for their efforts. Rugby football split acrimoniously into professional league and amateur union. Cricket compromised by distinguishing between amateur 'gentlemen' and professional 'players'. Association football permitted professionals, but amateur teams continued to thrive alongside them. The Corinthian Football Club was set up in 1882 to provide players capable of competing with the Scotland team. (Scottish footballers had been taking the game far too seriously; inventing the short passing game and regularly beating England.) Although they certainly played to win, Corinthians did so on their own terms. They were avowedly amateur, declining to 'compete for any challenge cup or prizes of any description', and their insistence on fair play meant that they even refused to take or defend penalties. 'Fair Play' and the 'Corinthian Spirit' achieved its apogee in Henry Newbolt's 1897 poem 'Vitaï Lampada':

> And it's not for the sake of a ribboned coat,
> Or the selfish hope of a season's fame,
> But his captain's hand on his shoulder smote –
> 'Play up! Play up! And play the game!'

The myth of a golden age before sport was tainted by money persists; a time when training and practice were considered to be 'trying too hard' and almost tantamount to cheating. As we have remarked before, when change occurs it can be difficult to remember the previous context accurately and so it is with the myth of the glorious amateur who was a 'natural' sportsman.

On Tuesday, August 24th 1875, Captain Matthew Webb breakfasted on bacon, eggs and claret before diving into the sea at Dover. After almost 22 hours of steady breaststroke (twenty strokes a minute, slowing to only twelve towards the end), having been fortified along the way with ale, beef tea, brandy and cod liver oil, he stood on the beach at Calais, the first person ever to swim the English Channel.

Several points need to be made.

First, Webb had been training for months and had already attempted the swim twelve days earlier.

Secondly, his diet and his use of breaststroke were deliberately chosen as the best suited for the task; a choice supported by the fact that the feat was not successfully repeated for 36 years and the time not bettered for an additional 23 years.

Thirdly, and to our mind perhaps the most surprising, he did it for money. Webb was a professional athlete who earned his living through his swimming. People paid to see him perform in exhibitions, stunts and races and they bought his books and merchandise. Sadly, he died in another, even more desperate stunt, swimming the Whirlpool Rapids below Niagara Falls.

Webb was a captain in the Merchant Service and so was not perhaps quite a 'gentleman' but if we go back a few more years we find another captain, who certainly was. Robert Barclay Allardice, the sixth Laird of Ury, was one of the most celebrated sporting figures of the early years of the nineteenth century. His most celebrated feat was in 1809, when he walked a thousand miles in a thousand hours for a thousand guineas. According to his contemporary, Pierce Egan, 'The Sporting pursuits of Captain Barclay are completely scientific; and his plans in general are so well matured, that his judgment, nine times out of ten, proves successful.'

Captain Barclay was also famous as a trainer of pugilists, in other words a coach. He took charge of Tom Cribb, the bare-knuckle champion, for his rematch with the upstart ex-slave Tom Molineaux, whom he had controversially (i.e. probably not) beaten the previous year. The training regime was hard physical labour, daily walks of ten to twelve miles and a strict diet. Underdone beef, grilled mutton and chicken were allowed; veal, lamb and pork were not. Fish, turnips, carrots and potatoes were too watery; butter, cheese and any fat or grease were forbidden as indigestible. Raw egg yolks, but not the whites, were allowed, as was vinegar, but little salt and no spices. Biscuits and stale bread were limitless but fluids were restricted to about three pints, usually of beer, a day. On September 28th 1811, after a breakfast of two boiled eggs, Tom Cribb duly defeated the under-prepared Molineaux by breaking his jaw in the ninth round. That was back in the days of the 'Fancy', before the Marquis of Queensbury Rules, when most sport was funded by gambling; even cricket being riddled with allegations of match fixing. The Victorian era cleaned up and regulated sport, making it a wholesome pursuit fit for both the public schools and the working classes, building both character and health. The 'golden age' was always more aspiration than actuality.

The reality, of course, was often somewhat different. By 1945, George Orwell was able to point out that 'Serious sport has nothing to do with fair play . . . it is war minus the shooting.'

While some took that sentiment to heart, it is true that both cricket and rugby still dwelt in a romantic glow. Both sports became professional in that they paid their players but were accused of remaining amateur in their organisation. The turnaround in fortunes started when the national teams agreed with club or county that certain chosen players would be made available to be coached as an élite squad.

(The idea of an élite squad is not new of course: in the Bible, Gideon's force is whittled down from 32,000 to just 300.)

In the case of rugby and cricket, both élite squads achieved their aims and celebrated accordingly. Both sports also suffered mighty hangovers. The England cricket team was humiliated 5–0 in the next Ashes and the rugby team started the next World Cup ranking a lowly seventh. Retirements and injuries exacerbated the natural break in continuity which comes with the conclusion of a triumphant campaign.

If we want *continuing* success, whether in business or in sport, there is much to learn from cycling. In Barcelona in 1992, Chris Boardman won Britain's first Olympic gold medal for cycling since 1920. And yet by 1996, the British cycling team was in danger of losing all funding. Performance director Peter Keen knew what the problem was; he referred to the glory days of another amateur sport, mountaineering: 'What Chris and I were doing in the early '90s was classic British alpinism . . . He was just another one-off success. Leave no ropes, leave no trail. *There was no system so there was no legacy.*'

The Atlanta games of 1996 saw only one gold for Team GB, leaving them 36th in the medal table. But in 2008, Great Britain came fourth with nineteen golds (eight of them in cycling); a position they had not held since 1924. Again this came as a surprise to many, this time even to team organisers, who found their target of ten to twelve golds far surpassed. But again it was not a complete surprise to the athletes – they knew how good they were; they had been building up to this. And it was not just a case of increased funding – the most successful teams, sailing and cycling, were those which had built a legacy of achievement with a system.

Under Keen's successor Dave Brailsford, British Cycling has formed an élite squad of athletes who have come to dominate the sport. The secret is the same as Clive Woodward's – to take care of every little detail. Woodward calls them 'critical non-essentials'; Brailsford talks about 'the aggregation of incremental advantage'. When all the little variables, diet, accommodation, equipment, etc., have been taken care of, all that is left is chance – the vagaries of sport – and even then you can usually play the odds. Where there is a culture of no blame there is also a culture of no excuses. Brailsford calls it 'ownership of performance' and it certainly brings results.

And for Brailsford and his team the system still creates the legacy. Speaking before the London Olympics, he was looking even further ahead, to Rio in 2016: 'Beijing was Beijing. London is a fantastic opportunity but life goes on afterwards . . . and it's a platform to build on, not the be-all and end-all in terms of performance' (BBC Radio 4, February 16th 2012).

Brailsford's approach to achieving 'personal excellence' has not gone unnoticed. After his track squad had won seven gold, one silver and one bronze out of the ten medals available to them at London 2012 he said: 'It's very nice to get offered different things... ...the model we've come up with and the way we work could be applied to anything really, the best lawyer, the best dentist, the best anything really, so I think there's a philosophy there that's quite interesting but like I say I know cycling and that's where I'll stay.' (BBC Television, August 8th 2012)

Even though they explain their methods quite clearly there is a tendency to suggest that the likes of Brailsford and Woodward possess some sort of secret, an almost magic touch. It was ever thus - here, speaking after the Battle of Trafalgar, is a considered evaluation of 'the Nelson touch' by his second in command Cuthbert Collingwood: 'everything seemed, as if by enchantment, to prosper under his direction. But it was the effect of system, and nice combination, not of chance.'

So what lessons can we learn from sport? Sports have taken business and management strategies and used them successfully because they are in an analogous environment – competition. And many would paraphrase Orwell: 'Business *is war minus the shooting*'. A word of caution, however – is winning really all that important?

At the Beijing Olympics, BMX world champion Shanaze Reade went into the final bend of her final race in silver medal position. She tried a difficult passing move, crashed and finished with nothing. 'I went into the race to get a gold medal, and I was going to do anything in my capabilities to get a gold medal. The race isn't over until you cross the finish line, so I don't regret anything that I did – I just wanted to win the gold.' Notwithstanding all the contributions of her support team, when it came to it, in poker terms, she 'bet the farm'. Which is all well and good, it was hers to bet – she 'owned' her performance. But what if an employee was to act that way? Isn't that what happened with Nick Leeson, the rogue trader who brought down one of the world's oldest banks – Barings – in 1995?

There is a great deal of difference between winning a tournament and winning the league. There are times when you might need to grind out a draw on a rainy winter's afternoon. When Sir Alex Ferguson presented Dave Bassett with an award commemorating one thousand football matches that he had managed, Bassett remarked that he had never, in all those matches, been able to field the team he wanted – he had always had to work with what he had got.

There is a parallel here with American baseball team the Oakland Athletics, who found themselves unable to compete with the wages paid by richer clubs. In 2002, they adopted a more sophisticated statistical measure of performance, which allowed them to recruit players that the big clubs missed. By the end of the season they had finished first in their league and achieved a record run of twenty straight victories. A book (2003) and film (2011), both called *Moneyball*, followed. The story illustrates what can be achieved by thinking clever, using superior, often counter-intuitive, metrics – until, of course, the others catch up; the richer clubs can afford better statisticians.

And yet in business terms there is much to be said for coming second. In the 1960s, CEO Robert Townsend took a lowly car rental company, Avis, from nowhere to the position of second only to Hertz. They made a virtue of their status: 'We Try Harder' was their motto. (Townsend was an innovator who credited Avis's accomplishments to positive management, believing that most employees are not inherently slothful but want to do well and should be trusted to do so – what was then called Theory 'Y' governance.)

And so there is a lot that business, sport and even warfare can learn from each other. But you need to remember that sport is entertainment, sport is also show business. 'Winning ugly' does not necessarily put 'bums on seats'. When we look for analogies, the 'solutions' we find are *general* and have to be applied carefully and tailored to *specific* situations.

In 2005, Clive Woodward became involved with Southampton Football Club; it did not work out. With hindsight it's easy to see that introducing a no-blame/no-excuses culture to Premiership soccer players was too much of a challenge even for a World Cup winner. Ironically, the professional culture of the Football League is far more resistant to innovation than the volunteer culture of amateurism, which draws on a much wider expertise. Performances at the 2011 World Cup show that English rugby has allowed Woodward's legacy to lapse, while Welsh rugby exceeded expectations through an increased professionalism. English cricket seems to have established a winning formula, while some involved in the game are returning to eighteenth-century roots of gambling and match fixing.

Other domains provide a multitude of solutions, but we mustn't limit ourselves to obvious analogies.

Say, for example, you run a small bakery and sandwich-making enterprise. Every lunchtime the line of people reaches out of the shop, blocking the pavement. The neighbouring shops don't like it but 'So what?' – they're just jealous, they'd love to have a problem like yours. On the other hand, you are so busy that customers are walking away because the queue is too long.

If you take this problem through Phase One of the Ingenuity Process (definition), one root cause is obvious quite quickly: it's the lunchtime rush! That is the *specific* problem; so let's identify the *general* problem. Again it is quite easy, the name gives it away: it is the rush, simply a surge in demand. You could respond in classic fashion by increasing supply (getting more staff and a bigger shop) or reducing demand (putting up your prices). But if you want to be a little more imaginative, you should look for analogies; responses to the *general* problem of surges are many and varied. How do power companies deal with the millions who all decide to boil a kettle during half time of the World Cup Final? How do the authorities deal with rivers that are prone to flooding? For that matter, how does an unmanaged river respond to flooding? What do Santa's elves do during the summertime? And very soon you start to see similarities. Could you increase your staff with part-timers or by redeploying; could you even increase your shop space temporarily? Rather than letting them overflow, could you control your tide of customers by speeding up the queues? You could alter your prices so that the need for change was reduced, or have a 'crawler lane' for large orders. Could you reduce the peak of demand with pre-ordering or even delivery? Very soon you will find you have an array of possibilities from which to construct *specific* solutions.

If your problem is organisational, look at organisations; if it's structural look at structures and so on. *To reiterate: from your specific problem identify your general problem area; look to general solutions for ideas that you can build into a specific solution.*

Ask yourself how your problem would be solved in another time, another place.

A quick example: temporary shelters. Now and in the past, every nomadic people in the world has had to face this problem. In different places and times, different solutions have been applied, dependent upon the materials available. And just as we saw with shipbuilding, the variety of solutions is amazing. Most of them involve a covered framework; since many of them have to be portable, the key dynamic is strength versus weight. Frameworks can be flexible or rigid; the coverings likewise. And so we see all the variety from felt-covered yurts on the plains of Central Asia to skin-covered tepees on the plains of North America. Some peoples manage simply by building anew every time. When new materials become available their use can be stretched beyond the original purpose; for example, corrugated iron, invented as a roofing material, proved so rigid that it was possible to do away with rafters as in the Nissen hut. And what about when it seems that there are no materials available? Human ingenuity provides an answer: the igloo, which is all the more remarkable for being a dome which is self-supporting during its construction. And so if you want to build a new type of temporary shelter, there is plenty of inspiration, especially when you introduce modern technology, e.g. aluminium for bamboo, PVC for animal hide, fibre-glass for willow, rip-stop nylon for canvas, plastic foam or breeze blocks for snow. And of course vice-versa, replacing man-made materials with natural.

It's not just nomads and campers who might find temporary shelters interesting – in a disaster area they are essential. As we have seen, problems and needs are also opportunities. In response to a design competition, students Will Crawford and Peter Brewin came up with the multiple award-winning Concrete Canvas Shelter, an inflatable structure made of cement-impregnated material which can be erected by two people in little over an hour. It is then sprayed with water and hardens overnight, leaving a sterile, secure building which ought to last for years. As they say: 'If you compare it to a tent it's more expensive and it's heavier, if you compare it to a permanent building it's lighter and quicker.' (BBC News, May 18th 2011) With hindsight, we could say that it is just a development of a technique to make puppet heads out of a balloon and plaster of Paris bandage but that would invite the question, 'Why didn't we think of it first?' and if we had done, 'Why didn't we do something about it?' Remember our definition of entrepreneurship – identifying an opportunity to bring value and taking *action* to bring it about.

If we are not bound in space or time when looking for ideas, neither are we bound by our own species. The words bionics and biomimicry are used nowadays to describe the application of solutions from the natural world to human innovation.

One of the most quoted examples is Velcro. In 1941, the Swiss engineer George de Mestral was removing burrs from the coat of his dog after a walk in the Alps. Being the sort of man he was, he was intrigued enough to examine the burrs microscopically to see what made them so sticky. Noting that the hooks of the burrs caught in anything looped, he set about developing a product which imitated the effect, coining the word Velcro from the French *velours* (velvet) and *crochet* (hook).

This story tells us as much about the nature of innovation as it does about innovation from nature. This innovation was by no means inevitable. The fact that 'burs, I can tell you; they'll stick where they are thrown' was known to Shakespeare when he wrote *Troilus and Cressida.* Teasels, which have similar hooks, have been and are still used in cloth manufacture to raise the nap of cloth as part of the finishing process. But no one had thought to use them as a fastener until de Mestral happened along.

Even though he wasn't looking for a new invention, he recognised one when it literally came and stuck to him and his dog. It still took around ten years of hard work before the Velcro became a practical proposition – a patent was finally granted in 1955. Even then the product did not take off until it had a champion (NASA) to bring it to a wider audience. That wider customer base of skiers, scuba divers and mountaineers, which led to sports fashion and children's wear, would never have been able to support the innovation without the space programme – unheard of in 1941. At any point in the story, the innovation could have been halted and the story would never have been told. As always, when recounting stories like this we have to be aware of the narrative bias.

Another example: when Percy Shaw invented reflective road studs, they quickly became known as 'cats' eyes', but were they actually inspired by actual cats' eyes? Percy could tell a good tale and on another occasion claimed that the first inspiration was the shiny tram lines running down the middle of the road.

The idea of insight from nature is not new: 'Goe to the Ant thou sluggard, consider her wayes, and be wise.' (*Proverbs* 6:6). Humans have always used the world around them for inspiration; after all there is nothing else to look at; for example, it is hard to believe that the inventors of plate armour had never seen a lobster.

The English ships known as 'race galleons', which defeated the Spanish Armada in 1588, were smaller, sleeker and faster than their floating fortress-like counterparts. A manuscript dated two years earlier, attributed to the Deptford shipwright Matthew Baker (1530–1613), illustrates the idea that the ship should have 'a cod's head and a mackerel's tail'.

An early example of biomimetics

George Iles' marvellous 1906 volume *Inventors at Work* includes a whole chapter on 'Nature as Teacher'. He does not limit himself to the straightforward lessons of the structural strength of plants and honeycombs, or the application of natural phenomena like sandblasting: he is far more imaginative in his analogies. He notes, for example, that nature tends to follow paths of least resistance, be it lightning bolts or rain water, and sees the application: 'When the surveyors of the first transcontinental railroad of America began their labors, they gave diligent heed to the trails of buffaloes in the Rocky Mountains, believing that these sagacious brutes in centuries of quest had discovered the easiest passes.'

He even finds inspiration for the metallurgy of (then) state-of-the-art gun-barrel manufacture in the structure of the animal heart. 'Its structure, made up of cylinders successively shrunk one upon another, resembles that of the heart, whose two inner parts have their fibres wound somewhat like balls of twine, these in turn being tightly compressed by a covering of other fibres.'

He sums up the approach: 'What nature has done, art may imitate.'

Perhaps the most familiar example of art imitating nature is 'viral' marketing, the term used to describe the deliberate spreading of concepts through social networks like the way a disease travels through a population. Although the term became popular in the American business community in the 1990s, the concept itself is, once more, a good deal older. A century earlier, French sociologist Gabriel Tarde, in his *Les lois de l'imitation*, described the different ways ideas spread:

Comparons un ouragan, une épidémie, une insurrection. A hurricane storms directly from one neighbourhood to another; an epidemic strikes to the right and left, sometimes missing one house whilst attacking others; an insurrection moves more freely still, jumping from city to city, workshop to workshop. Ideas like that can even be resurrected from past ages. *Parfois même la contagion vient du passé, d'une époque morte.*

To find ideas from the natural world, use the same technique as before: specific problem, general problem, general solution, specific solution. For example, imagine that you have identified your general problem area as one of temperature control. You may have arrived at this area from any number of specific problems; you could be an architect, a heating engineer or a clothes designer; for the purposes of argument the general area is temperature control. Look for analogies to your issue from the natural world. The architect should be interested in the air-conditioning systems of termite mounds; the heating engineer would be hard pressed to find a more efficient radiator than an elephant's ears; the clothes designer might study how pine cones react to moisture to make 'breathable' fabric.

Pioneers of aviation studied the flight of birds but the first successful machines were those that imitated the *function* of a wing rather than slavishly aping its structure; understanding what a wing *does* and *how* it does it rather than 'flapping about' copying wings.

Advocates of biomimetics point out with justification that natural solutions have been tried and tested for millennia in 'nature's laboratory' and so are not only proven successful but are also more likely to be sustainable. With literally millions and millions of species, there really ought to be plenty of possibilities to explore. Nature, however, will not provide parallels for every problem: you will have to look very hard to find a plant or animal with a wheel, but the whole field of biomimetics illustrates once more the importance of the multidisciplinary approach to idea generation. Proponents of biomimetics emphasise the conscious searching out of solutions from the natural world rather than waiting for them to happen along. This approach holds out enormous potential and is already providing innovative products.

Scientists at the ISTEC laboratory in Italy have developed artificial bone from wood; especially that of the rattan palm. The natural spongy structure of the wood is preserved but the carbon is replaced by bioceramic, resulting in a material which is so compatible with living tissue that it interacts; new bone grows into and fuses with the implant to the point where you can't see the join. Tests on sheep have been encouraging and human implants should go ahead by 2015. What is more, the mechanical properties of the new material could prove useful in domains far from medicine; for example, the turbine blades of aircraft engines.

For the layperson, it is surprising to think that a development in medicine might possibly have applications in industry but aerospace engineers have long been open to the idea of materials they haven't got. As long ago as 1957, NASA heard of the difficulties posed by 'the lack of a superior high-temperature material . . . dubbed *unobtainium*'. Engineers were using the word for the sort of material with the strength and resilience needed to cope with the engine power they knew they could achieve. Unobtainium is perfect for the purpose in every way, limited only by the fact that it does not exist.*

The word has come to mean any ideal material for a particular function that we can't have – at the moment. It may be too expensive; it might not have been invented yet; it may never be invented; or it may already be available *outside* our own knowledge.

It is sometimes said that the invention of the lightbulb must have upset the candle-makers of the world. But innovation nearly always comes from outside and it's ridiculous to expect candle-makers to invent the lightbulb. But imagine a candle-maker who wanted to stay ahead of the game. If he concentrated on what his product *does* rather than what it *is* he might see himself as a 'provider of domestic illumination'. As such he might be expected to be aware of any relevant new discoveries or ideas and would probably have a sideline manufacturing oil lamps and gas mantles and might even have discovered the lightbulb for himself. It is simply a matter of looking at things from a different point of view. That is what we will try to do in the next section.

> The old astronomers discovered and maintained much that was true; but, because they were placed on a false ground, and looked from a wrong point of view, they never did, they never could, discover the truth – that is the whole truth.
>
> (Samuel Taylor Coleridge, *Table Talk* 1831)

Remember the example of the mail coach: the developments that destroyed the coaching inns were simply not visible, never mind obvious, from the inn-yard.

---

*The concept has become a lot better known since being used in the film *Avatar* (2009).

Generate non-obvious ideas [Dance step two]

Followers of our fractals will realise that this is the central section of our problem-solving process and should be the most free-thinking, uncritical, and open-minded of all. It is the epitome of divergent production: finding multiple solutions. So if you think it's a bit vague and undisciplined, don't worry, it's supposed to be; we are picking up those childish things. Even if, like Alice, we can't 'believe impossible things', we ought at least to be able to suspend our disbelief for a short while – there will be time enough to tighten things up before we're finished.

Théodule-Armand Ribot was a great one for analogies, as we saw, but he identified their limitations: essentially they are still a sort of repetition through association and, if we are limited to association, truly novel creativity is impossible and we are imprisoned in routine: *'L'invention nous serait à jamais interdite; nous ne pourrions sortir de la répétition, nous serions emprisonnés dans la routine . . .'* But, says Ribot, there is an opposing faculty which frees us – dissociation: *'mais il y a une puissance antagoniste qui nous affranchit: c'est la dissociation'.*

Some dissociation occurs naturally and accidentally when we find analogies, but the type Ribot thinks is most productive starts with destruction. Images and concepts are not singular but joined in chains, woven into nets – dissociation breaks them into their constituent parts and reduces them to ruin: *'Les représentations ne sont pas solitaires; dans la réalité, elles font partie d'une chaîne ou plutôt d'une trame, d'un réseau, puisqu'en raison de leurs multiples rapports, elles peuvent rayonner en tous sens. Or, la dissociation agit aussi sur les séries les tronque, les mutile, les démolit, les réduit à l'état de ruine.'*

Ribot describes the process as similar to that which in geology produces new terrain from the breakdown of old rocks: *'C'est un travail analogue à celui qui, en géologie, produit de nouveaux terrains par l'usure des vieilles roches.'*

Dissociation is, of course, the very opposite of what we all think we are good at – it is the impossibility of Alice in Wonderland. The idea that we are going to try and generate more and more ideas that have progressively less and less to do with our preconceptions of what a solution might look like is profoundly uncomfortable but we are trying to imitate those times when we are not consciously engaged in problem solving. One is reminded of Vidocq looking at the stars by glances on page 64. A more prosaic way of looking at deliberate dissociation might be to describe it as similar to a rather inefficient effort at 'reverse engineering', whereby several similar objects or concepts would be deconstructed at the same time and something different made out of the bits.

It all sounds very airy-fairy and impractical, but we noted earlier the separation of art and science; the distrust that exists between those who credit imagination and those who insist upon the primacy of reason. There are areas, however, where the 'creatives' meet the 'bean-counters' – such as advertising.

The famously commonsensical Dr Samuel Johnson wrote: 'The trade of advertising is now so near to perfection, that it is not easy to propose any improvement.' (*The Idler* 1759)

Discovery

Johnson has been proved wrong (yet again) – advertising has been driven by the incessant demands of commerce to become more and more creative in manipulation. The most effective match Schopenhauer's definition of genius by persuading us to buy things we didn't even know we wanted. So much so that it would be a brave commentator who would now predict the end of innovations in advertising. It is therefore no surprise that creative idea generation is of supreme importance to advertising executives. 'How it works' is of far less interest to the advertising industry than 'that it works'.

James Webb Young asserts 'that the production of ideas is just as definite a process as the production of Fords; that the production of ideas, too, runs on an assembly line; that in this production the mind follows an operative technique which can be learned and controlled; and that its effective use is just as much a matter of practice in the technique as is the effective use of any tool' (*A Technique for Producing Ideas*, 1940).

As we said, the secret to creativity is that we are not limited in our search for material. We are not even limited by reality; imagination is just that: forming in our mind's eye images of things that do not even exist, at least not yet!

We have already seen how we can find a use for homeopathy which is well beyond reason and how, as a concept, unobtainium allows us to carry forward thought experiments and designs beyond our limitations.

- So called 'off the wall', 'out of the box', 'lateral' thinking is not new; think of the Judgement of Solomon: King Solomon decided a maternity dispute by pretending that he would have the baby cut in two, reasoning that the true mother would rather give up her child than see it killed (1 *Kings* 3:16–28).

A similar, less life-threatening plot device is found in a fourteenth-century Chinese play by Li Xingfu (李行道). The two 'mothers' each take an arm and attempt to drag the child from a circle drawn on the ground. The winner is in fact the one who deliberately loses in order to spare the child pain. *Hui Lan Ji* (灰闌記) or *The Circle of Chalk* is better known in the west as the basis of Bertolt Brecht's *Caucasian Chalk Circle*.

Lateral Thinkers: trickster-heroes and wise fools

We have already met the good soldier Schweik; he is part of a long tradition. The Trickster is one of the oldest archetypes of human culture. He is certainly one of the most widespread. In tribal societies he is often an animal and usually a shape shifter as well. In some traditions he also changes sex. He, or she, can be found all over the world in many guises; sometimes helpful, often malign, almost always mischievous and unexpected.

In Japan he is Tanuki the raccoon dog.

In China he's Sun Wukong the Monkey King.

He's the Greek hero Odysseus, who tricks the Trojans into demolishing their defences with the gift of a wooden horse.

He's the Norse god Loki; the Welsh wizard Gwydion.

He can trick a genie back into the bottle; he can put 'a girdle about the earth in forty minutes'.

He is legendary as well as mythical; Till Eulenspiegel is the hero of a cycle of popular stories who tricks and fools his way across medieval Germany.

Sometimes the trickster is a hero, sometimes the wise fool.

In the Islamic tradition, Mullah Nasruddin is both a wise man and a fool; Hershel of Ostropol serves the same purpose for European Jewry. The humour of these two is deliberately invoked by some teachers to create a mood where orthodoxies and presuppositions are questioned.

Nasruddin Hodja went to the bath-house one day. Because he looked poor, the attendants treated him badly, giving him rags for a towel. Despite this, Nasruddin tipped them a gold coin. On his next visit Nasruddin was treated like a king but only gave one small copper coin. The attendants were outraged at such small payment but Nasruddin explained, 'That was for the last occasion, the gold was for this time.'

Herschele Ostropole ordered cakes in the café. As they arrived, he changed his mind and asked if he could swap them for doughnuts. After his snack, he left without paying; 'What about the doughnuts you ate?' called the proprietor. 'I gave you the cakes in exchange.' 'Well, how about paying for the cakes?' 'But I didn't eat the cakes,' said Herschele.

In West Africa the trickster is Anansi the spider. The slave trade took his stories to the Caribbean and the southern United States, where he flourished under a variety of aliases including both Boy Nasty and Aunt Nancy. The Native Americans had their own trickster hero: Old Man Coyote. Anyone who can put one over on their masters is bound to be popular among the oppressed, but the tales were also adapted by white Americans, especially the poor ones. While Joel Chandler Harris was collecting Brer Rabbit stories in the southern states of the USA, Mark Twain published *Tom Sawyer*.

Chapter Two sees Tom whitewashing the fence when he would rather not. He tries paying a friend to do it but realises he cannot afford to: 'At this dark and hopeless moment an inspiration burst upon him!' He pretends to be enjoying the task so much that his friends actually pay for the privilege of taking turns until the job is complete, by which time, 'Tom was literally rolling in wealth . . . twelve marbles, part of a jews-harp, a piece of blue bottle-glass to look through, a spool cannon, a key that wouldn't unlock anything, a fragment of chalk, a glass stopper of a decanter, a tin soldier, a couple of tadpoles, six fire-crackers, a kitten with only one eye, a brass doorknob, a dog-collar – but no dog – the handle of a knife, four pieces of orange-peel, and a dilapidated old window sash.'

Bugs Bunny and Charlie Chaplin's little tramp are twentieth-century tricksters and it is no coincidence that Walt Disney portrays Robin Hood as a wily fox. Darker avatars of the trickster are found in Batman comics, The Joker and The Riddler. The trickster-hero is a stock character in Japanese Anime and is endemic in computer gaming.

Tricksters and wise fools sometimes form a double act and are even found in TV sitcoms; think of Sergeant Bilko and Private Doberman or Del Boy and Trigger.

If you are wondering what this has to do with entrepreneurship and creative problem solving, go to Wikipedia and think about Tom Sawyer and the whitewash.

- Jokes and riddles rely on looking from a different point of view. The moment you 'get it' is very like the moment you go 'Aha!' when you solve a problem; it is another of those moments when we are likely to use the word 'genius'.

- If new ideas are simply restructured old ideas then all we have to do to generate lots of extraordinary ideas is to take an ordinary idea and tweak it. Turn it inside-out and upside-down; reverse it, modify it; make it bigger, make it smaller; break it up and mess around with the bits; substitute, remove or add new parts; re-combine it in a different way.

- 'Brainstorming' is a group-creativity technique originally devised by advertising manager Alex Osborn in the late 1930s. The general objective of the technique is to produce a relaxed atmosphere where ideas bounce around freely and new and original concepts 'emerge' from collaboration rather than from individuals.

Osborn's 1948 book, *Your Creative Power*, remains useful despite the casual sexism.

> How big should a brainstorming group be? The ideal number is between 5 and 10. What sex or sexes? A group of men seems best; but our Vice-President, Mrs. Jean Rindlaub, has had great success with groups of young women. We have also found that mixed groups work well.

The titles of chapters 20–28 contain the essence of the technique:

To What Other Uses Could This Be Put?

What Can We Borrow and *Adapt* to Our Need?

Let's Look for a New Twist – Let's *Modify*

What If We Add, or Multiply – or *Magnify*?

Let's Subtract and Divide – Let's *Minify*

Let's Seek 'That' Instead of 'This' – Let's *Substitute*

Let's Change the Pattern – Let's *Re-arrange*

There's Lots of Good Hunting in *Vice Versa*

Your Creative Key May Be a *Combination*

Almost every one of Osborn's heuristics is illustrated in the history of the humble screw fastening. It derives from the screw thread, a simple machine which allows conversion between rotational and linear force. Leave aside all the engineering applications; leave aside the difference between screws and bolts, issues of manufacture and standards; let's focus on the sort of screws any of us might buy from a hardware store to fix some shelves on a wall. Every screw on display in the store is a variation on the basic theme, that has usually come about by a single 'tweak' of an older design.

Start with the oldest style, a tapered shank with a rounded head driven in by a slot screwdriver.

A parallel shank might be more useful if you need to undo the fixing from time to time; you could even make the screw tap its own thread into metal or plastic.

You might like a countersunk head, or even a mirror head which is disguised by a cover which itself screws into the screw.

A slot head is traditional but the crosshead is easier to use. Even then there are different crossheads; do you want the Phillips type which is so designed that the driver slips out once tightened, or the Pozidriv which allows you to drive a screw right through?

What about a tamper-proof screw which, once driven in, cannot be unscrewed? Or the double-ended screw, which is invisible?

How could a simple screw be improved by combination?

Well, you could combine it with a wall plug; you could even combine it with a drill. Finally, who said that screws had to be made of metal?

By a series of single steps you might arrive at the stunning invention of the plasterboard screw; this device drills its own hole, cuts its own thread, once fixed becomes the plug for another screw which actually bears the load, and, oh yes, it's made of plastic! A wonder of ingenuity, which is the result of creative answers to the easiest of questions: what happens if we modify, combine or substitute? Every man-made object has a story; even the most commonplace item illustrates the history of human ingenuity.

Brainstorming has been taken up enthusiastically by the creative industry. Osborn's four basic rules (to focus on quantity, to suspend criticism, to welcome the unusual and to combine/improve ideas) have increased with each new manifestation. Some of these expect a fairly rigid adherence to their rules in order to achieve free thinking. Recent researches suggest that brainstorming might not be quite as effective as its most zealous fans think; the biggest danger being 'groupthink', the exact opposite of what is desired. To which of course those zealots reply, 'That's because you're not doing it right!' The difficulty is that a great deal of innovation is carried out in competitive and hierarchical environments and it's sometimes difficult to see how strict rules and procedures can 'force' people to think freely.

There is one overriding 'rule' for free thinking, however, and that is to suspend your judgement. Here we can take some advice from the world of improvisational comedy. The essence of successful 'improv' is relentless positivity: for it to work, participants are simply not allowed to say 'no'. The comedian Neil Mullarkey, who runs creative-thinking workshops for business, explains the stultifying power of negativity:

> 'Yes, but that wasn't what I was thinking . . .'
> 'Yes, but that's not a good idea . . .'
> 'Yes, but we can't afford it . . .'
> 'Yes, but the bosses wouldn't like it . . .'
> 'Yes, but we've never done that before . . .'
> It's very easy to say, 'Yes, but' – why we can't . . . everything we hear before the 'but' is deleted when we hear the 'but'.
>
> (Speaking on BBC Radio 4, *In Business*, December 17th 2009)

If you keep saying 'Yes, but', people soon stop coming up with ideas. 'Yes, and', on the other hand, is far more encouraging. At this stage we are actually encouraging the confirmation bias that we were so critical of earlier because we are far more concerned with quantity and novelty of ideas generated rather than quality: if we judge them now we will stop the flow and fail to create that critical mass from which we hope truly original concepts will emerge.*

Genius and Madness

The term 'brainstorming' is now considered by some to be politically incorrect. It is true that the word was occasionally used long ago to describe mental disturbance but it has most often been used in the self-deprecatory sense that Norman Hunter used it in his creation of the absent-minded Professor Branestawm (1933), a man whose head was so filled with extraordinary ideas that he had no room for ordinary ones. The 'mad scientist' has become an icon of creativity from the fictional Dr Victor Frankenstein (1818) all the way to real-life 'boffins' like Sir Barnes Wallis (1887–1979).

The seventeeth century poet John Dryden is only one of many to voice the opinion that: 'Great wits are sure to madness near allied and thin partitions do their bounds divide.' He also thought that 'Imagination in a poet is a faculty so wild and lawless, that, like an high-ranging spaniel, it must have clogs tied to it, lest it outrun the judgment.'

*This relentless positivity will be curbed later on! One of the reasons 'improv' comedy isn't all that funny is that there's always more quantity than quality: it is work in progress.

And there is no doubt that certain of the traits we observe in brainstorming are also observed as part of the diagnosis of psychosis. Two types of 'thought disorder' have particular resonance.

'Knight's Move Thinking' is a term used to describe thought patterns which seem disconnected or tangential but reflect a logical sequence hidden from the casual observer.

'Flight of Ideas' is the rapid, almost unstoppable flow of thought, again often jumping from topic to topic apparently at random.

The only difference between madness and genius would seem to be that in the one we try to control the disorder whereas in the other we tolerate and indeed encourage it.

And so we should perhaps be sensitive if offence actually occurs but to replace brainstorm with 'thought-shower' shows a fundamental ignorance of the term. Thought-shower is not even a synonym. A shower is no substitute for a storm. We have mentioned 'gales of creation and destruction' and that is what brainstorming should emulate; taking concepts to bits and throwing them into the air to see where they land. The whole point is that 'we're not in Kansas anymore'. When we click our heels and return, we hope we have learned something. So tempests, hurricanes, tornadoes maybe, but definitely not a shower.

The overriding problem of studies trying to link genius and madness is one of definition. There is no commonly agreed definition of genius and likewise there is no commonly agreed definition of madness. This has not stopped people constructing arguments linking the two. Thus the poet *Emily Dickinson* and the painter Vincent Van Gogh are supposed to have suffered from bipolar disorder (manic depression). The problem is that despite being acclaimed as 'geniuses' today, neither Dickinson nor Van Gogh was successful in their time. And so we have a post-mortem diagnosis of 'genius' as well as a post-mortem diagnosis of 'madness'. Just as many people now look upon the word 'madness' as both vague and unhelpful, we may well find that the same applies to the word 'genius'.

Our basic advice for storming ideas would be to relax; at this stage there are no 'correct answers'. Don't criticise, don't judge, all contributions are welcome, unusual ideas especially as they are likely to send sparks in new directions. As ideas bounce around, see if you can't make some of them collide. If you get stuck, try some of the basic tweaking heuristics above. Write down *everything* however wild. Keep it short; you can always try again. If you're laughing, it's working.

A Chair is Not a Chair

In response to a challenge to explain 'storming', one of the authors undertook to demonstrate how easy it is for one person to generate a volume of ideas and concepts within fifteen minutes.

The general problem might be alternative seating provision (the specific problem may be anything from a waiting room to a theatre) and the default solution would be some sort of chair.

The central three bullet points of CPS are analogy, non-obvious ideas and quantity.

If we immediately encourage concepts of chairs we will limit ourselves to imitation, in other words incremental innovation.

To encourage radical innovation we can deconstruct the default concept – chair.

Thus we immediately have legs, seat, back – three ideas instead of one.

We can do this for analogous forms of chair from three-legged stool to La-Z-Boy recliners.

Very soon we have a whole raft of ideas, some of them non-obvious – three legs, two legs, no legs (bean bags or misericords). We have wood, leather, plastic; moulded, woven, screwed together, nailed together; temporary, permanent, collapsible, foldable, inflatable; privately owned, rented, disposable and so on . . .

The prerequisite is quantity. The above twenty or more ideas were generated in a couple of minutes. From this wide array of small ideas we ought to be able to construct novel concepts that may then be engineered into possible solutions. For example: *A one-legged stool (akin to a shooting stick) with a re-usable exothermic self-heating cushion and some sort of umbrella facility.*

The above is a concept (not a very good one, you might say, but remember Ribot's assertion that we ought to expect absurdity as well as originality) but it is really not that difficult to come up with several similar ones in a very short space of time, e.g. in three minutes:

A musical chair – when the music stops it collapses.

A puzzle chair – like a flat pack but deliberately difficult.

A DIY chair – the seat is knitted, the needles become the legs.

It should be noted that the above responses were to a *general* problem. The secret is not to be self-conscious, or attach too much value to them – they are not thought through and will not, by themselves, be a solution. But they may combine with or spark off other ideas, resulting in a concept relevant to the *specific* problem.

Obviously, but for some counter-intuitively, the more complex the problem, the easier it is to deconstruct. So we should be ambitious and generate large numbers of ideas and concepts – it's really not that hard.

There are conflicting opinions about the best methods of brainstorming. There is some evidence that generating ideas on your own is more productive than in a group, where issues such as self-censorship and groupthink are very difficult to overcome. UNIEI's response is to do both! Volume is what we're after. We tend to start, therefore, with a period of silent storming when participants have to come up with at least ten ideas each. Naturally, there will be duplicates but never mind. Next, participants are invited to build on each other's ideas – always 'Yes, and', never 'Yes, but'.

Idea generation is one of those areas of tacit knowing where there is a limit to explicit instruction. Even though we've suggested a few dance steps, there comes a point when you're on your own or, to return to the example of swimming, 'You have to get your feet wet.'

Nevertheless, the next best thing to doing it yourself is watching someone else splashing around in the pool of ideas. There follows an account of idea generation and evaluation of the type currently practised by the authors through the UNIEI.

Students were formed into groups, no less than four, no more than eight, and given problem areas in which to look for entrepreneurial opportunities. One group of students was looking for opportunities to reduce traffic congestion in a medium-sized city in the UK. At the end of the problem-definition stage, one of the root causes they had identified was that there were only 5,500 parking spaces in a city with 250,000 cars. They took this as a starting point for Phase Two: discovery.

This storming session was held in a large room along with other teams working on their own projects. Pens, paper, flipcharts, etc., were provided in abundance. Apart from the problem statement all the paper was blank. The students had all worked together previously and so were relaxed in each other's company. An egalitarian atmosphere prevailed, with each member at some point naturally taking the role of 'penholder' for the group. After thirty minutes or so, the ideas and the laughter tailed off and so they stopped and took a coffee break. Here are a few of the ideas generated in the first storm session:

More parking; less parking; underground parking; underwater parking; parking in the park; cut down all the trees; park in the sports stadium; park in the middle of the road; park on the sides of buildings; stackable cars; disposable cars; multi-purpose cars; giveaway cars; white bicycles; miniature cars; foldaway cars; free car parks; expensive car parks; auction parking places; eBay parking places; valet parking; time-share car parks; swap parking places; rent out your driveway; mobile car parks; ban driving; ban pedestrians; ban city centres; flexible opening; flexible working; flexible shopping; ban working; work from home; shop from home; remove the need for travel; better communications; better video to find places; GPS; automatic space utilisation; more taxis; personal taxis; corporate taxis; more trains; more buses; more bicycles/skateboards/unicycles; park and ride; ride and park; no lines in car parks; narrow lines in car parks; floating cars; abandon your car; driverless cars; homing cars; whistle for your car; intelligent car parks; lower roofs in multistoreys; transformers; expandable car parks; car racks; jigsaw cars; Ford only parking; odd number plates; lottery tickets for parking; mobile offices; work in your car; WiFi in the traffic jam; penalise large cars; ban deliveries; cheap night-shift parking; ban lorries; ban buses; ban everything.

It reads like a stream of consciousness, which it is – the consciousness of the group as they bounce ideas around, adding, subtracting, reversing and hitchhiking. As we mentioned, collective consciousness carries the risk of groupthink, another reason to keep it short, take a break and try again if necessary. We will return to them later.

Find as many ideas as possible [Dance step three]

- Don't forget the obvious.

We have already noted that the ability to communicate information accurately is one of the distinguishing characteristics of human ingenuity. Hand in hand with this faculty comes the desire to keep that communication secret. We see the development of codes and ciphers, secret writing and invisible ink, all designed to make messages intelligible only to the chosen few. Letter substitution is one of the oldest and simplest methods but is comparatively easy to crack by observing word patterns and letter frequency, so more and more sophisticated tricks are used to disguise the message. Code breakers tend to be mathematicians as well as linguists. The Enigma machine used a straightforward letter-substitution code but of such complexity of encryption that even if a word or phrase was repeated within the same message it would look totally different. It was assumed to be impossible to break because of the sheer size of the calculations involved. The story of the breaking of Enigma at Bletchley Park is essentially the story of a technological 'arms race' which led to the birth of computer science.*

There is a lesser-known account of ciphers that were *never* broken, the story of a more obvious solution, elegant in its simplicity.

It begins with an apocryphal tale of a British officer using an unsecured telephone during the First World War. When challenged, he replied that any potentially hostile listeners would be extremely unlikely to understand the language he was using – Welsh. We are on more substantial ground with the documented use of Cherokee and Choctaw speakers by Allied forces towards the end of the war in France in 1918.

*The code breakers of Bletchley Park famously included crossword puzzlers. Is it possible to speculate that there is a difference between solvers and setters – the former can find associations; the latter can also dissociate to generate the clues?

This simple idea was revived during the Second World War, most successfully with the recruitment of up to four hundred Navajo wireless operators in the Pacific theatre. The instigators of the plan estimated that only thirty individuals in the world outside the Navajo nation understood the language and that none of them were Japanese. Navajo is a complex, highly inflected tongue with no alphabet or symbols; listeners found it hard to transcribe, never mind decipher. Which ought not to be surprising given that it took a lifetime (or at least a childhood) to learn the language, which had developed over millennia. Because the language did not possess the military vocabulary, and as a further safeguard, a relatively straightforward substitution code was used which could be learned by all code talkers so that code books never entered the field. Navajo code talkers were used right up until the 1960s and their code was *never* broken. Presumably it has been replaced by something even more secure, which we may learn about in another thirty years or so. (The Modern Major-General's awareness of Babylonian cuneiform does not seem as ridiculous as Gilbert and Sullivan would have us believe!)

It's worth remembering that the American military would never have had Navajo to turn to if their forebears' attempts to integrate and 'civilise' had succeeded.

When we started school in 1929, we were forbidden to speak Navajo. But, when the government got in trouble with Japan in 1942, they called on us to use our language to help win the war. (Navajo code talker Teddy Draper)

It's strange, but growing up as a child I was forbidden to speak my native language at school; later my country asked me to. My language helped win the war, and that makes me very proud. Very proud. (Comanche code talker Charles Chibitty)

- Don't forget past solutions which became redundant; circumstances may have changed.

As we have seen with the windmill, redundancy need not be permanent. And we know that outdated ideas and lost or disused technologies remain at the back of the bookshelf, waiting to be rediscovered as they become appropriate once more, albeit in a subtly different fashion.

> The images of men's wits and knowledges remain in books, exempted from the wrong of time, and capable of perpetual renovation . . . they generate still, and cast their seeds in the minds of others, provoking and causing infinite actions and opinions in succeeding ages . . . [letters] as ships, pass through the vast seas of time, and make ages so distant to participate of the wisdom, illuminations, and inventions, the one of the other?
>
> (Francis Bacon, *The Advancement of Learning*, 1605)

We can see the to and fro of ideas in books themselves, specifically the printing trade. Johannes Gutenberg was voted one of the minds of the millennium in almost every poll at the end of the twentieth century. Gutenberg combined and refined several technologies in one for his invention of the printing press. He had to develop oil-based inks; he had to adapt the screw mechanism of olive and wine presses; but the greatest innovation was his use of movable type. Printing with the new process was considerably cheaper and more flexible than block printing and is widely thought to have provided the information technology at the heart of the Renaissance.

Movable type was the driving force behind the printed word for four hundred years, after which a curious reversal happened. The cost/benefit pendulum had swung back to the point at which movable type became more expensive than casting whole lines and pages of text. Linotype machines and cheap paper fuelled the newspaper revolution, which made the printed word so cheap that it became disposable.

The computer revolution has meant that 'hot metal' printing is all but extinct. With a computer in the home we can copy and print at will.

Copying in two dimensions, whether images or text, is now commonplace and raises the same sorts of issues as audio and video recording. But can we go one step beyond even that? What if we were all able to copy objects in three dimensions? One of James Watts's last and abiding projects during his semi-retirement was to build a sculpture-copying machine. He would surely have been impressed by the rapid prototyping machine RepRap. Extruding thermoplastic layer by layer, the machine effectively *prints* three-dimensional components. The open source project even allows the machine to copy itself! The day when replacement parts can be printed at will, at home or in a local copy-shop, may not be far away. Of course Watt was thinking of carving the image out of a block rather than building it up but the opposite is only one heuristic away.

Another to-and-fro example of ideas forming threads of consequence is fibre-optic technology. We have already met the Victorian scientist John Tyndall. He had an imaginative approach to popularising science and demonstrated internal light refraction to the public by use of coloured water fountains.

By the twentieth century, technology was advanced enough to use the principle to provide light for dentistry. The use of reflective tubes to transfer images was demonstrated in the 1920s and used for internal medical examinations in the next decade.

In the 1950s, the full potential of total internal refraction was identified by Narinder Singh Kapany. Combining his expertise as a physicist with his skill as an inventor and entrepreneur, Dr Kapany has become recognised as the father of fibre optics. The technology used to manufacture optical fibres progressed incrementally as the applications grew, but another revolutionary change is taking place. The latest

Discovery

technology uses diffraction along photonic crystal fibres, which for the cognoscenti is very different from 'traditional' internal refraction. It is difficult to imagine these new photonic crystal fibres being developed without the pre-existing optical fibre technology. Again we see the supreme importance of context.

But the principle of internal refraction can also be used on a macro scale. Reflective light tubes are used more and more to capture, direct and diffuse natural daylight into rooms with few or no windows. Running costs disappear and natural daylight is proven to be better than artificial.

Technologies can be lost altogether. Ancient building techniques spring to mind: that the pyramids were built by man is indisputable; precisely how is a matter of debate. The oldest continuing civilisations are capable of forgetting their own achievements; for example, the 'south-facing chariot' (a complex differential gearing) has been invented, lost and reinvented several times in Chinese history.

In our discussion of paradigm shifts we mentioned the loss of explanation which sometimes occurs between the old and the new. The new paradigm solves more problems than the old but not necessarily all of them. A similar thing happens after one of those 'gales of creative destruction'. A new procedure replaces an old one and, as we saw with the music industry, sometimes whole technologies are lost. So it might be worth looking to another time and another place to see how 'they' used to cope with similar situations when background conditions were different and different imperatives prevailed. We are not only looking at analogous problems but also analogous conditions.

We do not have to look that far into the past to see how quickly conditions and attitudes adjust. In 1983, David Braben and Ian Bell developed the computer game *Elite* while they were undergraduates at Cambridge. Game designers were severely restricted by the small memory of current machines. Games manufacturers were already surprisingly conservative, restricting themselves to arcade games like *Space Invaders* and *Pac-Man*. *Elite* offered 3D graphics in a game with eight galaxies, each containing 256 planets, to explore. Braben and Bell actually restricted the number of planets available to make the game user friendly.

So how did they manage to create whole galaxies on machines with only 14 kilobytes of memory? They used a technique related to the fractals we have already come across: 'procedural generation'. By initiating a sequence of pseudo-random numbers, they were able to create different 'worlds' without using much actual memory; each 'world' depended upon its immediate predecessor. The benefits of procedural generation – almost unlimited 'worlds' – outweighed the limitations, the sameness. Innovatively marketed, *Elite* was a great success. At its peak there was one copy of the game sold for every BBC Micro that could run it, 150,000 in total. The success of *Elite* contributed to the success of home computing in general, as a result of which computer memory has become incredibly cheap compared with the 1980s; so modern designers have little need for procedural generation.

To take another brief step sideways, it is interesting to note that procedural memory is observed in humans: the psychologist Oliver Sacks has written and spoken of the example of

> a musician and musicologist, Clive Wearing, who had his hippocampus systems wiped out by an encephalitis 20 years ago. He can't remember anything much for more than seven seconds. But this man is able to conduct a choir, conduct an orchestra, play the piano or sing long, complex pieces of music. His abilities to perform musically are entirely spared. If you ask him in terms of knowledge, 'Do you know such-and-such a Bach prelude and fugue', he will look blank or say no. But put his hands on the piano, sing the first note, and he's off.
>
> (In conversation at Columbia's Miller Theater, New York, on 6 November 2008)

In early modern times, a combination of increasing literacy and cheap paper, printed books with their indexes, and numbered pages meant that people no longer needed the memory skills of their forebears. The modern-day variety artist who performs astonishing feats of memory is demonstrating skills which were not quite so remarkable in ancient times. The techniques of memory training offered by self-help books today were known to Cicero in ancient Rome.

It is not just memory skills that are being threatened by technology: if everyone has satellite navigation, no one will need maps and the very particular skill of map reading will be lost to all but a few.

Sadly, one of the greatest areas of innovation and ingenuity has been the devising of quicker, cheaper and more efficient methods of killing each other. The devastating ballistic power of the longbow depended on a highly trained and practised militia; archery practice on a Sunday was as compulsory as churchgoing for centuries in England. But the longbow was replaced by the crossbow, which could be used by the meanest conscript with a minimum of training. By the eighteenth century, the musket was the tool of the infantryman, archery had more or less died out and 'fletcher' became a surname rather than an occupation, despite the fact that a well-trained archer could fire at least five times faster than the fastest musket man.

You can see the same phenomenon at work in metallurgy. The decline of edge weapons would have resulted in another lost technology but for the luxury trade in ornamental and ceremonial swords. The swordsmiths of the world have preserved astonishing expertise in producing metals that are both hard and flexible at the same time. The general principle is to combine two or more types of iron and steel in one. Pattern welding and damascening might seem arcane and irrelevant these days but the technique of co-extrusion of modern plastics addresses exactly the same problems.

Goods transportation is another good example. The packhorse was replaced by canal boats, which could carry goods safely and in far greater quantity. Scarcely had the canal system been built when it was pushed aside by the faster rail network, which is now under threat from the more flexible road-haulage industry. In simplistic terms, the driving imperative behind each change was different and at each change a loss occurred. The attraction of bulk transport favoured the canal system over the packhorse but there was a loss of flexibility and independence. Speed was the trump card of the railways but then the road-haulage industry reasserted flexibility and independence. (One response to the problems of goods transport has been containerisation, which we will return to later.) These changes happened against a background of cheaper and cheaper power. Manpower was cheap enough to dig the canals and later the railways, but when coal became cheap, steam locomotives replaced the horse. Road haulage would never have undercut rail transport without cheap oil. We have already quoted Matthew Boulton ('I sell here, Sir, what all the world desires to have – POWER') and it's worth remembering that it was power at a price the world could afford. What was seen as appropriate in the past is not necessarily appropriate now. We have to accommodate a world where carbon footprints and sustainability are the new imperatives. Ironically, perceptions of what constitutes pollution have also altered: at the turn of the nineteenth and twentieth centuries it used to be commonly remarked that the streets were far more pleasant now that nice hygienic motor cars had replaced those smelly horses that no one ever cleaned up after.

Although Wilbur and Orville Wright are accepted as the first to achieve manned, heavier-than-air, powered flight, they were unable to patent their 'Flyer'; confirmation, if it were needed, that their invention took place in a context of other people's efforts. What they were able to defend as unique was the 'wing-warping' technology that gave them control over the plane by changing the shape of the wings. It is said that Wilbur had first thought of the idea while idly flexing a cardboard box. With the limited power available to early aeronauts, the weight of the craft was all important and the spruce, fabric and string which made up the Flyer could cope with the strains imposed by the limited speeds attained in the early days. Wing warping was a short-lived technology, soon being set aside for more rigid fixed wings with ailerons. The development of stronger, lighter materials for aircraft building has gone hand in hand with increasing power from the aero engines which power them and rigidity has been the imperative. But modern materials can also have the flexibility to mimic the 'morphing' of birds' wings, even at speeds close to Mach One.

The technology may be about to make a return, to quote NASA:

The Active Aeroelastic Wing Project is researching an approach to flight control which is a modern outgrowth of the 'wing warping' technique used by the Wright brothers to maneuver their first aircraft. This active flexible wing concept uses traditional aircraft control surfaces, such as ailerons and leading-edge flaps, to twist or 'warp' a flexible wing to produce roll control. If these wing warping techniques for roll control are successful, wing weight for future military combat aircraft could be lowered, radar signature could be minimised and aerodynamic drag could be reduced at transonic speeds, increasing fuel efficiency.

- Explore to the edge of that bell curve of normal distribution.

We mentioned earlier the principle of least effort. It is the easy way but it is underwritten by the principle of adopting the first acceptable solution and that is exactly what we are trying to avoid. (If you google 'solution to all the world's problems', you will find millions of results; what are the chances of finding your particular solution in the first ten? We might need to refine the search or at the very least look at page two.) Remember we are looking for variety at the moment. We are looking for ideas to build on; we know that we cannot start from nothing.

We have seen how redundant solutions can become relevant once more if the background circumstances change; well, that works both ways: we can look for perfectly good ideas which, for a variety of reasons, have not been applied. The factors preventing their implementation may have altered. 'Failed' solutions are unlikely to have a high profile.

When American inventors Woodland and Silver filed a patent for what we now know as the barcode in 1949, they could see the potential. The bars were created by extending Morse code dots and dashes into columns and also into circles or bull's eyes. Unfortunately, the technology for reading the codes was simply not good enough at that time and it wasn't until 1974 that the first product (a packet of chewing gum, now on display at the Smithsonian Institute) was scanned in a supermarket.

Switch off and take a break – the importance of incubation

This is absolutely essential, even though it is sometimes the hardest thing to do. The anecdotal evidence is that some of the best ideas come when people are walking the dog, doing the housework, playing golf; in fact doing anything other than concentrating solely on the matter in hand.

Sir Isaac Newton was famous enough in his lifetime to be plagued by the question, 'Where do you get your ideas from?' According to Sir David Brewster's biography, 'His discoveries were . . . . the fruit of persevering and unbroken study; and he himself declared, that whatever service he had done to the public was not owing to any extraordinary sagacity, but solely to industry and patient thought' (*Memoirs of the Life, Writings and Discoveries of Sir Isaac Newton*, 1855).

Hard work, plain and simple, but what about the legendary apple? In the story an apple hits Newton on the head and he discovers the theory of gravity; for certain *that* never happened. The truth, as always, is more interesting. Perhaps the best account comes from William Stukeley's manuscript *Memoirs of Sir Isaac Newton's Life* (1752):

after dinner, the weather being warm, we went into the garden, & drank thea under the shade of some appletrees, only he, & myself. amidst other discourse, he told me, he was just in the same situation, as when formerly, the notion of gravitation came into his mind. "why sh^d that apple always descend perpendicularly to the ground," thought he to him self: occasion'd by the fall of an apple, as he sat in a comtemplative mood: "why sh^d it not go sideways, or upwards? but constantly to the earths centre? assuredly, the reason is, that the earth draws it. there must be a drawing power in matter. & the sum of the drawing power in the matter of the earth must be in the earths center, not in any side of the earth. therefore dos this apple fall perpendicularly, or toward the center. if matter thus draws matter; it must be in proportion of its quantity. therefore the apple draws the earth, as well as the earth draws the apple.

The problem of gravity had been on Newton's mind for some time, but it was when he was 'in contemplative mood' and noticed an apple fall from a tree in the garden that he realised *how* to frame the question.

In his autobiography, Charles Darwin recalled one of these occasions in relation to one of his problems: 'and I can remember the very spot in the road, whilst in my carriage, when to my joy the solution occurred to me'.

The physicist Leó Szilárd also recorded the exact time and place of an insight:

> I found myself in London about the time of the British Association meeting in September 1933. I read in the newspapers a speech by Lord Rutherford, who was quoted as saying that he who talks about the liberation of atomic energy on an industrial basis is talking moonshine. This set me pondering as I was walking the streets

of London, and I remember that I stopped for a red light at the intersection of Southampton Row. As the light changed to green and I crossed the street, it suddenly occurred to me that if we could find an element which is split by neutrons and emits two neutrons when it absorbed one neutron, such an element, if assembled in sufficiently large mass, could sustain a nuclear chain reaction. I didn't see at the moment just how one would go about finding such an element, or what experiments would be needed, but the idea never left me.*

As with Archimedes, insight does not necessarily *solve* the problem; it gives us a clue *how* to solve it. But some discoveries seem to arrive fully formed. One February afternoon in 1882, just as the sun was setting, Nikola Tesla was walking with a friend through the park in Budapest, reciting Goethe. He stopped as he suddenly visualised the solution to a problem that had plagued him for five years. 'Back in the deep recesses of the brain was the solution, but [until that moment] I could not yet give it outward expression.' That solution was the rotating magnetic field that lies at the heart of every electric motor using alternating current.

I could not demonstrate my belief at that time, but it came to me through what I might call instinct, for lack of a better name. But instinct is something which transcends knowledge. We undoubtedly have in our brains some finer fibers which enable us to perceive truths which we could not attain through logical deductions, and which it would be futile to attempt to achieve through any willful effort of thinking.

Nearly forty years later Tesla was resident in the USA and had refined the technique. An article he wrote, *Making Your Imagination Work For You*, is worth quoting at length:

Some people, the moment they have a device to construct or any piece of work to perform, rush at it without adequate preparation, and immediately become engrossed in details, instead of the central idea. They may get results, but they sacrifice quality.

Here, in brief, is my own method: After experiencing a desire to invent a particular thing, I may go on for months or years with the idea in the back of my head. Whenever I feel like it, I roam around in my imagination and think about the problem without any deliberate concentration. This is a period of incubation.

Then follows a period of direct effort. I choose carefully the possible solutions of the problem. I am considering, and gradually center my mind on a narrowed field of investigation. Now, when I am deliberately thinking of the problem in its specific features, I may begin to feel that I am going to get the solution. And the wonderful thing is, that if I do feel this way, then I know I have really solved the problem and shall get what I am after.

*It ought be noted that one of his colleagues doubted this tale as he had never seen Szilárd stop for a red light!

The feeling is as convincing to me as though I already had solved it. I have come to the conclusion that at this stage the actual solution is in my mind subconsciously, though it may be a long time before I am aware of it consciously.

> The inventions I have conceived in this way have always worked. In thirty years there has not been a single exception. My first electric motor, the vacuum tube wireless light, my turbine engine and many other devices have all been developed in exactly this way.
>
> (*American Magazine,* April 1921)

The year before Tesla's walk in the park, the French polymath Henri Poincaré published the first of his major contributions to mathematics (extremely complex issues in non-Euclidean geometry, which, thankfully, we do not need to go into). In his 1908 book *Science et méthode*, he reflected on the series of insights he experienced back then. One occasion he remembered was as he set foot on a bus in Coutances. 'At the moment when I put my foot on the step the idea came to me, seemingly without anything in my former thoughts preparing the way for it.' He was absolutely sure he was correct and only verified his calculations later *'pour l'acquit de ma conscience'.* Another occurred as he walked along the cliffs *'avec les mêmes caractères de brièveté, de soudaineté et de certitude immédiate'* (with the same characteristics of brevity, suddenness and immediate certainty).

Struck by the nature of this sudden 'illumination', Poincaré speculated that it might simply be the result of a short rest but that it was more likely the result of unconscious thought processes (*'travail inconscient'*) which had already been put in motion. But he insisted that such inspirations were only fruitful if preceded and followed by periods of conscious thought.

Poincaré's observations, together with those of German physicist Hermann von Helmholtz were used by Graham Wallas in his 1926 book, The Art of Thought*, to form one of the first and most widely quoted models of creative problem solving:

- Preparation
- Incubation
- Illumination
- Verification

Wallas's model adds 'verification' to three stages he quotes as first proposed by von Helmholtz in a speech in 1891, but he seems unaware of a somewhat similar model quoted by Ribot, published shortly afterwards. Ribot's source was an engineer who he knew had no inkling of psychological theory.

*Wallas has been out of print for many years but is of more than historic interest. We cannot but approve of a volume advertised as 'A book written with the practical purpose of helping the apprentice thinker to become a competent craftsman.' Wallas's ambition is based on his conception of 'the human organism as an imperfectly integrated combination of living elements, each of which retains some initiative of its own, while co-operating with the rest in securing the good of the whole organism. The aim of the art of thought is an improved co-ordination of these elements in the process of thought.'

We may, however, as far as regards mechanical inventions, distinguish four sufficiently clear phases — the germ, incubation, flowering, and completion.

By germ I mean the first idea coming to the mind to furnish a solution for a problem that the whole of one's observations, studies, and researches has put before one, or that, put by another, has struck one.

Then comes incubation, often very long and painful, or, again, even unconscious. Instinctively as well as voluntarily one brings to the solution of the problem all the materials that the eyes and ears can gather.

When this latent work is sufficiently complete, the idea suddenly bursts forth, it may be at the end of a voluntary tension of mind, or on the occasion of a chance remark, tearing the veil that hides the surmised image.

But this image always appears simple and clear. In order to get the ideal solution into practice, there is required a struggle against matter, and the bringing to an issue is the most thankless part of the inventor's work.

(Théodule Ribot, *Essay on the Creative Imagination*, tr. Baron, 1906)

Wallas also suggests a sub-stage of 'intimation' which occurs just before 'illumination' and writes of a 'fringe-consciousness' somewhat reminiscent of Poe's 'looking at the stars by glances'.

Incubation, intimation and illumination have fallen from favour since the 1920s, perhaps because they still defy accurate description and are redolent of mystical ideas of creativity, but it's worth recording that both Poincaré and Tesla were two of the most practical, no-nonsense individuals of their day, and that Ribot's engineer emphasises that the last phase, whether we call it verification or completion, is the hardest and most thankless.

That eureka moment revisited

Quite how an idea or concept 'emerges' to form a whole that is more than the sum of its parts is the great mystery of creativity; we are fairly sure *that* it happens; we just don't know *how*. It is remarkably difficult to track down the moment when new ideas appear, even when you ask someone who has only just had the idea. Anecdotal evidence often reveals more about story telling than discovery; it's that narrative bias again. Some of the most famous legends of discovery prove to be just that: legends. We have already noted the unreliability of the story of Archimedes but that was a long time ago. A more recent account reveals how little actual participants know about how they came up with their discoveries. Here is Alfred Russel Wallace's description of a malarial fever he suffered in 1858: 'There suddenly flashed upon me the idea of the survival of the fittest . . .'

However the phrase 'survival of the fittest' was not coined until 1861 (by Herbert Spencer), so Wallace's memory must have played him false. If the co-discoverer of one of the most influential concepts in human history doesn't know how he got the idea, what hope is there for the rest of us? But we are in good company; in a 1922 lecture entitled 'How I Created the Theory of Relativity', Einstein confessed, 'I cannot say exactly where that thought came from'. We can however garner some clues as to what is going on: Wallace uses the word 'flashed'; inspiration 'burst' upon Tom Sawyer. What is being described is an explosion of possibilities: the discoverer is bound to be more interested in where the idea is going than where it came from, and the seed is going to be very different from the flower. (This sounds very redolent of the 'Flight of Ideas' we came across in genius and madness.) It's only later that we try to reconstruct a narrative. But these explosions do occur under more observable circumstances. Here is John Tyndall on his contemporary Michael Faraday: 'When an experimental result was obtained by Faraday it was instantly enlarged by his imagination.'

Alec Jeffreys and his team sketched out the main implications of DNA fingerprinting within an hour. With Faraday and Jeffreys we know for certain where the idea comes from because they were conducting experiments; ideas that come to us when we are not consciously considering them are harder to study. Scientists are notoriously reluctant to study phenomena; they much prefer replicable experimentation.

'Emergence' is the term used to describe how complicated concepts and patterns arise from comparatively simple interactions. 'Strong emergence' is used when the new whole is not only more than the sum of its parts, but sometimes completely different from its parts. As mathematician Mark A. Bedau (1997) points out: 'Although strong emergence is logically possible, it is uncomfortably like magic.' Those of us who have witnessed creativity in action can only echo the sentiment.

Tesla used the word instinct, 'for want of a better word'; Poincaré wrote of unconscious effort. Michael Polanyi thought that long experience heightened the tacit element of knowing, leading to a state of 'connoisseurship' much like that of an expert wine-taster.

Some people use the word intuition in similar circumstances – knowing something without knowing how you know it. That sort of intuition is based upon deep familiarity with predictable situations. But as psychologist Daniel Kahneman writes: 'Claims for correct intuitions in an unpredictable situation are self-delusional at best, sometimes worse' (*Thinking, Fast and Slow*, 2011).

Concepts like intuition and instinct are ill-defined and very often used with hindsight. They are consequently difficult to study. But our ignorance of how something works should not lead us to reject the phenomenon, just as we need not invoke the supernatural to 'explain' it.

Sceptics should think of it as a 'power nap', studies of which suggest that short (20–30 minute) periods of sleep are the best way of preventing information overload. It may be that when we 'switch off' we slip into a different more contemplative way of thinking. It may be that when we return to a problem we see it from a different point of view. At the very least we may just need to rest and refresh ourselves. The secret seems to be to take a breather long enough to break your concentration but not so long that you totally forget where you were. To be honest, at the moment no one knows how this works or even if it works; most of the evidence is anecdotal but it is surely too strong to ignore. It is a field ripe for study.

Determine – realistic concepts begin to emerge

By now we should have generated lots of fuzzy ideas; this is the time when we try to identify patterns and threads, which we might be able to draw together into possibilities.

Reflect upon the nature and diversity of those ideas

This is an important point in our methodology. Maybe you haven't managed to come up with much variety; never mind, we shall sort that out. The danger is that you think you have found your solution. It has jumped out at you and you can't see the point of carrying on with the process. Recall what Tesla had to say about people who rush ahead and get engrossed in the details: 'They may get results, but they sacrifice quality.'

What is happening is that you are reverting to your old ways and rushing to judgement. But the solution you think you have found isn't even 'off the peg'; it's off the second-hand rail and it's never going to be as good as 'made to measure'. One of the commonest mistakes in social policy is to take a solution which has worked in one place and impose it elsewhere without making sure that it fits.

An analogy is a similarity in *some* respects, not *all* respects: you should not take them too literally. When we looked at sport and business we noted that both took inspiration from warfare. But it is still something of a surprise to see the works of Sun Tzu and Machiavelli on the Business/Management shelves of the bookshop!

Sun Tzu is the reputed author of a pre-second-century BC Chinese treatise usually entitled *The Art of War*. Long famed as a work of philosophy as well as strategy, it reached the west by translation into French in the late eighteenth century. It is *said* to have influenced leaders from Napoleon to Chairman Mao and now serves as a manual for managers. Next to it on the shelf we often find Niccolò Machiavelli an Italian civil servant who also wrote a book called *The Art of War.* But it was the posthumous publication of Machiavelli's *The Prince* which made his name a byword for devilment by the end of the sixteenth century. Some management sections even include *Vom Kriege* (*On War*) by the Prussian soldier and theorist Carl von Clausewitz (1780–1831). It is easy to suggest that volumes like these grace the bookshelf with the same air as all those pristine copies of Stephen Hawking's *Brief History of Time*, but that might be a little unfair: before the advent of large-scale industry the only models of management were military and political. The authors would only criticise the narrowness of choice. If your environment is similar to the warring city states of Renaissance Italy, Machiavelli may have something useful to say. If you require total dominance over your opponents Sun Tzu might be more appropriate.

If you are looking for analogies by moving from the specific to the general, military and political theory provides a wealth of often contrasting ideas to choose from.

For example: it was said that Napoleon Bonaparte was such a fan of meritocracy that every soldier in the *Grande Armée* marched with a (metaphorical/potential) Marshal's baton in his knapsack; promotion was there for the taking. But there were risks attached: in management terms there were high levels of burnout. In short, the troops were kept happy with promises despite, indeed because of, high staff turnover. Bonaparte boasted that he had an income of 100,000 recruits per annum.

On the other side we can see the Duke of Wellington, running a much smaller enterprise. The duke was certainly no fan of social mobility and opportunities for promotion were limited. But lacking Napoleon's 'income', he made sure that every soldier carried actual spare shoes in their knapsacks instead of an imaginary Marshal's baton.

There are limitations of the 'business is war' metaphor. Do you really want to 'crush your enemy'? We touched on game theory back on page 45. The simplest form of competition is the zero-sum game where players win to the exact degree that other players lose. This is the sort of war game that we associate with Sun Tzu. But as we saw with the prisoners' dilemma, it is perfectly possible to imagine outcomes where both players can win and both players can lose. It is also possible to sustain a career in sport or business by coming second most of the time. American academics Adam Brandenburger and Barry Nalebuff point out in their book *Co-Opetition* (1996) that 'In fact, most businesses succeed only if others also succeed' and 'Business is cooperation when it comes to creating a pie and competition when it comes to dividing it up . . . It's simultaneously war and peace.'

There are plenty of antagonistic analogies but why limit yourself to humans? You should be looking for models in the full range of competition, from sports to epidemiology.

The other thing to remember about analogies is that you can abandon them whenever you like; they are merely a source of old ideas that you might be able to restructure and re-present as new ideas appropriate to your situation.

Have all the permutations and combinations been explored?

That's an easy question to ask; harder to answer. How can we know?

Edison held over a thousand US patents but probably his greatest invention was the creation of the first industrial research laboratory at Menlo Park. With such a resource at hand he took no chances: he claimed to have tested over six thousand different materials in search of the right filament for the electric light bulb. That is what he was getting at when he said, 'Genius is one per cent inspiration and ninety-nine per cent perspiration.'

Tesla was not convinced: 'His method was inefficient in the extreme, for an immense ground had to be covered to get anything at all unless blind chance intervened and, at first, I was almost a sorry witness of his doings, knowing that just a little theory and calculation would have saved him 90 percent of the labour.'

If we accept (not difficult) that most of us are not as clever as Tesla and also accept (again, not difficult) that we cannot be as exhaustive as Edison, then we have to look for a middle way. Recalling the point we made way back that if this sort of thinking (solving complex problems in an uncertain environment) was easy then we wouldn't need a guide, we have to take the pessimistic view. Let us assume that no new concepts have emerged and further that any ideas which have sprung out at us are going to be sub-optimal. Let us assume that we are still short of that critical mass from which new concepts will emerge.

We have created a 'storm' of ideas, hoping that as they landed they would suggest new connections and combinations. If we don't like the way they have landed, then throw them up in the air once more. The students we looked at earlier came back from their break for a 'second storm'. This time they didn't come with a blank sheet of paper. They had lists of their own connections and combinations from the previous 'storm', which they passed around and discussed in turn. This is the point where you should be able to hitchhike on each other's ideas. Ideally, combinations are more than the sum of their parts: five plus five is ten whereas five times five is twenty-five. Again the mood is positive and non-critical but there is a bit more focus as we begin to try and engineer solutions.

If you get stuck there are always heuristics to fall back on. This is where the Internet once more comes into its own. Although it is an unprecedented resource, the Internet is of course also jam-packed with nonsense, but on this occasion that doesn't really matter – an idea is an idea and, as we demonstrated with homeopathic dance steps, can be useful even if it's wrong.

- What happens if you 'force-fit' two or more concepts? Just pick a couple of words or phrases from your first storm and google them. You can introduce totally random elements in the same way.

- Randomise your ideas. The cultural movement Dadaism was very taken with random ideas and the Internet provides several sites which will create Dada poetry from any prose you care to paste in.

Dada Poem:
trees; parks; travel; car mobile
better more more parks; parking;
stackable, giveaway, remove G.P.S. number
auction shop more ride; transformers;
parking places; ban park car
time-share everything; abandon racks.

- Similarly, sites like Wordle will create word pictures from text. These sites operate under the GIGO principle and will in fact highlight the quality and the preoccupations of the garbage we put in.

- It is important to remember that computers are best at associative tasks – they are far less effective at dissociation. One trick available to us is to use them deliberately for something they are not that good at:

- Translate your text into another language and back again; words appear that you did not use originally. For example the students' text when taken into French and then English changed the word 'ban' into 'prohibition', bringing a whole new flood of images of gangsters and bootlegging.

- Imagine the perfect solution. How could you achieve the direct opposite of what you want?

A group of postgraduates studying Health and Public Policy attended an Ingenuity CPS course at UNIEI. They were looking for new initiatives to combat childhood obesity. A 'standard' solution would be to increase the price of unhealthy food. The 'worst' solution would be to make it cheaper or even give it away. From this counter-intuitive idea came (again only recognisable in hindsight) the central feature of their eventual scheme – school-based cookery competitions with healthy food-related prizes.

Opposites can sometimes produce similar, although crucially different results, distillation and freeze fractionation, for example. Distillation is a method of separating liquids with different boiling points. Fractional freezing separates two liquids with different melting points. Distillation of fermented liquor will remove alcohol; fractional freezing will remove water: from the same ingredients, malted barley, water and yeast, you can produce whisky or ice beer. What use is this to problem solving?

Imagine that you have identified that the root cause of your particular organisation's problems is that it has become moribund; unwieldy, complacent and stale. Your strategy to deal with the situation is to look at options to downsize, focusing on core competencies, if necessary shedding some of your fringe interests. Using the analogy-finding technique described above, that is your *specific* problem; the *general* problem is one of how to concentrate something – increasing strengths and reducing weakness. Just *one* of the analogies you have come up with is the above, which in fact offers two *general* solutions: you can distil your strengths, throwing the rest away; or you can freeze out your weaknesses and retain the flavour. Quite how this is to be done, how we engineer *specific* solutions, is the subject of our last stage – determination. But there are dangers when a particularly blunt instrument is used.

Another cautionary tale

A corporate video for a well-known, multi-billion-dollar organisation explains the need for an innovative culture:

> Every year, every day, every week, you have to come up with new ideas, new approaches to the business. That's not easy, but I think

that if you can get the organisation in that mode it's a tremendous competitive advantage, a tremendous competitive advantage for the company.

It starts with good people, recruiting, retaining, motivating creative people, intelligent people who really have the capability of thinking about the world a little differently.

And if you have good people, and that environment, they start coming up with good ideas that work in the market.

We begin by attracting the sort of people who are more comfortable in an environment of change.

Diversity is good, diversity of ideas, diversity of backgrounds, diversity of people's opinion.

It's incredibly important that we encourage diversity of people and diversity of thought throughout our company worldwide.

All of which sounds wonderful. The same video reveals the sort of people they wish to attract: 'We are strong believers in competition'; 'some of your most creative ideas come from some of your newer and younger employees'; 'We have a lot of very aggressive people in the company . . . and that's great, because that's what you want.'

So how did this company set about creating this youthful, aggressive, competitive environment? How did they build on their strengths and eliminate their weaknesses? They used techniques based on what management consultants call a 'vitality curve' but is popularly called 'rank and yank'. When employees are evaluated, the highest ranked are rewarded and the lowest are 'encouraged' to leave. This particular company used the procedure to such effect that 15% of their staff was removed every year, while the top rankers were paid very well indeed.

This modus operandi seemed to work. The company was named by *Fortune* magazine as 'America's Most Innovative Company' for six years running.

Unfortunately, it was all too good to be true: much of the innovation occurred in the finance department. 'Creative accountancy' is often a euphemism for illegality and so it proved to be. Shareholders in the company, Enron, lost $74 billion dollars, well over half of which was attributed to plain fraud.

Of the speakers quoted above, one, then President and Chief Operating Officer Jeffrey Skilling, was fined $45 million and sent to prison for 24 years: the other, Chairman and Chief Executive Officer Kenneth Lay, died of a heart attack awaiting sentence.

In the aftermath, Skilling was quoted as saying: 'Are there things that now, in retrospect, with what I've seen happen to my company, would I have done some things differently? I think – I think we all would do – we would do a number of things differently.'

One of those things might be to recognise that the crude method of distilling from the top and freezing out the bottom led to a target-driven culture of ruthless individualism, massaged figures and back-stabbing.

Along with youth they got inexperience; aggression was accompanied by arrogance; competition was confused with ruthlessness; risk taking with recklessness.

The environment created was one where both knaves and fools would, and did, flourish.

Have enough ideas been produced for novel concepts to emerge?

As we saw with reference to swarm intelligence, iteration is the key to production.

- Every idea can be taken one step further, simply by applying an additional brainstorming heuristic. Some of the most remarkable 'breakthrough' inventions come about from a very simple 'tweak' of an existing concept.

There are plenty of examples. In 1901, the British engineer Hubert Cecil Booth was watching a demonstration of a new American cleaning machine. 'Have you tried sucking instead of blowing?' he said. 'It's been tried many times and it doesn't work,' came the exasperated reply. Booth, however, did make it work and invented the first practical vacuum cleaner.

The Centre Georges Pompidou in Paris depends upon the simple idea of turning a structure inside out. Placing all the services, stairs, lifts, cables, etc. on the outside gave designers Renzo Piano and Richard Rogers unprecedented freedom with the internal space of the building.

In the late 1940s, in response to a direct challenge to find a novel application of the ballpoint pen, Helen Barnett Diserens simply magnified the technology and came up with the roll-on deodorant.

Sometimes that simple change has fringe benefits. We saw how Emile Berliner enabled mass production of records when he replaced the wax cylinder with the disc. The sound still came from a groove; the only change was to the plane in which that groove revolved. But the new method also permitted a series of incremental improvements in terms of the plastics used. It even made it possible to press a 'B' side at little additional expense.

- Can you deconstruct obvious concepts and put them back together in a slightly different way? This doesn't just apply to physical objects.

There is a long-established tradition that stories should have a beginning, a middle and an end; but not necessarily in that order. The film *Memento* (2000) is a psychological thriller whose main character suffers from anterograde amnesia, which prevents him from storing new memories. It tells its story by the straightforward but rigid device of interpolating scenes of forward chronology (filmed in monochrome) with others in reverse chronology (filmed in colour). The result was enthusiastically hailed as one of the most innovative films of modern times, while also attracting praise from medical experts as an accurate exploration of the issues surrounding memory function.

- What can you add?

One way of improving a product is to add to its features. The old example would be the Swiss Army penknife; the modern 'must have' is the mobile phone, which, with its cameras and videos and Internet access, offers its owner far more than they perhaps asked for or indeed wanted.

- It is one thing to keep adding on, but what can you do without?

Great results can be achieved by keeping it simple, stripping away non-essential distractions, but we don't have to go as far as Sir Thomas Picton at the storming of Ciudad Rodrigo in 1812, who addressed his troops thus: 'Rangers of Connaught! It is not my intention to expend any powder this evening. We'll do this business with the *cowld* iron.'*

An early breakthrough in steam railways was the realisation that the wheels and rails did not need cogs – the weight of the engine provided enough friction. James Watt is recorded as confiding in his colleague William Murdock: 'It is a great thing to know what to do without. We must have a book of blots – things to be scratched out.'

For a hundred years most people's impression of a circus was of performing animals, star acrobats and clowns. There would be a Big Top, with a ring and a ringmaster; lion tamers, performing elephants, perhaps even dancing bears; at least one daring young man on his flying trapeze; all interspersed with various jugglers and clowns. By the 1970s, circus looked as if it was reaching the end of the line, the victim of sheer expense and changing attitudes to animal welfare. But the contemporary circus movement reinvented the genre by showing just what they could do without. No animals to start with; no star performers; no stagehands; not even a ring. Freed from these expensive constraints, they could afford to emphasise other elements such as music and narrative. The best known of the new movement is Cirque du Soleil, which now employs a staff of four thousand from forty different countries including a thousand cast members. They have performed to 90 million spectators in two hundred cities on five continents. It might not be circus as we knew it but it is certainly a success.

*They did, with devastating consequences!

More or less – hand-held electronics

In the 1990s, the Palm Pilot became the 'must have' device for anyone who wanted to be at the cutting edge. It was designed by Jeff Hawkins, who, in 1989, had been responsible for the first hand-held touch-screen computer, the GRiDPad, a miracle of engineering which was a market failure because, thought Hawkins, it was still too big. The design project was therefore predicated on making a device small enough to fit in a shirt pocket. To achieve that, they had to decide what to do without. Hawkins wanted to compete, not with computers but with paper (the Filofax was an enormously successful personal organiser), so the Palm Pilot concentrated on the basics – calendar, addresses and phone numbers, memos and to-do lists. The performance they sought was that users should be able to access information almost as easily as looking at their wristwatch. The Pilot held its own against the rush of copycats, all of which tended to over-complicate the original, but is now a museum piece along with its contemporary, the pager, all their functions being available on the cheapest mobile phone. The expensive mobile phones just keep adding more and more – an app for all occasions. But to include *everything* you have to go bigger. Hawkins actually carried a wooden mock-up of the Palm Pilot in his pocket for months to make sure he was comfortable with it.

Today's hand-held electronics combine several previously distinct products. This is more than simple addition and there is a great deal of novelty to be found in combinatory thinking.*

Novelty is not that difficult; it is *appropriate* novelty we are after.

You can, however, come up with some truly exciting ideas. What about this for an unlikely combination? The flying energy generator, which promises to convert the windpower of the jet stream into electricity, is in essence a combination of a turbine and a kite: a flying windmill. Sky WindPower's flying electric generator was named one of the fifty top inventions of 2008 by *TIME* magazine.

At the end of this phase you should be able to develop some of your wilder ideas into something more concrete: possibilities. A metaphor for concept formation is crystallisation. Before crystals can grow there is a period of nucleation; molecules of solute cluster together; unstable clusters redissolve but stable ones grow into crystals. What we need to do is cluster ideas together again and again until we recognise them as stable concepts which will grow. If not, take a break and repeat the process. Then switch off once more.

With luck we are now awash with ideas and opportunities and in dire need of another diversion – an opportunity to reflect on the role of chance.

*Reality TV provides a perfect example of entry-level combinational creativity. Anybody can mix and match at will from the following:

Amateur – Professional – Celebrity – Panel of judges – Survival – Jeopardy – Quiz – Talent – Makeover – Cookery – Design – Empowerment – Humiliation – Mental – Physical – Retro.

Unless someone gets really creative you will need phone voting and format franchising to pay for it. Until then we will have to rely on the likes of 'Celebrity Balloon Modelling on Ice'.

Discovery

INTERLUDE: chance and serendipity

During the last interlude we raised the idea of a multidisciplinary approach to problem solving; the fresh pair of eyes we need to check our conclusions from the definition stage. During the discovery stage we hope we have emphasised the importance of looking as widely as we can for possibilities rather than waiting for them somehow to drop into our lap.

Some inventions seem predestined, as Alec Jeffreys admitted: 'There are certain things in science that are historically inevitable, however. I was just lucky that I got to discover DNA fingerprinting. If I hadn't, someone else would have done it by now. I have no illusions about that.'

This is easy to understand; once a particular field of exploration is undertaken and continued it can only be a matter of time before all corners are discovered. Chance, therefore, is only a matter of *who* crosses the line first and so achieves greatness: the race is bound to be won by someone.*

But some of the most revolutionary innovations, the ones we look upon as most creative, have the most extraordinary origins; they seem to come from nowhere. They contain, in the words of the British Patent Office, 'an *inventive step* that is not obvious to someone with knowledge and experience in the subject'. A good many are so 'not obvious' that they seem to have happened by chance.

Penicillin, Velcro, Superglue, LSD, corn flakes, chocolate chip cookies, Cellophane, Teflon, the colour mauve, cyclamates, iodine, the microwave oven, the New World and even the planet Uranus are often said to have been discovered by accident.

As we mentioned earlier (p. 41), it is impossible to deny the part that chance plays in far more basic discoveries than these.

*On the other hand, there is the view that some are born great; they are bound to win some race or other. Machiavelli, when considering those who have risen to be princes through their own ability, makes clear that the only element of chance in their careers is when, where and how they arrive at their destiny: 'Studying their actions and lives you cannot see anything that they owed to fortune other than the occasion.' (*Ed esaminando le azioni e vita loro non si vede che quelli avessino altro da la fortuna che la occasione. Il Principe*, 1532)

The demise of the *Übermensch* is of course the occasion for others to achieve fame: 'The question is not when's he gonna stop, but who is gonna stop him' (DJ Super Soul talking about the last American hero in the 1971 film *Vanishing Point*).

Beveridge celebrates the role of chance and error, but takes a considered view:

> Although it is common knowledge that sometimes chance is a factor in the making of a discovery, the magnitude of its importance is seldom realised and the significance of its role does not seem to have been fully appreciated or understood.

> It is of the utmost importance that the role of chance be clearly understood. The history of discovery shows that chance plays an important part, but on the other hand it plays only one part even in those discoveries attributed to it. For this reason it is a misleading half-truth to refer to unexpected discoveries as 'chance discoveries' or 'accidental discoveries'.

> (*The Art of Scientific Investigation*, 1957)

To see what he means, we need to look at little more closely at some of those famous mistakes.

The story goes that penicillin was discovered in 1928, on a Petrie dish that had been left out when Alexander Fleming went on holiday. True – but far from the whole truth. Fleming did indeed recognise the antibiotic possibilities of penicillin and tried to produce a usable product but without success. It was 1945 before Fleming was awarded an equal share of the Nobel Prize 'for the discovery of penicillin and its curative effect in various infectious diseases' together with Howard Florey and Ernst Chain, representing the team of researchers at Oxford who devised a method of mass producing the drug.

Perhaps the key fact to remember in the story of penicillin is that in 1928 Alexander Fleming was a Professor of Bacteriology; furthermore, he had a history of interest in antibiotics based on his experiences of treating wounded men in the First World War. Interestingly, he had been very critical of the accepted wisdom of using antiseptics – they sometimes seemed to do more harm than good by encouraging superficial healing of deep wounds while sealing in infections. Fleming was certainly the 'right man' in the 'right place' for a happy accident, but the discovery itself looks, in the words of Alec Jeffreys, 'historically inevitable'. But 'Eminent Bacteriologist Interested in Antibiotics Discovers Fungi with Antibiotic Properties' does not make a good headline, especially when the punch line (the practical application of the discovery) does not appear for seventeen years!

Another case is that of Albert Hofmann and LSD in 1943. Hofmann absorbed the drug because he handled it without gloves and famously and dramatically discovered its hallucinogenic effects for himself. But what ought to be remembered is that Hofmann was employed as a scientist, investigating the pharmaceutical possibilities of various plants and fungi. Since the objects of his investigations were suspected to have psychotropic effects, it would surely be considered 'bad luck' if he had *not* discovered the drug, sooner or later. But, again, the headline 'Pharmaceutical Chemist Investigating Psychotropic Effects Identifies Active Constituents of Certain Psychotropic Plants and Fungi' fails to grab the attention.

When William Herschel discovered the planet Uranus in 1781, some astronomers called it accidental or even lucky. Herschel was outraged; his superior equipment and his painstaking method of sweeping the night sky meant that it was almost impossible that such a star could escape his notice.

Humphry Davy had some terse words to say about such critics: 'It suits the indolence of those minds which never attempt any thing, and which probably if they did attempt any thing would not succeed, to refer to accident that which belongs to genius.'

The story of Christopher Columbus, who sails for Cathay but discovers America, is often cited as the greatest chance discovery of all time. But in the context of exploration and discovery driven by the economic and political rivalries of late fifteenth-century Europe, the Americas were waiting to be found. They might have been an 'unknown unknown' but once Columbus set sail the discovery was inevitable. His intentions were clear, as stated right at the beginning of his commission from Their Majesties Ferdinand and Isabella of Spain: 'For as much of you, Christopher Columbus, are going by our command, with some of our vessels and men, to discover and subdue some Islands and Continent in the ocean . . .' (April 30th 1492)

Six years later, the Americas were certainly 'known unknowns'. The letters patent of Henry VII of England to John Cabot and his sons makes clear: 'to seeke out, discouer, and finde whatsoever isles, countreys, regions or prouinces of the heathen and infidels whatsoeuer they be, and in what part of the world soeuer they be, which before this time haue bene vnknowen to all Christians . . .'

Columbus and the Cabots are of far more interest to us if we see them as early entrepreneurs, hawking their projects around the courts of Europe, seeking funding, promising high returns and demanding high rewards – Columbus claimed 10% of everything he discovered: he never got paid.*

The fact is that Columbus would not have discovered penicillin any more than Fleming would have discovered America, even with a time machine: they made discoveries from a context within the range of their expertise.

Less inevitable discoveries are those unrelated to the field of interest of the investigator.

A story is told about American engineer and inventor Percy Spencer who was working on radar during the 1940s. He was standing by a functioning magnetron when he noticed that the chocolate bar in his pocket had started to melt. Out of sheer curiosity, he began experimenting with popcorn and even an egg. From his 1945 patent application to the first commercial model took less than two years.

*Nearly four hundred years later, Nikola Tesla was to have a similar experience when he inquired of Thomas Edison about a promised $50,000. He received the reply, 'Tesla, you don't understand our American humor.' But the laugh was on Edison; the great entrepreneur misjudged this particular opportunity: Tesla walked and, although he was never much good with money or people and died in debt, the fact remains that he made his greatest discoveries after he broke with Edison.

The microwave oven could be said to have been invented 'by accident', but there are other ways of describing what happened. Spencer is answering the title question of Alex Osborn's chapter 20: 'To What Other Uses Could This Be Put?' In the Kirk's Space description of innovation, Spencer would be found at the bottom right-hand side, next to Alec Jeffreys, with a clear idea of 'know how' to do something, but less certain of the 'knowing what' to do with it. And they are not alone – very often the *techne* precedes the *telos*.

> Just as invention does not occur in a strictly linear manner neither does science proceed according to strict inductive principles. Sometimes the science does indeed precede the technology; the discovery of electricity and the means of storing it in a battery (the voltaic stack) came before the electric motor. On the other hand, steam engines were puffing away for many years before the principles behind their actions were fully understood.

Isaac Asimov is sometimes credited with the observation, 'The most exciting phrase to hear in science, the one that heralds new discoveries, is not "Eureka!", but "That's funny"'.

During the Easter holidays in 1856, the young chemist William Henry Perkin was trying to synthesise quinine when he discovered the first aniline dye, which he named mauve. The discovery changed his life, and kick-started the modern dyestuffs industry. Perkin experimented; he sent samples to dyers and, by August of that year, at the tender age of eighteen, took out his first patent. Less than twenty years later, when he sold up and retired from business, he had become a very wealthy man and, by the time he died in 1907, he was a knight of the realm.

Both Spencer and Perkin perfectly fit our description of the entrepreneurial spirit. They recognise an opportunity, they take action and they bring value. You could argue that the properties of microwaves and aniline would have been revealed eventually, given the thrust of research in those areas, and the discovery (and the kudos) would have belonged to someone else. In both cases the value created translated into financial rewards but, as we said earlier, for some entrepreneurs money is not always a driving force.

This is the story of a man who should be regarded as a great entrepreneur not because he made a lot of money – he neither sought nor found financial reward – but because he saw an opportunity to bring value and took action to realise that value.

In 1829, Nathaniel Bagshaw Ward was practising medicine in the dockland area of London. Then, as now, it was the rough end of town, far removed from the rural idyll we might associate with a nineteenth-century gentlemanly curiosity about nature. But in his spare time Ward did pursue natural history as a hobby. He was especially keen on entomology and botany, although his beloved ferns failed to thrive in the polluted air of the East End. Ward put this down to *'deficiency of light*, the *dryness of the atmosphere*, the *fuliginous matter* with which the air of large towns is always more or less loaded, and the *evolution of noxious gases* from manufactories.' Entomology seemed more fruitful. In order to observe metamorphosis, he put the chrysalis of a sphinx moth, with a little earth, in a sealed bottle so that it could not escape when it hatched. Ward later described his rather quiet moment of serendipity:

> In watching the bottle from day to day, I observed that the moisture which during the heat of the day arose from the mould [earth], became condensed on the internal surface of the glass, and returned whence it came; thus keeping the mould always in the same degree of humidity. About a week prior to the change of the insect, a seedling fern and a grass made their appearance on the surface of the mould.

> I could not but be struck with the circumstance of one of that very tribe of plants, which I had for years fruitlessly attempted to cultivate, coming up *sponte sua* [of its own will] in such a situation; and asked myself seriously what were the conditions necessary for its growth?

Ward experimented, and found that he could keep plants alive for more than three years, 'during which time not one drop of water was given to them, nor was the cover removed', and in 1833 he was confident enough to announce his findings to the Linnaean Society. Even more confidently, he was bold enough to reveal that he had dispatched a case of plants to Australia in the care of his friend Captain Charles Mallard RN. How gratified he must have felt to hear that the plants had arrived safely. Mallard's letter, dated 'Hobart Town November 23rd 1833', ended thus:

> Allow me, in conclusion, to offer you my warm congratulations upon the success of this simple but beautiful discovery for the preservation of plants in the living state upon the longest of voyages; and I feel not a little pride in having been the instrument by which the truth of your new principle has been fully proved by experiment.

A second trial was arranged for the return journey:

> The cases were refilled at Sydney in the month of February, 1834, the thermometer then being between 90° [Fahrenheit] and 100°. In their passage to England they encountered very varying temperatures. The thermometer fell to 20° in rounding Cape Horn and the decks were covered a foot deep in snow. At Rio Janeiro the thermometer rose to 100°, and in crossing the line to 120°. In the month of November, eight months after their departure, they arrived in the British Channel, the thermometer then being as low as 40°. These plants were placed upon the deck during the whole voyage and were not once watered, yet on their arrival at the docks they were in the most healthy and vigorous condition.

Prior to Ward's discovery, plants were usually only moved large distances by sea when in a dormant state – seeds, roots and tubers, etc., carefully wrapped and waterproofed against the salty conditions. Transporting live plants was very difficult and could lead to real trouble: witness the 1787 attempt to take over a thousand breadfruit trees from Tahiti to the West Indies aboard the 90 ft long HMS *Bounty*. The determined Captain Bligh did eventually succeed in his mission four years later but the 'Wardian' case would have made his task a whole lot easier (although Hollywood would have been deprived of a couple of good films).

The first to exploit the innovation were the commercial nurseries. The Victorian passion for collecting exotic garden plants could not have flourished but for the Wardian case, and yet Ward made not a penny from his invention. He didn't apply for patent protection and was happy to give his invention to the world, although he wouldn't say no to some reward. His 'bottom line' is revealed in the last line of his memoir, *On the Growth of Plants in Closely Glazed Cases* (1842): 'as he desires no other reward for his labours than the means of increasing his acquaintance with his favourite science, he will be thankful for any addition to his herbarium or general botanical collection'.

Ward's discovery revolutionised the commercial exploitation of plants around the British Empire. In 1848, the Scottish plant hunter Robert Fortune was sent by the East India Company to China 'for the purpose of obtaining the finest varieties of the Tea-plant, as well as native manufacturers and implements, for the Government plantations in the Himalayas'.

He supervised the transfer of 23,892 young plants and about 17,000 seedlings, all protected by Wardian cases, together with eight Chinese tea growers and their equipment, who established what became India's greatest export industry.

The Royal Botanic Gardens at Kew were at the heart of the imperial enterprise: the British government broke the South American rubber monopoly when seeds were smuggled out of Brazil, germinated at Kew and transported to Sri Lanka as seedlings in Wardian cases. In one year alone, 1851, Kew sent plants to Guyana, India, Jamaica, New Zealand, Sierra Leone, Tasmania and Trinidad.

Ward's recompense was a network of friends and admirers who sent him their best specimens along with their best wishes and he undoubtedly enjoyed the fame. But the value to humanity of Ward's breakthrough is truly incalculable; if mankind ever leaves Planet Earth, it is probably safe to say that any plants that make the trip will be in the equivalent of Dr Ward's 'beautiful discovery'. Science fiction has already acknowledged this, in the 1972 film *Silent Running*, for example.

Spencer's, Perkin's and Ward's happy accidents are often described as 'serendipity'. The first use of the word was in 1754. The writer Horace Walpole coined it from a 'silly fairy tale, called The Three Princes of Serendip' to describe discoveries made by 'accidents and sagacity' while looking for something else.

Actually, Walpole's serendipity is subtly different from the gist of the fairy tale. To the amazement of all, the three princes are able to describe a lost camel despite never having seen it. The story is related to the tradition of teaching stories we mentioned earlier with reference to wise fools. The princes appear to be either liars or fools until they explain their reasoning. It's an example of Knight's Move Thinking. The device is also familiar to readers of Arthur Conan Doyle. Sherlock Holmes astonishes us with unique talents – in this case deducing from the state of Watson's boots that his medical practice is busier than usual.

> 'Excellent!' I [Watson] cried.
>
> 'Elementary,' said he [Holmes]. 'It is one of those instances where the reasoner can produce an effect which seems remarkable to his neighbour, because the latter has missed the one little point which is the basis of the deduction.'
>
> ('The Adventure of the Crooked Man', 1893)

A modern definition of serendipity is when you are looking for a needle in a haystack and come across the farmer's daughter (or indeed son) doing a spot of embroidery. But in fact the needle does not even have to be there.

Earlier we quoted Humphry Davy's disapproval of alchemy but he also repeated another, more pragmatic opinion, of Francis Bacon: 'Lord Bacon happily described the Alchemists as similar to those husbandmen who in searching for a treasure supposed to be hidden in their land, by turning up and pulverising the soil, rendered it fertile; *in seeking for brilliant impossibilities, they sometimes discovered useful realities.*'

Towards the end of his life, Davy had reflected that 'The most important of my discoveries have been suggested to me by my failures.'

> We learn wisdom from failure much more than from success. We often discover what will do, by finding out what will not do; and probably he who never made a mistake never made a discovery.
>
> (Samuel Smiles, *Self-Help*, 1859)

The German scientist Hermann von Helmholtz eloquently expanded on the same simple truth, writing in 1891:

I have been able to solve a few problems in mathematics and physics, including some that the great mathematicians had puzzled over in vain . . . But any pride I might have felt in my conclusions was perceptibly lessened by the fact that I knew that the solution of these problems had almost always come to me as the gradual generalization of favourable examples, by a series of fortunate conjectures, after many errors. I am fain to compare myself with a wanderer on the mountains, who, not knowing the path, climbs slowly and painfully upwards, and often has to retrace his steps because he can go no farther then, whether by taking thought or from luck, discovers a new track that leads him on a little, till at length when he reaches the summit he finds to his shame that there is a royal way, by which he might have ascended, had he only had the wits to find the right approach to it. In my works I naturally said nothing about my mistakes to the reader, but only described the made track by which he may now reach the same heights without difficulty.

American physicist Richard Feynman makes the same point in his Nobel Lecture of 11 December 1965: 'We have a habit in writing articles published in scientific journals to make the work as finished as possible, to cover all the tracks, to not worry about the blind alleys or to describe how you had the wrong idea first, and so on.'

So here we have some of the most eminent minds of the last two centuries admitting what all practical people have always known; that not only do we learn *from* mistakes, we also learn *by* mistakes. Also note the admission that the narrative does not always represent what actually happened.

But these accidents do not happen to just anyone; they tend to happen to people a bit like Archimedes and Newton. Millions of people have sat in the bath over thousands of years without having a principle named after them and how many of us have watched apples fall from trees without an original thought? These things happen to people of 'sagacity', who are already on the lookout for *something*. It is not just a matter of ability – there is also the matter of *attitude.*

In 1947, American schoolgirl Patsy O'Connell Sherman took an aptitude test. It indicated that Patsy was most suited to be a housewife! In those days there were different tests for girls and boys. Patsy demanded to take the boys' test, which revealed that chemistry was a possibility. Her determination paid off and in 1952 she found herself working as a research chemist in the labs of the 3M Company. The next year a seemingly trivial mishap occurred. A bottle of synthetic latex made by her colleague Samuel Smith was spilt on a pair of white canvas shoes. The colourless compound resisted all attempts to remove it, repelling oil, water and other solvents. Seeing this problem as an opportunity spurred the two scientists to invent what became the fabric protector Scotchgard – one of 3Ms most iconic and successful products. Sherman offered this advice: 'Keep your eyes and mind open, and don't ignore something that doesn't come out the way you expect it to. Just keep looking at the world with inventor's eyes!'

In the lecture quoted on page 41, Ernst Mach gives us a clue about the special character possessed by some of us when he points out that, of the facts behind the 'inauguration of momentous discoveries by accidental circumstances', 'unquestionably many were *seen* numbers of times before they were *noticed*' (original emphasis).

We have already seen De Mestral and Velcro. In 1854, Louis Pasteur remarked, *'dans les champs de l'observation le hazard ne favorise que les esprits préparés'* (in the field of observation chance only favours the prepared mind).

Beveridge is of course well aware of the value of 'inventor's eyes' and 'the prepared mind':

Although we cannot deliberately evoke that will-o'-the-wisp, chance, we can be on the alert for it, prepare ourselves to recognise it and profit by it when it comes. Merely realising the importance of chance may be of some help to the beginner. We need to train our powers of observation, to cultivate that attitude of mind of being constantly on the look-out for the unexpected and make a habit of examining every clue that chance presents.

The authors, however, would beg to differ as to our ability to evoke 'that will-o'-the-wisp, chance'. We would contend that as well as recognising opportunities when they drop into their lap, prepared minds which adopt an entrepreneurial mindset ought to be able to seek out actively those happy accidents which constitute serendipity. This is important because chance works both ways: there are chances taken and there are chances missed.

> Admiral Arthur Phillip led the First Fleet to Australia and landed, as instructed, at Botany Bay. It soon became apparent that a better place for settlement lay only a few miles along the coast.
>
> Port Jackson was not visited or explored by Captain Cook; it was seen only at the distance of between two or three miles from the coast: had any good fortune conducted him into that harbour, he would have found it much more worthy of his attention as a seaman, than that in which he passed a week. Governor Phillip himself pronounces it to be a harbour, in extent and security, superior to any he has ever seen: and the most experienced navigators who were with him fully concur in that opinion.
>
> (Arthur Phillip, writing in the third person, 1789)

The fact that the great Captain Cook had missed the greatest natural harbour in the world is of little consequence. Once the First Fleet set out, the discovery of Sydney Harbour was 'historically inevitable'. But some discoveries rely on chances that are only revealed with hindsight.

We noted William Herschel's confidence in the superiority of his telescopes. He would not have thought they came about by chance; he knew well how difficult it was to cast and polish the mirrors. With hindsight, we can see every development of his equipment as steps of the sort the reader should by now recognise. We see the development of lenses from the glass industry: put two together and you have a telescope. Good-quality lenses have always been expensive; the glass must be flawless and the grinding must be perfect. Large lenses are obviously much more expensive still. (Unless you get around the problem by using extremely small lenses like those of pioneer microscopist Antonie Philips van Leeuwenhoek, 1632–1723, whose secret method is now thought to have been to rely on the surface tension of molten glass to produce perfectly formed beads.) But similar results are obtained if, instead of looking through a curved lens, the astronomer looks at a reflection in a curved mirror and much greater magnification is possible because a large flawless mirror is easier to make than a large flawless lens.

When the first Jesuit explorers reached China, the telescope was the invention that most impressed the Chinese. The applications from astronomy all the way to the military were immediately apparent. But why had one of the world's greatest civilisations, with a known fascination with astronomy, have missed such an invention? Sun Tzu would have given several people's eye teeth for one. The answer may lie in the telescope's chain of inventive steps that started with a pre-existing glass industry. China had perfected porcelain as the high-quality drinking vessel of choice – it was far superior to glass and was arguably the first global luxury product. China went down the porcelain road; glass was the road not taken, and so the invention of lenses was virtually inconceivable – it was an unknown unknown.

Another example of the operation of chance in discovery emphasises the problem of uncertainty. On the face of it, James Lind (who we are about to meet) did everything right; he reached the right conclusion but the fact that he misunderstood the root cause of his problem allowed chance to delay implementation of his solution for half a century.

In 1740, Commodore George Anson set out with a squadron of eight ships and the best part of two thousand men to wage war on Spanish interests in the Pacific Ocean. Three years and nine months later he returned with only one ship, his flagship *Centurion*, and fewer than two hundred of his original crew. Almost all the dead had succumbed to disease – especially scurvy. The expedition would normally have been thought of as a complete disaster but for the cargo Anson had captured from the Spanish treasure galleon *Nuestra Señora de Covadonga*: '1,313,843 pieces of eight and 35,682 ounces of virgin silver, besides some cochineal and a few other commodities, which, however, were but of small account in comparison of the specie.' As commander, Anson received two-thirds of the prize money – the then fabulous sum of £90,000 – together with promotion to admiral. An ordinary seaman, whose normal wages were 1s a day, got about £300.

Scurvy was an accepted hazard of long sea voyages but Anson's casualties were shocking. James Lind, thirty-year-old surgeon aboard HMS *Salisbury*, was one of many interested in finding a treatment but he was more systematic than most. He conducted what is widely regarded as the first clinical trial in history.

On 20th *May* 1747, I took twelve patients in the scurvy, on board the *Salisbury* at sea. Their cases were as similar as I could have them . . .

Two were ordered to have a quart of cider each; two were given elixir vitriol to gargle three times a day; two more had vinegar gargles. Two were given sea water; two more were given oranges and lemon; whilst the final pair was given a mixture of spices including nutmeg, mustard, garlic and tamarind.

The consequence was, that the most sudden and visible good effects were perceived from the use of oranges and lemons; one of those who had taken them, at the end of six days, being fit for duty . . . The other was the best recovered of any in his condition; and being now deemed pretty well, was appointed nurse to the rest of the sick.

The evidence was overwhelming, so why was it another fifty years before citrus fruit juice gave the British the nickname 'limeys'? With hindsight, the answer is clear. Unfortunately, the results of the clinical trials were not replicated in practice, while other treatments seemed to work. Captain Cook, like Anson, took three years to circumnavigate the world but lost not one man to scurvy or any other disease. Cook was prepared for scurvy and carried various preventives: 'malt, sour-krout, salted cabbage, portable broth, saloop [a herbal infusion], rob of lemons, mustard, marmalade of carrots, and inspissated [thickened] juice of wort and beer.' Despite these efforts, an outbreak occurred in 1772 as they sailed into the ice of the Southern Ocean, being 'forced to live upon salt provisions, which concurred with the cold and wet to infect the mass of our blood'.

George Jackson, a carpenter, fell ill ten days after leaving the Cape; his gums were ulcerous, and his teeth so loose, as to lie sideways. A marmalade of carrots, which had been much recommended was tried, but without success, it having no other effect than to keep him open. Our surgeon, Mr. Patton, then began the cure with fresh wort, i.e. the infusion of malt, by which he gradually recovered, and in the space of a few weeks, was perfectly cured, his teeth fast, and his gums entirely renewed.

Cook was carrying James Lind's cure in the form of 'rob of lemons' [citrus concentrate] but it was not effective. With hindsight, we can see why. He had fallen into the error pointed out by Daniel J. Boorstin: 'The greatest obstacle to discovery is not ignorance – it is the illusion of knowledge.' Although Lind had identified an effective treatment, he was mistaken as to why it worked. In short, accepted medical opinion was that scurvy was a disease of putrefaction. Lind assumed that it was citric acid that provided the cure (rather than acetic or sulphuric, which he had also tested). To concentrate the active ingredient, therefore, he reduced the juice by boiling it – he could not know that the actual active ingredient, vitamin C, was destroyed by heat.

Lemon and lime juice was finally introduced after its efficacy had been demonstrated in ships revictualled in the tropics, where the fruit was cheap enough to be a common provision. But the mystery of scurvy had not been solved. Why, for instance, did the natives of the Arctic, who never saw a vegetable of any kind, not succumb to scurvy while the well-equipped European explorers did? The answer seemed to be connected with their consumption of plenty of fresh, raw (or barely cooked) meat. The 'root cause' of scurvy – vitamin deficiency – was only revealed in the 1930s, when vitamin C was isolated and named ascorbic acid for its anti-scurvy properties.

Two ironies:

First, it was thought at the time that the comparative good health of Admiral Edward Vernon's West Indies Fleet was due to his insisting that the rum ration be diluted to prevent drunkenness. His was nicknamed 'Old Grogham' because he wore a cloak of a coarse material called grogham – dilute rum therefore became known as 'grog'. With hindsight, however, we might note that sailors used lime juice to mask the foulness of the ship's water supply. Who would have thought that this eighteenth-century mojito would be such a boon to health?

Secondly, James Lind made his 'rob of lemons' by boiling the juice: if he had used freezing as a means of extracting the water, the cure would have worked.

The point of these stories is not to be wise after the event, although that's why we find them interesting. It is to demonstrate that chance is more complicated than most of us think and that 'serendipity' is far from pure chance. In the past, it was a truism that in order to invent the wagon you must first invent the wheel. China could not be expected to invent the telescope, just as James Lind could not have known of vitamin deficiency, never mind freeze fractionation – the relevant information was simply not in their context. But it can be in ours: although sometimes 'wheels' do appear by some sort of 'chance', we have demonstrated a mechanism (idea generation) which should allow us to seek out serendipity.

But having found a new path by some 'happy accident', will we be able to follow it?

We noted Ivan Petrovich Pavlov and his research into the physiology of digestion. His specific interest was in the chemical composition of saliva when he noticed the phenomenon he called 'psychic secretion' caused by food stimuli at a distance from the dogs on which he was experimenting. Because he found the phenomenon interesting, and more importantly because he *could*, he followed this new path and described for the first time conditioned reflexes. The right man, the right time, the right place – and the freedom to take action and follow his instincts.

Opportunity Recognition: problem finding

We have suggested that keeping a 'prepared mind' enhances our ability to recognise opportunities when they occur. If we recall Beveridge, 'although we cannot deliberately evoke that will-o'-the-wisp, chance, we can be on the alert for it, prepare ourselves to recognise it and profit by it when it comes'.

But it might be possible to improve the odds further by deliberately searching for the situations where happy 'accidents' can be made to happen, in other words *problem finding*.

Remember Schopenhauer's 'Talent hits a target no one else can hit; genius hits a target no one else can see.'

In 1948, another German philosopher, Eugen Herrigel, published a short book detailing some of his experiences while teaching in Japan. *Zen in the Art of Archery* is very much a westerner's interpretation of eastern philosophy and includes a famous description of a master archer hitting the target in the dark. This is *not* the sort of thing we are talking about. Problem finding in this regard is more like: 'What are you looking for?' 'I'll know when I find it.'

So how can we find something when we are not exactly sure what it looks like?

We mentioned that UNIEI students are expected to place themselves in the bottom left-hand corner of Kirk's Space, where 'We know there's a problem but we're not quite certain what it is and we are not especially sure how to solve it.'

Problem finding has to be done one stage earlier, indicative of the entrepreneurial spirit: 'That which identifies and creates opportunities and then takes actions to realise new ideas in an appropriate domain.'

At UNIEI, we assess such opportunities by asking questions such as:

- Is this a real problem?
- Will anyone pay for a solution?
- Can you make a good job of it?
- Can you make a return on your investment?
- Is the solution sustainable?

In short, 'Is this a problem worth solving?'

Problem finding is quite distinct from problem solving but, as we saw in 'definition', with problem solving we can borrow established analytical techniques from other domains.

- From the police – a crime has been committed.
- From the news media – an event has occurred.
- From medicine – the patient presents symptoms.

In situations like these, we can investigate, we can drill down, we can attempt a diagnosis. We have some sort of point from which to proceed, even though that point will change as our understanding of the problem deepens.

But what is our starting point to be? How can we set about looking for trouble?

One way would be to generate a mass of ideas and concepts by deconstructing a problem area using the techniques described in 'discovery'. Then examine this database – remember the car park full of cars on page 16. A full understanding of the array is only achieved by looking at it from all different angles, colours, manufacturers, engine sizes, number of doors, etc.

As before, we are going to suggest some 'dance steps', and once again we are going to use analogy – this time from cultural anthropology.

Ethnographers talk about a 'rapport' with the communities they are observing. You will begin to achieve rapport when you understand all the nods and winks, the in-jokes and asides that are an ever-present feature of the life of that community.

The American academic George E. Marcus introduced the idea of a multi-sited approach to research, 'designed around chains, paths, threads, conjunctions, or juxtapositions of locations' .

> 'Multi-sited ethnographies define their objects of study through several different modes or techniques. These techniques might be understood as practices of construction through (preplanned or opportunistic) movement and of tracing within different settings of a complex cultural phenomenon given an initial, baseline conceptual identity that turns out to be contingent and malleable as one traces it.'
>
> ('Ethnography in/of the World System: the emergence of multi-sited ethnography', 1995)

Marcus suggests a series of heuristics: 'Follow the People; Follow the Thing; Follow the Metaphor; Follow the Plot, Story, or Allegory; Follow the Life or Biography; Follow the Conflict.'

So, step one: deconstruct the problem area (however vague) into notes and phrases.

Steps two, three and more: arrange and rearrange the notes according to the heuristics: 'follow the people', etc.

These are heuristics for ethnographers; but there is no reason why others could not be tailored to any area. Detectives investigating crime are told to 'follow the money'. We can do the same: follow the market; follow the producers; follow the consumers; follow the leaders; follow the followers, etc. Establishing a rapport with the problem area by identifying all of its 'chains, paths, threads, conjunctions, or juxtapositions' should help would-be entrepreneurs to differentiate real from perceived problems – to identify those which are worth solving.

Opportunity

Such a procedure could be fruitful for any social domain. Imagine the 'chains, paths, threads, conjunctions, or juxtapositions' to be found using such a technique for one of our problem areas, alcohol consumption, say. Below is a response to a challenge to demonstrate the method in 'real time' similar to that on page 163 (A Chair is Not a Chair).

An Exercise in Problem Finding

If we take as a starting point the knee-jerk, tabloid view of 'binge drinking' in city centres in the UK that compares it with 'Mediterranean' culture, there seems to be a notion that if only 'we' were more like 'them'.

Using the techniques outlined above, let us take those city centres as the general problem area and examine it for a few minutes in more detail. Recalling Ribot, if we want to free ourselves from routine responses we need to dissociate; and so we will try to break apart the situation, using a simple series of questions:

- Follow the people: who is there? Young people, old people, couples, singles, women, men? What ethnicities? Who isn't there?

- Follow the thing: drunkenness and disorder. Where, inside or outside? What kind of inside or outside? Bars, clubs, cinemas, restaurants, theatres? On the street, on the bus, in the taxi rank?

- Follow the metaphor: what is the metaphor – loss of control? Who's in control? Which brings in another group of stakeholders: the police, the bouncers, the bus drivers.

- Follow the plot, story, or allegory: when did this start, how did it develop, how does it end? Which might bring in the health services, the street cleaners.

- Follow the life or biography: what are the individual 'stories'? Who are the groups?

- Follow the conflict: again, where and when?

Those are Marcus's heuristics; we can devise our own:

- Follow the money: who is spending, who is earning, who is making a profit, who is not, who is paying?

- Follow the market: where and when are these transactions taking place? From the pre-loaders to the freeloaders; from the businesses to the council-tax payers.

- Follow the producers: SMEs or chains?

- Follow the consumers: where did they come from, how are they getting home?

- Follow the leaders: what are the hot spots?

- Follow the followers: what is the latest fashion?

And then we can come up with specific heuristics to reflect our particular concerns: what are the health implications, the economic considerations, the social consequences?

If we use other heuristics from the definition stage of our CPS on these elements, looking for structures, interrelationships and root causes, we might begin to claim an understanding of the distinct 'ethnography' of a Saturday night in a Midlands town.

This problem area is not a case of complexity arising from iteration of simple rules. There are clearly multiple stakeholders with totally different points of view, so simply introducing single 'solutions' from an entirely different context is unlikely to be effective. But we can retain our perception of Mediterranean culture as an aspiration and come up with ideas which would bring value in those terms.

'Value' has very different meaning for different stakeholders and can be measured as anything from greater profits to fewer arrests. It is likely, but not certain, that projects which bring value to the widest constituency will have the most chance of success.

Also bear in mind that this exercise is done to gain a general understanding of the problem area. If we introduce a particular agenda, be it that of a bar-owner, a health-care practitioner or even a teetotal abolitionist, more specific criteria can be brought into focus.

Thus we can treat a Saturday night in a city centre a little like an (admittedly loosely structured) organisation and ask a couple of simple questions of each of the transactions and junctures we have identified:

- 'How can we do this better?' (Incremental innovation)

- 'How can we do this differently?' (Radical innovation)

We can be quite methodical about this and search until we find an opportunity to bring value. For example:

Package weekends for adults.

Almost every large town in Britain has enough attractions to while away an afternoon. Most can provide an evening's entertainment as well.

Adults have more money and are better behaved than most youngsters.

Therefore: book online from a range of recommended options.

Transport

Hotel

Restaurant

Theatre/cinema/concert/sporting event.

Download bespoke 'guide book' with directions to attractions: parks, museums, churches, ancient monuments, historic pubs, fashionable retail outlets.

Potential stakeholders in this solution would include all the attractions listed above, together with the local council and tourism offices.

This is not an original idea, but it is a half-formed business opportunity to encourage a more diverse night-time culture in city centres, produced by the authors in roughly the time it took to write it down.

As we said right at the outset of this book, most of us have the luxury of seeing problems as opportunities, and many of us enjoy the further luxury of choosing which problems/opportunities we care to address. That is the essence of entrepreneurial thinking.

PHASE THREE:
Determination

> The imagination must be active and brilliant in seeking analogies; yet entirely under the influence of the judgment in applying them.
>
> (Humphry Davy, *Consolations in Travel*, 1830)

This section is all about re-focus and synthesis; picking and choosing ideas from Phase Two, engineering them into practical, realistic possibilities and then assessing them rigorously.

As we said earlier, hindsight is a wonderful thing. What we need is a little foresight. To recap, the model of consciousness we have been using to construct our problem-solving process is one in which we continually perceive new experiences in the light of past experiences. When faced with the unfamiliar, we immediately look for something similar that we *are* familiar with. In this sense, we live in what Gerald Edelman calls a 'remembered present'. To take this one step further, while we are in the phase of productive thinking, re-presenting, restructuring our ideas, we also live in an 'imagined future'. Imagining what may happen when we finally get around to applying our ideas is the third and final stage of our problem-solving process.

Evaluating possible solutions rigorously is critically important; there is no point in coming up with creative, imaginative ideas that are totally impractical. It's worth re-examining our definition of creativity. 'Novel' and 'appropriate' were the keywords. But it is only when we actually apply a new idea that we can make a judgement as to whether it is appropriate or not. Until that time our 'creative genius' remains theoretical; and so:

Creativity generates ideas or concepts or associations between existing ideas and concepts, which, when applied, we judge to be both new and appropriate. In practice:

> 'Creative solutions have to be *new*, *appropriate*, and *applied*.'

The English writer and critic G. K. Chesterton said: 'Art is limitation; the essence of every picture is the frame.' Although we have been looking for solutions 'outside the box', remember that those solutions must fit 'back in the box', within the frame of constraints we set ourselves earlier on. If our ideas are so revolutionary that they break the frame, then we will have to take special care when planning how to introduce them.

This section is most applicable to products (including plans and decisions) rather than opportunities and discoveries – those need to be taken right back to the beginning to answer Alex Osborn's first question: 'To what other uses could this be put?' We keep saying that if we are to create the best innovations and make the best decisions, we might have to keep returning: it is an iterative process.

It is worth pointing out that we don't *have* to do anything – we can leave our discoveries and innovations to take care of themselves. The umbrella was introduced to London in the latter half of the eighteenth century by the travel writer, adventurer and philanthropist Jonas Hanway. Hanway is reported to have endured years of abuse from sedan-chair carriers and coachmen, who, quite rightly, saw the humble brolly as a threat to their trade – they accused him of being too mean or too poor – teasing him: 'Frenchman, Frenchman! Why don't you call a coach?' Despite resistance, the umbrella caught on. But there is no evidence that the eccentric Hanway cared one way or the other: he did not have that goal or *telos* we mentioned in defining entrepreneurs. His *telos* was not to make money, or even fame; he simply wanted to keep himself dry.

We are proceeding on the assumption that we want our innovations and decisions to succeed, so we use the word determination not only in the sense of judgement – determining the best solution – but also in the sense of resolve: the determination to go ahead with more certainty that we have identified the optimal rather than the acceptable. Most importantly, to determine whether our solution is appropriate.

Yet another cautionary tale – the WoBo

Sometimes an idea seems so self-evidently brilliant that we can see no reason why we shouldn't just get on with it, especially if we are rich enough and powerful enough to make it happen.

On a trip to the Caribbean in the early 1960s, the brewer Alfred Heineken noticed two things: first, that the poor people of the islands made shanty towns out of anything they could find; and secondly, that the beaches were littered with beer bottles (many of them his).

Back home in Holland, he and architect John Habraken launched a project to design a bottle with a secondary use as a brick. The WoBo (World Bottle) went through several prototypes before it was finally shelved as impractical.

The WoBo - an early take on corporate responsibility and sustainability

So why would such an elegant and simple concept fail? And might it be worth reviving in these eco-sensitive times?

- In the 1960s, glass bottles were much thicker than today. In fact most bottles were cleaned and re-used by the bottling plants.

- At least two different sizes had to be produced to turn corners and build windows and doors, without having to cut the bottles.

- You would have to drink an inordinate amount of beer to build even the smallest shack.

- People who are reduced to scavenging building materials rarely have the money to buy the mortar needed to fix the bottles together.

Finally, what would *you* say to someone living in a beer-bottle house?

So the strategies we adopt should be both pragmatic and attainable; there is no point in coming up with creative, imaginative ideas which are totally impractical.

We can of course assess our new ideas by applying them straight away, by simple trial and error; after all, we are going to have to test them out eventually. Trial and error might well be the easiest way of testing in some circumstances; for example, if you are thinking of opening your shop on a Sunday, you could commission some market research, convene a focus group or two, model some forecasts, or you could try it out for a couple of weeks.

Trial and Error

It is remarkable what has been achieved by such a simple method. The soaring Gothic cathedrals of western Europe were all built with techniques learned by trial and error. Notwithstanding their delicate and graceful appearance, most surviving medieval buildings are massively over-engineered – only the strong have survived. Very few cathedrals were built as one continuous venture: the money would run out periodically; wars would intervene; skills could be lost and towers or roofs might collapse; and when building recommenced it would of course need to be in the latest style. Architectural historians can trace the sequence whereby the limits of each style were reached through a succession of tower and roof collapses. For example, the unique octagonal Lantern Tower of Ely Cathedral is nothing more than an elegant solution to the problem caused by the collapse of the old central tower. Some were never finished. The engineer Jacques Heyman's study of the troubles trying to build Beauvais Cathedral concludes by quoting the Chapter's final acceptance that the project would not be completed: *'le temps n'était plus a bâtir des cathédrales'*. The time was past for building cathedrals; Gothic architecture was out of fashion – for a while.

In the year 1079 in the reign of King William I, a fine Romanesque cathedral church was begun at Winchester. In 1107, the tower fell down. William of Malmesbury, writing less than twenty years later, recorded that many attributed the collapse to the burial of the Conqueror's impious son William Rufus, who had been killed in the New Forest in mysterious circumstances some seven years before. Malmesbury declined to give a firm opinion on the matter, noting that the tower might have not been that well built. The replacement was the squat edifice which stands to this day.

At the start of the twentieth century, Malmesbury's doubts were remembered when the authorities called in the renowned civil engineer Francis Fox (one of only a few people in this story not named William) to investigate the fabric of the building. Cracks had appeared in several places and walls were definitely sinking into the marshy ground of the cathedral precincts. Digging down, Fox also found supporting evidence of another old tradition:

Bishop Walkelin found himself in want of timber (for building the Cathedral), and applied to the Conqueror to let him have as much timber as he could carry out of Hanepinges Wood in four days and nights. William at once granted the request. The astute bishop then collected all the woodmen in the neighbourhood, and they managed to cut and carry the whole wood within the appointed time (much to the surprise and anger of the king).

It was now clear what they had done with all that timber – the whole cathedral had been built on what was essentially a raft of enormous tree trunks. The logs had eventually rotted away and that was the cause of the subsidence. Times had changed, of course: Bishop Walkelin had been happy to knock down the ancient Saxon Minster once his replacement was finished; such a modern outlook now being considered vandalism, the decision was to launch possibly the first national fund-raising campaign for preservation and restoration. Fox needed to underpin the walls with thousands of blocks of concrete, but the trenches soon flooded. The solution was to employ one man, an experienced diver, to do the entire job. William Walker worked underwater, in zero visibility, for five days a week for six years. Walker was made a member of the Royal Victorian Order by King George V for having 'saved the cathedral with his own two hands'.

So we have two novel solutions separated by eight centuries – we ought to be well pleased if any of our solutions last as long. We might excuse a 'mistake' that takes eight hundred years to fail but in general trial and error can be very expensive – all those failures have to be paid for. Trial and error can use up the best part of the innovator's budget. It is an old business adage that 'It's the second mouse who gets the cheese.'

Determination

Trial and error might well be the easiest way of testing in some circumstances; without any faculty of foresight it is all there is.

Let's return to the ant and consider its ways. Ants exhibit complex behaviour through what is known as 'swarm intelligence'.

Take one aspect – food gathering. Every morning ants set forth in small numbers. If an individual finds a food source it returns, leaving a trail of pheromones that is followed by others who in turn leave a trail, which will dissipate in time. The strength of the scent thus indicates the popularity and consequently the size of the food resource. As the food source diminishes, the strength of the trail weakens and so foragers will follow other, stronger trails. As they depart the nest, the individual ants 'obey' two rules only: return with food and leave a trail. None of the ants sees the whole situation; the intelligence of the colony is not, of course, even discernible by the individuals. Simple rules plus feedback iterates into complexity. When we remember how trial and error played its part in cathedral development, it becomes easier to understand termite mounds and ants' nests – which have had millions of generations to perfect the system. By their very nature, computer programmes have comparatively little difficulty generating complexity from simple rules – the 'boids' we mentioned earlier are a prime example.

The ants' food-gathering behaviour is a strong, efficient, self-regulatory system based on just two rules. Imagine the possibilities for such a system in all those analogous areas of collection, distribution, indeed any communication. Here we have a biomimetic solution which might be applicable in another domain. The secret, surely, would be in designing the 'pheromone' that ensures the feedback: engineering your specific solution from this general one. You wouldn't be the first; computer algorithms based on this method are already being introduced in real-life situations as far apart as telecommunications and road haulage.

The inordinately snooty Pooh-Bah, one of the characters in *The Mikado* by Gilbert and Sullivan, boasts of his 'pre-Adamite ancestral descent'. He claims that his pedigree reaches back to a 'protoplasmal primordial atomic globule'. The slime mould *Physarum polycephalum* is just the sort of ancestor he would have been proud of. This remarkable organism forages across the forest floor by extending protrusions of protoplasm, locating and creating a network between food sources. Experimenters in Britain and Japan have found that slime moulds are extremely efficient. If a map is constructed in the laboratory using oat flakes to represent cities and towns and the mould let loose at the 'capital' city, it will quickly form a network surprisingly similar to those of railways in Japan and motorways in Britain. The mould's network is actually superior to the human version in some ways; it will maintain redundant lines in case of damage to the main routes. It is almost as if George Iles' herds of buffalo had been miniaturised and their millennia of migrations speeded up to a few days. The thing to remember about slime moulds is that they are very basic creatures indeed, being essentially a sort of colonial amoeba. They have no nervous system or brain – they have no CPU (Central Processing Unit) – but then again neither has a herd.

Slime moulds are multitalented: they are phototropic, for example, and have been physically incorporated into robots. Dr Klaus-Peter Zauner of the University of Southampton, which has developed one such, remarks, 'There was a time when people in hot-air balloons looked at pigeons and realised that there is a radically different solution to the problem of flight. Now we marvel at nature's molecular computers which tell us that there are radically different solutions to the problem of information processing.'

Most of our biomimetic solutions will have to be altered somewhat before we can use them. What we need to do is *translate* the concept from one appropriateness (the original) to another (ours). In 1681 John Dryden identified three types of translation that might give us a clue as to the different ways in which we could restructure what we have found:

1. **Metaphrase**, where an author/translator translates 'word by word and line by line'; this will convey the meaning but without the rhythm, perhaps a bit clunky.

2. **Paraphrase**, where an author/translator translates sense for sense; this makes the text more acceptable to its new audience. What Dryden calls 'translation with latitude'.

3. **Imitation**, where an author/translator takes 'only some general hints from the original' to create what might be a quite different work.

We have already seen the results of mistranslation with the thought-shower. Some ideas are easily transposed; e.g., one way of doubling the life of a conveyor belt would be to borrow from mathematics and convert your belt into a Möbius strip (not even a full twist!).

Most ideas, however, will resemble Dryden's distinctions one way or another. If you are an architect looking for ideas for buildings to withstand earthquakes, you may have come across Japanese pagodas, which seem to have lasted longer than you might have expected, despite their fragile appearance. Obviously, you are not going to build pagodas all over the place; you are going to find out how the pagoda's construction works and *imitate* it. 'Viral marketing' is *paraphrase*, the sense in which diseases spread is translated into the marketplace. The one that causes most trouble is *metaphrase* and it is difficult to find examples where it actually works. Even global brands like McDonald's and IKEA do not translate their concepts precisely 'word for word'.

If we are aware of the dangers of mistranslation, then fitting solutions into our box will be straightforward. If we correctly defined our problem back at the start of Phase Two, we ought to be on familiar territory. Solutions which are so revolutionary that they break the box are always going to be more difficult to assess – but now is the time to try.

Once again the fractal nature of this problem-solving process is revealed: a preparatory stage (**definition**) is followed by exploration (**discovery**) before refocusing on evaluation (**determination**).

Define – select and engineer potential solutions

Again illustrating the fractal nature of our process, this is a final iteration of the last section of Phase Two. The aspect of *preparation* is the arrangement (and rearrangement) of possibilities from the previous phase into *proto*-concepts that are capable of evaluation. As an introduction to idea generation, we used the analogy of homeopathic dilution as a 'dance step' to produce lots of ideas retaining a relevance, however slight, to our original problem. This is the final dance step: getting those bits of solutions to flocculate or crystallise together into something. It is a mechanism, however clumsy, to encourage that little understood phenomenon of emergence.

Sort and sift ideas into categories

The categories chosen will reflect what was discovered about the problem way back in Phase One. It may be that the ideas we have generated have caused us to reassess our original problem: we should not be afraid to return all the way back, redefine our problem statement and run through the process once more. And so we might find ourselves back here with a broader range of potentialities.

Or an altered sense of priority. Trevor Baylis, inventor of the wind-up radio, said that one of the great leaps forward in its development occurred when he realised that he did not need to make the clockwork electricity generator so small that it fitted in a 'normal'-sized radio. The idea of personal hand-cranked generators has since taken off to such an extent that what had been *unobtainium*, i.e. miniaturisation of the technology, now 'solves' Baylis's original problem. (An interesting contrast with the Palm Pilot, where success was dependent on size to the extent that function was sacrificed – technology now gives extended function while retaining the essential small physical size.)

We may like to offer ourselves more choice between strategies or time scales or budgets, for example.

- Bottom-up or top-down
- Gradual, step by step or all at once
- Stop-gap or permanent
- High-tech, lo-tech
- Top-price, mid-price or low-price.

Determination

Construct realistic possibilities

This is the point at which we start to separate 'good ideas' from 'lots of ideas', returning to an emphasis on *quality* rather than quantity.

Sometimes solutions emerge from the simple action of sorting similar ideas. The following anonymised example comes from a problem-solving workshop run by UNIEI as part of a business development course entitled 'Growth Readiness'. All participants were successful business people with proven track records in entrepreneurial enterprise. UNIEI workshops always try to use 'real' problems as case histories and sometimes elect to address one particular participant's 'problem' in order to teach our Creative Problem-Solving Process.

Mr Beevors has run a property management company in a large provincial town for over twelve years. His experience is such that he claims to be able to judge the moral probity of the nation by monitoring lettings to single men in January (after the Christmas break-ups). His firm manages both commercial and residential lettings for landlords but an increasing part of his business is the purchase of houses on behalf of buy-to-let investors. At the moment, he is buying at a rate of twenty houses a month and sees no reason to expect this to lessen. He regards the landlords as his customers: after all, they sign the cheques. The tenants are his clients. His problem, common to many growing businesses, is that he and his office staff spend a lot of time 'firefighting'. Despite detailed information packs about rights and responsibilities, his clients expect immediate attention to any and all household problems.

His team included an engineer, a builder and an IT consultant, all high achievers in their fields. The 'definition' stage of CPS necessarily involved Mr Beevors explaining his business to the other three 'fresh pairs of eyes'. The default 'solution' recognised by everyone was to employ more staff as the portfolio increased. However the team 'drilled down' to produce a more specific problem statement, which read: 'To develop a more effective method to manage clients' expectations and perceptions.'

In the course of two short storms the team generated well over a hundred ideas written down on sticky notes. These ideas were sorted and sifted under three headings: Products, Systems and Human Resources. The ideas placed under 'Systems' were:

Inform client of steps * Letter to client * Improve information * Welcome packs * Satisfaction questionnaire * Evaluate questionnaires * Reference number – contact details * Appointed callers * Robust and clear documentation * Rewrite contractors' contracts * Customer-feedback forms * Full repairing lease * Contractor relationship * Maintenance contract * Communication * Quality check sheets * Check list * Measure * Online reporting * Online system * Communication via online trainer * Online tracking * Outsource * Secret shopper * Obvious shopper * Computer intelligence * Management process * Sign-off sheets * Implement change * Reports * Management process * Manage change * Trackers * Automated systems * Programmes * Action list * Growth charts * Flow charts

The team's solution from this category was both elegant and simple. The status quo was that whenever the agency received a complaint from a client the appropriate contractor, plumber, builder or electrician, would be contacted electronically. The innovation was that at the same time the client would also be contacted by mail, text or phone with a reference number and timeframe for resolution and, crucially, the contractor's job reference number and the contractor's phone number. With hindsight, the solution arose from an answer to 'Whose problem?' What had been a problem for the client, customer and agent was shifted to the contractor. Mr Beevors could not see any barriers to immediate implementation. The software for the solution was already in place and the contractors would be left with little choice but to comply as the agency's work was highly valued – they might even appreciate the removal of a tier of bureaucracy. The agency would not need to take on a new, dedicated employee. Existing staff resources would be released. In Mr Beevors' words, 'I'm going to do it tomorrow.'

Feedback three months after the workshop confirmed that the solution worked: 'I am pleased to say that I did implement the idea the next day (well almost – it took me a few days to put things together), the change has definitely helped the business in its management processes, it has also helped our contractors' quality of workmanship.'

When this solution was presented to other teams at the end of the day, it was remarked by other participants that this obvious solution had not been obvious to anyone at the start of the day. That which now seemed such common sense had not been apparent from *within* the problem. It was also plain to see that the solution had not been on any single Post-it: it had *emerged* during the process of sorting and sifting.

One of the difficulties in describing creative problem solving is that the simpler the solution is, the harder it is to take credit for coming up with it. It is the problem of tacit knowledge transfer. Sceptics will claim that the answer must have been obvious to anyone with an ounce of common sense. To which we have to reply that two of the team members were distinctly sceptical at the start of the session and more than slightly surprised that they had not thought of 'it' at the end.

Ideas will often appear under two or more headings. Recall the car park full of cars that we used as a simple description of the same data being seen through different paradigms (p. 24). We can again use the multi-sited approach (p. 201). We may need to rearrange the same ideas several times to get a full appreciation of the possibilities. It may be, as in the case above, that single breakthrough ideas are so dramatically commonsensical that they can be implemented straight away, but most of the time we are likely to need to choose between alternatives.

Select three or four different concepts for final evaluation

While the emphasis is on the practical and pragmatic, we should not be afraid to give seemingly eccentric ideas a proper assessment. That's what creative problem solving is for.

Again the easiest way to demonstrate the principle is to look at an actual example, so let's revisit our students with 45 cars for every single parking place.

They decided to sort and sift into hi-tech solutions, lo-tech solutions and those requiring a degree of social engineering. Some ideas fitted into more than one category. For each of these categories they engineered a possibility.

Their lo-tech possibility was the mobile car park, a little like a car transporter; once full, the car park would be removed until the end of the day.

The hi-tech solution was yield management of car parking: the car park would match subscribers to empty places using wireless technology, essentially linking a central database to individual's satellite navigation systems.

The solution requiring social engineering was to ban all heavy goods vehicles and other non-commuter traffic from the city centre during designated hours.

Discover – investigate the alternatives, find the best solution

This stage is concerned with applying rigorous analysis across the breadth of possibilities that we have discovered.

The double Nobel Laureate Linus Pauling (1901–1994) is quoted as saying: 'If you want to have good ideas you must have many ideas. Most of them will be wrong, and what you have to learn is which ones to throw away.'

The choices we make at this stage should be determined by our decisions about the nature of the problem to be solved. To do that we must recall what we concluded at the end of phase one, definition: we need to anchor our concept on the vertical axis of Kirk's Space or it is liable to drift away.

Recall your criteria from the problem definition stage

Because we have been exploring the widest range of options (or so we hope), it is essential to confirm that we are proposing to solve the problem we originally identified, within the constraints that we set ourselves.

- What were the criteria for success?
- What were the constraints in both time and resources?
- What were the priorities?

Finding a solution to a different problem is not necessarily a *bad* thing, but it is a *different* thing: you may have to return to the start. To show an example from 'real life', here is a case study from a UNIEI creative problem-solving workshop.

Shakeel represents a large, highly automated bakery in Birmingham. They bake approximately three million pittas per week! He is extremely well informed about his market, including international possibilities. He has identified a particular product – sangat/songat flatbread – which is extremely popular but has defied machine manufacture, largely because it has very high moisture content. His problem, as he initially stated it, is how to develop a machine to bake this bread with all the qualities of the handmade version and be first to this enormous and growing market. He is aware of progress in this field in both Germany and Iran.

His team partners in the workshop were an IT training and online education provider and a director of a large firm of contract joiners/shopfitters.

The team soon decided that Shakeel's case was more of an opportunity than a problem and that his underlying problem was of how 'to continue to grow in a growing market', so they addressed that as well as his R&D issues.

The team spent a lot of time coming up with 'new' products to extend the range and be pro-active in product development, rather than waiting for distributors to lead. It was also decided that R&D partners could be sought outside the bakery business by looking for machines which dealt with similar problems: high moisture content; low viscosity; stickiness, etc. These might be found in areas not in direct competition, e.g., confectionery; but also outside the food industry, e.g., plastics, glues and mastics, even carpet underlay. And so Shakeel was given at least two coherent strategies with which to move forward.

Most interestingly, however, the team came up with a surprising piece of radical creativity. They identified and went some way to realising a model of manufacturing and distributing real handmade bread at a scale to rival machine manufacture, albeit as a more expensive product and at a lesser volume than the bakery was aiming for. While rejecting this 'solution' as inappropriate, they recognised that rivals could quite easily make inroads if they were to 'discover' it. It might be best to investigate the possibility of launching a premium product/service to complement the existing mass marketing. All of which goes to show that the title of the course – 'Out-thinking the Competition' – means accepting that you might be uncomfortable with what you find.

Compare the alternatives

This is one of the points at which we are most liable to make mistakes. Rational choice is difficult to achieve; we have already noted that any salesman, confidence trickster or conjuror can exploit our unreasonable reason. The chief dangers here are groupthink and confirmation bias. Having forced ourselves to get to the root causes of the problem and having looked at a wide range of possibilities, we find ourselves with a favourite solution; perhaps it's a eureka moment and we can't wait to put it into action.

But as we noted, trial and error can be very expensive if we get it wrong.

Problems can be made worse by guessing.

Snap decisions are not always the best.

Opportunities can be squandered by ill-judged over-enthusiasm.

Again none of this is new – several of Aesop's Fables have 'look before you leap' as a moral. Although we may be 'built for speed' in our decision making, as we have repeatedly shown, there are relatively few occasions when there is no time at all for considered judgement. Our difficulty now is to assess our alternatives as dispassionately as we can.

A wide range of formal decision-making tools has become available. From the simplest list of those for and against to the most complex cost/benefit matrix, there is plenty of choice. As we noted with problem solving and idea generation in general, there is a tendency for formal processes to become more detailed and specific as time goes on. Our purpose is not to replace or reject any of these established techniques but to reference them while trying to provide a broad guide for clearer thinking.

For an overview of the general principles, let's once more take our own advice and look back to see how decision making works in another place and time. Here is a letter from one of the great minds of the Enlightenment, Benjamin Franklin, to an up-and-coming colleague, Joseph Priestley:

London Sept. 19. 1772

Dear Sir,

In the Affair of so much Importance to you, wherein you ask my Advice, I cannot for want of sufficient Premises, advise you what to determine, but if you please I will tell you how. When these difficult Cases occur, they are difficult chiefly because while we have them under Consideration all the Reasons pro and con are not present to the Mind at the same time; but sometimes one Set present themselves, and at other times another, the first being out of Sight. Hence the various Purposes or Inclinations that alternately prevail, and the Uncertainty that perplexes us. To get over this, my Way is, to divide half a Sheet of Paper by a Line into two Columns, writing over the one Pro, and over the other Con. Then during three or four Days Consideration I put down under the different Heads short Hints of the different Motives that at different Times occur to me for or against the Measure. When I have thus got them all together in one View, I endeavour to estimate their respective Weights; and where I find two, one on each side, that seem equal, I strike them both out: If I find a Reason pro equal to some two Reasons con, I strike out the three. If I judge some two Reasons con equal to some three Reasons pro, I strike out the five; and thus proceeding I find at length where the Ballance lies; and if after a Day or two of farther Consideration nothing new that is of Importance occurs on either side, I come to a Determination accordingly. And tho' the Weight of Reasons cannot be taken with the Precision of Algebraic Quantities, yet when each is thus considered separately and comparatively, and the whole lies before me, I think I can judge better, and am less likely to make a rash Step; and in fact I have found great Advantage from this kind of Equation, in what may be called Moral or Prudential Algebra. Wishing sincerely that you may determine for the best, I am ever, my dear Friend, Yours most affectionately

B Franklin

In other words, 'I can't decide for you, I don't know enough about it; but I can tell you how I make difficult decisions. Why not give it a try?'

Several points are noteworthy in Franklin's 'Prudential Algebra'. It is not just a sheet of paper with a list of pros and cons to be totted up straight away; Franklin emphasises the need to weigh each point individually before considering the overall balance. He also insists that the process should take several days in order to reflect the widest consideration.

We have already remarked on the tendency to confuse good decision making with rapid decision making but, unless considered judgement actually has a negative effect, then snap decisions will *always* have a lower success rate than well-thought-out ones.

Lest it should be thought that Benjamin Franklin was some cautious eighteenth-century 'gentleman scientist and philosopher', we should recall that apart from being a diplomat and statesman he was also an innovator, being responsible for the first public library in America, and the first fire service in America. He funded his interests by being a highly successful businessman and entrepreneur in printing and publishing. As for risk taking, he not only was prepared to fly a kite in a thunderstorm, he also took the greatest risk of his century by signing the Declaration of Independence in 1776. What his 'prudential algebra' allows is *calculated* risk. If a man of Franklin's prodigious achievements thinks it's important to take a little time to answer big questions, then it ought to be good enough for the rest of us.

Dependent upon the nature of your problem, some decision-making methods may be more suitable than others. Franklin's method judges a single proposition. Paired Comparison does exactly what its name suggests. A Decision Tree is a diagrammatic extrapolation of successive options, which can be constructed to suit each particular problem. The Pugh Method allows several possibilities to be progressively eliminated and is of particular benefit when assessing options against an existing 'solution'. There is no reason why you shouldn't run your solution through several different matrices; if they agree, all well and good; if they disagree, perhaps you need to think again. It is still possible to be creative at this stage by asking the simple question, 'How can we turn this negative into a positive?' and running the changed version through the matrix again.

Assessing possibilities in this manner should help to identify negative aspects of your proposal that cannot be eliminated. It may be that you can take the attitude that 'What can't be cured must be endured,' but some negatives are so strong that they become 'deal breakers'. Recall that, however well they were explained or justified, the payments proposed in the *Eames Bradley Report* were simply not tolerable to some particularly vociferous parties in Northern Ireland and this one negative swept away any consideration of the positives of the rest of the report.

To return once more to our car-parking example: the students assessed their alternatives using a simple advantage/disadvantage matrix. Their judging criteria formed the rows; the solutions were the columns. Each cell was then marked plus, minus or not applicable. The table below represents a final iteration of the matrix:

As the table shows, the high-tech solution scored highly and was chosen as the one to be taken forward as a concept whose implementation can be planned with a very real chance of success. The remaining negative – complexity of implementation – was considered to be a price worth paying.

Criteria	Mobile Car Park	Banning heavy traffic	Intelligent yield management
Start up cost	+	+/-	+
Market potential	+	NA	+
Profitability	-	NA	+
Acceptance by consumers	+	-	+
Acceptance by government	+	-	+
Complexity of implementation	+	+	-
Acceptance by existing suppliers	-	-	+
Effectiveness to solve the problem	-	+	+

Intelligent yield management has proved to be a very successful concept. At about the same time as our students were storming, a computer engineer named Eugene Tsyrklevich came up with a similar idea on the other side of the Atlantic. The difference is that he acted on it and founded a company called Parkopedia which now (2013) allows users to access over 28 million parking spaces in over 6,000 towns in forty countries.

As always, with the benefit of hindsight, we can look back at the array of brainstormed ideas and trace the development of successful concepts, but that is to misunderstand the nature of idea generation. The most creative solutions *emerge* from a range of possibilities in a manner which cannot necessarily be forecast.

It is worth recalling that there are no single, correct answers to any given problem. It must have been a similar array of ideas which led MIT (Massachusetts Institute of Technology) to propose their City Car: a shareable, rechargeable, *stackable* solution to the same problem that our students were addressing.

Choose your optimal solution

- We have to make a balanced judgement between the optimal and the acceptable. If we return for a moment to the restaurant where we were arguing about the bill, the *optimal* choice of wine to accompany the fillet steaks might have been the 1966 Gevrey-Chambertin, but the *acceptable* choice lies somewhere between that and the house red. A very swift cost/benefit analysis may be the best way of deciding on the most *appropriate* bottle.

For most projects we are comparing the start-up costs with the market potential, but costs are not only expressed in purely monetary terms. In effect, we need to assess the effort required to achieve the success we desire.*

- How do the solutions match up to your goals?

Exceeding your goals may bring other problems when it comes to implementation. We shall be looking at the risks of unintended consequences a little later but for now it is useful to note that some decisions have *intended* consequences – they solve two or more problems at once. For instance, in Tudor times, Queen Elizabeth's attitude to religion was far more tolerant than either of her siblings – she claimed that she had 'no desire to make windows into men's souls' – and yet she strictly enforced fasting. It was an *intended* consequence that the English fishing industry should be supported, with the additional benefit of a ready supply of practised sailors to man the fleet. From this distance in time it is hard to see which came first.

- Which solution has the most realistic chance of success?

Now is a good time to take risk into account. Risk taking is not a prerequisite for success. The fact that lots of entrepreneurs take risks does not mean that all risk takers are entrepreneurs. This is a resurgence of one of the oldest logical fallacies known to mankind, i.e., if all 'A' are 'B' then all 'B' are assumed to be 'A'. It is easy to see the folly of this assumption by using one of the simplest of our problem-solving techniques and looking at the question from a different point of view. If we focus on risk takers rather than entrepreneurs we can see that the whole spectrum of risk taking includes gamblers and bankrupts. Risk taking is clearly not the defining characteristic of entrepreneurship.

> To understand successes, the study of traits in failure need to be present. For instance some traits that seem to explain millionaires, like appetite for risk, only appear because one does not study bankruptcies. If one includes bankrupt people in the sample, then risk-taking would not appear to be a valid factor explaining success.
>
> (Nassim Nicholas Taleb, 2004)

Risk is an extremely complicated business: it is not a simple matter of odds. For example, we saw with Meadow's Law that some people think that lightning will not strike in the same place twice, totally ignoring *why* it struck in a particular place the first time. In fact, lightning is more likely to strike the same place twice; if it was random, we wouldn't have lightning conductors.

*Venture capitalists use the colloquialism 'Death Valley Curve' to describe the period from the initial funding of a project to the point at which revenues begin to flow back. When passing through this period, the project is most susceptible to cash-flow problems while being least likely to raise extra finance. Again this is relevant to any budget: when your credibility is all used up before the promised benefits arrive, an extra input of trust is hard to come by.

Determination

Risk assessment and risk management are the subjects of an ever-growing literature beyond the remit of this book but they may offer useful insights, especially when the stakes are high. Taking the time to examine problems and possibilities at this stage should reduce the chance of failure, but it will never be removed completely. Acceptance of risk necessarily implies the inevitability of occasional disappointment. In the knowledge that failure is always more expensive further on down the road, *minimising* that risk constitutes foresight.

The writer and cryptographer Herbert O. Yardley spent most of his leisure time playing poker and winning consistently. He recorded his technique in *The Education of a Poker Player* (1957), stating at the very beginning, 'I do not believe in luck – only the immutable law of averages.'*

In his 2004 book *The Medici Effect*, Frans Johansson relates the advice of a successful poker-playing friend: 'It has less to do with reading the other players around the table or figuring out if they are bluffing or not. It may help, but it's not the key to winning. The key to winning is to stay disciplined. Make sure to bet big when you have good cards and stay low when you don't. Because it is all about winning more when you win and losing less when you lose.'

He observes that 'people make riskier bets when things are going poorly, but lock in a win early when things are going well. They are the people who end up losing in the long run.'

Yardley's trust in 'the immutable law of averages' brings us to measurable probability. For all the image of purity in certain subjects like mathematics, advances are often driven by utility. In 1657, the Dutch mathematician (and inventor of the pendulum clock) Christiaan Huygens published the earliest study of probability theory, examining the place of reason in games of chance in *De Ratiociniis in Ludo Aleæ*. Shortly afterwards this was translated into English by the polymath Dr John Arbuthnot and prefaced with the following:

> The Reader may here observe the Force of Numbers, which can be successfully applied, even to those things, which one would imagine are subject to no Rules. There are very few things which we know, which are not capable of being reduc'd to a Mathematical Reasoning, and when they cannot, it's a sign our Knowledge of them is very small and confus'd; and where a mathematical reasoning can be had, it's as great folly to make use of any other, as to grope for a thing in the dark when you have a Candle standing by you.
>
> (Of the Laws of Chance, or, a Method of the Hazards of Game, 1692)*

*Yardley is eminently quotable with regard to business and decision making. For instance, on 'sunk costs' and the 'Death Valley Curve': 'A card player should learn that once the money is in the pot it isn't his any longer. His judgement should not be influenced by this. He should instead say to himself, Do the odds favour my playing regardless of the money I have already contributed?'

And on 'blue oceans' and 'second mover advantage': 'Never stay in a poker game unless there are at least three suckers. If possible, let them do your betting for you.'

Arbuthnot's opinion is echoed by the physicist William Thomson, Lord Kelvin:

> I often say that when you can measure what you are speaking about, and express it in numbers, you know something about it; but when you cannot express it in numbers, your knowledge is of a meagre and unsatisfactory kind; it may be the beginning of knowledge, but you have scarcely, in your thoughts, advanced to the stage of *science*, whatever the matter may be.
>
> (Lecture on 'Electrical Units of Measurement', 1883)

Two voices, two centuries apart, illustrating Isaiah Berlin's view (p. 105) of the 'particular twist' of the Enlightenment that reason can be brought to bear on almost every field of study and therefore understanding of anything is dependent upon its measurability.*

This stance is also found in the old adage that you cannot manage what you cannot measure – you have to measure what's important (the key indicators) and then monitor them.

Key indicators can be useful. It is said that the progress of an economic recession can be followed by monitoring lipstick sales. The theory is that at times of hardship women will cut down on costly luxuries, but still allow themselves relatively inexpensive 'treats' such as lipstick. Some people spend a considerable effort trying to identify the 'Leading Lipstick Indicator' for their particular business. This is all very well, as long as the indicator is accurate and not subject to interference.

But we have already seen what happened at Enron, where they identified trite key indicators and measured them clumsily.

The American social scientist Donald T. Campbell (1916–1996) is responsible for 'Campbell's Law', which describes what happens when the measure becomes more important than what it is supposed to be measuring:

> The more any quantitative social indicator is used for social decision-making, the more subject it will be to corruption pressures and the more apt it will be to distort and corrupt the social processes it is intended to monitor.

The cost/benefit analyses of game theorists, behavioural economists and psychologists are necessarily as uncomplicated as possible but they have to exclude all that is not measureable. For example, we now realise that the difficulties of analysing the prisoners' dilemma (p. 45) arise because mutuality (the fear of consequences) is not articulated in the original problem, perhaps because it is difficult to measure.

---

*Critiqued by Einstein's comment (p. 46), 'It would be possible to describe everything scientifically, but it would make no sense; it would be without meaning, as if you described a Beethoven symphony as a variation of wave pressure.'

Determination

One reaction to that is to try to improve your measurements. It is quite easy to go down this path, measuring and monitoring all the possibilities and constructing predictive models of what might happen.

Over-reliance on detailed predictions of what *should* happen can have its own pitfalls. Scientist James Lovelock, himself never afraid to make predictions, warns:

> Gradually the world of science has evolved to the dangerous point where model-building has precedence over observation and measurement, especially in Earth and life sciences. In certain ways, modelling by scientists has become a threat to the foundation on which science has stood: the acceptance that nature is always the final arbiter and that a hypothesis must always be tested by experiment and observation in the real world.
>
> (*The Vanishing Face of Gaia*, 2009)

The same applies to all our projects. Sooner or later we have to face up to the real world.

In March 2006, eight male volunteers were taking part in clinical trials of a new drug, TGN1412, at Northwick Park Hospital in London. One after another they were given intravenous infusions a matter of minutes apart. About an hour later it was clear that something was going terribly wrong. Six of the men started to suffer severe headaches, fever and shivering, back and stomach pain, diarrhoea and vomiting. Blood tests revealed that their white blood cells were fast disappearing; the direct opposite of what was expected in the trial. Two lucky volunteers were unaffected, having received a placebo as control. By the end of the day, the other six were in intensive care fighting a 'cytokine storm' – the potentially fatal uncontrolled reaction of the immune system. By day two, all were suffering multi-organ failure. No lives were lost, although the long-term effects remain to be seen.

After investigation of the incident, one particular recommendation was made that, with hindsight, but even to the layman, seems blindingly obvious – that the drugs should have been administered at greater intervals and in increasing dosages so that the trial could be stopped if there were adverse reactions: 'The dose calculation would have been lower, the drug would have been given sequentially with a gap between each volunteer and it would have been given more slowly. One person might have been affected, but more mildly.'

So why did the volunteers receive the drug in the way that they did? The short answer is that there was no reason to expect that anything would go wrong – as part of the preliminary animal testing no adverse reactions had been observed in macaque monkeys with 500 times the dosage. All the protocols had been followed.

It has been suggested that the reason why the drug induced the cytokine storm is that the drug was so specific to humans that it would not have any effect on monkeys. As always, mistakes point the way forward; which is of little comfort to the six volunteers. Nor is it of any consolation to TeGenero AG, the pharmaceutical research company behind TGN1412 – despite being exonerated, they filed for insolvency within months, finding it impossible to attract further investment.

As Robert Burns pointed out, 'The best-laid schemes o' mice an' men gang aft agley.' Even if our measurements are really detailed and accurate, we cannot measure that which we are not aware of – we are back with those 'unknown unknowns'.

To bring this into focus, let us quote two economists who might not be thought to agree on very much. First, let's return to American economist Frank Hyneman Knight previously quoted on p. 131, who emphasised 'the fact that the risk involved in entrepreneurship is not and cannot be a known quantity'.

But:

> The term 'risk,' as loosely used in everyday speech and in economic discussion, really covers two things which . . . are categorically different. The essential fact is that 'risk' means in some cases a quantity susceptible of measurement, while at other times it is something distinctly not of this character; and there are far-reaching and crucial differences in the bearings of the phenomenon depending on which of the two is really present and operating. There are other ambiguities in the term 'risk' as well . . . but this is the most important. It will appear that a *measurable* uncertainty, or 'risk' proper, as we shall use the term, is so far different from an *unmeasurable* one that it is not in effect an uncertainty at all.

Second, John Maynard Keynes writing in 1937: 'About these matters there is no scientific basis on which to form any calculable probability whatever. We simply do not know!'

A certain irony may not have escaped the readers' notice: the very area of uncertainty, knowledge of which is 'very small and confus'd' and 'meagre and unsatisfactory', has since become of enormous interest to the mathematicians and physicists so highly regarded by Arbuthnot and Kelvin. We have already touched very lightly on Chaos Theory – we will not be going anywhere near Heisenberg's Uncertainty Principle – but it is important to realise that the incalculable cannot be dealt with simply by turning it into an abstract concept, giving it a name and carrying on as usual.

From our point of view, problem solving, an 'unknown unknown' is, by its nature, impossible to predict and so in order to proceed we could rely on being lucky or, more sensibly, we could supplement luck with a contingency plan.

There are many situations where it is nigh on impossible to calculate the odds on anything.

Let's suppose that we are at a magic show. The magician gives us a sealed pack of cards, which we open and, having discarded any jokers, etc., shuffle. We then pick a card, return it to the pack and shuffle again. What are the odds of the magician finding our card in the pack? One in 52, says the statistician. But hang on a minute – we are at a magic show, so maybe it should be a 100% certainty that he will find it. But hang on a further minute – that wouldn't be much of a trick for a professional magician, so maybe it should be a 0% chance of finding it in the pack, because the 100% certainty is that it will be found somewhere else, somewhere inconceivable. But hang on one last minute – who is to say it isn't a comedy act à la Tommy Cooper or a hidden camera show? Not only can we not be sure where the card will be found, we cannot be positive that it will be found at all – that's uncertainty, and that's the attraction of the show.

Damon Runyon gives his unique outlook on the absolute certainty of the highly improbable in his story 'The Idyll of Miss Sarah Brown' (better known in its musical manifestation, *Guys and Dolls*). Sky Masterson's father gives him this advice: 'Some day, somewhere, a guy is going to come to you and show you a nice brand-new deck of cards on which the seal is never broken, and this guy is going to offer to bet you that the jack of spades will jump out of the deck and squirt cider in your ear. But son, do not bet him, for as sure as you do you are going to get an ear full of cider.'

Determine – look to the future

This is the final part of our problem-solving process. After all that exploration and wandering around, we have to refocus our minds and concentrate on that 'imagined future'.

We quoted Robert Burns about the best-laid plans going awry but the worst-laid plans are almost bound to fail.

In 1946, the British government authorised the expenditure of £25 million to promote the growing of peanuts in East Africa. The plan ticked several boxes: there was a ready market for vegetable oil in post-war Europe – rationing was still widespread – and it would be an example of a new type of colonialism, bringing modern agriculture and economic development. By the early 1950s, when it finally fizzled out, the Groundnut Scheme, as it was known, was a byword for disaster.

The conclusions of the relevant chapter of a modern study for the think tank the Institute of Economic Affairs cannot be bettered as a summation:

The very concept of mechanisation (replacing cheap labour with expensive capital) was totally inappropriate for East Africa; the notion of economies of scale with such variable conditions over a wide area was misplaced; infrastructure requirements were grossly underestimated; and the failure to arrange for a pilot scheme was an extremely expensive mistake.

At a more down-to-earth level, there was inadequate data on rainfall, insufficient analysis of the soil and failure to appreciate the many problems in clearing the ground. For a large agricultural project these are rather serious shortcomings. A widespread scientific research programme was to follow, not precede, the large-scale implementation of the scheme.

Finally there was a costly delay of two years before the government admitted the plan was hopeless. This may have been genuine incompetence, but more likely it represented the minister's attempt to save face.

> Overall this grandiose project was a complete fiasco, well deserving its place in our folk memory more than half a century later. The cost was large (£1,150 million) and it is hard to point to any offsetting benefit at all.
>
> (*They Meant Well: government project disasters*, D. R. Myddelton, 2007)

The Groundnut Scheme is sometimes cited as an example of the inherent failings of socialist government planning. So, by way of balance, we should also note a less well-known but similarly disastrous scheme of the arch-capitalist Henry Ford, recounted in Greg Grandin's 2009 book *Fordlandia*.

By the late 1920s, Ford wanted to secure his own supply of rubber for the millions of tyres for the hundreds of thousands of cars rolling off his production lines. To that end he purchased a large tract of land in Brazil and established 'Fordlandia', which he hoped would become the largest rubber plantation in the world. His vision included exporting the American lifestyle – he built neat rows of tin-roofed houses and self-service canteens dispensing hamburgers (and presumably apple pie). In return, he expected regular hours and no alcohol. In 1930, the workers rioted, but labour relations were the least of Ford's problems – his rubber plants were also refusing to conform to 'Fordism'. Although native to the region, they were not suited to monoculture. The rubber plantations in Asia that Ford was emulating thrived because they were an alien species, having been removed from the Amazon's indigenous pests and diseases. A British journalist visited in 1931 and reported in the *Indian Rubber Journal*: 'In a long history of tropical agriculture, never has such a vast scheme been entered in such a lavish manner, and with so little to show for the money. Mr. Ford's scheme is doomed to failure.'

In 1933, Ford bowed to the inevitable and hired a botanist.

Ford never actually visited the site but his friend Walt Disney did, producing *The Amazon Awakens*, extolling the scientifically balanced meals, the schools and day nurseries, the hospital and the golf course. The film claimed that 'two million acres of jungle are being converted into a highly modernised plantation, capable of producing rubber on a large scale'. But the truth is that they never produced anything approaching their targets. The scheme limped on heroically until 1945, by which time rival synthetic materials had removed any remote chance of ever making a profit and the land was sold back at a token price.

Neither the Groundnut Scheme nor Fordlândia was an original concept. We have already touched on the 'breadfruit scheme' as implemented by Captain Bligh and the *Bounty*. That enterprise followed a successful series of experiments in the South Seas. Bligh had sailed with Captain Cook, who distributed seeds of melons and pineapples during his voyages, not from solely altruistic motives. On the subject of Tahiti, he wrote that 'it does not produce any one thing of intrinsick value or that can be converted into an Article of Trade; so that the value of the discovery consists wholy in the refreshments it will always afford to shipping in their passage through these seas; and in this it may be greatly improved by transporting hither horned cattle, etc.'

William Selkirk (the inspiration for *Robinson Crusoe*) survived his four years on the island of Juan Fernandez courtesy of the descendants of goats that had been deliberately introduced by the island's eponymous discoverer.

Such introductions were simple trial-and-error ventures – there was no cost after the initial investment in seeds or livestock.

The American entrepreneur John Osher listed seventeen mistakes entrepreneurs need not make. Failing to spend enough time researching the business idea to see if it's viable comes top. 'This is really the most important mistake of all. They say 9 of 10 entrepreneurs fail because they're undercapitalised or have the wrong people. I say 9 of 10 people fail because their original concept is not viable. They want to be in business so much that they often don't do the work they need to do ahead of time, so everything they do is doomed. They can be very talented, do everything else right, and fail because they have ideas that are flawed.'

We have used the word hindsight a lot in this book – inevitable when we study the past – and in many ways hindsight is the only sight we've got. Much of the time failure is self-defining; it's easy to spot and easy to be wise after the event. When sitting in judgement on the mistakes of the past, it is easy to remark that 'They didn't think it through.'

In 1935, the Australian government introduced the cane toad (*Bufo marinus*) to the sugar plantations of Queensland as a biological control for native cane beetles. The effects have been far reaching: the toads have had a still unquantifiable impact on Australian biodiversity, spreading into New South Wales and the Northern Territory. They are now regarded as a serious pest, along with feral foxes, rabbits, camels and goats, all previously introduced without too much thought for adverse consequences. But the cane toad was not released without forethought. It had been introduced to the sugar plantations of Puerto Rico over fifteen years previously and adjudged a great success. It had also been used in Hawaii and the Philippines. Moreover, the widespread release of toads in Queensland was delayed for a year while a trial introduction was observed. With hindsight, it's easy to be critical but 'It seemed like a good idea at the time' can be a reasonable defence. And the general principle of biological pest control has been very successful when developed with foresight and proper trials. For example, nematode worms, which prey on a range of pests, can be bought by the general public in garden centres or by mail order.

Some unintended consequences can occur a long way from their source. For example, the predominance of private health care in the USA might well be the result of the government-sponsored wage freeze after the Second World War, which encouraged employers to offer medical insurance in lieu of a pay rise.

Another instance is even less foreseeable. Road safety has appreciably improved since the 1970s, leading to a dramatic decrease in the number of accident victims available to donate organs for transplant. As a consequence, the quality threshold of organs obtainable has been reduced and the average donor age has increased from around 30 to 45 years.

Another example from the area of health and safety illustrates that the best-meaning of initiatives may not achieve their goals, even though initial figures seem encouraging. Cycling is generally considered *good* – for health and fitness as well as for the environment. Head injuries are generally considered *bad.* Therefore: compel cyclists to wear helmets and there will be a reduction in head injuries. And so it proves to be – head injuries *are* reduced, but largely as a result of *fewer* riders taking to the road, which reduces the overall health benefits of cycling.

A study by Piet de Jong, 'The Health Impact of Mandatory Bicycle Helmet Laws' (2010), concludes:

> In jurisdictions where cycling is safe, a helmet law is likely to have a large unintended negative health consequence. In jurisdiction [sic] where cycling is relatively unsafe, helmets will do little to make it safer and a helmet law, under relatively extreme assumptions may make a small positive contribution to net societal health. As such, helmet legislation appears to be a distraction from the main bicycle related health issue: the safety of the bicycling environment.

And what about this as a problem waiting to happen? The Human Genome Project promises enormous medical progress. According to Richard Dawkins: 'discoveries are providing clues to novel therapies to treat inherited diseases which are currently incurable' and 'Your genome could now be fully sequenced in just three weeks for less than £10,000. It will not be long before it will cost no more than a hospital scan. A complete genome test may become part of our routine health care within the next ten years.'

The development of novel therapies sounds good but must be preceded by the identification of such inherited conditions: what are the implications of such knowledge for health insurance, for example? It could be said that data protection will prevent insurance companies from denying cover to those prone to inherited illness but are we thereby to forbid those who pose less of a risk for insurers from seeking a discount?

We ought to accept that people in general are neither malign nor wilfully stupid, although as we discussed right at the start with reference to the tragedy of the commons, conflicting interests and short-termism can make us pretty gloomy.

The German philosopher Hegel said of the study of history in general, 'that peoples and governments had never learned anything from history, nor acted upon any lessons they might have learnt from it'.

Maybe it is too much to ask that the instigators of the Groundnut Plan should have had a subscription to *The Indian Rubber Journal* and read the criticism of Fordlândia, but they should have been aware of other attempts at introducing 'modern' methods. As we have seen, individual innovators through the ages *have* learned from their own and others' mistakes and, in the light of our studies, the chances of success, whatever the project, will be enhanced by a decent appraisal of the probable consequences of our actions.

Present your chosen solution as a clear proposal

- A formal proposal acts as the benchmark for your implementation plan – it sets the final agenda.

   (This is the **definition** of our final fractal; next we will **explore** likely barriers to implementation before at last we **determine** our course of action for the future.)

Your solution may exceed your criteria for success or it may only be a partial solution. Does this affect the resources you need? You may need to address this as a separate problem, taking it right back to the beginning. We don't want to leave any unanswered questions. Most importantly, if our solution answers the needs of more than one 'stakeholder' in the problem, we ought to recognise the possible complications.

Triumph or disaster – the Aérospatiale-BAC Concorde

On the one hand it was a triumph: by the time it started scheduled flights in 1976, it had seen off its American and Russian rivals. Concorde flew for 27 years, consistently outperforming subsonic airliners, exactly as it was designed to do. Apart from the terrible crash in July 2000, which effectively enforced its retirement, it had an enviable safety record. Today it takes around seven and a half hours to fly from London to New York; Concorde could do it in less than three hours.

On the other hand it was a disaster: only twenty aircraft were ever built, at stupendous cost, subsidised and underwritten by the French and British governments at every stage. For the average taxpayer, who could never afford to fly with it, the undeniable thrill of seeing it in flight was the only return on the billions of pounds the whole project cost.

One way of deciding whether it was triumph or disaster is to pose the type of questions we have asked throughout our problem-solving process.

What was the problem/need/opportunity that Concorde was built to address?

What were the criteria for success?

Who were the 'stakeholders' and what was the outcome for them?

The key to understanding Concorde is identifying the stakeholders.

For the aerospace industry it was an opportunity to show what they could do – a challenge to their technical abilities not unlike that faced by their contemporaries at NASA.

The politicians had different needs – jobs and national prestige were important, but one of the underlying drivers behind the project was a belief among some British leaders that an Anglo–French venture would assist Britain's entry to the European Economic Community, which French President General De Gaulle had vetoed in 1963.

As for the airlines and their passengers, strange as it seems to say, no one thought to ask them! It would seem that no market research was carried out at all; the general assumption was that speed was the way forward.

So what was the outcome for each of these?

For the engineers and test pilots it must have been a project that they were very proud of, and the problems they faced and overcame must have taken their industry forward to the wider public good.

For the politicians (and the taxpayers) it must be accounted a failure – De Gaulle used his veto once more in 1967. Furthermore, although both governments knew that costs were out of control and at different times desperately wanted to cancel the project, they were unwilling to take the blame by actually pulling the plug themselves.

For the airlines and passengers we see now that numbers, not speed, were the future.

Concorde was not actually as fast as all that – hours in the air are only part of the trip. With transcontinental flights asking passengers to check in three hours before take off and time taken before you even get to the airport, the time saved by flying supersonic is far less than half of the total journey time. Concorde was designed for transatlantic flights – longer journeys requiring refuelling meant that a Boeing 747 would be able to fly from London to Sydney faster than Concorde.

Knowing what we do about the difficulties of foretelling the future, we might be tempted to accept that Concorde 'seemed like a good idea at the time'. They had no evidence at all, however, to back that assertion.

The 1989 film *Field of Dreams* has the central message, 'If you build it, he will come.'

Magic realism is all very well in Hollywood but, in the 'real' world, pre-concept thinking ought to mean that we don't have to rely on blind faith.

There are hazards even in projects with several disparate stakeholders whose goals *are* clearly defined at the outset. Failure in one department may be excused or disguised by success in another; over-achievement may lead to an unplanned expansion in another department, throwing the whole venture out of balance. We might say someone has moved the goal posts; the military expression is 'mission creep'.

Examine possible barriers to acceptance

It is hard to think of any innovation that has been welcomed with completely open arms; quite apart from vested interests that may be threatened, there are always others who only see the downside. So airbags and seat belts in cars are said to be dangerous because, among other things, they give drivers an exaggerated sense of safety. Sherbet lemons turn out to rot your teeth. Even penicillin is said to be bad for us because over-prescription of antibiotics leads to resistant strains of bacteria.*

We have already noted the way that innovation eventually becomes 'common sense'. Physicist Max Planck is quoted as saying, 'An important scientific innovation rarely makes its way by gradually winning over and converting its opponents: it rarely happens that Saul becomes Paul. What does happen is that its opponents gradually die out and that the growing generation is familiarised with the idea from the beginning.'

William Beveridge records this distinction: 'It has been said that the reception of an original contribution to knowledge may be divided into three phases: during the first it is ridiculed as not true, impossible or useless; during the second, people say there may be something in it but it would never be of any practical use; and in the third and final phase, when the discovery has received general recognition, there are usually people who say that it is not original and has been anticipated by others.'

(This tripartite description exists in various versions: Beveridge attributes his to Scottish cardiologist Sir James Mackenzie, who, among many other achievements, invented the polygraph – so it must be true!)

American sociologist Ron Westrum (*Technologies & Society*, 1991) categorises what he calls the 'Rhetoric of Denial':

1. The proposed invention is impossible because it violates scientific laws.

2. The would-be inventors are not competent; true experts have already given up the possibility of the invention.

3. Even if the invention were developed, it would have only academic interest because routine use would cost too much.

4. If the invention were developed, it would have side effects so negative as to render it worthless or even dangerous.

5. Alternative lines of development that would meet the same needs seem more promising and are already being pursued by competent authorities; many of these improvements are made to current, well-understood systems.

---

*One novel solution would be to rotate the use of different antibiotics in order to create 'firebreaks'. Such firebreaks could, perhaps should, have been introduced at the outset – the bacteria are evolving in precisely the manner predicted by theory.

With hindsight, after the innovation has 'won through', it becomes difficult to imagine how we managed without it, whatever it might be. And it appears that it has always been so: 'We who lived before railways, and survive out of the ancient world, are like Father Noah and his family out of the Ark. The children will gather round and say to us patriarchs, "Tell us, grandpapa, about the old world." And we shall mumble our old stories; and we shall drop off one by one; and there will be fewer and fewer of us, and these very old and feeble' (W. M. Thackeray, 1860).

Luckily for us, Thackeray and others recorded their stories and it is possible to track backwards through generations of discontent.

The building of the first rail network is often thought of as a great enterprise, which revolutionised transport, but it wasn't always seen as such at the time. Monsal Dale in the Peak District National Park is a famous beauty spot. Thousands of motorists, walkers and cyclists enjoy the peace and quiet of the Derbyshire countryside. If they take a photograph it is often of the picturesque Monsal Viaduct built, despite protest at the time, in 1863.

The critic John Ruskin did not mince his words about the 'enterprise': 'You Enterprised a Railroad through the valley — you blasted its rocks away, heaped thousands of tons of shale into its lovely stream. The valley is gone . . . and now, every fool in Buxton can be at Bakewell in half-an-hour, and every fool in Bakewell at Buxton; which you think a lucrative process of exchange — you Fools Everywhere.'

Ruskin was not alone in his dislike of that sort of progress. Here is Sir Harry Smith recalling his Spanish wife's first experience of England: 'The delight of our journey to and from Bath is not to be described. Everything was modern, novel, and amusing to my wife . . . No brutal railroads in those days, where all are flying prisoners. We dined where we liked; we did as we liked.'

We have noted that coach services were efficient and reasonably fast. But in their day coaches had not been universally welcomed as progress. Here is John Aubrey's account of the opinion of Thomas Tyndale, 'an old Gentleman that remembers Queen Elizabeth's raigne and Court': 'He hath seen much in his time both at home and abroade; and with much choler inveighes against things now :–Alas! O' God's will! Now-a-dayes every one, forsooth! must have coaches, forsooth! In those dayes Gentlemen kept horses . . . In Sir Philip Sydney's time 'twas as much disgrace for a Cavalier to be seen in London rideing in a Coach in the street as now 'twould be to be seen in a petticoate and wastcoate.'

Ironically, much of the railway network of Britain lasted little more than a century. Enthusiasts who regret the passing of the old technologies might find their view of 'living' engines being replaced by impersonal diesel and electric trains remarkably similar to those of Thomas De Quincy in 1849, although he was talking of their beloved steam: 'seated on the old mail-coach, we needed

no evidence out of ourselves to indicate the velocity'. 'But now . . . iron tubes and boilers have disconnected man's heart from the ministers of his locomotion . . . and the trumpet that once announced from afar the laurelled mail, heart-shaking when heard screaming on the wind and proclaiming itself through the darkness to every village or solitary house on its route, has now given way for ever to the pot-wallopings of the boiler.'

Many of the old routes, including the one through Monsal Dale, are now used as footpaths and cycle tracks. Some have even been reinvented as bridleways: it would be nice to think that Thomas Tyndale would approve, but some people are never happy.

Here is one of those rare acknowledgements from critics that they might have been mistaken: on July 17th 1969, the day after *Apollo 11* was launched, the *New York Times* published this 'correction':

On Jan. 13, 1920, Topics of The Times, an editorial-page feature of The New York Times, dismissed the notion that a rocket could function in a vacuum and commented on the ideas of Robert H. Goddard, the rocket pioneer, as follows: 'That Professor Goddard, with his "chair" in Clark College and the countenancing of the Smithsonian Institution, does not know the relation of action to reaction, and of the need to have something better than a vacuum against which to react – to say that would be absurd. Of course he only seems to lack the knowledge ladled out daily in high schools.'

Further investigation and experimentation have confirmed the findings of Isaac Newton in the 17th century and it is now definitely established that a rocket can function in a vacuum as well as in an atmosphere. The Times regrets the error.

In the course of an article about the Internet in 1999, Douglas Adams suggested, tongue only slightly in cheek, that you could use his threefold system to reckon your own age:

1. Everything that's already in the world when you're born is just normal;

2. Anything that gets invented between then and before you turn thirty is incredibly exciting and creative and with any luck you can make a career out of it;

3. Anything that gets invented after you're thirty is against the natural order of things and the beginning of the end of civilisation as we know it until it's been around for about ten years when it gradually turns out to be alright really.

The accelerating pace of change means that people like Thackeray find it harder and harder to hold an audience. Recalling our example of the recorded music industry, most of us have lived through the complete life cycle of several innovations.

Bearing in mind the paradox of the overtaking spacecraft, we must be aware of a dynamic between 'early adopters' – those who jump on the next spaceship first – and those who hang fire and wait to see how the new innovation goes. No one wants to be stuck with Betamax or Windows Vista.

The history of innovation is littered with stories illustrating the rhetoric of denial; the worst of which dismiss new ideas in the fashion of Maréchal Ferdinand Foch, when he was Professor of Strategy at the École Supérieure de Guerre. He is reputed to have said, 'Les avions sont des jouets intéressants mais n'ont aucune utilité militaire'. (Aeroplanes are interesting toys, but of no military value.)

What we rarely hear with such stories is the context in which the offending comment is uttered. Sometimes the context seems to be wilfully ignored. Take, for example, this widely quoted remark of one of the Warner Brothers, Harry, when he was presented with talking pictures in 1927: 'Who the hell wants to hear actors talk?' The isolated phrase makes Warner sound stupid but when you are given the full sentence – 'Who the hell wants to hear actors talk? The music – that's the big plus about this' – and reflect on the coming heyday of Hollywood musicals, the comment makes a lot more sense.

Sometimes we have no context because there is none: there is, for example, no evidence at all that IBM Chairman Thomas J. Watson ever forecast a world market for computers of only five – it's simply an urban myth.

So what's going on? Why is it that so many stories of innovation, from Archimedes in his bath, through Newton and the apple tree all the way up to the computer age, don't stand up to scrutiny? We shall return to this question later but for the moment it's worth checking our sources before taking anything we hear too seriously. The search is often revealing.

It is widely repeated that a group of US senators to whom Samuel Morse demonstrated his telegraph thought that he was 'deranged'. The source of the story is quite easily tracked down; it is found in the reminiscences of Senator Oliver Hampton Smith.

The full story reveals a far more interesting tale. Smith had a run in with an obviously disturbed visitor earlier that day: 'He [the previous visitor] was evidently deranged, and I looked upon Prof. Morse, and his wild talk about electricity, and the certainty of the success of his plan, in the same light, and I was assured by the other Senators after we left the room, that they had no confidence in it.' The very next sentence reveals why they had no confidence: 'There was not at that time a mile of stretched wire for telegraphic purposes in the United States.'

Smith then lyrically praises the worldwide success of the telegraph before disclosing why he has told the tale: 'The object of this sketch is to show the reader the skepticism of good minds, after full explanations on this great invention.' He is telling the story *against* himself and the other senators to explain that a group of supposedly intelligent men in full possession of the facts were unable to imagine the future in the way that Morse could.

Westrum accepts that some of the rhetoric of denial may be reasonable but points out, 'There is a flaw in this calculative rationality, however, and the flaw is the assumption that the rest of the world will remain the same, so that the conditions under which the technology works will never change much.'

Conditions can change beyond the imaginations of inventors themselves. In 2005, Steven Sasson, the inventor of the digital camera, was asked whether he foresaw one of the now omnipresent applications of his creation. He replied, 'Didn't even know about mobile phones back then, so no. We did some initial thinking about looking at the different technical elements of the chain but those other developments were beyond my thinking back in 1975.'

The first telephone call using a portable hand-held device had been made in 1973 by Marty Cooper of Motorola – he called his great rivals at Bell Laboratories. In a recent interview he admitted, 'We had no idea that in as little as 35 years more than half the people on Earth would have cellular telephones, and they give the phones away to people for nothing,' and 'In fact we had a joke that said "in the future, when you were born you would be assigned a telephone number and if you didn't answer the phone, you were dead".'*

Of the many serious predictions made by optimistic innovators, some will be fulfilled, some will not. How can we tell which were accurate and which lucky guesses? And could anyone have predicted the success of cupcakes in modern western culture? Some innovations take *everyone* by surprise.

Then of course there are those who 'just don't get it' even when they really should. When Braben and Bell tried to sell their totally revolutionary computer game *Elite* to Thorn/EMI, one of the companies most able to take it forward, they received a rejection letter that completely missed the point: 'The game needs three lives, it needs to play through in no more than about 10 minutes, users will not be prepared to play for night after night to get anywhere, people won't understand the trading, they don't understand 3D, the technology's all very impressive but it's not very colourful.'

*This was a light-hearted prediction, which may yet turn out to be true. There are, of course, many instances of predictions coming true, although rarely by the same people who brought them about. Arthur C. Clarke famously forecast the communications satellite in 1945, two decades before it became a reality.

A less well-known instance is the artist Sir Hubert von Herkomer (1849–1914), whose astonishing prediction was reported in the *New York Times* (December 21st 1912):

The cinematograph has already shown itself to be a potent factor in daily life and possibly the day will come when one film will take up form, color and sound and reproduce all these simultaneously; when a cinematograph will be laid in every home as your gas or electricity is now laid; when the world's stories will be brought to you in pictorial and dramatic form such as one has not yet dreamed of; every child will be taught geography, natural history, and botany by screen pictures rather than by books; actors and singers be recorded for all time; the progress of any great engineering feat be recorded accurately. In short, the feature will be made of recorded facts.

I will not venture to say it is all for the good of mankind; but man is getting more and more subjective, and his inventive faculties lean altogether that way.

The word seminal is not hyperbole when used for *Elite* – just about every modern computer game with role-play, three-dimensional graphics, flight simulation or open-ended play can be traced back to *Elite*.

We can see that change is nearly always resisted in one way or another, very often in a wholly predictable manner. If our plan fails to convince, it is not the fault of those it fails to convince; it was *our* plan, not theirs, and the failure is therefore not theirs but ours, however unfair that might seem.

Although we might come to expect criticism, there is of course one last reason why we hear the rhetoric of denial and that's when our ideas genuinely are rubbish!

> The fact that some geniuses were laughed at does not imply that all who are laughed at are geniuses. They laughed at Columbus, they laughed at Fulton, they laughed at the Wright Brothers. But they also laughed at Bozo the Clown.
>
> (Carl Sagan, *Broca's Brain*, 1979)

We have used the analogy of solutions as products being brought to a marketplace. It is not too fanciful to think of that marketplace as an ecosystem – a complex interrelationship of many disparate and often competing factors. When we introduce our product we hope for an effect. We are not in a vacuum and, if our actions are to be meaningful, they will cause a reaction.

Earlier in the book we noted the enormous consequences of the 'butterfly effect' and contrasted it with a 'drop in the ocean'. We have seen the disastrous results of the too-successful introduction of rabbits, foxes and cane toads into the unfamiliar ecosystem of Australia; while the foreign invaders of Fordlândia and the Groundnut Scheme were repelled by the very nature they thought themselves superior to.

Some innovations are so successful that they invite imitation: the Million Dollar Homepage spawned several copycat ventures but none of them made as much money. As Alex Tew said, 'The idea only works once and relies on novelty.'

The same words can be used to describe another internet phenomenon of the same time: 'one red paperclip'. Through a series of fourteen online exchanges starting on July 14th 2005, Canadian blogger Kyle MacDonald traded up from the eponymous paperclip to a three-bedroom house in a small town in Saskatchewan.

This sort of project is never quite repeatable because the context in which they succeeded has been altered by that very success – to whatever small degree, *a paradigm has shifted*, the ecology has changed.

It's hard to see how an idea like the Nullabor Links could be repeated exactly, but in the case of the Netflix Prize the new context might very well lead on to further fortune: Netflix Two was announced in 2009 but later cancelled because of security concerns.

The electronics multinational Cisco Systems has overcome intellectual property and other concerns and held two I-Prize competitions.

Lock-ins and Path Dependence

Successful innovation can result in a particular domain becoming 'locked in' to a pattern which is not necessarily the most efficient, because the benefit of changing is outweighed by the cost, making the domain extremely resistant to change. Breaking this 'path dependence' is one of the greatest barriers to implementation.

Probably the most quoted lock-in is the QWERTY keyboard.

The inventor of the typewriter, C. L. Sholes, designed the keyboard in the way he did in order to get around the problem of keys jamming. (The fact that you can type the word 'typewriter' using only the top row must also have been helpful to salesmen.) It was considered important enough to be included on the 1878 patent drawing for the Remington Number Two (the model which really took off).

By the 1930s, advances in manufacturing technology led Professor August Dvorak of Washington State University to attempt the ultimate arrangement. But, so the story goes, by this time QWERTY was so entrenched that the Dvorak Simplified Keyboard was unable to make headway despite its manifest superiority. The argument still rages, especially on the Internet, with all the fervour of the boiled-egg eaters of *Gulliver's Travels*. Jonathan Swift's satire tells of the tensions between the inhabitants of Lilliput and Blefuscu over which end of a soft-boiled egg should be cracked open – the big end or the little end. (Levels of irony are always difficult to detect on the Internet, where 'flame wars' are conducted between devotees of big- and little-endian number ordering.)

It's all a bit of a storm in a teacup; it seems that speed of typing has more to do with practice than keyboard configuration. Also QWERTY has proved adaptable enough to tolerate all the eths and umlauts of the various western alphabets. Several modern languages manage quite well without Q, W or Y. For example, we find AZERTY, QWERTZ and QZERTY as the first six letters of Franco–Belgian, Czech and Italian keyboards respectively.

The idea that QWERTY has held back innovation seems overstated; nevertheless it has left a long trace and continues to hold its own in the extremely dynamic world of text messaging.

The pace of change has meant that some recent lock-ins have been short-lived. The VHS video-cassette achieved market dominance over the Betamax system, but is already on the verge of complete extinction. The ubiquitous compact disc is now so cheap that it is given away but is unlikely to survive. Windows appears to have inherited the earth, but for how long? (In May 2010, Apple overtook Microsoft to become the world's largest technology company by market value.)

Some paths of dependence go back a very long way. One urban myth attributes the standard railway gauge to the width of Roman chariots. Measurements of the ruts in the pavements of Pompeii were said to be very close to 4 foot 8 inches. More significantly, so were the ruts in the stones of Housesteads Roman Fort in the north-east of England, close to the workshops of George Stephenson, who used the gauge on the world's first passenger railway, the Stockton & Darlington. Unfortunately, a little investigation undermines the story: chariots were largely confined to the races, and similarities in width are far more likely to be the result of the structural limitations of timber axles as well as the admittedly variable standard of One Horse's Backside.

Stephenson added a half inch to the internal gauge for the Liverpool & Manchester Railway (to prevent binding on curves) and this was imposed on all new railways in Britain by Act of Parliament in 1846. Even the genius of Isambard Kingdom Brunel could not resist the standard and his Great Western Railway finally succumbed in 1892.

Around the world, however, many engineers had no compunction about ignoring such an arbitrary standard and a multiplicity of gauges resulted, although exports of British design ensured the popularity of 4 ft 8½ in. It was only when long-distance networks started to join up that problems arose. Breaks of gauge could be dealt with by adopting three rails or three wheels, or more often by transfer of passengers and goods.

European and Asian countries found breaks of gauge convenient for strategic purposes: the prospect of a trainload of enemy troops steaming straight through your territory was a sobering reality for much of the twentieth century. The problem of changeover remains, with wheel-changing technology the likeliest solution.

In the USA, railroad development was instrumental in opening up the country. Rivalry between companies and pure chance resulted in the adoption of many different gauges. In the 1850s, the city of Erie passed ordinances ensuring that different gauges were used to the east and west of the city, reasoning that business would flourish at the changeover point. Factions formed, the 'rippers' against uniformity and the 'shanghais' for it. Tracks and bridges were ripped up by the authorities, resulting in a seven-mile break in the line, which lasted for three months before order was restored.

By the Civil War, however, the North was predominantly 4 ft 8½ in. As the war ebbed and flowed, some tracks were destroyed and re-laid to different gauges several times. The end of the Civil War marks the point at which railroads really came into their own – a statement supported by the fact that it was the same time that Cornelius Vanderbilt sold his final shares in steamboats, which had made his fortune, and invested in railroads, which made him an even bigger one. The major Southern railroads finally agreed in 1886 to standardise and embarked on one of the greatest logistical exercises of the age.

From 30 May until the end of the year, up to 13,000 miles of track were altered. The Louisville & Nashville Railroad Company was reported to have changed 1,806 miles in a single day by deploying 8,763 men.

Two or more systems can often co-exist, as long as they don't overlap. Where they meet, there has to be either a 'change-of-gauge' or the adoption of a single standard. Driving on the left- or the right-hand side of the road is a case in point. In Britain the costs of changing to the right are far greater than the benefits: the English Channel is a big enough break-of-gauge already. Sweden, however, with its land borders, felt an increasing pressure to change. And so September 3rd 1967, was named Dagen 'H' (right-hand traffic day), despite the misgivings of many (mostly elderly) Swedes. In an operation to rival the American railroad engineers, all the road signs were altered in a matter of hours. As a matter of interest, once things had settled down, there seemed to be no change in the number of accidents.

Change, however is not always one way: on September 7th 2009, the Pacific island of Samoa changed from right to left, despite the fact that most of their cars and buses were left-hand drive, and the change was very unpopular. It was a deliberate policy to discourage environmentally unfriendly imports from nearby American Samoa, while encouraging the import of second-hand motors from Australasia and Japan, which drive on the left. (Samoans have continued to be bold in their policies. They cancelled Friday, December 30th 2011, moving the International Date Line to bring themselves into the same time zone as their preferred trading partners.)

The advantages that the citizens of Erie sought from transhipment have of course always existed wherever there are changes in modes of transport. In those days the change from sea to land was the most significant. Vested interests, from hotels and restaurants servicing passengers to dock workers and taxmen looking after freight, will always tend to resist innovations which speed up transit. And so it was with the development of containerisation.

Containers had long been used in rail transport and attempts made at standardisation, but it was not until the 1950s that the idea really got going.

The container revolution in intermodal transport was the inspiration of American trucking entrepreneur Malcom [sic] McLean. Abandoning his first idea of rolling trailers on and off ships, McLean realised that detaching the trailer body from its chassis would save space and allow the body to be transferred securely and easily between road, sea and rail. As with early rail development, the boom in the new freight-handling method resulted in a multitude of completely different and incompatible sizes and designs. By 1970, however, global standards were introduced and as much as 90% of all non-bulk international cargo is moved by container.

It was said that Brunel resisted the 4 ft 8½ in gauge because it was unscientific, and it was such a sentiment that had led King Louis XVI of France to ask some of his leading advisers to determine new standard measurements. Unfortunately for him, Louis was not so forward thinking in other matters and he was swept away along with the *ancien régime* of measurement by the Revolution. (The revolutionaries' attempts to decimalise time turned out to be a leap too far.)

While it is understandable that Britain would prefer its traditional standards, based upon things like the distance between King Henry I's nose and outstretched thumb, to such 'continental' aberrations, quite why the otherwise fiercely republican USA rejected such rationality is unclear. The British Imperial units were defined in 1824, but even they failed to replace many local sizes, and historical anomalies remain. For example, using nineteenth-century measures, it is easy to fit an English quart into a Scottish pint pot.

In 1960, the introduction of the International System of Units (abbreviated to SI from the French *Système international d'unités*) sought to impose uniformity in science, while for wider applications we rely on the International Organization for Standardization (*Organisation internationale de normalisation*), commonly known as ISO, not an acronym or initialisation but from the Greek *isos* – equal.

But standards still echo the past. Because of the involvement of the US military in their introduction, ISO containers are measured in TEU (Twenty-foot Equivalent Units) and are now so universal that any change to metric is unlikely. One consequence is that container-ship architects have to work to unusual standard sizes, the 'malaccamax', for example – the largest ship capable of fitting through the Straits of Malacca.

As we have seen, different systems can happily coexist as long as they mind their own business. But even the greatest of enterprises can be undone by the simplest of mistakes.

On September 23rd 1999, after a ten-month flight, the Climate Orbiter spacecraft crashed into Mars at a cost of $125 million. The root cause of the disaster was confusion between some members of the team using the imperial 'pound force' and others using the metric 'newton'. The newton is of course named after the English, and definitely pre-metric, Sir Isaac Newton.

Produce an implementation plan

This is the final stage of the final stage of our problem-solving process; it is the last piece of pre-concept thinking. The implementation plan represents the concept we wish to take forward.

If our solutions represent the *product* of our thinking, we can use the analogy of consumer packaged goods (CPGs) as an indication of success rates in one particular domain for which figures are available. Every year literally thousands of 'new' products appear on supermarket shelves. In marketing terms, the vast majority (estimates vary between 90% and 99.5%) are 'line extensions'; in our terms they represent incremental change. Many of these 'new' products are destined for a short life – inexorably replaced by 'new and improved'. If you return to a hi-tech retailer in three months it is quite likely that many of the products on display today will no longer be there – turnover is that quick.

Radical innovations are very much the minority. How many of these products can be judged as successful is even harder to quantify. No one likes to talk about failure, even though most people accept that their best lessons have been learned through failure. Figures vary widely among different industries, depending upon how one defines a new product and what amounts to failure. It is hard to assess statistics when figures swing from zero to one hundred per cent but, for what it's worth, the average failure rate of new products is around 33%.

That is the failure rate at the *end* of the innovation process – *after* the product is launched. It does not include all those new product ideas which have fallen by the wayside long before launch but have often incurred almost as much time and effort and expenditure. Again figures vary but suggest that around one in ten product ideas survives the development process. Perhaps the most alarming statistic is that 'an estimated 46% of all resources allocated to product development and commercialisation by U.S. firms are spent on products that are cancelled or fail to yield an adequate financial return' (Booz Allen Hamilton, quoted by Robert G. Cooper, *Winning at New Products*, 1993).

The price of failure is not just financial either – staff morale and performance is bound to be affected, as is the organisation's credibility: confidence is vital. But the same study reveals that some 30% of firms achieved a more respectable 80% success rate: 'It is possible to outperform the average, and by a considerable margin.'

So on the plus side, remember once more that all the work we have done so far is still 'pre-concept' – we have still expended little more than brainpower. We have spent nothing on design and development and our budgets of goodwill and credibility remain intact. Way back at the end of our definition stage, we advised a fresh pair of eyes to review progress – it may be time to call on these once more.

Towards the end of Ingenuity workshops at UNIEI, we often split groups who have been working together all day and ask them to present their ideas to each other, as critical friends who will then work in these new groups to try and turn negatives into positives. Obviously, this can present difficulties when working on confidential projects or those with intellectual property sensitivities, but the dangers of groupthink need to be addressed before we enter the final stage of presenting a fully thought-out concept.

Canadian academic Roger Martin (*The Design of Business*, 2009) visualises a 'knowledge funnel' of problem solving/innovation from a 'mystery' through 'heuristic' to 'algorithm'. The heuristic is derived from abductive thinking, a.k.a. intuition or hunch – the exercise of the imagination. (In our terms this is the movement from problem/need/opportunity through exploration and discovery of alternatives towards possible/potential solutions.) An innovation becomes successful once the heuristic (the working solution) has been developed into an algorithm, a reliable, consistent, measurable and repeatable method of exploiting a new concept. (In Martin's terms, our implementation plan looks very like the moment when that algorithm is proposed.)

A successful algorithm can be implemented, monitored and rewarded easily, and is quick and efficient.

He quotes McDonald's as the classic case. The *mystery* (how to satisfy the market for eating out in California) was addressed by the McDonald brothers, who developed their concept of fast food, the Speedee Service System, with a limited menu of burgers, shakes and fries. It was Ray Kroc who saw that this heuristic system could be rolled out across the country. He bought the business and changed the heuristic into an algorithm: 'He simplified the McDonalds system down to an exact science, with a rigid set of rules that spelled out exactly how long to cook a hamburger, exactly how to hire people, exactly how to choose locations, exactly how to manage stores, and exactly how to franchise them.'

Such algorithms are successful because of the massive increase in efficiency – wastage and uncertainty are eliminated – but their rigidity means that they are not conducive to change. If and when circumstances alter, a once-dependable algorithm can become unreliable and the larger and more successful the organisation is, the slower it may be to realise that the game has changed. Again the example is McDonald's, whose tried and tested menu was left looking tired and unhealthy as the world moved on.

Martin contrasts the uncertainty of innovative thinking with the presumed certainty of inductive and deductive reason, noting that although the former may be *valid* (i.e. proved correct with hindsight) the latter is considered *reliable*.*

*This sort of reliability relies on the algorithm being 'correct'. We have already seen how James Lind's trials identified a treatment for scurvy – citrus juice. But this heuristic was changed into an incorrect algorithm (because it was not fully understood) and therefore the innovation failed. It is helpful to know the science behind a technology but it is not essential. The science behind the steam engine followed the technology – as steam engines improved, so did the understanding of how they work. The opposite is the case with regard to the electric motor – the work of scientists such as Swammerdam and Galvani towards understanding electricity preceded the work of engineers like Tesla in finding practical applications by some considerable time.

The ultimate algorithm might be a computer code, automated stock market trading, for example. On 6 May 2010, the US equities market dropped by around 10% in ten minutes. About ten minutes later the market had recovered. So what caused this 'flash crash'? High-frequency trading, where firms use computerised algorithms to trade automatically at incredibly high speed, was at fault. Many such firms stated that immediately the market started falling they turned off their systems; whether they started the crash or not, it exposed a clear cause for concern. The markets have responded by improving their 'circuit breakers', short time delays on trading key stocks which exhibit sudden rises or falls, to try to prevent computerised meltdown. The actual time lag may be as little as five seconds for humans to intervene before the automated trading recommences. The problem with such algorithms is that they have to operate in environments which are far from benign: 'guerrilla' algorithms will try to disguise a trader's presence in the market by carving large orders into smaller unobtrusive packages, while 'algo sniffers' will seek out the opportunities that come with such information. (Incidentally, analysts continue to argue about what caused the flash crash – since they fail to agree about what *has* happened, why should we have any confidence in their predictions of what *will* happen?)

Martin asserts that most businesses follow a common path: the company is born of a creative act which solves a problem (converts a mystery into a heuristic through intuitive thinking). The business then hones and refines that heuristic through analytical thinking into an efficient algorithm. This is a movement from *exploration* to *exploitation*. The focus changes from the *creation* of business to the *administration* of business. Successful exploitation means that the so-called 'reliable' culture may become self-perpetuating. Reliability is easy to measure; therefore it is, according to received wisdom, easy to manage. We have seen how organisations will identify key indicators and monitor them, and reward those who deliver. The algorithm comes to be seen as the 'cash cow', from which all fortune flows, and encourages the very culture which is in fact incapable of coming up with the innovation in the first place. Indeed, since the success of the algorithm depends upon its being capable of being used by personnel far removed from its originators, there is a tendency to create vested interests which are resistant to change.

This helps us to understand one of our earlier examples, why the leading players in the fresh and new world of computer gaming were so swift to reject *Elite*: they had moved from exploration to exploitation. It is only surprising how *quickly* gaming adopted a conservative mindset. We could speculate that they took their model of a computer game from the amusement arcade, where the likes of *Pac-Man* and *Space Invaders* were the logical heirs to the *proven* success of the pinball machine, not realising that the real revolution was not the technology so much as where it was located; after all, not many people had a home pinball machine.

In due course, a competitor comes up with a better heuristic to address the mystery and either supplants the original, or forces a reappraisal – a journey back to the beginning of the knowledge funnel. Martin's concern, which we will return to, is how to maintain a flow of innovation and so avoid the obsolescence which threatens those who live by exploitation alone.

Q: What do telescopes, pigeons, railways and fibre optics have in common?

A: All are technologies that have been used by stock-market traders to gain an edge in time.

There is a plaque on the Campanile di San Marco in Venice to commemorate the day in 1609 when Galileo Galilei demonstrated the telescope to the Doge. Galileo went on to observe the moons of Jupiter and overturn the Ptolemaic model of the universe but, with all due respect to the good people of Venice, it was not cosmology that interested them. Galileo wrote to his brother-in-law that numerous gentlemen and senators had climbed the highest bell towers more than once to witness that ships at sea could be observed two hours or more before they became visible to the naked eye. Such information could be worth good money on the Rialto.

In 1850, Paul Reuter, founder of the news agency, was using carrier pigeons to outpace the postal service and get the latest stock prices from Paris and Berlin before anyone else.

The ticker-tape machine reduced message times to minutes, while the computer age brought so called 'real time' trading. But today the unit of trading time is measured in milliseconds and microseconds and competitive advantage may depend on nanoseconds. The fastest message presumably would transmit at the speed of light, but here's a problem: the fastest overland optical cable is still liable to follow the railroad – rights of way have already been negotiated. The path of least resistance for a railway was determined by herds of buffalo not crows flying. Even the time it takes to bounce a signal from a satellite could be a factor.

The 'Northwest passage', a sea route linking the Atlantic and Pacific oceans in the far north, had been sought ever since the New World was discovered. Countless expeditions tried and failed before Roald Amundsen finally found a way through in 1906. Even so the route was impractical, being frozen over for most of the time. And so the story came to be looked on as an example of the glorious futility of some undertakings. But the explorers' sacrifices may not have been in vain. Climate change might make the voyage passable in the near future but more immediately at least three projects are underway using the route to lay submarine cables which will allow high-frequency traders to gain crucial milliseconds on their rivals.

This is, obviously, in the tradition of Schumpeter's 'creative destruction'. The 'reliable culture' is also in accord with Kuhn's 'normal science'. A new 'algorithm' in science will prove itself effective – and as it is applied to new problems it will reinforce its power. The kudos and the funding will go with the new orthodoxy. It too is a cash cow and creates a vested interest of those who benefit from the reliable returns. But there comes a time when questions that the formula does not address become more insistent. The puzzles and anomalies that Kuhn talked about keep mounting up until the paradigm becomes unsustainable; 'normal' science has to be overturned.

Martin's model comes from the background of free-market capitalism, which tends to be 'red in tooth and claw'. He observes that the deleterious effects of a reliable culture increase the further it is away from the customer but, whether fast or slow, the market ought to have the final word. Consider those domains, however, where the bottom line is less clearly defined, or even lost sight of.

In Britain in March 2009, the Healthcare Commission's investigation into Mid Staffordshire NHS Foundation Trust was published. Concerns had finally been addressed that, between 2005 and 2008, mortality rates in emergency care were between 27% and 45% higher than would be expected, which translates into between 400 and 1,200 deaths. The report makes disturbing reading:

> Although board members assured us that the care of patients was their top priority, this was not apparent from the minutes, or from the decisions they took.

> Decisions were divorced from the reality of care for patients in A&E or on the wards where emergency patients were treated. The trust board was aware at this time that a high proportion of their own staff would have no confidence as a patient in the care at the trust.

> We noted that much of the discussion at the board was dominated by finance, targets and achieving foundation trust status.

> Despite a system that looked good on paper, the trust did not have a clinical governance structure or audit process that worked. It had no effective system for monitoring outcomes for patients and so failed to identify or understand the cause of high death rates among patients admitted as emergencies.

> This was a serious failing. When the high mortality rates were drawn to the attention of the trust, it looked primarily to problems with data as an explanation, rather than poor care.

In June 2010, Andrew Lansley, the British health secretary, concluded that 'The events at Mid-Staffordshire were a tragic story of targets being put before clinical judgement and patient care, focusing on the cost and volume of treatment not the quality.' He announced 'a full public inquiry into how these events went undetected and unchallenged for so long', asking the following questions:

Determination

Why did the primary care trust and strategic health authority not see what was happening and intervene earlier?

How was the trust able to gain foundation status while clinical standards were so poor?

Why did the regulatory bodies not act sooner to investigate a trust whose mortality rates had been significantly higher than the average since 2003 and whose record in dealing with serious complaints was so poor?

Two phrases, 'a system that looked good on paper' and 'it looked primarily to problems with data as an explanation', could have come from our earlier account of Enron. Crude targets and inaccurate measurements leading to a ruthless culture divorced from reality, having a tendency to deal with bad news by shooting the messenger; culminating in disaster – in the case of Enron, $74 billion worth. In Mid Staffordshire the price was paid in hundreds of lives.

This almost unconscious change from exploration to exploitation, with a corresponding emphasis on reliability rather than validity and an increasing distance between those who devise the algorithm and those who implement it, makes it essential that we get it right. Whatever else the managers at Mid Staffordshire may have done, they certainly seem to have done as they were told.

If a plan challenges the priorities (and budgets) of some organisations, then implementation can be variable. In July 2010, Louise Casey, commissioner for victims of crime in England and Wales, described the official code for the treatment of victims as a 'maybe' service: 'Police may ask you if you need support, you might get a visit and you might or might not then get help.' Help on offer varied from none at all to too much: 'If you have had your lawnmower stolen, you probably don't need three phone calls from Victim Support which is struggling to provide support for children who have been abused. The system is based on process and managing it, rather than the needs of victims and witnesses.'

Way back at the beginning, we asked whether box ticking and target setting were a substitute for trust. The answer could be that, if you are *absolutely certain* of your algorithm and want consistency above all else, then go ahead and insist that all the boxes are ticked and the targets met: measure and manage; it worked for McDonald's. But if you have any doubts, then flexibility, initiative and pragmatism should have a place. We need to produce an implementation plan that not only looks good on paper but is capable of dealing with issues which challenge the plan if, or more likely when, they arise.

Having looked at the intended consequences and made ourselves aware of the possibility of unintended consequences, what can we do about them?

Once more a series of questions:

- What about the competition, how will they react? We used the analogy of an ecosystem into which we are trying to innovate. If our introduction is going to have any impact, it is bound to cause a reaction. Remember the negative reaction to the Volstead Act, which banned alcoholic drinks in the USA: the prohibitionists seem to have assumed that everyone would share their high regard for the law – they were mistaken.

Two contrasting reactions can be found in the case of Concorde. A crude generalisation is that the Soviets quickly produced their own supersonic airliner, the Tupolev Tu-144, nicknamed 'Concordski' because of its similarity to the original (not surprising since espionage almost certainly played its part). Although the prototype flew first (the Soviet five year plan had decreed that it would!), it was inferior in many ways and was cancelled by 1978. The Americans, by contrast, launched a competition for a rival, bigger and better design. In response to rising costs and environmental concerns, however, government funding for the winner, the Boeing 2707, was cancelled in 1971. Opposition to American supersonic passenger flight was then turned on the Anglo–French version and Concorde had to go to court before being allowed to fly into the USA. The practical response to the reality of a supersonic service was easily achievable – cheaper fares, an extra in-flight movie, a couple of complimentary drinks and a bag of nuts.

- Do you need to protect your Intellectual Property? There is plenty of advice to be had about the different types of IP – patents, trademarks and copyright – and the legal options to safeguard your investment.

Patent laws have existed since medieval times, originating in a desire to encourage innovation by protecting what we now call 'first-mover advantage' for a specific length of time, after which the innovation becomes 'public domain'. There are pros and cons. On the one hand, a patent will allow an inventor a reasonable head start but, on the other, patents may actually hold back innovation by discouraging other, perhaps more able, people from pursuing a particular line. Also it is possible for inventors to patent far more concepts than they could ever develop simply to deter competition. The World Wide Web, being perhaps the greatest paradigm shift since printing, has of course changed everything. Access to the web through the Internet challenges national and legal boundaries at almost every step. Is it open source or is it piracy? We have already noted file sharing of music; the collaborative competition of the Netflix Prize; and obviously a book such as this could not have been produced without online open content – there simply isn't a library big enough or searchable enough. The open source/piracy debate is enhanced by the remark of free software pioneer Richard Stallman that 'free speech is not the same as free beer'. The dust from these storms of creative destruction shows no signs of settling.

The American inventor Benjamin Holt spent a great deal of effort buying and challenging patents relating to continuous-track technology for his tractors, although arguably his best piece of IP was in 1910 with the trademark 'Caterpillar'.

The prolific engineer Sir George Cayley patented his 'Universal Railway' back in 1826 but precedence for the technology probably goes to a glorious character, Anglo-Irish statesman, writer and inventor Richard Lovell Edgeworth, who in 1770 invented a continuous track which unfortunately had no practical application and so was forgotten, languishing in innovation limbo, until the start of the twentieth century. Edgeworth was a member of the Lunar Society but seemed to lack the practical money-making talents of some of his fellows. He invented both a wind-powered carriage and a one-wheeled, horse-drawn carriage, neither of which troubled wider society.

- How will you monitor implementation?

Many modern CEOs might recognise the truth of Marshal Marmont's comment, 'With 12,000 men one fights; with 30,000 one commands; but in great armies the commander is only a sort of providence which can only intervene to ward off great accidents.'*

- Have you the resources to cope with likely obstacles?

It seems only just that the originators of any innovation should reap the benefits, the first-mover advantage. If, however, the creator is not able to capitalise on this advantage, the initiative passes to the 'second mover'. In other words, 'It's the second mouse that gets the cheese.'

- Will you have the flexibility to react to feedback?

Feedback *will* happen and it will have an effect. Feedback is a lot more complex than merely positive or negative. For example, there might just be the reaction (as imagined by Tolstoy) of Field Marshal Mikhail Kutuzov 'If in doubt, my friend, do nothing.' (*Dans le doute, mon cher, abstiens-toi.*) His motto, 'Time and patience', saw him wait for his opponent's plans to fall apart and served the Russians well in 1812, when he may have sacrificed Moscow to save his army but soon took it back again as winter approached.

- Have you a plan B or even a plan C?

Have you told anyone? If they know you have a plan B, are they less likely to agree with plan A? Are we bold enough to echo the officer leading some of those troops with unloaded guns at Ciudad Rodrigo, 'If we do not do the business with the bayonet, we shall not be able to do it at all.'

So much for the opposition. What about the effect on those on our side?

*If there is one domain that loves plans, tactics and grand strategies, it is the military. The observation that 'no plan ever survives first contact with the enemy' originates in the writings of Prussian Field Marshal Helmuth von Moltke. The 'fog of war', which captures the uncertainty following that contact, comes from his compatriot Carl von Clausewitz .

- How will the solution affect you and your organisation?

The greater the transformative power of the initiative, the more aware we need to be that *our* world is going to change as well. This is a problem that can be overlooked in the flood of enthusiasm. We have seen that there is a difference between exploration and exploitation – the circumstances and talents that brought an organisation, or indeed an individual, to a particular point of accomplishment may not be the same as those needed to take the project forward. The people who own the solution may not, out of pure, understandable self-interest, wish to find themselves training their cheaper replacements. We have already noted the reluctance of some artists to discuss their talents; others in possession of high-performing heuristics (know-how) may be similarly reticent about passing on their secrets.

- How can you 'sell' your solution to your colleagues?

Many organisations have their own vested interests, 'Kutuzovs' who will simply refuse to join in. How are you going to deal with them? Some organisations run like 'well-oiled machines', each part knowing its function and being easily replaceable off the shelf, but most are a collection of individuals with their distinct qualities and foibles, differing talents and ambitions. It is beyond our remit, but we ought to reference a wide literature concerned with the way organisations react to change. Since we noted earlier the limitations of the 'brain as computer' model, a good start would be Stafford Beer's 'Brain of the Firm'.*

One old tactic is to convince people that they thought of it themselves – a newer tactic might be to involve them at an earlier stage.

This is an anonymised example from a UNIEI Creative Problem Solving course. Two participants were partners in a firm which was growing at 15% per annum. Their problem was how to reorganise their existing staff in response to similar projected growth for the next year. They were reaching the end of our process, when they packed away their work on their provisional implementation plan and started on a new document. When the authors asked what was going on, they replied that, although they were sure they were on the right track, they had realised it might be difficult to sell to their employees. So they were making a list of key personnel to go through CPS themselves. They were even going to be bold enough to absent themselves from the 'discovery' sessions. They were confident that they had identified root causes and constraints and so could welcome either confirmation of the direction of their solution, or indeed something better. They had recognised that, when solutions emerge from a context, they are 'owned' by the group rather than any individual. It is always going to be easier to implement change when the solution has common ownership.

- How will *you* adapt to the new situation?

*Watch out that you don't google 'Beer Brain of the Firm'.

This is where it gets personal. Remember Schumpeter's description of the entrepreneur as someone engaged in an act of entrepreneurship. Once that act is accomplished, the person reverts to being a businessperson like any other; we have already noted the change in mindset that accompanies the move from exploration to exploitation.

- What sort of time scale does your 'solution' entail?

If we bear in mind Dirac's advice that 'one must always be prepared that various beliefs one has had for a long time may be overthrown', we ought to ask what is the likely 'shelf-life' of our project. We may embrace the inevitability of Schumpeter's 'creative destruction', but in some cases we might not like to go down with the ship. Are we going to man the pumps or man the lifeboats? John Osher's final mistake that entrepreneurs need not make is the lack of an exit strategy: 'Have an exit plan, and create your business to satisfy that plan.'

Finally, an odd one:

- Could you cope with runaway success? Will you be able to satisfy demand without compromising quality?

It can happen to the best. In February 2010, Akio Toyoda spoke publicly about safety concerns which had resulted in the recall of millions of cars and trucks around the world as well as a brief suspension of production and sales. 'Toyota has, for the past few years, been expanding its business rapidly. Quite frankly, I fear the pace at which we have grown may have been too quick . . . Toyota's priorities have traditionally been the following: first, safety; second, quality; third, volume – these priorities became confused and we were not able to stop, think and make improvements as much as we were able to before . . . we pursued growth over the speed at which we were able to deliver.'

Roger Martin's *The Design of Business* is a compelling description of innovation in business, which we can extrapolate into our wider discussion of creative problem solving, effective decision making and entrepreneurial innovation in general. His description of long-running algorithms is crucial: 'What organisations dedicated to running reliable algorithms often fail to realise is that while they reduce the risk of small variations in their businesses, they increase the risk of cataclysmic events that occur when the future no longer resembles the past and the algorithm is no longer relevant or useful.'

Reliable cultures, however long running, are essentially short-term cultures – they thrive on predictable returns. But as we saw with Bertrand Russell's chicken and Taleb's turkey, past performance is absolutely not a guarantee of future performance. One last bird analogy: the life cycle of the dodo was a long-established algorithm of proven reliability until the day came when the future no longer resembled the past.*

*A note to fans of biomimetics: although biomimetic solutions have been tried and tested for millennia, they too are short term, demanding a return every generation. They are not, and have not been, immune to cataclysmic events – to them an asteroid is an unknown unknown; for us the impact of an asteroid or the destruction of our electric infrastructure by a solar flare would certainly be a *shock* but, knowing what we know, it would not be a *surprise*.

The trouble is that most of us, most of the time are running long-established algorithms, and the reason that we are 'doing what we have always done' is not because we are reckless or wilfully stupid. It is the same reason that we tend to jump to solutions. It is because it works, it is *reliable* (for most of the time). Most of us, most of the time are engaged in exploitation; we have to be – that's what pays the rent. And as a society we tend to acknowledge, with rewards of power and money, those who are best at it. But it is when we realise that long-established behaviours are nearly always short term in nature that we begin to understand why they are resistant to change and how prone they are to disaster.

For example, is it possible that the short-termism which caused the recent banking crisis thrived because banking is itself short term in nature and so, whatever banks might say, they find it very difficult, if not impossible, to take a long view? We are right back to the tragedy of the commons. Management theorist James G. March, back in 1991, wrote that 'Adaptive processes, by refining exploitation more rapidly than exploration, are likely to become effective in the short run but self-destructive in the long run.' He is surely echoing Schumpeter's contrast between the adaptive response and the creative response which will sweep the old world away.

All of which emphasises the purpose of this book – the need for clear thinking, an awareness of what might happen and some thought of how to deal with it. Remember that we are dealing with *wicked* problems, which are complex, where very little is certain or measurable, and there may not be a single, correct answer. It may well be that wicked problems are not conducive to rigid solutions.

Earlier in the book we talked about knowledge transfer – the difference between tacit and explicit knowing – and we used the analogy of cookery. Our implementation plan could, without too much of a stretch, be described as our *recipe* for success. And as we said in relation to cookery books, explicit recipes, as long as they are carried out correctly, will produce the same results every time – just like scientific experiments, or fast-food franchises. They rely on the formula being correct in every detail and, as we said before, users will never discover anything new, except by accident. The algorithm/recipe/formula works all very well as long as the world does not alter. But if certain ingredients run out, or become more expensive, the recipe will have to be adjusted accordingly. What happens when the oil, as an ingredient for cooking with or as fuel for cooking on, runs out?

The other sorts of recipes are much less prescriptive; they rely more on trust that the users possess the skills to make them work in a world where 'the future no longer resembles the past'. The results will almost always be different – some will be worse, but crucially some will be better.

The implementation plan should represent determination and resolution in both senses: as a final expression of this pre-concept process and as the first step in the next.

At the end of this phase, you should have a practical response to the questions posed by your problem definition. The problem has not yet been solved but we should have a good idea of a solution and how to apply it. We should have balanced our *telos* and *techne* and moved to the top right-hand corner of Kirk's Space. We have *finally* arrived at the point where we have a concept to take forward – and, we hope, a far better-quality concept than had we jumped to one as we all too often do – one which is worthy of being developed, designed and finally deployed.

If not, you should not be afraid to reframe, restructure or split your question into parts and re-engage with an earlier position in the light of new insights. To repeat: creative problem solving is an iterative process. The authors assert, however, that our CPS process will always move us forward, towards a solution or towards a deeper understanding of the problem.

One final cautionary tale – this time with a happy ending

Even when conditions seem perfect, the road of innovation can be longer than you might expect.

Foremost among the attractions of the London Borough of Enfield is a small plaque commemorating the opening, on June 27th 1967, of the world's first automatic telling machine (ATM) by the then slightly better-known comedian Reg Varney.

The inventor John Shepherd-Barron recalled the genesis of the project in a speech in 2007. He had been late to visit the bank one Saturday morning in 1965 and had had to cash a cheque at his local garage. In those days it must be remembered that most people were paid in cash; cheque books were only issued to 'trustworthy' bank depositors. Musing upon the inconvenience later that night in his bath (shades of Archimedes), he put together the basics in his mind: an adaptation of the chocolate machines so common on railway stations of the time, together with a security system and six-digit personal number. It was his wife who suggested the next day that a four-digit number would be better. By the following Monday, he had a contract with Barclays Bank.

From an idea in the bath to a contract with one of the world's leading banks in nine days seems almost unbelievable unless you understand the context.

John Shepherd-Barron was CEO of De La Rue Instruments, which manufactured banknote counting machines for their parent company, which had been printing playing cards, postage stamps and cheques for well over a hundred years. Shepherd-Barron was also chairman of another De La Rue company, Security Express, and it was at one of his regular meetings with Barclays that he was able to sell the concept.

The 1967 machine was one of an initial order of six and was very different from today's ATMs. It was simply a cash dispenser exchanging a wrapped ten pound note for a special voucher, impregnated with radioactive carbon 14. The voucher was retained by the machine to form part of the paper trail of traditional accounting.

The technology of the 1960s certainly did not allow for automatic debiting.

The Enfield ATM was popular enough to start that process of continuing incremental innovation which leads directly not only to modern ATMs but also to the whole concept of out-of-hours banking. The notion of 'hole-in-the-wall banking' had occurred independently to the highly successful Armenian–American inventor Luther George Simjian. In 1939, he registered some twenty related patents but trials were discouraging and the development was abandoned. In this instance, the lapsing of patent protection allowed other innovators the freedom to pursue the idea. Plastic cards and magnetic strips; computer networks giving instant balance statements were the developments which sent ATMs all over the world.

So here was the right man with the right idea in the right place at the right time and it still took another two years before the acorn planted in such fertile ground grew into the sapling inaugurated by Reg Varney.

In fact the only original feature of the Enfield machine to survive is the four-digit PIN.

A window of opportunity

Any opportunities we have identified can be taken through the whole process later; we shouldn't confuse our original issues by diverting our efforts. We quoted Linus Pauling saying words to the effect that to have good ideas you must have lots of ideas and reject the bad ones. The principle of selection ought to have been made clear by the end of Phase One and by the end of CPS we are bound to have lots and lots of ideas that simply didn't make the cut. Among these are some that are undoubtedly *good* ideas, but they are not the *right* ideas for our specific problem. For these ideas there are at least three options: we can try to sell them; we can give them away; or we can stick them in our back pocket for another day. Two other options – ignoring them or forgetting about them seem less than sensible – so WRITE IT DOWN!

Innovation is not inevitable – potential is not always realised. The time may not be right, the place may not be right, the people (including us) may not be right. We may be lacking one essential ingredient for success. It may be that we are unable to make our solution pay – because we can't protect it or we can't make a good enough job of it.

Marking the fiftieth anniversary of 'the pill', Carl Djerassi, the chemist whose work underpinned the development of oral contraception, asked whether technocrats and technophobes alike credit the means with more influence on the ends than is justified? Is it not equally likely that the 15-year window of opportunity for the development of oral contraceptives as a practical means of birth control was created by the confluence of two seemingly separate movements in the 1960s: the women's movement and the then geopolitically fashionable focus on the population?

Determination

The window opened and then closed:

> If we had done our chemical work 15 years later, in other words instead of 1950 but in 1965, the biologists would have then done their work in 1968, and the clinicians in the early 1970s, and you would have no pill.

Opportunity recognition: what are the driving forces of innovation?

We started this book with a somewhat pessimistic observation that we are only staying ahead of catastrophe by our ingenuity. As problems arise they have been solved, with the implication that invention is driven by need. We have noted the correlation between crises and opportunities.

'Necessity is the mother of invention' is the phrase used over and over.

> Depend upon it, sir, when a man knows he is to be hanged in a fortnight, it concentrates his mind wonderfully.
>
> (Dr Samuel Johnson)

This quote, as so many others, is rarely placed in context. On February 19th 1777, William Dodd, an Anglican clergyman, stood trial for the capital crime of forgery. His defence was that he always intended to repay the money: 'I leave it, my lords, to you, and the gentlemen of the jury, to consider, that if an unhappy man ever deviates from the law of right, yet, if in the single first moment of recollection, he does all he can to make a full and perfect amends, what, my lords, and gentlemen of the jury, can God and man desire further?'

The jury took only ten minutes to find him guilty but recommended clemency. Dodd's case became a *cause célèbre; Samuel Johnson wrote pamphlets and a petition attracted thousands of signatures; Dodd issued a sermon entitled* 'The Convict's Address to his Unhappy Brethren'. Johnson made his famous remark when asked whether he or Dodd had written the sermon. Despite the campaign and the efforts of his *city friends, who stood by him and raised money to try and bribe the Newgate turnkey, on* June 27th, at Tyburn, Dodd became the last person in England to be hanged for forgery.

Johnson felt absolved of his obligations to Dodd and later admitted his authorship to Boswell with the words, 'I did not *directly* tell a lie: I left the matter uncertain.'

So, despite suggesting that Dodd's talents might have been enhanced by his imminent demise, Johnson knew full well that Dodd was in no fit mental state to craft a sermon and that the necessity was for someone else to plead his case.

Johnson had previously stated his view of linguistic invention:

> Thofe who have much leifure to think, will always be enlarging the ftock of ideas; and every increafe of knowledge, whether real or fancied, will produce new words, or combinations of words. When the mind is unchained from neceffity, it will range after convenience; when it is left at large in the fields of fpeculation, it will fhift opinions; as any cuftom is difufed, the words that expreffed it muft perifh with it; as any opinion grows popular, it will innovate fpeech in the fame proportion as it alters practice.
>
> (Preface to his *Dictionary*, 1755)

One might argue that necessity in language is a little too easily satisfied to compare with other forms of creativity, especially technology or business, but the idea that progress is made by 'Those who have much leisure to think . . . when the mind is unchained from necessity' tallies exactly with no less a man than the father of modern economics, Adam Smith. Division of labour enables individuals and societies to satisfy their necessities efficiently and thereby create a surplus:

> And thus the certainty of being able to exchange all that surplus part of the produce of his own labour, which is over and above his own consumption, for such parts of the produce of other men's labour as he may have occasion for, encourages every man to apply himself to a particular occupation, and to cultivate and bring to perfection whatever talent or genius he may possess for that particular species of business.

> (*An Inquiry into the Nature and Causes of the Wealth of Nations*, 1776)

Economic development is built, therefore, *not by satisfying necessity but by exceeding it* – remember: 'The stone age did not end because of a lack of stone.'

Fifteen or twenty years ago there was no 'necessity' for everyone to have a mobile phone, yet nowadays people feel naked without one. Why, back in the 1990s, did nobody express this 'necessity'? Was it that they didn't know that they needed mobile phones or was it that they couldn't conceive of them as a possibility?

An early user of the phrase was Daniel Defoe and the immediate thought might be: of course, Robinson Crusoe; stranded on a desert island, he has to invent everything from a lamp to an umbrella.

But actually he first used it in the first thing he ever published: in 1697, an essay all about enterprise and invention. For Defoe, necessity is certainly the mother of invention and it is the personal necessity of individuals which is the most potent driving force. He takes a broad view of what constitutes invention. The most desperate will 'turn open thieves, house-breakers, highwaymen, clippers, coiners, &c., till they run the length of the gallows'.

'Others, being masters of more cunning than their neighbours, turn their thoughts to private methods of trick and cheat, a modern way of thieving every jot as criminal, and in some degree worse than the other, by which honest men are gulled with fair pretences to part from their money.' Here he is referring to the new invention of the stock market and he speaks with experience. But, 'Others, yet urged by the same necessity, turn their thoughts to honest invention, founded upon the platform of ingenuity and integrity.'

Defoe was one of the great optimists of his age and entrepreneurship and innovation were things he was most enthusiastic about. He didn't use those words – innovation had been used in a religious context but had fallen from use, while entrepreneurship hadn't even been coined. He used the word project. All quotes are from *An Essay upon Projects* (1697).

The best people for projects are certainly not the aristocracy – they do not feel the necessity; neither are they scholars or clergymen, or lawyers or even tradesmen – they all have nice safe jobs with guaranteed incomes. For Defoe it's businessmen: 'it is in the merchandising part of the world, who indeed may more truly be said to live by their wits than any people whatsoever'. Every deal, every transaction is a project or invention – enterprises through which business 'converses with all parts of the known world'.

This makes businessmen, and merchants in particular, 'the most capable, when urged by necessity, to contrive new ways to live'.

> The honest projector is he who, having by fair and plain principles of sense, honesty, and ingenuity brought any contrivance to a suitable perfection, makes out what he pretends to, picks nobody's pocket, puts his project in execution, and contents himself with the real produce as the profit of his invention.

Daniel Defoe's reputation nowadays is as a writer, but the literary world of the time thought of him as an unprincipled hack journalist, pamphleteer and spy; he had spent time in both pillory and prison for, among other misdeeds, sedition, libel and debt. But he was far more than that: he was at other times a tax-collector, wine merchant, stocking salesman, brick and tile manufacturer – a businessman. If he were alive today he would call himself an entrepreneur – we would probably call him a 'chancer'. But he did deserve his fame – there are many who say that he invented the novel, in the form of *Robinson Crusoe*, which went through six printings in four months in 1719 and pirated translations all over Europe in the next few years. Up to the present day there have been hundreds of editions in over a hundred different languages, not to mention countless stage adaptations, pantomimes and films. Unfortunately for Defoe, he had no copyright protection and probably died while hiding from his creditors.

The fictional hero Crusoe lives on but one of Defoe's real-life heroes is largely forgotten: William Dockwra, who in 1680 introduced the London Penny Post: 'so fine a thought, that had both the essential ends of a project in it (public good and private want)'. So here we have perfect invention – something that satisfies both necessities.

The Post was launched with a fanfare in the newspapers: 'There is nothing tends more to the increafe of Trade and Businefs than a Speedy, Cheap and fafe way of Intelligence.' The service offered would rival any modern courier: 'To the most remote parts [of London] Letters fhall be fent at leaft Five times a day. To Places of quick Negotiation within the City . . . at leaft Fifteen times a day.'

The advertisement ends with this exhortation:

> Therefore we fhall leave all the Ingenious to find out wherein our invention may be ferviceable to them and refer all people to be convinced by Time and Experience,
> The True Touch-ftone of all Defigns.

The ingenious did indeed find the invention serviceable, but rival couriers and the General Post Office were less impressed by these upstarts. Dockwra had known there would be opposition: 'But in this Age it is not to be expected that any New Defign can be contrived for the Publick Good, without meeting many rafh Cenfures and Impediments from the Foolifh and Malicious.'

Ironically, what happened was that the service was so successful that the chief beneficiary of the GPO, the Duke of York (the future King James II), fined Dockwra for breach of monopoly and took over the business. After the Glorious Revolution of 1688, which removed James from the throne, Dockwra regained control but he was dismissed in 1700 following an investigation into his conduct. It turns out he was little better than Defoe at actually translating his ingenuity into hard cash.

The better-known nationwide Penny Post of the 1840s was a reinvention by another 'projector', Sir Rowland Hill, which succeeded through a simple tweak. Hill reduced labour costs by *insisting* on payment in advance, offering customers a further convenience, the option of pre-payment – the self-adhesive Penny Black postage stamp. The GPO's business increased fivefold in ten years and was copied all around the world, the first practical communication technology that operated over distance at an affordable price for the common man. And the business world took full advantage of the possibilities, not least Rowland Hill's brother, who invented an envelope-folding machine.

The success of the Penny Post was based on a very simple premise. Both William Dockwra and Rowland Hill 'aimed for performance through reducing complexity, going for a very simple solution'.

Those are not their words, they are the words of Steve Furber, principal designer of the ARM 32-bit RISC microprocessor, which revolutionised hand-held electronics to the extent that 95% of all mobiles use ARM-based chips – around 20 billion – and he was describing the genesis of that product. RISC stands for Reduced Instruction Set Computing and it works on the principle that simple instructions, executed very quickly, will outperform slower, more complex algorithms; exactly what Rowland Hill achieved with the postage stamp.

The ARM microprocessor was only one factor in changing the mobile from a house brick to a more manageable and affordable product. Other factors are miniaturisation, battery technology and of course economies of mass production. But mass production needs a mass market and which comes first and how each feeds the other are arguable. A comparatively small 'necessity' (or demand) can become a large demand (or necessity). Eric Hobsbawm quotes the car industry as an example: 'It is not the demand for motor-cars existing in the 1890s which created an industry of the modern size, but the capacity to produce cheap cars which produced the modern mass demand for them' (*The Age of Revolution*, 1962).

Mobile-phone usage took off very differently in different countries – in Europe before the US, probably because of infrastructure, which must be linked initially to population density. Once the market is established it can expand into areas of lower population densities, with coverage and unit price as drivers. Mobile-phone infrastructure is, of course, easier to put in place than other infrastructures that we associate with 'civilisation' and so countries can leapfrog our traditional notions of development to the position where everyone has access to a mobile phone *before* they have running water or a sewage system.

In the US during the 1990s, the pager was the gadget of choice. It was used as a plot device in films and sitcoms; there was a whole sub-culture of codes and abbreviations. It was the big thing and it was profitable.

In 2001, there were forty million pagers in the USA but that was the very moment that Orange withdrew its pager service in the UK. Why? Because everything a pager could do and more had been added on to the mobile. The irony is that teenagers in the UK were used to thinking of the USA as trend setting but, while their American counterparts were able to drive their own cars, they were still using pagers!

The technology that enabled text messages to be sent had started out as a deliberate project but the ambitions were limited – engineers; deaf people; later, customer alerts, etc., so it was easy to offer as an add-on. The idea that ordinary people would develop the skill and dexterity to compose messages on a dozen minute multi-function buttons was never part of that project. But for young people, the cheapest way of using a mobile was to text. It was also the quietest; you could do it anywhere. So what was initially an add-on became, for many, the dominant form of usage; and for the phone companies, 'the nearest thing to printing money'. On Christmas Day 2006, over 205 million messages were sent in the UK alone.

Add-ons have become an easy marketing tool for the phone industry; the product consistently gives you more than you ask for, or indeed want – games, cameras, music, video – and the ability to send them to each other. And once again the consequences have been far reaching and in some cases profound.

The product is now inextricably linked with the Internet – YouTube is filled with grainy images taken on phones. The SMS lives on as Twitter.

The point is that none of these innovations have been driven by a pre-existing demand, a perceived necessity: in no way were they born of crisis, nor have they been driven by some far-sighted genius (whatever they might tell us now). But that's not to say they came about by accident: they came about because they could; because someone recognised an *opportunity*, and it may well be that opportunity is a far more important factor in innovation than necessity.

We know that crisis engenders opportunity, but such opportunities are limited:

> I am enthusiastic over humanity's extraordinary and sometimes very timely ingenuities. If you are in a shipwreck and all the boats are gone, a piano top buoyant enough to keep you afloat that comes along makes a fortuitous life preserver. But this is not to say that the best

way to design a life preserver is in the form of a piano top. I think that we are clinging to a great many piano tops in accepting yesterday's fortuitous contrivings as constituting the only means for solving a given problem.

(Buckminster Fuller, *Operating Manual for Spaceship Earth*, 1968)

Crisis-determined choices are always going to be sub-optimal; the array of choices is limited but the lowered risk-aversion makes them acceptable. On top of this we must remember that one man's crisis is another man's opportunity. Machiavelli used the word '*occasione*' for opportunity and there are plenty of his admirers out there waiting for the occasion to take advantage: 'Only a crisis – actual or perceived – produces real change. When that crisis occurs, the actions that are taken depend on the ideas that are lying around. That, I believe, is our basic function: to develop alternatives to existing policies, to keep them alive and available until the politically impossible becomes politically inevitable' (Milton Friedman, *Capitalism and Freedom*, 1962).

Although we have shown the first part of Friedman's statement to be incorrect, the latter part, together with the Machiavellian design, is only too practical. As we suggested earlier, at times of crisis, as well as being aware of opportunities, we should be wary of opportunists.

Nevertheless, we have also seen that opportunities exist independently of crises, so it ought to be possible to look for them, as Dr Johnson said, 'when the mind is unchained from necessity'. Then we might aspire to achieve what Defoe called 'both the essential ends of a project . . . public good and private want'.

Conclusions and Suggestions

> The last chapter is merely a place where the writer imagines that the polite reader has begun to look furtively at his watch.
>
> (Walter Lippmann, 1922)

Underpinning our approach throughout has been that very human faculty that Artificial Intelligence researchers define as common-sense reasoning:

- Reasoning with knowledge that we cannot *prove*.

- Reasoning rapidly across a wide range of domains.

- Being able to tolerate uncertainty in our knowledge.

- Coming to conclusions without complete knowledge and being able to revise those decisions or beliefs as better knowledge becomes available.

It is a method that has emphasised the unreliability of what we think we know and the uncertainty about what we think will happen.

How can such a self-doubting style be consistent with the 'guide for clear thinking' style of our book?*

Practical Common Sense (in Theory)

In an 1878 article entitled 'How to Make Our Ideas Clear', American polymath Charles Peirce introduced a very practical way of thinking: 'Thus, we come down to what is tangible and practical, as the root of every real distinction of thought, no matter how subtle it may be; and there is no distinction of meaning so fine as to consist in anything but a possible difference of practice.'

In a lecture twenty years later, William James explained the reasoning:

> To attain perfect clearness in our thoughts of an object, then, we need only consider what conceivable effects of a practical kind the object may involve – what sensations we are to expect from it, and what reactions we must prepare . . .

> It is astonishing to see how many philosophical disputes collapse into insignificance the moment you subject them to this simple test of tracing a concrete consequence. There can be no difference anywhere that doesn't make a difference elsewhere – no difference in abstract truth that doesn't express itself in a difference in concrete fact and in conduct consequent upon that fact, imposed on somebody, somehow, somewhere and somewhen. The whole function of philosophy ought

*We also promised to raise more questions than answers.

to be to find out what definite difference it will make to you and me, at definite instants of our life, if this world-formula or that world-formula be the true one. [Original emphasis]*

This emphasis on consequences fitted the mood of America at the start of the twentieth century perfectly: 'The test of theories must be found in practise [sic]. The pragmatic philosophy is a renewed emphasis of this truth. It is a philosophy of doing, and of knowing, only in relation to doing. It is a philosophy of work, of activity, of enterprise, of achievement' (Henry Heath Bawden, 1908).

Our definition of creativity was a pragmatic one – new, appropriate and applied. We only call something 'creative' with hindsight, when it has been shown to work. A creative thought is not the same as a creative deed – its nature is only confirmed when it is applied.

Our definition of the entrepreneurial spirit is similarly pragmatic – it insists on action, action whose effectiveness is judged by the value it brings.

'The truth is that which works' sums up the pragmatism of the American philosopher John Dewey (1859–1952). That truth is not of itself certain and immutable, but for the moment it works. This insight allows us to deal with the problem of paradigm shifts; that a new worldview may not necessarily explain everything that the old one did and that there may even be a loss of explanation (p. 23).

This is not to suggest that science is just another social construct. As Peirce puts it:

> On the one hand, reality is independent, not necessarily of thought in general, but only of what you or I or any finite number of men may think about it; and that, on the other hand, though the object of the final opinion depends on what that opinion is, yet what that opinion is does not depend on what you or I or any man thinks. Our perversity and that of others may indefinitely postpone the settlement of opinion; it might even conceivably cause an arbitrary proposition to be universally accepted as long as the human race should last.

Walter Lippmann coined the word 'stereotype' to describe how we construct our worldview and he puts pragmatism in plainer language: 'Our stereotyped world is not necessarily the world we should like it to be. It is simply the kind of world we expect it to be . . . The way in which the world is imagined determines at any particular moment what men will do. It does not determine what they

---

*Pragmatism has its limits: it cannot deal with concepts which have yet to make a difference, and maybe won't actually make a difference, a 'lost opportunity', for example – we know it existed because we missed it, but cannot be sure what difference it might have made. Thankfully, along with the mathematics of emergence, the finer points of philosophy are well beyond our remit (and competence!).

will achieve. It determines their effort, their feelings, their hopes, not their accomplishments and results.'

He describes the problem of a too rigid adherence to any particular model of the world, in this case the 'economic mythology' of his day.

> The myth is, then, not necessarily false. It might happen to be wholly true. It may happen to be partly true. If it has affected human conduct a long time, it is almost certain to contain much that is profoundly and importantly true. What a myth never contains is the critical power to separate its truths from its errors.

> For the distinguishing mark of a myth is that truth and error, fact and fable, report and fantasy, are all on the same plane of credibility.

> It is only when we are in the habit of recognising our opinions as a partial experience seen through our stereotypes that we become truly tolerant . . .

> Without that habit, we believe in the absolutism of our own vision, and consequently in the treacherous character of all opposition. For while men are willing to admit that there are two sides to a 'question,' they do not believe that there are two sides to what they regard as a 'fact' . . . when the real difference between them is a difference of perception.

> But if our philosophy tells us that each man is only a small part of the world, that his intelligence catches at best only phases and aspects in a coarse net of ideas, then, when we use our stereotypes, we tend to know that they are only stereotypes, to hold them lightly, to modify them gladly. We tend, also, to realise more and more clearly when our ideas started, where they started, how they came to us, why we accepted them.

William James called pragmatism 'a new name for some old ways of thinking'. He might have approved of a remark from our old friend Han Fei Tzu: 'The sage neither seeks to follow the ways of the ancients nor establishes any fixed standard for all times but examines the things of his age and then prepares to deal with them.'

We noted, near the start of the book, the way in which stargazers, faced with myriad dots of light, formed them into constellations which reflected their worldview.

Samuel Taylor Coleridge pointed out, way back in 1830, that when searching for principles you have to have a principle of selection yourself: 'You must have a lantern in your hand to give light, otherwise all the materials in the world are useless, for you cannot find them; and if you could, you could not arrange them.'

And so we are always bound by hindsight; we will always find what we are looking for because our 'lantern' only shines on certain 'dots'.

The lantern used by Thomas Carlyle in 1840 picked out fame to determine the driving force in the world: 'The history of the world is but the biography of great men.'

And there is a great deal of material, including academic studies, about innovation, creativity and 'genius' consisting of stories of these great men and how they made their famous discoveries. Presumably, if we can identify and explore the particular qualities which make up those people, maybe we can emulate them.

First, of course, we have to define those 'great men' and, as we know, 'genius' is hard to define, let alone measure.*

Although attractive, a narrative history of connections between 'hero inventors' and 'heroic discoveries' is deeply flawed: we are only able to take into account those inventors and inventions that we know about. We cannot tell who invented the loom or who first domesticated corn. We know nothing about the 'genius' who invented the wheel, so are forced to leave the greatest invention of mankind out of our studies. We are left with that preponderance of 'dead white men' to represent the ingenuity of the whole of humanity. Actually we do know at least one thing about the inventors and developers of the wheel: they were not in possession of the Protestant Work Ethic. Similarly, whoever it was who realised the therapeutic qualities of quinine it was certainly not the Duchess of Cinchona, who was merely the first notable westerner to be successfully treated for malaria by it and so had the tree named after her. Nor can we identify various 'primitives' in different parts of the world who found out how to extract digestible starch from plants like cassava, sago palm and cycads – some of them toxic when untreated.

Even where there are accounts of invention from earliest recorded times, they do not necessarily bear scrutiny. Recent archaeological discoveries have provided evidence of sericulture in the Indus valley at roughly the same time as it was legendarily discovered by a Chinese empress: silk might not be a purely Chinese invention. We cannot seriously study innovation through mythology.**

*However entertaining it might be, a considered critique (actually a thorough debunking) of attempts to measure 'greatness' and 'genius' in both the dead and the living is sadly beyond the remit of this book. Suffice it to say, psychometrics is not a universally respected discipline.

**A considered critique of narrative in the study of innovation is also beyond the remit of this book but it ought to be noted that any criticism of historical narrative is not to deny that history, and life in general for that matter, is diachronic (in other words, 'one damn thing after another') – it is to suggest that causes and effects are not as simple as they sometimes appear.

The American historian Hayden White expounds the problem of narrative:

> Narration is a manner of speaking as universal as language itself, and narrative is a mode of verbal representation so seemingly natural to human consciousness that to suggest it is a problem may well appear pedantic. But it is precisely because the narrative mode of representation is so natural to human consciousness, so much an aspect of everyday speech and ordinary discourse, that its use in any field of study aspiring to the state of science must be suspect. For whatever else a science may be, it is also a practice that must be as critical about the way it describes its objects of study as it is about the way it explains their structures and processes.
>
> (*The Content of the Form*, 1987)

White hits the nail on the head with this last distinction between explanation and description. Narrative comes to us so naturally that we are tempted to use it uncritically as a means of communication to *explain* innovation but it is just as untrustworthy to *describe* the process. This is not to deny the power of narrative but to temper our use of it. Nor is it to deny that the dynamics of society are constructed from the interplay of personal narratives – the psycho-ecologies in which we find problems and have to fit solutions.

From a business standpoint, we could say that narrative is a marketing tool rather than one for R&D. We should be using the power of narrative to 'sell' rather than to create our innovations.

Innovation in context

Throughout this book we have looked at creativity, decision making and discovery as responses to problems. The 'lantern' we have used throughout is change – those eureka moments when discoveries are made and paradigms shift. And if we study the context of each of those moments we gain a broader understanding than we find in a simple diachronic string of causes and effects.

Certain conclusions can be drawn from looking at innovation in context:

Innovation is not inevitable; it does not proceed from necessity alone but requires opportunity.

Radical innovation is not evolutionary; nature does not seem to have invented the wheel: it is revolutionary in more ways than one.*

We have shown that innovations *emerge* from an array of 'old' ideas and concepts, which we use as building blocks to construct 'new' concepts – the wider the array,

*The wheel and axle is a combination, which defies the existing topology of autonomous organisms; it is difficult to conceive of an intermediate stage in its development. Nature does provide examples of combination in symbiosis and parasitism but, conceptually, perhaps the nearest it has yet come to a wheel might be where an organism combines with an inanimate object, e.g. the hermit crab!

the greater the possibilities. And so we should not be surprised that a similar array will produce similar innovations, be it the development of agriculture or the invention of the motor car – in this regard innovation is the inevitable product of the 'Zeitgeist'; there's 'something in the air'.

'Chance' can be regarded as the sudden injection of elements into the existing array, which cause an expansion of that array, consequently increasing the possibilities.

So what? The above is a description of the way innovation works and has worked, with a reasonable degree of success. Despite the gloomy forecasts, there is little doubt that in terms of nutrition, health, life expectancy and material possessions there has never been a better time to be alive. But as in Defoe's time, there have been mistakes and over-enthusiasms – bubbles.

The Venezuelan neo-Schumpeterian economist Carlota Perez describes modern creation and destruction:

> Investment in the new industries is carried out by new entrepreneurs while the young financial tycoons create a whirlpool that sucks in huge amounts of the world's wealth to reallocate it in more adventurous or reckless hands: some for speculation in real estate or in whatever is amenable at the time, some for buying existing assets and some for new investment. A part of this goes to new industries, another to expand the new infrastructure, another to modernise all the established industries, but most of it is moved about in a frenzy of money-making money, which creates asset inflation and provides a gambling atmosphere within an ever-expanding bubble. Eventually it has to collapse. But when it does, the changeover has been made. New industries have grown, a new infrastructure is in place; new millionaires have appeared; the new way of doing things with the new technologies has become 'common sense'.
>
> (*Technological Revolutions and Financial Capital: The Dynamics of Bubbles and Golden Ages*, 2002)

Some people revel in the process, e.g. Bob Metcalfe, Professor of Innovation at the University of Texas: 'I think bubbles are a good thing. I think bubbles are a tool of innovation. They are a way of attracting capital to a promising area, and social networking is a revolution and a promising area that needs investment capital. So the bubble is a way of attracting resources and it serves a purpose in accelerating innovation' (BBC *Newsnight,* 4 April 2011).

As Perez remarks, however: 'It is all achieved in a violent, wasteful and painful manner.'

The grave of Karl Marx bears the legend 'The philosophers have only interpreted the world in various ways. The point, however, is to change it.' And the stakes have never been higher:

> The future of everything we have accomplished since our intelligence evolved will depend on the wisdom of our actions over the next few years. Like all creatures, humans have made their way in the world so far by trial and error; unlike other creatures, we have a presence so colossal that error is a luxury we can no longer afford. The world has grown too small to forgive us any big mistakes.

(Ronald Wright, *A Short History of Progress*, 2004)

But:

Reasons to be Cheerful

1. We are beginning to understand how we solve problems

We call ourselves *homo sapiens*, implying a certain amount of wisdom, or at the very least the ability to think, but it is only in the last hundred years or so that we have started to study exactly how we make decisions and solve problems.

We, the authors, are working with the presumption that creativity is an everyday faculty of humanity, as natural as breathing; that just as we do not learn how to breathe, we do not learn to be creative – it is an ever-present element of our consciousness and what we call 'genius' is one end of a continuum. ('Genius' is a word which may be better used to describe a moment than a person, a moment of creativity which takes us by surprise through its sheer quality.) Just as singers and sportsmen sometimes have to re-learn their breathing techniques to improve their performance, we should be able to enhance our natural abilities with practice. For our purposes, the potential for improvement is so vast that any distinction between nature and nurture becomes a question of academic rather than practical significance. Every one of us ought to be capable of moments of 'genius'. As our understanding of ingenuity increases, so should our ability to make use of what we know to be our greatest resource – the human mind.

2. We have an unprecedented new technology

Creativity depends upon two things: the generation of an array of possibilities and the ability to evaluate them.

An individual human (or indeed any conscious organism) is limited to its own experience and its ability to recall that knowledge.

Communication between individuals increases the available memory; language must be seen as the first great leap forward.

Trade and barter between individuals probably developed hand in hand. The account-keeping that accompanies trade seems to be a vital stage in the development of physical records from the cuneiform clay tablets of Mesopotamia to the knotted strings (quipu) of the Andes. (There is a case to be made that the invention of double-entry bookkeeping is a greatly underestimated step change in civilisation.)

The alphabet has been the dominant technology of connectivity, but not the only one: recordings of any kind, whether oral transmission, pictures, musical notation, the postal service, the telegraph, movies, radio and television are all technologies for storing and accessing information.

Each technological leap increases the connectivity.

The latest and biggest such leap (at least as big as printing) is the World Wide Web. (It must be significant that its abbreviation takes longer to say, but less to type.)

> My goal for the web in 30 years is to be the platform which has led to the building of something very new and special, which we can't imagine now.
>
> (Tim Berners-Lee, BBC *Newsnight*, 2005)

We talked right at the beginning of the book about the Internet being the collective brain of humanity. A couple of observations suggest that it is a development in connectivity we are only just beginning to come to terms with.

Nowadays reading and writing tend to be taught together. It was not always so. Reading, writing and reckoning were exclusive skills not thought necessary for all. Even when literacy became more common, there was a distinction between consumers and producers; the attitude seemed to be that the lower orders and women might be taught to read 'improving texts' but ought not expect to be able to write themselves – that would suggest that they had something worth saying.

Most previous information technologies have been largely under the control of those in power, those who could read or write or count, those who could afford pen and ink – or a printing press or multi-media empire. This technology is different.

The American writer Clay Shirky uses the phrase 'cognitive surplus' to describe the way people are no longer spending all their time in front of screens consuming, but are actually producing material. And social entrepreneur Iqbal Quadir has said that 'In the past technology has been driven by business – nowadays the unit of business is the individual consumer of technology rather than the producer.'

How the powers that be react to this flood of user-generated content remains to be seen. Governments would like to control it; multinationals would like to charge for it. But for problem solvers and innovators the implications are incalculable. (For a start, a book such as this would not have been possible ten years ago.)

3. We have a strategy to improve our success rate

The imperative to innovate is ubiquitous in the modern world; it is the only thing upon which both the doom-mongers and the cornucopians agree. There are many voices speaking about the need to innovate; this book adds to the considerably lesser number that provide concrete suggestions as to *how* to do it.

A methodology like ours is open to the criticism that it is 'creativity by numbers'; a mechanical process cannot match the organic creativity of a human being. To this, there are two responses: first, anything transmitted by digital technology is reproduction by numbers – most of our sense data are digitised these days (Mr Deeds was not pixilated in the film but is certainly pixelated in the DVD). Secondly, and critically, the moment any digital data hits the human mind it undergoes a sea change – remember Baldwin: 'The individual thinks and imagines in his own way. He cannot give back unaltered what he gets, as the parrot does. He is not a repeating machine. His mental creations are much more vital and transforming. Try as he will he cannot exactly reproduce . . .'

To recap: the subject of our book is problem solving; it consists of material collected using the 'lantern' (principle of selection) of change; and the framework we have used to display our materials is our Creative Problem Solving methodology, a methodology that we believe helps select optimal solutions from the widest range of possibilities.

It is a method that seeks to restore the link between imagination and reason in problem solving and decision making.

By improving the quality of ideas 'pre-concept', we ought to reduce the violence, the waste and the pain of change itself.

By emphasising opportunity as a vital element in innovation, we ought not to have to wait on chance. Entrepreneurial thinking encourages us to recognise opportunities and take action to 'bring value'. Every one of us is capable of moments of 'genius' if, like the entrepreneur, we recognise them and take action to realise them.

Bibliographical Note
(actually a final diversion)

Right at the beginning of this book, we directed the reader to leaner expositions of the ingenuity process. Those readers who have stuck it out may even have begun to suspect that this is a 'lean work larded with the fat of others', to paraphrase the seventeenth-century writer Robert Burton.

It was Ralph Waldo Emerson who, in 1849, remarked that whenever writers broach the subject of immortality they begin to quote. His own (much-quoted) response was: 'I hate quotations, tell me what you know.'

And this is where we have a dilemma: if we were to tell you what we have found and not mention where we found it, it would be thought that we were trying to take credit where it was not due. The French essayist Montaigne pointed out the problem: *'Comme quelqu'un pourroit dire de moy que j'ay seulement faict icy un amas de fleurs estrangeres, n'y ayant fourny du mien que le filet à les lier.'* (Some might say that all I have done is to make a posy of other men's flowers, my only contribution being the thread that binds them together.)

If we venture an opinion, we ought not to deny readers an earlier and usually more elegant expression of that argument. Would that be to gather 'gaudy flowers of speech from other men's gardens' as Geoffrey of Monmouth wrote at the very moment (1136) that he claimed his *Historia Regum Britanniae* (History of the Kings of Britain) was a translation of a 'certain very ancient book' now conveniently lost or mislaid? (Now that's enough of the layers of ironic nods and winks, quoth the plain people of Myles na gCopaleen.)

Adelard of Bath, who we met earlier, stridently proclaimed the primacy of reason over authority and had harsh words for scholars of his generation, who were possessed, he said, of the great fault that they never believed anything which did not enjoy the burden of classical learning. And so in his day it had become routine to make public your own discoveries by attributing them to one or other more respected authorities. The credulous, who did not rely on their own reason, were liable to be led around by the rope and halter of often spurious 'authority' like brute animals.

You can of course be quite subversive. The multi-talented American Elbert Hubbard (who died aboard the *Lusitania* in 1915) had a lot of fun describing and classifying what he called 'kabojolism', 'the antithesis of plagiarism'. 'Kabojolism in the second degree,' he wrote, 'consists in stating things tinted with risque [sic], for which you do not wish to stand sponsor, but which you feel should be said in the interest of the Higher Criticism. Therefore, you say them, and give another credit.'

Reverse plagiarism, both conscious and unconscious, is as common today as it has ever been.

It is easier than ever to ransack the libraries of the world to give a semblance of authority. The bibliographical note to A. G. Macdonell's *Napoleon and his Marshals* (1934) could not be more appropriate:

I am profoundly suspicious of almost all bibliographies. Nothing is easier than to hire someone to visit the British Museum and make a most impressive list of authorities, which will persuade the non-suspecting that the author is a monument of erudition and laboriousness.

I propose therefore to confine myself to the simple statement that every single detail of this book has been taken from one or other work of history, reference, reminiscence or biography.

The authors would only add that, apart from UNIEI case studies and anecdotes, almost all the facts, figures and quotations in this book are freely available online, so readers are urged to check sources and take nothing on trust. Someone* once said that statements like "'I think it was X who said . . .'" followed by some plausible but obscure quote' were no longer acceptable in the modern world. 'That hoary old stunt, ignorance posing as knowledge, is done for. Now we read it and think "Well, why not look it up, then, you fool? Five seconds on Google is all it takes."'

*Actually it was Michael Bywater in his excellent 2004 book *Lost Worlds*, and the quote is not, at the time of writing, googleable, but you get the drift . . .

We have tried to demonstrate that where ideas come *from* is not nearly as important as what we can *do* with them. Appropriateness trumps provenance every time. And so it ought to be plainly stated that, while this book is littered with quotations, what is important is not *who said what* (that's really just a question of common courtesy), but the *value* of what is being said.

And it is our interpretation of these arguments that is crucial. We have used them as building blocks to construct a creative problem-solving process which, as we said before, stands or falls on whether or not it works. As Montaigne said, the posy may be made of other people's flowers (how could it be otherwise?) but the thread that holds them together is our own.

And remember, context is everything. Question: what did Nelson Mandela describe as the greatest day of his life? Answer: meeting the Spice Girls!

The Spice Girls travelled to South Africa in 1997. During a photo opportunity, Nelson Mandela said, 'These are my heroes . . . this is one of the greatest moments in my life.' Prince Charles, who was also there, stated it was 'second greatest, the first time I met them was the greatest'.

Sometimes people are just having a laugh.

INDEX

USERNAME:
REGENERATED

THE RETURN OF THE **SUGG SQUAD!**

MINDY LOPKIN IS RESPONSIBLE FOR ALL THE COOL SPEECH BUBBLES, EFFECTS AND LETTERING.

AMRIT BIRDI IS THE GUY BEHIND THE INCREDIBLE ILLUSTRATIONS IN THE USERNAME SERIES.

JOE SUGG CREATED THE STORYLINE AND CHARACTERS AND DIRECTED THE PROJECT TO MAKE THE BEST GRAPHIC NOVEL SERIES POSSIBLE.

MATT WHYMAN IS THE PERSON WHO TOOK THE STORY AND CREATED A GRIPPING NARRATIVE TO ACCOMPANY THE ARTWORK.

JOAQUIN PEREYRA BROUGHT THE IMAGES TO LIFE WITH HIS AMAZING COLOURING.

IN TIME YOUR MOTHER WILL BELIEVE ME.

... A-DADA.

SHE'LL SEE WHAT I'VE CREATED FOR YOU, AND ALL WILL BE WELL.

CREAK

IN FACT, MAYBE THAT TIME IS *NOW*.

MAMA...

SHHH!

9

10

13

15

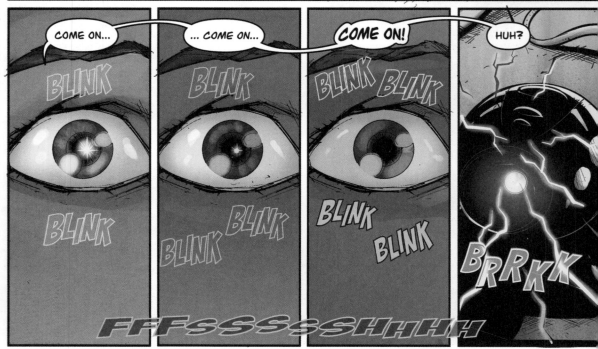

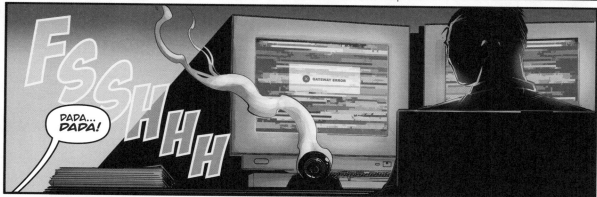

21

PART ONE

RIGHT NOW

THEY COME AS I SLEEP...

... AND BREAK INTO MY DREAMS.

WHEN I OPEN MY EYES, THEY'RE GONE.

JOE & CASPAR HIT THE ROAD

ONCE UPON A TIME, SUCH A PLACE WAS JUST A MOUSE CLICK AWAY.

NOW, BOTH MY DAD AND THE SANCTUARY HE CREATED ARE HISTORY.

I'M SO TIRED OF THESE NIGHTMARES.

WHAT I NEED IS SOME PLACE I CAN GO TO GET AWAY FROM IT ALL.

EVIE:

E.SCAPE ESCAPEE. RESTLESS SOUL.

SHHRIP

INCLUDING EVERYONE IN IT.

I THINK ABOUT YOU SO MUCH, BUT NEVER KNEW YOUR NAME.

YOU SACRIFICED YOURSELF SO I COULD COME BACK. BUT IT DOESN'T FEEL LIKE HOME WITHOUT YOU.

IF I COULD RETURN TO E.SCAPE, I'D GO IN A HEARTBEAT. BUT WHEN DAD SHUT DOWN THAT WORLD TO START IT AFRESH, JUST MOMENTS AFTER I GOT OUT, IT COOKED SOMETHING IN THE SOFTWARE.

I CAN STILL LOOK IN...

E.SCAPE

BRRK

... BUT ONLY FROM AFAR, IT SEEMS.

I CAN'T WALK THROUGH THE GLADES, BREATHE THE FRESH AIR OR EXPERIENCE THE FREEDOM DAD CREATED FOR ME.

THAT CONNECTION HAS GONE, ALONG WITH MY FATHER...

... AND I MISS IT MADLY.

E.SCAPE IS OVER, EVIE, AND WE'RE LUCKY TO HAVE GOT OUT WITH OUR LIVES.

WE BOTH KNOW YOUR HOTSHOT BUDDY DIDN'T MAKE IT, BUT YOU HAVE TO FACE FACTS.

HE WAS JUST PART OF THE VIRTUAL LANDSCAPE. A STRING OF DATA WITH A FACE...

DON'T SAY THAT.

A CUTE FACE, MAYBE, BUT IT'S TIME TO STOP BROODING AND MOVE ON.

THAT'S EASIER SAID THAN DONE WHEN IT FEELS LIKE HE'S STILL WITH ME IN SPIRIT.

I GO TO SLEEP THINKING ABOUT HIM, MALLORY.

"I EVEN DREAM ABOUT THOSE THINGS HE TOOK ON TO SAVE US. EVERY TIME IT SEEMS SO REAL. THEN I WAKE UP HERE ... AND WISH I WAS STILL THERE. WITH HIM."

LET IT GO, EVIE...

B-DING

B-DING

WHY NOT FOCUS ON SOMEONE CLOSER TO HOME?

Hi Evie.

How are thongs?

TODAY 17:21

I mean THINGS!

How are things with you?

TODAY 17:22

27

28

29

LIONEL

BLAP

MALLORY, THAT WOULD JUST MAKE ME FEEL WORSE.

ALL YOU'RE DOING IS FEEDING THIS DAYDREAM THAT YOUR HOODED HERO WILL MAKE EVERYTHING BETTER.

WE ALL KNOW IT'S BEEN TOUGH FOR YOU LATELY, BUT DON'T LOSE SIGHT OF THE GOOD THINGS YOU'VE GOT GOING HERE.

LIKE ME, FOR STARTERS.

IT'S ALL ABOUT MAKING THE EFFORT, AND CREATING A GOOD TIME RATHER THAN THINKING YOU'RE MISSING OUT ON A BETTER ONE.

WE CAN'T ALL STRIKE LUCKY AND DATE HOT, RIPPED GUYS, RIGHT?

HOW IS JASPAR?

I'M ABOUT TO DROP ROUND AND FIND OUT.

LET'S HOPE HE LIKES MY NEW LOOK.

THERE'LL BE TROUBLE IF HE DOESN'T.

TOO RIGHT!

THINK ABOUT WHAT I SAID, EVIE.

A CRUSH CAN BE FUN, UNTIL IT BECOMES A MONSTER.

THEN IT'S TIME TO GET A GRIP.

MALLORY WAS RIGHT. BUT HOW COULD I JUST SHUT DOWN ON THIS GUY? BACK IN E.SCAPE, HE HAD BEEN THERE FOR ME WHEN I NEEDED HIS HELP.

SWITCHING OFF JUST WASN'T AN OPTION.

BRKK BLIP BRKK

NOT WITHOUT A PROPER GOODBYE.

I'D LOST COUNT OF THE TIMES I'D TRIED TO RETURN.

ON EVERY OCCASION, I'D FIND MYSELF THERE...

BRKK BR

BUT NOT THERE.

EVEN THOUGH I COULDN'T CROSS OVER FOR REAL...

... IT ALWAYS HELPED ME TO FEEL CLOSER TO HIM.

HERE WAS A WORLD THAT HAD BEEN GIVEN A FRESH START. A PARADISE LOST, BUT CODED TO REGENERATE JUST FOR ME.

EVERY VIRTUAL ATOM WAS PROGRAMMED TO PICK UP ON MY PRESENCE, AND YET SOMETHING IN THIS PROGRAM HAD BROKEN.

SOMETHING THAT STOPPED ME FROM TRULY CONNECTING.

IN THE YEAR SINCE I'D SCRAMBLED FROM E.SCAPE, ALL I COULD DO WAS LOOK BACK IN FROM A DISTANCE.

DAD'S REBOOT HAD LAID WASTE TO A CORRUPTED LAND, AND YET I HELD OUT HOPE THAT THE VIRTUAL SOUL MATE I FOUND HERE WOULD BE WAITING FOR ME.

NOW MALLORY HAD BROUGHT HOME JUST WHAT THIS WAS DOING TO MY HEART AS MUCH AS MY HEAD. IT WAS TIME TO GET REAL.

IT'S LIKE YOUR MIND'S BEEN ELSEWHERE LATELY.

I'M FINE.

OK, I'M TRYING TO BE FINE.

BUT THANKS FOR YOUR CONCERN.

I JUST WANT YOU TO KNOW THAT I'M HERE TO HELP. ANY TIME...

I KNOW I'M NOT THE KIND OF GUY WHO CAN MAKE THINGS BETTER, BUT IF THERE'S ANYTHING I CAN DO, JUST ASK.

DON'T DO IT. MOVE ON, LIKE MALLORY SAID.

ACTUALLY, THERE IS ONE THING.

OH, EVIE!

MY HEAD TELLS ME TO WALK AWAY.

IF MY HEART IS WRONG HERE, I'M DEAD AGAIN.

GRAAAGGHHH

BUT YOU SOUND LIKE YOU'RE IN PAIN, AND I CAN'T IGNORE THAT.

THE WAY I SEE THINGS, IT ALL COMES DOWN TO TRUST. I SET YOU FREE. YOU CONTROL YOUR INSTINCT TO CRUSH MY SKULL. DO WE HAVE A DEAL?

MURHH.

GOOD!

UNLESS THAT GRUNT IS A NO?

I GUESS THERE'S ONLY ONE WAY TO FIND OUT.

JUST HANG IN THERE BIG GUY AND CHILL OUT. SERIOUSLY.

GRAGGH

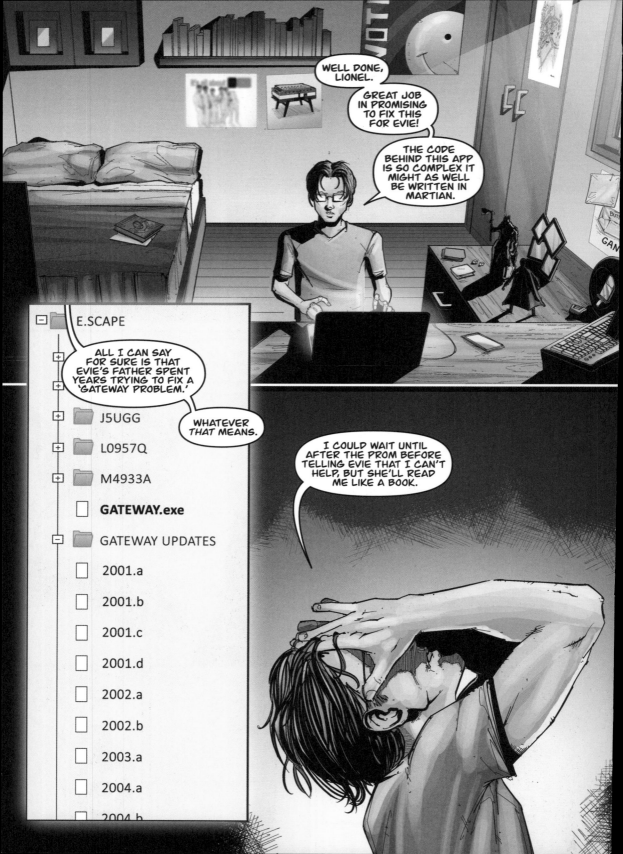

SO, WHAT'S CHANGED EXACTLY?

...?!?!

B-DING

SAVED BY THE BELL.

THAT BUYS YOU TIME TO HAVE A LITTLE THINK.

GIRL, WHAT HAVE YOU DONE *NOW?*

EVIE

I should've listened to your advice. Now I think I've made things worse...

TODAY 19:38

TROUBLE?

EVIE'S PROMISED TO BE LIONEL'S PROM DATE IN RETURN FOR SOME HELP WITH HER LAPTOP.

B-DING

SAYS SHE COULDN'T HELP HERSELF.

B-DING

APPARENTLY HE'S JUST TEXTED TO SAY HE HAS SOMETHING TO TELL HER.

TAKATAKA CH-CH-TAK

LIONEL IS BESOTTED, BUT WAY OUT OF HIS DEPTH.

IT ISN'T THE ONLY FANTASY RELATIONSHIP ON HER MIND RIGHT NOW.

SHE HAS TO PUT LIONEL OUT OF HIS MISERY... AND NOW IS THE TI--

I'VE JUST WORKED OUT WHAT'S DIFFERENT ABOUT YOU... NEW NAIL COLOUR, RIGHT?

NO, WAIT -- YOUR EYEBROWS ARE DARKER!

I FELT TERRIBLE.

72%

19:27

LIONEL
MESSAGE RECE

Evie, I need to tell
something...

≥SIGH≤

JUST THEN, THE APP NO LONGER MATTERED TO ME.

MALLORY HAD JUST SPELLED IT OUT TO ME: YES, I WAS ABOUT TO MAKE LIONEL FEEL BAD...

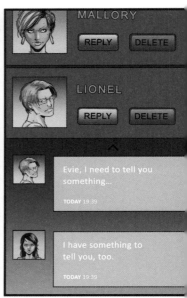

MALLORY
REPLY   DELETE

LIONEL
REPLY   DELETE

Evie, I need to tell you something...
TODAY 19:39

I have something to tell you, too.
TODAY 19:39

BUT IF I SAID NOTHING, WENT AHEAD WITH THE DATE AND HE WORKED OUT I WAS USING HIM TO FIX E.SCAPE, THAT WOULD JUST MAKE THINGS WORSE.

DELETE

LIONEL

REPLY

DELETE

Evie, I need to tell you something...
TODAY 19:39

something to too...

IT WAS NOW OR NEVER...

B-DING

REPLY   DELETE

LIONEL
REPLY   DELETE

I have something to tell you, too.
TODAY 19:39

This isn't an easy thing for me to say...

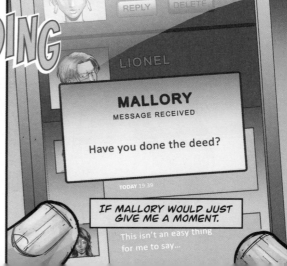

REPLY   DELETE

LIONEL

MALLORY
MESSAGE RECEIVED

Have you done the deed?
TODAY 19:39

IF MALLORY WOULD JUST GIVE ME A MOMENT.

This isn't an easy thing for me to say...

THE LAST THING I NEEDED RIGHT NOW WAS DISTRACTION.

MALL

REPLY

Have you done the deed?

TODAY 19:40

LIONEL

REPLY   DELE

Just trying to find the right words to bail from the date. Between us, Lionel makes me feel suffocated, but I can't be that brutal

TODAY 19:42

TAP

THUMB

TAP

WITH MALLORY OUT OF THE WAY, IT WAS TIME TO DO THE RIGHT THING...

SEN

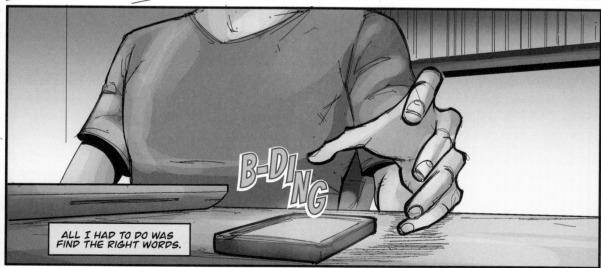

B-DING

ALL I HAD TO DO WAS FIND THE RIGHT WORDS.

...?!?!

EVIE

MESSAGE RECEIVED

INSTEAD, I WENT AND BROKE IT TO HIM IN THE WORST POSSIBLE WAY.

OH NO... OH, LIONEL. THAT WASN'T MEANT FOR YOU.

♪DIDDLE DAH DAH♫
♫DIDDLE DAH DAH-DEE♪

PICK UP, LIONEL. PICK UP!

I'M SO SORRY. I CAN EXPLAIN EVERYTHING.

PLEASE... LET ME HEAR YOUR VOICE.

OH, LEAVE ME ALONE!

HOW COULD YOU DO THIS TO ME, EVIE?

♪ DIDDLE DAH DAH ♫

♪ DIDDLE DAH...

FWOOSH

KRIK

YOU *USED* ME! AFTER EVERYTHING I TRIED TO DO FOR YOU...

WELL, WHATEVER YOU WERE HOPING I COULD FIX, IT ISN'T A PROBLEM ANY MORE!

M4933A
GATEWAY.exe
GATEWAY UPDATES

2001.a
2001.b
2001.c
2001.d
2002.a
2002.b
2003.a
2004.a
2004.b

M4933A
GATEWAY.exe
GATEWAY UPDATES

DELETED

LIONEL, WHAT ARE YOU NOW? A VICTIM OR A VANDAL?

☐ E.SCAPE

⊞ 📁 F34301E

⊞ 📁 G7959R

⊞ 📁 J5UGG

⊞ 📁 L0957Q

⊞ 📁 M4933A

☐ **GATEWAY.exe**

⊟ 📁 GATEWAY UPDATES

EMPTY

≑PHEW!≑ OK. THE ORIGINAL VERSION IS STILL THERE. WHATEVER THOSE UPDATES WERE TRYING TO PATCH SHE CAN FIGURE IT OUT HERSELF.

I'VE GOT BETTER THINGS TO DO WITH MY LIFE!

LIONEL WAS SO KIND, AND I HAD CRUSHED HIM.

ALL I WANTED TO DO WAS LOCK MY BEDROOM DOOR AND HIDE AWAY.

AND THAT MADE THE DESIRE TO RETURN TO E.SCAPE ALL THE MORE INTENSE.

JOE & CASPAR
HIT THE ROAD

JUST THEN, I FELT SHUT OUT FROM BOTH WORLDS.

I FIGURED A MOMENT LOOKING IN ON MY LOST PARADISE WOULD HELP ME TO FEEL BETTER.

CLICK

A BROKEN CONNECTION. THAT'S ALL I EXPECTED...

... BUT THEN MY SENSES TOOK ME BY SURPRISE.

... AND FEEL SUNSHINE ON MY FACE.

I COULD BREATHE THE AIR, HEAR BIRDSONG ON THE BREEZE ...

WHATEVER LIONEL HAD DONE TO THE APP...

PART TWO

SO, OUR MAIN MEAL IS SORTED, AND I'M HAPPY TO COOK, WHICH LEAVES JUST TWO TASKS ON THE LIST.

YOU'RE IN CHARGE OF DESSERT...

... AND WASHING UP.

OK, SO I'LL WASH UP AFTERWARDS.

SOME FRUIT WOULD BE GOOD, CHIEF.

SEEING THAT YOU CAN REACH SO MUCH HIGHER THAN ME, IT MAKES SENSE FOR YOU TO DO IT.

WE MIGHT BE ALONE IN THIS WORLD, BUT WE'LL ALWAYS HAVE EACH OTHER... AND DESSERT.

WHAT ELSE DO WE NEED?

I'D LONGED TO RETURN TO E.SCAPE FOR AGES. THE MOMENT I ARRIVED, THERE WAS JUST ONE PLACE I WANTED TO BE.

IN A WORLD IN BLOOM ONCE MORE, FLOWERING FROM THE RUINS OF THE LAST, I WASN'T SURE WHAT I'D FIND WHEN I REACHED MY DESTINATION.

BUT EVERY STEP OF THE WAY, I CLUNG TO THE HOPE THAT IT WOULD HELP ME FIND WHAT I WAS LOOKING FOR.

AND THAT STARTED WITH A CHANCE TO FEEL CLOSE TO MY DAD ONCE MORE.

THE LAST TIME WE SAID GOODBYE,
I SENSED IT WAS FOR GOOD. I COULD
JUST IMAGINE MY DAD HITTING THE
SWITCH TO REBOOT THIS WORLD,
KNOWING HIS DAUGHTER WAS SAFELY
HOME, AND THEN STEPPING OUTSIDE
FOR ONE LAST LOOK.

SO, I DIDN'T EXPECT TO FIND HIM HERE.
BUT AS THIS WAS THE HEART OF HIS
VIRTUAL CREATION, BURIED IN THE HEART
OF A MOUNTAIN, IT SEEMED LIKE THE
RIGHT PLACE TO COME.

IT WAS A CHANCE TO GATHER MY
THOUGHTS, CONSIDER MY NEXT
STEPS... AND TAKE IN WHAT
DAD HAD LEFT FOR ME.

February 22nd 2002

I'm a good man at heart, but I've done a very bad thing. As a result, my dear wife is lost in a virtual wilderness, and I must face the consequences. Every day, I look at our daughter and see my reflection in her eyes: a fool guilty of placing too much faith in technology. Now that Evie can speak, she sometimes asks after her mother. In response I show her pictures from a happier time. She's too young to know the truth.

February 27th 2002

The gateway into e.scape is the problem. The original build just wasn't ready. I had been so focused on patching the code to prevent digital natives from slipping into our world that I neglected to realise that it was never primed to let humans return. The update successfully locked out unwanted visitors as planned, but now my dear wife has crossed over and we've all paid a terrible price. I just hope the key is close at hand.

March 30th 2002

Every update I code to unlock the gateway ends in failure and despair! I can't even restore a visual connection, just so we can see each other again. Meanwhile, our beautiful daughter is denied her mother. But I refuse to give up on my family. We will be together some day. I have to make it happen.

October 31st 2003

On many occasions, I've thought about crossing into e.scape in search of my sweetheart. Even with no chance of returning, it's a powerful draw. Then I consider our little girl, and know that her mother would insist I remain at her side. Yes, I could take Evie with me, but what future would she face in a virtual wilderness? This world was intended as a break from reality, not a sentence without end. All I can do is be a good father, while devoting my life to pursuing a fix for this terrible mistake I've made.

December 24th 2003

The festive season is upon us once again. Unlike the last dark years, I'm hoping the surprise I have in store will light up Evie's life. For I've created a chat interface that might just connect us to her mum. It's a long shot, but I can only think that every day my wife must return to the place where she arrived in escape - hoping to come home. The virtual laptop she'll find there won't bring her back just yet. Even so, she can open up a message window on my screen so we can chat - and take comfort in the fact that we're with her in spirit.

March 7th, 2004

Another year and this nightmare continues. The message window is permanently open on my screen. I dream of the moment that letters and words appear as she types them from her virtual keyboard. I am ready to reply, but the cursor just blinks and blinks - marking every second of this seemingly endless sentence that keeps us apart.

September 13th 2005

Evie started school this week. I'm so proud of her (even if she did get on the wrong bus on her first day) and know her mum would feel the same way. When I'm not working on the gateway, I find myself blending photographs of how our daughter looks today with images of me and her mother from our time together. Some are so good that for a moment I'm convinced they're real. It comes as a comfort, until my attention returns to the accursed code. I will crack this!

April 9th 2006

'Is she dead?' asked Evie yesterday, which took me completely by surprise. I couldn't answer her for tears, which told her everything I would wish her to know right now.

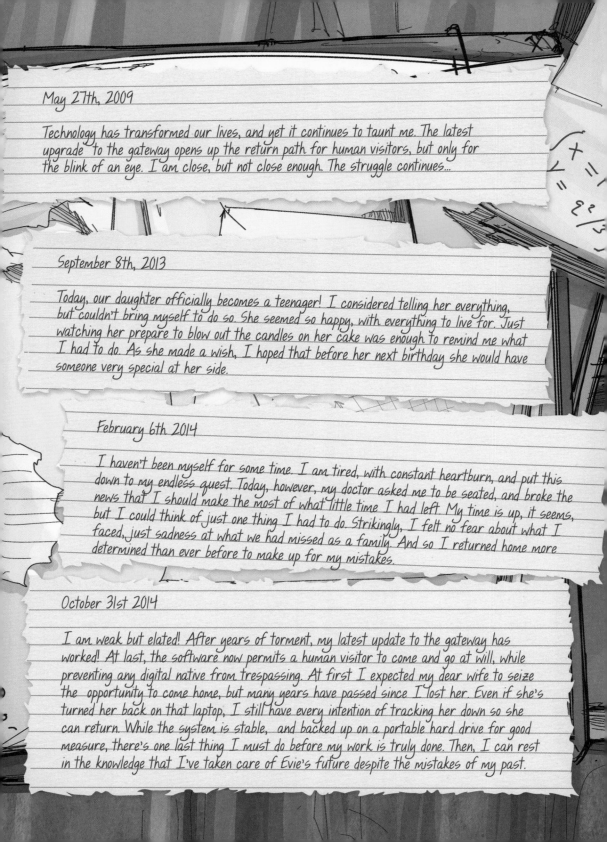

May 27th, 2009

Technology has transformed our lives, and yet it continues to taunt me. The latest upgrade to the gateway opens up the return path for human visitors, but only for the blink of an eye. I am close, but not close enough. The struggle continues...

September 8th, 2013

Today, our daughter officially becomes a teenager! I considered telling her everything, but couldn't bring myself to do so. She seemed so happy, with everything to live for. Just watching her prepare to blow out the candles on her cake was enough to remind me what I had to do. As she made a wish, I hoped that before her next birthday she would have someone very special at her side.

February 6th 2014

I haven't been myself for some time. I am tired, with constant heartburn, and put this down to my endless quest. Today, however, my doctor asked me to be seated, and broke the news that I should make the most of what little time I had left. My time is up, it seems, but I could think of just one thing I had to do. Strikingly, I felt no fear about what I faced, just sadness at what we had missed as a family. And so I returned home more determined than ever before to make up for my mistakes.

October 31st 2014

I am weak but elated! After years of torment, my latest update to the gateway has worked! At last, the software now permits a human visitor to come and go at will, while preventing any digital native from trespassing. At first I expected my dear wife to seize the opportunity to come home, but many years have passed since I lost her. Even if she's turned her back on that laptop, I still have every intention of tracking her down so she can return. While the system is stable, and backed up on a portable hard drive for good measure, there's one last thing I must do before my work is truly done. Then, I can rest in the knowledge that I've taken care of Evie's future despite the mistakes of my past.

June 17th, 2015

Evie knows I'm dying now. I can't hide that from her any more. Even so, she's determined that life at home goes on as normal, which is exactly as I wish it to be. I'll always be with her in spirit, just as I am with her mother. And soon I hope the time will come when Evie feels closer to us both. I have now recorded instructions that will guide her to e.scape when she's ready. There, in a realm programmed to reflect her personality, she will find a sanctuary. A place to rest and recharge so she might make the most of her life in the real world.

$\int d^2$

September 10th, 2015

Until now I've always kept this journal safely tucked away under the water tank in the loft. Evie will read it one day, no doubt, but that has to be in the right time and place. And so, having stashed the portable hard drive in my favourite hiding place (for I'm no longer a man who takes risks), I now find myself facing the webcam with the book in my lap. The undertaking has exhausted me, but I'm ready at last to make my final journey. I've left instructions for Evie, but I won't say goodbye. Why? Because we will see each other again.

I just hope that I can say the same thing about my poor, beloved wife. For she has to be out there somewhere - adrift in a virtual world - awaiting a connection.

Final update

Time moves differently here in e.scape. It feels like I have been here for an eternity, and yet I know the end is near. Evie has arrived, but a corrupting influence followed her. No doubt her cousin, Mallory, will change for the better on their return, but it leaves me to take drastic digital measures. We've said our goodbyes, and in a moment from now I must wipe all life from the surface of e.scape in order to reboot it. Even if it means letting go of those she found here, my final wish is that my daughter might come back one day - and find the sun shining again.

For with light, there is hope. And should you find yourself reading these last words of mine, Evie, maybe you will understand why I never gave in to darkness.

Dad X

I'M HERE TO WELCOME YOU BACK, EVIE; TO PROVIDE COMFORT AND GUIDANCE.

THAT'S HOW YOUR FATHER PROGRAMMED ME.

IT'S BEEN A LONG TIME, NO?

APART FROM THE TEARS, YOU'RE LOOKING GOOD! NOW, WHY DON'T YOU GIVE ME A HUG?

BUT... BUT HOW? WHERE ARE YOU?

A MOMENT LATER, DESPITE EVERYTHING THAT HAD GONE WRONG, I WAS REMINDED WHY DAD FIRST CREATED THIS WORLD FOR ME.

YOU'RE NEVER ALONE IN E.SCAPE, EVIE. NEVER ALONE...

...AND ALWAYS LOVED.

YOUR FATHER MADE THE ULTIMATE SACRIFICE WHEN HE RESET THIS WORLD.

HE KNEW HE WOULDN'T SEE IT REGENERATE, BUT IT MUST BE COMFORTING TO KNOW THAT HE BELIEVED YOU'D COME BACK AND FINISH HIS SEARCH.

BUT DAD WIPED OUT EVERYTHING ON THE SURFACE OF E.SCAPE. IT WAS THE ONLY WAY TO STOP THE CORRUPTION FROM SPREADING.

HE SAID SO HIMSELF.

IF MUM REALLY WAS HERE, SURELY SHE'S GONE NOW?

WITH LIGHT...

... THERE IS HOPE. I KNOW THAT NOW.

WHERE WOULD YOU BE WITHOUT IT?

BACK IN MY BEDROOM MOST LIKELY...

... FEELING SORRY FOR MYSELF NO DOUBT.

AND NOW YOU'RE BACK, THANKS TO YOUR FATHER, WITH A CHANCE TO MAKE SENSE OF YOUR FEELINGS.

THIS IS A JOURNEY OF DISCOVERY, EVIE. WHATEVER HAPPENS, I GUARANTEE YOU'LL LEARN MORE ABOUT YOURSELF ALONG THE WAY THAN STEWING ON THINGS AT HOME.

UNITY, AS MUCH AS I APPRECIATE YOUR WISE WORDS, I'M JUST PLEASED YOU'RE HERE...

... AND HOPE YOU KNOW YOUR WAY AROUND THESE SCREENS.

IF MUM IS HERE, SHE'LL SHOW UP SOMEWHERE...

YOUR FATHER TAUGHT ME EVERYTHING ABOUT HIS CREATION.

NATURALLY.

WE COULD BE DOING THIS FOR SOME TIME, COULDN'T WE?

YEP.

≥SIGH≤

YOU JUST HAVE TO BE PATIENT.

OR LOOK AT THINGS IN A DIFFERENT WAY?

... ?

ALL THIS TIME, I THOUGHT MUM HAD PASSED AWAY. NOW I SEE THINGS FROM A NEW PERSPECTIVE, AND YOU KNOW WHAT? AS MUCH AS IT HURTS, I UNDERSTAND WHY DAD KEPT THINGS FROM ME.

SAY NO MORE, EVIE. I KNOW WHERE THIS IS GOING.

IT'S ALL ABOUT THE BIGGER PICTURE, RIGHT?

MASTER CAMERA

OVERGROUND

UND

79

FOR ONCE, I HAD A CHANCE TO APPRECIATE MY DAD'S LIFE WORK.

I JUST COULDN'T IMAGINE THE TORMENT HE HAD PUT HIMSELF THROUGH, KNOWING THAT MUM WAS TRAPPED IN A MIRACLE OF HIS CREATION.

I COULD ONLY THINK HE'D SCOURED THIS LAND AS WE WERE NOW:

HOLDING OUT HOPE AGAINST ALL ODDS, BUT ENDING UP WITH NOTHING.

IF ANYONE KNEW HOW TO LOOK AT THINGS DIFFERENTLY, IT WAS DAD.

HE WAS A DEEP THINKER ALRIGHT.

UNITY, *THAT'S IT!* ONCE HE'D CHECKED OUT EVERY PIXEL ON THE SURFACE, MY DAD WOULDN'T HAVE STOPPED THERE.

YOUR FATHER NEVER GAVE UP, FOR SURE.

EXACTLY! HE'D SIMPLY TAKE THINGS TO ANOTHER LEVEL!

WHAT'S MORE, IF I WAS MUM, THERE'S ONLY ONE THING I'D DO WHEN LIFE STACKED UP AGAINST ME.

LOCK YOURSELF AWAY IN YOUR BEDROOM?

IN A SENSE, YES...

OVERGROUND

UNDERGROUND

I'M TALKING ABOUT GOING TO GROUND.

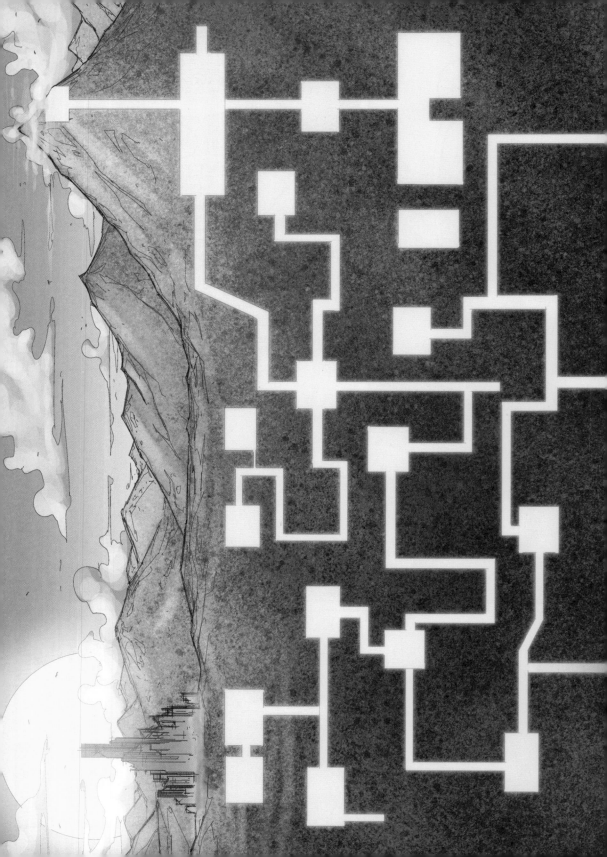

OK, THAT'S DEEP THINKING.
DAD WAS FORCED TO WIPE OUT LIFE ON THE SURFACE OF E.SCAPE. HE NEVER SAID ANYTHING ABOUT LIFE ***UNDERNEATH*** THAT SURFACE!
WHICH IS WHERE HE'D TAKEN HIS SEARCH, IT SEEMS.
ONLY IT LOOKS LIKE HE NEVER FINISHED THE TASK.
LOOKS A LITTLE DARK DOWN THERE, EVIE.
YOU'RE RIGHT...
BUT AFTER EVERYTHING MY DAD DID FOR ME -- AND WHAT HE PUT HIMSELF THROUGH FOR MUM -- I WON'T REST UNTIL I'VE SHONE A LIGHT THROUGH EVERY LAST TUNNEL DOWN THERE.

MALLORY, GO AND TELL YOUR COUSIN HER SUPPER IS ON THE TABLE. SHE CAN'T GO TO PROM NIGHT HUNGRY.

EVIE DOESN'T HAVE A DATE. SHE'LL HAVE PLENTY OF TIME TO FILL UP ON BUFFET SNACKS LATER. WHAT ELSE IS SHE GOING TO BE DOING?

DO AS YOUR MOTHER ASKS. *NOW*, MALLORY...

BUT I'M ON A TIGHT SCHEDULE HERE. I NEED TO EAT AND THEN DO MY NAILS.

MAL!!!

UNBELIEVABLE!

OI! EVIE! DINNER IS ON THE TABLE!

SHE SAYS SHE'S ON HER WAY. AT LEAST I IMAGINE SHE DID. MOST PROBABLY GOT HER EARPLUGS IN –

– HAVING A LITTLE CRY TO HERSELF.

86

RUNG BY RUNG...
IN MY TIME I'VE MEDITATED ON MOUNTAINTOPS, AND DRIFTED ACROSS DESERTS LOST IN THOUGHT. THIS IS NEW, AND I MUST CONFESS A BIT SCARY.
... WITH MY HEART HAMMERING...
WHATEVER HAPPENS, AT LEAST WE GAVE IT A SHOT. THAT'S WHAT COUNTS, RIGHT?
I'VE TAUGHT YOU TOO WELL.
... I DESCENDED INTO THE ABYSS...
... WITH UNITY CLOSE BEHIND.

IN DARKNESS, THIS DEEP DOWN, WE SOON LOST TRACK OF TIME...

SQUEEEE

SQUEEE

SQUEEEE

SQUEE

SQUEE

SQUEEE

SQUEE

... AND ANY SENSE OF JUST HOW FAR WE'D TRAVELLED.

SQUEEE

94

I'VE SEEN THIS BEFORE. IN ANOTHER LIFE, PERHAPS?

... OAK?

WHAT HAS HAPPENED HERE?

COME BACK, WHEREVER YOU ARE.

BLINK

BLINK

... HUH?

BLINK

E SCAPE

G7959R

SUGG

L0957Q

M4933A

GATEWAY.exe

EMPTY

BLINK

BLINK

BLINK

BLINK

BLINK

BLINK

SO WHOSE BRIGHT IDEA WAS IT TO WALK TO THE BIGGEST EVENT OF THE YEAR?

MY FEET ARE KILLING ME IN THESE HEELS.

OH, I KNOW... MY *BOYFRIEND!*

LIMOS ARE FOR LOSERS, BABE. NOBODY CARES HOW YOU GOT HERE. WHAT MATTERS IS THE ENTRANCE YOU'RE ABOUT TO MAKE.

THIS IS US, REMEMBER? THIS YEAR'S GUARANTEED PROM KING AND QUEEN.

MALLORY AND JASPAR.

THAT'S JALLORY... NO, *MASPAR.*

NOT TONIGHT IT ISN'T. UNLESS YOU INCLUDE YOU KNOW WHO...

WELL, LET ME SEE. *LIONJALLORY* ROLLS OFF THE TONGUE.

DID YOU HAVE TO BRING *HIM* ALONG WITH US?

EVIE LET HIM DOWN BADLY.

THE NEW MALLORY TAKES CARE OF THE HOPELESS CASES.

JASIONORY... LASPOREL...

BUT HE'LL CLING TO ME LIKE A LIMPET. WHAT WILL PEOPLE THINK?

JASPAR, LOVE ME, LOVE THE LOSERS IN MY COUSIN'S LIFE. THAT'S THE DEAL.

MALLSPARNEL! TOTALLY NAILS IT.

WHERE IS EVIE ANYWAY?

WELL, I CHECKED OUR FRIDGE AND SHE ISN'T IN THERE...

... SO I CAN ONLY THINK SHE'S FOUND A WARMER PLACE TO HIDE OUT UNTIL THIS WHOLE SHAME STORM BLOWS OVER.

ALL YOU HAVE TO DO NOWADAYS IS PRESS ONE WRONG BUTTON AND *BOOM* -- YOUR WORLD TURNS INSIDE OUT.

ON THE UPSIDE, THANK GOODNESS IT DIDN'T HAPPEN TO ME.

JASPONEL--

LIONEL, DON'T EVER SHIP MY NAME WITH YOURS, OK?

WE'RE *UNSHIPPABLE.*

OK, BOYS, RUN AHEAD AND HOLD THE HALL DOORS OPEN FOR ME. IF I HAVE TO SHOW UP WITHOUT A LIMO, YOU HAD BETTER MAKE THIS MEMORABLE.

SHRIEEKK!!!

WHAT IS THAT THING?!

SOMEONE CALL THE POLICE!

JUST TAKE MY PURSE BUT DON'T HURT ME!

KLANG

KLUP

MURRGHHH!

SPRING

WHUMP

≋WHIMPER≋

UNITY WAS WARY, BUT I DIDN'T WANT TO SHOW MY TRUE FEELINGS IN CASE IT MADE THINGS WORSE.

SPLOOSH

I COULDN'T AFFORD TO BE AFRAID OF THE DARK OR THE UNKNOWN, BUT ONE THING TERRIFIED ME – THAT ALL THIS MIGHT COME TO NOTHING.

I JUST HAD TO BELIEVE THAT MY DAD WASN'T CHASING A DREAM TO MAKE UP FOR THE NIGHTMARE HE HAD CREATED FOR HIMSELF. IF I STARTED TO DOUBT THAT MUM WAS DOWN HERE SOMEWHERE, MY COURAGE WOULD QUICKLY DESERT ME.

SPLOOSH
SPLISH

BRING IT IN QUIETLY, UNITY.

SPLOOSH

SKREEEP

SORRY!

RIGHT NOW I SHOULD BE REVELLING IN THE SOLITUDE AND SILENCE.

BUT THE FACT IS I FEEL LIKE WE'RE BEING WATCHED.

STAY STRONG, UNITY. STAY STRONG AND STAY FOCUSED.

IN TRUTH I SENSED IT, TOO...

JUST THINK HAPPY THOUGHTS AND WE'LL BE FINE.

WE WEREN'T ALONE.

FFT

FFT

NOTHING BAD CAN HAPPE--

OW!

YELP!

ALL I COULD DO WAS CLING TO HOPE.

EVEN AS THE LIGHT WENT OUT.

PART THREE

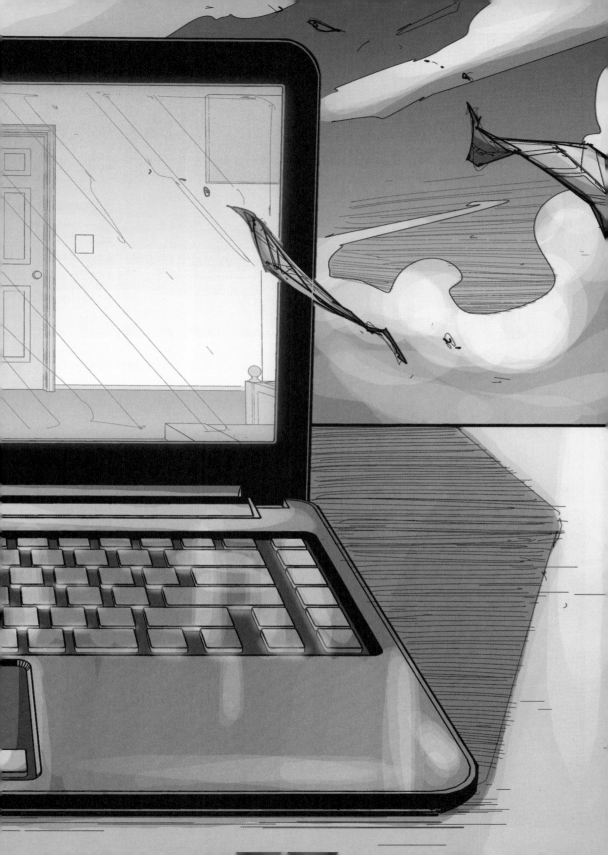

106

SO, I HAD LOST A FRIEND...

... BUT I WOULD FIND HIM.

!?!

VRROOOOM

HONK

EVEN IF I HAD TO GO TO THE ENDS OF A STRANGE, HOSTILE WORLD.

IN THIS URBAN JUNGLE, WHAT I NEEDED WAS A VANTAGE POINT.

♪ WHUMP WHUMP TSSHH... ♪

AND A CHANCE TO ASSESS THE ENVIRONMENT.

MY CREATOR WOULD EXPECT NOTHING LESS FROM ME – CODED AS I AM TO CONNECT WITH MY SURROUNDINGS...

♪ B-DOM DOM BLARE ♪

... AND NEVER, EVER GIVE UP ON THE PEOPLE IN OUR LIVES.

108

WILLIAM AND ARDEENA --

CONGRATULATIONS, GUYS! COME UP ON STAGE FOR YOUR CORONATION!

OH, GOSH! WILLIAM AND I JUST WANT TO SAY HOW THRILLED WE ARE.

WE'D LIKE TO THANK YOU GUYS FOR SUPPORTING US, OUR PARENTS...

OUR TEACHERS...

... AND, ARDEENA, LET'S NOT FORGET THE PANDAS. I HOPE THE MONEY WE RAISED WITH OUR CAKE SALE MAKES THEM JUST A LITTLE BIT LESS ENDANGERED.

COVER ME, PAL. I NEED SOME SPACE RIGHT NOW.

JASPAR! WHY DIDN'T YOU THINK OF THE PANDAS? IF ANYTHING IS ENDANGERED RIGHT NOW, IT'S OUR RELATIONSHIP!

WOOHOO
CLAP
YEAH
CLAP
CLAP
CLAP

SHE STILL LOOKS SLIGHTLY MURDEROUS.

DON'T EVEN CATCH HER EYE, MAN.

♫ WHUMP CHH! WHUMP BFF! WHUMP! ♫

♫ WHUMP TSHH WHUMP WHUMP ♫

SHE'LL CALM DOWN IN A WHILE.

BOOM BAP BANG WHUMP! ♫
♫ TSHH TSHH TSHH WHUMP

JASPAR, I DON'T WANT TO BE RUDE, BUT YOU'RE KIND OF, WELL...

... HOLDING ME BACK. DO YOU MIND IF I?

ARE YOU SERIOUS?

OH! SURE. DO YOUR THING.

HAHA! HAHA! HA! HAHAHA!

HA! HA!

OK, THAT'S ENOUGH.

I SAID THAT'S ENOUGH!

FOR ALL WE KNOW, THIS PAIR COULD BE SCOUTS AHEAD OF A TOPSIDE INVASION!

ARLO, GUARD THEM WITH YOUR LIFE WHILE I RAISE THE ALARM.

WHOA! REALLY?

THAT JUST MEANS YOU DON'T MESS UP, ALRIGHT?

GOT IT, KNOX. YOU CAN RELY ON ME.

OK, HE'S GONE. TIME OUT, MY FRIENDS!

THESE GUYS AREN'T GOING ANYWHERE.

BESIDES, KNOX IS ALL MOUTH.

HEH HEH!

UNITY, D'YOU HEAR ME? THESE KIDS ARE CRAZY. WE COULD BE IN TROUBLE HERE!

WHAT HAPPENED?

I'M MORE CONCERNED ABOUT WHAT *MIGHT* HAPPEN IF WE HANG AROUND ANY LONGER.

IT'S ME. EVIE! YOUR DAUGHTER...

?!?

... EVIE?

I CAN SEE SO MUCH OF ME IN YOU.

YOU HAVE THE SAME EYES.

THE SAME VOICE.

THE SAME HEART.

THE SAME SOUL.

A LONG TIME AGO YOU RISKED EVERYTHING TO SAVE ME. I'M HERE TO DO THE SAME FOR YOU.

BUT I DON'T NEED SAVING.

...?

HERE WAS MY MOTHER...

... A WOMAN I HAD NEVER DREAMED THAT I WOULD MEET...

... AND YET SHE SEEMED SO... DISTANT.

123

GROWING UP, I USED TO TREASURE DAD'S MEMORIES OF MY MOTHER. I HAD NO REASON TO CONSIDER WHAT SHE HAD BECOME.

EVIE, PERHAPS WE SHOULD LEAVE?

OK, IT'S TIME WE TURNED OUR ATTENTION TO FOOD. WHO IS ON FOOD GATHERING DUTY?

SHE WAS A DETERMINED WOMAN, ALL RIGHT.

I COULDN'T IMAGINE HOW TOUGH IT MUST'VE BEEN FOR MUM TO EMBRACE HER NEW LIFE HERE. ALL I KNEW WAS THAT IT HAD CHANGED HER.

NOW I'D BEEN GIVEN THIS CHANCE, AND IT FELT LIKE COMING FACE TO FACE WITH A STRANGER. WE HAD BOTH MOVED ON, I REALISED. TWO SURVIVORS LIVING DIFFERENT LIVES.

IT WAS TIME TO GO HOME.

WILL YOU DO ONE LAST THING FOR ME?

...?

WHEN I FACE THE WEBCAM, I'D LIKE YOU TO BE AT MY SIDE. IT'LL FEEL LIKE A PROPER GOODBYE.

BUT THAT MEANS SURFACING.

I HAVEN'T BEEN TOPSIDE FOR YEARS.

IT'S A WHOLE NEW WORLD UP THERE. TRUST ME, I'VE SEEN IT.

YOU MIGHT BE PLEASANTLY SURPRISED!

125

WELL, THAT WASN'T THERE WHEN I ARRIVED!

SOMEONE'S BEEN HERE.

BEEN AND GONE BY THE LOOK OF THINGS.

BUT THE GATEWAY'S SECURE NOW. DAD'S FINAL UPDATE FIXED EVERYTHING.

THAT MIGHT BE SO...

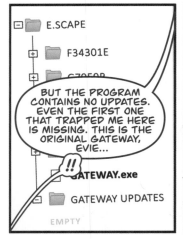

📁 E.SCAPE

⊞ 📁 F34301E

⊞ 📁 C7OF9B

BUT THE PROGRAM CONTAINS NO UPDATES. EVEN THE FIRST ONE THAT TRAPPED ME HERE IS MISSING. THIS IS THE ORIGINAL GATEWAY, EVIE...

‼️ GATEWAY.exe

📁 GATEWAY UPDATES

EMPTY

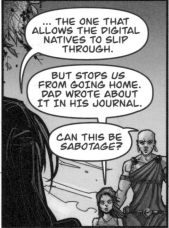

... THE ONE THAT ALLOWS THE DIGITAL NATIVES TO SLIP THROUGH.

BUT STOPS US FROM GOING HOME. DAD WROTE ABOUT IT IN HIS JOURNAL.

CAN THIS BE SABOTAGE?

ONLY ONE PERSON HAD ACCESS TO THE CODE, BUT HE'D NEVER DO SUCH A THING. NOT DELIBERATELY. I'M NOT EVEN SURE HE KNEW WHAT HE WAS DOING WHEN HE TRIED TO FIX IT, WHICH MEANS...

... OH.

OK, SO NOBODY SABOTAGED THE SOFTWARE... BUT SOMEONE MIGHT'VE MESSED UP.

BOSS, OVER HERE...

WHATEVER WENT THROUGH IS MASSIVE.

IT'S A BRUTE, MA'AM. MAKE NO MISTAKE.

THOSE AVATARS ARE PROGRAMMED TO PACK A PUNCH.

LET ME TAKE CARE OF THIS. I CAN BRING IT BACK.

OUT OF THE QUESTION.

?!?

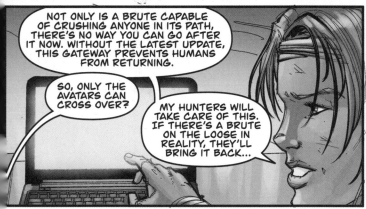

NOT ONLY IS A BRUTE CAPABLE OF CRUSHING ANYONE IN ITS PATH, THERE'S NO WAY YOU CAN GO AFTER IT NOW. WITHOUT THE LATEST UPDATE, THIS GATEWAY PREVENTS HUMANS FROM RETURNING.

SO, ONLY THE AVATARS CAN CROSS OVER?

MY HUNTERS WILL TAKE CARE OF THIS. IF THERE'S A BRUTE ON THE LOOSE IN REALITY, THEY'LL BRING IT BACK...

... DEAD OR ALIVE.

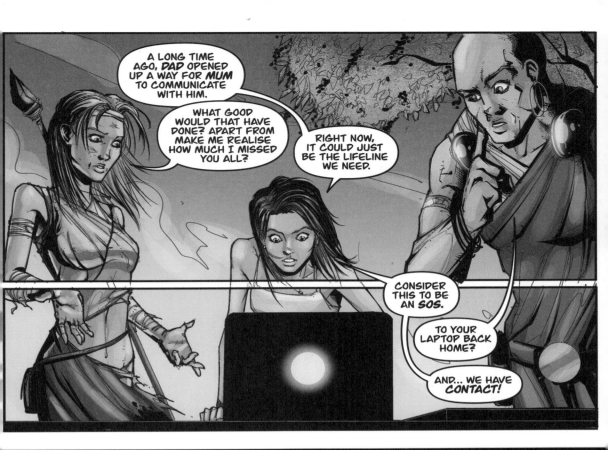

A LONG TIME AGO, *DAD* OPENED UP A WAY FOR *MUM* TO COMMUNICATE WITH HIM.

WHAT GOOD WOULD THAT HAVE DONE? APART FROM MAKE ME REALISE HOW MUCH I MISSED YOU ALL?

RIGHT NOW, IT COULD JUST BE THE LIFELINE WE NEED.

CONSIDER THIS TO BE AN *SOS.*

TO YOUR LAPTOP BACK HOME?

AND... WE HAVE CONTACT!

DAD HAD DREAMED OF THE MOMENT A MESSAGE FROM E.SCAPE BEGAN TO FORM ON HIS SCREEN. I'M SURE HE NEVER IMAGINED THAT I WOULD BE BEHIND IT...

TO: Mallory@email.com

SUBJECT: I need yr help!!

OK, this is going to sound rly weird, but you migh just be the one who saves the world fro disas |

SEND

I JUST HOPED HE'D BE PROUD OF THE FACT THAT...

... I WAS ABOUT TO USE IT TO REACH OUT EVEN FURTHER AND RAISE THE ALARM.

MURGGHH!

I'M JUST AS TIRED AND HUNGRY, OAK, BUT YOU HAVE TO TRUST ME HERE.

WE'LL RETRACE OUR FOOTSTEPS AND BE HOME IN NO TIME.

NEE NAH NEE NAH NEEE NAHH NEE NAH NEEEE NAHH

I'M GONNA NEED YOU TO BE INVISIBLE, BIG MAN.

MURRGGHHHH....

NOT LITERALLY. JUST TRY NOT TO ATTRACT ATTENTION TO YOURSELF, OK?

I REALISE THAT'S EASIER SAID THAN DONE, BUT I WON'T LET YOU DOWN.

EVEN IF THAT MEANS CALLING UPON OLD FRIENDS TO HELP US OUT.

♪ DMF DMF BIP DMF BIP BIP DMF ♫

WELL, I THINK THAT WENT OK.

THREE PHONE NUMBERS IS NOT A BAD HAUL FOR A FIRST ATTEMPT.

♪ BIP BIP DMF DMF BIP DMF BIP ♫

WATCHING YOU STEP IT UP JUST THEN WAS A THING OF BEAUTY, LIONEL. THOSE GIRLS *ADORED* YOU, AND THE PHOTOS I TOOK WERE MADE TO GO VIRAL.

IT'S CERTAINLY GIVEN ME AN APPETITE, I'LL SAY THAT!

B-DING!

♪ DMF BMF ♪ BLMP BIP ♫

FINALLY...

♪ DMF B....IE BMF ♫

IS THAT WHO I THINK IT IS?

MAYBE.

I HAVE TO GO.

EVIE
CHAT MESSAGE RECEIVED

...can't get home without the update. It's stored on a portable hard drive, taped under the water tank in my old cottage.

Mallory, I'm relying on you! E XXX

WHERE? AT LEAST LET ME FINISH MY SANDWICH.

MALLORY, *WAIT!*

WHAT'S GOING ON?

LEAVE IT, LIONEL.

IT'S A FAMILY THING.

SO, THIS IS ABOUT EVIE! WHERE IS SHE, MALLORY?

SHE CAN'T HAVE MISSED THE PROM JUST BECAUSE OF ME. C'MON. I WANT TO HELP!

IS THERE ANOTHER GUY? BE HONEST WITH ME, MAL.

IT'S MORE COMPLICATED THAN THAT.

EVIE IS INVOLVED WITH....

... ANOTHER WORLD.

?!

SHE'S TALKING ABOUT A PLACE I CALL HOME.

WHAT THE...? *YOU!*

BUT I CAN'T GET BACK WITHOUT YOUR HELP.

THIS IS A PRIVATE CONVERSATION, PAL.

DON'T HIT ME.

IT'S OK, LIONEL. HE'S ONE OF THE GOOD GUYS.

YOU MAKE IT SOUND LIKE THERE ARE BAD GUYS OUT THERE.

ACCORDING TO EVIE, THERE COULD BE LOTS OF THEM HERE AT ANY MOMENT, WHICH IS WHY SHE NEEDS MY HELP.

SO, IT SEEMS THAT WE AREN'T THE ONLY VISITORS TO HAVE CROSSED OVER.

CROSSED OVER FROM WHERE?

WHO'S 'WE?'

YOU SAID 'WE' AREN'T THE ONLY VISITORS.

WHO CAME WITH YOU?

UM... CAN YOU GUYS KEEP A SECRET?

OAK? IT'S ALRIGHT, BUDDY. YOU CAN SHOW YOURSELF.

SO, WHAT ARE WE LOOKING FOR HERE? A KITTEN?

OMG!

OK, NOT A KITTEN.

THE LAST TIME EVIE AND I SAW ONE OF THOSE, IT WAS KINDA FURIOUS.

THIS IS OAK. YOU HAVE MY WORD THAT HE'S HARMLESS.

AND HARD TO HIDE, RIGHT?

ALL I WANT TO DO IS GET HIM HOME.

LIONEL, SEEING THAT YOU'RE ALL ABOUT PUSHING BOUNDARIES TONIGHT, I NEED YOU TO COLLECT A HARD DRIVE FROM MY COUSIN'S OLD COTTAGE.

BUT OTHER PEOPLE LIVE THERE NOW...

THEN TAKE IT TO EVIE'S BEDROOM – WITHOUT ALERTING MY PARENTS BECAUSE YOU DON'T WANT TO LOOK LIKE A CREEP – AND UPLOAD THE FILE TO HER LAPTOP.

MAL, UM, ARE YOU CRAZY?

NEE NAH NEE NAH

UNLESS YOU TRY, WE MIGHT NEVER SEE EVIE AGAIN.

?!?

THINGS MIGHT NOT HAVE WORKED OUT BETWEEN YOU, BUT SHE'D DO ANYTHING FOR YOU AS A FRIEND.

WHAT ABOUT YOU?

THESE GUYS NEED A FRIEND, TOO.

BLINK
BLINK

DO YOU REMEMBER OUR PROM NIGHT?

HOW COULD I FORGET?

BLINK
BLINK
BLINK

IT WAS ALL ABOUT COURTING IN THOSE DAYS.

≈CHUCKLE≈ WE HAD A FINE TIME.

BLINK BLINK
BLINK
BLINK

NO DOUBT THINGS ARE VERY DIFFERENT NOW.

I JUST HOPE THAT WHATEVER'S GOING ON WITH THE GIRLS THEY LOOK BACK ON WHAT SHOULD BE A HIGH POINT IN THEIR TIME AT SCHOOL.

IF MALLORY AND EVIE HAVE ANYTHING TO DO WITH IT...

"THE HARD DRIVE'S TAPED UNDER THE WATER TANK IN THE LOFT...

... YOU'LL BE IN AND OUT IN NO TIME."

YEAH, RIGHT. LIKE BREAKING INTO HOUSES IS A BREEZE.

GRRR

OK, SO TALKING TO GIRLS TOOK GUTS, BUT I NEED MORE THAN THAT HERE...

... STARTING WITH A SANDWICH.

THERE YOU GO, BIG BOY. FRESHLY MADE FOR THE SCHOOL PROM.

EVIE, IF YOU COULD SEE ME NOW...

CRASH

THEN I'M NOT A VANDAL, OK? JUST A KID TRYING TO DO THE RIGHT THING FOR A FRIEND.

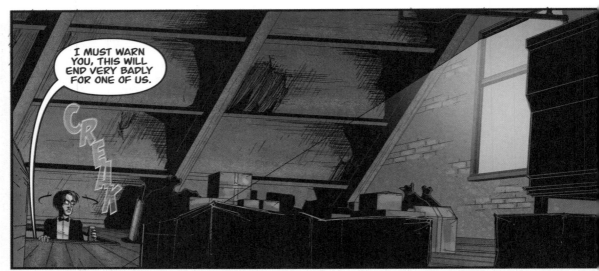

I MUST WARN YOU, THIS WILL END VERY BADLY FOR ONE OF US.

CREAK

AND I DON'T INTEND IT TO BE ME.

CREAK

I SEE YOU!

STOP! WHATEVER YOU'RE DOING. I AM HEAVILY ARMED, SO JUST GIVE IT UP RIGHT NOW!

I'M SORRY, SIR. I CAN'T DO THAT RIGHT NOW.

THERE'S A GIRL TRAPPED IN ANOTHER WORLD WHO... OH, NEVER MIND!

JASPAR, IF I MEAN ANYTHING TO YOU RIGHT NOW, YOU WON'T FREAK OUT ON ME, OK?

I WANT TO INTRODUCE YOU TO A COUPLE OF FRIENDS.

THEY'RE A LONG WAY FROM HOME, AND NEED A PLACE TO LIE LOW FOR A SHORT WHILE.

LIE LOW? ARE THEY BANK ROBBERS?

JUST BE COOL, OK? PROMISE ME THAT.

BABE, I ALWAYS KEEP IT TOGETHER. YOU KNOW ME.

OK, GUYS, COME IN BEFORE SOMEONE SEES YOU OUT THERE.

THIS IS RIVER.

HE'S FROM A DIGITAL WORLD CREATED BY EVIE'S DAD BEFORE HE DIED.

AND THIS IS OAK.

HE WOULDN'T HURT A FLY.

MALLORY'S HOUSE

ISN'T IT QUIET WITHOUT THE GIRLS?

ENJOY IT WHILE IT LASTS. THEY'LL BE BACK SOON, NO DOUBT.

DRAINPIPE, DON'T BE THE ≶PUFF≶ SECOND ONE TO ≶GRUNT≶ LET ME DOWN TONIGHT...

HNGHH!!

KLUP

EVIE, WHEREVER YOU ARE...

...WHATEVER'S GOING ON IN YOUR LIFE...

...AT THIS MOMENT IN TIME...

...I'M HERE FOR YOU.

JUST ABOUT...

SO, THESE WOULD BE THE GATEWAY UPDATES I TRASHED. WHOOPS! WELL...

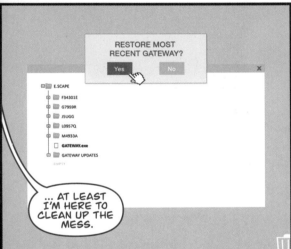

RESTORE MOST RECENT GATEWAY?

Yes   No   X

E.SCAPE
F34301E
G7959R
J5UGG
L0957Q
M4933A
GATEWAY.exe
GATEWAY UPDATES
EMPTY

... AT LEAST I'M HERE TO CLEAN UP THE MESS.

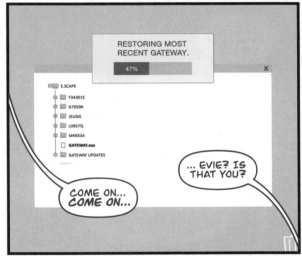

RESTORING MOST RECENT GATEWAY.

47%   X

E.SCAPE
F34301E
G7959R
J5UGG
L0957Q
M4933A
GATEWAY.exe
GATEWAY UPDATES
EMPTY

COME ON... COME ON...

... EVIE? IS THAT YOU?

EVIE? ARE YOU HOME? WE DIDN'T HEAR YOU COME IN.

!!!

COME ON DOWN, SWEETIE.

JUST ONCE THIS EVENING, I'D LIKE TO LEAVE A HOUSE THROUGH THE FRONT DOOR.

RIGHT NOW, I SHOULD BE AT OUR PROM NIGHT...

... BUT I MADE A MESS OF THINGS WITH A BOY WHO DESERVED BETTER.

YOU DON'T STRIKE ME AS THE TYPE TO GIVE UP THAT EASILY.

I IMAGINE THAT'S WHAT YOU THINK OF ME.

TURNING MY BACK ON YOUR FATHER LIKE THAT, DESPITE EVERYTHING HE DID TO BRING ME HOME.

SOMETIMES, EVIE, THE RIGHT PATH ISN'T THE EASIEST ONE.

I KNOW THAT.

IT'S WHY I'M HERE, HOLDING OUT HOPE THAT I CAN GET HELP FROM HOME.

MUM AND I? WE WERE WORLDS APART IN EVERY WAY. I HAD LOVED ONES I COULD COUNT ON, AND SO DID SHE.

BUT IF I DIDN'T GET BACK TO THEM SOON, HER ADOPTED FAMILY RISKED CAUSING GRIEF AND SUFFERING THAT NOBODY DESERVED.

B-DING

I MADE IT! I MADE IT!

A-LANG-ALANG-A-LANG-ALANG

IF ANYONE SEES US, WE'RE DOOMED!

SHHHH!

CLICK

WHAT ABOUT "OH, LIONEL! THANK GOODNESS YOU MADE IT BACK IN ONE PIECE! YOU'RE SO BRAVE..."

... SORRY.

THE GOOD NEWS IS THAT EVERYONE OUTSIDE HAS GIVEN UP WAITING FOR THE FIRE BRIGADE AND GONE HOME.

THEN WE SHOULD GET GOING BEFORE THEY ARRIVE.

THE BAD NEWS IS THAT SINCE LIONEL SHOWED UP I FEEL LIKE WE'RE BEING WATCHED.

ARE YOU SURE YOU'RE NOT JUST IMAGINING IT?

PSSHHH

OK, WE'RE BEING WATCHED!

TARGET DOWN!

GOOD SHOT.

I KNEW IT! DIDN'T I TELL YOU?

AS SOON AS I SPOTTED THAT KID SNEAK IN WITH HIS CLOTHES ALL SHREDDED, I SENSED SOMETHING WAS AFOOT.

HE'S TANGLED UP WITH THE BRUTE, AM I RIGHT?

YOU DID WELL, ARLO. FOR ONCE.

SO, IS THAT MONSTER IN THERE? D'YOU SEE HIM?

COVER EVERY ESCAPE ROUTE...

ON MY WORD, WE GO IN FOR THE KILL!

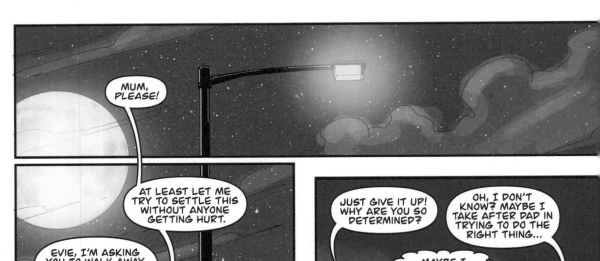

MUM, PLEASE!

AT LEAST LET ME TRY TO SETTLE THIS WITHOUT ANYONE GETTING HURT.

EVIE, I'M ASKING YOU TO WALK AWAY AND PRETEND THIS NEVER HAPPENED!

THAT MIGHT'VE SUITED YOU IN E.SCAPE...

... BUT IF SOMEONE IS AT RISK OF GETTING HURT IN THIS WORLD, THEN WE SHOULD FIGHT TO PROTECT THEM!

WILL THE PAIR OF YOU SLOW DOWN!

I'M DESIGNED FOR MEDITATION, NOT MARATHONS!

JUST GIVE IT UP! WHY ARE YOU SO DETERMINED?

OH, I DON'T KNOW? MAYBE I TAKE AFTER DAD IN TRYING TO DO THE RIGHT THING...

MAYBE I SHOULD'VE KEPT MY DISTANCE.

... AND NEVER GIVING UP HOPE.

HE RAISED YOU WELL. THAT MUCH IS CLEAR.

THEN GIVE ME THIS CHANCE...

GRAAAGGHHHHH!!

NOT SO LONG AGO, I HAD FOUND MYSELF ADRIFT IN A WORLD WHERE IT FELT LIKE EVERYONE HAD TURNED AGAINST ME.

IT MEANT I KNEW JUST WHAT THAT POOR CREATURE WAS GOING THROUGH RIGHT NOW...

... AND I WASN'T GOING TO LET HIM FACE IT ALONE.

WELL, NOBODY PREDICTED THIS FOR PROM NIGHT...

JASPAR, IF YOU STAND UP TO THIS LIKE LIONEL, YOU CAN STILL BE MY KING.

EVIE, TIME IS RUNNING OUT!

HEY, I'M ON IT! JUST GIVING HIM A HEAD START...

OAK, STAY CALM!

BUDDY, WE'LL TAKE CARE OF YOU.

HOLD YOUR FIRE!

MY FRIEND HERE MEANS NO HARM!

OH, MUM!

EVERYONE COME DOWN HERE THIS INSTANT!

KNOX, YOU HAVE DEFIED ME...

JUST THEN, I KNEW THAT NOTHING WOULD COMFORT RIVER. HE HAD LOST A TRUE FRIEND. A SOUL MATE THAT COULDN'T BE REPLACED.

I MIGHT'VE SPENT A LONG TIME LIVING WITH FEELINGS FOR HIM, BUT THAT WAS BASED ON NOTHING MORE THAN A FANTASY.

THIS WAS REAL. AND HEARTBREAKING TO WITNESS.

I'M SO SORRY. IF THERE'S ANYTHING WE CAN DO.

WE TRIED OUR BEST...

173

NEE NAH NEE NAH NEE NAH NEE NAH NEEE NAHH

EVIE, WE HAVE TO GET OUT OF HERE, AND FAST!

FLY NOW, CRY LATER. RIGHT, MAL?

GIVE ME STRENGTH!

NEEE NAHH NEE NAH NEEEE NAHH SCREEECH

I GUESS THIS IS ONE PROM NIGHT WE'LL NEVER FORGET, RIGHT?

I THOUGHT THAT FROM THE MOMENT LIONEL GOT THOSE GIRLS' PHONE NUMBERS.

DID HE? NO WAY!

GUYS, CAN WE DISCUSS THIS LATER?

AND THERE WE TOOK OFF INTO THE NIGHT...

SO, DOES THIS MEAN YOU TWO ARE FRIENDS AGAIN?

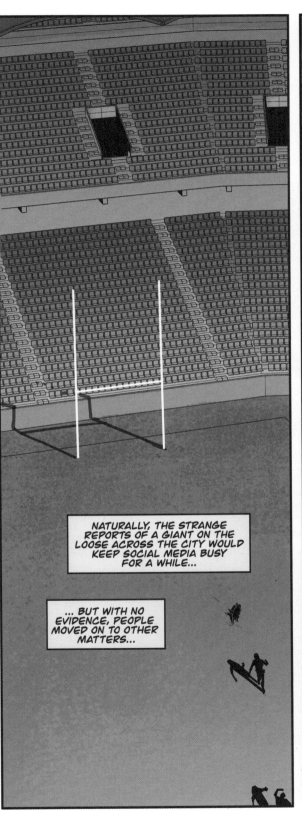

NATURALLY, THE STRANGE REPORTS OF A GIANT ON THE LOOSE ACROSS THE CITY WOULD KEEP SOCIAL MEDIA BUSY FOR A WHILE...

... BUT WITH NO EVIDENCE, PEOPLE MOVED ON TO OTHER MATTERS...

... AND LIFE RETURNED TO NORMAL.

Mountain Road,
Late at Night

Alan Rossi was born in 1980 in Columbus, Ohio. His fiction has appeared in *Granta, Missouri Review, Conjunctions, Agni,* and *Ninth Letter,* among others. Rossi was named the New England Review/Bread Loaf Scholar for 2017 and his stories have been awarded a Pushcart Prize and the O. Henry Prize. He lives in South Carolina with his wife and daughter. *Mountain Road, Late at Night* is his first novel.

Nathaniel observed – alternating between varying degrees of clarity and confusion, doubt that resolved into certainty, which in turn morphed into questioning – his central role in the numerous discussions among the family members about where the boy should live, who would best serve as replacement parents, who had the necessary parental acumen, who had the finances, who would be dedicated, whose lifestyle the boy would most easily fit into, who was young, who was old, who had been parents, who hadn't, who was willing to do it again, who wasn't, who knew the wishes of the boy's parents and who only thought they knew, who was closest to the now-gone family itself – the parents both dead in a car accident – and finally, who would make the boy immediately feel safe. None of these discussions yielded clear answers for Nathaniel, the dead man's brother, or anyone else. All the accumulated arguments were like an uncertain sea of information, Nathaniel thought, one point swelling into a wave of what felt like fact only to have another point wash out that wave with its own relevance and truth. In this way, rather than revealing who could best help the boy, the debate among the family members in the first days after the accident left the continual, implied, unasked, but deeply felt question: what did the boy want and need? The answer was both too simple and too impossible to approach: Jack wanted his parents. Nathaniel felt that all that these conversations were doing, and what they would continue to do, was serve as a way for the family to act out their scripted roles without any of them seeing what was right in front of them.

Nathaniel received a phone call from his dead brother's mother-in-law the day before. She called to tell him that she had started driving Monday night and would continue for the next four days, since it was over a thirty-hour drive from Boise, and that she would arrive on Friday. She was sorry she couldn't be there sooner, but see no one thought to tell her, you know, the *mother*, that her *daughter* had been in this accident, and plane tickets were way too expensive at this point, to which Nathaniel wanted to explain that there'd been a mistake, that he believed she'd been notified by the police, but before he could say anything this Tammy woman had said, It is what it is and it doesn't matter now. She said she was on her way and would pick up the kid on Friday afternoon in order to drive him back home, asking Nathaniel to please have a suitcase packed with a week's worth of clothes, whatever toys Nathaniel felt the boy needed or would want. He could ship the rest to her later, and then she ended the phone call by saying that she was appreciative of Nathaniel taking the time out of his schedule to look after the boy, appreciative of Stefanie as well, please tell her that, she knew that children weren't in their plans so it was really great that for the past week they'd moved in and stayed with the boy in the house he knew, but not to worry, she'd be there soon and they could go back to their apartment and their lives. Nathaniel had then explained to Stefanie, his wife, that Tammy – a woman he had met only once and with whom he had never had a real conversation before – this woman didn't even say *hello*, she just began *talking*, telling him that she was coming to pick up the *kid* with barely any acknowledgment that Nathaniel was even on the line, and *then* she gave him *instructions* for packing. Nathaniel told Stefanie that the mother-in-law basically patronized *both of them* by implying that these few days with Jack had been a burden for them. He told Stefanie that his brother's mother-in-law conveyed this information to him with such flippant urgency, almost an annoyance at having to convey it to him, so that he'd felt reproached and stupid, like he should've somehow known this information, and he hadn't known how to react and therefore hadn't reacted, except to say, Okay, that all sounds great. Thanks, Tammy.

Now, a day after that call, thinking about when to call this Tammy woman back and what he would say to her, Nathaniel watched Stefanie looking through the cabinets for what she said was 'a strainer.' They were in the kitchen of Nathaniel's brother's cabin-like home. They had driven nearly three hours from Charlotte where they lived and worked, driven into the mountains, to be there with Jack in the home that Nicholas had built. Besides the appliances, the kitchen itself – the wood floors, the wood cupboards and drawers, the counters of poured concrete – had been constructed, like the rest of the house, by Nicholas. Every place Nathaniel looked, every space he occupied in the house, he felt his brother. He didn't know how many times he'd cried. He remembered being in the bathroom a few days ago, and how he dropped his toothbrush and was reminded that he'd helped Nicholas lay the tile and how Nicholas had eventually kicked him out of the bathroom because it was too small for both of them to be working in, and when Nathaniel had stood up in an annoyed hurry, he'd smacked his head against his brother's chin as he was standing, hit his brother's chin so hard with the top of his head that he could hear the clack of Nicholas's teeth and when Nicholas uncovered his mouth and spit into his hand, Nathaniel had seen both blood and maybe a quarter of Nicholas's tongue. They had to go to the ER, where a doctor sewed the tongue back on. When he had dropped his toothbrush all this moved through his mind, making him see something other than what he was seeing, which was also what he was doing now standing in the kitchen with Stefanie – seeing something other than what was right in front of him, being somewhere else. In order to correct this, instead of thinking about dropping the toothbrush and remembering how that caused him to remember Nicholas's tongue, now, in the kitchen with Stefanie, he tried to look at everything without letting it remind him of anything, to just see what he was seeing.

Out the windows above the kitchen sink, a constant rain fell, a sound that was at once one sound and many: a padding sound on the grass, a tinny sound on the roof, a thudding sound on the wood of the porch. Stefanie had failed in finding the strainer and was now cleaning potatoes at the sink, potatoes she had picked from the garden, scrubbing them with a little wire brush which caused mud to streak through the running water in the porcelain sink. For the first couple of days, they'd gotten by on sandwiches, but now she wanted to cook. She told Nathaniel, while she scrubbed the potatoes, that he had to call this Tammy woman back. He said he couldn't call her back, what was he going to say? I can't remember a single time I've ever addressed the woman by name, he said. I've only met her once at Nicholas's wedding, where she told me that her daughter had almost married a guy who lived in California. Some guy named Desmond, who was now in the Secret Service. She told me she had no idea why April had chosen to be with my brother, but she had, so she was going to support her daughter, though, Come on, she'd said: Secret Service or anthropologist? Stefanie shook her head, her dark hair, which was in a ponytail, swinging.

Jack, Nathaniel's four-year-old nephew, was napping in his bedroom. Nathaniel walked down the hall and looked into the boy's room. Jack was still sleeping, his breath deep and steady, his body turned away, covered, his black hair messed from sleep. Out the window, a stream flowed beside the cabin. The steady rain that fell from the slate grey sky muffled the sound of the stream, so that Jack, if he woke, wouldn't even notice the sound of the running water, Nathaniel thought. Nathaniel felt the privacy of the rain, like a blanket enclosing the cabin. A half mile away, there was a barn where his dead brother did his carpentry, had once done, Nathaniel thought, and further along the property, a greenhouse and larger outdoor garden, all of which Nathaniel, standing at Jack's bedroom door, had forgotten about to some degree until arriving – it felt nearly impossible, how exactly Nicholas and April and Jack lived – but more than anything, Nathaniel had forgotten how quiet his brother's place could be, how quiet the nearby town was. Even the rain, the reverberating thunder, felt as though it emphasized the quiet of the mountain rather than negating it.

He went back down the hall to the kitchen and stood at the kitchen island, leaning against it, watching Stefanie cleaning potatoes. He could hear, just under the rain, the stream that passed by his brother's cabin, and as the rain lessened, the two different sounds of water created one sound, both seemingly issuing from the underlying silence, and Nathaniel felt he was on the verge of sensing something significant: how that one watery sound – the combination of the rain and the stream – meant something else entirely. The stream trickled and gurgled over rocks, over logs, through grasses, numerous sounds creating the sound of the stream, and the rain that fell into the stream also con- tributed to that watery sound he was hearing, almost a humming sound, and the many things the stream once was went down the mountain as one thing, where it became a larger river, and merged with another river that ran through the town, which then came out of the mountains, and moved toward the coast, where it became the Atlantic. Many things changing into one thing. One thing changing into another. Or was it simply that the river was already the ocean? Nathaniel's mind tried to grab onto something – he didn't know what – as he stared out the window. He'd been doing this, he'd noticed: his brother was dead, he had to take care of Jack, but he kept thinking of other things. Now it was this: what was he feeling about this mountain rain? Was he feeling the force of coming from the city to the countryside? He knew the natural world was there, but he'd forgotten it, somehow. Mountains and fields and rural life, clouds moving in the still cold spring wind, and trees, just budding, obscured in fog each morning, and rain falling or simply materializing as mist in the air, and the air itself cold and crisp in the morning, slowly warming during the day, still damp, and then temperatures dropping again at night, everything wet, muddy, just becoming green again, everything in balance with itself, a peacefulness that was undercut by something quietly haunting and dreamlike, all of which Nathaniel felt at the fringes of his perception, like he was just a child, learning how the world worked again.

Stefanie finished cleaning the potatoes and said, Okay, back to the original mission, and after opening a few cupboards and moving pots and bowls around this time, she found the strainer. A *colander*, she now said, it's called a colander. She went back to the sink, grabbed a potato from the counter, and peeled the skin into the colander. Nathaniel stopped looking out the window, turning off the natural world like turning off a switch, and watched Stefanie, the potato skins making a quiet slapping sound as they occasionally missed the colander and hit the sink. Stefanie reiterated that Nathaniel needed to call this Tammy woman back and explain to her that this wasn't how things were going to go. I don't like that solution to this particular problem, Nathaniel said. Because it involves me confronting a person and you know I hate doing that. Nathaniel asked if maybe he should get a second opinion, and Stefanie rolled her eyes and said, Go ahead, call your parents. That's not fair, Nathaniel said. No, that's completely fair, Stefanie said. You and your family have to have little conferences before anything gets decided. Your parents call you with detailed travel plans before they visit us. They outline down to the hour how long they'll stay. You call them with questions about your work, your financial situation, and now you're going to call them about this woman. It's not a judgment, but my family isn't the same. That's what you learn coming from divorced parents. You're on your own. You guys are a little committee. Except Nicholas. The one that broke away. That's so hyperbolic I can't tell if it's mean or not, Nathaniel said. You know you're going to call them, she said. He looked at her and said, yeah, he was.

He picked up the phone and thought for a moment of this Tammy woman driving from – where was it again, Omaha or something, somewhere in Idaho, was Omaha in Idaho? – and how she was so sure she was going to be picking up Jack in just a few days. What was he going to say to her? Then he realized that maybe his father would know how to approach the situation, like he knew how to approach so many. When his father answered, Nathaniel said that he wanted to talk to him and to Mom, forgetting, of course, that his mother had decided to take a vow of silence earlier in the week. Before he could say anything, his father was explaining, once again, solemnly, that it'd just have to be him because his mother was still deep in her grief about her son's death – his father actually used the phrase 'her son's death,' which was the kind of overt formal use of language that his father often employed in moments of seriousness, but which also, especially in this moment, came across as insensitive, as though Nathaniel didn't know that his mother's other son was dead – and she was currently going through a period of total silence, no talking at all, which she'd conveyed on a notepad a few days ago, writing out that she wouldn't be talking for some time in order to fully experience her son's leaving this world. Nathaniel said that his father could stop, thanks, he'd just forgotten, and he remembered now, Mom wasn't talking. He thought of how his mother had essentially remained in the hotel in town, not visiting the cabin, and that alone felt distancing, and along with the complete silence, she felt even more cut off from him and the rest of the family. At the same time, it all also felt like a kind of performance, the exact sort of thing his mother would do. The performance of being alone with her sadness: not only was she not leaving her hotel room, she was also now not speaking, and how profound, Nathaniel thought, immediately disliking that he'd thought such a thing. She's still writing little notes and communicating though, his father said. So I guess she might text you. But she won't speak. Right, I know that, though I don't understand the difference, Nathaniel said. His father immediately replied that neither did he but it wasn't for either of them to understand, this was how she was grieving her son's death. Nathaniel knew that what this actually meant was that his mother was grieving her *favorite* son's death and wanted to fully experience her *favorite* son's leaving this world. Then, again, Nathaniel felt mean for having such a thought, even though it wasn't particularly untrue. Nicholas was the son who had left home, who had made his life entirely different from the life of his parents and from Nathaniel's, and who was not only a craftsman, but also an intellectual – teaching botany and anthropology courses at a liberal arts university about thirty miles from his cabin – while Nathaniel was just a chef, didn't have beautiful and ardent thoughts about life, and had once been, for a period of time that was now over, a burden to his parents, who had to bail him out of jail twice for admittedly minor indiscretions, but still, and had to help him finish his high school degree, and then had to support him after college when he decided to forgo grad school and go to culinary school, which had nothing to do with his communications major, and which he knew they had doubted he could really be successful at, but he'd done it. He was not his brother, but he was doing okay: he was married, was an up-and-coming chef, according to a local magazine, and owned a condo with Stefanie. On the phone, after his father was finished talking, Nathaniel explained what had happened with Tammy and what Stefanie thought he should do. He asked if his father thought that was a good idea or not, if he should call Tammy back. Stefanie stopped peeling potatoes and was looking over her shoulder at Nathaniel. His father said, Stefanie's right, you need to call the woman back immediately, to which Stefanie, who apparently could hear his father, mouthed to Nathaniel, Told you, then went back to the potatoes. His father began to say something about how he wanted to talk to Nathaniel about another issue, though, if he had a minute, and Nathaniel replied by saying, Dad, no, I don't have a minute. I have to call this crazy person back.

Stefanie had stopped peeling the potatoes and Nathaniel felt her looking at him. He went to the door, grabbed his jacket, and stepped out onto the porch. He was struck by a sort of fungal, muddy odor of plant and land. He was so accustomed to the sterilized environment he was usually in, or the intensely pleasant smells of garlic and onion and oil and herbs or intensely unpleasant smells of garbage where he worked, that he often forgot the world could have this odd, not bad, smell of dirty freshness. He surveyed the land and mountains as a way to survey his thoughts, annoyed that his father had confirmed what he already knew his father would confirm, that he had to call Tammy back, and now had to figure out how to say what he had to say. He thought of the fact that his dead brother and his dead wife had chosen this town, and this place in particular, for its remoteness. He looked down the mountain as though looking through the trees and fields to the town itself, which he couldn't see, but which arose in his mind as a series of images, like a PowerPoint presentation: a small town of nine thousand people in southern Appalachia, home to a liberal arts university of around a thousand students, beside which was the town proper, a little crosshatch of streets: Main and Church and Broad, all parallel, crossed with Spring and Henry, many of the old buildings still in place, one cobblestone road a reminder of some other period, like an expression of the town's memory. Whenever he and Stefanie visited, they walked downtown with Nicholas and April and Jack, almost always in the summer, almost always with Nicholas or April pointing out things about the town, though he and Stefanie had visited before. Jack would always walk next to Nathaniel, making faces at him, his blue eyes contrasting with dark hair, his striking little boy's face, a face of playfulness and sincerity that wanted the sincerity of playfulness returned, and Nathaniel returned it: listening to his brother, and making adult 'hmm' and 'oh' sounds while giving Jack, in asides, weird, exaggerated faces that Jack giggled at.

Nathaniel was always eventually pulled into his brother's world, and he couldn't help noticing that since moving to the town, his brother had changed. He was someone Nathaniel didn't recognize. He was at once more distant and more open, Nathaniel thought. Nathaniel couldn't tell if this was because of the place, if the remote cabin and the forest and the mountain had changed his brother, or if his brother had changed first and had felt himself out of place in the city where Nathaniel still lived. His brother walked through the town, pointing out spots – family doctors and pediatricians, dentists, two chiropractors, a holistic healing doctor, a yoga studio, one meditation center (also one on a farm outside town), a new/used bookstore, several restaurants – but more than the actual places, he said that the doctor was Dr. Shelly, she was a good one, lots of homeopathic stuff, and the chiropractor was Dr. Nick, the meditation center run by a little Cambodian guy who everybody called Ted because it was easier to say than his name, the manager of the restaurant was Davis, etc., etc. Nathaniel had never known his brother to have any interest in other people, his brother barely had any interest in Nathaniel. And the fact that he lived with his family alone on the mountain seemed contradictory. Did he really know these people? Nicholas would eventually tell them that the town was associated with three nearby state parks, and along with a small art community that arose from the liberal arts college, there was an aspect of the community that was interested in outdoor sports, hiking, kayaking, rock climbing. He'd explain that there was no mall, no nearby fast food places, two gas stations, two garages, a body shop, a farmers' market twice a week that brought in the rural community who lived outside the town proper. When Nathaniel had asked him why this place – Jack tugging on his hand to tell him a joke or get him to listen to what he had to say – his brother had said the college gave him a tenure track job, and when Nathaniel said he knew his brother could've gotten a job at a big state school and made more money, so why here, Nicholas had said, I like it here because there's space to be a person alone and a person not alone, and that's what April and I want for Jack. And when his brother said this, Nathaniel had at first laughed, then saw his brother wasn't joking and wondered if Nicholas was aware of the contradiction of wanting to be alone and yet somehow suddenly having more friends, or acquaintances or whatever they were, than Nicholas ever had in the city.

Standing on the porch, Nathaniel could see the town in his mind: the old buildings set in the Blue Ridge Mountains, a part of Appalachia that was just slightly distanced from authentic Appalachia, a place mainly for middle- and upper-class white people, a destination for travelers who wanted sweeping vistas of blue mountains in the summer, achingly beautiful trees shifting shade in the fall, snow-capped peaks in the winter, and relatively few foreigners, brown people, Nathaniel thought. Nathaniel and Stefanie both noted that when she was in town, she was looked at: dark hair and dark skin and while it was overt, it wasn't malicious. White tourists visited the mountain town for its smallness, its safe quaintness, its Americana-ness, which Nathaniel hated a little, but which Nicholas seemed to have bought into. The two major streets of the town offered a view of Bear Mountain rising in the distance, blue and fog-cloaked, and then on the other side of Main, the river valley and rolling hills stretching away toward the piedmont. Nathaniel understood the idea of giving Jack some remoteness from city life, or just life in a fast-paced suburbia, but he didn't understand the wanting to be near rural depression, or limiting cultural experiences, in particular, for him, like food. Where was Jack going to eat real Indian, Italian, Cambodian, Vietnamese? Sure, there were a couple of Thai restaurants, but those weren't real, and where would he interact with the people who made these foods? At the time Nathaniel had felt sad that this chance to interact with people from all over the world, through food, and through him, Nathaniel, wasn't going to be part of Jack's growing up. It was disappointing that Nicholas had done much of his research in South America and still didn't feel the need to give something more to Jack than a privileged view of white rural-ness. But Nicholas was his brother, and Nathaniel knew there had to be something else Nicholas wasn't fully saying. He wondered if Nicholas's friends at the school knew what it was. He wondered how many of them were thinking of Nicholas now.

It seemed that almost all of the inhabitants of the town knew of the car crash. At the grocery store, the coffee shop, a restaurant he and Stefanie went to, people offered heart-felt condolences. Over the course of a couple days, Nathaniel noticed that the townspeople shared more than just condolences: they shared their knowledge of Nicholas, of April, of the boy. They seemed to want to let Nathaniel know that they knew his brother, understood him even. They told Nathaniel information that was not necessary for him to hear: we all loved Nicky so much, did you know his book about plants from the rainforest, I mean, you're his brother, you must know, but apparently his book about nature containing a hidden intelligence was a big hit. A woman said he was like their mini-celebrity. He performed public readings of the book, not just in the town, but in other actual cities. Chicago and New York. I had no idea he lived in Peru until I read his books. It must be wonderful having such a fascinating brother. Oh god, I'm sorry, the woman had said. I'm so sorry I said that. I wasn't thinking. Another had asked, Have you looked his books up on Amazon? They have hundreds of reviews. He's gonna be here even after he's gone. That's important to remember in this trying time. It made Nathaniel feel odd, even lonelier, this try at connection, this mock understanding of his brother, and it made him sense that he couldn't be for Jack anything close to what Nicholas was, not only not a biological father, but also not a person of interest. Because of the smallness of the town, Nathaniel realized after a few days, because many people knew of his brother before he died, knew of his family, the townspeople felt they had some ownership. They liked talking about Nathaniel's brother as if he was theirs. They seemed to like talking about all of it because it was such a tragedy, and it was *their* tragedy, part of them now. Nathaniel, now sitting on one of the porch rocking chairs, wondered if they'd also like talking about it even more once they learned that there was a custody battle going on, that this Tammy woman, the mother-in-law, was staking her claim. He thought the phrase, The mother-in-law is staking her claim. Fascinating and sad, they'd say. And the poor inept brother having to handle it all. But maybe they'd think good things about the situation. He imagined the townspeople, as they conveyed to each other – at decriminalizing marijuana meetings, after Hot Yoga, as discussion for meditation class, in the faculty cafeteria at the liberal arts university, at the two Thai restaurants, amid the folk rock of two small music venues, quietly in a used bookstore, too loudly in the coffee shop, in the aisle of the organic grocery, at the vegan café, among the art of local art galleries, on the trails of the state park, and at various other meeting places in their Blue Ridge mountain town in southern North Carolina – some version of the idea that it must've been so hard for the family, for the boy, of course, but also particularly for the brother, Nathaniel, who instead of simply missing his brother, had to clean his brother's house, go through his brother's and his sister-in-law's things, box up those things, set up the services, call people, accept condolences and engage in what probably felt like rote, empty sentiment, and in addition to all this, somehow find some place in himself that wasn't grieving and wasn't distracted from grief for his brother's four-year-old boy, Jack, his nephew, who the townspeople knew the brother loved so much, they'd seen him visiting often, more often than the grandparents on either side of the family, and how hard for the brother, and also for his wife.

Nathaniel looked at his phone, the phone number from the Tammy woman. He didn't want to call. He thought that if he just waited something would occur that would allow him not to call, though he knew this was not an actuality and that he'd have to call. He enjoyed imagining how the townspeople saw his own suffering, though he knew it was a selfish thing to consider at the moment, yet he did like it, there was a weird pleasure there, knowing that people knew you were going through something painful and doing it gracefully, and in thinking this thought, Nathaniel thought that he wasn't doing it gracefully, he was imagining what people were thinking and saying and his brother was gone. Yet even this realization did not stop him from further imagining a townswoman, a person who'd served him at the coffee shop, named Meredith, and what maybe she was saying to friends and family about Nathaniel, Nicholas and Jack, the situation itself. Maybe she was saying that the boy must have found it totally confusing that his aunt and uncle were now living in his family's house, sleeping in his mom and dad's bed, cooking in their kitchen. Maybe she'd tell people that she had seen the uncle and the boy at the grocery store, the uncle probably just taking the boy out so he could feel normal, and the uncle had picked Jack up, the once-happy boy now with a fearful and stunned look in his blue eyes, a sadness through his whole being. She'd explain all of this at the pro-marijuana-legalization meeting, telling the members at the meeting how she'd seen how the boy did not want to be away from the uncle, who'd ordered himself a coffee and Jack a hot chocolate, and told her something so sad. Nathaniel remembered explaining it to her: this Meredith woman had asked how the boy was doing and Jack had sort of hid from her behind Nathaniel's leg. He'd told her that Jack was sleeping next to him in his brother's bed during the night, always holding onto him very tight and often clutching his t-shirt. During the day, Jack's thumb was almost always in his mouth, and he followed Nathaniel through the house, his small hand gripping Nathaniel's pantleg even when they sat down to read a book. Nathaniel had told this Meredith person all this and imagined her now telling it to others, and he found himself thinking of how others saw his suffering, his care, his possible neglect, ineptitude, and wondered if they knew anything about him, if Nicholas had ever in conversation conveyed what a fuck-up Nathaniel had once been. He wished he hadn't said anything to this woman, but he'd kept talking, telling her that Jack not only did this holding on thing with him, he also did the same with his aunt, holding onto the black curls of his aunt's hair when she held him, or her skirt, and not only that, but Jack had actually crawled under Stefanie's skirt one afternoon when a friend recognized the boy in the bakery and came by to offer condolences and tried to say hello to Jack, had tried to say, Hi Jack, do you remember me? Ms. Katie? I'm a, I was, I mean, a good friend of your mom's. How are you?, and Jack had at first hid in Stefanie's skirt and then had actually crawled inside it, between Stefanie's legs, and the Ms. Katie woman had apologized, quietly, in a whisper, and said she hadn't meant to say that, she didn't know what possessed her to say that, and she actually began crying in the bakery, and Stefanie had told her it was fine, also in a whisper, and the woman had left, and Stefanie had had to get her order of bread and croissants from the baker by walking up to the counter with Jack clinging to her legs. Nathaniel imagined this Meredith person passing this information on to others in the town, and he knew they all probably were looking at this tragedy askance, like not wanting to turn your head to look at what you know is just a coat on a chair but feels like the silhouette of a person watching you. And though they maybe felt like they were looking at it – both the deaths of the parents and Jack's heartbreak as well as his yearning for some kind of safety, certainty – directly, inwardly, unconsciously, he knew that if they paid too much attention to these clear expressions of not wanting to lose anything more, of learning to hold so tight on to what he didn't want to lose, that it could keep them from doing anything. Because they would see the uncertainty in their own lives.

Just as he himself felt in those moments when Jack held on to his pantleg or gripped his shirt in bed, that he couldn't do anything either, couldn't possibly know what to do amid such clear and powerful impermanence. When moments like talking to this Meredith person arose in Nathaniel's mind, he sensed his distance from himself, as though he was trying to judge his actions and suffering from some outside perspective, which he knew wasn't helpful in any way, and which he also knew was a kind of romanticizing of the pain he was in, the romanticizing serving to distance himself from it, to turn it into a story he could tell himself and understand and pity, rather than doing what he should be doing, though he didn't know exactly what that was. Jack was asleep, after all.

The wind picked up, Nathaniel felt a spray of rain on his face, and he noticed a deep, damp cold move through his body. He pulled his unzipped jacket together over his chest and then went back inside, gently opening and then closing the front door so as not to wake Jack. Stefanie was dumping the potato skins in the trash. He knew that his main job here should be to find some way to help Jack, but when he thought of how he might do that, he didn't know how: was he supposed to help Jack understand where his parents were now? Were they anywhere? Did he invoke God? Was that something his brother had talked to Jack about? Did he go with a more scientific view that in nature energy cannot be created or destroyed, it can only change forms, and so Nicholas and April had simply changed forms, and were, actually, everywhere? Jack wouldn't get that though. Or would he? Would Nicholas have said something more like that? It sounded a little like Nicholas, though he and his brother had stopped having those conversations years ago, and recently, in the last year or two, what they mainly talked about, or what Nathaniel mainly questioned Nicholas about, was when Nicholas was planning on returning to the real world, which Nicholas almost always deflected. They occasionally got into arguments, matters of perspective, with Nathaniel claiming that Nicholas had retreated from life, not just from society and thus community, which Nathaniel argued Nicholas could make change in, but also from the problems of the world: you've created your own little utopia in the mountains while everyone else suffers, Nathaniel had told Nicholas. Nicholas claimed, in his cryptic, unrevealing way, that he didn't feel that was the case at all, that he wasn't looking for some separate peace, that this was his attempt to speak from his inmost intention, for his inmost intention to manifest as action, to which Nathaniel had said that it seemed selfish, and that, actually, it had all been April's idea anyway, and he was only following it out and seeing how some different life might feel. Nicholas had then quoted some old Japanese writer to Nathaniel, had actually sent Nathaniel an email, which had said, I think this explains my position best, though it hadn't explained his position at all. Nathaniel had not understood and still didn't, though he thought of it often and looked at the email often, looked at the quoted words like they were foreign objects from some other universe whose purpose and meaning he glimpsed intuitively, but with clear thinking he could not see: 'Because the blue mountains are walking they are constant. Their walk is swifter than the wind; yet those in the mountains do not sense this, do not know it. To be "in the mountains" is a flower opening "within the world." Those outside the mountains do not sense this, do not know it. Those without eyes to see the mountains do not sense, do not know, do not see, do not hear this truth. They who doubt that the mountains are walking do not yet understand their own walking.' Nathaniel had read the passage so many times he had it memorized, and he had asked Nicholas about it several times, only for Nicholas to respond that they'd talk about it in person when Nathaniel visited next, but that never occurred. Was it something about knowing nature, being close to nature, Nathaniel thought now? Something about people's oneness with nature? He thought of Jack, again, of what Nicholas would say to Jack now. It was impossible to know his brother's mind. Could he say to Jack that his parents had gone away, but they would return, in another form, as grass or trees or a dog, or as the mountain, born again? But that didn't make sense. What did *he* even think? To him, his brother was just gone, so was his brother's wife, April, who Nathaniel liked in theory, but not always in practice. That's all he felt – both were just gone. And he hated it, he didn't want them gone, especially his brother, but that's all that was left in their place: a goneness. The cabin, the cupboards of this kitchen, the small farm his brother had made, all of it was just things. Was he supposed to simply help Jack let go of them, his parents? But how could he do that, he wondered, when he knew that all he wanted to do was also hold on to his brother? Something tightened in Nathaniel's chest when he realized he had no idea what to do with or for Jack, and now, standing in the kitchen watching Stefanie rinsing some carrots, he tried to refocus on getting everything done so that he could understand clearly how to help Jack, and to begin doing it, because so far it felt a little like he'd been putting it off.

Nathaniel thought that all week he'd had to ask Jack to go away, when all the boy wanted to do was hold on to Nathaniel: telling Jack he wanted him to play with Stefanie in the backyard or could Jack go to the greenhouse to get some basil or sage, fill this basket, telling him these things so that Nathaniel could have a few moments alone on the phone with a local estate attorney, with the funeral home, with the bank, who he had to call twice, because he didn't have the death certificates, calling the department of health to ask how to get the death certificates, on the phone with his brother's school to figure out what insurance he had so that Nathaniel could figure out how life insurance was supposed to work, and also setting up cancelation dates for things like utilities and the postal service, all phone calls that required him to say that he was calling on behalf of his brother and sister-in-law, who had recently passed away, which he didn't want Jack hearing over and over again, and all of which he wanted finished so that he could just focus on Jack. Yet now, standing in the kitchen with Stefanie, wondering why she was cleaning carrots and potatoes at ten in the morning, Jack napping because he'd gotten up so early and had worn himself out, there was now his brother's mother-in-law, Tammy, in addition to everything else, and after listening to Stefanie tell him again, now slicing the potatoes, that he needed to call this woman back right now, no more waffling, that this was the most important thing, more than anything else now, he said he got it and told Stefanie that okay, he understood, he had to call.

From the boy's bedroom, he heard Jack begin to make half-crying noises as he woke up. They looked at each other, unmoving for a moment, as if some game, waiting for the word that would unfreeze them. They had learned that these half-crying noises didn't mean he would wake up fully. He would cry some, then talk a little at the mobile that Nicholas had made, which hung above the bed, the mobile fashioned out of wood, little birds that Nathaniel's brother had carved that bobbed up and down on three separate 'branches' of the mobile. After talking at the mobile for a few minutes, both Nathaniel and Stefanie listening, Jack stopped and fell asleep again, and, it felt to Nathaniel, he was free to operate in the world, and in his mind, again. Again, the stream and the rain emphasized the quiet around them, and after Jack was quiet, Nathaniel decided to do it.

He told Stefanie, in a moment of clarity, that he was going to call Tammy on speakerphone and he wanted Stefanie to grab her phone and record the call, so he could share it with his father, the lawyer, to see if this woman had any actual legal rights. He tapped the woman's last incoming call on his phone's screen and then hit the green button. He reminded himself to speak in a low voice, not quite a whisper, so that he wouldn't wake Jack. The mother-in-law answered her cell phone, and Nathaniel said hello, it was Nathaniel, to which he and Stefanie heard (Nathaniel's phone was sitting on the counter. Stefanie also had her phone out and was holding it close to Nathaniel's phone on the counter in order to record the call), I know who it is, what's up, which made Nathaniel pause. They could hear her driving, that monotonous sound of static behind her voice – the hollow white noise of a car traveling over road, and then behind that sound, Nathaniel heard what must've been rain. It was raining where she was too. Nathaniel took a short breath and continued by saying that he was sorry to call back, to be bothering her here, but he maybe hadn't heard correctly, but did she say that she was coming to pick Jack up on Friday? She told Nathaniel he had heard her one hundred percent correctly. She was on her way, and it was what, Tuesday now, so she would arrive Friday morning, and then would drive Jack back that afternoon or the next day. They could arrange for all of Jack's things to be boxed and shipped to her whenever was convenient for them, but not too long, because she wanted Jack to feel at home with her. Stefanie's eyes went wide and she shook her head when she heard this information, as though hearing it for the first time. Nathaniel said that he didn't want to be rude, but he wanted to ask why Tammy thought that she would be taking the boy. Well then ask it, the mother-in-law said. What? Nathaniel said. You said you wanted to ask it, the mother-in-law said. So ask it. Okay, Nathaniel said. Why are you—. I'm just fucking with you, the mother-in-law said, and sort of snort chuckled at this and then said, in an annoyed and almost vacant voice, Who else is going to take him? You? I know neither of you wanted kids. April and I talked. Spoke words on the phone. Conveyed information to each other. Plus, I talked to April about it all when Jack was born. He's coming with me. Nathaniel and Stefanie made confused-looking faces at each other, and Nathaniel leaned into the phone resting on the counter, and said that that was, you know, he didn't think certain, you know, things pertained, since, actually. He stopped, composed himself, as if finally realizing the reality of what he was encountering, and said that look, all that sounded odd because he was told that in the event that both Nicholas and April should pass away, that guardianship would pass to him and Stefanie. Nathaniel heard himself saying this in his most cordial, most warm voice, a voice that, he felt, asked for understanding. The mother-in-law said that that's not what she was told and that wasn't what was happening anyway – she knew about both of them and there was no way Jack was going to *live the rest of his life* with them. I mean, do you get that: you think he's going to live until he's an *adult* with you, Nathaniel? There was a pause, as though the universe was stretched on a taut line between the past and future, the present suddenly unavoidable in its tension, and this tension was expressed, Nathaniel felt, in the way she had used his name, as though he himself was an indictment of himself. He asked if Tammy had any documentation of her guardianship, or did she only *speak* to April, see, because that wouldn't constitute *legal* guardianship. Stefanie was nodding, her eyes still wide, her hand still holding her own cell phone and recording the call. The mother-in-law said that she didn't have any *documentation*, no, but that even a *will* wasn't binding, only a court could grant *legal guardianship, Nathaniel,* though if there was a will, she'd abide by it, and actually, she thought that there probably was one, and it most likely showed that *she* was to be the guardian, and she was really sorry, here, but the truth was she knew she was meant to be the guardian and knew that probably pissed off Nathaniel and Chiquita Banana over there – Stefanie stepped backward, as though the absurdity of the remark contained a physical force, and threw her arms up and let them flap at her sides in apparent disgust – but they'd just have to get over it because this is what April wanted, she knew that for a fact, *Nathaniel,* and it was better for Jack anyway to have an experienced parent. Just because he and his brother were Mr. Educated didn't mean she was a moron or that he could push her aside, she had her rights, she knew them, and she was on her way to pick up the kid, and unless he could prove otherwise, she was just really sorry, but *she* was the guardian here.

Nathaniel had begun to say that well maybe they'd have to talk about this together when she arrived, and would she, but as he was saying it, Stefanie was shaking her head, indicating that Tammy had hung up. Nathaniel looked at her, his mouth slightly open, and Stefanie said, Chiquita Banana. Really? Because my dad is from Mexico? That doesn't even make sense. Nathaniel nodded his head and said they needed to remain calm here, which was what he believed Nicholas might say. He continued by saying that it was very important not to do anything rash or emotional that could jeopardize Jack's chances of being with them, which was the sole goal here, suddenly a very important goal that Nathaniel hadn't even thought was going to be a goal or even thought was going to be a real problem he had to deal with. The problem had somehow not felt *actual* until being confirmed by his brother's mother-in-law, this Tammy woman. I'm not not calm, Stefanie said. I'm just saying that woman is a racist bitch. I think that's exactly right, Nathaniel said calmly, aware that he was acting calm. He added that he supported the notion that this Tammy woman was obviously a racist, there was definitely no questioning that, though maybe bitch was too much, he said, feeling it was a very composed thing to say, but that wasn't the point here, he went on, the point was about Jack, they needed to figure out how Jack could stay with them, and, Nathaniel wondered, there had to be a will or something somewhere in here, so they'd just have to start going through some of the boxes they'd packed, go through the boxes again, and see if they could find it. He said he'd call his father – the *lawyer*, he said in a deep baritone that was supposed to be funny but elicited no response from Stefanie, probably, Nathaniel thought, because he shouldn't be joking – who had been coming over each day for a few hours to help pack, and see if he wanted to come and help them with this new problem, this woman.

He went down the hall to his brother's small office, really just a guest room, with a desk and a twin-sized bed, which he and Stefanie had squeezed into when they visited in the past. They'd packed up much of the room, and now Nathaniel began looking through the papers again, to see if he could find a will. Rain was still falling outside the cabin, a steady, calming sound. A mutter of thunder moved over the cabin. He'd looked through all these papers already, knew the will wasn't there, but he shuffled through a box again, not really paying attention to what he was doing. He opened an accordion folder and looked through the papers there. Drawings that Nicholas had made of plants and trees, with short descriptions, scientific and common names. Their mother had liked these drawings, and had had several framed and hung in her office at the university where she taught, as well as in her home. Nathaniel listened to the rain falling on the trees of the early springtime mountain, and thought that the rain, based on the radar he'd looked at on his phone, would soon move to the town proper some ten miles southeast. There it would become more sporadic yet maybe somehow drearier.

His brother had once told him of a group in town called CALM-AA, and he'd actually met a member of the group before, who was in one of Nicholas's grad classes, a woman named Maddie Dobenstein. CALM-AA stood for Citizens for A Less Materialistic and Apathetic America and met in the basement of the Unitarian Church, and at first Nathaniel thought it sounded like some kind of joke, but apparently it was real, they met and had conversations much like the pro-marijuana group. Nathaniel thought that even those who felt apathy and ambivalence toward all things would be moved to note that the deaths of the boy's parents, and the situation with the rest of the family, was particularly poignant. He put some folders back in a box and thought that Maddie Dobenstein might comment on the sad affair at the next group discussion. He knew from Nicholas that the members of CALM-AA shared either their emotionally numb responses to the state of the materialistic culture they lived in and their disappointingly materialistic part-hippy part-bohemian part-bourgie lives, or noted, with hope, that they were again feeling something, could see beyond the sad materialism and rote-ness and vapidity of their American lives, and he wondered what they would think of this. He pictured all the members of the group suddenly feeling a kind of interest they had not felt in some time when Maddie, normally one of the most bored of the group, asked if everyone had heard about the boy's parents who had died on Smoky Mills Road, which would draw nods from the circle of CALM-AA, and which would then allow her to relate that she had heard about the mother of the dead son. Had anyone heard about her? None of the members had heard, Nathaniel imagined. All of them shook their heads, though Tom, who some suspected of being not really apathetic, deluding himself about his uncaringness, would say No, he hadn't, what about her? Listening to the steady rain, Nathaniel thought of Maddie telling how she'd heard that the mother of the dead son, the grandmother of little Jack, had taken a vow of silence. This mother would not speak again until she had fully accepted the fact that her son was dead, was what Maddie would convey, and that this process could take who knew how long, but the mother had not spoken for a week. Nathaniel saw this Maddie person explaining that she herself had seen the mother one day, ordering sandwiches from the Vegan Café, and in order to do so, this mother and grandmother had written her order on a legal pad she carried with her (which was something that Nathaniel's father had told him his mother had done, which embarrassed Nathaniel, but which he knew he shouldn't be embarrassed about, or maybe simply shouldn't be concerned about his embarrassment), and what devotion, Maddie would tell the group, didn't everyone think? What a reverence for things, what an act to make. Nathaniel could see this Maddie Dobenstein person saying something like she had to admit that she found this particularly moving, one of the most moving things that she had witnessed in a long time, one of the most real things, and she hated the way people used this word, real, that people said things like 'it was real' or whatever, as though there were a certain number of moments in one's life that were real moments and that all the rest were just unreal capitalistic, consumerist bullshit moments, like somehow watching reality TV,

31

which was clearly fake, was somehow less real than say staring at a tree. The problem, Maddie might add, was that every moment, every life, was immersed in complete and total reality, and it was just that people didn't want to deal with that, that was too hard. They didn't want to experience the actual reality of watching a reality TV show, which was that it was a complete waste of time, a numbing, in the same way that a drug addict doesn't want to see the reality of their life, which is that it is a waste, in the same way we here at CALM-AA don't want to really look at the reality of our apathy, which is that it's pointless, and so what people do is they construct 'real' moments and call the rest bullshit, and Maddie really hated that. But watching this mother was such a real thing, Nathaniel could see this Maddie person saying about his mother, like his mother had chosen some real way to express her suffering. This mother's actions felt completely and wholly real, as if everything else around it was only sketched, and that was because this woman, this mother and grandmother, was attempting, Maddie would explain, to live out every moment as though it was completely real. What this mother highlighted, Maddie would explain, was that the people around her did not want to do this. They didn't want to take part in reality in this way. They only wanted to take part in a capitalistic process covered over in some faux-peaceful hippy philosophy, and Nathaniel, in what he understood as the sweeping final drama of this imagining, saw Maddie now saying that in particular she was going to stop going to her yoga classes because going to those classes was not about yoga, it was about who was getting something, who was being something, who was more devoted, who was better, and who was going further and pushing harder, and what bullshit, more fakery, but this mother, Maddie would say – this woman wasn't bawling her eyes out as was popular when sons died on television, she wasn't frantic or hysterical with grief, she wasn't displaying her grief for anyone, she wasn't making it about who had more grief or who suffered more or who was feeling deeply in their lives. This woman, Maddie would explain, she wasn't doing anything for anyone else or anything else, not for other people and not to fit into some prescribed form of progressivism or liberalism. She was simply allowing herself, as far as Maddie could tell, to feel something fully. Allowing herself the time and the silence to do that. Nathaniel saw this Maddie person, now crying a little in the CALM-AA meeting, say it was like a great lightness opened in herself and she'd cried and felt things, all kinds of things, that she couldn't remember feeling in just a long, long time, and in imagining this, Nathaniel felt himself moved, and then remembered that his brother was gone, that this thing he had made up was a fantasy, and his brother was gone. Just gone. And who knew what his mother was doing anyway? He wasn't even sure why he was doing this imagining – it was just something he'd always done, he'd always imagined people's responses to his food, his failures, his appearance, his family, trivial things and meaningful things, like how they saw him right now, if they believed he was being unselfish, self-sacrificing, a good brother, son, godparent, in the same way he wondered what they felt about Stefanie, about his mother and father – and he knew he should stop, but he began thinking of other members of CALM-AA, members who might feel that his mother was actually being deeply narcissistic, show-offy, and therefore selfish, but before he could continue he heard something from the kitchen and he realized he didn't know how long he'd been in the room, staring vacantly at some papers, not really looking at them. Out the window, the rain had stopped and patches of blue began to show in the sky through the grey and white cumulus.

Nathaniel closed the box full of papers and folders that he wasn't really concentrating on, though he hadn't seen a will, he was pretty sure he hadn't seen one, and walked to the kitchen to investigate the sound he'd heard, but then was overtaken with the thought that the rain had stopped and the eastern side of the mountain would be a patchwork of sun and shadow, making it appear, if one were viewing the side of the mountain from the valley, as though the trees were slowly undulating toward some new destination, moving wavelike, heaving slowly forward. He'd witnessed this once when driving up the mountain to Nicholas's place. The small cabins that populated the mountainside appeared to be moving under the shifting shade and sun. He knew that if one were looking at the cabins on the mountainside, Nicholas and April's place would be seen as a glint of sun off the tin roof and solar panels. The property was well-maintained, trails clearly visible overhead, the barn also tin-roofed, the garden and greenhouse well-kept, a stream running by the main cabin. All would appear exactly as it should be, and it was nothing Nathaniel himself could have constructed, and the life inside the cabin, before Nicholas and April had died, was not one he could ever recreate for Jack, he thought. From a certain point of view far away from the cabin, Nathaniel knew that none of the discussions, the analysis of the situation, the reanalysis, the hesitation about what to do, the lack of hesitation, the need for clarity amid the uncertainty, none of what was occurring on the inside of the cabin would feel a part of reality at all, and no one looking at the cabin would know anything different was occurring there, but it was, he thought.

In the kitchen, Nathaniel focused on what he should be focusing on, telling himself to pay attention, and asked Stefanie if maybe they were acting a little too impulsively here. If maybe it wasn't a great idea for Jack to be with them. After all, Nathaniel wasn't exactly in a good place financially. When are you ever? Stefanie said. Oh, haha, Nathaniel said in a mock-annoyed manner, to which Stefanie did an aware-of-how-stupid-the-joke-was-toothy-grin. But seriously, he told her, his job didn't pay enough, did it? To support a child? How much did children cost, exactly? They hadn't thought about that. He could Google it but his brother didn't have internet on the property, and while there was a cell signal, it was weak. Not only this, he said, but he also wanted, no, he needed his own restaurant, it's what he'd been working for for so long, and certain things were finally coming into place. They had a little money saved up, and he didn't want to be working for a rich family his entire life. He wanted to, you know, make an impact, he said. A food impact, Stefanie said. Jamie Oliver shit, she said. I mean, sort of, he said. Whatever. The job itself as a private chef for this ridiculous family was already difficult, he thought. He drove nearly an hour on Thursday, to Greensboro, stayed at the Camerons' Thursday night in the guest house so that he could prepare Friday's dinner, then stayed again Friday night so that he could wake up and prepare Saturday's dinner, and then stayed again Saturday night so that he could wake up very early on Sunday to prepare brunch for the entire Cameron family, a group of around twenty people, depending on the weekend, so that he often arrived home Sunday evening so tired he couldn't do anything other than stare at the television, and then it was back to work on Monday prepping at the country club, a second job that he truly hated – a rote menu with rote flavors. And yet cooking, the simple act of it, not being a chef, but being a cook, was not only finally something he was good at, but also something that he felt made an actual impact on the world. People need to eat, Stefanie said. And they need to eat high-quality local foods prepared rustically. Okay, the mocking thing is hurting my feelings a little, he said. She walked over to him in the kitchen, squeezed his arm, and said, I love your food, don't be so uptight. Nathaniel said but that was exactly the thing: he was uptight. He was a seriously uptight person. He was so uptight that his brother died a week ago and he was worrying about his job in relation to his nephew – that was the definition of uptight. He was hating himself a little bit that he was thinking about himself here and his career, which was an admittedly superficial concern, he knew that, but it was something he had worked on for so long, and he didn't like how he was saying all this, that he might be implying that Jack was somehow going to mess that up, that's not what he was implying. What are you implying then? Stefanie said. Because it sounds like all you're doing is being worried about things you can't control. I'm worried we won't be good parents to Jack, he said. And you're right, maybe that's not a thing we can control, but we should think about it. We have to, he said. For Jack's sake. Because maybe what he had failed to acknowledge, maybe what this Tammy woman had *revealed*, was that while he loved Jack, maybe they weren't exactly in a position to take him, maybe Tammy was right, maybe this was an opportunity they should really look at?

Stefanie looked at him as she was putting the sliced potatoes and carrots into a Tupperware bowl. She put on the lid and then put the bowl in the refrigerator. After a moment she asked if maybe he thought he was doing more than thinking about just Jack's welfare here? Maybe he was being actually selfish. She went to the front door and put on her raincoat and told him that if he really wanted to continue this conversation, they could, but he knew the answer was pretty simple. I don't know that the answer is simple at all, he said. She said that he knew what Nicholas wanted, she herself knew what April wanted, they were the godparents. Even if this wasn't public record, Nicholas and April had asked *both of them*, at the same time, at Jack's first birthday actually, if they would be the guardians. Simple. She put on a pair of rubber boots she kept outside, near the door. Nathaniel was hobbled over, getting his boots on as well. The bottoms of both pairs were covered in mud. Nathaniel looked at their bootprints of dried mud, that moved off the porch, down the steps, and then into the yard, which wasn't a yard, but was just the mountain. The traces of their coming and going. And we accepted, Stefanie said.

She stepped off the porch with Nathaniel following, Stefanie walking fast, her arms crossed across her chest against the wind, which was moving the clouds above relatively quickly across the sky. Her body's quick movements, quick pace, conveyed her slight irritation toward him. Nathaniel caught up to her and pulled on her coat a little and she glanced at him, relaxed her arms. They walked side by side to the garden, a mile away on the property. Stefanie held her phone in her left hand, and on it, a feed from Jack's room monitor. She showed it to Nathaniel and made a he's-so-cute face – it was both audio and visual, but was extremely pixelated and blurry because it was connected to such a weak cell signal, but they could still see the boy in his bed, in black and white – the image seeming almost like a negative of a photograph – sleeping on his side in his bed, with what they both knew was a blue blanket bunched up near his chin and face, his left hand cupping his left ear, a thing the boy did when he slept or in moments of what they deemed 'worry.' The cat slept on a chair in the corner. Stefanie put the phone in her pocket – the phone would vibrate if he moved – and said that Nathaniel didn't need to bring his self-doubt to this. Please don't do that, she said. He brought it to everything else. He brought it to his life with her, he brought it to his job, he brought it to his existence as a person, and every time he did, it made her feel like shit, because it meant in some way that he wasn't content with her.

Their boots made squishing noises on the dirt, now mud, path. It was still cold in the mountains, spring defrosting rather than warming, and yet small wildflowers, the size of bees, grew along the trail. They were in a pocket of sunlight that broke through the trees and was highlighted by mist rising from the ground, then they were in the shadow of a quick-moving cloud. Nathaniel told her that he didn't want her to feel that way. He didn't mean to bring any doubt into this, he just wanted to know if Stefanie really wanted to do this. No, that's not it, she said. You understand that this is going to be a fight of some kind, and you want to run from it. You don't want to engage in it because you think that you're above it in some way. You're just like your brother in that respect. For a moment, neither of them said anything. Nathaniel felt the force of the absence of the dead brother, of April, too. As though his name conjured both his presence and his absence at once, and the confusion between those two things. Here and gone, Nathaniel thought without willing himself to think it, like the thought wasn't his. Where did a thing come from and where did it go? All this in his mind in the space of a moment felt like the reality of the moon reflected in water: the moon is there, in the water, and also not, and in the same way, these thoughts existed in his body and also not, and you were here for a short time in the world and then you were gone, and this coming and going seemed to contain some hidden message, like the coming and going itself was attempting to say something, as though everything was trying to tell itself something, though he didn't know what. He thought of Jack and felt a pressure rise through his chest and into his head and stopped himself from crying by biting his cheek hard. Stefanie said she was sorry – she shouldn't have said that about his brother. Her hand briefly touched his and in the touch, he felt a small release. Nathaniel shook his head and quietly said it was okay, it was fair, she was being accurate. He did think Nicholas ran away to some degree – that was the meaning of his moving out here. His brother couldn't deal with certain things. They were the same in that regard, they didn't like to fight. Even when younger, they didn't fight as kids. Or rarely did. Not like other brothers he knew. After a moment he said that he missed Nicholas. Stefanie moved her body close to his and in the way bodies communicate their own actuality, he accepted wordlessly, and they held each other standing under the trees on the trail.

Nathaniel said okay, okay, and they continued walking and after a moment he thought that Stefanie was right, that he didn't want to fight with this Tammy woman. So much of his existence was fighting. His career took getting good reviews and getting noticed and creating new things not solely because he wanted to be creating dishes, but because that's what the industry demanded, and there was a certain kind of 'new' that was acceptable, there was a certain kind of creation that was immediately obvious as creative, and in this way, he'd realized over time, he was in a kind of box — there were things he had to do, this wasn't purely creative — and it made the thing he did less in some way, corrupted in some way, and Stefanie was right, he was a little like his brother, he was tired of fighting so much for what he wanted. Had he not proved himself? Did he even need to? He'd worked under one of the best chefs in the city, he'd helped open two new restaurants, he'd been featured in the local magazine as a chef to 'watch out' for, and yet he couldn't get help starting the kind of restaurant he wanted to start. It was like he was going backward. He was a private chef. He knew he was selfish. He was selfish and idealistic about his job, which was a thing he didn't think he should have to fight for, the fighting ruined some part of it, and he knew that she knew this made him, often, like now, feel shitty. Like maybe he wasn't actually good at what he did — maybe he was just lucky even to work for the Camerons. And because of all this, he thought, maybe the clear answer here was to just let Tammy have Jack because he already had to go back home in a few days and deal with the fallout from a mediocre review of his spring menu at the country club, a review which had called the menu theoretically interesting, but almost too interested in the small things, in pure tastes, so that everything was a little bland. As though Nathaniel had any real choice in that menu. He had to go back home and deal with that on top of the ever-pervasive stigma about vegetarian food in the first place, as though good vegetarian food can't be rustic and elegant, can't be simple and complex, can't taste great and be affordable, that it's either plates of mush or salads. Nathaniel said, I don't know, maybe this is wrong, maybe we can't do it. How are we supposed to raise Jack and live our lives? Stefanie stopped walking and asked him what were they supposed to be talking about here? Fuck, he said. I know. See, that's evidence itself though. All I do is think about myself. I've been having these terrible moments where I imagine what the town is thinking about all this. She told him to stop. She didn't want to hear about the existential crisis of his career or whatever right now, she didn't want to hear his food philosophy again. She knew his food philosophy. She was on board with it. She didn't need to hear it again. He said that she was right, he was done, sorry, he just had to get that out.

They came to a part of the trail that crossed a stream – Nicholas had built a wooden bridge some years before, complete with a handrail. He'd built it, Nathaniel remembered, when he had moved himself and April to the property, before he had cleared part of the woods for the garden and greenhouse. Nathaniel had helped him construct the bridge, which basically meant that he held boards in place while Nicholas hammered and constructed. They walked across, the bridge now bowed, moving gently above the rushing stream. Nathaniel thought of the things Nicholas could do well, things which came easily to him while he himself could barely do one thing well, he could barely be a good husband to Stefanie, be a decent chef, be a somewhat involved son, and also do other things he cared about like working in some hiking and tennis from time to time, he could barely even approach the idea, he was so busy, about how to actually be a decent person, so how was he going to be a parent? In an effort to stop thinking this, he said that what it came down to was that he was very anxious now that this Tammy person had said her piece. Stefanie agreed.

The garden emerged, through trees and fog, set in a large clearing. It had recently been planted, small green sprouts coming up in places, the neat rows of dirt still noticeable. In the back of the garden, some larger plants, winter vegetables. Nathaniel watched Stefanie walk around the garden to where potatoes and carrots grew. She began to dig up carrots and turnips from the ground. She seemed so capable of doing, of completing tasks, he didn't know how, though at the same time he thought that there was no reason to be out here getting vegetables. She'd peeled and cut up potatoes and carrots already. What did they need more for? As the carrots and turnips came up from the wet dirt, Nathaniel collected them where they lay. She told him that his problem, which had always been his problem, was that he had lost his original intention in all of this, he had allowed himself to be influenced by others and by himself. She said that that was the difference between their two families: his family was a family of people who overthought everything, though his parents had improved now that they were nearing retirement, as he himself had described, and Nicholas had apparently entered some way of life that was unfathomable to them both, but Stefanie had parents who taught her to just do things. When you have a father in Mexico and mother in Dallas, you learn to just do what you have to do. She said that wasn't he happiest when he was just making food, making a dish, creating, wasn't that the thing? Why add all this extra onto it? She didn't like the phrase 'man up' because they were living in a culture that was still stupidly patriarchal, and obviously 'grow some balls' was insensitive, so maybe she'd use the thing the pilot says in *Raiders of the Lost Ark,* 'show some backbone.' Seriously, she said. Show some backbone. Nathaniel was gathering the vegetables and he said, Okay, okay, yeah, I got it, you're right, and Stefanie was saying that she knew she was right. She knew she was right because she was the kind of the kid who got left at home when her mother used to go to the bar. She was seven and had to make dinner for herself. She was eight and had to set her alarm, make her lunch, and walk to school by herself. She took care of her father when she was twelve and thirteen and he refused a hospital. She didn't want to do it. But she also didn't get to think about it. She just did what she had to do. Nathaniel was picking up the vegetables behind her, now saying, I think that's enough, that's plenty of carrots. Didn't you already cut a bunch of carrots up? Stefanie pushed the spade into the dirt and looked at Nathaniel. I'll say when there are enough carrots, she said in a mock-dad voice. He stood up and nodded his head and said she was right, he got it, and said,

I'm done, I'm over it. We can do this. She quickly kissed him on the cheek and said, That's better.

They walked back to the cabin and when they arrived, Jack was just waking, and when he was fully up from the nap, Nathaniel watched him walk from his bed toward him and immediately grab his pantleg. He sort of combed Jack's black hair into place, Jack's wide blue eyes briefly looking up at him and then back down. Want to read a book? Nathaniel said. Jack put his thumb in his mouth and nodded. They went down the hall and into the small family room. Nathaniel picked Jack up so he could choose a book from what was a sturdy, probably oak bookshelf that Nicholas had constructed. Jack pulled a book about a bear in a toy store, whose overalls are missing a button. The bear, convinced that a new button will help him find a home, has an adventure at night in a department store. Nathaniel had read the book to Jack what seemed to be countless times since they arrived – and when reading it the first time, unfamiliar with the book, he felt so moved he almost wasn't able to complete it without his voice wavering and had to take several breaths and then cough in order to compose himself. Now Jack held the book while Nathaniel held him and when Nathaniel sat him on the sofa, then sat next to him, Jack immediately stood up on the sofa, and sat on Nathaniel's lap, holding, with his left hand, the sleeve of Nathaniel's shirt. Jack handed him the book, and Nathaniel said, Okay, you turn the pages, and Jack opened the book, and they began, and Nathaniel tried to be fully there for Jack, but he was thinking about how Jack might be thinking of how Nicholas read the book, or how April read it, how they probably read it with different inflections, how they emphasized parts that Nathaniel maybe didn't know to emphasize, and along with this, since he'd now read the book several times, he knew to distance himself from the sentimental story he was a reading, a story about a bear wanting a family, feeling outcast, left out, alone, a story which would be trite and amusingly, maybe even warmly, clichéd at any other time, but that was now, Nathaniel couldn't help but feel, exactly what Jack was feeling, a book chosen because it mirrored Jack's own feelings, and was probably Jack's way of indicating, over and over and over, in a child's way, his longing to be with his family, to have a family, and if Nathaniel allowed himself to think about it too much, to consider this barely coded message and to really be there with Jack and therefore with the book, he would start crying. So he read it distantly, thinking of the Tammy woman, of how to figure out that situation, while Jack turned the pages. When he finished, and Jack closed the book – he always closed it – he turned it over and looked at Nathaniel and said, Again. Nathaniel said, Yeah, one more time, then we need to eat lunch, and when he said it, Jack sat up higher in his lap and hugged him around the neck briefly, then opened the book again.

After reading, Nathaniel fed Jack lunch and played with him on the kitchen floor and in the afternoon they went on a walk. The day passed quickly, quicker than Nathaniel was used to. Jack was quiet and sullen, but Nathaniel so sensed a wish in his small body for physical expression. Nathaniel played a wooden block game with him, he kicked the soccer ball with him in the muddy yard, they read another couple of books, thankfully not the bear book. Nathaniel watched Jack, his play withdrawn, and Nathaniel thought his play seemed to be more of an attempt at play than actual play, which if he allowed himself to think about, just like when he thought about the story the boy wanted read to him over and over, made it impossible for Nathaniel to engage, so he tried to stop thinking about it.

That evening, Nathaniel made pan-roasted chicken, with the vegetables on hand and a mushroom cream sauce. For Jack, homemade mac and cheese. They ate quietly in the kitchen, Jack watching them and looking away in the same way Nathaniel felt he was observing Jack. Nathaniel watched Jack, and watched Stefanie, thinking about how he could never be Nicholas, how Stefanie couldn't be April – they would always and only be substitutes. He thought of April, how when he first met her, he didn't know how to talk with her, she was so quiet. It unnerved him. She watched. Yet when she finally spoke, he found her easy, kind, and also full of her own anxieties that he hadn't seen. She wasn't this observant, perfect person, and this understanding – Nathaniel remembered now while eating dinner, watching Jack brush his long hair out of his face while spooning mac and cheese to his mouth – endeared her to him, and thinking of it now, it made him feel like maybe he and Stefanie could do this, that their flaws weren't an inescapable problem. There was a piece of macaroni on Jack's face and Nathaniel reached across the table with his napkin and wiped it off, as though symbolically proving to himself that he was capable, that he could do this. He ate a piece of chicken and thought of April, knew from Nicholas that people found her odd, and he did, too, at first, and though he wasn't sure he liked her, he did feel an odd admiration of her, that she was okay being considered odd and wasn't going to change herself to fit some more prescribed idea of normal. She didn't do any social media, didn't even look at the internet, had influenced Nicholas not to look at the internet, almost never drank, though she claimed she didn't dislike drinking, and was impressed when Nathaniel told her he was a vegetarian chef, but was also distant when he revealed he himself ate meat, as though she was judging him, but he'd learned, over maybe a half a year or so, that she wasn't, she was only observing. Nicholas had told Nathaniel that the townspeople thought April was odd, he told Nathaniel he could just see it. Nathaniel imagined that probably no one disliked her, no one thought she was a bad person or that there was anything malicious in her, they just thought she was strange, maybe they mistakenly thought she was a little dim, all that quietness: Nicholas had explained that her fellow teachers at McComb Montessori had learned that, along with the weirdness surrounding technology, she had a shaman she met with occasionally, and that while this was not terribly strange for their town (many people in the town had gone to one of the two Peruvian shamans for a cleansing), what was odd was that April invited the shaman to her and Nicholas's cabin on the mountain. The shaman had stayed for several days. This was all sometime in her sixth month of pregnancy, and while the shaman himself didn't reveal any of what had gone on during those days, April did, Nicholas had told Nathaniel. She had told her friends, or supposed friends at the school, that the shaman took the whole family on a cleansing journey. Nathaniel remembered how Nicholas explained that the other teachers asked April what she meant by whole family, since it was just her and Nicholas at that point, and she'd replied that she meant

Jack, too, of course. Nicholas just knew that the other teachers at McComb Montessori glanced at one another, out of comedic suspicion, because apparently this woman believed that her unborn child had also entered the dream dimension with her and Nicholas, and sure, the whole shaman thing was acceptable for adults, many of the townspeople would've thought, but it was of course just a psychological trick, a way of meditating maybe, all that drumming meant to bring one into a trance-like state which could thereby allow a person to see into their own idiosyncrasies and flaws and be accepting of those things, possibly learn from them, or, alternately, if there were drugs involved, the drugs opening a person to some unseen aspect of themselves, but to think that an unborn child also experienced this journey was a little superstitious. Nicholas had said he could just see that to the Montessori teachers this all was a little superstitious, and also sort of dumb, and therefore, he'd said, that's how they saw April.

Stefanie was cutting some of her chicken for Jack, Nathaniel noticed, and though he'd been aware of Jack asking for some chicken, he hadn't actually been seeing what he was seeing because of his thinking, though now he saw it because the pieces of chicken seemed too big. Cut it a little smaller, Nathaniel said. Stefanie looked at him. They're small enough. Jack do you want the pieces smaller? Nathaniel asked him. Jack looked between the two of them and Stefanie said, They don't need to be smaller. They're fine. Don't be so controlling, I know what I'm doing. Nathaniel looked at her and tried to convey with his eyes that he wasn't trying to be controlling. The boy took the pieces from her and began eating them without any trouble.

Nathaniel saw, for a moment, that this was what it would be like: he would have one idea of how to care for Jack, Stefanie would have another, and they'd be at odds, the gap would only get bigger. In the same way that, when April claimed that she had seen her unborn son's face in whatever astral-dreamscape the shaman had brought her to, the other teachers couldn't help but laugh, already constructing stories for their spouses and friends, and she'd been at odds with them. In the same way that the Tammy woman thought she knew what was best for Jack, and now Nathaniel and Stefanie were at odds with her. Everyone was always thinking they knew the right way to live, Nathaniel thought, eating some of his potatoes. The other teachers at McComb Montessori thought they knew better than April what was the right way to live, that her way was strange, stupid, and this was what caused isolation. Nathaniel knew from Nicholas that April didn't talk much with the other teachers, the shaman thing being one of the first stories she'd told after moving to the town. Nicholas had told him that all April had wanted from this journey with the shaman was to open up a calm, loving space for the child to come into because she was experiencing some anxiety about the pregnancy. This was what Nicholas had told Nathaniel on the phone, this was what Nicholas told Nathaniel that April wanted, a simple thing, and Nicholas said he knew the story had gotten around, and though he didn't care, he cared that it was isolating April and making her feel like her worries weren't real. She was thirty-six after all, and this was their first child. She and Nicholas hadn't been able to get pregnant before, and now she was able to, and what might that mean? She was a little scared, sometimes more than a little,

Nathaniel remembered Nicholas telling him, but how could you make that clear to people? You couldn't. And so, Nicholas had explained, he knew that the story had gotten around town, and all he could hope was that when people gossiped about how she wouldn't allow plastic toys in her house, how the family didn't have television, how there was no internet connection on the property, how they grew and ate their own vegetables and built their own house, which they all probably thought was commendable and sustainable, but also a little wild, and how weird they all thought the shaman thing was, maybe they would also think, initially out of guilt and shame but then out of actual conviction, that she was just trying, you know. Like us all.

Jack asked to be excused, and Nathaniel looked at him. His plate was partially finished, and Nathaniel felt a small guilt for not paying attention while eating, not talking to Jack, but then Stefanie hadn't either. Come here, Nathaniel said. Jack came over and grabbed Nathaniel's pantleg. Ice cream? Nathaniel said. Jack smiled, and Nathaniel stood and picked him up. They had some dessert and by the time Stefanie put Jack to bed, and Nathaniel read him one more book, Nathaniel's mind felt full of a cloud-like feeling, stuffed yet also empty, and when he got into bed he couldn't remember falling asleep or thinking anything on the way to sleep which was what normally happened at home in their condo.

The next day was Thursday, the day before Tammy was supposed to arrive, another day of intermittent cloud and sun and rain, the temperatures very cold at night, in the high thirties. The cabin was warmed with wood burning from the two iron stoves, the insides of the stoves glowing and hot and sending out a smoky cedar smell, still cold in the early morning when Nathaniel made Jack pancakes from scratch and used the syrup that Nicholas harvested from the maple trees on his property, Nathaniel's mind just beginning to orient, as it did every day, into rain-like, unremitting thought. While cleaning the dishes and pans from breakfast, Nathaniel observed Stefanie reading Jack a book, holding him on her lap, and he tried to assess the boy's mood, if it was improved, if he was even the slightest bit happier, all while feeling the futility of the attempt. After reading, Jack followed Nathaniel around the house wherever he went – to do laundry, to put more wood in the stove, to make more coffee, and it felt good, doing nothing all morning except doing – and Nathaniel, at one point, walked into the bedroom on the pretense of folding a load of laundry, then ran to the other side of the bed and hid. Nathaniel then slowly raised his head over the edge of the bed, feigning looking around to see if anyone knew where he was hiding, caught Jack's eyes, the boy's thumb in his mouth, then ducked back down. When he did it again, Jack smiled at him. Nathaniel got up, ran past Jack out the bedroom door, ran down the hall, and hid behind the sofa in the family room. He heard Jack's feet running clumsily behind him, padding nicely on the wood floor. Nathaniel again popped his head up, scanned, found Jack's eyes, and the boy smiled again, his thumb still in his mouth, and Nathaniel again went running by the boy, hiding in the bathroom, again hearing the boy's feet run after him. Nathaniel did the same scanning, found Jack's eyes in the same way, but this time there was no smile. Nathaniel came out of the bathroom and ruffled the boy's hair, something that felt right and an affectation, or maybe it was practice.

After putting Jack down for his nap, a more normal nap time, Nathaniel waited on the porch and then, after a few minutes of thinking about what he had to do when he got back home – the cat litter, vacuuming, calling in to work – he watched his father's car drive up the dirt road toward the house. Nathaniel looked at his watch and thought that his father of course arrived almost exactly on time, his arrival coordinated to occur, like the phone calls of the previous day, during Jack's nap around two which could last forty-five minutes to an hour or two, depending, and was of course perfectly executed by his father. It was warmer outside, though wet. The rain system had gotten trapped in the mountains on the way to the Atlantic, Nathaniel had read on his cell phone. Nathaniel watched his father shake out his coat on the porch, take off his shoes, and enter the cabin, all without addressing Nathaniel, so that Nathaniel followed behind, saying internally in a sarcastic voice, Hi Dad, how're you? Oh, I'm good. Good to hear. His father sat on the family room sofa, got out a little green notebook and pen, and immediately asked Nathaniel what exactly had been said on the phone, the pen poised in his right hand for note taking. Nathaniel told him he didn't need to take notes and his father replied that if they really wanted his help, this was how he helped, so please tell him what had happened because this woman was going to be here tomorrow. Nathaniel looked at Stefanie, who'd joined them, then began recounting the phone call. He told his father that luckily he and Stefanie had thought to record the call, so his father could listen to it if he wanted. The woman,

Nicholas's mother-in-law, Tammy, had used racist language, and Nathaniel, already sidetracked, said that maybe that was something they could use in court, if it went there, which he hoped it wouldn't, but it seemed like it might, this woman, she's pretty determined, she called Stefanie 'Chiquita Banana,' she told me to have the boy packed and ready, like she's going to show up, pick up the kid, and then disappear into middle America. His father stopped writing and said, Chiquita Banana. Do they still make those? Nathaniel said that that was sort of beside the point, the point was, shit, he'd lost his train of thought here, what was the point he was trying to make about the phone call, he asked Stefanie. She was standing in the kitchen, which was directly next to the family room, and now stepped into the family room and said the point was that this Tammy person was not who April or Nicholas had wanted to be Jack's guardian.

She said to Nathaniel's father that she personally knew from April that April would not want Jack with her mother. Nathaniel's father was now intermittently writing notes and also looking through nearby boxes that Nathaniel had pulled down from Nicholas's attic, presumably looking for the will. He asked how Stefanie knew that April didn't want Jack with this Tammy person. Nathaniel watched his father adjust his reading glasses on his face and poise the pen over the notebook. He observed Stefanie watch him slump back in his chair, and he tried to indicate to her how grateful he was. Stefanie said that April routinely complained about her mother, confiding in Stefanie more than once that her mother was a cynical, bitter person, and it had made April very sad that this was the case, that she couldn't talk to her mother without hearing something negative about the world, something vaguely racist, or something negative about the way she and Nicholas were raising Jack. Like, Stefanie said, when Jack was first born, she remembered April telling her this, it was so clear, she remembered that April told her that her mother came to visit and she didn't hold the baby, didn't change the baby, didn't even interact with him at all because April had told her mother that she and Nicholas were co-sleeping with the child, and her mother said that if that was really the choice they were making here, the mother didn't want to get too close to the kid only to lose him in a month's time when he suffocated in his sleep. She'd be glad to help out around the house, but she wasn't going to form a connection with a death sentence, Stefanie explained April had told her. April's mother had actually left the next day and said when the kid was sleeping in its crib then she'd come back, but until then, April and Nicholas would have to fend for themselves because she wasn't going to have a hand in putting a newborn in such a dangerous situation, basically a death trap, and that if the kid lived, it'd be through luck alone. I mean, that was the first week Jack was here, Stefanie said to Nathaniel's father who was writing notes in his notepad. Nathaniel watched his father, who was nodding his head in a lawyerly manner, such a practiced affectation that Nathaniel could only barely discern the grief beneath his father's poise. When Jack was a toddler and sleeping in his crib, Stefanie said, her mother visited again. This was just the second time since Jack was born, Stefanie explained. *The second time*. Got it, the father said. Second time. Okay, Stefanie said, so I guess what happened was after April's mother put a regular diaper on Jack, from a pack she had brought as a gift, April asked her mother to please use cloth diapers next time – you know Nicholas and April. Ecologically mindful. So April said this, very politely, showed her mother where the cloth diapers were, how to use them, etc, and then she guided her mother through the house, showed her the toys Nicholas had carved out of wood, the quilts she herself had made, the crib Nicholas had built, the cloth diapers, the balms she'd learned to make at her holistic healing class, picture frames she'd made with old pieces of metal and wood, and all kinds of stuff, and her mother stopped at one point, I guess, and just looked at her. Gave her this stare, is what April told me. And then walked out of the house. She came back an hour later with her SUV filled and like five hundred dollars of plastic toys and Pampers and a tub and wipes and plastic spoons and bowls and sippy cups and all kinds of shit, all of this stuff that Nicholas and April were completely against, and the mother said to April: you're teaching him to think he's better than everyone else. Well, he's not, and you're not either. This is the country you live in, and you're teaching him that other kids are doing something wrong and he's doing something right. This woman told April that April was going to mess up Jack in every imaginable way.

Nathaniel watched his father stop writing and, putting his notebook down and pulling a stack of folders from a box, carelessly leaf through the papers inside, and then toss the folders back into the box. He said, That can't have really happened, right? He looked at Nathaniel. Nathaniel shrugged, feeling grateful to not be talking, to be fully listening. He felt pulled out of himself by Stefanie's words, which was what she did for him, over and over, and momentarily, feeling again the presence of Nicholas's absence from the world, he felt a sort of gratitude. He wanted to tell Nicholas thank you, though he didn't know what for, in the same way he wanted to tell Stefanie thank you. He closed his eyes, as though searching for the source of this thank you that had suddenly arisen in him. He opened his eyes and saw out the window that more rain had begun. He heard it sweeping spattery gusts onto the tin roof. Nathaniel, watching his father stand, crossed his legs in the desk chair his brother had made, and though he'd never heard the particular information that Stefanie had related, he told his father that it was definitely true, this Tammy woman was really rooted in her ideas of what being a good American was, and she really thought that meant going to Toys 'R' Us or wherever. Still though, Nathaniel said to both his father and to Stefanie, wanting to sort of aid her, they shouldn't be completely unfair here, and that it might be a helpful tack to attempt some flattery or praise in order to appease her – for instance, Nicholas had told him many times that the mother-in-law also said that the baby was lovely, and posted pictures of him on Facebook where she was definitely a proud grandmother, and, Nathaniel remembered, April said that she did eventually apologize about all the toys, which Nicholas accepted in a way only Nicholas could, thanking her for the gifts and, after she left, donating all of it to charity. But apparently she did apologize for acting the way she did, Nathaniel said. Nicholas told me that she had told April that she just wanted her grandchild to fit in and be liked and not be viewed as some backwoods weirdo and to please keep that in mind and let the kid have some normal toys and normal books and normal everything. Nathaniel said that maybe they could use that when talking to her, like show that he and Stefanie weren't as, you know, far out as Nicholas and April. Maybe we could invite her to our place? Make her feel like she has a hand in this? Nathaniel took a contemplative pause, though he already knew what he was going to say, and then he said he thought it was important that they approached the situation in as even-handed a manner as they could, which was what he imagined Nicholas might say in a similar situation, and then he continued by saying that, on the other hand, maybe he was wrong and such a tack wouldn't work. After all, he did remember when April had first gotten pregnant and all the drama that had attended that event. According to Nicholas, he said, April's mother told her to end the pregnancy, so that's something we could use as well. Nathaniel's father pulled his phone from his pocket, read a text message, sent a text back, and then shook his head, said that he was sorry to cut the trip short, but that was all he could do today, he had to get groceries for Nathaniel's mother. Thank you, he said, he'd call tomorrow, he really had no idea, now, what to do, but he'd think about all this. He closed his notepad, hugged them both, listened at the hallway for Jack, as though saying goodbye through telepathy, then told them good luck with Tammy and stepped out of the house and put on his shoes and coat and went walking down the stone path toward his car.

Nathaniel again began looking through boxes they had packed, searching for the will, thinking that he just needed to search for the will and find it and then everything would be solved. Stefanie helped, going through dressers and shelves and cupboards even. After spending a few minutes looking through boxes that he had already looked through, and knowing that he'd find nothing there, he went to the second bedroom, opened the center drawer in the desk, and pulled out Nicholas's laptop, carried it out to the living area, and put it down on the coffee table and said, We're probably going to have to get into this, right? Feeling, as he said it, that it was a violation, that not only did he not want to search through his brother's computer for some document, he also didn't want to take it into a computer store and ask them to crack the password or whatever they might do, it all felt a little too much, like why couldn't Tammy be reasonable? When he asked Stefanie what they were supposed to do with this, did they take it into a computer store if that's what it came to, she looked at him and said, A computer store isn't going to crack the password. Nathaniel then started trying passwords, typing and re-typing, knowing that there was no chance that he was going to guess one, and when Stefanie said it, You're never going to guess it, and as he turned his head to say he knew, he saw Jack was standing in the hallway, watching both of them, Nathaniel trying to open his father's computer, Stefanie going through his parents' things. For a moment Jack stood there, little jeans on, the socks on his feet loose and worn, dirty-looking, his sweater maybe a bit too tight, his eyes looking not at Nathaniel but at the computer. He began crying. Nathaniel closed the computer, stuffed it behind a pillow, and went over to him and picked him up and told him that it was okay, buddy, everything was okay.

After calming Jack, after telling him it would be okay, after telling him they were here, after Jack had asked again why they were putting all of his mommy and daddy's things in boxes, after Nathaniel tried to put him down for a nap, but couldn't, he'd just napped, after he stopped crying and was staring vacantly and holding Nathaniel's pantleg as they walked around the house, after Nathaniel quietly looked at Stefanie above Jack and shook his head to convey that he didn't know what they were doing, they didn't know what they were doing, after she went to the bedroom and he could hear her own muffled sounds of crying, after taking Jack to another part of the house so he couldn't hear, after thinking again that he didn't know what to do, that this Tammy woman would be here sometime tomorrow and would be wanting to take Jack away with her that afternoon, or the following day, which he couldn't let occur, wouldn't let occur either that afternoon or the following day, but what about the day after, and the day after that, after sitting with Jack and singing with him on Nicholas's guitar and trying, again, to not think about his own loss, his brother gone, and trying to be there for Jack, after spending the afternoon with him, taking a cold walk out on the trails, telling Jack maybe they'd see a turkey or a coyote, after Stefanie prepared lunch, Jack still hovering against his leg, after they ate, after Nathaniel kept thinking of the town, what they thought about all this, what they would know and wouldn't know when it was all done, what people would think about him, if he could do this or not, was he like Nicholas or not, whether his father believed he could do it or not, after all this the early evening still hung in a grey fog of rain, a rain that Nathaniel once thought acted as a sort of cloak, a privacy for them, but which now he felt was obscuring things, like a veil pulled over the world, so that he couldn't see clearly. Later, Tammy called and said she was stopping for the night but would arrive tomorrow morning and would pick up Jack then if that was okay, and when Nathaniel had said to her that he hoped she knew she wasn't going to just take Jack tomorrow, that they were going to talk about this, Tammy had said, Whatever gets you to sleep at night, Nathaniel, he's coming with me. After this phone call occurred at around five in the afternoon, Nathaniel's father called again.

He was calling from the hotel. He asked Nathaniel if maybe he should call Tammy and talk to her. Nathaniel sat up on the sofa and looked at Stefanie, hand over mouthpiece, and said, quietly, the lawyer. He replied to his father by saying that he could do that if he really wanted to, but he didn't have to, that Nathaniel had already been talking with her, and it had ended amicably enough, and she was going to arrive tomorrow, Nathaniel told his father on the phone. Maybe it would be good, his father said, for the mother-in-law to know that there was another group on the same side, that maybe that would discourage her from making a claim of guardianship when she saw an entire side of the family against her. Actually, yes, Nathaniel would be really grateful to his father for that. He didn't want her here in the morning just trying to haul off Jack.

There was a pause on the line then there was the sound of sweeping, gusting rain on the roof of the cabin, the wind suddenly picking up, a very strong gust, seeming to increase the longer it went. Nathaniel told his father to hold on a second. He listened, though he wasn't sure why he was listening. From the upstairs bedroom loft (once Nicholas and April's bedroom), he heard Stefanie and Jack talking.

He climbed the ladder to look into the loft and could see the blue glow of Stefanie's laptop lighting the room. Stefanie was sitting cross-legged on the bed and Jack was sitting in the space between her bent legs. Stefanie was playing him music and singing quietly. Then, from the back of the property, he heard a crack, like the snapping of a giant's bone, then the resultant crash of limbs and leaves. The wind picked up again, spraying rain on the windows below the porch.

Nathaniel backed down off the ladder and said sorry and reiterated that it'd be great if his father let the Tammy woman know that she was outmatched here, thanks for doing that. There was another brief pause on the line then Nathaniel's father said that that wasn't exactly what he had in mind. What he had in mind was to construct a sort of compromise, the compromise being that Jack would stay with him and Katherine, the grandparents. Nathaniel stood up, said hold on to his father, and ran to the bottom of the loft ladder, whispered for Stefanie to get down here, and put his father on speakerphone. She climbed down the loft ladder, leaving Jack listening to music, and Nathaniel said, Is he sleeping? She said yes, he's out, and then Nathaniel mouthed to her, holding the cell phone away from his face, I can't believe this shit. He told his father he was back and his father told Nathaniel, before he got upset, to hear him out, to think about the goal. If the goal here was what was best for Jack, then please consider his position, because look, to be perfectly frank, this woman had a clear argument against Nathaniel and Stefanie becoming the guardians, especially if they didn't find a will, which was looking more and more likely to be the case. Nathaniel had a record, for instance – he'd been arrested and convicted of possession of marijuana and driving while intoxicated, and yes, while all that happened eight or nine years ago, it was still something Tammy was undoubtedly going to bring to court with her. Stefanie wasn't a natural-born citizen. I'm an American citizen, Stefanie said, that's such bullshit. But not a natural-born one, Nathaniel's father said, hi Stefanie. So I'm on speaker, okay. So, yes, you're an American citizen, but a naturalized one, since you were born in Mexico. I have no idea if that might be a factor, but it could be. I'm just asking you both to hear me out here. And look, the important thing that's going to come up is that Stefanie, I don't mean to be insensitive here, but Nathaniel told me that you had an abortion. Dad, Nathaniel said. His father continued, saying, Yeah, okay, that was some time ago, yes, but you still had an abortion, and you two, you both travel for work. You're both gone all the time. Nathaniel, you're gone four days a week. How's that going to look? Nathaniel said that they'd have to think about it, and his father said he wanted him to think about one other thing, before they started thinking about it. Think about it like this: look at them and look at April and Nicholas – so different. Wasn't it true that Nathaniel and Stefanie didn't want children? Hadn't Nathaniel conveyed that he felt himself to be too selfish a person to have kids, and also didn't want to be tied down by kids, wanted to travel and do exciting things and go see the world, which was what they'd been doing for the last few years. Look, Nathaniel's father explained, did Stefanie and Nathaniel consider how April and Nicholas had been raising Jack? Nicky and April didn't even own a television, Nathaniel's father said over the phone. They took those things very seriously – your brother literally thought television and media in general was something that kept people from experiencing real life. They only owned a computer because Nicky had to write his articles, but they didn't even have internet at their house. Nicky drove up to work to email people. Every day he drives to work, even when he isn't teaching, checks his email, and if he doesn't have a class, he drives back home, Nathaniel. Drove, Nathaniel said. He doesn't do any of that anymore, drove. There was another pause on the line and his father continued, saying, they don't have a dryer for god's sake. His father wanted them to consider that Jack had been living this very particular life. What's going to happen when he goes to your house and you watch Netflix every night, or you're home at three in the morning from the country club restaurant, or Stefanie is out of town twice a month? Nathaniel felt a sort of blankness in himself, an inability to respond – his anxieties being presented to him as though through slideshow – but then he said that it wasn't as though his father and mother were some better option. They didn't live like April and Nicholas, they had a dryer and a TV and internet, come on. But we're finished with our careers, his father said. We have time to devote. Plus, your mother, this would mean so much to her. She hasn't spoken for over a week, and I think this silence is okay at first, but at some point it's selfish, and she needs something to pull her out of it. She's writing these little notes, so she's talking, but she's not talking out loud, and she needs something. Nathaniel said that was completely backward thinking, that you couldn't use Jack to help Mom, and his father said that wasn't what he meant, and Nathaniel said that this was of course what his father would do, take a situation that was about something entirely different, and turn it into something he had to solve, his parents' selfishness was so glaringly obvious, he wondered how a person as intelligent as his father couldn't see it. His father said, Nathaniel, this is a conversation, just a discussion, it's not the end, I just wanted to present it to you, it's not set in stone, it's the beginning, and Nathaniel said, No, it definitely wasn't, and hung up the phone by pushing the little red button on the screen. Stefanie said she didn't know what to do now. She said they just had to stick by what they knew, what April and Nicholas really wanted, they had to consider that this was a difficult situation for his parents, too, not just them, and that this was just a bump, they'd come around. Nathaniel thought of the text first, then wrote it, which read, I don't understand why you wouldn't talk to me first, and then sent it to his mother, who, after a moment, wrote back a text that read, I don't know what you're talking about. I'm about to call this Tammy person. Will let you know how it goes. Nathaniel showed the texts to Stefanie and, feeling a brief anger that resolved into confusion, which in turn slipped into a hesitant understanding, said, My dad didn't even talk to her about this.

By the time the cold day ended, Nathaniel observed that there was more rain, so light it almost seemed to rise from the trees on the mountain rather than fall from the sky. An almost full moon slid between quickly moving clouds. He imagined the eastside of the town, his father and mother, where they watched television in the hotel they were staying at, a room on the second floor – his father described it to him, needlessly Nathaniel had thought – which overlooked a small ravine where a river flowed, kudzu curling around trees. He wondered what his mother and Tammy had spoken about, but was tired, and didn't try to conjure it – what was the point, he thought. He pictured the downtown, the mother-in-law maybe arriving late in the afternoon and settling into the Bed and Breakfast he had arranged for her, eating Baby Ruths and reading one of the six *People* magazines she had brought. He saw the town, people exiting their yoga classes, sweaty and red-faced, smiling and open, people eating dinner on the patios of restaurants, students readied in their dormitories and apartments for the coming night, drinking beer and rolling joints, the streets emptying of noise and people going home or leaving home, the surrounding mountains alive with unseen animal life, and the mountains seeming to hold the town, which was how Nathaniel always saw it, like a hand holding a hand, pulling dark toward all beings, the slow erasure of the myriad things in existence.

In his dead brother's house, Nathaniel carried Jack from the loft to the boy's bedroom. Nathaniel read him a book, the bear book again, and when he finished reading to Jack, the boy fell asleep for the night, asleep once more, as though sleep was the boy's response to loss. Nathaniel watched him, and then lay down next to him. Jack was wearing just his blue underwear and a white shirt, his hair was fine and soft, very dark, and his closed eyes, with long lashes, appeared woven shut. Part of Nathaniel wanted Jack to stay peacefully asleep forever and part of him wanted to tell him something, though he didn't know what, and he kept thinking of what he wanted to tell him, thinking of the night he received the phone call, the phone call which had come after several years of Nicholas convincing both the families to visit together, since Jack so rarely got to see his grandparents or aunt and uncle, Nicholas tempting all of them with visions of springtime mountains, hiking on wooded paths, batcaves, hot springs, waterfalls, organic foods, the impressive meals Nathaniel would make, and not only that, but their nephew, Jack, who was really growing up pretty fast. Both sides of the family had waffled about dates and travel until all finally relented and the visit had been scheduled, a weekend in the spring, certain food items bought for April's mother and for Nicholas's parents, other items that Nathaniel asked to have on hand so he could make a couple nice meals, the house was cleaned, cold spring rains swept through, and five days out, Nathaniel received the phone call, which he couldn't keep from visualizing, as if compelled to by some alien source: Nicholas and April were involved in a car accident on a winding mountain road in the rain, late at night, after a beer tasting and dinner party for Nicholas's tenure, a party which, Nathaniel learned from the police, the couple had left very late, and coming down the winding mountain road, it was speculated that his brother had been tranced into a brief sleep – rain on windshield, wind in trees – his eyes closing, and when he woke, the car was heading off the road into the trees and Nicholas had overcorrected and the wheels slipped on the wet asphalt and the car went into a tailspin that caused it to careen directly toward the dividing concrete abutment, which the car hit and then skipped over like a stone, all soundlessly in the quiet rain on the mountain, sending the car airborne until it again landed, flipping three times, literally rolling down the mountain road in the wrong lane, and both the brother and his wife were killed (the wife probably

died instantly, the police said, the brother later in the hospital). The police on the scene noted that three deer were
eating grass near the car. Nathaniel thought about the accident going unreported for some hours, imagined Nicholas
trapped, ensuring his death, and leaving behind a blue-
eyed, dark-haired, happy four-year-old boy who could not
stop crying in Nathaniel's car on the way back from the
hospital, saying repeatedly, Where's Daddy? Where's
Mommy? Lying next to Jack now, all Nathaniel wanted to
do was go back in time, if not to when his brother was still
alive, which his mind couldn't compute, then back to the
moment sitting in his car with the boy, back to the moment
he had first held Jack again after several months, the boy
crying, back to the moment when he had known exactly
what he had to do.

KATHERINE

Thought after thought, do not become attached. [. . .]
Whether it's a past thought, a present thought, or a
future thought, let one thought follow another without
becoming attached. [. . .] Once you become attached
to one thought, you become attached to every thought,
which is what we call bondage. But when you go from
one thought to another without becoming attached,
there is no bondage.

—*PLATFORM SUTRA*

Our life is shaped by our mind; we become
what we think.

—*DHAMMAPADA*

Louis Walters had a mole on his cheek, which, if he didn't shave, grew long, curling hairs from it that, Katherine had noticed in the past, were thicker than his facial hair. One of the hairs was white and coarse. Katherine had pulled it out with tweezers once, declaring an experiment. Two weeks later, it was growing back, and in his guest room – Louis Walters' wife was out of town, which she often was – Katherine rolled on top of him and, squinting, had said, Let me see. Jesus, it's an unstoppable hair. Terminator hair. If you just let that thing keep growing, I bet it'd turn into a fingernail.

Katherine could see the hair now – slightly longer than the rest of his facial hair – in the Skype window on her computer screen. Louis Walters wore wire-frame glasses and his head was shaved bald. In his forties, he was in extremely good shape, tall, very fit, and his eyes, dark green, were set in his face in a way that, coupled with his baldness, made him appear somewhat bug-eyed, which the glasses helped, making him appear handsome even if he wasn't exactly handsome. He was wearing a grey checked button-down, his upper body and head on the screen. She'd contacted him – in the space of time David had left to go on a hike, to clean out his mind, he'd said, and to pick up some groceries for the room – because she wanted to discuss their

71

situation with him. This was what they called their affair: their 'situation.' It'd begun as a kind of semantic denial of what they were actually doing, then it became a joke. She often said things like, I'm not sure if the situation we're in is sustainable. I'm not sure we can keep using up our own inner resources on each other. We have to protect some for those we're already with. They talked about the relationship, their situation, in environmentally apocalyptic terms, which seemed apt. She didn't know how it'd happened. You melted the glacier of my heart, she'd once said to him, mocking a woman in a romantic comedy. The problem with that, he'd said, is that it'll make the ocean of your understanding overflow and flood the land of your life. They'd been in his office that time, and she'd looked at him and said, Oh, good one. There was the sense of accident about it all, as though she'd somehow tripped into the situation, like tripping on a sidewalk into an easy and mindless trot. But it had all colored darkly when she learned about Nicholas, when Nathaniel called her and through tears – she could hear them – told her that Nicholas was gone. Now she felt she had to end this thing with Louis Walters. Nicholas being gone somehow clarified how awful she was being. She couldn't take it anymore, that's what she was going to tell him.

Louis Walters was saying something, his face slightly blurred and pixelated on Katherine's laptop's screen, about how he wished he could be there with her, that he was glad she had contacted him, because he wanted to be there for her and this way – meaning through the computer – he got to be there for her. He hadn't called or tried to message her, he said, because obviously she was around David a lot and also he didn't want to complicate an already difficult thing, so he'd been feeling just totally and completely helpless. He was so glad she'd called. He wanted to hug her through the screen, hold her close.

She typed that she felt like shit for contacting him. Real shit. She continued to write, without looking at his face, that she hated that she'd contacted him so much, actually, that she was going to log out of Skype right now, after she said her piece. Which was this. She shouldn't be doing this. They shouldn't be doing this. This was something they shouldn't be doing and they should've both known they shouldn't be doing it, she wrote. Doing what, he said quickly. Doing what, exactly? Because I hope you're not saying what I think you're saying, and if you are saying that, I think you need to just give it a little time. This is a stressful time for you. He cleared his throat, swallowed. A very stressful and difficult time, I understand that, and you shouldn't be making, you know, rash decisions.

She picked up her coffee, which was lukewarm. It had been made in the little Keurig machine supplied by the hotel. She knew that the plastic of these Keurig cup things was somehow dangerous for her health, cancerous or something, as well as being ecologically unsound, but it was just for a few days. Plus, the package, the Keurig cup thing, said hazelnut mocha on it, and the picture of a hazelnut mocha in a ceramic mug on the foil of the little plastic cup had looked so good. Also, she'd thought while staring at the cup, what wasn't cancerous and ecologically unsound? She looked at Louis Walters while drinking her coffee. He was probably cancerous and ecologically unsound, she thought. Then, without immediately noticing, she laughed, and then noticed she had laughed outwardly, when Louis Walters said, What's funny? She shook her head. Since she wasn't speaking, she could take as long as she wanted to reply. She looked at the rest of the room. The laptop was angled in such a way that she could view the entire room, but Louis Walters couldn't. He could see the wall behind her, maybe some of the window. She wrote, Hold on, then she sipped the coffee again and watched him reading her words. Let me help, he said. Let's think about something else. Tell me about the town or something. She wrote that she'd been there for less than a week and she disliked the town more than ever, in the same way she disliked herself right now. She wrote that the problem with the town was the same as her own problem with herself: it was in the middle of nowhere, destitution and rural decay all around, mountains cutting it off from everything else, in the same way that she was alone in her life, the mountains of thoughts in her mind finding no expression or understanding in other people, cutting her off in the same way the mountains isolated the town. Except me, Louis Walters said. You find understanding in me. She just looked at him. I can feel me understanding you, he said. So you must feel it too. Just barely, she wrote. Plus, I shouldn't even be talking to you. We shouldn't be talking at all.

She put the mug down feeling as though she was doing something right, finally. Louis Walters made a pained face and she typed out an apology. You don't have to apologize, he said. And you're not cut off. I want you to know that. And you're understood. I understand you. Her own small face hovered in the corner of the Skype window, the cliché of grief: her hair wild, her face appearing old, no make-up, washed out in the dull light coming through the hotel window, her eyes far off, red. It looked like she'd been in the woods all night on the run from an insane serial murderer, whose chasing and murderous intentions toward her in turn made her insane. That she had this thought, and many others, that she was even talking to Louis Walters, that she was doing anything when Nicholas was dead seemed like a kind of betrayal, like what she should be doing, somehow, was being in constant mourning, in non-stop grief, which she was, sort of. She didn't know anymore. She didn't know where her mourning stopped and her life began, as though the two could be separated. But it felt that way: it felt like, here Katherine, these are moments supplied for grief, and here, these other moments, don't forget, they're your life. She knew this was a falsehood, yet she felt it. She pulled her hair back in a ponytail, which made her look worse, her face even more tired. She rubbed her cheeks for a moment, reddening them, then looked at herself in the Skype window again. She was wearing her Professor Sweater. David called it that. I see we're doing Professor Sweater with jeans, David liked to say. Very professorial of you. Immediate profundity. A presence of ever-refining knowledge. Cute, too. The thought of David out in the world, her in here talking with Louis Walters, made her wince, close her eyes. When she opened them again she couldn't understand why she was talking to Louis Walters when she didn't want to be talking to him, didn't want to be hurting David, didn't want to be doing any of this. Yet she was. It sometimes felt as though the universe had given her her life in the form of a puzzle, and she'd dumped the box, spread the pieces, turned them over, and slowly started fitting the pieces together, but when the picture became too clear – there she was! – she began forcing pieces into her neighbor's puzzle, messing it up purposely. Who wanted to complete a picture they already saw, already knew? And now that Nicholas was gone, it was as though she was again looking at the puzzle she'd started long ago, and then had abandoned. A little layer of dust covered all the pieces, obscuring what had once been clear.

Katherine watched Louis Walters on the screen. His face was larger than it seemed in real life, and somehow more unattractive. Then she thought that this *was* his face in real life. It was just on a screen. She watched him read her message again and then watched his nodding head and him say, Just get out of there. I don't see why you're staying. There's nothing you can do there, really. If I was there, I'd tell David there was no point in the both of you staying there. What's that going to do? Why is it when something terrible happens people believe that proximity to the event matters? We have phones, we have computers, we have automobiles, planes, what the hell. I don't get it.

She looked at his speaking face and wrote, It's not about Nicholas. Or being close to Nicholas. We have to help pack the house and get everything cleaned up. It's also Jack. It's about who will take him. Louis Walters read, nodding, then shaking his head, then was saying, I know, I know, but why can't that be accomplished with a phone call, a text, an email, then a quick drive into rural depression and a quick drive out. Part of the reason you feel so shitty is because you're in a shitty place. She put a finger up, stopping him. The mother-in-law is supposedly coming, she wrote. April's mother, I mean. That's why. She called Nathaniel and told him. Apparently she started Monday night, and was now driving across the entire country. Four full days on the road, staying in motels, and eating junk food. It's, what, Tuesday, so she'll be here by the end of the week. Why else would she be driving out here from South Dakota or wherever she's coming from? Huh, Louis Walters said. I mean, wow. Does she have any legal right? Katherine wrote to him that she didn't think so, and then, after pausing a moment, wrote that David believed that they had to present the seriousness of their concerns through the seriousness of their presence. Also, he wanted to help Nathaniel pack, so we're here, she wrote. That sounds like David, he said. She wrote, David seems to have closed his mind to the fact that we will never see Nicholas again. He's being who he is – focused on the problem at hand, what to do with the material possessions, the house, the distribution of things, and to some degree, what to do with Jack. He's being the distant observer and eventual fixer of all situations, the lawyer, the mediator and moderator of all conflicts and problems and emotions into the simplicity of fact. I can't stand it.

The last line was unnecessarily mean. After all, David was the one who was trying to take care of things, he was the one who was out, first to help Nathaniel pack some boxes at Nicholas and April's house and then to look for the will just in case this Tammy woman was thinking she had some right to guardianship, and then he was going to pick up some essentials for their hotel room's small refrigerator because Katherine couldn't stand meeting any more people from the town. David was doing all this and here she was typing to Louis Walters that she couldn't stand him. David was taking care of her, trying to, and maybe it was all a little overdone: you stay here – I'll get some groceries,

I'll help Nathaniel pack, and when the time comes, if it comes to it, I'll meet with this Tammy person. You don't need to even think about it. Plus, maybe this Tammy person just wants some of her daughter's things – that might be it, too, he'd said. Let's wait until we find out what she's doing, though Katherine had thought that if she was driving over thirty hours, it probably wasn't for some clothes. She'd written to David on her phone, while he stood waiting, that she wasn't going to miss talking with this Tammy woman, if it came to that, but then she'd thanked him and said she felt bad and frustrated at herself that she couldn't do anything, couldn't go out and deal with the people in the town again. It was as though her annoyance at herself translated into annoyance with him. Before leaving for the cabin, he'd asked her if she would be okay alone. Because I don't have to help Nathaniel pack today? he'd said. I can stay here. She'd typed to him, on her phone's screen, that she'd be fine, please, go. He'd gathered his wallet, put on his shoes, and went to the door, only to step back into the room. I shouldn't go, he said. It feels wrong. She typed on her phone, GO. I can't see it, he said, stepping back into the room. Go, he said. Go, then I'll go. Are you sure? She looked at him, raising her eyebrows. Okay, he'd said. The message I'm getting is that you're going to be fine, you could actually use a little time alone, and I can go? She'd looked at him flatly, coolly. I'm going, he said. Then, as soon as he was gone, she'd wished she hadn't sent him away.

She told Louis Walters that she'd be right back, and got up to make another Keurig thing. She stood before the machine, debating about whether to use it again, and thought of how this time in the hotel room was the first time she'd been alone except for maybe the bathroom or the shower, completely alone with the idea that Nicholas was now dead, he had died in a car accident last week, nearly a week ago. She felt confused, as though time was working in some way she no longer understood. Every other moment, there'd been someone there with her. Back in Charlotte, David was in the house with her, Nathaniel and Stefanie had stopped by on their way out of town to go be with the boy and to start packing up Nicholas's house, and the next day her sister came over and stayed a night. Her sister had taken her on a walk through the neighborhood. On the walk, the neighborhood had seemed changed, seemed to lack depth, as though she were on a sound stage, and that if she went into any of the houses all she would find was the wood supports holding up the faces of houses, and behind that, barren land, no lives being lived. She told as much to her sister, Margaret, who told her, It's just because it's so new. It'll stop feeling like that. Walking next to her sister, unreal houses around them and tree branches creaking in the wind, Katherine had said, You don't understand. It's felt like this for years. She felt her sister look at her. Then they'd walked on without any more speaking and Katherine had felt mean, unreceptive. She'd given her sister a hug when they got back to the house, thanked her. She told her sister, Thank you for getting me out of the house, though as she said it, she was aware she was saying it without meaning it, saying it because she knew it was what her sister believed she was doing for her, and so, Katherine had tried to return this consideration to her sister, and said this clichéd thing – thank you for getting me out of the house – in an attempt to be considerate of a clichéd attempt by her sister. Anything you need, her sister had said, as though she were being given the line from a director behind Katherine's head.

In the first few days after Nicholas died, people seemed to huddle around Katherine like she was some delicate, slightly old animal, whose fur wasn't so thick anymore, was a little ratty in fact, and it was cold out. People seemed to believe she was in need of cocooning or deep hibernation, covering her in blankets and bringing her food. Eat, they seemed to suggest, and then sleep for a couple months, and once you wake, you won't have to deal with this at all. It'll all be gone. Hibernation Therapy. Eventually, people left, and she went into her office at school to be alone. She stepped into her office, left the light off, closed the door, and took a breath. She sat at her desk and turned on her computer. She didn't know what else to do. She checked her emails. There were several from colleagues. Condolence emails. A moment later, there was a knock. Colleagues came by with kind, understanding words, withdrawn and pained body language. Some came with flowers. One came with chocolate, which she couldn't understand. Apparently David had alerted them. The younger faculty members didn't come by. They were the ones who sent their condolences as emails, a distancing Katherine almost admired. She also knew they couldn't come by. Young men and women who, while intensely intelligent, had not seen death in their lives. She barely had time to see it herself – Nicholas was dead, a car accident, and all she kept thinking from that first moment was, That's not possible. She was a faculty mentor to one of the lecturers, one of the ones who'd emailed her a note of personal sorrow and sympathy. Kylie

Newman. She wore vests, a grey, a black, a green one over a starched shirt. She'd once said, This is my lesbian uniform. She had dark hair, short on the sides and long on top. Vigilant, semi-aggressive, hip hair. Hair that it seemed you could have a conversation with and might be more interesting than the person beneath it. This hair, coupled with the vests and starched shirts, jeans, and weirdly, cowboy boots, made Kylie Newman look like a dorky version of a gunslinger. Katherine liked her. Thirty or so, intelligent, her work focused on digital media, of course, and yet Katherine saw the child in this woman still. Everything about her was still at play. Katherine thought that Kylie Newman knew sadness only as a romantic reaction to actual suffering. It was a game still. She'd broken up with her girlfriend, she once confided to Katherine. They'd been talking about the election of a conservative governor, how this deeply worried Kylie and the girl's eyes had become far off, glazed, the vest and the entire persona she presented to the world appearing like a costume. She told Katherine that her girlfriend, now ex-girlfriend she corrected herself, had gotten into a graduate school in Illinois and it made more sense to separate than to try to do a long-distance thing. She told Katherine that her girlfriend, now her ex-girlfriend, had said that they were either going to pony up and get married, or it was time to move on. Kylie Newman had said it was something about the phrase 'pony up' that had allowed her to see with clarity that this wasn't the person for her. It was so hard, and she was afraid of being alone, but she'd done it. Jesus, Katherine had said. Luckily, Jesus has nothing to do with it, Kylie Newman had replied, which seemed to Katherine yet another occasion to exclaim 'jesus.' Still,

Katherine envied the ease of this separation, the un-actualized suffering of it. Something as simple as moving to another state, an off-putting phrase, could cause it. Katherine found herself secretly missing, as Kylie Newman relayed her breakup, her more careless days. Friends that came and went, boyfriends, too – time didn't seem to exist then. It was as though she'd once been living in a kind of Bob Dylan-y heartbreak album, where the world had a rhythmically structured sadness that contained a little note of hope or defiance: the sadness of people leaving! But it'd be okay, there were always more people to get to know/to meet, bars to drink in, mountains to hike, countries to see, and people she didn't, couldn't know! When Katherine was young, everything had been enriched by the uncertainty of her future: would this person merge with her, become part of her, or would he leave her? Who was this man, what was his existence like, would he really see her? What about this friend, was she a real friend, an authentic person? Anxiety and worry about the future now seemed like a gift, and whatever difficulties Kylie Newman had, Katherine knew that there was a deeper suffering there that she hadn't even touched, and she knew this was true because she longed for Kylie Newman's type of pain. If she could have that anxiety and worry again, that uncertainty about life. That uncertainty seemed to be endless, until it wasn't.

Katherine lifted a corner of the tinfoil lid of the Keurig cup. The coffee inside emitted almost no odor. She tried to smell it like a Folgers commercial, the one where the robbed mother around Christmastime seems physically warmed by the act of smelling. Yet now she smelled very little, a scratch-and-sniff of actual coffee smell. She held the plastic cup containing ground coffee. How long had the coffee been in this plastic entrapment? She placed it in the machine, turned it on. Water gurgled and began to move. She considered why the world had changed for her. There had been a kind of subtle shift in her understanding and perception – so subtle it might not be there, like tremors you believe you're imagining – that had permanently altered the ground upon which she viewed the world. It wasn't marrying David that had done it, it wasn't having children, it was some time after that, some time she could not precisely discern. A slow transformation, like a jagged rock rounded after years in a stream, and after that, ever more eroding away, until that rock was a small, smooth pebble, and then that pebble a grain of sand, washed away. Driving on a freeway out of town no longer meant experiencing the open country, an easy freedom. The summer no longer meant the feeling of endlessness, time seeming to stop, of everything bloomed and alive as though it would never change. Drinking too much didn't mean the loss of inhibition, it meant an escape from her anxieties and worries, often about Nathaniel and Nicholas and their respective families. Her children were no longer the incredible beings who, as babies, pooped their diapers and giggled about it, who as toddlers fumbled hilarious nonsense into the world, who as children found awe in everything: a tree, a cat, a cloud, a bottle cap. They were now men whose lives seemed to be made much like hers: repetitive days of certain frustrations, certain anxieties, their own worries, their worlds reduced in the same way she felt hers was reducing every year, year after year. She looked back at Nathaniel with a kind of surprise: she'd found him such a troublemaker when he was in his teens, rebellious and unkind, drinking, smoking, getting frequent speeding tickets, almost in trouble for stealing the Nelsons' car, but luckily Janey Nelson had been in the car with him, pleaded with her father that it was her idea. While maybe he got a little nicer after high school, he continued doing stupid things in college: arrested for drug possession, failing out of classes, not even going to classes according to his dorm mate. Katherine had been so scared for him for so long, but then he'd found cooking and things had changed. Music, sports, books, he'd always liked these things, but he was never any good at them. She told him to become a teacher, but he laughed at her and told her he had no interest in going back into what he'd hated for so long.

The coffee mug was halfway full, the coffee smell now stronger, as though water had brought the grounds to life. She looked back at her computer on the desk, near the window. The computer was facing away from her. She felt a strange aloneness – a person was just on the other side of a piece of metal, in the room with her and not – an odd separation. She wondered vaguely what Louis Walters was doing while he was waiting for her. She thought of how so much of what she was thinking she would not communicate with him, how she was alone with her thoughts, as she was so frequently. She remembered how culinary school came next for Nathaniel, and they paid for it in the same way that they paid for college, part of his grad school, and there was a fear that he would just drop out of culinary school as well, turn into a drifter, a drug dealer, a homeless person, maybe a mental patient, but he didn't drop out. He flourished. He was a good cook, a chef, really, he was a chef. The first meal he cooked for her was one she would not forget: a simple grilled turbot with white wine emulsion, cabbage and carrot puree. Later, he moved exclusively, and she thought, riskily, to vegetarian food. He wanted simple, elegant, and also affordable, and also, humane. She couldn't believe she still bragged about her children: well, Nathaniel's a chef now if you can believe it. He's been written about in two magazines. Oh Jesus, she had spoken the words of a television mother. In the years after this, though, she found that, strangely, he was her last tie to the world of youth. At the time, Nathaniel's 'existential crisis,' as David had put it, had been an inconvenience in her life, a deep worry. Yet he had also enlivened her life. There had always been Nathaniel to think and worry about, and now that he was doing fine, she saw that both her worry was overdone and at the same time her worry had given the world an uncertain quality that allowed her access to kindness and care and, eventually, awe at the fact that Nathaniel was succeeding. For some time she couldn't see an outcome for Nathaniel, now she could. For some time she couldn't see his life, now she could. Her worry and anxiety, which still arose in her mind like a practiced emotion, was no longer connected to anything, to Nathaniel, and certainly not to Nicholas, who'd shunned what she deemed ordinary social life in order to take his family off the grid. She missed both of them, but didn't worry about them in the same way. And couldn't be awed by them in the same way. In the same way she couldn't be awed by David. By herself. She understood it all too much, understood her life too easily. It was as though she'd figured out the math equation of her life and the answer was unbelievably banal: C equals twelve. She had been a girl, she had been a young woman, she became a woman, a mother, a professor, and now she was whatever she was, it didn't seem to matter anymore. She had fulfilled her evolutionary duty. The universe seemed to have sensed Nathaniel was going to figure it out, watched with close attention, then had patted Katherine on the head, gave her a little certificate, checked off her duties for existence, and was finished with her. We're ready for you to die, the universe seemed to say. Thank you for your service.

The coffee finished. The last drips fell into her mug. She didn't want to go back to the computer, to the glowing Apple logo. She didn't want to continue talking to Louis Walters, continue distracting herself from this situation with Nicholas's son, from Nicholas himself, from Jack. She looked out the window: the mountain in blue morning mist. She considered how she and David used to hike almost every weekend. She remembered a time, years ago now, they were walking, and she'd said, We're on a planet in the universe. Yes, he'd said. Be aware of that. Let's be with that idea this whole hike, no talking. Yes, she agreed. No talking. Or, a little talking. Yeah, a little talking's fine, David had said. They'd hiked some, their feet crunching leaves, mist moving between the autumn trees, leaves coming down in the wind, hanging in the air, deep oranges and browns and reds, the burned colors of the season, a shedding of life, the smell of dirt, fungus, crisp, colder wind, rush of the breeze through trees, swirling, the cries of hawks, their bodies warming to the walk, breath visible in the morning air, she felt her own being emptied out, cloudlike, as if being dispersed. It was beautiful, really beautiful, then she sort of started thinking about Nicholas, Nathaniel, wondering how they were doing, her once-young boys out in the world, then her job. I'm good with just general talking now, David had said after a little while, breathing harder. It's been like fifteen minutes, she'd said. I feel we've done our duty. We got it pretty clearly, David said. We're on a planet in the universe. Duly noted. There was a playfulness, a kind of easy letting go into the world, or an easy receiving of the world, occasionally complicated with anxiety and worry. Now though, walking in the woods was walking in the woods. She could not pull up any of the prior tran-scendence, if that's what it had been. She wondered if David felt it too. They were just on a walk. The trees were trees, the leaves had fallen.

In the hotel room, her coffee ready, she went back to the computer and Louis Walters' waiting face. She sat and blew on her cup of coffee then put the mug down. She wrote that she'd just been thinking of Kylie Newman who'd written her an email, one of those condolence emails. She wrote that she'd been recalling the time she'd been envious of Kylie's breakup with her girlfriend. I remember feeling the world must have opened up to her again in her sadness. I thought, Katherine wrote, that soon it wouldn't open like that anymore. Things would be what they were. A girlfriend leaving was just a person exiting your life. Your son's death was not mysterious or strange. It was what the world did. There was nothing else to it. Louis Walters said that he wasn't sure it was that simple and that they were sort of getting off point here. So what if we're getting off point, she wrote. Maybe that's the point, to get off point. Good point, he said. Not funny, she wrote.

She wrote to Louis Walters, who was both in the room with her and not, present with her and somehow not, how she remembered being in her office and getting the email from Kylie Newman that read, *I'm so sorry for your loss. I don't know what else to say beyond that, so I'll just end with this quote, from Tolstoy, which I've found comforting in my own difficult times: 'The meaning of life is life itself.'* In my office, I'd almost guffawed, both at the quote itself and the idea that it came from Tolstoy, in front of the computer, Katherine wrote. Then, inexplicably, I cried. I remember it with startling clarity because it was the first time I really cried hard since learning he was gone. I had my phone on the desk, my face in front of my computer, the light of it almost palpable on my face, that heat, you know, Kylie Newman's weird email staring at me, a bunch of colleagues had been by and had given me little half hugs, shoulder hugs, and full hugs, dropped off flowers, and I cried. What was I doing in my office? I remember thinking. I couldn't stop. It was all suddenly there: Nicholas was gone. Along with his goneness, I sensed that part of the reason I was crying, beyond my own sadness for myself and what and who I had lost, was for this Kylie Newman person. She hadn't felt real suffering yet, the banality of it, the confusion of that banality. Of course, she knew it to be a fact of existence, certainly, knew, most likely, it was coming for her, but she had never touched it, and thus, it had never touched her. Her girlfriend had left her, she was heartbroken. But there was a certain sort of sense, a logic to a leaving girlfriend, the separating. There was no logic with Nicholas. He was here then he was not. I cried because I was in my office. Because of this email from Kylie Newman. Because of everyone who stopped by. Because Nicholas was gone. Because I couldn't convey to anyone what this meant to me. Because I don't understand what it means. I want to understand. That's why I'm not talking, and also because I can't take talking with people.

Katherine stopped typing. She remembered that she had been in her office to be alone and was crying in front of her computer, her door still open because colleagues had been visiting, and she couldn't get up to close it, she was crying, just crying, and feeling as though she was falling a little. The shadow of a person, Mark Feltzer, had walked by, then he had slowly backtracked, stuck his head inside her door, and asked if she needed anything. There were flowers on her desk, a box of chocolates, her computer glowing in the dark room, a room in which she hadn't turned the lights on, and now her phone was also glowing with a call from David. No, she'd said. Just close the door please. He did, with a contemplative little nod and lips pursed in understanding. She thought of this Kylie Newman person and felt sick knowing that this playful person would be slipped out of herself when certain realities arose. She felt a deep sympathy for her: she hoped it wouldn't happen. Then thinking of Kylie Newman transmuted into thoughts about Nicholas, which she could barely stand. She remembered how Nicholas had seemingly slipped from the world, years before, too young, she often thought, his alienation present from a young age, distant from people, even as a boy watching people, thinking about them, much like herself, she thought now. She cried for this and for Kylie Newman and for the fact that Nicholas was gone. She cried for his past self and his gone self, for herself and for Kylie Newman, for the people who had brought her gifts, had mumbled only partially felt sympathies, no less sincere for it. In the hotel, sitting before the computer, waiting for Louis Walters to say something, she remembered crying for herself, for her son, for this other person she barely knew.

Before Louis Walters could say anything else, she wrote to him that she remembered feeling and thinking all of these things in front of her computer, crying, when he arrived at her office. You opened the door and immediately shut the door behind you, pulled a chair next to mine, and held my shaking shoulders. I remember, Louis Walters said. She looked at Louis Walters, and wrote, Why don't I feel any different? He read the message and seemed to think, opened his mouth, and then said he didn't know. Concerning what? Concerning us? She shook her head and wrote that that was maybe the most selfish thing she'd heard in a long time. He said, Okay, so concerning Nicholas. Well, I didn't know you didn't feel any different. You hadn't told me that until now, and I actually can't understand how that could be true. So that's why I asked concerning us. But, to answer your question, Louis Walters said, I think you're probably still too close to it. You're trying to look at yourself and figure out who you are now, now that, you know, he's passed away. She put a finger up, stopping him, and wrote, Say 'died.' I don't like passed away. It implies he went somewhere. He didn't go anywhere. He didn't pass. He isn't away. He's dead. Just gone. Not away. Away feels like he was once in this way, and now is in this other way. Away. He's not. He's dead. Louis Walters read and said, See, just that there, just you talking about it like that. I think you haven't had any time alone to digest this. Why the food metaphor? she

wrote. Why, when we're talking about understanding something, do we say we need to 'digest' it, or let it 'marinate,'
or say that we're 'stewing in our juices'? You're right though,
I need to roast on this a bit. Haha, Louis Walters said. She
sat back in her chair. I need to sign off, she wrote. I don't
like this. This, talking with you, this is me trying to bring a
normal something from my life in order to feel normal and
not feel the change of things. I'm distracting myself. Louis
Walters said he wouldn't characterize it like that at all. She
wasn't distracting herself, she was afraid of being alone and
right now, she shouldn't be, he said.

She looked away from the laptop and saw a text message
lighting her phone's screen. David. Doing okay? it said. She
looked at the computer screen and wrote to Louis Walters,
One second. She picked up her phone, hesitated, then
replied, All is well. After a moment, another text arrived,
which read, Artisan wheat or Tuscan bole? She could barely
comprehend the question and wanted, for a brief moment,
to write back, Sunbeam White. You choose, she wrote. She
put the phone back down and thought that Louis Walters
was wrong in the same way her husband was wrong. She
knew she needed to be alone. She could feel the information being conveyed to her as though in alien code, through
telekinesis or something. Be alone and know, this intuited
information seemed to say, repeatedly. But know what? The
hotel was the first time that she'd had the chance to be really
by herself in over a week. With David gone, before she'd
contacted Louis Walters, she had tried to just sit in the hotel
room, to just sit there with the fact of it, feeling only the
fact of Nicholas not being there, as though calling up the
experience in her office, to feel authentically devastated, but

sitting alone in the hotel room – two plastic cups from the night before on the dresser, one about half-filled with water, the other empty, smudgy fingerprints on the plastic, orange peels next to the cups, David's overnight bag on his side of the bed, opened, a shirt hanging out, her bag zipped closed in a corner, the small refrigerator clicking on, the heater clicking off – she couldn't understand it, couldn't recall any sadness, felt only a sort of blankness. She had gone to the window, which she was staring out now, not looking at Louis Walters.

The mountain loomed out the window, mist gently rising from it, dispersing, and below, the town's main street was empty in the early morning. If the mist wasn't moving she could've been looking at a postcard of a rural American town. She thought of when she had still been speaking, maybe three days after, still in her own house, and she'd told David that she didn't understand. She knew Nicholas was dead, but the world seemed no different. The world isn't different, he'd said. *Your* world is. She hadn't been able to withhold her frustration at the comment. How thoughtful of you, she'd said. How intelligent. Philosophical even. David sat next to her in the breakfast nook and said he was sorry, this was just how he thought about these things. Sunlight came through the window and fell against the wall in the elongated shape of the window. He pulled his chair close to hers. He'd put his arms around her, hugging from behind and the side, very much like how Louis Walters had the previous day in her office. And because of this, she hadn't wanted David touching her anymore. She felt as though he'd be able to sense this other man on her, some psychic connection would flash in his mind, and he'd know she'd already been comforted in this same way. And he'd know it at the worst possible time. This same hugging, she irrationally thought, could lead to David feeling this man's presence in other ways. Moments like this had occurred before. If she watched television after being with Louis Walters, she couldn't do that with David at home. If she ate food with Louis Walters at work, she took her dinner into the family room, claiming that her back hurt. If she drank a glass of wine with Louis Walters, she didn't have one in the evening with David. And in the moment David comforted her by holding both of her shoulders, almost like picking up a child from behind, she withdrew from him. As she did it, she also wanted David's tenderness, his warmth, his body next to hers, and his words, whatever they might be. She wanted his comfort *and* she didn't want him to touch her. In the space between these wants, she felt frustration and annoyance at herself, which immediately she had directed at David with her sarcastic reply. After a moment of composing herself, she had told him as gently as she could that she understood what he meant, her world was probably different. She just didn't feel it yet. She apologized. She was just easily frustrated, that was all. He got up to make coffee, she remembered now as she watched the clouds drift up the mountain. Her annoyance at him, at herself, had also been a dispersing cloud in the sky: there and then gone. And after the annoyance was gone, she had considered this thing David said, turning the phrase over in her mind like turning over a moon rock: *Your* world is different.

She considered it again now. *Your* world is different. Before Nicholas was gone, she woke in her house, or she had before coming to this town, and she still did that. She woke in a room. Before, she had opened her computer. She had read the news, emails. She had drunk coffee. She had urinated, defecated, showered. After he died, she did all of these things, still. Everything was exactly as it had been except now she noticed that fact: everything was exactly as it always was. It was not monotony she was noticing. Long ago she knew some perspective on the world had been lost, some vital seeing of it. This was worse than monotony, that growing banality of her life, the clear understanding of it. This was worse and it was nothing she could pin down. Before Nicholas was gone, she did certain things. After he was gone, she continued doing them. Yet now she saw that she was doing things with the accompanying thought of why do this thing: there was, suddenly, an awareness of the arbitrariness of what she was doing. Whereas over the past however many years, starting in her early forties and pro-gressing to now, when her boys were no longer boys, her husband was more of a roommate than a husband or lover, the world had slowly drained of both meaning and mystery, this was something utterly more stark: Nicholas was dead, yet she had to have a bowel movement. Things will become more different, David had said the evening before they drove to the small town where Nicholas lived, had once lived. She had said to him that she hadn't been able to exercise. That was something different. He'd nodded his head. He said, I know that's sarcastic, but things will feel more different and then they'll feel more the same. Or more normal, he said. You'll get used to it, I mean.

Louis Walters asked her if she wanted to talk about Nich-olas. She'd nearly forgotten he was there on her screen. She looked at the computer and shook her head, not bothering

to write. She took a sip of coffee and then typed to Louis
Walters, asking what he would do if his daughter died, how
did he think he would feel? She honestly wanted to know,
and she was sorry it was such a morbid question. Louis
Walters immediately said that it was nearly impossible to
imagine, he would, he would feel, devastated, thoroughly
devastated. That probably doesn't help. She wrote that it
didn't. I would, he said. I don't know. He paused, picking
at a napkin on his desk with both hands, tearing little shreds
off it. Katherine thought that he had no idea. He had no
idea, for instance, that he wouldn't be interested in eating.
She hadn't been interested in eating and still wasn't interested in eating, though she ate. She thought of how two
days after she sent and responded to several emails, informing other faculty members at the university that she would
be gone for some indefinite amount of time, and could
anyone take her classes for a short while, she had then written an email in which she explained that her son had died
in a car accident, that he'd been driving on an isolated, rural
mountain road, late at night, in the rain, and had somehow
lost control of the vehicle. He and his wife had died. She
wrote that she wanted to write this email so that people
wouldn't be gossiping and spreading false information, that
this was the true information. Writing the email she could
barely understand why she was writing it. She had felt both
oddly comforted by writing the facts in the email, as though
she had some clear handle on the situation, and completely
distant, as though the woman typing was not her, that this
was not even close to the action she should be taking. She
had signed off by saying that she was thankful for the
department and her friends there and their support, though

she didn't particularly feel that at all. After writing that email, she had responded to one student, who asked for an extension on a paper. One week, she'd written, slowly typing out each letter, as if watching her mind form the thought, the reply. Then she had gone into her office, stupidly, to be alone, and her colleagues visited one by one, except the younger ones, and she'd cried, they'd witnessed her crying, she was inconsolable, of course. She'd even forgotten that she'd written the strange email about her son. She thought that maybe David had alerted her colleagues. No, it'd been her, and she'd gone in and cried, ridiculously. Louis Walters had pulled up his chair and hugged her from behind, awkwardly, as her husband did a day later. Louis Walters had told her to take the semester off. She had been, and still was, having an affair with him. She was doing things though she didn't care to do them. Looking at his face now, the cliché of their situation, the fact that he was a male in a position of power and she was his inferior, was almost beyond belief. Yet, at sixty-two years old, she had been talking with him, sleeping with him, meeting him in his office, locking the door. It had been a little antidote to the poisoned monotony of her life. It was a terrible, definitely a mean, selfish thing, yet she had done it. What Nicholas's death brought into stark relief was this: she was doing it still. She couldn't believe how completely foolish she was.

She sat forward and wrote to Louis Walters that it felt as though behind each action were both the space Nicholas had left behind and Nicholas himself, as though pointing at her life: her memories of him as a baby, as a toddler and child, an adolescent, a young man – all memories which were so much like dreams they barely seemed to have an existence, barely there in her mind, but which she often tried to sharpen and make clearer, like digitally enhancing surveillance footage – and then as a father himself, then as nothing, a person suddenly ended. In this endingness, a revealing of herself. Louis Walters read the message and said that she was proceeding through the stages of grief from what he could tell, and from what he could tell, this was depression she was experiencing. She wrote to him that if he said another thing about the stages of grief she wasn't going to talk to him anymore. He put his hands up, nodded, and said, I don't know what to say then. I shouldn't be talking to you anyway, she wrote. You've said that enough, he said. I can sign off if that's what you want. I'll disconnect. She looked at him, his sad, hurt face, and she wrote, Don't, if only to not create any more hurt.

Katherine thought that it was impossible to explain to someone who hadn't experienced it, which was why Louis Walters had just been so dismissive: how in each of her actions – putting on shoes, tying the laces, standing from a chair – she felt the unfairness of this double Nicholas, the one who was there and the one who was not. There was an anger at his being gone, and underneath that anger, a sadness that sometimes overtook the anger, like a wave overtaking another wave. Both anger and sadness could flare up, matchlike, into heated intensity, a feeling in her body, and then wisp out. Reality itself seemed both clearer and more remote: like nothing much at all, like she was experiencing her life as though it were a book, a thing she was reading and interpreting, but barely experiencing, except in brief moments. There seemed to be a veneer of thought over everything. The walls in this room were walls, they were called walls, there were four corners, no, more than four, she counted, six, six corners, called corners, in this room, which was called a room. The window was a window, a word. The pane of glass, the air outside, inside, the mountain looming, the streets below, all first thought of, then there. Even now the only thing that felt real was this thought. She was first a character in the book that was her life in her mind before she was a real person. She knew that her life before this moment was like this, too, that everything she experienced was her experience of experiencing it. It was as though she was narrating her life while living it – this was the narration of her life, she was doing it now, again and again, moment after moment, and couldn't stop. The thing she was attempting to do with this thinking, she thought, was find a way to access Nicholas again, and through him, herself. But with Nicholas gone, could one really have a thought about him, who was an absence? It was like trying to paint on the air. When considering Nicholas's absence, her thinking and feeling couldn't locate the object of that very thinking and feeling – there was no ground, nothing to grab on to, nothing upon which to contemplate or judge or perceive, and maybe this was the falling feeling she had felt in her office, some groundlessness.

A car pulled into the hotel parking lot, which at first she thought was David's, but upon closer inspection was a Jetta and not a Passat. She watched it move ghostlike in the foggy morning air, soundless and smooth. It pulled into a spot and an Indian man and child emerged. Not a child, she thought, an adolescent. Visiting the college, she thought. What's wrong? Louis Walters said. Talk to me Katherine. Just talk. No writing. She looked back at the screen, rubbed her eyes and cracked her neck, and then wrote that she thought David's car had pulled into the parking lot. Has it? Louis Walters said. I can go. She typed that it wasn't his car, she was mistaken. Like I am about so many things, she wrote. Now that's being dramatic, Louis Walters said. Look, if you really feel guilty, then let's talk when you get home. But pretending you don't want to see me anymore because you feel lonely, because you're with Mr. Distant, who won't even openly talk about Nicholas's passing, I mean, it's hard to blame you. You need someone to talk with. Please stop, she wrote. Let her think. And don't use the word 'passing.' She needed to think about what she needed to do. Once again, she wrote, what I really need to do has gotten lost. It's not lost, Louis Walters said. There's nothing you *need* to do. There's only things you can do, and you can speak, and that's what will help you, talking this out.

Another text arrived from David, which said that he'd be home soon, but he wanted to stop at the patisserie. Did she want a croissant or something? She needed to eat. She held her phone up, showing Louis Walters her typing to her husband, no longer hiding it from him, a thing she had done initially, as though she had to hide Louis Walters from David, and David from Louis Walters. No, she wrote to David. Then, Thank you. She didn't like that Louis Walters had used the phrase 'Mr. Distant' to describe David. Not that it was inaccurate, but she was the one who called David that, Mr. Distant. She hated that she'd told this to Louis Walters, because now he used it, like it was his, or theirs together, when it wasn't. Louis Walters would ask about Mr. Distant, ask if she and Mr. Distant were ever, you know, intimate anymore, a slight jealousy that crept into their situation. He'd ask if Mr. Distant was still talking to College Sweetheart. This was another thing, regrettably, that Katherine had told him: one afternoon, David had inexplicably left his iPad open to his personal email, and she couldn't help but pick it up and swipe through. Startlingly, she'd found that he'd been conversing with a Laura Moser. Frequently. This was not another teacher in the law school, she didn't think, no name that she knew, yet she did know the name, somehow, though she wasn't sure how. She couldn't help but click on one of the emails to find out who this person was. She wished she hadn't. Laura Moser wrote, in the particular email that Katherine had opened, that she couldn't imagine being married for so long, that she'd divorced twice, would never get married again, though she wanted a partner, a companion, and a lover. But more than anything, Laura Moser wanted the freedom to be herself, something that'd been kept from her by her previous husbands, who were controlling traditionalists with the thoughts of liberals and the actions of nuanced, complicated, subtle misogynists. What Laura Moser really wanted was an open relationship, the freedom to take lovers and friends without jealousy or pain, and that was exactly what she was doing. She was living out her life exactly as she wanted, doing what she wanted, and you know what she'd found? Getting what you wanted did make you happy. Katherine had to quit reading, closing out the email, though she had then gone back and read through all of them, little pieces of nostalgia from both David and Laura Moser, sentimental, about how much they were in love in college, and trying to figure out exactly what happened, why they'd parted, David, in one email, writing that he often thought about their lovemaking – he actually used that word – and said it'd been something that'd never left him, that no one had ever been as good as her, as uninhibited and free, and that, he was embarrassed to admit, he still used these memories. He used her thighs, her breasts, her hands, her hair and eyes, even her feet. The word 'used' had made Katherine want to vomit. This Laura Moser woman, in a subsequent email, confessed the same thing, and had been so embarrassed about it for so long, she didn't know people in their fifties, no, she thought, sixties, still fantasized about sex with old lovers, but she did, and now she could openly share her fantasies with her current lover. Sure, occasionally there were issues, but mostly things were completely smooth sailing. In one email, Laura Moser claimed that she often thought of the time when she and David found a house being built and used it as a place to escape the dorms, how easy it was in those days to sneak into places: cemeteries at night, houses still under construction, the restaurant she worked in, after hours. No thought of consequence. Then came a string of emails in which they detailed their favorite sexual memories, which nearly caused Katherine to destroy the iPad, but she'd composed herself, read on, and then even worse, a string of emails that detailed their most tender memories, and after that, comical emails about their past arguments. David shaking Laura Moser out of her sadness on the campus green one night, telling her a guinea pig's just a guinea pig, dammit, I'm a person! In an act of what she viewed as complete composure, Katherine had sent all the emails to herself, forwarding them, then sent them to David, who was at work, teaching a class, one by one. Eighty or ninety emails filling his inbox. He'd had no explanation when he got home, and merely said, Yes, I've been talking with her, but that's it. Just talking. Nothing more meaningful. And anyway, we're just reminiscing. About fucking, Katherine had said. Oh come on, David had said. Aren't we over all the jealousy by now? No, Katherine had said. We're not. Then, several months later, she'd met Louis Walters. The emails were not the cause of her affair, but they opened things up for her, allowed her some space that might not have been open otherwise, allowed her to view herself as capable of being someone else, as capable of being with David and not. She eventually told Louis Walters about the emails, about David – who he'd met in person at department parties – and about how he was Mr. Distant. When Louis Walters used them in conversation, it felt as though he was accessing some part of her life that she felt should've been closed off, easily red-taped, though she knew it was her fault, since she brought them up. And she'd probably brought them up to make herself feel better, to let Louis Walters know that she wasn't the type of person who would just cheat on a person, there had to be some pain there first, so she portrayed David as a remote man, Mr. Distant, which she called David to his face as a little joke, a playful thing – they did a kind of comic superhero joke, like when they were eating dinner and he'd suddenly completely tune out of the conversation, then suddenly return, and say something like, I just thought of the moment my mother, when I was a young boy, hit me with a switch. It only occurred one time, and I had a scar for years, and Katherine had said, Mr. Distant, with the powers of staying visible but being completely gone. It was a passive-aggressive joke, with an element of truth, she knew, added in, and which she knew David knew. But then that was why it was funny. In addition to the Mr. Distant thing, she also portrayed David to Louis Walters as having emotionally cheated on her, a phrase she actually used – I know David didn't cheat on me cheat on me, but he sought out emotional connection with another woman, and that would be bad enough, but he sought, and found, it should be noted, this emotional connection with another woman who was once a lover or girlfriend or whatever – and she had told this to Louis Walters, she knew, so that she wouldn't feel so bad doing what she did with him, but also as a way to present to Louis Walters that her cheating with him was not something she did casually: she had to have a reason for it, some kind of inner damage that she and Louis Walters were treating, like a course of antibiotics for some infection in her existence.

Louis Walters asked her if she knew she'd just been holding her coffee cup and staring for the last couple of minutes. It looks like it's getting cold, he said. There's no more steam. She put the mug down, then picked it back up, sipped it, and then put it down again, and wrote, Yes, I knew that. I did it on purpose, to see if you thought it matched your image of what a person in mourning should look like. He smiled a little. Does it? she wrote. I suppose so, he said. She wrote that if she wanted to hold a cup of coffee without drinking it, letting it get cold, that's what she was going to do, and if she wanted to stare at nothing and feel nothing, that's also what she was going to do, and if he didn't want to do that, he didn't have to and could sign out. I understand, he said. I just thought you should know you don't have to hold a coffee cup for all eternity. There are tables available. Surfaces upon which to place items we don't always want to be holding. She nodded without giving any recognition to his little joke and thought that the worst part about telling Louis Walters these things was that she had liked, for years, that David was a remote man. She liked his distance from the world, as though he were an alien sent to observe and watch. It was a fascinating trait, one which served to relocate Katherine's own perspective on the world, served to show her the advantages of watching, of distancing in order to understand, a distancing from oneself as much as from the world. What was even more fascinating was that David could be pulled from his distance like a tethered astronaut slowly pulled back to the ship. She could do it with a hand on his thigh, a cool look, playing with the curls of his hair. She liked being able to turn him from mind to body with the ease of flicking a light switch, and additionally she liked his mind, which scrutinized everything, but which was also fair, generally kind, just poetic enough. Bringing him back to his body had become more difficult, though. He taught two grad school law courses at the state university, reticently moving toward retirement, and in this transition, which she felt might bring him back to the world, and to her, he'd simply found (beside the email situation, she thought) another solitary activity: gardening. He said it reminded him of being a boy, of growing up on a farm, before his father had sold it. He liked working with dirt. I like digging up the back corner of the yard, he said. My hands. Jesus, I forgot they were here, he said. Look, he waved his hands, put them on her body, look, my hands, he'd said. Arms and hands and head. He'd gently headbutted her, and she'd laughed and slapped him away – all this before she knew about the emails, before Louis Walters. She'd liked to watch him in the garden. Pulling out the rocks, digging, tilling the ground, bringing manure from the hardware store, constructing a small fence around the vegetable garden, a garden that was already quite large – neighbors commented that it took up most of their backyard – and got larger every year. He made and remade the fence each spring, citing wear and tear from rain and animals. The fence was a small wooden thing, which allowed him to anchor chicken wire, covering over the small plants, and then some kind of veil-like covering for the herbs. He wore work boots and jeans when gardening, a loose flannel. He was in decent shape and looked so much like Nicholas. When he came inside for water, there were patches of sweat around his neck and armpits. Sweat on his face and arms. He smelled like a mixture of his sweat and deodorant. He didn't wear aftershave. He watered the garden, weeded, cut the plants back, sprayed organic sprays to rid the garden of pests. He brought in leaves from the plants with small holes in them: beetles. He looked up photos, compared. He brought in roma tomatoes with blackened ends: end rot. He brought in leaves with their ends gnawed off: slugs. He inspected the leaves of plants and soil in the same way he inspected the vegetables themselves, with care and concern for what he was growing. He sometimes brought in a jalapeno chili and would hold it up, like holding a tiny baby kitten, turn it around in the sunlight, then take a bite, eating the whole thing raw. She'd never seen him do such a thing. She understood two things then: he'd found something else to pull him out of his distance from the world, to pull him into some connection with his body. The other thing was that

David cared about what he was doing. She'd almost forgotten what that felt like. When she commented one afternoon on the fact that David looked like Nicholas out there, she almost, for a moment, hadn't been able to tell the difference. There was Nicholas, she'd said to him. Then there was Nicholas and you at once, and then just you. Hmm, he'd said. Then, You mean he looks like me? She'd been surprised by the question and the force of its actuality and logic. Yes, she said. That is what I mean, I guess. It makes me feel closer to him, doing the work, David had said. He was referring to how Nicholas had built his own house, had his own, much larger garden, an acre. A greenhouse. To both the boys, really, he'd added. They talked with Nicholas infrequently on the phone, a landline, which she couldn't believe still existed, in his cabin-like house. He reported on the land he was clearing, then burning, for a garden, a little farm. He reported on the barn he was turning into a workspace, in order to build a greenhouse and additions to the house, to be able to take the house completely off the grid, using solar panels on the roof. It'd be a lot of work, he told them on the phone, but he liked the work, which was so different from his job teaching anthropology classes. It was more like his fieldwork in the Amazon, he said, where he both examined the culture and role of drugs in the indigenous experience and also, tangential to the project, had helped build houses in the nearby village with a missionary group, just randomly joining up with them, he hadn't cared they were religious. They listened to him on speakerphone, his voice both his and not, somehow different, though she didn't know how, exactly. He called with reports, not to talk. Not to share, as he once did, his internal world. She never knew how he was feeling anymore. If he felt April was right for him, if he genuinely liked the small town he was living in, if he was happy. Nathaniel, Nathaniel would talk to her for hours about his troubles, his anxieties, his new vegetarian dishes, his idea for a restaurant that he couldn't get a good enough loan for, his care for and grievances concerning Stefanie, occasionally apologizing for what a shit he'd been in high school and college, and she loved Nathaniel for this, but she missed Nicholas. He'd gone and never returned, even when he did return physically. When he was building the cabin on the mountain, April, pregnant, had stayed with Katherine and David, and Katherine had occasionally overheard April talking with Nicholas, Nicholas saying something about how he was starting now, and she'd heard April say that he still had to text her even if they didn't speak for a week. Katherine hadn't known what to make of this, but April was in the kitchen, so she had to ask, she couldn't not ask, couldn't pretend she hadn't heard. I'm sorry for overhearing, Katherine had said. But why aren't you talking for a week? Are you having a disagreement? April had been holding her belly, which was not large yet, only about four months pregnant, and she'd said that they weren't fighting or anything, but that Nicholas spent a week in silence each year. Since when? Katherine had said. The last three years at least, April said. To what end? Katherine had asked. April said just to be quiet, just to shut up, at least that's what Nicholas had said. It has something to do with the idea he got from a shaman, though I don't know what exactly, that it's language that can open things, and language that can close things, and too much language is a prison. That's what he said. You should ask him, April had said, and then poured herself some tea. When Katherine told this to David in bed that evening, he'd said, Hmm, sounds like Nicholas. She'd wanted to talk about it more, but didn't. David had picked up his book, as he always did at night. Sitting in front of the computer, not talking with Louis Walters, she didn't even know if David knew that part of the reason she wasn't speaking now was to feel something about Nicholas, though she didn't know what. She didn't know how to be quiet. Of course she was tired of speaking to other people, but what did Nicholas see in this quiet? she wondered. She sometimes felt as though he'd located some secret, in the space of his silent weeks, she imagined he'd discovered something unfathomable, the truth of existence or at least his own, but now that she wasn't speaking, all she really felt was that she was still speaking internally. She had no idea how to be quiet.

Her phone buzzed, which caused Louis Walters to seemingly glance at the area of his screen from which he heard the buzzing sound. She felt the strangeness of the effect: she felt that everything in her room was unavailable to him somehow, that they were in separate realities, that the screen defined this separation, and yet now she remembered that wasn't true. He was there with her and not at the same time. She picked up her phone, read the text from Nathaniel, that said, Mom, the lawyer is acting strange. Can I talk with you in private? She read the text and when Louis Walters asked what was it, she wrote, My son. Give me a moment. The lawyer is acting strange, Nathaniel had written. It was their little joke about David: the lawyer. She almost wrote, when isn't he? But didn't. After all, she wasn't even speaking. She thought of how this week of silence that Nicholas did once a year had seemed so out of the ordinary to her, but to David it was just another Nicholas thing. He'd easily dismissed it, or not dismissed, not accepted either, but just assumed normalcy. Didn't look at it too long. This was the routine they followed, too: she taught at the university, she met with students, she wrote a paper or two each year, which were accepted and published in journals that no one read except her colleagues, who greeted her small success with pleasure undercut by an obvious jealousy, and this was what she did, while David did his thing. They spoke to their sons, mainly Nathaniel, met with Nathaniel a couple times a month, and maybe saw Nicholas twice a year, not looking at anything too much, certainly not the idea that they were aging, that their children were gone from them, into the world, that they didn't really know Jack, their lone grandchild, that well, and death was closer. She and David discussed their separate lives over dinner, occasionally meeting in the middle of the relationship, shedding their singular selves, but not looking too closely. They went to a movie twice a month, they drank coffee in coffee shops, they watched television, sometimes many hours of it, they walked their dogs, they talked about how Nathaniel and Nicholas were doing, Jack, too, occasionally April. David told her he wanted to try growing a rare heirloom tomato next year, it grew very small, very red, didn't require much water, was intensely flavorful. Very hard to grow. She had told him something like Nathaniel would love to have some of those, that she would too. He told her that was exactly what he was thinking, wouldn't it be neat if Nathaniel could visit for a weekend and just choose things to make from the garden, like his own personal farm-to-table thing. Again and again

David surprised Katherine with his thoughtfulness – it was surprising because he could be so distant, and so cruel, as with the Laura Moser emails. She told him that sounded like a good idea. If I can grow them, he'd said. Katherine thought now that there'd be these small occasions of coming together that barely even counted, separated by larger spaces in which it seemed almost no real communication occurred, then a fight. David occasionally claimed that she didn't do any laundry, didn't help with meals, didn't help with the house, and she, in turn, claimed that she never saw him, he was always in his office or in the garden, he seemed to take no interest in her or her life. Though as they had these fights, she wondered if she wanted anything to change. She liked that she could leave for a weekend, attend a conference with a co-worker, she liked that she could go to her feminist book club alone, and talk with the other women there, that she could go on a hike alone, walk the dogs alone. At night, in front of the television, streaming some detective show, there was still David on the sofa with her. Nothing had been lost really. He'd rub her feet while watching the show. He'd absently comment on the contrivance of an episode. They'd laugh. She felt no passion from him, no desire from him for her, certainly, but there was some comfort she didn't want to disrupt. There was comfort, and directly below that comfort, a danger in the comfort itself. She didn't know why exactly. Maybe it was that while she seemed to feel things emptying in the monotony of their lives, David was able to find one or two things that supplied meaning. He was able to find some meaning within the monotony that she could not. Gardening every day. She wondered if Louis Walters was in her life simply because she wanted something new. Loneliness was the accusation she often directed at David. She sat inside while he worked in the garden, she watched television while he researched old cases to present to his classes, she called Margaret, her sister, and they complained about their jobs, she called colleagues to see if they wanted to meet for coffee. She was free in her aloneness and didn't want to be alone but still wanted to be free. This felt irreconcilable, some cage of language and wants she couldn't see out of. She enjoyed her freedom, and she did feel alone, but she also knew that she was using the accusation of feeling lonely almost as a preemptive measure. There was something other than aloneness there, but it felt unreachable, unknowable. If he ever found out about Louis Walters, of course, she could use it, her loneliness and David's distance, in conjunction with his little email affair with College Sweetheart. It was an accusation she cultivated in the same way he tended to the plants in his garden, so that if she was ever found out, she could point clearly: I told you I felt alone. But in her most shameful moments, she was afraid she was only bored, bored with David, bored with herself, bored with her life.

She typed to Nathaniel, Is he looking for the will? If that's what it is, don't worry about it. We're just not sure why this Tammy person is driving across the country and want to make sure our ducks are in a row. She had no idea why she typed that phrase. She couldn't imagine what else David could've said or was doing that would've offended Nathaniel or been strange in a way that was beyond David's usual strangeness. Maybe he was worrying Nathaniel by making up some battle that was going to happen with this Tammy person, but even though the police had bungled that, even though no one had contacted this Tammy person until four days after the accident, even though she'd been in, in David's words, a serious rage when he finally contacted her and told her, Katherine knew that even if this woman put up a fight, she had no legal rights. Jack was Nathaniel's charge now, everyone in the family had to know it, and she was glad for it. He was the right person, despite the troubled years of his youth that, in retrospect, felt almost banal. She put the phone down, and looked back to the computer screen, where Louis Walters said that they hadn't really been talking anyway, but that he'd be right back. He was going to leave his computer on, he wasn't leaving her alone, but he had to take the dog out very quickly. He now held up a Shih Tzu, and said that Morten had been circling his feet, just give him like ten minutes and he'd be back. She began writing that this was probably a good time to sign off, but he said, I'm not saying goodbye. Right back, he said, and left the room. She saw him carry the dog out of the room, his back to her momentarily, then there was only the room where Louis Walters had been sitting. His desk chair swiveled slightly to the right, turning around with the motion of him getting up and leaving, the remnant of the act. The chair soon stopped moving. The Skype window showed bookshelves behind him, a side table covered with what appeared to be papers he was grading for his classes. Several stacks in different manila folders. A coffee mug on top acting as a paperweight. Another coffee mug on top of the bookshelf. Morning sunlight came slanting into the room, cut neatly by the blinds, then jaggedly lying across the uneven surface of the shelves and books. There were two framed photographs on the bookshelf, in which she could see both his wife and daughter. In the photograph of the daughter, she was holding Morten. In the photograph of the wife, there was Louis Walters. His bald head, smiling face, slight bug eyes hidden by glasses. He was moderately good looking, intelligent, and successful, though who among her and her husband's friends weren't? Hovering behind these thoughts, like a haunting of them, was Nicholas, Nicholas's life, his absence, that she would never see him again. There were sketches of further thoughts and feelings at the remote corners of her consciousness, which her thoughts of Louis Walters, and other things, covered, repeatedly, over and over, the thought, for instance, that there would never now be a new photo of Nicholas like there could be a new photo of her, or David, or Louis Walters, just as the photo of Louis Walters with his wife that she was looking at now through her laptop screen was a picture of a Louis Walters that had been and was no longer, and there would never be a photo of Nicholas now that was a photo of him that could possibly contradict his presence. She looked at the photo of Louis Walters and his wife and wondered who he was to that woman.

She thought that what Louis Walters was to her, mainly, was younger. A younger person, a man, a romantic interest who'd taken an interest in her when that had not occurred in so long, had seemed like it maybe couldn't occur again. So long, in fact, that at first, she hadn't even noticed his advances, like she'd deprogrammed herself, years ago, from noticing romantic advances. Oh, she could still flirt, but if someone else did, she couldn't see it, couldn't believe it. She had spilled her coffee one morning in the sociology department's parking lot. She had pulled in, set the coffee on top of her car, and then pulled out her bag with her laptop, the day's lectures, papers that needed to be handed back. When she shut the door, she did it hard, unthinkingly, and the mug had sort of flipped off the car, hit the ground, the lid cracking, the mug rolling away and spilling all the coffee. Fuck, she'd said. Louis Walters happened to be walking by, and he'd waved at her. He'd given her a kind of weird look, an unhappy or confused smile, and kept walking. Later that day, he'd left a coffee on her desk in her office, and then she thought, Okay, maybe I wasn't giving the guy enough credit. That was nice. She sent a thank you email. After that, he walked with her each morning into the building, having learned they both arrived for teaching at the same time. She caught him sitting, waiting for her in his car one morning when she was late. He pretended to be shuffling papers into his briefcase, also just arrived, so that they could walk in together. He bought her lunch, on the department. He left occasional lattes, banana bread. She began to get it. It'd been so long. Is this real? she thought. Or is my sex software failing? Then he called her into his office for her annual review and not only found no faults with her teaching, but said something about the fact that she was the most elegant person in the department by far. He made comments on the two papers she'd published that semester: 'The Bechdel Test and Social Networking' and 'Voting Against Oneself: Why Rural America Is Blind to Itself.' He said that he loved that she brought the Bechdel test into everyday life as a way to challenge its descriptive nature and association with mere pop culture, and that in doing so, she basically questioned its usefulness, and she'd replied with the idea that she wasn't questioning the test's authenticity, she was

merely attempting to figure out if it had any practical applications beyond being used in film and other narratives, and
that, somewhat lamely, of course it didn't, it couldn't. I said
hello to a woman today when buying my coffee – does that
mean I interact with enough women? Is the narrative, the
film of my life, complete, full? That's really the difficulty I
discovered with the Bechdel test, she'd said. That if two
women can say 'Hey, how's the weather,' the movie somehow passes the test. This is meant to show, Hey, look how
patriarchal and misogynist movies are. Two women can't
even talk about the weather, but I can't help but feel that
the test is actually granting too much space, and confusing
some people about a film's or story's overall openness by
leaving out the idea of 'meaningful' conversation. So its
mere descriptiveness acts as a confusing factor in a way.
Yes, yes, he'd said. That's exactly it. He'd continued the
meeting, commenting on her body of work, and then said
that on a personal note he liked watching how she moved
in front of a class, her presence in the classroom. There was
a quiet power, a certain elegance to her movements, as
though she were dancing through the lecture. She almost
couldn't reply, until she said, That's more than slightly
exaggerated. He'd then said, See, it's that directness that I
never see anymore. It's so refreshing. I know you're not
bullshitting me. I have no idea if you're bullshitting me,
she'd said. There it is again, he'd said. Who says that to
someone? Especially their boss. Later that week, the end of
the semester, she went to his office – she'd scheduled a
meeting – sat in the chair across from him and asked him
if he was making advances toward her. Yes, he'd said. I am.
Good, she said. I want you to be. That began it. They made

love in his office, she gave him a blowjob like a naughty secretary, they met at his house when his wife was away. His youth served as a doorway to her past, her own youth, her own passion, her carelessness – some thrill of living. It was difficult to even think of how clichéd this was, that because she was dissatisfied and bored in her own life, with herself, with the fact that she was aging, was, in fact, old, or deemed by society as old, at sixty-two, that she had accepted the advances of a man younger than her, as though this could really do anything, change anything. She hoped this wasn't true. She hoped that she was, in actuality, lonely, but she was afraid that she wanted to be young again, didn't want to be growing old. As a young woman, she'd been terrified of not being pretty enough, smart enough, interesting enough, but in this anxiety the world presented itself forcefully, fearfully. This feeling had returned with Louis Walters: how could this younger man find her so attractive, she wondered, while sitting in front of her computer. He desired her with a certain hunger. He went down on her in his office, propping her in his office chair, her feet on his desk. She walked out of his office with a buzzing feeling of secrecy. Passing her colleagues in the hallway, her students, she felt as though the world had transformed into a mysterious place again: no one knew what she'd just done, no one knew who she was, no one knew, including her, what would come next. Maybe he'd come into her office, tell a student that he would have to meet with her another day, send the student away, then bend her over a desk like a scene out of a noir film. She was free to be desired again. So maybe that was why Louis Walters. It wasn't that David made her feel alone, it was that he made her feel ignored. Though when she thought this, which she had thought before in the same way she was thinking of it now, as though it was the narrative of her life, the recursive theme of her thinking, which she constantly ignored and then re-approached: did it actually matter what the motivation was if the act itself was a hurtful one? Was she simply distracting herself from what she was actually doing by thinking that there was some way that what she was doing could be justified?

Louis Walters arrived back in his office. He was wearing a jacket now. He unzipped it, hung it on the back of his chair, and then still standing, said, Shit, be right back. Forgot my tea. He ran back out of the room, returning a moment later, with a steaming cup of tea in his left hand. He sat at the desk, the glow of the screen paling his face some, and then blew on the tea and said, Thanks for waiting. I have one thing I want to say, then I'll let you go. I'm guessing David will be back soon. She wrote to Louis Walters that she knew she'd said it, but she felt bad for communicating with him when she was supposed to be here with her family. This is, she wrote, an admittedly small amount of what I'm actually experiencing right now, but I can't do it anymore. Not now and not ever again. Look, can you just speak out loud? he said. I feel weird sitting here reading your messages waiting for you to write something while I talk. It feels odd. I'm okay with silence, but I'm not okay just hearing my own voice. It feels like I'm having a conversation with no one, with myself. It makes me feel a little nuts. So, here's what I'm going to do. I'm just going to sit here. I'm going to just be here with you. There was a pause. And as a last note, he said, I really can't believe David left you alone.

117

She looked away from the screen, out the window, to see if she could see her husband's car. He would come back soon with a few things to put in the mini-fridge: bread, salami, cheese, fruit. Also wine. She'd told him she couldn't go out into the town again, couldn't bear going to dinner, being seen, or seeing anyone who might have known Nicholas. When David arrived back in the hotel room, Katherine knew she wouldn't tell him about Louis Walters, and she further knew that she wouldn't end things with Louis Walters. She looked into the parking lot, which she could view out the window, over her laptop. If she were to see David's car pull up, she would tell Louis Walters goodbye, close out the Skype window on the computer, open up a web page, something from the *Washington Post* about climate change, the protesting of the Kodiak pipeline, the indigenous people who were protesting there. Maybe an article about the raid on an Iraqi city to free it from terrorists. Perhaps a video about posture, about how proper posture can correct bowel problems, though David might take that as a passive-aggressive comment about his own posture. Maybe something completely ignorable, some new recipe, a quiche, which she baked every Saturday morning – to show that she was being normal, she was getting back to normal. Or maybe something more to the point: How This Mother Dealt with Her Son's Death. Or, maybe something that would make David think of things: How My Son's Death Made Me Realize I'm Afraid of My Own. He'd say something about the fact that they had plenty of good years left, almost half a lifetime. She hated that it would be something, that she would choose something to cover over what she was doing, that she couldn't just stop talking to Louis Walters right now.

She looked at Louis Walters' face, which was supposedly just sitting there for her, just being with her, but which she really knew was waiting for her to type something. She saw herself in the small corner of the Skype window: tired, her face washed out by the cold light coming in the window, make-up-less, her hair a little out of control even though she had pulled it back into a ponytail. When had she done that? It had been all down and wild around her face, and sometime in the conversation with Louis Walters she'd tied it up, yet she couldn't remember doing this at all. How long had it been? How long has it taken, all of this, sitting here? What other parts of reality were excised, deemed unimportant?

She watched herself seeing herself, the twoness of her: there she was, in the same hotel they'd always stayed in when they visited Nicholas and April, and eventually Jack. I don't want to be talking to you anymore, she wrote. I'm going to sign off now. Katherine, Katherine, Louis Walters said in the Skype window, look, this is the last thing. I don't think this silence is healthy. I think it's good for you to talk. For you to get out what you're really feeling. You need to express it. Get it out. You'll feel lighter, better. She felt an anger rising in her, the same anger that had been present, along with the sadness, since learning of Nicholas's car accident, an anger and sadness that arose in her mind like a wave, then settled into a still, glassy surface. I won't feel lighter, she wrote. You can't reduce everything down to a psychological concept, as though pain's something we can shed like skin. You can't talk me into feeling better. Do you want to know what I'm doing right now? What I'm doing right now is this: my husband left to get some groceries, and for the half-hour or so that he's been gone, I decided to text you, Skype you, and talk with you because I didn't feel like being alone. I felt like distracting myself, and I did this knowing that I'd feel worse doing it, because we're doing this thing that is both hurtful to my husband, and by extension the rest of my family, and I know your wife would be devastated too. So, I knew that I'd feel worse by contacting you, but I didn't know in what way, so I did it because since I didn't know in what way I'd feel bad, maybe there was a chance it could make me feel good. There was some safety there, in not knowing exactly how I would feel bad, like the feeling bad couldn't happen if I couldn't locate the specific of it, like it would remain in abstraction, but now I do feel bad, specifically because now I feel alone, whereas before I didn't. I wanted to see you to make myself feel less alone and now I feel more alone because all this shows about me is that I don't want to actually deal with whatever's going on. I know I was the one who contacted you, but I can't talk to you right now, she wrote, and probably never again.

She watched Louis Walters' pinched and hurt face. She'd hurt him, she'd wanted to hurt him, and she was viewing it now. After a moment, she wrote, I'm sorry, writing it more because it was what she was supposed to do than because she really felt it. Or, maybe, she did feel sorry, but she also didn't – part of her wanted him to be complicit in her shame, to be shameful together, another kind of intimacy, another kind of deceit. I shouldn't have written that, she wrote. No, you're right, he said. You're right. I know you're

120

supposed to feel bad. To feel, you know, terrible. I mean, I guess I don't know. My kids are both alive. That sounds really insensitive. This is hard. Me talking, you not talking, this is bad. I feel it's revealing bad things about me. There's an imbalance to this that I don't like – your not talking, it allows me to say too much. It's like you can see more of me and I don't like it.

She looked at him without acknowledging him. She felt it, what he was talking about, this imbalance. He was right. She'd felt it with others. With strangers in the coffee shop, with colleagues at the college. With David, all the time. She sensed people were uncertain how to react to her silence. Of course, first there had to be the realization that she was the mother of the man who died. But that almost always occurred quickly. This town, everyone knowing each other, it was a reason she hated it, but not the sole reason.

The first night in town – away from her house, her job and colleagues, away from Louis Walters, away from her life except for David – they'd eaten at a local place, and she had felt a grateful anonymity through the meal. A space in which to be genuinely sad, genuinely lost. She didn't have to be the grieving mother, as she had to be at her school, in her neighborhood, with her family. She could just sit and eat food and feel whatever she felt. And she did that. She ate her locally sourced trout and grits. She drank a glass of house chardonnay. She ate some bread. David sat across from her, not talking, occasionally glancing at his phone, then at her, as if to say, What's wrong, but knowing that, finally, for once, he couldn't say that, couldn't ask it. He knew what was wrong. Yet in the space of that dinner – the hanging lamps above each table lighting the place only

121

dimly, the dark of the outside streets, old-style streetlamps, an imitation of gas lamps coming on – she'd felt she could just eat, not be noticed, not be anyone, not be the mourning mother momentarily. Then the owner had paid for the meal. It's taken care of, their waitress, a middle-aged woman said. David had looked around. Katherine kept her own eyes on the table, on her wine. She took a sip. Then the manager came over. He had a beard, was a big man, had been speaking earlier to some other customer of the numerous handcrafted beers on draft, and when he came up to the table, he put a big fist there, gently pounding the table, like a mime might, and said, I can't understand what you're going through, but I want you to know that we're all here for you. Your son and his family meant a lot to this community. He'd been looking down when he said it, then he looked up, giving Katherine a deeply pained look, his lips pursed hard into a frown, and his head nodding with profound understanding. She'd done her best to close her eyes and not glare at him. He was only trying to be kind, she'd thought. When she opened her eyes, he'd still been standing there, looking around awkwardly, as though he should be congratulated for his empathy. She couldn't believe he was still there. Thank you, she'd said after a moment. David had put a hand on her hand, which was holding the stem of her wine glass. She wanted to ask them, David and this manager, to please, could they just stop and watch what they were doing, because, none of it, nothing, it seemed, felt anything other than rehearsed, scripted, the outward gestures of grief, a performance, an attempt at mimicking some inner feeling. Then she'd thought, maybe that was grief: that one could come to view oneself from such a distance that one was no longer in one's life, but was watching it, completely separate from others and one's self. Then he'd gone.

Afterward, she and David had walked the few blocks to their hotel. David stopped in the old-timey drugstore to get bottled water and mixed nuts for the evening. She'd waited at the front of the store, felt herself staring vacantly at a stand of Corn-Nuts, thinking of what this man had expected from her. Had he wanted her to reach out, take him by the shoulder, and thank him for finally acknowledging her suffering? She knew this was an awful way to think, and that she should push it from her mind – the man was only trying to be kind, she repeated to herself, an echo of the thought she'd had in the restaurant, only fainter, less compelling. David had come back to the front of the store with the bottled waters and mixed nuts and they went to check out with the clerk, a young woman, homely, probably from a local farm, Katherine remembered thinking now, and in the middle of scanning the nuts, the clerk had looked up and said that she'd lost her sister when she was little, so she knew exactly how they felt. God bless.

Katherine looked at Louis Walters' waiting face and typed to him that what caused her to stop speaking was this: after eating dinner in the town, and hearing all these sympathies that felt empty, that night, she wasn't able to sleep. I thought, she wrote, did Nicholas really know these people? He never spoke of them. The only people he spoke of were April, Jack, and two people from the college, sometimes his students. The next morning, we, David and I, went to breakfast at a diner, where the waitress, a girl named Amanda, after taking our orders and getting us coffees and waters, finally recognized us, or realized who we were, or was told who we were. She said, Oh my god, you're the grandparents. During her speech, I watched this girl, wondering if she'd come to the realization on her own, if our grief was that apparent, or if someone had told her. I'm so sorry for your loss, she said to us. Nicholas and April and Jack sometimes came in here. We all loved them so much. It's such a tragedy. Poor Jack. Poor little thing, I can't imagine. I have a boy who's four and a little girl, just one a few weeks ago. I can't imagine it at all. They're my heart. Katherine wrote to Louis Walters that she remembered the way the waitress had stood there holding their plates of food, an early bird special and a vegetable omelet. I decided right then I wasn't doing this, she wrote. I wouldn't suffer the inanities of an entire town's superficial sympathy. I looked coldly at the girl, feeling my anger like a kind of force field around me. I wanted to project it out, to touch this Amanda woman with it. David saw this I think and to interrupt me he said, Thank you for that, Amanda. Now, I think our breakfast is getting cold. And the woman, startled, had said, Oh my god, I'm so sorry, and set our plates down. Whenever she returned, to fill up water, or coffee, she did that same sort of sad, pursed lip understanding face the manager at the restaurant had made the night before, the same one that all people had been making in order to convey their sadness and understanding. Eventually I stopped drinking the coffee and water, stopped eating. I just wanted to leave. When we finished the breakfast and went to our hotel, David asked why I hadn't said a word through breakfast. He asked if I was all right. I pulled a pad of paper from the desk, wrote on it that I was now in a period of silence, I didn't know for how long. That's what started it. Even writing this now feels like a cop-out.

Katherine stopped writing. She remembered how David had looked at her, his mouth open, then he nodded, swallowed, and said, I understand. He'd walked over to her, held her, fully pulling her into him, and she'd cried. She wanted Nicholas back so bad was what she wanted to say to David, but she only cried into his shoulder, resolved to her task. Then she remembered Nicholas spending a week a year in silence, and she realized that that was what she was doing. She hadn't done it consciously, but she was going to now. Not to find out anything about Nicholas, not to honor his memory, but just to do something that he'd done, to feel close to him and to one of his actions. She didn't feel any closer. David had released her and begun unpacking, and for some amount of time, she'd felt that her original intention, which was to avoid the stupidity of the townspeople, could be transformed into something more meaningful if she allowed herself to do it: it would force her to confront the actuality that her son was gone, she thought. That she would, also, one day be gone. That was better, she thought. She didn't dislike the town in its entirety, but the sort of detached, hippie view of things, the hip-Appalachia façade, coupled with the Cracker Barrel aesthetic of the surrounding rural areas, was more annoying to her than anything she encountered in the medium-sized city she lived in. Everyone here was so 'authentic': musicians, artists, outdoorsmen, hunters, academics. A weird little mix of a community. She didn't want anyone in the way of her grief, she wrote to Louis Walters, and yet they were already all over it, representing it to her. She wanted to meet it alone, without distraction. So I choose silence.

Yet even now, in the room waiting for David to return, not talking to Louis Walters, only writing to him, she knew she was finding distractions from this confrontation, and every time she came back to the realization that Nicholas was gone, she felt the pain as though newly beginning again. Every time her mind reconstructed her reality for her, and that reality first began with Nicholas and then the negation of Nicholas, and the same in turn for April, it was like experiencing the news all over again. She looked at Louis Walters, who was now smoking a cigarette on the screen – it was something she didn't like about him, but he was free to do what he wanted. He sat there, waiting for her, and she sat in front of her computer, alternately looking out the window at the view of Church Street, the farm-to-table restaurant she'd eaten at twice, a bookstore, some small boutique, and then, above the street, as if floating above it almost – the clouds and fog were so thick – there was the mountain, some indiscernible distance away.

Do you want to know the other reason I'm not talking? she wrote. He nodded his head. I'm not talking because I keep finding ways not to look at what is happening, because there are so many distractions from what is happening. You know my other son is with Jack right now, she wrote. When Nicholas made him Jack's godfather, I thought: What a nice gesture. It felt like the right thing, but I never thought it'd have consequences. It has consequences. It's Nathaniel. This is the chef? Louis Walters said. Yes, she wrote, the chef. It's not that I don't think he's the right person, or that he and Stefanie aren't right for Jack. I think they are. But I'm worried for Jack's way of life. It'll be so different with Nathaniel. The same if he comes with David and I. I think the real reason I'm not talking, she wrote, is because of Jack. It's obvious to me now. I learned a while ago that Nicholas spent a week in silence every year. Which was what he wanted Jack to be able to do when he was old enough too. I think that's actually where this is coming from, she wrote, though I didn't realize it right away.

Almost simultaneously, David's car pulled into the parking lot and her phone buzzed with a text message. She looked at the text, a number she didn't recognize, and then read the text, which said, We need to talk, and not understanding who this text was from, she quickly typed to Louis Walters that she had to go. As she typed it, she looked up the area code of the phone number, saw that the number came from an area code she didn't recognize, and realized this was April's mother contacting her. We need to talk, the text read. Louis Walters was saying something, but Katherine wrote, Please don't try to contact me. She'd contact him if she felt she could. She thought about saying that she missed him – if only because she might want to see him again – but she didn't. Suddenly this was clear. She missed his hands on her, his mouth on her, his body making her body feel like a young body again, but these were all things she also had come to hate, and in this way, she did not miss him at all. She missed the pleasure he provided, a momentary pleasure, and everything else, she felt, which was beneath the pleasure, was her sickness. Some brief pleasure was what she got from Louis Walters, and the rest, none of which she really liked and almost all of which made her feel bad, she did to herself, and so she wrote, Bye,

Louis, and closed out the Skype window, and searched for an article about how to make quiche with goat cheese, and texted April's mother back: Let's all meet when you get in on Friday so we can discuss exactly what is going to happen.

TAMMY

Flowers fall even though we love them; weeds grow even though we dislike them. Conveying oneself toward all things to carry out enlightenment is delusion. All things coming and carrying out enlightenment through the self is realization.

—DOGEN, *GENJOKOAN*

Your mind is [. . .] always attempting to leave here and now, to look for purpose or meaning beyond itself.

—DAININ KATAGIRI

There were accidents along the way, stupid people, Tammy thought, driving recklessly, making it harder for everyone else, but most annoyingly, there was one not two hours from her house, right at the beginning of her drive across the country. Good omen, she thought, sitting in the traffic. She felt some generalized anger at everything in her perception – at the flashing lights of police cars passing her on the shoulder, at an ambulance, a fire truck, the red tail-lights of other cars and trucks and semis, the steady rain, the people inside the cars, even the buildings and restaurants off the side of the highway, the night sky polluted by city light, a sickly grey-orange, the leafless trees – and this anger shifted to an annoyed boredom, a sort of wispy feeling of wishing stupid people out of existence. The world might be better then. If there was something some mad scientist could slip into the water that only affected stupid people, causing them to Facebook themselves to death or something, uploading pictures of themselves and their pets for days on end without eating or drinking, growing sickly and tired, eventually falling asleep in front of their webcam, dying a selfish and peaceful death, feeling loved by themselves and their pit bulls. Tammy thought the headline in the paper the next day would be, FB Users Die in Front of FB, Immediately Improving the World.

For a moment, she thought of April, whose house she was driving to, who she kept thinking she'd be seeing, but wouldn't be seeing. There'd only be Jack, and she knew this was her one opportunity, a chance not only to correct mistakes she'd made as a parent to April, but also to give Jack the kind of life he deserved and to show everyone that she was capable of doing this. And she was driving to the boy to do this despite the fact that she hadn't been told that her daughter had been in a car accident, had actually died in the car accident, until four days after the crash and she was driving there now, four days later, despite the fact that the other side of the family barely registered her existence, that they didn't like her, and despite Steve's disapproval. Yesterday, when they had first learned about the accident, Steve had been his usual caring, considerate self. Like her, he also couldn't believe it'd taken her four days to learn about the accident. It had occurred early Wednesday morning, and the wreck wasn't discovered until Wednesday at daybreak. And yet she didn't find out until fucking Sunday. The story was the authorities contacted Nathaniel and that side of the family, but hadn't contacted her because April didn't have the same last name, had no will, no contact information for her mother, then some mix-up occurred where supposedly someone from the other side of the family was supposed to contact her, but never did. She got a bunch of apologies and we're so sorries from David after (somehow, who knows fucking how, Tammy told Steve) he finally realized she hadn't been contacted. She heard David's explanations that the other side of the family had forgotten, they'd all forgotten, in their grief it had all gotten mixed up, and the police or whoever hadn't done their damn jobs, and he was so sorry, this father of Nathaniel and Nicholas had said, apologizing over and over to her. But his apologies counted for nothing, she'd thought. Steve had said that it was bullshit was what it was, and after doing some bitching together about how small-town police cut corners, but really that it was this other side of the family that was worse, she'd then said she didn't even want to think of any of it anymore. And she didn't want to. She wanted to think of April, of Jack.

She told this to Steve, and he agreed that that was what she should be thinking about. He had said that he too had lost someone close, a thing she already knew, but so he knew what she was going through. She'd watched him speaking, watched him talking about himself, not with surprise, but with curiosity. Was he really talking about himself at this moment? They'd only been seeing each other seven months, but he had already moved in, they had already shared whatever they typically hid of their pasts, they were too old to do any testing of the relationship, and so moved in together easefully if only half-enthusiastically. It felt to Tammy like a kind of maturity. Steve had told her many times about the old girlfriend, and he did it again after news of the accident. How he'd been driving on a country road after being at a bar. Back when he was still drinking too much. He'd seen a green light turn yellow too late, the car skidded through and they were hit by a truck. His old girlfriend, who was in the passenger seat, she was the one hit by a truck. She died instantly. While telling her this, Tammy was always amazed at how easily he could take a situation and make it about himself while at the same time forgetting that he'd told her all this several times, once right when they began seeing each other, and then a few months later when her cousin died. He even told her some version of the story when her mother got sick and had to have her gallbladder removed. There were always slight changes to his story: one time, they were drinking beer, one time, whisky, one time, it was raining, one time, it was only misting. The one thing that didn't change was the way the story ended. With the notion of the guilt he carried around and that the accident was his rock bottom, that made him quit drinking, that made him take responsibility for himself and his life. At first, Tammy had admired this, had admired him. She still did. But in the last month or so, she'd begun to pity him. He seemed a man consumed by his past. An event that happened over twenty years ago shading the rest of his life. She felt she could never replace the dead woman who she only recently realized he was sort of romanticizing. When Steve learned April was gone, he'd said, I know what you're going through. It's like, you know, they tell you they're dead, but you can't help but think you'll see them tomorrow, or in a few hours. It's almost like you want to say, Yes, I know she's dead, but then you wait for her to show up at your door. And I bet your daughter was just like Sloane for me. You're afraid of forgetting the perfect things this person did. The way she'd cut off her split ends while sitting on the sofa and then there'd be hair everywhere. Or how every Thursday was fresh gulf shrimp. She just had to have it. Stuff you didn't even notice before, but that you now saw were the perfect things about these people. Tammy'd listened to him, feeling both the loss of April and the loss of Steve, finally realizing just how much he hadn't moved on, how much he felt, but almost never said aloud, that he killed the girl, and that made her feel like he was pathetic, made her hate him some, and made her want to take care of him too. But mostly it made her pity him and wonder what he would've been like had he never met this woman, or at least if their relationship had ended in a normal way. Though what was normal? she'd wondered. At least you can see it as just one of life's things though, Steve had added. You have no guilt in this. You didn't cause it. It was as close as he'd come to it, saying it this way. Partly in order to make him stop talking, to stop him thinking about himself, she'd looked at him and said, Jack's coming to stay with us. Steve had sat back from her on the sofa then stood up. He went to the kitchen, got a cup of coffee for himself, for her. His typical measured movements. Careful. Considerate. He wanted to appear considerate, she knew. She hated that she'd said Jack was going to live with them as a way to take him a down a notch. You want to make this about you? she'd thought. Let's see what this looks like when you're actually involved. When you're forced to stop thinking about yourself. At the same time, she knew the boy needed to be with her, that she alone among both sides of the family knew what the boy needed. She'd been an overworked, overstressed young mother, who hadn't paid enough attention to April, and she knew this, this alone – attention and care, really being there – was something she could give Jack. She knew it because she'd failed at it. And she didn't trust Nathaniel or Stefanie, she didn't trust Jack's grandparents on the other side, simply because things had come too easily for them. Jack would be there, but would they really be there for Jack? In addition to this, she was afraid, she could acknowledge that, that these other people would push

135

her out, or at the very least would neglect her, ignore her, and she wouldn't know her grandchild, and that wasn't happening. Steve brought her the coffee and told her that he understood what she was going through, he knew that pain, that loss, but getting the boy wasn't going to make that loss go away. Trust me, he told her. I tried so many things to make that pain and loss go away. You can't. Plus, look at our lives. We can't look after a four-year-old. That wouldn't be fair to him. You have to think about him, Steve had said. Tammy had taken the coffee, drunk it and tried to appear satisfied. Tried to appear pleased with his point of view. She was careful not to say anything though. Just drink your coffee, she remembered thinking. Then do what you know is right, which was what she was doing now, in the car, on the way to Jack, the only real option there was. She hadn't even told him she was going. The last thing he'd said to her was something like, Let's think about it and then we can talk about it in a couple days when you're more clear-headed. He had also said, Maybe I was wrong earlier, maybe this is something we could pull off, but let's sit on it first. Tammy had agreed, gone to work, and left around five in the evening, well before her shift was over, asking Dolores to cover for her, and then, only a couple hours into the drive, hit the accident she was sitting in now.

She tried to sit up and look down the highway, but could see only the taillights of cars reddening the road and her windshield. There was a soft humming from the car's heater, so different from her own car, an old Jeep Cherokee from the nineties. The heater in the Cherokee rattled, like there was a squirrel working a tiny unicycle that fanned the air toward her. Tammy had even told this once to April. She liked picturing it, the little squirrel in there, but then April tore off two of the vent things one day trying to find him while he was napping. Tammy told her he'd nap or go grocery shopping when the car was stopped, but six-year-old April had broken the vents and so Tammy had to tell her the truth, which ruined the thing for her, too. The game was gone not just for April but for Tammy too. She turned up the heat in the car now. She sometimes forgot new cars were like this one, which was a Jetta, with a lighted, digital display, the phone connected to the speakers through Bluetooth. Her own Jeep no longer had a glove box door, a headrest was lost long ago when April was still young, just a teenager – a fight they'd had in which April calmly pulled the headrest off Tammy's seat and dropped it out her window. The brakes had started to grind, again, too, and the wheel pulled hard to the right if Tammy let go. She sometimes felt like she was fighting the Jeep, that what it really wanted to do was turn around and go home, like an old dog on a walk. But this rental, this car, felt like if she were to let go of the wheel, it would convey her to where she needed to go. She'd been going, moving easily and smoothly in the car, barely driving it seemed, like a capsule through the night in a futuristic movie, conveying her toward the kid. Then she hit the traffic.

She called her sister Jeannie for something to do and told her that she was stuck in a traffic jam and needed some advice about Steve. Jeannie asked what she meant and Tammy told her that Steve didn't want Jack to stay with them. Not only that, but she was driving now to North Carolina and hadn't even told him. He thought she was at work. He would not be happy when he found out what was actually happening. There was a quiet moment on the line before Jeannie said that she hadn't realized Tammy was the guardian. Tammy said that she wasn't necessarily the guardian, that no one was necessarily the guardian, that April and Nicholas had never stated who the guardian would be, but she had to be. It couldn't be the other side of the family. She'd never see Jack then. She told Jeannie that she didn't necessarily want to be doing this, she just had to. For Jack. That was how it was for her: part of her didn't want to do a thing and another part had to. A constant fighting in herself. Did her sister ever have that? It felt like that was her entire life, fighting with herself and the world. Not only was she fighting Steve, not only was she going to have to fight the other side of the family just to get Jack in the place he should be, she was also fighting the damn traffic. It was how her life always was. Same as always. Just turn around, her sister had said. What's the point of driving? How long is that drive anyway? Fly out or something. Her sister said that this was a hard enough time for Tammy without having to drive across the country. Do herself a favor, turn around, go home, talk to Steve, tell him whatever you need to tell him, and then buy a plane ticket. Tammy told her sister that she knew she didn't have money for a ticket, even with the bereavement rate. Plus, she had no choice. She'd gotten off a few days from the hospital now, this week, and that was all they were going to give her. She couldn't drive back now and walk in and say, Hey, I'm going to take my shift after all, Dolores, thanks for coming in though. But hey, I'm flying out tomorrow night, so could you cover these new hours instead? Please. That wasn't happening. Plus, if she wanted to be part of Jack's life, she had no choice but to go now. The other side of the family was already there. They were already making plans. Without her. So, she had no choice. She was going. Also, Jack was the one chance she had, she said, to make things better. To correct some wrongs, and to finally feel right about her life. Just like Steve, these people didn't care about that though, she explained to her sister. They were all probably figuring out the nicest way to tell her she wasn't going to get to see Jack ever again, she told Jeannie. They're probably debating how much money to give her that would equate to a grandmother's relationship to a four-year-old boy. That's not necessarily true, Jeannie said. Don't think like that. I don't understand how that's helping anything right now. You're not there. You don't know. Maybe just try to be open to whatever happens.

Tammy paused, watching another police car pass by on the shoulder, the siren off but the blue lights flashing momentarily in her car, then lighting, strobe-like, the windows of the cars in front of her. Each of the thousand drops of rain on the windshield of her car flashed with the reflected blue light then were wiped away. She explained to Jeannie that she didn't know these people, she only knew what April had told her, and sure, they appeared all nice on the surface, but underneath that surface they wanted what they wanted and they got it. It's how the world was for them, she told her sister. It was the only way they knew the world. It gave them what they wanted. Plus, they had money to get what they wanted, and if you were both lucky and had money, you didn't need anything else. Really, Tammy said. Maybe money was luck. I'm not talking about these people I've never met anymore, Jeannie said. I'll talk about something else, but I won't do this gossip thing with you about people you barely know. Like you wouldn't be thinking the same shit, Tammy said. What Tammy wanted to say was that she had called Jeannie for some support, for someone to be on her side, but now that she saw Jeannie wasn't, she said that Jeannie couldn't understand. She'd never been in this position before. And because Jeannie didn't have kids, she never would be in this position. But thanks for the help, Tammy said. Jeannie said she was sorry, but she understood, this was a difficult time – stop saying that, Tammy said, you don't understand. Jeannie said she didn't know what else to say. After a moment, Jeannie said that, look, dinner was just finishing and Randall was hungry. It'd been a long day. I gotcha, Tammy said, feeling self-pitying and frustrated with herself. Say hello to Randy, Tammy said, in an obvious mocking of bright and happy. Jeannie said she'd call back after dinner to see how Tammy was doing and hung up.

Sitting in the unmoving traffic, now without Jeannie's voice coming from the speakers in the car, surrounding her, almost blanketing her, she felt the force of her aloneness. She equally felt the force of her not moving, of not having anything to do, of being confronted with just sitting there for who knew how long. Her car moved slowly forward and for a moment she thought the traffic was going to open up, but it didn't. She pushed hard on the brake pedal before nearly rear-ending the Nissan in front of her. She thought of Jeannie in her house in Florida and wished she was there with her. Jeannie said that what she liked to do when life presented her with a dilemma was to consult her cards. Tammy knew that Jeannie would prepare a joint, light the candles, and then get out the tarot deck. Tammy pictured

Jeannie, on her sofa, legs curled up to her, in her little apartment, with this new black boyfriend, Randall, maybe in the kitchen. He was apparently a good cook, and Jeannie'd be there in the darkness of that apartment, the wood slatted shades always drawn, the sound of the ocean waves out the window, the oil paintings on the wall all painted by Jeannie, her dreams, she said, not very good paintings, but strange enough that Tammy was always surprised by them: a cracked moon reflected in a puddle, which itself, you came to realize, was reflected in an eye. She felt a momentary longing for Jeannie's life even though she knew she judged it. She saw her sister as a faux-mystic, a pretend-gypsy, and underneath all the tarot and palm reading and scarves and dark dresses and long hair, Jeannie was just a pothead. Still, to live on the beach, to feel some easefulness in life, to not have to work every day, to be as carefree as Jeannie presented herself to be. And yet when she and Steve learned about the fact that Jeannie was dating a black guy, they told each other it'd last six months, was a novelty, that they were too different. At that point they'd only seen pictures of the guy through Steve's FB (I thought you hated this shit, Steve had said when she was looking, to which Tammy remembered replying, Not now I don't). He was not a big guy, not a small guy, just an average black guy. Average black guy, Tammy had said to Steve. He's definitely no football player, Steve had replied. She couldn't get one of those? Help this family out. She sometimes felt a snap in her mind when Steve referred to the family as his, as though he was fully a part of the family in the time they'd been together, as though she hadn't plucked him from complete anonymity, but then, who was she? Just a person with a sister, parents, and a daughter, and now, potentially anyway, a black brother-in-law. Still, she had people. Steve didn't have anyone. She knew it must be hard, so she let Steve have this, she granted it to him: it's your family too, she told him once, and he'd looked at her, not understanding why she said it. She didn't explain. She wondered if Jeannie had granted this to Randall as well. He was newer though, so maybe not yet. Her parents, who were now great-grandparents, certainly hadn't. She even suspected news of Randall was a contributing factor in one of her father's recent strokes, that left his face droopy and his words muttery. You're kidding? Steve had said. Oh no, Tammy told him. I can just see my dad seeing a picture of this guy, asking Mom, is this Randall, and her nodding and then a part of my dad's sphincter squeezing so tight and hard that it scrunched shut a pathway in his brain. Knocked him out cold. Jesus, Steve had said. Hey, he survived it, Tammy had told him. She knew her parents wouldn't even consider the thought that Randall might be part of the family, but Tammy got it, if this black guy did it for Jeannie, if jazz and Tyler Perry and smoked pork butt or whatever did it for Jeannie – all of which she knew were clichés and stereotypes, but whatever – then good, she deserved something decent. Someone in the family did. Plus, maybe he was an understanding, thoughtful person. Maybe Randall was the type of person that would be okay with having a boy unexpectedly have to come live with Jeannie and him, unlike Steve, who was a different type of person.

Her phone buzzed with a call. It was Steve. She didn't want to answer it. She wondered if he knew she wasn't at work, but decided it was just his normal phone call during her nightshift at the hospital's front desk. Yet, if he somehow had found out, she didn't want to hear him attempt to convince her that her heart was in the right place, but logically speaking, practically speaking, this was not her place. There were other family members better suited to this than them, which had seemed to be his primary argument, along with the idea that she was reacting in a selfish way, and that what she should really be doing is grieving her dead daughter. Her phone continued its buzzing and instead of answering it, she ignored the call, let it go to voicemail, and put the car in park and got out. A light rain fell. She pulled up the hood of her windbreaker and walked toward the accident, stretching her legs and observing the line of cars, some angled off toward the concrete barrier separating their side of the highway from the other side, the cars on the other side moving freely and easily. The angled cars were people trying to get a look, to see how far ahead. It doesn't matter how far, a trucker yelled down at her. Every lane is closed. She smiled at him and he told her to climb up, that it'd be awhile. She ignored the comment and kept walking. A gust of wind made her pull her windbreaker around her and tighten her hood over her head. She glanced to her left, where a man in some kind of Nissan was staring at his phone. Behind her, a woman was in a Ford, staring at her phone. She noticed that around her, almost every person in their car was looking at their phone, their faces framed in a strange glow of blue light, making them all appear ghostly and unreal. But they were real, with real lives, different from hers, some better, some worse, there was no way of knowing which. She imagined Jack, and his being with her making her own life better. No, not better, she thought, more real.

143

So often she felt like a ghost in her own life. She went to work, she filled out insurance forms, people treated her as though she herself was a form, she watched television with Steve, she occasionally went for a drive through the cornfields, everything the same, every day repeating itself, just like every row of corn, every block of field. She imagined Jack eating breakfast with Nathaniel and Stefanie. She imagined how lost those two probably were, how when she arrived, it might take Jack a minute, but then he'd remember her, the toys she'd brought him, maybe some subconscious memories of the times she'd fed him a bottle when he was little, and he'd eventually sit next to her on the sofa, like he did the night April had been reading to him and he'd just stood up with the book, walked over to her, and sat on her lap. No words. No asking. He just came over to her and wanted her to read like he'd felt that she was family, not that he'd been told it. And she'd read to him with April watching. She remembered wanting April to see it. To see her. She'd wanted April to see that Jack could feel they were related and that she knew what she was doing, despite the fact that April, and Nicholas, thought she didn't because she hadn't been the perfect mother to April. But they didn't take into consideration how difficult things were for her then. An eighteen-year-old girl, trying to do it all alone, April's father not there to help. She imagined that Jack would do the same thing now. She would arrive, pull up in her rental, walk up to the cabin, and when Jack saw her, he might hesitate at first – he only saw her once a year, after all – but then he'd remember the times she'd read to him, the times she'd swung him in the swing, the times she'd sung to him, the times she'd made him French toast, and most importantly the feeling of family he'd gotten from her, and he'd come to her, take her hand, and it would all be clear. If only April could see that, that Jack chose her, not the rich kids. It was a disgusting thought to have. Her daughter was gone and she was thinking of how she'd show April, and everyone else, that she was the right one for Jack. Not only that, but that it would be his choice. She shouldn't be thinking it. Out of respect for the dead. But she couldn't help the glimmer of a thought that said that maybe April hadn't done a good job of reminding Jack that she was family too, that she mattered, that she was part of Jack's life, that April was wrong. It wasn't only Jack's choice though that mattered. She would have to come up with an argument, something to convince Nathaniel and Stefanie, the other side of the family, that Jack belonged with her.

The cars started moving again, and she jogged back to her rental, shook off the rain, got in, and she was driving. Another phone call from Steve. She again ignored the call and after a few minutes of moving slowly, maneuvering to the far left lane, she passed the SUV, motorcycle, and F-150, which looked destroyed, as though a boulder had been dropped on its hood. She noticed herself register that there were people standing on the side of the road, heads down, soaked by the rain. Two women, a younger and older woman, sisters, or a mother and daughter. Their hair lank and wet. Then another body, a man, on a stretcher being put into the back of the ambulance. She watched, her head turning as she drove by. A movement in her, like a hand inside her chest trying to unclench and pry apart another hand that was in a fist. She closed her eyes and breathed, then remembered she was driving here. The highway began to move by her. She saw these people momentarily in her rearview, growing smaller, their bodies against the enormity of the highway, the rushing cars, the world around them. Then she couldn't see them anymore and she was driving, watching the rushing freeway. The visual illusion was still something that she enjoyed – that when in a car one could feel like the entire world was moving by, the rush of pavement, the buildings and trees, the concrete abutments, the moon and clouds, a grey nighttime moving outside, while remaining still. While thinking this, driving, her headlights made almost tangible by the mist and rain, solid beams of light into the night, she thought of April, how she'd heard about her daughter's death, how it was so different from the accident she'd just passed. Everyone had survived the accident she'd just passed. Even the man on the stretcher, or gurney, or whatever it was called, he was moving, he was looking around, she could see him. He'd be okay. The lives around him, he'd join again, like a fish pulled from the stream and then tossed back. That man on the stretcher didn't have to be envious of the faces that were watching him, didn't have to feel that they'd go on without him. But April had been alone on a mountain road. No other cars. They weren't even found till the morning. It'd be worse to die on a highway, Tammy thought, hitting another vehicle, seeing other faces, all these other faces that were going to outlive you, lying on the pavement or stuck in an ambulance and knowing that everything was going to outlive you. That other worlds would remain complete, intact. These other people, the world was going to stay there for them, they were going to stay in it, however good or bad it was, but you were not. Not only were you dying but you also had to try not to feel envy that other people were not dying. But you would, she thought. You definitely would. You'd feel envious that everything was going to keep going without you. That you were the most insignificant part of the world in that moment. Your death was the proof of that. Your own death was so small that the world took no notice, and the pain of it, whatever pain April'd experienced, whatever fear, the fear that you would never be in the world again, that the world was gone for you, was also completely insignificant: there and then gone. Dying on a highway, you'd see passing cars, people looking in at you, the lights of buildings, restaurants maybe, a gas station, and you'd know that you were soon to be nothing, while the something that was everything else went on like the stupidity it was. She thought of how maybe April got to see Nicholas, though he was supposedly unconscious, so that didn't really count. That was better anyway, being alone. Being alone when you died was the best way to die because it was how everything was: you were alone. Maybe you had friends when you were a kid or a teenager, maybe you had a family, maybe you had everything you wanted, but when you were dying you realized you were utterly alone. That you always had been, Tammy thought. People didn't know that. People thought you went to some perfect place or that you went back to the universe or that you were reborn, but that wasn't it. It was just finished. You were done. You would never see, feel, think, be anything again. It was why Tammy was fine with however hard her life was, because it showed her that loneliness was banal, boring even, nothing to be that afraid of. When she died, she hoped it could be like April, completely alone. Being completely alone in that moment was even better than being with maybe one person who wouldn't make you feel like they were just going to go on without you. There were so few of those people in anyone's life, Tammy knew. She had once thought that maybe Steve was her person, but he wasn't. He was just another unmoored soul. The person, she knew, was Jack. When she was older, after she'd sent him to school, or maybe even after she homeschooled him, anything but the Montessori school that April and Nicholas sent him to, after she'd helped him learn a trade, maybe something with cars, after she helped him get into a decent little state school, maybe a partial scholarship, after she'd got him set up in the world, he'd be the one that would come to her when she was going to disappear into nothingness. He'd hold her hand, tell her he loved her, would thank her. Before April's death, she'd thought that person would be April, but now she knew her witness would be Jack. If you were lucky, you got a witness, you got one person to watch you die and say, This person was here. This person affected something in this world, and that something is me. She felt almost nauseated that April hadn't had this from her, but as Tammy well knew, you did not get what you wanted. You got lucky or you didn't, that was all, though it helped to arrange your luck. And with Jack she got a new start: both to be there for someone and for someone to be there for her. Some disconnection had occurred between her and April. Something was missing. Something had been missing for a long time. Or maybe was always missing, she didn't know. Like those model airplanes and cars April used to get, which had infuriated Tammy some. She had wished April was doing something a little more feminine by ten. Though still, Tammy had helped. They'd build the plane or whatever it was, and inevitably, it seemed, as the thing took shape, it never looked quite as real as on the box, never looked like an actual plane or battleship. That was their relationship: it was only the semblance of the thing itself. Some incomplete mother–daughter model, missing some key piece, from the beginning of April's life, as though Tammy, in not wanting the child initially, despite doing what she thought most mothers did when their baby finally arrived, which was feel a complete and utter love, had somehow created the lack, as though she was the model maker and had willfully misplaced some key component of the model. This only intensified throughout April's life, falling into the background in certain moments, when she was a young girl, then becoming more obvious again as a preteen in her hatred of her mother's boyfriends (who were, admittedly, often idiots, just as Tammy was often an idiot), then turning into April's identification not with other young teenage girls, but the sports boy crowd, so that she dressed and acted like an afflicted teenage boy, which was infuriating to Tammy and which April seemed to delight in infuriating Tammy with, only for April to change again, in college, into an intellectual, taking philosophy and psychology classes and treating Tammy herself with a sort of openness that felt ironic in its sincerity. And then the final change, Tammy thought, was the most obvious move in explaining the distance between them and what was missing between them: after Nicholas and April met in grad school, after they married a year later, they moved far away from the Midwest, into the mountains, isolated and alone, and lived a life that Tammy knew April felt was a sort of rejection of everything that Tammy had taught April: to fight for oneself, to try to move up in the world, to live with family even if you disliked them, which was what Tammy had tried to do herself when she was a young mother. She wouldn't let any of this happen with Jack, and that was exactly what Steve didn't understand.

A car came up behind her, in the middle lane, and tailed her closely. Tammy signaled to change lanes and then did, the BMW speeding past. She watched it weave between a truck and an SUV, moving into the left-hand lane. She observed, with mild annoyance and the vague thought that the driver was probably on a cell phone, the BMW moving fast and swervingly. The rain was falling harder, she now noticed, and she increased the speed of the wipers by bumping the wand next to the steering wheel upward. She called Steve back and before she could say anything, he said, I've been calling and calling you, Tam. I called your work. Dolores said she's filling in for you. He was surprisingly calm. She had a hard time understanding if his calm and concern were real or not, if he was using it, as she'd begun to learn he used calm and concern, as a way to manipulate her, in the same way he'd seemingly tried to manipulate her in their earlier conversation when she told him she wanted Jack to live with them, by telling her that she was still in the grieving process and could not possibly make that decision and to give it a few days. On the phone now, she told him she was driving to North Carolina. He said that that was what he was afraid of, and he wanted her to know that more than anything that was disappointing to him because obviously she felt she couldn't tell him. Oh, that's disappointing, she said. No, no, that's not what I meant, he said. It's disappointing, I mean, I'm disappointed in myself. What he meant was, the fact that she didn't tell him made him feel bad because he didn't want to be the type of person who she had to hide things from, he didn't want to be the type of guy who told her she shouldn't go get her grandchild or something like that, or that she shouldn't be the guardian, and he was sorry if he put that in her head, or if what he'd said came off that way. That was not the way he wanted it to come off. He was disappointed in himself because obviously he'd put that in her head and he didn't want to do that. If she wanted Jack to live with them, he would definitely, fully support that. But Tam, he was just sharing a concern, and that concern was based on his own experience. When he lost Sloane, that was one of the most confusing moments of his life. He didn't know up from down. He quit his job working construction because it reminded him of her, how she'd bring him lunch at work and they'd eat on a picnic table or under a tree near whatever building he was working on. She'd bring a thermos with coffee and whisky in it and share it, and he'd go back to work with the warm feeling of her inside him. What he should've done was take the two weeks his boss wanted to give him, but he'd quit, and gone on a bender instead and nearly killed himself in *another* car accident. He realized her situation wasn't the same, but. Stop, Tammy said. Stop talking. For one fucking minute stop. There was quiet on the phone. Then she told him she didn't want to hear about Sloane. In fact, one month, she didn't want to hear a Sloane story for one month. Or maybe they should just start with a week. How about that? One week without Sloane coming up. She felt an anger that she'd been suppressing become centrally focused, like a glowing coal in her throat, that allowed her to say what she needed to say to him. In fact, it seems like I know everything about you and Sloane, I know your past, I know your lowest point, I know your recovery, but you know almost nothing about me and my past. And that's because you never ask. I mean, sure, I shared things, but you don't really know. You don't know me and April. You don't know why I'm doing this. Why I'd want to. Because it's always Steve and Sloane. As though no one else has had hard times. As though Steve and Sloane were the real Bonnie and Clyde, but in this version, only Bonnie dies, and Clyde goes on to live a guilt-ridden and self-pitying life with a boring woman named Tammy. There was silence on the line and Tammy felt the heat in her throat cooling, as though expressing these words was like cold air settling gently over the burning coal. After a moment, she said she was sorry, and Steve said that no, she was right, she was definitely right, he knew he made things about himself and he knew he had a problem, his past was his problem, and he was the one who was sorry, he should've done a better job just listening to her or whatever it was she needed, but see, instead, part of him gave advice, probably because he'd been in AA for so long and he was a sponsor, as she knew, and people were always asking him for advice. So, he had that habit of making things about himself and giving advice, but he really didn't mean to try to convince her one way or the other. Tammy said that he was doing it again, was he aware he was doing it again? Fuck, Steve said. Yes, I see it, he said. I'm done now. I'm stopping.

The highway was becoming hillier, and the bunched trees, set back from the road, seemed like black malignant growths along what had once been a flat, clean skin of land.

The rain was slowly thickening on the windshield, changing to sleet, and the cars around her, she noticed, had decreased speed. She was in the right-hand lane, but was passing all the other cars, and she touched the brake gently, slowing the Jetta from eighty, to seventy-five, to seventy. She was surprised at how easily the outside world could disappear. In talking to Steve, she'd barely even seen it, she'd barely even remembered she was driving. Now though, with the sleet, she felt a danger that made her pay attention. She saw a sign showing upcoming cities, Salt Lake City in forty miles, and she knew the mountains were coming, leaving Idaho and entering Utah and Wyoming before moving on to the flatter plains of Nebraska and Iowa. Billboards along the highway, lit up in the sleeting rain, advertised for McDonald's, Shell, BBQ, Fireworks, Adult SuperStores, the Bible, the miscellaneous array of stupid American rural life that she knew she was a part of, that was her heritage.

Steve said that he wanted to know what she was going through and to please talk to him, he was ready to listen. That was his problem, he knew, that he was always wanting to fix things, and he said he would try not to do that, a thing he knew he sometimes did, and would just listen, if that's what she wanted. He said he knew that he could be a selfish asshole and he was sorry, but please explain to him so that he could understand why she wanted Jack to live with them. Not that she shouldn't want that, or that she should have to have some explanation, but just so, so that, he said, hesitating, confused now, stammering. I get it, Tammy said. Just hold on a minute. After thinking for a moment, she told Steve she thought it started from the very beginning: when she had April at eighteen, her parents insisted they live with them. The arrangement had slipped Tammy out of needing to be a mother. She became a worker, not a mother. Her father demanded it. There had been, Tammy said now, a strange relief: she'd been frightened of being a mother, and while she felt a joy she had never experienced when April was delivered safely into the world, the fact that she wouldn't be doing this alone and would, in fact, have to be a worker, could leave the house, would have help, even though it was her parents helping, was a sad relief. She felt guilty for feeling it, she said.

In the car, the sleet-rain increased its ticking onto her windshield. She thought of when her father told her that what was going to happen here was he and her mother were going to take care of April until Tammy saved enough to get a place of her own. She was the one who'd fucked up. He wasn't going to pay Tammy's way, she wasn't going to leech off him, but he'd help. Along with feeling secretly relieved, then ashamed at this relief, she'd also been surprised even at that offer of help. Her father wasn't a man who did such things. Suddenly the trees dropped away on her right and there was open farmland, fields broken apart by barbed-wire fencing, and in the distance, set in rolling hills, farm houses, barns, with hazy lights seeming to struggle against the sleet and rain. She told Steve that when she had April, her father had changed. She remembered seeing him in the kitchen, she said – making bacon, flipping bacon, his beard greying and long, lumberjack-like she'd thought – and holding April at the same time he was making breakfast, singing to her, and she remembered clearly seeing that the baby had aged him, caused him to grow older, and also softer. This helpless thing, smiling and happy, had opened him up. She witnessed less drinking and smoking from her father. There was a new No Smoking rule in the house. He'd implemented it one night over dinner, maybe two weeks into April being there with them, sleeping, or often not sleeping, in her crib, and Tammy's father, while passing a bowl of potatoes or something, said that there'd be no more smoking in the house, and that when it was cold, if you needed to smoke, then people could smoke in the garage, but no more in the house, and though Tammy'd wanted him to state the reason, wanted to ask him why he was saying this now, even though she basically knew the reason, she hadn't had to ask because he then said, It's not fair to the kid to smoke in here. She told Steve that she and her mother had sat quietly, a little stunned, and then finished their meals. She told Steve that maybe Jack could do something like that for them. She said that when she was with Jack, she also felt again the possibilities of what she herself could be. Like her father years ago, she wanted a change, was ready for a change, was tired of being in an ugly world that was only against her, that didn't allow her to care for anything, and here was a chance to care again. Just like when she witnessed her father hold April, sing to April, make faces at April, give April a bottle and let her sleep on his chest, she wanted that again with Jack. She knew part of it was selfish. But part of it was for Jack. She knew the right way to take care of him because she'd done it the wrong way for so long. Just like her father seemed like another person with the new baby, like he'd been taken aboard an alien craft, her father's self removed, and then the aliens had implanted some other being inside his skin, she wanted to feel new again, and she wanted the world to also feel new again.

Steve told her that he understood that, understood wanting all that. He said that there was nothing wrong with wanting that, but the problem was, it seemed to Steve, that that was just Tammy wanting Jack so that, you know, her life would be better. I feel like that's not taking into account certain practicalities, Steve said. Like clothing, shoes. Diarrhea. Sickness. Also, this isn't a baby. This is a four-year-old kid. He's not going to want to be sung to every night. Tammy said that she understood that, that she was just using an example – she didn't think Jack was going to magically change everything. What she was trying to say was that maybe a change in her life would be a good thing. Maybe having to care for someone else would do her good, in the same way it did her father good. That was all she was saying.

Driving in the sleeting rain and not actually seeing the rain, or hardly seeing it, only some mechanical part of her driving the car, she remembered how she drove to work, at nineteen, leaving April at home, and cried in the car, thinking of her father holding her baby. The image of her father holding her baby didn't move her because of its beauty. She remembered crying because she was witnessing a kindness that was never afforded her. A kindness that she didn't even know existed in him and was now easily available, as though he'd been saving it up for someone more worthy, and that more worthy person was her daughter, who Tammy had not even wanted. She spoke toward the phone in the stand near the digital display and told Steve that for the first two years of April's life, she worked two jobs, two shifts – one at UPS, and another bagging groceries. She eventually became a clerk at the grocery, then assistant manager. She saved money. She found the apartment. She didn't want to leave completely, but she didn't want to be in the house with her parents anymore. She couldn't deal with this new father anymore. A father who was finally a father, she told Steve. Something he had never really been to me. Her parents, her father, took care of April during the day, feeding her and clothing her and changing her diapers and wiping her spit up. Her mother knitted and read the Bible. Her father walked the baby through town in a stroller. When Tammy came home, exhausted in the evening, or in the morning, if she worked a nightshift at UPS, she'd hold April and the baby would cry and cry. She didn't feel like a mother, or a caregiver. She had loved April, of course, but she didn't feel the love was the right love. There was something in the way of it. She knew now it was her father, and she also knew, she explained, that the reason she was driving across the country was because if she didn't do something, there would be something even bigger in the way of her and Jack, that there already was something in the way, and she had to do her best to knock it down.

Steve said that he remembered some of this. Hadn't she told him at some point that her parents would not help with April when Tammy was in the house? That's right, Tammy said. Steve said that, see, he really did listen, and that she had told him some of these things. She rolled her eyes at the boy-like comment, but was also pleased. She didn't remember telling him and yet he was saying that he remembered her telling him that when she came home from a late shift, maybe it was one of the first times she'd come home late, after a shift at UPS, he thought, he wasn't sure, and the baby crying, spit-up on the baby's shirt, a wet or pooped diaper, and she tried to eat some dinner and hold the baby at the same time. Her mother had come up to her to take the child, possibly to change her, and soothe her while Tammy had a meal, and her father came into the room, standing in the kitchen. You told me, Steve said, that your father said something like, Not if she's in the house. We don't help if she's in the house. This is her responsibility. Your mother tried to argue against your father but he took the baby and handed her to you. I mean, I remember you telling me that and thinking that that was just awful. Tammy said that wasn't all. That there was more to it than that, that she had withheld this from Steve because she was afraid of what he'd think of her. Her father, while not helping when she was in the house, still corrected Tammy as he'd always done. No, he'd say about the way Tammy held April. Like this. Your forearm under her butt, that's how she likes it. Stable base. And if you bounce her, well, don't. Don't bounce her. She doesn't like being bounced. And he'd hold her and April would be soothed, contented, and this man, who had been no real father to her, was being, suddenly and unexpectedly, a good father. So many moments of turning away, gritting her teeth, wanting to scream, Tammy told Steve. She told him that she knew now, and probably knew years before, realized it years before, but felt it more now that April was gone, the shame of what she felt: that her father had made her envious of her daughter. Her father had made her resentful of her own baby because her baby got from her father the exact thing she knew she wanted. In this way, she told Steve, she'd come to understand that her father had made her fight herself, fight these feelings in herself, and she worked hard to keep herself aware that none of this was April's fault, and she worked hard as a worker, to keep her mind on the goal of getting out, which had become at the time a bigger goal than Tammy had ever had, maybe, she told Steve now, the only goal she had ever had, really, and filled with a sort of cosmic significance: leaving home meant being a mother, and she felt that same significance now: getting Jack meant correcting the mistakes she'd made with April. She said into the phone held neatly in the little stand near the Jetta's digital display screen, I want to be able to sit in the family room with Jack, to teach him things, now that I have time. We can do flashcards. We can learn to make models together. I know what Jack likes. I've been with him, taken him to movies, to playgrounds, on bike rides, I know how he likes to play during the afternoon and then sit and read in the evening. Nathaniel and Stefanie don't know these things. And I know what I failed to do with April, and what I failed to feel. Or what I felt that was wrong. That won't be there with Jack. I was hoping you'd want to do that, that you'd want to be a part of that for Jack. Steve said that that made sense, he didn't realize any of that, and he wanted to answer her, but let him think for a moment because this was not something he'd considered, how could he have. As he was saying it, as her car was ascending, moving steadily upward toward the mountains, the call dropped.

In the distance, through the rain, Tammy saw the lights of a police car and thought there'd been another accident, but as her car approached the flashing lights, she saw that it was the BMW that had passed her fifteen minutes ago, pulled over. Rain like a thin veil over the car and two men. The driver was being given a sobriety test, the cop shining a flashlight at the man. The beam of the flashlight made clear by the rain. The driver, in a long raincoat and dark clothes, had his hands extended, like a man walking a tight-rope. The cop wore a bulky jacket over his uniform and a little plastic covering over his hat. All passed in a moment, gone, the blue lights behind her. Sleeting rain ticking on the car and windshield with more intensity that, along with the rushing sound of her car over the highway, created a white noise of weather and road. In the space of time in which she passed by the sobriety test Tammy unwillingly recalled the time her father forced her to drink a bottle of whisky. She'd come home late from a party when she was a sopho-more, drunk, driving the car drunk, and when she arrived at her house, every light was on. She knew her father did it. So she'd know. So when she pulled the car into the drive-way, she'd know. So she'd feel his anger before she even saw him. She turned off the car and got out and walked up the path to the front door and went in, quiet and head down, not wanting to meet his eyes. She didn't have to look up to know he was there in his recliner, sitting up in it. He had a beer belly then (which he lost a good deal of after April arrived), and always smelled of cigarettes. He told her to sit. When she didn't move, he'd said, Is there something about the word sit that you don't understand? She'd moved then, into a chair he had out, right in front of the coffee table. The bottle of whisky was on the coffee table, and he told her to pick it up. She didn't move. If you want to drink, he'd said. Pick it up and drink. She'd looked at the bottle and heard him say, Now. She picked it up and drank. Then put it down. He reached across the table, took a swig, and put the bottle back down. There were small beads of liquid in his beard, like there often were when he drank anything, something that bothered Tammy, like why couldn't he drink in the way everyone drank and not get it on his face. Now you, he said. They finished the bottle like that and when she was vomiting in the backyard, on her hands and knees she was so drunk, the frozen ground and grass hard and cold beneath her knees and hands, she heard his calm lecture: If this is what you want, that's fine with me. But I want you to know what this really is. This is what it is. You will turn into this person, on hands and knees. Or you'll turn into what I am – I drank half that bottle and feel nothing. I don't feel a thing. And that I don't feel a thing is disgusting, but what you're doing is even more disgusting, and you should feel disgusted by it. It was a discipline beyond discipline, conveying her toward her own eventual meanness, she thought. And yet, even at the time, very drunk and vomiting what she'd had for dinner that night, a cheesesteak and French fries – she could see undigested chunks of bread and fries, thinking she'd never eat a cheesesteak again – even at that moment, repulsed at her father and herself, she detected a message of love in what he was doing: he didn't want her to be like him. It worked, she thought, driving through the sleeting rain. She never drank again. She could still very clearly remember the cold ground of the backyard, frozen and hurting her knees, and the smell of alcohol and vomit and also of cold, clean air. It was so strange, that deeply unpleasant, repulsive smell mixed with that crispness of cold pine and snow, as though even the gross things in life – one's body and garbage and the smell of skunk or a dead dog on the road – had their own pristine quality, something beyond good and bad, all just what it was. She experienced that basic banality years later when April was in the world, pooping ridiculous green slime or runny peanut butter-looking liquid, and while unpleasant, Tammy didn't care, wasn't repulsed, could see such things only as another example of something she should be grateful for, which was weird. Of course then when she saw a disgusting or ugly person, she'd forget all this and feel repulsed, but she tried to remember April as a baby, pooping everywhere, out the top of diapers, onto shirts, onto Tammy, and when older, vomiting on Tammy when she ate too quickly, and when out in the world, feeling repulsed at some ugly person, she'd check herself momentarily, and try not to be like her father, try not to see things, supposedly ugly things, as ugly, to know that there was a person there. Uglier were the pretty ones, the Facebook perfect ones, the ones who didn't acknowledge their animalness, Tammy thought now. The supposed disgusting things were not what was unpleasant, what was unpleasant was other people, their selves, what they thought, their self-righteousness and stupidity, not their bodies. Her father never saw that, but she did. She remembered feeling years later – when her parents were taking care of April while she worked, then not taking care of April when she entered the house again – that April would never know these things about her father, never know his cruelties. Part of her was grateful for that. Part of her was grateful to her father, she thought driving now in the rain, but another part of her was envious and resentful and that part of herself she hated. She hated that she was resentful that her father hadn't thought to treat her, his own daughter, any better, which in turn translated into Tammy being envious of April, her daughter, whose life, she had immediately seen at the time – like the world had stamped its approval on it and forlornly handed the certificate to Tammy for safekeeping – would be easier than her own. She wanted her own life to be easy, she remembered thinking, to be like this car through the rain, effortlessly passing through the unpleasantness of other people and the world, but it was not like that, so she worked hard those two years while living with her parents, not really being a mother to April, in order to get out and get to some easier place in her life. She might not get to be young again, but she could at least be a mother to April. She worked hard and was proud of that, she thought in the car without feeling as though she was in a car, or anywhere at all, and after two years, she'd made enough and left. She remembered thinking that she wouldn't be indebted to them, to her father, and she most especially wouldn't watch this man give to her daughter what he never gave to her.

A car cut her off even though she was in the right-hand lane, and she felt a heat in her chest. Fucker, she said. The highway suddenly materialized again, her car moving swiftly, and she felt a sort of danger: she hadn't even been seeing the road and in its place she'd been freely thinking about April, of her father, though she hadn't wanted to be, as though something in her was preparing her for motherhood again. As though something in her was reminding her of mistakes so that she wouldn't make them with Jack. Like she had a shock collar on and each time she wanted to venture into the world freely, the thing went off, reminding her that she wasn't free. And yet, she knew, there was no shock collar: it was just her. It was just herself reminding herself, which made Tammy want to shout at this other Tammy, this annoying double of her: shut the fuck up. She knew that nothing she did could undo what she'd done. Her life was saturated with what she'd done. Jack was the only way to correct any of it. She saw images of him in bed, reading or singing him to sleep, images of him at the dinner table with Steve, Steve cutting his food into small bites, images of the boy on a rope swing once they found a little house, some place with a yard for the boy, images of him when she had to discipline him, but not in the way she did with April, not the shouting and arguing she did with April, a more controlled, motherly version of herself, and then, when the boy got older, images of him looking through her records, listening to old music, classic rock and Motown and jazz and her telling him the meaning of these songs to her, images of Jack growing into a young man, maybe he'd forgo college and join the Navy, maybe he'd become a pilot, images of him holding her hand as they walked across the street to the grocery store, images of her younger self once again a mother, but this time focused and patient and understanding and wise, and then these images reduced themselves to a single image, as though the images of Jack growing into a man were suddenly rewound into just Jack as she knew him now. A four-year-old boy, alone in his bedroom. His aunt and uncle with him, but April and Nicholas gone, his mother and father gone. She suddenly recalled that the only information she knew had come from a very brief phone call from Nathaniel when he'd said that Jack was okay, just sleeping a lot, and thinking of this, she began to cry. A moment after this, her phone buzzed with a call from Steve, and she saw that again she had service. She took several deep breaths, composed herself, though she didn't exactly know why, why she'd want to hide the fact of her crying from Steve, but she did, and she hit the green glowing button to answer her phone.

Before he could say anything Tammy told him that he was right, that she shouldn't be driving there, that she shouldn't be doing this. She told Steve that he was right. She was making this about herself. Instead of thinking about Jack, she was thinking about her past, she was thinking about how things had been hard for her, about the fact that she didn't want to be pregnant at eighteen and had missed out on so many things, and she thought that wanting to correct the mistakes she made wasn't a bad thing to want, and she thought that wanting to be a better version of herself wasn't bad either, but wanting to use Jack to do it was. It was no reason for the boy to live with her, no reason for her to be the guardian, she said. Streetlamps lit the highway in cones of light. Highway signs were beginning to crust over in sleet. Tammy saw more billboards for an upcoming exit and told Steve that there were gas stations and fast food places coming up and she was going to stop rather than keep driving because the sleet was getting intense. Steve told her to hold on a minute, don't do that yet, just slow down, drive safely, because he wanted to tell her that she had been right earlier. He hadn't been just trying to make her focus on the grieving process, focus on April, or whatever he'd said before. *She* had been right. He hadn't wanted her to go get Jack. All he'd really been doing this whole time was waiting to convince her that her wanting to take care of Jack was all caused by Tammy's grief-stricken state, and then once he'd done that, he was going to try to convince her that he really did want Jack to come live with them, it was just that he didn't think they'd be able to do it. He said he was going to say that they were too busy, that they didn't live in a good area, that Jack would think they were too old, he was going to say that he himself thought they were both too old, he was going to say that neither of them had savings or anything to put into a college fund for Jack, he was going to point out that he was diabetic, and while generally healthy, this wasn't ideal, and Tammy too had had her own health problems. Steve said that he actually had more than this, though he couldn't remember it all right now, and he was planning on subtly bringing each of these things up, but what had changed his mind was how Tammy'd spoken about her own father and April, and he got it. He really did get it. And while Tammy was now saying she felt she was selfish, he wanted to tell her that he didn't think that. Tammy hung up the phone. She wanted to pick it up and throw it out the window, but knew that such a childish act would be counter-productive. She saw the exit approaching, the glowing lights of gas stations and fast food places, the signs on enormous poles like canes for giants, towering above the mountainous land, the trees, her car, making her feel small. A blinking cell phone tower beaconed her toward the exit and she took it. She took the off-ramp to the right, not caring which place she went to, and finally pulling into a place called Dina's Country Diner rather than one of the fast food places.

She parked and got out, jogged to the front and inside. There was a sign next to the hostess stand asking her to seat herself and she took a booth that overlooked the road, and in the distance, the highway, the mountains, the sleet and rain. On the ground in the grass, the sleet gathered, a speckled whiteness on the grass, but nothing was accumulating on the roads. Her phone buzzed in her pocket with a call she knew was from Steve, and she pushed the button on top of the phone to stop its buzzing. She was no longer angry. Well, she was, she thought, but she wasn't. What else could she expect from him? Of course he wanted what he wanted, just as she wanted what she wanted, and of course both of them were going to try to get it despite the other. That was how things were. The problem now was that she didn't even know what she wanted. She didn't know now if Steve had manipulated her into somehow believing that she shouldn't go get Jack or if she had come to that on her own, and now, in trying to decide if she'd decided to not get Jack, in trying to decide if she was acting selfishly in wanting to bring him to live with her, in wanting to raise him, in trying to decide if she was somehow using Jack as a replacement for April and was not, as Steve had mentioned, properly mourning April, she couldn't see clearly where she had been manipulated and what she really felt. This felt like a new suffering, a sicker kind: her own confusion at what to feel and how to feel it, her own confusion at what was real and what wasn't, and yet, she wasn't mad at Steve so much as disappointed by him, and she wasn't mad at him because she herself had felt herself manipulating him, maybe not consciously, but she wanted him to feel guilty and ashamed by his initial response to her, and she knew she'd formed her responses to him in a way that she hoped would make him feel that way, and that itself, she knew, was a shameful thing.

A waitress, Tammy's age, overweight, with almost grey skin and what appeared to be no demeanor, as though life had failed to give her a personality, came and asked what she wanted. Tammy said she didn't have a menu. The woman didn't sigh or complain at this. She just walked to the hostess stand, grabbed a menu, handed it to Tammy, and said she'd be back in a minute. Tammy looked at the menu, not really hungry, and quickly decided on a bowl of soup and coffee. She glanced around the restaurant, which also had a lunch counter. A man, who Tammy believed must be a truck driver, sat there reading a newspaper. For a moment she felt she was living twenty years in the past. He had reading glasses on and was alternately peering over them or reading through them. When the waitress returned, Tammy ordered and the waitress said, Don't order the soup. Tammy almost asked why not, and then figured it wasn't worth it, and then said, What should I order on a night like this then? The woman looked out the windows, her eyes widening, as though seeing for the first time, in surprise, that there was a world beyond the diner. Brisket sandwich, she said. She took the menu back and said she'd be back with Tammy's coffee presently. The word presently surprised Tammy, like it was some kind of joke, some word this woman had heard in a Bond movie and was trying out in her own life. It was also evidence, just barely, of some kind of personality behind the tired, grey, dope-eyed face. Tammy felt again the phone in her pocket and this time she pulled it out and turned it off entirely. She tossed it on the table, where for a moment, the sound of the phone hitting the tabletop seemed the only sound in the restaurant. It made Tammy glance up, to see who was looking at her, and three booths away, a young man, eating soup and grilled cheese, was looking at her, then away. Then he looked up again, put his spoon down, and said, Did she tell you not to get the soup? The man had a soft, boyish face, freckled, and red hair that was cropped very short. He wore a flannel shirt. Tammy told him the waitress did say that. I wonder why I didn't get that advice, he said. Tammy shook her head and after a moment, the man said, It doesn't taste bad. I just hope they haven't done anything to it. The person, she realized, was the sort of person who wanted to talk, who could not, when around other people, observe silence. I'm Caleb, he said. Do you mind if I just. He got up, picked up his plate of soup and sandwich, put it in the booth next to hers, then went back, and grabbed his Coke, and sat down. Tammy looked at him and his face, which three booths away looked like a man's face, but, closer now, actually appeared to be a boy's. He was twenty, she thought, couldn't be more. He said, If I'm intruding, I can go back, and she shook her head. You shouldn't throw your phone like that, he said. That's a good way to crack the screen. Even the back of it. I know it's in one of those safety cases, but it could crack the back of it too. Tammy thanked him and said she'd be more careful and he said that sometimes old people didn't know exactly how to treat the new phones. His own mother had once thrown one across the room when she was in an argument with his father and she had to drop nearly two hundred bucks to get another and have all her data transferred. I get how phones work, Tammy said, though thank you for noting how old I am. The boy-like man held his hands up and said he was sorry, he didn't mean it like that. He ate, dipping the grilled cheese in the soup, just as Tammy imagined Jack doing in her kitchen. For a moment, she saw the young man as Jack, a grown-up Jack, and wondered what this boy's life had possibly been like. After a moment, Caleb asked where she was headed and Tammy hesitated, considered saying, To bury my daughter, or just, To a funeral, though there wasn't going to be a funeral, but those things sounded too dramatic, and so she said that she was going to see her daughter and grand-child. The man-boy said that it wasn't a great night to be driving alone and then asked if maybe her husband was out in the car and rather than take it as an offensive, overly intrusive question, Tammy said she was divorced and liked driving at night. I like that, the boy said, who seemed more like a boy every passing moment. You don't need a big man to do your work. That's how it ought to be. He told her that that wasn't the way his father saw things for sure, and that actually, he came from a broken home, too, just like Tammy and her daughter. He said that his father, whenever they went on a trip, insisted on doing all the driving, and when there was work to be done around the house, his father did it. Fixed the toilet, the roof, built an addition when his brother came along, never made his mom lift a finger, except for the cooking and laundry. He was glad things were changing, he told her, because the other thing his father didn't let his mother do was talk. He remembered plenty of nights she got a lick to the face for even expressing an opinion. She eventually was done with it all, he said. I haven't seen her for nearly two years, and I'm happy for it, he said. It must mean she found something better. He told her that there was no way he could change anything between his parents and he didn't want to, and there was no way to change his view growing up that his father was like a kind of god, because to him and his brothers, and to his mother, he was, but he could see now that that was all basically bullshit and that his mother figured it out. He told her that he still had to check himself on certain things and that sometimes he got confused, like for instance once he was on a date with a girl and he'd not held the door open for her, he did it on purpose, he thought that she'd probably want to do that herself, in fact, his friends at the community college told him as much, that girls now didn't want to be herded around like cows was the exact words they used, and so he didn't order her drinks at the bar, and he didn't make any suggestions about food and especially didn't order for her, and then later in the night, when they were finishing the date, and he was, he admitted, a little bit drunk, not drunk, buzzed, you know, a lot of beers over several hours, a couple shots, well then we went to my car and I just wasn't thinking and I opened the passenger door for her. Right when I did it, I remembered, and thought, damn, messed that one up, but that's when she said, Looks like it takes you getting drunk to become a gentleman. The boy laughed to himself and glanced up to see if Tammy was smiling and she was, a little, and she nodded at him to indicate she understood. She wondered where this boy grew up – his voice had a rural, almost Southern quality, though they were nowhere near the South, and she pictured his friends at the community college as being first-generation college kids, coming from farm families, blue-collar families, and the boy himself looked like he wasn't a stranger to hard work. He was endearing. Here he was, trying to be some kind of modern man in a world that wasn't sure if that was what it wanted, and he was getting it confused. Tammy herself got it confused.

The waitress brought her food. Tammy looked at the sandwich, a dry roll between which were slabs of meat, French fries on the side. She pushed it away and took the coffee, put cream and sugar in, stirred with a fork. She told the boy that she had a difficult father as well, but she told him the difference between her and him was that she was now a difficult mother. The boy asked if she and her daughter didn't get along, and Tammy said that was one version of the story. She told him that she sometimes got caught up in telling herself this story about her and April – your daughter, he said, and Tammy nodded – and about how there was something dividing them. Stop telling yourself this story, she said she tried to tell herself, but it was difficult, when she'd been telling it to herself for so long. She'd been driving to visit her daughter and she'd been doing it again, she said, telling herself the story, about how they were going to argue, not see eye to eye, not feel like mother and daughter, not agree about what was best for Jack. The boy nodded knowingly and then finished his grilled cheese in three successive dip-bites and said, I think that's what my mom figured out. That she was in this other person's story and she wasn't going to do it anymore, she had her own to make up.

Tammy thought that while she was lying, there was a way what she was saying was true somehow, that there was a story she was telling herself and it was one she couldn't escape: the fact that she hadn't been a mother to her daughter for those first two years was a story, was the beginning of the story about a battle between her and April that lasted for as long as April was alive, that was still going on, even though April was gone, and the fact that they'd grown closer when April'd finally left home, sort of became friends, she thought, and then weren't anymore, was also a story. It was not the full truth, somehow, and was not something she could ever figure out. So why think about it, why try to figure it out? It was like people talking about movies or television shows incessantly online. In two weeks none of these people would remember the shows or their neat little theories and they'd be on to the next thing. That was the best way to be. Move on. Next thing, and try to make it better than the last thing. That's a thing she'd tried to teach April. Move on. Next thing, better thing. That's what she had imagined she was going to do with Jack now, though even that might be wrong. Just like leaving her parents' house with April, to get to something better, you had to make the next thing better. The world didn't help you. The world was something you had to try to wrestle into place like wrestling a sibling into submission. So that you could impose your story. The story you wanted. Just like this boy's mother did. Some people couldn't do it. She, for instance, for most of her life, hadn't been able to. It was exactly what her own life lacked, knowing what to wrestle and when. But now, this thing with Jack, this was the thing she knew she had to fight for. Still, her conviction that this was the right thing, both for her and Jack, she was now doubting.

The boy in the booth seemed to follow her eyes, through the windows and out to the parking lot. He asked which one was hers, nodding at the cars. It was a question asked in order to go on talking and she didn't necessarily want to do that, but she answered him anyway.

Tammy told him that she was driving that Jetta out there in the parking lot. The boy looked out at the car, now covered in a layer of sleet. She didn't tell him she usually drove an old Jeep Cherokee, a car that April had called the White Trash Mobile when she was in high school, but she'd say it in a way that showed she liked the car. Recently though, whenever Tammy picked her up at the airport in the last few years April'd say that Tammy needed to get a new car. Tammy would ask if she didn't like the White Trash Mobile anymore, and April'd shake her head – once their joke, now something she could tell April was ashamed of. Tammy had called April after she'd first married Nicholas and said, So what does the husband think of marrying into a white trash family? April had asked her not to say that, that that's not what she was, not what their family was, and not what Nicholas thought. Tammy told April that she knew what April thought of her, she knew what April thought of where she came from. I know why he's taking you to some isolated place in the mountains, away from our side of the family, Tammy had said. April'd say to Tammy that Tammy was one of the smartest people she knew, she just hadn't refined that intelligence, and she should take some classes, and they'd argue and argue on the phone, and hang up angry and hating each other. Tammy thought that part of the problem between her and April was that both of them forgot the good times. There were years in the small apartment they first lived in, after leaving her parents' house, that she often wanted to go back to. That small place, almost no decorations, a few pots and pans and plates and bowls in the cupboards. Dinner was chili mac or sloppy joes or just popcorn. They didn't have much money, but they were together. Tammy was the mother and April was her daughter. And Tammy was finally on her own, away from her family. Her family was only twenty minutes away, but she was still gone from them. She had her own family. April and her were now a family, and she could make what she wanted of it. She could construct a new story. They could. They did. There was a kind of effortlessness to their days, an easy freedom. Tammy drove April to daycare. They sang songs on the way. She picked her up in the evening and they practiced rhymes. She made them dinner, and they played games – Memory and I Spy, and then when she was a little older, six, seven, eight, they sang Creedence Clearwater songs, Neil Young, Carole King, Stevie Wonder. Tammy was educating April, in her own way, her own unique way. Rhyming games turned into Tammy giving April a verse to remember every day at preschool or kindergarten. Then they'd practice the verse on the way home. When they got home, April put the record on in the family room and they sang together while Tammy made a taco kit dinner or warmed up half a rotisserie chicken and potatoes. They did math, flash cards, adding and subtraction. Tammy felt some desire to go back to school, to become a teacher. She felt she was doing well. She felt like a mother and a teacher. She checked her annoyance in those years with the control of a good Samaritan checking on the flaws of the citizenry, governing herself through herself. When April broke something or spilled something, and Tammy felt annoyance, she recalled her father, and in this way, she didn't let him in their apartment. Her parents, her father in particular, they saw on holidays, and Tammy met her parents on the holidays with the same carefreeness she and April met the world with:

they didn't need anyone else, they didn't need the world, it was just them, and this was a nice stop, thank you for the meal, but soon they'd be gone, gone, gone, and no rules about how to behave in the house, where to eat, when to turn on the TV, how loud, no shoes inside, the heater not above sixty-seven degrees, coats hung here, that was her father's chair, that her mother's, none of these little rules had anything to do with her and April. They observed them and then left them behind, free. Tammy felt that she conveyed to her father by her very actions and living: I am finally out, away from you, who for so long kept me from some happiness. April was hers. She was April's. They were for each other, like the song. She tried to convey this to her father, indirectly, but it didn't touch him. Or she couldn't tell if it touched him. These holiday visits allowed her to keep her parents, and her father in particular, at a safe distance, and yet, eventually, as if sensing Tammy's plan, her father began just dropping by to see April. And when her father was around April, he was this happy and kind man that Tammy didn't recognize. Tammy couldn't believe her father's way around April. Holding her hand, taking her on walks, kicking the soccer ball with her. On her father's visits to her apartment, he'd come into the place as though he owned it, as though there had never been any problems between him and Tammy, as though he didn't know, didn't realize, that Tammy was purposefully keeping herself and April away from him, and he'd say she needed pictures or paintings up or more lamps and that he could buy some of these things if she wanted, which she always declined. He'd also ask how Tammy was, how her job as a dental assistant was going, if she thought she'd go back to school, which he thought might be a good idea, which he thought might be good for April, for getting April a better life, and when Tammy told him it wasn't on her mind at all, she didn't want to be in school ever again, she liked the job, she made good money, she was even saving a little money, he told her he was glad she was doing well and knew she would be. But see, she just had to fuck up first. He had to make her see that she was fucking up, so that she could know how to avoid it. Still, she could always be doing better. Things could be better if she tried harder, but this was good for now, pretty good. In these moments, she would recall images of him shaking his head at her, yanking her dog out of the house once when the dog had peed on a rug, putting a stake in the yard, tying the dog to it, never letting him inside again, and telling a seven-year-old Tammy that she'd lost the privilege of a dog. Now he was giving her backhanded compliments about her work and her parenting. But compliments nonetheless. She was pulled toward and away from him, and this very pulling she felt encroach on her life, cause some hidden tension. She'd wanted to tell him that there was no need to come by, but she didn't want to fight with him either, or she didn't want April to see her fighting him, since April had completely endeared herself to him: she saw the good grandpa! The fun grandpa! The funny and loving grandpa! So Tammy had no choice, like she had no choice in so many things: she let him in, let him be this person she didn't know. She sometimes imagined subtle ways of pulling out his anger, to show April, so that she'd also see the meanness, the calm and almost effortless cruelty, the distance, his man's mind. But she didn't let herself do that, she told the boy. That would've been unfair to

April. If this was what he was now, then she'd accept it. April wouldn't know, her father wouldn't know, but Tammy knew: she accepted, forgave. In those moments, she'd look at April and know that April wouldn't know the hardship that Tammy knew, wouldn't know the cruelty, wouldn't really know this man, and in her acceptance and forgiveness of her father, she was both happy for her daughter and envious. Jealous, really. Jealous again that she saw in her father now the father she'd never had. She'd hated the return of this feeling she thought she'd escaped. Her father conjured it in her so easily, and she worked hard to hide it from April, from her father, and from herself. From herself, too, she said. She didn't want to look at it and she sometimes thought that in not looking, she made it worse. It was the one thorn in those good years with April, the one thing she wanted to wipe from her experience but couldn't. She imagined that if she could let it – her father, her jealousy, her anger – sink from her mind, like a ship sinking on the horizon, she could feel that everything was right, that her life with April in the apartment was complete, but she felt it always there, like the annoying hangnail of her well-being.

Tammy watched the boy finish his soda and seem to accept that she didn't want to talk with him. In case he made another attempt, she picked up her phone and turned it back on and saw several texts from Steve. Each text was a version of an apology, with one text asking her to call him back, and another saying that he'd wait up until she called him back and that she should call him back, or not, whenever she felt like it, if she felt like it at all, and he'd understand either way, and was sorry for not being more up front with her. When she looked up, the boy was standing over his booth, laying down money on top of the tab. He told her good luck and then said that he had a feeling that things would work out in the best way possible for her and her daughter and then he smiled at her and went out to the parking lot. Through the windows of the diner, she watched him get into a pickup truck, reverse the truck, and then drive out onto the road. She imagined it was Jack's truck, that Jack had bought it cheap and basically broken down at a local used-car dealership, and then had fixed it up himself and got it running again, and that Tammy had taught him the lesson of working for the things you wanted and needed because no one else was going to help you out.

After finishing her coffee and eating a few French fries, she paid her bill, left a large tip, and then went out to her car without knowing what to do. The sleet had turned back to rain and was lessening, and before she got in the rental, she surveyed the diner, the parking lot, the road leading to the highway, and in the distance, cutting between what Tammy now could see was a forest, the sweep of cars on the highway, taillights going one way, headlights moving another. Something about the stillness of the forest against the constant motion of the cars momentarily disoriented her. The forest seemed to emphasize the futility of the travelers in the cars, as though wherever any of them were going was not a final destination, but just another place that they wouldn't find home. She got in the car and pulled out, got on the road that connected to the highway, and continued driving toward Jack. Her car, among other cars and trucks and SUVs and semis, was soon up on the mountain road, on a flat, elevated stretch of highway, which widened to three lanes. She felt that being in her car on this cold night was the proper expression of how things were. If she looked to her right or left, as she passed a car or as a car passed her, she might see the face of the driver, might see a young man, an old woman like her, or she might see a husband and wife, children in the back of an SUV watching some cartoon. She liked that, even in separate cars, when she looked, people could feel it, and they'd look, they'd see her in her car, alone, separate, being conveyed to wherever. All were going to different destinations, all alone, like the boy she'd met in the diner. That was why trains were a lie, why the car, that American invention, was the proper expression of how things really were: separate and alone, and cars drew the division. I see you, but I'm not with you. We're, none of us, going to the same place – that was what the car represented. Isolation and separateness, in the same way the trees were separate from the grass, the highway was separate from the mountains, the mountains were separate from the sea, and human life, cities, separate from nature, and you had to either fight your way through all these things that had nothing to do with you or let people pass. A car merged into her lane like some kind of symbolic action she couldn't quite decode, though she gestured at the car as evidence of what she was thinking. For a moment, the rain and sleet seemed to stop, then a gust of wind brought down more. She hadn't noticed it until now, but there were pine trees now along the road, rather than the deciduous trees she'd been seeing. The icy rain gave the pines a white sheen. Her phone lit up, and she saw another call from Steve. She decided to answer and told him she was in mountains. She glanced to her left – toward where? the west? she didn't know – and saw the drop-off of a cliff, the valley below populated with the tiny lights of so many separate lives, lives that would never really know one another, lives distant as galaxies, separated by light years. Steve asked how she was doing. In front of her car, in the right-hand lane, was a semi, and on the left another semi came up beside her and boxed her in. She told him that she was fine, though there was too much time to be thinking, and she'd just gotten boxed in by a couple of semis so she had that to deal with. He asked what she was thinking about and she said, What I'm thinking is what are you going to say now. What are you going to say to try to convince me to not get Jack. Are you going to say that now you're on my side and you think that I should do this, and hope, somehow, by saying that, that I'll become reasonable and think that he shouldn't live with us? Steve said that he wasn't going to say anything like that, and that yes, maybe he hadn't been fully honest with her at first, though he'd been at least partially honest. He did think, for instance, that she needed to be dealing with her sadness about April, he thought that was important, but he was wrong in using that to keep her from the idea of wanting to get Jack. If she thought Jack should live with them, then he shouldn't stop that, and not only that, he wanted to say that he didn't think she was being selfish, that wasn't fair of him, and he was sorry for saying that, but she did really need to think about how their life would change, and while he had planned to say certain things about how time would change for them and how their jobs would make raising Jack difficult and that their age would make it difficult, and while he was going to say these things to sway her, to try to make her see that maybe they weren't the right guardians for Jack, now he didn't want to sway her, but he did want her to think about these things because these things were worth thinking about, worth considering, he said. Tammy asked him if he thought that she'd not thought about these things. He was quiet, and she continued by saying that if he didn't think she'd thought about these things, then he must also think she was stupid. Did he think she was stupid? He mumbled a quiet no and she said that was good because while they hadn't been together very long, she was beginning to think, based on the last few days, that he thought she was stupid, and she'd have to kick his ass out if that was the case. She explained that she didn't like treating him like a child right now, but she sort of figured that's what he deserved because he'd thrown everything she was doing into doubt and he had, she realized now, from the beginning, for completely selfish reasons. It made her wonder if he was only with her because he could maintain the lifestyle he wanted, he could basically be single, he could go out to bars, he could go to his job, he could hang out with his friends, and he got to come home to a roommate, sometimes a date-mate, sometimes a sex mate, someone who occasionally made dinner and did his laundry, she was beginning to wonder if everything he did wasn't for some selfish reason. Hold on, hold on, he said, that wasn't fair. It wasn't fair to take this one example and to then turn it into something bigger. He knew he was selfish, he was well aware, and sometimes he was selfish and he wasn't even aware he was doing it, and he was sorry for both things, for when he knew it and for when he didn't, but he wanted her to know, right now, that he was done, he wanted her to do what she thought she should do concerning Jack, and if that meant the boy living with them, then that was okay with him, no, it was more than okay, he'd support her and he'd help raise the kid to the best of his abilities, though she knew he'd never had children and never really had any intention of having children, but still, he'd do the best he could.

Behind her, another car's headlights appeared, so that she was nearly completely boxed in. When the semi to her left didn't change lanes for some time, she pushed the gas and tried to make the semi in front of her change lanes faster, but it stayed steady, in the same way the semi on her left held his speed. She felt a tightness in her chest, a clenching of her shoulders. The semi in the left-hand lane, which seemed to have been ready to pass the truck in front of her, now was riding right along next to her, and she looked in her rearview and saw headlights were still only in the distance, so she slowed, let the semi to her left pass by, and then got behind him, signaled into the far left lane, and went around both, feeling herself breathing again. She had a brief image of cutting back into the center lane, but not moving ahead of the semi far enough, changing lanes without looking in her rearview, and the back of her car clipping the front of the semi, sending them both into a near-fatal slide toward the guardrail, where they would both crash, the semi flipping and crushing her car. While he was talking, Tammy thought of Steve at home, Steve on the road for days at a time for UPS, how she was often alone in their apartment, how when he was home they sat together and watched television, ate in front of the television. She tried to insert Jack into this picture, like a hologram of the boy superimposed over images of their life. Trying to think of Jack with them made her aware that her own life was barely

183

even there. She was a ghost in the house, looking for something to eat, staring in the fridge, the cupboards, wanting to be somewhere else. When Steve fell asleep early, which he often did after a long couple days on the road, or if he was gone, she sometimes drove through the nice neighborhood nearby late at night, not able to sleep. So many nights she didn't sleep, her mind going and going, though thinking about nothing in particular: work the next day, something April said on the phone, her father's failing health. She'd get up on those nights and drive, and she wondered, Would she take Jack with her on one of these drives if the boy couldn't sleep in the new house? She'd drive into the neighborhoods with two-story houses, three and four bedrooms. Garages. Lawns and trees. Pools in the backyards. The houses lit by landscape lights. A second-story window with a light on. She saw herself driving slowly so she could see the people inside, who were almost always white. She sometimes saw glimpses of bodies. A man, a woman, a child. She hated them a little. For getting what they wanted. For the world giving it to them. Maybe Jack would be in her passenger seat and when he was older, she'd tell him that these people didn't have to work for what they had, and that it was better to have nothing than to have things you didn't deserve and hadn't earned. What had these people done, she sometimes wondered? What weird portal opened in their existence, like an alien door presented to them by some sorcerer, that led them to easeful lives? Of course, they were also the worst consumers and materialistic people in existence, but still, they had something she had lacked, and they'd found a way to it: ease and comfort.

She told Steve that he didn't even understand what this was all about. What this really was about was that Jack needed someone who could devote their life to him, and the other family members, they had full lives. She didn't. She and Steve didn't. Their life was barely there, so unreal compared to these other lives, as though it existed in black and white: an apartment, an old car, an unsalaried job, the scarcest of healthcare, no retirement. She told Steve that they talked a little over dinner, a television show, and there wasn't a lack of communication, there wasn't miscommunication, there wasn't wondering what was going on with Steve, there wasn't the unknowability of this other person. There was just another person there. Just Steve. Just Tammy. She knew what he was, he knew what she was. There was nothing to talk about, there was no communication that needed to occur, their life was barely there. At some point, there was barely even loneliness, she told him. There was the empty space – like a clearly missing book on the shelf of life – where their life should have gone, and with Jack, there'd be a purpose again.

Ahead, brake lights lit up and dimmed in the night, lit up again. Traffic slowing as the flat elevated highway gave way to another downward slope. Tammy thought that the last time there'd been a clear purpose in her life was at another point in her life, when she had felt the need to save April. Now she felt the need to save Jack, but years ago she'd done something similar. Except then it had been her fault. She remembered that in the apartment with April, when April was finally older, eight or nine, Tammy had begun to feel some unease. She felt like a mother, but she also felt a little starved for adult communication. It'd been years since she'd even thought of dating, but there was another dental assistant at work, a man. She'd thought it was time. She told the male dental assistant (which was what she called him since she'd known him) to take her for drinks, a burger. He did, but he also didn't last long: when she brought him home the first time to meet April, he'd almost been shocked the kid was real. At work, she'd told him she had April, and he seemed fine with it. Then he was presented with the reality, an actual child. The reality of this child put him off, and she had seen, suddenly, how hard getting what she wanted was going to be. In addition to this, whenever Tammy went out, April moped a little. When Tammy began seeing other men from the restaurant-slash-bar she went to after work, April gave the guys a hard time. She quizzed them on US history, multiplication, their intentions, and, most pryingly, their families: How many girlfriends have you had in the last year? Do you have parents who are still together? How old are your siblings and what do they do now? The guys took it as good fun, but April also thwarted their efforts. She was a force. Tammy knew the men thought she was a handful. So when things seemed to consistently not work out (almost every man claiming that they'd had a lot of fun with Tammy, but hey, they just weren't in the dad business), Tammy then resented April for it. She found one guy who delivered Fedex to their neighborhood and house, when April was about to be in high school. He had a beard and long, brown hair. He wore flannels. He worked every day, and April'd finally sort of given up on interrogations. She actually seemed to like him. They dated for several months. He spent the night. He watched movies with them, popped popcorn, made meals. But it didn't work out, as so many

186

things in her life didn't, and it was no one's fault, really, if she honestly considered it, no one's fault at all, just a thing that occurred in the circumstances of her life, which were, as they had always been, not exactly right. Just not right enough. Not wrong, entirely, but not right, either. One night, after Tammy went to bed but he and April stayed up to finish some horror movie, Tammy woke and went to the kitchen for water and she found the Fedex man massaging April. That ended that and when Tammy discussed this with April, asking why she'd let him do that, April told her that it wasn't the first time, that he did it at least once a week and that he had told April that if she told Tammy that she wouldn't understand. Tammy had called the guy then, told him that she was filing a report and he would be arrested tomorrow, so be ready, but she never did it. Instead, she moved them away, to a different part of the city, changed phone numbers, gave them a new start, she'd finally had the means to do it, though all April'd said was that she'd moved her away from her school and friends, beginning the divide between them that would eventually carry April away to North Carolina. April hadn't appreciated Tammy, and neither would Jack, Tammy knew, but in time he might, and anyway, she thought, Jack's appreciation or gratitude wasn't necessary. He was too little for it. He just needed a safe space, and that was what Tammy was going to provide.

Steve was saying that he hadn't realized Tammy believed their life was so boring, and that he was glad to be at a steady and settled place in his life. He liked eating dinner and watching television together. What was wrong with that? He told Tammy he sometimes wondered if she felt this way because she didn't get to have a proper youth. He sometimes wondered if she wouldn't resent so much, or take so much for granted, if she'd been granted some wildness. Then maybe she could appreciate quiet things, simple things, like he did. Her car slowed to a stop, a winding trail of cars down the mountain. She said she didn't think it was that. She wasn't resentful. She just wanted something that was hers, and she'd messed that up with April. She told Steve that if Nathaniel and Stefanie took Jack into their lives, she'd never see him, and she'd never get the opportunity to correct some of the mistakes she'd made, along with April's own mistakes with Jack. I don't know, Steve said. I understand, but I don't know.

Her car was coming out of the mountains, and she could see the city she was approaching, which appeared to be huddled around a river. She told Steve that he didn't know because he never had a kid. He never had a girl who at seventeen had stolen his car. He'd never had a son say, I can't wait to get away from you. He'd never had a child, maybe fifteen, try to get out of his grasp after an argument about his boyfriend, a guy some seven years older than her, and how a pair of scissors one of them was holding slipped, and cut him deep through the forearm. He'd never sat with a daughter, both of them sitting on the sofa, not talking, eating Subway, not knowing at all what was going through his kid's head, but he'd also never watched his kid in the kitchen making grilled cheese sandwiches for dinner for the first time. He'd never played Risk on the dinner table for hours, drinking tea and eating pretzels. He'd never shared colds. He'd never had a son slip into his room after watching a horror movie to sleep with him. He'd never watched his kid begin lessons on the piano, an old one a friend had given them, and then finally, after years, watch that same child actually start getting good, singing and playing songs they'd sung when April was a girl. He'd never seen the little feeling of pride in that kid when they knew they were playing well, and how that feeling radiated outward, like a warm light, over himself. Maybe Steve was right, she told him, though not in the way he thought. It wasn't that she needed some wildness or missed her youth, but maybe it was that the bad moments in her life were so much larger than the good ones, that she'd taken so much from those moments, that she applied what she felt in those moments, the jealousy and resentment and anger, and applied those same feelings to the normal things, and in doing so, she'd lost what made things good. She wasn't going to do that with Jack, and knowing this, this made her the right person for the boy, she was certain of it, and there was nothing Steve or anyone else could say to change her mind on that. She'd doubted it, but she knew it again. And tomorrow or maybe the next day, she was going to call Nathaniel and tell him that she was coming to get Jack. She wasn't going to give him a chance to say no, so she was going to wait until she was closer, until the trip was almost over.

Ahead on the sloping road, Tammy saw the old city growing larger, with more and more distinct buildings and lights. It was far down the mountain and appeared to be spread across both sides of the highway. She could see a car, flipped on the other side of the highway, two police cars surrounding it, and a long line of headlights stretching down the mountain road. On her side of the highway, two cars cutting off two lanes, police cars and an ambulance near them. Who were these people? Sitting in traffic, she began crying, thinking of people down there driving somewhere. Thinking of herself driving somewhere. Thinking of April alone on the road at night. She'd be thrown from the car. Her body in the woods. She thought of April and Nicholas and Jack, and she thought of her thinking of them, which equaled her treatment of them, and felt like wanting to admit something to someone, though she didn't know what. The cars in front of her advanced against the rainy night. The black of the pavement ahead of her was mirror-like and shining in the rain. The headlights of the on-coming cars were reflected right below those same cars, as though there was another world just below and opposite this one.

She told Steve that she was going to tell Nathaniel that this was what April wanted and he said that if that's what she wanted to do, okay, and after saying goodbye and telling him she'd call him when she decided to stop for the night, she hung up. She continued through the town. She passed a plant of some kind, lighted and blinking in the night, near a river, probably polluting it, Tammy thought. Then neighborhoods of old houses set on a hill near the river, the houses close together, small yards, working class. On the other side of the river, as she went over a bridge, she could see the old city, town hall. The river was covered in fog, which moved eerily, giving the city a ghostly unreality, as though it could evaporate with the fog. The rain had stopped, she noticed. Her shoulders hurt and she loosened her neck, rolling it around, and in this recognition, she felt the tension in herself, and wanted to loosen it, but couldn't. The city was behind her and again the car was going into the mountains. She thought she'd find a smaller town, one where the hotels would be cheaper, and stay there the night. Welcome to the Wasatch Range a sign said, flashing green in her headlights off the side of the highway. She didn't know how many mountains, rivers, towns, cities, long and boring stretches of farmland she'd have to pass through, but she remembered the mountain range near the end of the journey, the Blue Ridge. Even when April and Nicholas had bought her plane tickets and flown her in, they still had to drive through the Blue Ridge. She wondered why the word blue? The mountains weren't blue at all. They were green or brown or grey, depending, but they weren't blue. Another lie, she thought. Another way the world was trying to convince you it was one way, it was some dream, some beautiful place, when really it was against you, or at the very least it was just there. And you were just where you were, isolated from it. Driving alone in a car through the night to a place full of people who were going to be against you, going to fight you, who didn't know you and didn't want to know you and never would know you, and whose lives were, in all their stupidity and selfishness and privilege, completely separate and unknowable to you, too, and which you didn't want to know, and yet you kept driving through the night toward these people who didn't want anything to do with you at all.

NICHOLAS

Yunmen said to the assembly, 'All people are in the midst of illumination. When you look at it, you don't see it; everything seems dark and dim. How is it being in the midst of illumination?'

—*THE TRUE DHARMA EYE*, CASE 81

There was the ticking of the car's engine and the sensation of falling awake in the dark. The grey outlines of the interior of the car slowly materialized in the darkness – steering wheel and dash and airbag and frame that once held the windshield. Then he felt himself, felt his head pressed against a flat, almost carpeted surface, which he knew, after something in him made an adjustment, was the roof of the car, and that he was upside down in it, still in his seat, held by the seatbelt. In and through the grainy dark, the splintered windshield lay flat on the ground, grass flattened beneath the cracked glass. The ticking of the car's engine slowed. A humming of pain from some distant source, like a tuning fork struck gently, grew louder and more intense. He felt himself falling into himself to the sound of the ticking engine. His vision darkened and he closed his eyes, and after a moment, opened them. The darkness undimmed again, and there was the steering wheel, the deployed airbag, a pulsing pain behind his eyes that sent brief flashes of white into his vision, which slowly faded. Beyond the flattened and splintered windshield was the muddy ground, grass, leaves and brush outside the frame of the car, and further out, the forest. It was dark, but he could see, and suddenly he knew that the forest was lighted by moonlight, almost held by it – that silvery light. That humming pain grew louder. He closed his eyes, opened them again, and now saw the deflated airbag hung upside down from the steering wheel and was wet with blood and swayed gently. It felt like there was an optometrist clarifying his understanding of reality with each closing and opening of his eyes. The airbag swayed noiselessly, a drip of blood hanging from a corner. It occurred to him that the bag hung upside down in the same way he hung upside down from the seatbelt, and yet he was still compactly in his seat, almost squished in it, and he realized through a wave of pain – suddenly the hum of pain crescendoed – that moved up his abdomen and back and into his neck that the roof of the car had been collapsed in the accident, and he had almost been smashed. He felt his breathing get faster, shallower, trying to remember the accident, trying to not feel his body, which suddenly seared with heat and ache. The passenger seat, he could see by moving his eyes but not his head, was empty. He observed his body try to move almost without his will and then tried to think it into movement to get out of the car, as though getting out of the car would get him away from the pain, but he couldn't move his head or his left arm, which the crushed-in driver-side door had trapped somehow. He tried again to move his left arm and a ringing coldness radiated from his shoulder into his neck and back and chest and down, or was it now up, his arm into his fingers. He sensed himself thinking that his arm felt like it was his and not his at once, and behind this thought, he felt himself sensing that he was unsure he was thinking this thought, feeling this thought, or feeling feeling. He felt himself to be at some distance from himself, still falling into himself, as though he hadn't fully materialized yet, as though he was slowly resolving into physical manifestation – just as the car and physical world had done in his vision – like a slowly resolving and clarifying image on a screen. Cold air swept into the car and felt like thoughts from some other mind, which was watching from stillness: the symmetry of the cold air and the cold pain in his arm produced a strange synesthesia, as though his attempt to move his arm and the coldness he felt there had produced the cold air. He observed his mind think of this strange synesthesia, in order to get away from feeling the pain, feeling as though he hadn't produced the thought. Then the thought was gone as well as the synesthesia and he was just cold, shivering. He felt momentarily confused considering all this and his head involuntarily tried to tilt, cock, like a dog's head when considering human words, a habit which was completely mechanical, unthought, and that involuntary movement sent a flash of stabbing pain down through his chest and abdomen, which hit something in him and reverberated back up toward his head along his spine with the force of a physical blow, causing a heat to rush up into his head in a flashing that wiped everything to white.

Sometime later gathering through wide spaces of dark to his waking self again. Like spilled water collecting itself back into a toppled glass, which righted itself again. His eyes did the same slow readjustment to the dark. He closed his eyes hard and opened them wider in an effort to wake himself up. For a moment, he believed he had woken from the bad dream of the accident, but then realized that it hadn't been a dream. A lone cricket was now chirping in the forest among a sea of quiet humming sound. He could still feel a strange pulling into his body, as though parts of himself were still gathering back into him from the various places they had been dispersed to. This gathering feeling made him know that whatever was in him could be dispersed again and that he was about to die and this was his being gathering itself into him again in order to divest itself of his body – as though his being was one final inbreath and outbreath. It wasn't an entirely unpleasant sensation, but then the gathering into himself changed somehow, like he could hold what was gathering, and it made him know that he was just here in the car again. He squinted his eyes closed then opened them wide, trying to see and trying to stop from shivering in the cold dark. The shivering of his upper body made something in his neck pulse and hurt. He inwardly told himself to breathe, breathe, just be cold, and to his surprise, it helped some and lessened the shivering and pain in his neck, though then, through breathing cold air and steadying the shivering, he felt other pain more distinctly: a searing and pulsing in his left leg and left shoulder and along his chest, sternum, and neck, the different parts of his body individuated by pain, making it clear that something had happened to his left shoulder, maybe a broken collarbone, that maybe he'd cracked some ribs or his sternum, and the new pain in his left leg, which when he tried to look at he couldn't and when he tried to move he couldn't, something holding him there, the lower part of the dash collapsed or maybe the drive-side door pinning him somehow. His body was these individual areas of pain, shoulder and chest and neck and legs, and everything else, the rest of his body, felt like a blank white space, as though it wasn't there at all. Then with his one free right hand, he felt the stickiness of what he knew to be blood along his abdomen, and it was the blood that made him feel in real danger, and the thought arose again that he was going to die here, that he needed to get out. He searched his chest and stomach and along his ribs with his free right hand but couldn't find any lacerations or open wounds and knew that the blood that was soaking through his shirt must be coming from his legs, which were above him. Blood from his legs was seeping down his body. He pushed lightly on his upper body and felt that his shoulders and ribs and stomach were sore but okay. He was okay, he thought, though the blood was not good because it was still night and he couldn't move, so if he was still bleeding, that meant he would keep bleeding, he would bleed out, he would die here. He wanted to move his head to see the blood or its source and assess how serious the bleeding was and maybe put pressure on it with his free hand, but he remembered not to move his neck, that he'd already done that and it had caused him to pass out.

Then the dark was undoing itself again: out the frame that usually held the windshield there were the trunks of trees and further in the woods full trees and weeds and smaller plants on the forest floor, already, or still, green. Again not seeing April beside him and knowing without thinking that she'd been thrown through the windshield and then a wavelike pain, like an instant fever, ran through his body, making him convulse with shivers, which in turn made his entire body seem a clenched ball of deep discomfort. He felt himself sweating though he was freezing.

Something in him told himself to breathe. He recognized the voice, though it wasn't his voice, didn't seem like his voice, but he recognized it, a voice he felt he'd been hearing in glimpses intermittently as long as he could remember and occasionally came in clearly, like a suddenly tuned transistor radio, during his project on the mountain. It reminded him vaguely of a thing April had once done for him when he'd broken his leg playing soccer. As she drove him to the hospital, he'd nearly gone into shock, the muscles in his arms and legs stiffening, making the pain worse, and she'd told him he was hyperventilating and to breathe slower, slower, slow down, deep breaths – and this voice too had not seemed like hers, like he was hearing it from out of the depths of a cave – and he'd followed the force of those words then in the same way he did now. Eyes closed, steady in and out. He opened his eyes again. For a few minutes, lightheadedness caused his mind to move toward and away from waking consciousness and again he felt himself expansive and large: images of trees and dense wood and second growth timber and weeds and damp, decaying leaves, and the smell of mud, fungus, a burned rubber smell and gasoline or oil, the creak of the trees in wind, a sliver of moon through the trees and among the clouds, all as if being in a dream. He told himself to wake up, thinking it over and over like a chant – this is a dream, this is a dream, the thought stretched out and slow. Then there was a strange sensation – like a record player that had been lagging suddenly moving again at the right speed – and he felt his thinking accelerating, himself slipping back into himself fully, that gathering that occurred slowly and strangely before, now occurred instantaneously, and what for a moment was expansive compressed suddenly: he was in a car, trapped, unable to move, needed to get out.

He reached with his right hand across his body and put his hand on the driver-side door handle. He could see now that the door was buckled inward. The handle moved, but the door didn't. He jiggled the handle and shook it and pushed against the door, but nothing happened. He took a breath and pushed against it across his body with his right hand, pushed as hard as he could, but still the door wouldn't move. It was crushing his left arm, keeping him stuck in place, and wasn't going to move, wasn't going to open. He let the handle go and noticed that the digital clock on the dash was still working. It was nearly one thirty in the morning. He tried to remember the last time he noticed time, and he thought it must have been leaving the house where the party was, sometime around midnight. So he hadn't been passed out long. If he could get out, he could help April. He pulled at the belt and felt wrenched back into place, a screaming pain through his body, which was his own scream. Then, the pain pulling back like a wave receding back into the ocean, the voice telling him to stay calm, to breathe. He thought that he didn't want to be doing this, he didn't want to be in here alone, trapped in this car alone. He had the realization that he hadn't tried the seatbelt. It passed through his mind as a kind of boyish excitement, like a kid finding five dollars in his winter jacket from the previous winter. He reached down, or up, he thought, up, with his free and uninjured right hand and pressed the button thing but the belt didn't unlatch, or unbuckle, he thought, unbuckle. It was a thing his seatbelt did sometimes – he'd once had to slither out of his seat and then mess with the buckle until it'd come out of the latch – and now it was doing it again, sticking, and he pushed and pushed the button, but nothing happened, and in his right hand he felt a new hot pain from pressing, though the pain wasn't unbearable. He pressed the button again and again and the stinging pain in his hand dulled some and he pressed as hard as he could through gritted teeth and he heard a click and he felt a huge relief, like the process had begun, like this was the first indication that he wasn't going to die here, he was going to get out of this car. But somehow, though he'd heard, or maybe felt, the buckle click, the seatbelt was still in the latch, it wasn't coming out. His breathing felt freer, but when he tried to move his body he still couldn't, and he thought that he really didn't want to be doing this, he wanted to be doing anything but this. Then, as if conveyed to him by some reluctant god or alien being, he again thought of April. That this wasn't only happening to him. That this was happening, had happened, to her, too. And she was out there alone. He thought of her on the road. Or her body on the forest floor among the trees. Wet, maybe, due to the rain, which, he now registered, fell in a gentle humming static. Had it just begun to rain and he hadn't noticed? The sound of the rain made him feel as though he wasn't paying close enough attention, that if he just paid close enough attention, he could understand how to get himself out of this position. After a moment of listening, he thought of the rain covering April's body as a kindness, though he didn't know why, like the thousands of raindrops that fell on her were thousands of tiny hands holding her. He called out to her. Not loud the first time, then louder, like he had to gather her name in his mouth and try it first in order to make the action real. He called again and again, now shouting her name. He screamed it as loud as he could. He waited. Only the rain in response.

He pulled at the seatbelt, but it was somehow stuck in the latch, still holding him upside down, and it wouldn't move. Fucking shit, he said. Thinking of April made him think of Jack – that this was not only just happening to him and April, but to Jack as well – and for a panicked moment he tried to look in the rearview mirror to see the boy in his car seat – a sudden visual montage in his mind of Jack hurt in his car seat, arm broken, tossed about the car during the accident and lying motionless in the backseat, hurt or dead – but then he knew that Jack was with the babysitter, he was in bed, he would be sleeping until morning, which made Nicholas look at the digital clock again and see that only a few minutes had passed. He didn't know exactly how long ago the accident occurred, though it couldn't have been too long, and he didn't know how long he'd have to wait for help, how long April would have to wait but at least he did know that Jack was with the babysitter and safe, his little boy was okay, and in this inward expression he felt what he perceived to be a deep warmth and gratitude move through him, which he told himself to focus on, to stay right there with it. Jack in bed, asleep. Reading a book to Jack. Jack hiding his stuffed animals in the woods around the cabin. Nicholas finding them. Nicholas hiding them for Jack to find. But not too difficult, April said. Don't make them too hard to find, or too high. Nicholas looked out the car window and understood that when he and April weren't home by midnight the babysitter would attempt to call April. A phone call would be coming. The babysitter was going to call April. He knew for sure that a phone call would be coming – maybe he'd even hear April's phone, which he knew to be in her jacket pocket, go off, and he'd be able to locate her by sound – and when that phone call wasn't answered, people would know something was wrong, someone would find him, they'd know where he and April had gone for the night, they'd retrace where they'd been, they'd call friends, they'd find him on Smoky Mills Road and he'd be alive, and so would April, and they'd get home and Jack would still be asleep, as though none of this had occurred, and at the same time he thought this, he also thought that April might not pick up her phone again and might never speak to anyone, not to Jack, not to him, ever again, and he felt his heart nearly pushing against his ribs upside down in the car, and he shouted her name again, waiting, and when he heard nothing, he told himself to calm himself – though it was not the distant voice, he was aware, that spoke this, but his own mimicking it – and then he felt the ridiculousness of telling himself to calm himself when he was upside down in a crashed car and bleeding and cold in freezing temperatures and sweating and could die and April was in all likelihood not alive, she was dead, and yet there it was again, some competing voice in him telling himself to calm himself, this time distinctly not his voice, some voice from some distant place telling him to calm himself, to think of what he needed to do, what do you need to do, which after asking it of himself he knew was to do only what he could do, and to understand that Jack was okay and safe, that the babysitter would attempt to call April, was probably already attempting to call April, and was not getting April, and would eventually call the police, and he'd be found and then be back with Jack. But April wouldn't be, he thought. There was the competing urge to be both utterly honest with himself and to feel that she was still alive. He felt some knot of tension in his chest, which made his chest hurt, and then tears and he mumbled aloud that he didn't know anything to be true or not true, you don't know anything. He thought that maybe she was only unconscious. Maybe April was out there in a soft pile of leaves or maybe she'd been thrown in such a way that she'd rolled and had hit her head and was now passed out, though the delusional nature of this thought was almost too apparent, and his fight against what was actual felt almost stupid, like playing tug of war with a rope securely attached to a wall, though then he considered that maybe she'd walked away from the accident. Maybe she was on her way to get help. Maybe he'd been passed out, and she'd woken up, looked at him, tried to wake him, and then had left and was walking, or running even, jogging, right now into town. How long would that take her? If the babysitter fell asleep, she might stay asleep until the morning came, until her own parents woke and realized she wasn't there, so it could be hours before anyone found him, but if April had walked away from the accident, someone would find him. She'd turn off this old, isolated road, get onto one of the old farm roads where surely someone would be driving by, some farmer maybe, would pick her up, she'd call the police. Maybe she already had. Though none of that made sense. Her door was closed, her seatbelt recoiled, she'd left no indication that she'd gone for help, and if she was okay, why hadn't she just called the police? But maybe she was okay and looking for help and had called the police and they were on the way and had called the babysitter, what was she going to do, leave him a note, she probably rushed away as fast as she could to get him help, and if her cell phone had been damaged, or lost, she could still be walking and it could take hours to get back to town on foot, he thought. Maybe it wasn't such a ridiculous thought after all.

The rain increased, a near hissing sound off the forest floor, and now that his eyes had adjusted to the darkness, he saw both the rainfall and spray of rainfall as it hit the ground, as well as a soft mist moving between the trees. Because the car was on a slope, he could look down into the forest as it moved down the mountain. A scattered light reflected on the corner of the flattened windshield, and he couldn't understand what light it was, then knew it was the moon reflected there, fractured into glints of light. A single ant was walking along the cracked windshield. It seemed to rise up on its hind legs for a moment to survey Nicholas. He half wanted to ask it for help. He called April's name again, then again, louder, and heard only the rain on the trees and leaves of the forest floor. He felt afraid to say her name and then said it, quietly, and then yelled it. The rain seemed to increase as if in remorseful response. It was not helpful to think that April was alive and walking toward help in the same way that it was not helpful to think that April was dead simply because he couldn't see her or hear her, or that she couldn't hear him. He told himself that he couldn't know anything for certain. He grabbed onto the steering wheel with his unstuck arm and tried to pull himself out of the stuck seat and horrifying pain like ripping occurred in his left leg and he stopped immediately. In order to not feel the echoing pain, he made himself recall that he'd actually witnessed an accident once in graduate school when he and April had been driving to see her mother, they were driving on the highway, and in front of them, maybe two hundred yards, a truck's tire blew out and the truck flipped several times and he'd seen a girl inside the truck sort of fly out of a window like a crash-test dummy, her body seeming not real at all, and her body kind of did two strange rolls, half-summersaults on the side of the road into a sitting position. He'd barely been able to believe that the girl sitting there had survived. Like other people, he and April had pulled onto the shoulder of the highway and stopped and gotten out of their cars and rushed over to her. The girl's eyes had been glazed and she appeared to be looking down through some telescope at her hands and body, a little cross-eyed almost, her head unsteady, as though she was not in control of herself. But she was okay. They all asked, What hurts? Are you okay? And she'd looked up at them and down at her hands and said, I'm fine. I think I'm fine. Then she said to them when they asked if she was okay again, she said, directly to Nicholas, Where's Mark? Mark was her boyfriend and he was back in the truck, which was flipped over, and he too was okay except for a cut on his forehead, a bruised thigh. Nicholas thought now that maybe that was like a precursor to this moment, that maybe him witnessing that accident was proof not to be despairing now, that maybe April was okay, and so maybe was he, though he then considered the idea that another person's life, this girl, whose name he never learned, and this Mark person, they were not blueprints for his life, they were not signs or symbols, they were real people, who didn't necessarily have anything to do with him. So maybe just take it as evidence that people survive, he thought. Then he wished he had a phone, wished he hadn't taken what now felt like a somewhat stupid stand against certain technologies, refusing to ever have a phone, and in this wishing, he looked at the center console, near the gearshift, thinking that's where it would be if he had a phone, but then remembered he and the car were upside down and his hypothetical phone could be anywhere, might not even be in the car. The digital clock said that it was just before two in the morning. Only twenty minutes, he thought. How long was this going to take?

The rain held a steady rhythm and he now began to feel some drops hitting his face and arms, which at first he didn't understand, how it could be raining on him, then realized the drops were warm, that he was bleeding on himself, from his legs. He was panicked a moment, desperately wanted out of the car, and he pulled with his free right arm on the steering wheel, pulling harder than before, pulling his entire body toward the open windshield. Pain throbbed through his still stuck left arm and in his legs. It moved up his body in a hot and cold light. It blurred his vision. He heard himself sort of whimpering and sobbing, breathing quickly, and saying, Okay, okay, I won't, I won't move, as though he was talking to his own body from outside it. He tried to make himself very still and breathed and breathed and tried to slow himself down, just like he'd been practicing on the mountain. He suddenly understood that this was an opportunity to view things as he'd been trying to view things, without any positives or negatives, but just to constantly be learning from his existence, and to be able to calmly approach all situations, and yet, despite this understanding, he felt himself trying to not think that he was stuck here, trying to not think that he was not only stuck but trapped and could die here, trying instead to allow the part of himself that believed that he could get out to take over his thinking. He'd just have to do it slowly, carefully. It couldn't be some rushed and unthought thing. He'd have to get his body out of this car with great care, he thought. In fact, he'd have to do it in stages, like with the seatbelt buckle. First free his left arm. Then one leg. Then another. With care for each part of his body in order to keep pain at a minimum. He could do it if he did it in slow increments.

His project on the mountain had been to slow his life down in order to teach himself to be content and easeful with all situations, with all life, even negative moments, to be always in aware repose, like a tree accepting its divestment of leaves every winter, and he thought this situation now couldn't be more negative and that his fighting against it was purposeless. He had to accept it, be with it, and with a calm awareness, he'd get himself out of it. But he couldn't hate it or fight it. He'd wear himself out, pass out, or, if he wasn't careful, he'd hurt himself more. He almost started moving his left arm, then stopped himself, and inwardly repeated to himself to wait, just wait. He needed to let the pain subside, needed to allow his body to get back to a sort of stable base of non-pain, or less pain, because freeing the arm would be excruciating, and he was still feeling a hot tingle in his spine and legs, sweat on his forehead though it was very cold. Rain began falling harder, and a little distance from the car, there was a spiderweb shimmering in the rain and wind and moonlight. The web had no insects in it, no spider, it looked abandoned. He could see where the web connected at several points to a branch of a small tree, and then on the other side, to the stem of a weed. A circular pattern at the center of the web. He didn't want to be doing any of this, he thought again, but he was, and next he had to figure out some way to free the arm that was stuck, and in doing so, he knew he had to feel that pain again, which was not something he wanted to do, then he would have to take a rest, then feel more pain freeing the left leg, he thought, then rest, then more pain, then rest. Again, something in him viewed this from some distance, something far from himself communicating to him that all things were this, suffering, then no-suffering, then suffering again. He told himself it was as simple as this: pain, rest, pain, rest, and he could do it now again, just as he did anything, even though he didn't want to and some other part of himself told himself that it was not possible, he was trapped here. So much of his life, he reflected now, was determined by what he wanted to do and how he wanted moments to be as good as they could possibly be. And he was dissatisfied by so much of his life, as though he had failed, over and over again, to get the message that his wanting to do something and make it exactly how he wanted it to be did not equate to any kind of satisfaction. In fact, this wanting was often starkly against his own satisfaction. He'd learned this in numerous ways, and he thought now, it was only in the last few years that he'd actually begun to try to live by it, in a slow, stunted manner, like an android first learning it was not a human but an android and speaking again, for the first time, its millionth word.

He thought that he'd wasted so many years wanting things to be different than they were, wanting himself, others, to be different than they were, and it was only Jack who he'd never felt this way about. But everything else, he thought, he was constantly wanting to be different. He closed his eyes and blinked several times in order to get sweat that was running down his forehead to stop pooling near his eyes. If he blinked fast, he could get the sweat to move around his eyes. The burning sensation from the salt slowly subsided, and he was again listening to the quiet rain. For a moment, the physical world – rainfall, woods, tree trunks, the slip of dark sky he could see, the rising crescent moon, damp mud and fungus-y earth smell, mist moving between the trees, the spiderweb vibrating in the rain – manifested itself as a stronger reality than his mind, and he tried to let himself go out into it, and he felt something in him pulling outward.

He told himself he needed to stop thinking and start doing something. He needed to get out of this car now, and with his right arm, he pulled at his left arm a little, felt a streak of hot-cold pain, and stopped due to the pain and felt cowardly. Then, he focused on his right leg, which he could move some, and he reached down, which was up, with his right hand and felt around his right thigh, then under his thigh, felt only a small amount of pulsing in his lower back, and then with his right arm pulled on the thigh. It didn't come loose, but he felt it move to the right. It was too dark to see up into the floor of the car, but he reached again, and grabbed his right leg behind the knee, pulled and wiggled it at the same time, and it wiggled, loosening, and he realized he needed to slide it. He slid it toward the center console, toward the passenger door, moving it along the seat and whatever was pinning it in place, and as he slid it, it suddenly lurched free and fell toward him. He waited a moment, then moved the leg, and he could. He could move it. He was doing it, he thought. He was getting out. Now, feeling that he had this under control, he knew what to do, he reached across his chest to his left arm, and tried to jiggle it like he'd jiggled the leg and when he tried that again the same stabbing sensation screamed through him, and he stopped and said, Okay, not that, not doing that. The stabbing pain slowly dissipated and he breathed, deep breaths. He thought, in what he knew was a self-pitying way, that if he just hadn't been driving on this road then this wouldn't have occurred – he wouldn't be trapped in the car, April wouldn't be on the road somewhere, Jack wouldn't be alone with the babysitter waiting for them. Images arose in his mind like a sort of indie movie cliché, complete with opening credits – his name playing himself, April's name playing herself – over the slow-motion capture of a simulated accident, and yet this was no simulation, this was not a movie, not a drama. He felt the force of the cliché's actuality, that if he'd just said no to the tenure party like he'd wanted to say no to it and not let that other part of him that wanted recognition win out, if he'd just said that he wouldn't have another beer and not let that part of him that told him to get drunk tonight, whatever, win out, if he hadn't listened to April saying that this was something his colleagues wanted to do for him and he should be both accepting of and grateful for their respect and kindness and then let the sincere part of him also have its say, as though he suddenly saw that he wasn't going for selfish reasons but because it was actually kind of him, a kindness and respect shown to his colleagues, if he and April hadn't been arguing on the way home about the fact that Nicholas had been talking to Nora Evans in the kitchen, an argument he hadn't wanted to have, but which he definitely wanted to win, then none of this would've happened. If he could just have been one person at any one moment, he thought, then none of this would've occurred.

He took several deep breaths and tried to roll his head. He tugged a little at the seatbelt and it slipped up his chest some, which allowed him to maneuver his right arm so that he could slip it out from under the belt, but the belt stayed in place, now wrapped around the outside of his left arm, holding him in the seat. He tried to get the belt around the outside of his left shoulder but couldn't. Shit, he heard himself say, even more confined than before. He pulled his arm across his abdomen, tight against himself, without moving his upper body at all, afraid that it might hurt his left arm if he did, and was able to slip the arm under the belt, so that it was back into the original position, free of the belt, but still the rest of him stuck. He then noticed that his freed right leg hung uncomfortably toward his chest. The leg pulled on his lower back and made something ache there, so he pushed the leg back down, wedging it under part of the collapsed dash. He made sure he could easily free the leg again, and he could, and then put it back in under the dash, which relieved some pressure on his lower back. He noticed himself breathing hard, like he'd just climbed several flights of stairs in quick succession. Not wanting to move his left arm, not wanting to do this at all, he thought again of the ride home, and suddenly understood with a kind of paralyzed horror that barely allowed him to fully form the thought and wouldn't, for a moment, let him go beyond the thought, that the argument he had with April might be the last communication he had with her. Momentarily unable to move, to think, to do anything, until his mind began again moving toward what he didn't want it to move toward, which was their argument, and more specifically what led to their argument in the car, he felt a deep shame and regret. The impression of the car ride home – like a kind of emotional signal from a distant star, not definable and clear until he was able to decode it – arose in his consciousness, and in that impression he recognized their worst selves: April at her worst, him at his worst. He felt nauseated and for a moment his mouth began to water as it did before vomiting and he told himself to breathe, breathe, and after a moment, the feeling subsided. In the car driving home, he recalled, April had said she'd noticed him talking with Nora Evans for quite a while in the kitchen tonight. She'd said it off-handedly, an affect he hated, like she didn't really care. But he felt it – her jealousy, a kind of held-in energy that she was ready to direct, negatively, at him, like a weapon. As soon as she said it, he'd interrupted her by saying that he'd been trapped there in the kitchen, he hadn't wanted to be talking to her, and anyway, Nora Evans was the one who was talking to *him*, asking *him* questions, *he* wasn't talking to *her*, and also she was mainly asking about the two of you, he'd added. As he was saying this, though, he was also aware that when Nora Evans had begun talking to him, he'd liked it, he'd wanted it to happen, he'd been happy this pretty woman wanted to speak with him, yet he didn't say this to April. He'd told April that whatever she thought had occurred with Nora Evans probably hadn't come close to occurring in the way she was thinking it had. He remembered saying to April in the car that Nora Evans had actually asked about April and Jack, saying that she so much liked the idea of all of us, you know, whatever she called it, living on a sustainable farm and attempting to go off the grid. There's nothing to be jealous about because Nora Evans was asking about you, he had said. And Jack. She wanted to know how you two both liked living in the woods. She said it like that, *living in the woods*. I mean, she was asking about you two, about our life. She said things like how she admired that we were making no small attempt to do our part, to live beyond the confines of late capitalist ideology, and that she admired it very much, our lives, and the way we were raising Jack to have these alternative values, and she'd said that she too had these values, that maybe they weren't even alternative anymore, what intelligent person didn't have them, we all wanted to save the planet and not hurt animals, but who actually lived it, and from her perspective, she said, no one really lived it fully but that we made a decent attempt at least. Nicholas remembered himself saying things like this, though they sounded better in his head now, and he couldn't be sure what was real or not, though he did clearly recall not wanting to engage in an argument with April, but also at the same time wanting April to try to argue with him so he could show her how wrong she was. He recalled that he had been a little drunk, that he hadn't wanted to get drunk, or to drink at all, but he had, he had gotten drunk, and now, upside down in the car, he realized that part of the reason his head was aching and his mouth was dry and he had to pee was because he was hungover and the little stream of water running by his face was tempting him, his own blood running copper through the water. He stuck his tongue out to try to reach the water but it was just beyond him. He tried to nudge his head forward against the ceiling of the car and though he moved, the water seemed no closer. He glanced at her empty seat.

He told himself to think of something else, of good times with April, with Jack, of how Jack was the present moment around which he and April moved and were pulled into. They'd discussed this maybe when Jack was a year old, the way in that first year he pulled them to immediacy and away from their own private lives with ease. He was a quiet baby, a good sleeper mostly, a good eater, though when he got constipated he had made strange faces that had scared both Nicholas and April, then made them laugh, faces like he was going to explode either himself or the room, like this little baby was actually some kind of magician gnome, but then, after some time of strange, wrinkled, occasionally evil-looking faces, they'd hear the poop, and then smell it, which caused Jack to smile tiredly, like he'd been making some enormous effort, which he had been, he had, and they then were brought into action. After already being in the action of laughing, they were now in the action of diaper change. They noticed that their days, which they had once categorized as good, okay, great, bad, boring, no longer could be contained in such a way. There was less time to judge, for one, but what they both felt was that any judgment couldn't contain Jack. Jack crying all night, which was rare, was not bad. How could it be? It was only exactly what it was. It was exhausting, frustrating, but the designation of 'bad night' didn't even have a chance to exist. In the morning, it was just another day. Jack playing quietly by himself for the first time was exactly what it was: Jack playing. His deep screams when he wanted food were just that: a screaming baby. And their own exhaustion was just that: tiredness.

Of course they got annoyed, frustrated, but it seemed to happen after the fact, later, upon analysis, and only ever at each other. In the evening, when Jack was asleep for the night, they argued about when he should be taking naps, when he shouldn't, when he should be going to bed, getting up, when he should be starting more solids, what types of solids, should he eat baby food, or the same food they ate just cut very small, they argued about how it was frustrating that one of them let him sit in a wet diaper too long, that's why he had a rash now, or one of them thought baths every other day were okay, or that they should be using organic disposable diapers less and washable cloth diapers more, though Nicholas couldn't now say which side he'd fallen on in any of these arguments, just that he had. Stupidly, they both had. They'd quietly argue, blame, judge, accuse, retreat, apologize, attack again, claim tiredness, claim con-fusion as excuses, apologize again, wait, get quiet, tell each other that this was where they were, they had to keep some-thing for themselves, and it couldn't just be their exhaustion and frustration. Then, when Jack was with them again, it was as though their frustration had been some kind of game – unreal – and they were there for him. It was sad, Nicholas thought now, that they saved their annoyance for each other, though after a couple years, as the boy became more capable and independent, this frustration dissipated and they found space to be themselves again, to be there for each other, too, and not just for Jack. They'd almost forgotten what that was like, and Nicholas was glad to return to some version of it, him and April together, with Jack, yes, but together alone, too, once again getting to be just what they were. Nicholas thought that those first two years with Jack had taught him something indispensable. In any given moment with Jack, there was only what there was to do: feed the baby, put him down, be tired, burp him, change his diaper, clean his spit-up, talk to him, laugh with him, walk him around the yard, sing to him, be spit-up on, be peed on, be interrupted while doing work, listen to his cries, unrelenting and sometimes causing him to vomit, all perfectly as it was. There was no chance, April said, when with Jack to make analysis of how life was going and wish for something better or wish things were different if not better – there was no better, no worse, and even the one medical scare that year, they only did what they could do, which was take him to the doctor, give him the medicine, be concerned, be wary, hold him in a gentler manner, speak more softly. It was later that they thought and argued and complicated it all, but in the moment there was only what they were doing. How to make all life like that? Nicholas thought. To just do what one had to do.

Beneath this thought Nicholas felt the other thought about the argument with April and felt his mind wanting to go there, to think of the argument, but he didn't allow himself to do it. He tried to stay with Jack, and April too, and not find too much meaning in this one argument, though he felt the pull, wanting to analyze, wanting to see why it occurred, why it happened, why the fight came into existence, but he made himself think of when Jack played as a toddler. His little tongue stuck out in the corner of his mouth, at play with great seriousness, and it was the same when he got older and began reading little books and drawing and doing chores around the cabin. Everything he did was what he was doing right there, and though Nicholas and April had wanted to move to the mountain for the quiet and isolation, for the opportunity to find again the moment that they were constantly rushing from, it was their child who revealed what this actually meant, that even in rushing there could be presence, that even in difficult moments, there was immediacy, and Nicholas thought now in an effort to not think about his and April's argument, that what Jack revealed to him was that he'd mistaken being present for every moment being good. What he feared most for Jack was that he'd lose this, the ease of not living in any world except the one right in front of him. Nicholas thought of how he'd worked so hard to try to be able to do that again, to live without any obstructions, and it only rarely worked, or he only rarely felt the depths of where that might lead, but on the mountain he'd been moving toward it. There were small moments, glimpses, when sawing a table was sawing a table, not sawing a table and thinking about work, and worrying about an article he needed to write, and worrying about what April said earlier, or what to say to a male student he knew was gay, and who kept coming to his office hours with throw-away questions in order to flirt with him. He just sawed the table. There were moments when he just walked on the mountain path, just planted the garden, just played with Jack, just changed him, just fed him, just read him a book – this thing he'd wanted and was trying to access was only accessed through this other being, who he'd been afraid he could not be a good father to. Jack made things for both him and April simple again, even in the chaotic, exhausting moments of parenting, it was still simple, the focus of their life was simple, obvious, clear, what one needed to do was clear: be there for Jack, and even this formulation, he thought now, itself was lacking, didn't actually come into existence in the moment, it was only afterwards in analysis of the situation that it came into being, which made it an imperative, which it did not feel like. He, like April, didn't think, Be there for Jack. It just occurred, arose of its own accord, like a seed that had always been inside him manifesting itself as a tree, without any will. But with the exception of Jack, he rarely brought this same kind of awareness and attention to the rest of his life. Even now in the car, he thought, he wasn't living in the moment because he didn't want to be: because the moment meant pain, diffuse throughout his body, and it meant mental pain, the recollection of this last conversation with April, which he didn't want to think about, but which he could feel under his thoughts about Jack like a virus infecting his memories of his little boy, Jackie. Jackie, he'd say, gimme a big big nug-hug. Jackie, he'd say, what are the words on page four of *I Am a Bunny*? Jackie, he'd say, what do the bees who don't collect honey do, just to hear the ridiculous answer, which had something to do with being traitor bees who showed bears where the honey was located. With Jack everything was not easy, but easeful, whereas in the rest of his life there was some discord, some divide between how he wished things would be and how they were. As he was thinking this, he suddenly had the competing thought that maybe things with Jack weren't perfect or easeful, but were only that way in retrospect, and that he was idealizing his time with Jack, was doing it, right now, constructing a fantasy past, a delusion. The idea that Jack was some force of immediacy that brought him and April into the present moment and wiped away their delusions was maybe itself a delusion, in the same way that thinking about Jack now was avoiding this moment of pain and suffering that he didn't want to suffer through, deluding himself.

He closed his eyes and gritted his teeth and something distant in him told him to breathe. He opened his eyes and looked at the digital clock, which neared three a.m., and he wondered again where April was, why no one had found him yet, and how long he'd have to wait, and he felt a tiredness that was more than being sleepy, he felt weak and drained, literally drained, the blood in him going out still, and he wondered if someone didn't find him soon, if April wasn't walking to get help right now, who would take care of Jack, and like the thought of April and him arguing in the car, he didn't want to think of him and April not being there for Jack, and he willed the thought to stop, and what was waiting there behind it seemed to wake and come into being, and he again thought of what April had said in the car, Yes, I heard her talking to you. She was talking to you and being all flattering, Oh, Nicholas, what a brave forestman bringing his family to the forest to live a life of forest people among the bears, please show me what a big forestman does please, she had said. Nicholas remembered saying that he couldn't believe she was eavesdropping on his conversation, what a ridiculous and untrusting thing to do. I can't believe that after eleven years together you still don't trust me with a woman who you deem to be somehow above you. April had said that was the most ridiculous thing she'd ever heard, and yes, she felt bad she'd eavesdropped. Nicholas told her to just wait, just hold on a minute, because he wasn't finished, he wasn't going to, you know, he wasn't going to let this happen, he wanted to finish this fight before it began. Oh, you're going to finish it, big forestman, she said. Nora Evans wasn't interested in him, he had continued, and he wasn't interested in Nora Evans, it was all just happenstance, he'd said to April. April had said that she was going to interrupt him now in the same way he had interrupted her, and then she added, Watch the road. She was quiet for a moment, testing him, he knew, to see if he'd say anything more, if he'd fill in the silence with more explaining, which he knew was an indication to keep quiet and also a temptation: he wanted to speak. Then, when more quiet passed than he could stand, he said, Say whatever it is you actually think, feeling a quick anger in his body extending from mind to arms and chest and legs, which were clenched and tight. April said he just couldn't shut up, could he? You're drunk, he'd told her, you did that on purpose and I know you did. And yet you couldn't not talk for fifteen seconds, she said. Try it now. Fifteen seconds. I'll count. He'd waited, counting in his head in the same way he was counting now, then told himself to stop counting, annoyed at her. After a moment, she said she was just going to say one thing, and that one thing was that whatever Nora Evans had said in the kitchen with him, that's just what she was *saying*. What she was *doing* was giving you fuck-me eyes. And you were playing along. And what really bothered me about it, was she was using me and Jack, but mainly I was pissed that she was using *me, using* me, to do it. The comment caused Nicholas to say to April that that wasn't fair, that wasn't fair both to him and to Nora. He didn't think anyone would be that brazen about something like that. Nora wasn't a bad person. Upside down in the car, he recalled feeling a little insane when he was talking, as though the beers and drinks had loosened his mind enough to let it spill forth unreservedly: he recalled the clear feeling that much of what he was saying he didn't really mean and didn't feel very convincingly, it was just glancing thoughts, like the white noise of his mind, that he simply allowed to slip out without any real investigation or care.

Additionally, he remembered adding – unable to stop the random thoughts and words and seeming to view himself from outside himself, as though his words were tuned to some disparate source of annoyance and anger but his actual being was observing from some distant place in the cosmos, calm and dispassionate – that it annoyed him that if he was talking with a woman, any woman, the first thing April went to was that he was, in some way, flirting with said woman, a statement that he understood to be utterly false, and yet which he said in order to make April angry. April replied by saying that she hadn't said that Nicholas was flirting, she had said that Nora was, but that it wasn't the flirting that had annoyed her, and actually, she wasn't even that annoyed, she'd wanted to talk to Nicholas and instead he was being an asshole, but what annoyed her was Nora Evans was flattering Nicholas and using her and Jack to do it, like he was the big man of the family and took care of April and Jack and fended off bears and invested their money and taught them how to live in accord with nature, like I'm your little housemaid of a wife and Jack is going to take over the family one day and become an intellectual Navy Seal. It was gross. Nicholas said, Look, Nora was a gender studies professor. He didn't think she'd think that. April said that she didn't think Nora thought any of that shit was true – it wasn't the flirtation itself that bothered

April, it was the nature of it, which was to flatter his manliness. It was disgusting. And what was doubly disgusting, though mainly annoying, was how easily Nicholas got sucked into it, blushing and looking away in his deep flattery, swimming in flattery. That is really all that April wanted to say, why couldn't they just have a conversation, why was Nicholas defensive, which Nicholas recalled now had caused him to say that he wanted to go back a minute, to the idea that maybe it was just Nora flirting and not him, maybe that was the case, but then why bring it up? I understand now you're saying you just wanted to chat with me about it, but if she didn't suspect him, or if she knew that he wasn't participating in the flirting then the idea that she just wanted to have a laugh about Nora or whatever seemed weak, like why she really wanted to bring it up was because it really felt like she thought he was in some way participating and that she was subtly attacking him here, or wanting to fight or something. It wasn't him wanting to fight, it was her, she was the one doing it, he'd told her. He had tried to keep what he felt was a clenched anger – all his thoughts and energy compressed to a singularly dense frustrated point, which he was fighting to not let explode out, like trying to hold in a universe which would explode out from him only to create more anger and resentment and fighting – down and unexpressed. He had always been able to do this: to view himself and his anger and his emotions as though at some remove from them, both engaging in them and somehow some other part of him acting as the passive observer. April had replied that she wasn't attacking him, that she hadn't been, and wasn't now, but she felt jealousy, insecurity, and yeah, it was annoying, this woman, him giving so much of his attention to this woman, but what she didn't like now was that if Nicholas had nothing to do with this flirting, well, his defensiveness showed her that maybe that wasn't the case, that maybe he wasn't being completely honest here. Nicholas had gone quiet. He had paid attention to the mountain road, the slow rain, the slow wind, the trees slow in their rocking, in an effort to let his anger pass. He'd thought in the space of their quiet that April was right: he had in fact enjoyed the presence of this other woman. He *had* noticed, at some point, that Nora Evans was flirting with him, and while he didn't feel as though he engaged with the flirtation, he hadn't stopped it either. He didn't like this, he didn't want it to be the case, he was arguing with April as much as he was arguing with himself, for indulging in the flirtation. Yet, there was something more there, he knew. He remembered being in the kitchen, and in remembering it, he recreated it, being in the kitchen, whose faucet was dripping slowly, enjoying this other woman talking to him and possibly flirting with him and him possibly flirting with her, her being impressed by something he'd written in one of his books, which April maybe hadn't been eavesdropping on yet, her looking different than April, her face different from April's, her eyes not grey-green, but brown, her hair not sandy blonde, but dark, her face not oval, but round, her upper lip fuller, though her lower lip not as full as April's, the rest of her body different, slightly younger, maybe more in shape, maybe her breasts a little bit smaller than April's, her fingers slightly longer than April's, her breath different from April's, the recognition of her different body instantly manifesting as sexual attraction, him briefly wanting her (and, secondarily, annoyed that he was wanting her, annoyed that something in him was attracted to her, and annoyed that, once again, his biology was taking over, compelling him, this other side of him he associated as being the negative, selfish, probably more primitive side), her voice different, her opinions different, her thoughts and feelings different from April's, her interest in him newer and different and in all likelihood caused because she didn't actually know him. At the same time that he felt and sensed all of this and both enjoyed it and wanted her with some part observing that he didn't want her, and feeling a little repulsed by his own wanting, he also was listening to the dripping faucet. The drops of water spaced perfectly, like the metronome of his thoughts. Something about the slow drops slowed his mind, slowed Nora Evans speaking, slowed his occasional looking past Nora Evans to the party in the other room, everything moving slower, even his sudden wanting of her moving slower, so that he could see it. Suddenly a drop of water in the sink seemed to reverberate like a bell through his mind, rippling out and settling the surface of the water of his mind into a glassy stillness so that the kitchen and Nora Evans and the party and everything almost rippled to a stop, and while waiting for the next drop, the moment in the kitchen slowed so much that he suddenly saw, and saw again, his wanting this person as purposeless and selfish and completely biological and as only leading to dissatisfaction – which, in some way, was exactly what it led to: the fight in the car – and saw Nora as somehow being the same as April. That April's body was not new only to him. That April's voice, her habits, her actions, her interests, were only not new to him. That because he knew April so *fully*, this other person he didn't

know created some sexual attraction in him due to her newness, which when he allowed himself to see clearly, as Nora
Evans spoke, he saw as specter-like, and which he recreated
again now, recreating the moment, the thoughts of the
moment, the intuition and understanding of the moment,
and he imagined that her beauty and his attraction dispersed as a cloud might. The force of his attraction undoing
itself like a mist clearing, and in the space of the moment
before the next drop of water from the kitchen sink, he felt
this all clearly and simply, and then he observed April in a
surrounding room, talking to one of his colleagues, about
to eat what appeared to be a piece of cheese on a cracker.
He then saw April's immediate freshness, her always newness, everyone's, Nora the same as her, not the same person,
but both of their newness in each new moment complete
and whole, and what replaced the passing sexual attraction
for Nora Evans was a gentle and open seeing of Nora Evans
no longer as a sexual body, but just as a body. Which he
was too. Which April was. Each in their difference the same.
All of this had materialized in his mind, he thought and
reconstructed now, in the instant a drop of tap water fell
from the sink: he felt it all move through him and understood it with the intuition he'd developed over four years
living in the woods and living in complete silence for a week
at a time each year. He'd thought, standing in the kitchen,
that this moment wouldn't have been possible if he hadn't
learned to pull from himself the inner feeling that often got
covered over in his stupid and selfish wants: some distant
voice inside him that spoke as though from the depths of a
cave – your wanting isn't you. Yet, he hadn't been able to
tell any of this to April in the car on the way home, he

hadn't been able to explain any of it, it was too complex, the way his feeling about the situation with Nora Evans and how it had transformed was too complexly intertwined with his perceptions, his view of himself, his opinion of April, of Nora, of the water dripping from the faucet, of how he wished he was and how he actually was, how he wanted to be and how he actually was, and so he hadn't said any of it. Feeling an intense pain behind his eyes now, like a sudden migraine arriving, he hated that he hadn't said any of this and he tried to think if their last conversation had really been this ugly or if he or she had said anything more, and at the same time he tried to think if they'd said anything more, he also didn't want to think about it at all, and then he wondered what was more real: his attraction to Nora Evans or his sudden unattraction, his fight and annoyance at April or his care and concern for her, his thinking and recreating these moments in his mind in the car or his body in pain in the car. It was impossible to tell, he thought, what was real and what wasn't, and he thought that his problem was that he thought some moments were real and some weren't, that some moments appeared to be real and some appeared to be a dream that needed to be woken from.

His cheek was smashed against the roof, and his neck was bent and growing sore and stiff. He moved himself a little, readjusting his neck with careful movements, rolling his neck so that his face was off the roof of the car and his ear was pressed against it, muffling the sound of his breathing. It felt good to move and when he felt no pain, he thought he'd try again in a minute, feeling in this new position like he could go to sleep, though he was thirsty. The sound of thunder reverberated through the car. He felt it in the ground, and heard the rain increase, and then felt rainwater running under him, as though the thunder had loosened some pocket of water somewhere. The little stream went right by his face and he moved his neck to lap at it, his mouth so dry, and what he tasted was water mixed with his own blood, and he momentarily became lightheaded again and nauseated. A flickering of dizziness and nausea that made the world reconfigure: the trees and forest and interior of the car all blurred into a flattened visual field. His body and the pain in it pulsed and then seemed diffuse and amorphous and bodiless and not there, and his hearing became confused, as though the sound of the rain, breathing, the running rainwater, the wind in the treetops all became voices speaking an alien language to him in order to coax him from himself. He closed his eyes and breathed and tried to make it stop, and his senses gathered inside him again, and the pain that had dispersed momentarily returned, and his body was the different parts of his body again, pain in arm and left leg and neck, and he opened his eyes, grateful it was back, though now he felt an extreme exhaustion. He thought there was no way he was getting out of this car, he was so tired – he looked at the clock nearing four in the morning. Why hadn't anyone arrived? Why had no one found him yet? He reached down with his right arm and felt around his left leg. There was sticky blood there making his pants feel thick. He explored what he could of his thigh, knee, and when he moved his hand up his leg, maybe mid-thigh, there was a searing sensation that made him stop touching the leg for a moment, and then after the sensation faded, he reached down again and felt around the knee, noting that there was less pain. He reached

229

across himself toward the outside of the left knee and then pulled a little, felt only a dim ache, and then pulled harder, and the knee moved some. Maybe that was it, he thought. Slide the leg toward his right leg, away from the crushed-in door, just slide it carefully. He took a breath and reached across his body again and grabbed the outside of his knee and pulled it. Instantly a stabbing pain in his thigh, but he kept pulling, and the knee and leg moved a little, and gritting his teeth and yelling he pulled hard one more time and the leg slid a bit more and then the pulsing and stabbing moved up his spine into his head and his vision flashed in and out and he stopped and breathed, breathed. More sweat dripped down his temples, he could feel some sweat getting into an ear, tickling it annoyingly. He breathed and waited, was so tired, so glad to not have to move the leg for a minute. He'd done something, he thought. It'd moved some. He felt his legs shifted, both aimed now diagonally toward the opposite side of the car, away from the crushed door. He could still get out. He was doing it. He was getting out, untrapping himself, slowly, just as he pictured it. Take your time, he told himself. The leg would come free. It was nearly free. He could feel it under the dash, the dash still holding it, but looser. It was just the arm now that would hurt. Take your time. Take a little break. Rest.

After a moment of getting his breath back, of hearing the rain outside and the wind in the trees, he suddenly had the feeling that he was more alone than he'd felt in a long time, maybe than ever before, as though he was experiencing loneliness again for the first time. There was no one else. Just rain and wind, just this crushed car, his body. He tried to think of when he had felt the least alone, or when he didn't even consider loneliness, when it didn't even enter into his being, and knew that the answer was when Jack arrived, when it felt like the first time in their lives that their life was not about them: the force of the sleeping baby's presence on his chest, the connection of the baby to April's breast, milk and spittle on their clothes, soupy diarrhea in cloth diapers and on Nicholas's own clothes, washing the boy's clothes and hanging them on the line that the mountain wind dried crisp and fresh smelling, the baby growing from a baby into a toddler, slowly learning consonants: Nicholas thought that these bas and das and mas were the complete expression of this little, helpless being, stating exactly what it was: I'm here, I'm here, I'm here. But not only that. I'm with you. You're here. You tell me, what is that, what is that, what is that, like a mind awakening to everything and everything in turn inviting it to awaken. At nine months, pointing to everything: ba. I'm here, you're here, what is that. April sitting on the floor in the small family room, the windows of the cabin open, rolling a ball toward the baby. Jack reaching for Nicholas by constantly grabbing the air and flapping his hands toward Nicholas. Reading books in the low, yellow lamplight. Holding objects for the baby, slinging him over his shoulder. The baby crawling toward Nicholas as he worked on an article, as he cooked dinner, as he vacuumed, swept, cleaned, and everything pausing for the immediacy of Jack. The first time Nicholas felt a warm energy move from his head to his heart and expand through his chest like a kind of gentle electricity, he'd been holding April in a parking lot after an argument. In the parking lot, it occurred to him that the thought of Jack, of April, of both of them, of him with both them, made him aware that this energy – not an emotion and not a conceptual feeling, but a sensation in his body, his chest – had always been there and was only waiting to be awakened.

Upside down in the car, not wanting to move again but knowing he had to move, he suddenly felt this vacillation between not wanting and having to as a principle of existential import: if he didn't do this thing he didn't want to do – move his arm – he wouldn't live. Trapped in the car, he suddenly saw a strange convergence of what he deemed the two competing sides of himself: he wanted to live, but he didn't want to experience any pain. This, it suddenly seemed, this being trapped in the car, sweating and cold, his own blood occasionally falling on his face, this moment felt symbolic, as though his life itself was metaphorical, the convergence of a story, as though there was some abstraction behind the reality he was experiencing, but that the abstraction was just reality itself, no abstraction at all, that wanting and avoiding were not two separate things, that death and life were not two separate things, that he would die. He felt confused and fought against this thought with the suddenly urgent need to get out of the car and he pulled hard on the steering wheel, so that his neck lifted momentarily off the carpeted ceiling, and he took a breath and tried to extract himself like extracting a deeply embedded thorn from a toe, from the seat. He felt hot pain in his left arm, which pulled and wrenched him back in place, making him yell in pain. He stopped and sat and felt sweat running down his face and his body breathing. Something in him telling himself to breathe, keep breathing, calm down, and after a few minutes, his breathing steadied, though there was still a searing pain in his arm. That was so stupid, why'd you do that, he thought. Now he'd have to wait again until the pain subsided and try to get out slowly, you moron, do it in steps. Another rumble of thunder through the ground and up through his body. Another moment of thinking of the last conversation with April. The thunder moved through the ground, the vibration holding him momentarily. He told himself to breathe and watched another rivulet of rainwater stream by his face, watching the rivulet grow larger, waiting for it to get big enough again so that he could take another drink, and through breathing he told himself to rest, to let his eyes close, he was so tired, to think of something else, to not reduce his entire relationship with April to one argument, to think of the good moments, cooking dinner with her, talking with her, hiking with her, being Jack's parents together with her, think of something else, he inwardly related to himself, which caused him to remember the days that he and April used to smoke lots of marijuana when they were both in grad school and then sit around and self-analyze in order to figure out things about themselves and their relationship. He opened his eyes as though what was there might not be there, as though he might only be in bed, but he wasn't, and he remembered how they'd have these discussions, very stoned, as though they were holding each other up for the other to look at, and they knew it was a kind of indulgence, a privilege to have the job that gave them the money that allowed for the time for them to do this, not to mention to have been educated in a way that allowed them to do this, but Nicholas remembered that at least they were doing it, maybe that analysis was better than no analysis at all, maybe, though privileged, they were using their privilege to at least attempt to better themselves, they asked each other. Was that what they were doing? They agreed that they felt they were sculpting their lives into the shapes they wanted, the figures they wished to be, and that it was their view of it that was important, and Nicholas accepted that. He could feel them somehow becoming intertwined, as though their minds in these discussions became one mind, as though they were two cells on a slide under a microscope that bump each other, for a moment separate, and then slip inside one another, a whole new existence, two and not at the same time, a new life. And yet he'd never, no matter how aware he was, and no matter how aware April was, neither had been able to end this feeling that there was division in them, between them, and now, Nicholas thought, what did any of that feeling of connection matter if he was going to pass out of existence here alone? And then the immediate competing and contradictory thought that all that he had just thought had only been possible because of April, because of Jack: they were inside him, they were him. He felt he could let himself fall into this thought, this feeling, a warm dark – he was moving toward it, it enveloping him, it was happening slowly, gently, moving toward it, it moving toward him – and then he opened his eyes. No, he thought. He couldn't do that. Don't fall asleep. He opened his eyes wide, and wondered how much time had passed. He blinked hard several times, waking himself, telling himself to wake up, to stay awake.

In the periphery of his vision he saw what at first was only a flash of shadow moving quickly, he thought at first a person, but he heard wings and a small noise, and he knew it was a bird. Out the passenger-side window where

April's profile should've been, shifting his head ever so slightly, he saw, on the road, directly in the middle of the road, what appeared to be a hawk. He closed his eyes and opened them and looked and saw the bird was not a hawk, but an owl. He saw the animal in profile, its round head, wings like hunched shoulders, claws on the ground, all visible in the moonlight. The owl stood and slowly rotated its head with its hooked beak and large eyes like a cat's. It looked into the car at him. The owl's entire body turned, though its head stayed facing him, and it seemed to lean over and stretch forward, to see him. He didn't know if this was real, or if he was dreaming, and the owl's head seemed to move in response, as though it was confused by his thoughts, and then his eyes and the owl's aligned and he felt a rushing toward the animal and it moving toward him, though the same space separated them, as though the animal's eyes were pulling him out of the car and himself, and for a moment he seemed to see his own face, the eyes with which he watched the owl the same eyes with which the owl watched him. Then the owl lifted its wings and flew to a branch of a tree, its body completely in silhouette against the moonlit sky. He couldn't tell if it was still watching him or not, or what it was doing here, or why it had landed on the road and looked at him. It was now a two-dimensional figure on a tree branch, completely quiet, and its silence reminded him of his own failed attempt, of the cultivated quiet and isolation in his family's life that he hoped would allow him to see clearly what he was trying to do. To change the narrative of his thoughts, to see through the seeming validity of his personal fiction. But he hadn't changed anything, he thought.

Nicholas closed his eyes in an effort to stop the pulsing in his head and his continuing thoughts, which he both wanted to stop and wanted to keep having, because what if these were his last thoughts? He opened his eyes again and saw that it was nearing five in the morning. What if this cold air here was his last breath? What if this heartbeat, this view out the frame of the car into the forest was the last thing he would see, the last sound the sound of the gentle rain? He wanted to keep seeing and experiencing and thinking, he wanted to apologize to April and feel her body pressed to his, he wanted to pick Jack up from his bed and carry him into the kitchen and share a bowl of organic Sunny-Os, he wanted to bite his lip and be annoyed while eating too fast, he wanted to pop a perfect whitehead on his chin, he wanted to take a piss or crap in the morning, he wanted to have a fever and feel himself changed after it, he wanted to hold Jack's hand crossing the street or surprise April with a kiss, he wanted to fight with her, manipulate her, feel her manipulating him, feel bad for manipulating her, attempt to be sincere, feel her wanting to be sincere, apologize, begin again, he wanted to keep being alive no matter if he was confused or clear or selfish or mean or kind or dumb. He just wanted to keep doing it, he just wanted to keep being himself and wanted the pain to stop. He didn't want to think of freeing his stuck left arm. Being stuck in the car, shivering with cold, no longer sweating, he felt an enormous force in him explaining that in every moment he was deeply divided between what he wanted and what he didn't, as though what he'd always thought about himself was being confirmed now, as he was dying, that yes, he was a deeply divided person, and now that he was not going to live anymore, he was going to experience that divide on the most physical and painful level: he didn't want to die, yet he was. The pressure in his head that had been increasing for some time, both from being hungover and from being upside down, and from, he thought now, the loss of blood, began to make him see spots of flashing white, as though the material world was de-pixelating, coming apart. He again had an urgent need to pee and felt himself clench down there and it hurt. At the same time, again the thought arose to move his arm, to do whatever he had to do, he'd moved his legs, it was just this last thing. He was so tired, he told himself, and then something in him told him it didn't matter if he was tired, he had to free the arm. The drips of blood that had been hitting his face and cheek and nose at what felt like random intervals were now hitting him more frequently. He tasted his own blood again, though he couldn't tell if this came from dripping down his face into his mouth or came from inside him, and that made him afraid. It was time to try the arm, he told himself. He told himself it was time to free the arm, over and over in order to make the action one he was prepared for. What he knew would be pure pain. The rivulet of water running through the car still wasn't close enough, and in complete exhaustion, he thought he needed to move his arm, get his left arm free, and when he pulled it now he felt a wave of pain, and he stopped again, feeling the effort was futile, watching the rivulet of rainwater become larger and larger, until it was so close that he could drink it, lap it up finally, a great reprieve. He drank the water with his tongue and sort of sucked at the rivulet moving by, coughing occasionally due to the dryness of his throat. The water in his mouth was momentarily just the water in his mouth and everything in him was this drinking. He drank and drank, the water tasting of dirt, but it was lovely and clean somehow. He tried to push his face into it even though he was very cold and shivering. He wanted the blood off of his face. No, he thought. You want to free your arm. You're getting tired. You have to do it now.

He observed that the pain in his arm had lessened, he was breathing steadily, he'd rested for a while, the pressure of the blood in his head because he'd been flipped over for so long now was constantly intensifying. He pulled with his upper body, pulling his left shoulder forward and seemed to be able to feel a string of pain along his arm and into his neck, but it wasn't unbearable. His left arm, which was behind him a little, jammed in place by the door, he pulled forward gently, and when the arm didn't move, he pulled more forcefully, then he jolted forward, in frustration, and he heard a horrific cracking sound, then a bell-like ringing of hot energy that quickly morphed into excruciating pain, and he said aloud fuck fuck fuck, jesus. He tried to focus on his breathing, but couldn't: shallow and halting and quick breaths, which his heart followed. There was no sweat on his brow now, his mouth was dry even though he'd just had water, his eyes felt sunken in his face, and the ringing pulse in his left arm made it feel as though the arm was inflated and large, made of shattered ice. After a few long moments, it settled, his body quieted its shivering. And while the pain was still intense and the arm still stuck, he thought the arm was looser, not quite as stuck, and he told himself good, maybe he'd broken it, but it was looser, he could get it out, and he breathed and inwardly related to himself to calm down and try again and just wait a little and then try again. He tried to regulate the pain through his breathing. Then, in attempting to re-shift his upper body in order to reach his left leg, he moved his left arm and a ringing pain moved up his spine, causing a lightheadedness, his vision flashing white, like a camera's flash right in his face, and then the world slowly resolved again. Stop, he told himself. Don't pass out now. You can't pass out now. He breathed, breathed in again, as deep as he could, little points of pain firing all around his body with the deeper breaths. He breathed in again, slowly, and tried to let it move through him and then out of him, then breathed in again. He moved his head against the ceiling of the car. He didn't experience the same sharp pain in his neck, and he felt a brief reprieve, being able to move his head, adjusting his neck and right arm, and though the pressure of the blood in his head made him dizzy, it felt so nice to roll his head like this even against his own sticky blood. For a moment, just from being able to move his neck he thought that he'd be okay, that there wasn't something seriously wrong with his neck, it was just sore from being in the same position – and in this lack of pain, the momentary feeling that he wouldn't die here, he'd get out, he'd talk to April again, he'd get another chance. He moved his head again, kind of rolling it against the ceiling of the car in order to stretch his neck, feeling sticky blood pull away from his face and hair when he moved from the ceiling, and then stopped, breathing heavier, resting. The dim thought that it was just the leg now, just that that had to be completely freed from under the dash.

More rainwater passed by his face, and he drank for a few minutes and stared thoughtlessly, exhaustedly into the dark forest, which was now in a heavy fog. It made him think that morning was approaching, the world beginning again. Maybe April was near town, but that thought was stupid, he knew. She wasn't walking anywhere, and the last conversation they'd had was one in which they'd argued. He stopped drinking and closed his eyes hard and opened them and the urge to pee became too strong and he allowed himself to pee and felt it warm running down his stomach and chest and down his neck and he turned his head so that only a little got on his chin and face. The warmth was momentarily comforting. It made him sleepier and he told himself to rest for a minute, just a few minutes, and as he closed his eyes he again reconstructed the scenario, standing in the kitchen with Nora Evans, her talking to him, him talking to her, and eventually a strange space opening that allowed him to recognize this Nora Evans person as a person, in which he'd felt clarify in him the simple intention to go find April, which was what he had done, telling Nora Evans that it was nice talking to her. He remembered after the party driving home in the car with April, thinking that he'd wanted to convey all this to her. That he'd come to find *her*, and what had allowed that to occur was the confusion of his selfish wanting to flirt or be near this other person, that the dispersal of the wanting awakened the actuality of this other feeling, which was not a feeling, but a self, another story: not wanting April, but just being with her, just being there. But to be able to explain that properly, he remembered thinking, he'd have to admit the sexual attraction first, which had led him to this other feeling, this other intention, this clearer recognition of the others around him and himself, and he didn't want to have to do that because he knew it'd both hurt April and make her angry and cause an argument. Though they'd eventually argued *anyway*, in the car, the argument he'd wanted to avoid somehow manifesting itself, and the most painful part of the argument was that the clear intention he'd thought he'd found in the kitchen was once again lost, was once again dispersed in his feeling that April's implied accusation was unfair, unjust, mean-spirited, and that he didn't want to be doing this, and in feeling that he didn't want to be doing this fight with April, he felt clearly he was against April and her fighting, fighting her, trying to wrestle through words to his own rightness and to the end of the argument, and he had then thought, hands on the wheel, that the only thing he really knew now with any certainty was that he didn't want to be doing what they were doing, which was arguing, he only wanted to stop arguing, though he also felt he wasn't wrong, there was nothing wrong with his actions at the party, so he kept arguing with her, explaining to her that she was simplifying the situation in a way that was frustrating, and that she'd be frustrated by it too if she really thought about it. Then he remembered, at the sort of climax of the fight, that she'd said that she was upset not because of the flirting and not only because Nora Evans was using April as part of her flirtation method, but because Nora Evans had said something about Nicholas bringing the family off the grid, and he hadn't corrected her. In fact, he'd gone along with it. When the whole thing was my idea, she had said. It was my suggestion to get you out of that job you hated. My suggestion to move some place quieter, slower. My suggestion to get out of the city. I know you remember that I told you that maybe you needed a place where you could see what you were doing again, I know you remember that, but what I remember thinking was that I was getting sick of you bitching about how everything was wrong, the fast pace was wrong, driving in cars was wrong, TV, social media, publishing, your job, and I framed it like that, move to some place quieter because I was sick of hearing you complain. That's not fair, Nicholas had said. You were just as annoyed with the traffic, the commute, the loss of our time getting to some place we didn't want to be, don't give me bullshit about how you did it because all I do is complain, to which Nicholas imagined her saying in his memory that of course she wanted something different, too, but that, see, what he wasn't understanding even now was that she had to frame it in this particular way, she had to frame it like maybe doing this would help his work, would help him do what he was always saying he needed to do, live in the present, and you took that and ran with it, but really I just wanted you to stop complaining about everything, and now you're talking to this Nora Evans woman like you dreamed up another way of life for me and Jack. Such bullshit. Nicholas thought of how he'd shaken his head, saying that it'd just been easier, he was just moving the conversation on, and to please think about it, and April had said, Oh, I'm thinking about it, she'd said. And what I think is you're a selfish asshole. She had gone quiet on the ride home but in the continued conversation in his mind, she said, What I think is that you're a selfish asshole, and what I think is you've always done this shit, why would it be any different now? You always eliminate Jack and me. You always say, I live in the mountains of North Carolina. I live off the grid. I took my family off the grid. But you wouldn't have done any of that had I not shown you the books and the websites and introduced you to some people to help us do it. It was *my* idea and you make it seem like you grew a beard, put on a flannel, grabbed an axe, and created the entirety of our life by hewing thatch huts for us to live in. Nicholas imagined himself saying that that was all maybe true but that he really wasn't even trying to do that, he wasn't trying to eliminate her and Jack, it was just easier in conversation to talk in this way, and he knew that April would say that that was exactly her point, it was easier to talk about him, it was easier to make everything about him, it wasn't malicious, she realized, she wasn't saying he was evil, she was calling him an asshole, and that's what an asshole was, a person who made everything about himself, and that was exactly what he did, she thought maybe Jack arriving would change it, and to some degree it had, but after Jack grew up some, Nicholas was back to being the way he'd always been, which was self-concerned with his own self-improvement or investigation or whatever he was calling it these days, his project, she guessed that's what he was calling it now, his project, and it left her and Jack out, except when it was convenient for Nicholas.

He opened his eyes. Listening to the rain, he wondered if this was the last word she'd spoken to him. They often reached a point in their arguing when they'd stop, and they'd both relent, and then both claim that they'd attacked the other, that the attack wasn't really how they felt and thought about the other, but this time there had been nothing more. In remembering the argument with April, Nicholas now wondered if everything he'd ever done had been a selfish delusion, if nothing in his life was truly done for another person, but was always done with some thought of self-gain: make a nice dinner for April and she'd massage his back later, play and sing with Jack because he wanted to be seen as a caring and attentive father, publish articles and become slightly well-known in his field to impress his colleagues and parents and old friends, live off the grid to show his moral superiority to everyone else, thereby impressing them. It made him feel self-pitying and ashamed at his self-pity, just another selfishness, another way he put his pain before anyone else's. In an effort to not keep thinking in this painful, though possibly true way, he decided it was time. One more pull and the arm would be unstuck, then he'd do the legs. Do it now, he told himself. He thought that he had to move in order to at least have an attempt to correct this last conversation. He wanted the chance to make it so that his last interaction with someone on this planet was not one of meanness and ugliness and selfishness. He breathed in and breathed out, steadying himself, waiting for the moment, and in the waiting he thought the last thing she'd said to him was that he was an asshole – the word like an echo – and he thought that this couldn't be the last conversation they'd have, then, in a kind of horrified understanding, realized it was, knew it was, and attempted to think of what else he'd said, what else she'd said, had either of them said anything more? The conversation couldn't have ended with April saying this and him feeling angry and guilty and mean. He couldn't remember anything else though. He remembered not talking after that, and he feared for a moment that this was maybe the actual expression of who he was. That this last thing that April had said, maybe it was the truest thing, the realest thing about him, was the most banal and stupid thing one could be. Maybe the universe had designed his living to inevitably lead up to this moment when he had nearly died and April presented to him what he actually was, as though through April's mouth, the universe had said: selfish asshole. And in hearing this message from either the universe or April, he thought now, he had no choice but to face the idea that he was an asshole. Was essentially an unkind, uncaring, selfish, idiotic person despite whatever intellectual successes and understandings he'd had. Then he thought that he was turning April into a message for him, another selfishness, and he made himself stop. Was life a designed teaching or was it happenstance? Were there real messages behind things or were things things themselves, or were they not even that? What was real and what was delusion? Trying to keep breathing steadily and deeply and to let go of the pain that was pulsing in his arm and shoulder and dully in his neck and back, he thought that what he felt he'd been doing in supposedly cultivating clarity, in coming to the mountains, in attempting to live in a sustainable way, in attempting, with April, to live again in balance with the world, in attempting to extricate their lives as much as possible from the patriarchal, materialistic, corporately driven, consumerist, competition-based culture that inundated everything in their country and was oppressing not only minorities in the States, but was exploiting people in other counties, the poor and indigenous, as well as exploiting land and plant and animal, maybe in moving to the mountains and in building the little cabin and taking it off the grid and attempting to create a garden they could live on, maybe what he'd been doing was actually nothing. Maybe what he was actually doing, maybe all he was really doing, rather than getting rid of his stupidities, rather than seeing into and listening closely among the quiet to his better self, rather than dropping what he had come to see as cultural selfishness, he had become, as April indicated, selfish in a different way. Maybe they both had. Maybe they'd just created a little island of selfishness. Maybe what he thought they'd done in order to be less distanced from each other and the nature of things was merely create a space where they could more easily fight one another, more easily see how they were in the same room and yet were not, were there and not there, were with each other and somewhere else. Maybe all they'd really done was given themselves a space to see just how alone, how distanced from each other, from their family and friends, from society, and from even themselves they were.

Out the open frame of the windshield, the now gentle rain continued falling in a pattering rhythm that seemed to regenerate itself through sound. He thought that it was probably raining where Jack was sleeping. He looked at the digital clock nearing six in the morning, and out the window through the trees, the small space of sky he could see was just lightening. In his exhaustion, he thought that he'd never say goodnight to Jack again, never get to sing him a new song, never show him the movies and albums he wanted to show him when he got older, never argue with him when he became a teenager, never feel like he was losing him when he left, never feel old himself due to the youth of his kid, never have a falling out and reconnect, and his little boy would always be the little boy whose parents had died, and someone else, over time, would become Jack's real parents, and what had been real for Jack would become unreal.

Just like it was doing for Nicholas now. What was real became unreal and what was unreal became real. He hoped it'd be Nathaniel and Stefanie, and he thought for a terrifying moment of April's mother wanting Jack and how he and April had never made a will, and the poor boy being fought over by the entire family. He tried to think of Nathaniel and Stefanie, like thinking of them taking the boy could somehow create the reality. He closed his eyes and tried to construct the thought from some sourceless depth inside him in an effort to make what was unreal real. When he opened his eyes, viewing the dark woods in the rain, he didn't know why someone hadn't found him yet, why someone hadn't called April's cell phone and realized something was wrong, and he began crying, and said in his mind to Jack that he hoped he would be okay and he was sorry for not being there, for the fact that he might not be there again, he was sorry he'd been stupid and was stupid, he apologized for not being able to say goodbye, he apologized to April, though he knew she was no longer alive. He apologized to his parents, to his brother. He apologized to the rain falling in the woods, and felt his consciousness slip toward the woods, move away from his body, and he seemed to be looking at himself, his face a pale light in the dark of the upside-down car, staring out, but not seeing out of his own eyes, seeing into them, and then he seemed to be viewing himself from up on the branch of a tree, like he was seeing out of the owl's eyes and viewing himself from above, feeling himself move away from his slumped and upside-down body, now above the car, and a part of the woods, the rain, the mist moving through the forest, and he felt as though he was the mist, as though he was gently moving over the earth, and in watching himself grow smaller (he could somehow see himself through the bottom of the car) and now that he was more distant from himself through the trees, he felt a gratitude for his life, and instead of apologizing, he thought the words thank you to the same people he apologized to a moment before and then said thank you to what was everything else. Then there was a sharp pain in his ribs and he was back in his body in the car, looking out. The owl was there looking in at him through the opened frame of the car. A brief moment of feeling dispersed and bodiless slipped away, and was replaced by utter fear, which in turn was replaced by the thought that he needed to understand right away if he and April had said anything else after this argument they'd had. Then, in both fear and awe, he observed his mind slow down and his thinking become abstract, as though his identity was dropping away and he was a representation of one half of the universe, male, though he felt also female, and the female in him was April, was his mother, was other women he knew, and the male in him was his father, Nathaniel, Jack, that existence was divided, that everything was separate and alone so that it might know itself, divided on some vast continuum between male and female, divided between myriad other forms, plant, land, water, animal, air, and myriad other forms of mind, clarity, confusion, boredom, excitement, lust, love, greed, giving, kindness, hate, each complementing each, each forming each, nothing its own existence, selfishness and selflessness, all the same thing, all in him, and his face became some other face that he both knew and didn't know hovering right behind his own face. He didn't see the face so much as become it, which made him breathe in shallower, shorter breaths. Not even become. He was it. This other face that wasn't other. Then he perceived the female face, that also was not fully female. Both faces were looking unwaveringly at each other, and in his fear at observing these faces that were his and not his, he began crying, at the understanding that these thoughts he'd been having were not him, they were not April, not Jack, not his mother, father, Nathaniel, that all of them and everyone were beyond his thinking of them. He closed his eyes to make the faces go away and opened them again and saw them behind the rainy forest. It was as though his mind had become intermingled with the forest itself, had become a physical thing. He could not tell if it was his mind or the not speaking faces that he lightheadedly perceived that conveyed to him that what he'd been learning on the mountain with April and Jack was that what he knew was insignificant compared to what he didn't know, both about others and about himself. He didn't know himself or anyone. Everything was shining beyond knowing. I'm dying, he thought. The lack of knowing was a gift that he'd always been hesitant to accept, afraid to accept.

His vision darkened from the outside in, making a sort of tunnel of looking out the empty frame of the car into the rainy woods. He closed his eyes – a bright pulsing star of light behind his lids – and opened them. The seatbelt suddenly slipped off his left shoulder and hit his ear as it slipped around his head and jolted, retracting back into place, and in an equal and opposite reaction, his body lurched forward and he fell from his sitting position and his right leg came unstuck, and all except for his left leg was loosed onto the ceiling of the car and heard himself yell in pain. The moaning understanding that he'd unbuckled the seatbelt, but it had remained latched, and it had suddenly let go fully and retracted. He was splayed across the ceiling of the upside-down car, his left arm broken and limp above him, his right knee coming down, and the left leg was still stuck beneath the dash, but the entire leg now outstretched, his entire body pulling on it, a burning, pulsing pain through the whole leg. He reached up and tried to move his left arm into a more comfortable position but there was a stabbing jolt against the side of his body and he stopped moving. He felt warm liquid hit his face and knew it was his own blood and knew that he needed to get the stuck leg out now. If he could get the stuck leg out, he could then get out the car – an image of him crawling out from under the car, through the open windshield, over the cracked glass, into the rain and ditch, free. He reached down across his body with his right hand down below the dash, to his left knee, and he felt up and down the knee and thigh, the lower part of his thigh smashed by the dash, and he reached down again to the knee, in the space between seat and some part of the dash, and pulled hard against the outside of the knee, sliding the leg under the dash, the thigh resisting, and he pulled harder and the entire leg slid along the seat, between the seat and dash, a fire burning up and down his leg and up his back and into his neck – the faces behind and beneath everything hovering in his mind and vision. When he closed his eyes, the faces were there, and when he opened them, they were there. He whimpered in pain, heard himself whimpering, half crying, then breathing deeply, trying to make his shallow breathing deeper. Rainwater was now gathering in pools inside the car, on the ceiling of the car, and running over the windshield in small streams. He waited for the burning pain in his leg to settle and he breathed and breathed and told himself to breathe deeply and he heard his breathing quivering. It was just a few more inches, he thought, it must be, slide the stuck leg just a little further, and it'd fall on top of him and he'd be able to get out. He could look at his legs now, he noticed – the faces behind everything seeming to be watching him with distant and neutral curiosity, as though they were the filmmakers of the universe – and he moved his neck and head, and through streaks and sparks that filled his vision, when he looked into the dark below the steering wheel and blood-soaked airbag, he saw his pants ripped and left leg bent strangely at the thigh under the dash, and for a moment he felt he might vomit and then did, watery bile, onto the ceiling beside him. He looked away. The seat where he'd just been was soaked in blood and now he felt the stickiness on his head as well and again thought that this couldn't be the way he died. He couldn't die in a ditch trapped in a car after arguing with his wife about some stupid moment at a party. The faces in his mind, or that were his mind – he was trying to understand – were there. He could not tell if he thought it or if the faces conveyed that he was nothing, was not even a he, and he fought against this and said aloud that he was getting out of this car, he was just drained and tired and hallucinating and told himself to not pay attention to anything his mind was making up and he shifted on the ceiling of the car, moving his torso and trying with his good right arm to reach his stuck left leg, but he couldn't reach it now without a new, sharp pain in his back, that made him take quick breaths, and then he forced himself to do it and through screaming pain pulled and slid his left leg beneath the dash and felt it come loose when he pulled sideways and then the entire leg fell on top of him – his vision bursting in sparks and stars of convulsing energy that was pain – almost feeling as though it was dangling right above the knee, and he had his left thigh in his right hand, his entire body flipped on itself. After a moment, he propped the leg against the steering wheel so it wouldn't fall, and then he looked out the open frame of the windshield and pulled with both arms toward the opening and scooted his upper body, his legs falling down, his left leg on fire, and pulled his body out from the car and then out from under the hood, pulling himself and almost growling through a clenched jaw, pulling onto wet leaves away from the car, and then he was looking back at where'd he'd been trapped and saw something like the impression of his body in blood in the upside-down car seat. He moved himself to lie on his back and had to hold his left thigh to do it, and he felt, in his thigh, bone coming through muscle and skin and jeans, and newly moving blood. When he had flipped onto his back his body remained a pulsing center of pain and for a moment he didn't register the rain, until he did, and told himself to breathe, and took a deep breath, which eased his body momentarily.

Rain was falling gently through the forest onto his body, and he saw now, looking back about ten feet, that the car had gone into the forest some, was actually beyond the ditch near the side of the road, and had broken a tree. He looked around for April, but didn't see her. In exhaustion he let his head fall back on what he assumed were wet leaves, and again took a deep breath, which seemed to come into him slowly. Being free of the car made it feel as though his body was not his and was expanding, and with a slow-moving in-breath, the rain falling on his body slowed, and he looked up on the out-breath, which proceeded from him even slower, and he could see each raindrop that was falling and behind each drop of rain another drop, his eyes barely open, and the warmth of blood running down his leg, the brief vague thought that he shouldn't have moved it, that it was pinned and something had been stopping the bleeding, but nothing was stopping the bleeding now, and the faces he'd seen in the car emerged again more clearly and force-fully, behind the trees and mist and rain, and then the rain stopped and the paused rain was now a ladder, each drop a drop proceeding up, outward, and each drop led toward the faces, which were both of his faces, his face merely an aspect of these other faces, and felt himself go into them, which was himself, but not himself as he knew himself, and so he was no longer he, and he saw time moving beyond him, time that was no longer his time but was Jack's, Jack with him and April on the mountain, then Jack with Nath-aniel and Stefanie, Jack amid conversations and argument between the family members in the cabin, the entire family discussing and questioning and propositioning and debating in the cabin, Jack alone in his room, Jack crying, a decision finally made, promises and compromises and intentions presented, to include all, to allow Jack to know both sides of his family, and Jack leaving with Nathaniel and Stefanie, Jack in an apartment, Jack in a new room, Jack crying, Jack going to a new school, Jack alone, Jack sitting with Nathan-iel, with Stefanie, Jack watching TV, Jack playing soccer, Jack running around the house while Nathaniel chases him,

Jack sitting in a chair while Stefanie cuts his hair, Jack helping Nathaniel make bread, Jack helping Stefanie in the urban garden, Jack having friends over, Jack spending weekends away, Jack sitting between Nicholas's father and mother and watching a movie, Jack playing with Tammy, who'd moved across the country, Jack doing flashcards with her, Jack showing her videos of Nathaniel cooking online, Jack growing taller, Jack with his friends, Jack moving to a new house in the suburbs, Jack with new friends and girl-friends, Jack through his life thinking of Nicholas and April, Jack missing them, Jack wanting them back, Jack seeing his father in Nathaniel, his mother in Tammy, Jack missing his mom and dad, Jack wondering who they were, where they were, if they could hear him, if they couldn't, Jack talking to them, Jack no longer talking to them, Jack forgetting them, Jack becoming Jack, Jack's life moving in a slow bloom outward like a flower opening and all the people around him doing exactly as he and April had done, trying, despite their selfishness, to be there for him, to be there for him in his sadness at losing his parents, to be there for him at his first soccer game, to be there for him when he hated them, when he loved them, when he felt cared for, when he didn't, when he wanted them, when he didn't, when they thought he was being difficult, when he was, when he wasn't, when they were too busy to be there for him, when they weren't, when they held him, punished him, thought they knew how to raise him, didn't know, when they judged, blamed, accused each other, when they didn't, when they needed each other, when they each wanted to do it alone, when they were right, wrong, open, closed, considering Jack, considering themselves, when they gossiped behind each other's backs and Jack heard and felt alone amid the fighting and arguing, when he felt the family members, on a car drive, on a walk, while eating pizza, subtly suggesting that this person was not good enough, that this other person was, when they relented to each other, when they all saw beyond themselves, when they failed to, when they remembered that they had all agreed to do it together, when they all did it together, for Jack they all did it together, whether they wanted to or not, when Jack felt it, when he didn't, all their concern and neglect and selfishness and judgment and greed and delusion and kindness and care, all exactly as it was, his face and all of their faces merging into the two faces in his mind and Jack's face merging there, too, all held by each other. His breath still slowly moving out from him and breathing them all out, up the drops of rain, up through the mist, beyond the mist up through the treetops with just sprouting leaves, up beyond the treetops – his body lying on the ground bleeding – up into the raincloud, a grey growth on the sky, up beyond it into the dark blue night and beyond the moon swiftly passing by, planets, beyond the solar system into some deep darkness and then a galaxy and the faces behind it and further – the flashing image of the body on the ground – a gaseous cloud that was passing through faster into the blackness toward the two faces which slowly merged into one expressionless and calm face which at the same moment dispersed into being the web of the universe which was a mind and every mind and yet also there was the body on the ground trying to hold a hand though there was no hand to hold watching the rain fall from the treetops and being afraid the neutral and calm mind itself afraid through the wet trees a crescent moon in the now lightening sky beyond and moving so fast that galaxies and stars passed by in streaked light, the light also rotational, the streaking light seeming to rotate or spiral inward and outward at once to the neutral face and mind which was the face and mind that was also on the ground feeling an enormous fear that was the fear of itself inviting itself to be itself and then again breathing on the ground feeling the rain hit the body and in each breath the raindrops fell on the body as the face and mind of everything moved up into the body and breathed in and out and this mind that was everything rose up through the body and breathed in just as it ever did and that mind despite its calm acceptance of everything it gave rise to felt fear and awe and foolishness and gratitude as it once again breathed in and out and collapsed in on itself once again, and the first flashing blue lights lighted the treetops.

ACKNOWLEDGEMENTS

Thank you to my family, my mom and dad, former teachers, and friends, who have offered support over the years, in particular Eric Kocher and Patrick Whitfill. Thank you to Seren Adams for seeing something when no one else did, for her brilliant editing, and for all her hard work and kindness. Thank you to my publisher, Picador, in particular Gill Fitzgerald-Kelly and Ravi Mirchandani, for caring about this book. Most importantly, thank you to Emily Rossi, for never failing to see me, even when I haven't been able to see myself, and for all that she has given - her endless and unconditional support, kindness, advice, and time – so selflessly: this is for you.

CIVILIZATION
AND ITS DISCONTENTS

SIGMUND FREUD, M.D., LL.D.

AUTHORIZED TRANSLATION
BY
JOAN RIVIERE

Martino Publishing
Mansfield Centre, CT
2010

Martino Publishing
P.O. Box 373,
Mansfield Centre, CT 06250 USA

www.martinopublishing.com

ISBN 1-891396-25-0

© *2010 Martino Publishing*

Cover design by T. Matarazzo
Printed in the United States of America On 100% Acid-Free Paper